D1269329

CHAOS & NONLINEAR DYNAMICS IN THE FINANCIAL MARKETS

Theory, Evidence and Applications

Robert R. Trippi
Editor

IRWIN
Professional Publishing®

Chicago • Bogotá • Boston • Buenos Aires • Caracas
London • Madrid • Mexico City • Sydney • Toronto

This publication is designed to provide accurate and authoritative information in regard to the subject matter covered. It is sold with the understanding that the author and the publisher are not engaged in rendering legal, accounting, or other professional service.

ISBN 1-55738-857-1

Printed in the United States of America

BB

1 2 3 4 5 6 7 8 9 0

CB

TABLE OF CONTENTS

PART I—FOUNDATIONS

LIST OF TABLES

LIST OF FIGURES

To my wife, Cecilia, with love

PREFACE

In recent years the theories of nonlinear systems in general, and chaotic systems in particular, have received a great deal of attention in the financial community. A "chaotic" process in this context is one that, although deterministic, generates time paths of variables of interest that give the appearance of being generated by some random process. Historically, the study of complex dynamics has its roots in the physical sciences. However, the notion of the existence of at least some deterministic component to the dynamics of prices has great appeal to those interested in forecasting the time paths of market prices of investment assets. The hope for many is that such determinism, although perhaps elusive to most conventional statistical tests constructed on linear hypotheses, may be susceptible to being uncovered through more sensitive and sophisticated methodologies. To the extent that nonlinear dependence exists within or across asset price time series, an understanding of the form of the underlying mechanism could, at least in theory, lead to a greater degree of predictability than is possible under the more conventional statistical models.

This book deals with both theory and empirical results related to determinism in the dynamics of asset prices. Its chapters address a broad spectrum of how's, what's, and why's of nonlinear dynamical phenomena of interest to finance professionals. Theoretical properties of various chaotic processes are explored in depth, along with the performance of statistical tests that have been developed specifically to detect the presence of chaotic behavior. The more empirically oriented articles generally frame as hypotheses whether or not actual or measured price movements or asset returns appear more to be generated by a purely random process or by a process which includes a chaotic deterministic component.

The organization of this book is as follows. The first section, Foundations, is a collection of papers on the theory underlying chaotic processes.

Taken together, these chapters can provide the reader with a sufficient understanding of the statistical and economic interpretations of nonlinear data-generating processes to appreciate the empirical issues addressed in subsequent chapters. The next three sections, Stock Markets Evidence, Commodity Markets Evidence, and Money Markets Evidence, contain mostly empirical papers dealing with the detection and significance of chaotic processes within time-series data from these respective markets. Several chapters include results from one or more of the markets represented by other sections. In such cases, chapters were somewhat subjectively assigned to the section for which the empirical results seemed most important. The last section of this book, Methodological Issues, focuses on statistical methodology and measurement issues associated with the assessment and characterization of chaotic behavior, including newer methodologies such as neural networks.

An easy-to-use Windows software package, *Chaos Explorer*, accompanies this book. *Chaos Explorer* illustrates graphically the behavior of several of the chaotic processes that are mentioned throughout the book. This software makes it quite easy for the user to visualize the transition of a system from stable to unstable states, and from chaotic to cyclic behavior and back again, through the use of suggested example parameters. Operating instructions and other documentation are included within the software's help menu.

It is my hope that a collection of papers such as this, dealing exclusively with issues associated with the application of chaos theory to the behavior of prices of financial instruments such as stocks, futures contracts, and currencies, will prove to be a useful addition to the libraries of financial analysts, economists, statisticians, and other professionals wishing to keep abreast of developments in this field, as well as portfolio managers interested in exploring whether chaos theory can make a positive contribution to their investment operations.

I wish to give thanks for their generous encouragement in this endeavor to all my friends in the Department of Economics and the Graduate School of International Relations and Pacific Studies at the University of California, San Diego. My thanks also go to Carol Klein and Carol Barnstable of Irwin Professional Publishing, who managed the production of this book.

Robert R. Trippi

SOURCES AND ACKNOWLEDGMENTS

Chapter 1 "Nonlinear and Chaotic Dynamics: An Economist's Guide," by Michael D. Weiss. This article originally appeared in *Journal of Agricultural Economics Research*, Vol. 43, No. 3 (Summer 1991), pp. 2–17, and is in the public domain.

Chapter 2 "When Random Is Not Random: An Introduction to Chaos in Market Prices," by Robert Savit. This article originally appeared in *The Journal of Futures Markets*, Vol. 8, No. 3 (June 1988), pp. 271–289. Copyright © 1988 by John Wiley & Sons, Inc. Reprinted by permission of John Wiley & Sons, Inc.

Chapter 3 "Adaptive Learning and Roads to Chaos: The Case of the Cobweb," by Cars H. Hommes. This article originally appeared in *Economics Letters*, Vol. 36, No. 2 (1991), pp. 127–132. Reprinted by permission of Elsevier Science, S.A., Switzerland.

Chapter 4 "Chaos Models and Their Implications for Forecasting," by William J. Baumol and Richard E. Quandt. This article originally appeared in *Eastern Economic Journal*, Vol. 11 (1985), pp. 3–15. Reprinted with permission.

Chapter 5 "Structural Shifts and the Volatility of Chaotic Markets," by Sherrill Shaffer. This article originally appeared in *Journal of Economic Behavior and Organization*, Vol. 15, No. 2 (March 1991), pp. 201–214. Reprinted by permission of Elsevier Science, B. V., Amsterdam.

Chapter 6 "Testing for Nonlinear Dependence in Daily Stock Indices," by Thomas Willey. Reprinted by permission of Elsevier Science, Inc., from *Journal of Economics and Business*, Vol. 44, No. 1 (February 1992), pp. 63–76. Copyright 1992 by Temple University.

Chapter 7 "A Chaotic Attractor for the S&P 500," by Edgar E. Peters. Reprinted with permission from *Financial Analysts Journal*, Vol. 47, No. 2 (March/April 1991), pp. 55–62, 81. Copyright 1991, The Association for Investment Management and Research, Charlottesville, Virginia. All rights reserved.

Chapter 8 "Evidence of Chaos in the S&P 500 Cash Index," by Robert M. Eldridge, Christopher Bernhardt, and Irene Mulvey. This article originally appeared in *Advances in Futures and Options Research*, Vol. 6 (1993), pp. 179–192. Reprinted by permission of JAI Press, Inc.

Chapter 9 "Investor Preferences and the Correlation Dimension," by Steve Satchell and Allan Timmermann. Printed with permission of the authors.

Chapter 10 "Modeling Structured Nonlinear Knowledge to Predict Stock Market Returns," by Ypke Hiemstra. Printed with permission of the author.

Chapter 11 "Evidence of Chaos in Commodity Futures Prices," by Gregory P. DeCoster, Walter C. Labys, and Douglas W. Mitchell. This article originally appeared in *The Journal of Futures Markets*, Vol. 12, No. 3 (June 1991), pp. 291–305. Copyright © 1991 by John Wiley & Sons, Inc. Reprinted by permission of John Wiley & Sons, Inc.

Chapter 12 "Chaos" in Futures Markets? A Nonlinear Dynamical Analysis," by Steven C. Blank. This article originally appeared in *The Journal of Futures Markets*, Vol. 11, No. 6 (December 1991), pp. 711–728. Copyright © 1991 by John Wiley & Sons, Inc. Reprinted by permission of John Wiley & Sons, Inc.

Chapter 13 "Nonlinear Dynamics of Daily Futures Prices: Conditional Heteroskedasticity or Chaos?" by Seung-Ryong Yang and B. Wade Brorsen. This article originally appeared in *The Journal of Futures Markets*, Vol. 13, No. 2 (April 1993), pp. 175–191. Copyright © 1993 by John Wiley & Sons, Inc. Reprinted by permission of John Wiley & Sons, Inc.

Chapter 14 "Measuring the Strangeness of Gold and Silver Rates of Return," by Murray Frank and Thanasis Stengos. This article originally appeared in *Review of Economic Studies*, Vol. 56 (1989), pp. 553–567. Reprinted with permission.

Chapter 15 "A Low-Dimensional Attractor in the Foreign Exchange Markets?" by Dominique M. Guillaume. Printed with permission of the author.

Chapter 16 "Implications of Nonlinear Dynamics for Financial Risk Management," by David A. Hsieh. This article originally appeared in *Journal of Financial & Quantitative Analysis*, Vol. 28, No. 1 (March 1993), pp. 41–64. Reprinted with permission.

Chapter 17 "Chaotic Behavior in Exchange-Rate Series: First Results for the Peseta–United States Dollar Case," by Oscar Bajo-Rubio, Fernando Fernández-Rodríguez, and Simón Sosvilla-Rivero. This article originally appeared in *Economics Letters*, Vol. 39, No. 2 (June 1992), pp. 207–211. Reprinted by permission of Elsevier Science, S.A.

Chapter 18 "Nonlinearity in the Interest Rate Risk Premium," by Ted Jaditz and Chera L. Sayers. Printed with permission of the authors.

Chapter 19 "Using the Correlation Exponent to Decide Whether an Economic Series Is Chaotic," by T. Liu, Clive W. J. Granger, and Walter P. Heller. This article originally appeared in *Journal of Applied Econometrics*, Vol. 7 (December 1992), pp. S25–S39. Copyright © 1992 by John Wiley & Sons, Ltd. Reprinted by permission of John Wiley & Sons, Ltd.

Chapter 20 "A New Test for Chaos," by Claire G. Gilmore. This article originally appeared in *Journal of Economic Behavior and Organization*, Vol. 22, No. 2 (October 1993), pp. 209–237. Reprinted by permission of Elsevier Science, B. V., Amsterdam.

Chapter 21 "Measuring Complexity of Nonlinearity by a Relative Index with Application to Financial Time Series," by M. A. Kaboudan. Printed with permission of the author.

Chapter 22 "Nonlinearities and Chaotic Effects in Options Prices," by Robert Savit. This article originally appeared in *The Journal of Futures Markets*, Vol. 9, No. 6 (December 1989), pp. 507–518. Copyright © 1989 by John Wiley & Sons, Inc. Reprinted by permission of John Wiley & Sons, Inc.

Chapter 23 "Chaos, Taxes, Stabilization, and Turnover," by Sherrill Shaffer. Printed with permission of the author.

Chapter 24 "Neural Learning of Chaotic Time Series Invariants," by Gustavo Deco, Bernd Schuermann, and Robert R. Trippi. Printed with permission of the authors.

CONTRIBUTORS

Oscar Bajo-Rubio, UPNA, Pamplona, and Institute for Fiscal Studies, Madrid

William J. Baumol, Princeton University

Christopher Bernhardt, Fairfield University

Steven C. Blank, University of California, Davis

B. Wade Brorsen, Oklahoma State University

Gustavo Deco, Siemens AG

Gregory P. DeCoster, Bowdoin College

Robert M. Eldridge, Southern Connecticut State University

Fernando Fernández-Rodríguez, Universidad de las Palmas

Murray Frank, University of British Columbia

Claire G. Gilmore, St. Joseph's University

Clive W. J. Granger, University of California, San Diego

Dominique M. Guillaume, Catholic University of Leuven

Walter P. Heller, University of California, San Diego

Ypke Hiemstra, Vrije Universiteit Amsterdam

Cars H. Hommes, University of Amsterdam

David A. Hsieh, Duke University

Ted Jaditz, U.S. Department of Labor

M. A. Kaboudan, Pennsylvania State University

Walter C. Labys, West Virginia University

T. Liu, Ball State University

Douglas W. Mitchell, West Virginia University
Irene Mulvey, Fairfield University
Edgar E. Peters, PanAgora Asset Management Ltd.
Richard E. Quandt, Princeton University
Steve Satchell, University of Cambridge
Robert Savit, University of Michigan
Chera L. Sayers, University of Houston and Marymount University
Bernd Schuermann, Siemens AG
Sherrill Shaffer, Federal Reserve Bank of Philadelphia
Simón Sosvilla-Rivero, FEDEA and Universidad Complutense de
    Madrid
Thanasis Stengos, University of Guelph
Allan Timmermann, University of California, San Diego
Robert R. Trippi, University of California, San Diego
Michael D. Weiss, U.S. Department of Agriculture
Thomas Willey, Central Missouri State University
Seung-Ryong Yang, Korean Rural Economic Institute

PART I

FOUNDATIONS

Nonlinear and Chaotic Dynamics: An Economist's Guide

By Michael D. Weiss

In the past two decades, the world of science has come to a fundamentally new understanding of the dynamics of phenomena that vary over time. Grounded in mathematical discovery, yet given empirical substance by evidence from a variety of disciplines, this new perspective has led to nothing less than a reexamination of the concept of the predictability of dynamic behavior. Our implicit confidence in the orderliness of dynamical systems, specifically of *nonlinear* dynamical systems, has not, it turns out, been entirely justified. Such systems are capable of behaving in ways that are far more erratic and unpredictable than once believed. Fittingly, the new ideas are said to concern *chaotic dynamics*, or, simply, *chaos*.

Economics is not immune from the implications of this new understanding. After all, our subject is replete with dynamic phenomena ranging from cattle cycles to stock market catastrophes to the back-and-forth interplay of advertising and product sales. Ideas related to the notion of chaotic behavior are now part of the basic mathematical toolkit needed for insightful dynamical modeling. Agricultural economists need to gain an understanding of these ideas just as they would any other significant mathematical contribution to their field. This chapter is intended to assist in this educational process.

What exactly has chaos theory revealed? To address this question, let us consider an economy, subject to change over time, whose state at time t can be described by a vector, v_t, of (say) 14 numbers (money supply at time t, inflation rate at time t, and so on). Formally, this vector is a point in the 14-dimensional state space $\mathbf{R}^{14}$ (where $\mathbf{R}$ is the real number line). Suppose that the economy evolves deterministically in such a way that its state at any time uniquely determines its state at all later times. Then, if the initial position of the economy in $\mathbf{R}^{14}$ at time 0 is v_0, the evolution of the economy through time will be represented by a path in $\mathbf{R}^{14}$ starting at v_0 and traced out by v_t as time, t, moves forward. This path, called the *orbit* generated by the initial position v_0, represents a "future history" of the system. Questions about the behavior of the economy over time are really questions about its orbits. We are often interested not so much in the near-term behavior of orbits as in their eventual behavior, as when we engage in long-range forecasting or study an economy's response to a new government policy or an unexpected shock after the initial period of adjustment has passed and the economy has settled down.

Fractals, Sensitive Dependence, and Chaos

Scientists long have known that it is possible for a system's state space to contain an isolated, unstable point p such that different initial points near p can generate orbits with widely varying long-run behavior. (For example, a marble balanced on the tip of a cone is unstable in this sense.) What was unexpected, however, was the discovery that this type of instability can occur *throughout* the state space, sometimes actually at every point, but often in strangely patterned, fragmented subsets of the state space—subsets typically of noninteger dimension, called *fractals*. Once investigators knew what to look for, they found this phenomenon, termed *sensitive dependence on initial conditions*, to be widespread among nonlinear dynamical systems, even among the simplest ones. Though technical definitions vary, systems exhibiting this unstable behavior have generally come to be called "chaotic."

For chaotic systems, any error in specifying an initial point, even the most minute error (due to, say, computer rounding in the thousandth decimal place), can give rise to an orbit whose long-run behavior bears no resemblance to that of the orbit of the intended initial point. Since, in the real world, we can never specify a point with mathematically perfect precision, it follows that practical long-run prediction of the state of a chaotic system is impossible.

Attractors

For a dynamical system, perhaps the most basic question is "Where does the system go, and what does it do when it gets there?" In the earlier view of dynamical systems, the place where the system went, the point set in the state space to which orbits converged (called an *attractor*), was usually assumed to be a geometrically uncomplicated object such as a closed curve or a single point. Economic modelers, for example, have often implicitly assumed that a dynamic economic process will ultimately achieve either an equilibrium, a cyclic pattern, or some other orderly behavior. However, another discovery of chaos theory has been that the attractor of a nonlinear system can be a bizarre, fractal set within which the system's state can flit endlessly in a chaotic, seemingly random manner.

Just as an economy can have two or more equilibria, a dynamical system can have two or more attractors. In such a case, the set of all initial points whose orbits converge to a particular attractor is called a *basin of attraction*. A recent finding has been that the *boundary* between competing basins of attraction can be a fractal even when the attractors themselves are unexceptional sets. A type of sensitivity to the initial condition can operate here too: the slightest movement away from an initial point lying in one basin of attraction may move the system to a new basin of attraction and thus cause it to evolve toward a new attractor.

Chaotic behavior within a working model would be easier to recognize if all orbits initiating near an erratic orbit were also erratic. However, the potentially fractal structure of the region of sensitive dependence can allow initial points whose orbits behave "sensibly" and initial points whose orbits are erratic to coexist inseparably in the state space like two intermingled clouds of dust. Thus, simulation of a model at a few trial points cannot rule out the possibility of chaotic dynamics. Rather, we need a deeper understanding of the mathematical properties of our models. Nor can chaotic dynamics be dismissed as arising only in a few quirky special cases. As we shall see, it arises even when the system's law of motion is a simple quadratic.

The Discovery of Chaos

Recent years have witnessed an explosion of interest and activity in the area of chaotic dynamics. What accounts for this new visibility, which extends even beyond the research community into the public media? To provide an answer, we briefly trace the historical development of the subject.

The first recognition of chaotic dynamics is attributed to Henri Poincaré, a French mathematician whose work on celestial mechanics around the turn of the century helped found the study of dynamical systems, systems in which some structure (perhaps a solar system, perhaps—as now understood—an economy) changes over time according to predetermined rules. Poincaré foresaw the potential for unpredictability in dynamical systems whose equations of motion were nonlinear. However, neither the mathematical theory nor the imaging techniques available at the time permitted him to explore his intuitions fully.

Following Poincaré's work and that of the American mathematician G. D. Birkhoff in the early part of this century, and despite continuing interest in the Soviet Union, the subject of dynamical systems fell into relative obscurity. During this period, there was some awareness among mathematicians, scientists, and engineers that nonlinear systems were capable of erratic behavior. However, examples of such behavior were ignored, classified as "noise," or dismissed as aberrations. The idea that these phenomena were characteristic of nonlinear dynamical systems and that it was the well-behaved, textbook examples that were the special cases had not yet taken root.

Then, in the 1960s and 1970s, there was a flurry of activity in dynamical systems by both mathematicians and scientists working entirely independently. Mathematician Stephen Smale turned his attention to the subject and used the techniques of modern differential topology to create rigorous theoretical models of chaotic dynamics. Meteorologist Edward Lorenz discovered that a simple system of equations he had devised to simulate the earth's weather on a primitive computer displayed a surprising type of sensitivity: the slightest change in the initial conditions eventually would lead to weather patterns bearing no resemblance to those generated in the original run.

Biologist Robert May used the logistic difference equation $x_{n+1} = rx_n(1-x_n)$ to model population level, x, over successive time periods. He observed that for some choices of the growth rate parameter, r, the population level would converge, for other choices it would cycle among a few values, and for still others it would fluctuate seemingly randomly, never achieving either a steady state or any discernible repeating pattern. When he attempted to graph the population level against the growth rate parameter, he observed a strangely patterned, fragmented set of points.

Physicist Mitchell Feigenbaum investigated the behavior of dynamical systems whose equations of motion arise from unimodal (hill-shaped) functions. He noticed that certain parameter values that sent the system into repeating cycles always displayed the same numerically precise pattern: no matter which dynamical system was examined, the ratios of successive distances between these parameter values always converged to the same constant, 4.66920 ⋯. Feigenbaum had discovered a universal property of a class of nonlinear dynamical systems. His discovery ultimately clarified how systems can evolve toward chaos.

Thus, as these and other examples demonstrate, while mathematicians were developing the theory of nonlinear and chaotic dynamics, scientists in diverse disciplines were witnessing and discovering chaotic phenomena for themselves. Ultimately, researchers learned of one another's findings and recognized their common origin.

The role of the computer in the emergence of the contemporary understanding of dynamical systems is difficult to exaggerate. As we now realize, even the simplest systems can generate bewilderingly complicated behavior. The development of modern computer power and graphics seems to have been necessary before researchers could put the full picture of nonlinear and chaotic dynamics, quite literally, into focus.

The Mathematics of Chaos

We now explain some of the basic mathematical ideas involved in nonlinear dynamics and chaos. We also adopt a slightly different perspective. In the above discussion, we have implicitly portrayed dynamical systems as being in motion in continuous time. However, the equations of motion of such systems typically involve differential equations, and a proper treatment often requires advanced mathematical machinery. It is generally much easier to work with (and to understand) discrete-time systems, in which time takes only integer values representing successive time periods. Let us shift our attention to these systems.

When the law of motion of a discrete dynamical system is unchanging over time, the movement of the system through time can be understood as a process of iterating a function. To establish this point, consider a typical dynamic economic computer model, M, having k endogenous variables. To start the model running, one enters an initial condition vector, v_0, of k numbers. The model computes an output vector, $M(v_0)$, containing the new values of the k endogenous variables at the end of the first time period. The model then acts on $M(v_0)$ and computes a new output vector, $M(M(v_0))$, describing the economy at the end of the second time period. Successive output vectors are computed in the same manner. Note that the model itself, the law of motion, remains unchanged during this process. In effect, M acts as a function, mapping k-vectors to new k-vectors, applying itself iteratively to the last-computed function value. The state space of the economy is the k-dimensional space $\mathbf{R}^k$, and, for each initial condition vector v_0, there is a corresponding orbit, v_0, $M(v_0)$, $M(M(v_0))$, $M(M(M(v_0)))$, $\cdots$, describing the future evolution of the economy.

More generally, consider any function f. If f maps its domain (the set of all x for which $f(x)$ is defined) into itself, then, for each x_0 in the domain of f, the sequence x_0, $f(x_0)$, $f(f(x_0))$, $f(f(f(x_0)))$, $\cdots$ is well-defined and may be considered an orbit of a dynamical system determined by f through iteration.

Henceforth, for brevity, we denote by:

$$f^n,$$

the nth iterate of a function f. Thus, $f^1(x) = f(x)$, $f^2(x) = f(f(x))$, $f^3(x) = f(f(f(x)))$, and so on. By convention, $f^0(x) = x$. Of course, f^n is itself a function. It should not be confused with the nth *derivative* of f, which is customarily denoted:

$$f^{(n)}.$$

Orbit Diagrams

Fortunately for expository purposes, many of the important features of dynamical systems are present in one-dimensional systems. In fact, one of the important findings of chaos research has been that discrete dynamical systems generated by iteration of even the most elementary nonlinear scalar functions are capable of chaotic behavior. Thus, we shall concentrate on functions that operate on the number line.

For such functions, there is a particularly convenient technique for diagramming orbits. Consider a function f and an initial point x (see Figure 1-1). Beginning at the point (x, x) on the 45° line, draw a dotted line vertically to the graph of f; the point of intersection will be $(x, f(x))$. From that point, draw a dotted line horizontally to the 45° line; the point of intersection will be $(f(x), f(x))$. From there, draw a dotted line vertically to the graph of f; the point of intersection will be $(f(x), f^2(x))$. Continue this pattern of moving vertically to the graph of f and then horizontally to the 45° line. The resulting display, called an *orbit diagram*, shows the behavior of the orbit originating at x. In particular, the orbit may be visualized from the intersection points marked on the 45° line; the dotted lines indicate the direction of motion of the system. Of course, the points (x,x), $(f(x), f(x))$, $(f^2(x), f^2(x))$, ... only *look like* the orbit. They reside in the plane, whereas the actual orbit, consisting of the numbers x, $f(x)$, $f^2(x)$, ..., resides in the state space, that is, in the number line.

Figure 1-1

Construction of an Orbit Diagram

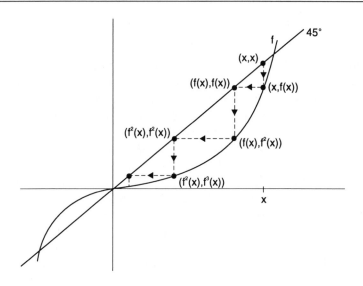

Dynamics of Linear Systems

Though the basic focus of this chapter is nonlinear dynamics, examination of linear systems provides essential intuition about nonlinear ones. Thus, we begin with an exhaustive treatment of the linear case.

Choose any numbers a, b, and consider the function g defined by $g(x) = ax + b$. To compute a typical orbit of g, observe that:

$$g^2(x) = a(ax + b) + b$$

$$= a^2x + b(1 + a),$$

$$g^3(x) = a\left[a^2x + b(1 + a)\right] + b$$

$$= a^3x + b(1 + a + a^2),$$

$$g^4(x) = a^4x + b(1 + a + a^2 + a^3),$$

and, in general, $g^n(x) = a^nx + b(1 + a + a^2 + a^3 + \cdots + a^{n-1})$. If $a = 1$, then

$$g^n(x) = x + bn.$$

However, if $a \neq 1$, the formula for the sum of a geometric series gives:

$$g^n(x) = a^n x + b\left[\frac{1-a^n}{1-a}\right]$$

$$= a^n\left[x - \frac{b}{1-a}\right] + \frac{b}{1-a}.$$

Note that when a is nonnegative, a^n remains nonnegative, while when a is negative, a^n alternates between negative and positive. In particular, when a = –1, a^n alternates between –1 and 1. When a ≠ ± 1, the distance between a^n and 0 either converges monotonically to 0 or diverges monotonically to ∞ as n → ∞ according to whether | a | < 1 or | a | > 1. Using these facts, we now analyze the behavior of all the orbits generated by g, according to the various possibilities for the structural parameters a and b and the initial point x. We shall find it convenient to organize our analysis around the possible value of a. We distinguish seven cases: (1) a < –1; (2) a = –1; (3) –1 < a < 0; (4) a = 0; (5) 0 < a < 1; (6) a = 1; and (7) a > 1. Within each of these cases, we consider all possible values of the remaining structural parameter b and the initial point x, and we determine the long-run behavior of the orbit originating at x when g has structural parameters a and b.

Let us first dispense with the case a = 1. In this case, if b = 0, then every x is a fixed point of g (that is, g(x) = x), and (since then, also $g^n(x) = x$) the system always remains at any initial point. In contrast, if b ≠ 0, then no x is a fixed point of g; indeed, for any initial point x, $g^n(x)$ diverges monotonically as n → ∞ to either ∞ or – ∞ according to whether b > 0 or b < 0.

In discussing the six remaining cases, that is, the cases in which a ≠ 1, I take b to be an arbitrary number. In these cases, g has exactly one fixed point, b/(1–a), and any orbit originating there remains there. I next examine the behavior of orbits originating at points other than b/(1–a). For this purpose, I assume that the initial point x is an arbitrary number distinct from b/(1–a).

If a < –1, then $g^n(x)$ has no finite or infinite limit. Rather, it eventually alternates between positive and negative numbers as its absolute value diverges monotonically to ∞.

If a = –1, the fixed point b/(1–a) equals b/2, and:

$$g^n(x) = (-1)^n (x-b/2) + b/2$$

$$= \begin{cases} b-x & \text{if n is odd} \\ x & \text{if n is even.} \end{cases}$$

Thus, $g^n(x)$ alternates endlessly between the (distinct) numbers b-x and x.

If $-1 < a < 0$, $g^n(x)$ converges to $b/(1-a)$ while alternating above and below it.

If $a = 0$, then, for all n, $g^n(x) = b$. Thus, the system moves from the initial point directly to b and remains there.

If $0 < a < 1$, $g^n(x)$ converges monotonically to $b/(1-a)$. The convergence is from above if $x > b/(1-a)$ and from below if $x < b/(1-a)$.

Finally, if $a > 1$, then $g^n(x)$ diverges monotonically, to ∞ if $x > b/(1-a)$ and to $-\infty$ if $x < b/(1-a)$.

The possible behaviors of orbits in the one-dimensional linear system are illustrated in Figures 1-2(a) through 1-2(h). From these figures and the preceding discussion, two lessons emerge. First, the fixed point is often at the "center of the action": it is to or from this point that orbits typically converge or diverge. Second, the slope parameter, a, plays a pivotal role in determining orbit dynamics. These two principles hold as well for nonlinear systems.

Fixed Points and Periodic Points

It is not a coincidence that, in the linear system, convergent orbits always converge to a fixed point of the underlying function. In fact, this property holds in general. To establish it, suppose a continuous function f has a convergent orbit $x, f(x), f^2(x), ..., f^n(x), ...$ Let L be the limit. Then:

$$f(L) = f\left(\lim_{n \to \infty} f^n(x)\right)$$

$$= \lim_{n \to \infty} f^{n+1}(x)$$

$$= L,$$

so that L is a fixed point of f. Thus, in partial answer to our guiding question, "Where does the system go?" we can reply: if it converges to any finite limit, that limit must be a fixed point. Correspondingly, if an economy converges to an equilibrium, the equilibrium state must be a fixed point of the system function.

Closely related to fixed points are points whose orbits may leave but later return (see Figure 1-2(b)). A point x is called a *periodic point* of f *with period n* if $f^n(x) = x$. The smallest positive n for which the latter equation holds is called the *prime* period of x. It can be shown that any period of x is a multiple of the prime period.

Every fixed point of a function f is a periodic point of f of prime period 1. It is also true that every periodic point is a fixed point (though not of the

---

Figure 1-2(a)

Orbit Diagram for Linear Function (a < −1)

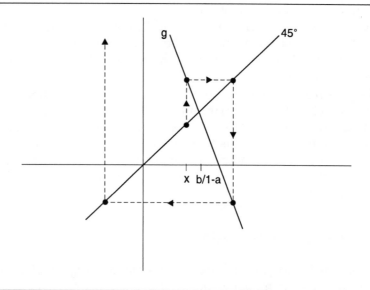

Figure 1-2(b)

Orbit Diagram for Linear Function (a = −1)

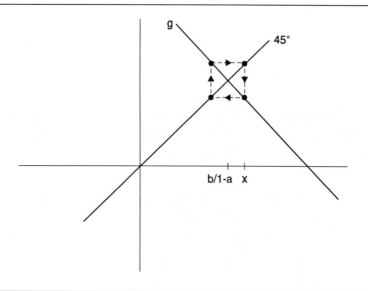

Figure 1-2(c)

Orbit Diagram for Linear Function (−1 < a < 0)

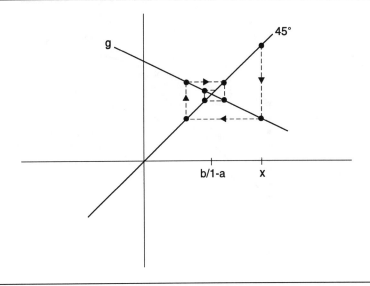

Figure 1-2(d)

Orbit Diagram for Linear Function (a = 0)

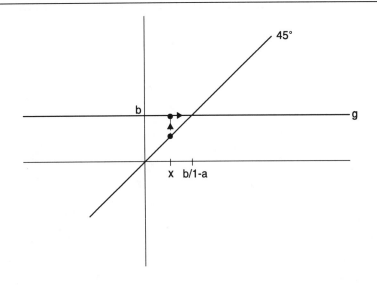

Figure 1-2(e)

Orbit Diagram for Linear Function (0 < a < 1)

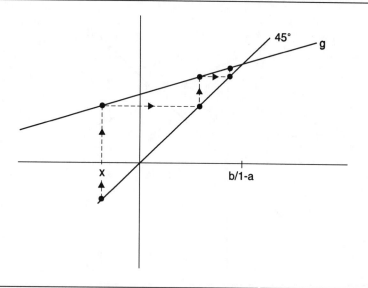

Figure 1-2(f)

Orbit Diagram for Linear Function (a = 1, b = 0)

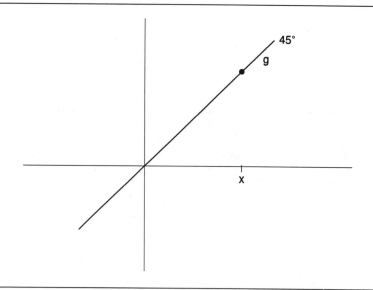

Figure 1-2(g)

Orbit Diagram for Linear Function (a = 1, b ≠ 0)

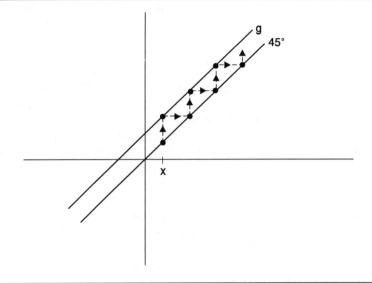

Figure 1-2(h)

Orbit Diagram for Linear Function (a > 1)

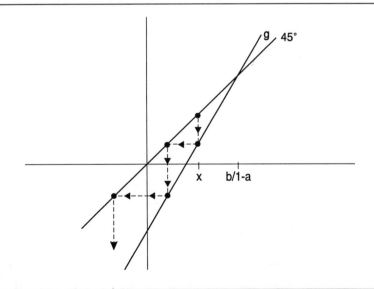

same function), since the periodicity condition $f^n(x) = x$ is nothing but the assertion that x is a fixed point of the function f^n. Thus, properties of fixed points have counterparts for periodic points, and vice versa.

If x is a periodic point of f having prime period n_0, then necessarily,

$$f^{n_0+1}(x) = f(f^{n_0}(x)) = f(x),$$

$$f^{n_0+2}(x) = f(f^{n_0+1}(x)) = f^2(x),$$

and so on. It follows that the orbit of x reduces to a finite set consisting of the distinct points x, $f(x)$, $f^2(x)$, ..., $f^{n_0-1}(x)$, through which the system endlessly cycles. (Such an orbit is called a *cycle of length* n_0.) As a consequence, whenever a system with a computationally tractable law of motion is initialized at a point known to have a small period, the system's entire future evolution can, as a practical matter, be calculated.

In recent decades, there have been some remarkable discoveries concerning when the existence of a cycle of one length implies the existence of cycles of other lengths. Li and Yorke (10) show that if f is any continuous function mapping an interval J into itself, and if some point in J is periodic for f with prime period 3, then, for every positive integer n, there is a periodic point in J having prime period n.[1] In brief: if there is a cycle of length 3, there must be cycles of all lengths.

The Li-Yorke Theorem is actually only a part of a more general result of Sarkovskii [see (6)] that may be described as follows. List the entire set of positive integers in the following manner:

$$3,5,7,...,$$

$$2\cdot3,\ 2\cdot5,\ 2\cdot7,\ ...,$$

$$2^2\cdot3,\ 2^2\cdot5,\ 2^2\cdot7,\ ...,$$

$$2^3\cdot3,\ 2^3\cdot5,\ 2^3\cdot7,\ ...,$$

$$\cdot$$
$$\cdot$$
$$\cdot$$

$$2^n\cdot3,\ 2^n\cdot5,\ 2^n\cdot7,\ ...,$$

$$\cdot$$
$$\cdot$$
$$\cdot$$

$$...\ 2^3, 2^2, 2, 1.$$

This list is called the "Sarkovskii ordering" of the positive integers. Observe that the odd integers exceeding 1 are listed first, followed by the various positive powers of 2 times the odd integers exceeding 1, followed finally by the pure powers of 2 in reverse order. Now, suppose f is a continuous function mapping the number line into itself. Then, Sarkovskii's Theorem states that, if f has a periodic point of prime period k and k' is any integer appearing later in the list than k, then f also has a periodic point of prime period k'. One consequence of this result is that if f has any cycle whose length is not a pure power of 2, then f must have cycles of infinitely many different lengths. Thus, for example, if an annual iterative economic model with one endogenous variable exhibits a business cycle of length five years, then (for other initial points) the model must be capable of generating business cycles of infinitely many other lengths. While Sarkovskii's Theorem pertains only to functions of one variable and thus would be directly applicable to, at most, a limited class of dynamic economic models, it does serve to illustrate the thesis that nonlinear dynamical systems are liable to impose unobvious but empirically relevant mathematical restrictions on economic behavior.

Hyperbolic Points

Examination of the linear system reveals that, whenever $|a| < 1$, all orbits converge to the fixed point $b/(1-a)$. However, it is clear from Figures 1-2(c), 1-2(d), and 1-2(e) that, if a curve (that is, a nonlinearity) was introduced into the graph of the function g at some distance from $b/(1-a)$, any orbit originating near enough to $b/(1-a)$ would still converge to $b/(1-a)$. Such local convergence does not depend on the slope of the graph of the function far away from the fixed point; what matters is only the slope, that is, the derivative, in a neighborhood of the fixed point. In fact, less obviously, but as we shall see momentarily, it is really only the derivative at the fixed point itself that matters.

Similarly, all orbits in the linear system originating elsewhere than $b/(1-a)$ move away from $b/(1-a)$ whenever $|a| > 1$. If a nonlinearity was introduced into the graph of g at a distance from $b/(1-a)$, any orbit originating sufficiently close to (but not precisely at) $b/(1-a)$ would still move away from $b/(1-a)$, at least initially (the possibility of an eventual return is another issue). Again, for such local "aversion" to $b/(1-a)$, it turns out that only the derivative at $b/(1-a)$ itself matters.

These observations lead to the following definitions. A fixed point p of a function f is called *hyperbolic* if $|f'(p)| \neq 1$. When $|f'(p)| < 1$, p is called *attracting*, while when $|f'(p)| > 1$, p is called *repelling*. These adjectives are justified by the following two propositions, which are readily established: (1) If p is an attracting hyperbolic fixed point, there is an interval containing p such that any orbit originating therein converges to p. (2) If p is a repelling hyperbolic fixed point, there is an interval containing p such that any orbit originating therein (but not at p itself) eventually leaves the interval (at least temporarily). For the function shown in Figure 1-1, 0 is attracting hyperbolic while the other two fixed points are repelling hyperbolic.

In the literature, a periodic point x of f of prime period n is defined as hyperbolic if $|(f^n)'(x)| \neq 1$. The meaning of this definition becomes transparent once it is recalled that x is a fixed point of f^n.

In higher dimensional systems, the notion of the derivative at a point is expressed in terms of a Jacobian matrix, and a periodic point is defined as hyperbolic if none of the eigenvalues of this matrix has complex modulus one (that is, if none lies on the unit circle in the complex plane).

When a fixed point p is hyperbolic attracting, the system can be considered stable at p with respect to changes in initial conditions. If the system is initialized at p, it will, of course, remain there. More important, though, the system will converge to p even if it is not initialized there, as long as it is initialized sufficiently near p.

In the same vein, a hyperbolic repelling fixed point p can be considered a point of instability of the system with respect to changes in initial conditions. While the system will remain at p if initialized precisely there, it will move away from p whenever it is initialized sufficiently close to, but not at, p.

Structural Stability

The stability property enjoyed by an attracting hyperbolic point concerns the effect of a slight change in the initial condition; the underlying model, however, remains fixed. We now discuss another notion of stability, structural stability, which concerns the effect of a slight change in the model itself.

In essence, a model is structurally stable if small changes in the model's structure leave dynamical behavior qualitatively unchanged. To understand why this property is important for empirical work, suppose that, from a collection of economic models sharing the same functional form and differing only in their values of some structural parameter vector w, we were to attempt to select the model M_{w_0} that truly described reality. Suppose further, though, that there existed parameter vectors w arbitrarily close to w_0 whose corresponding models M_w had dynamical behavior differing from that of M_{w_0}. Then, as a practical matter, we could never confidently determine the true economic dynamics of the situation, for even the slightest error in econometrically estimating w_0 (such as due to computer rounding) would leave us vulnerable to having arrived at a dynamically inequivalent M_w. What we would prefer is for our parameterized collection of models to satisfy the condition that, whenever w is sufficiently close to w_0, M_w must be dynamically equivalent to M_{w_0}. This property, structural stability, is probably implicitly assumed by most economists engaged in computer modeling of dynamic economic systems. However, as we shall soon see, even the simplest nonlinear systems can be structurally unstable. Thus, structural stability cannot be taken for granted.

To make these ideas more concrete, let us consider the meaning of structural stability for discrete one-dimensional dynamical systems. We first need to clarify what could be meant in this context by "a small change in the model's structure."

Since these systems are entirely determined by the function being iterated, it makes sense to interpret a small change in the system as meaning a small change in the underlying function. But, to change a function slightly really means to introduce a new function that is, in some sense, near the original. How, then, can we measure the "nearness" of two functions? In the theory of structural stability, the following method has proved effective. Suppose f and g are r-times differentiable functions defined on an interval J. Usually, one assumes also that $f^{(r)}$ and $g^{(r)}$ are continuous, so that f and g are r-times continuously differentiable and thus belong to the set C^r of all such functions.[2] Define the "C^r-distance" between f and g as

$$d_r(f,g) = \sup_x \max \{ |f(x){-}g(x)|, \ |f'(x) - g'(x)|,$$

$$..., \ |f^{(r)}(x){-}g^{(r)}(x)| \},$$

where the supremum[3] is taken over all x in J. (For each x in J, there is a corresponding maximum of absolute values as shown; the supremum is over this set of maxima.) Then, f and g are considered "C^r-close" when $d_r(f,g)$ is small, that is, when f is pointwise close to g and the first r derivatives of f are pointwise close to those of g. Figure 1-3 shows two functions that are C^0-close but not C^1-close.

Our next step in making precise the notion of structural stability is to clarify what is meant by the dynamical "equivalence" of two dynamical systems. Toward this end, suppose f and g are continuous functions mapping an interval J into itself. By a *homeomorphism*[4] of J we mean a

---

Figure 1-3

Functions C^0-close but Not C^1-close

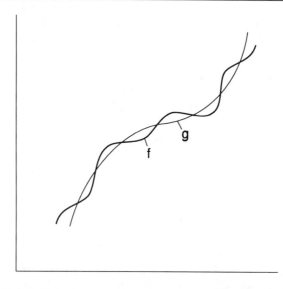

---

continuous invertible function mapping J onto itself. Thus, a homeomorphism of J is a one-to-one correspondence between J and itself such that nearby points are sent to nearby points. Since the inverse function of a homeomorphism of J is itself necessarily continuous, this "preservation of nearness" operates in both directions. As an example, the function h defined for all x in the interval $[-1,1]$ by $h(x) = x^3$ is a homeomorphism of this interval.

We say f and g are *topologically conjugate* if there exists a homeomorphism h of J such that, for each x in J,

$$h(f(x)) = g(h(x)).$$

What this condition expresses is that, whenever f sends a point x to f(x), g sends the point corresponding to x (namely h(x)) to the point corresponding to f(x) (namely h(f(x))). Thus, the behavior of g corresponds in a continuous one-to-one manner to the behavior of f.[5]

When two functions are topologically conjugate, each precisely replicates the dynamical properties of the other, and the dynamical systems they generate may be considered equivalent. To illustrate this point, suppose f and g are topologically conjugate by means of a homeomorphism h. Also, suppose f has an orbit originating at x and converging to p. Then:

$$h(p) = h\left(\lim_{n \to \infty} f^n(x) \right)$$

$$= \lim_{n \to \infty} h(f^n(x))$$

$$= \lim_{n \to \infty} h(f(f^{n-1}(x)))$$

$$= \lim_{n \to \infty} g(h(f^{n-1}(x)))$$

$$\cdot$$
$$\cdot$$
$$\cdot$$

$$= \lim_{n \to \infty} g^n(h(x)),$$

that is, the orbit of g originating at h(x) converges to h(p). Similarly, suppose y is a periodic point of f of period m. Then:

$$g^m(h(y)) = g^{m-1}(g(h(y)))$$

$$= g^{m-1}(h(f(y)))$$

$$\cdot$$
$$\cdot$$
$$\cdot$$

$$= h(f^m(y))$$

$$= h(y),$$

so that h(y) is a periodic point of g of period m.

A precise definition of structural stability is now within reach. Let f be an r-times continuously differentiable function mapping an interval J into itself. Then, f is called C^r–*structurally stable* if there exists an $\varepsilon > 0$ such that any r-times continuously differentiable function g that maps J into itself and satisfies $d_r(f,g) < \varepsilon$ is topologically conjugate to f.

While verifying structural stability can be difficult, examples of structural *in*stability are not hard to find. Define f by:

$$f(x) = x - x^2,$$

and, for each $\varepsilon > 0$, define g_ε by:

$$g_\varepsilon(x) = x - x^2 + \varepsilon/2.$$

Note that, for each r, the functions f and g_ε are r-times continuously differentiable and map the number line (here playing the role of the interval J) into itself. A simple computation shows that, for every r and ε, $d_r(f,g_\varepsilon) < \varepsilon$. However, examination of the equations $x - x^2 = x$ and $x - x^2 + \varepsilon/2 = x$ immediately establishes that f has only one fixed point while each g_ε has two. Thus, for no $\varepsilon > 0$ can g_ε be topologically conjugate to f. It follows that f cannot be C^r-structurally stable.

If there is a moral for agricultural economists in this discussion, it would seem to be that greater emphasis should be placed on confirming the structural stability of a dynamic model prior to its econometric estimation. In the absence of structural stability, estimation of a model would only single out one of a number of dynamically inequivalent approximations. It would therefore serve no clear purpose.

An Example of Chaotic Dynamics

To gain a qualitative understanding of what is involved in chaotic dynamics, we now examine in detail the class of functions F_μ ($\mu > 1$) defined by:

$$F_\mu(x) = \mu x(1-x).$$

Using functions from this class as the law of motion of a discrete dynamical system, I shall investigate the long-run behavior of all orbits, following the notation and approach of (6).

First, some basic facts (see Figure 1-4). Let $p_\mu = (\mu-1)/\mu$. Then, $0 < p_\mu < 1$, and p_μ is a fixed point of F_μ. Another fixed point is 0. Since $F_\mu(1) = 0$, the orbit originating at 1 goes immediately to 0 and remains there. Finally, it is easy to show that any orbit of F_μ originating at a point less than 0 (such as the point x_0 of Figure 1-4) or greater than 1 (such as the point x_1 of Figure 1-4) diverges to $-\infty$.

Next, suppose $1 < \mu < 3$. Since $F_\mu'(0) = \mu > 1$, 0 is hyperbolic repelling. On the other hand, since $F_\mu'(p_\mu) = 2-\mu$ and $-1 < 2-\mu < 1$, p_μ is hyperbolic attracting. One can show that the basin of attraction of p_μ is precisely the open interval $(0,1)$; any orbit originating in this interval (such as at the point x_2 of Figure 1-4) converges to p_μ. We have thus determined the long-run behavior of all orbits of F_μ for all values of μ in the range $1 < \mu < 3$, and we have found nothing unusual in the dynamics arising in this parameter range.

Figure 1-4

Orbits of F_μ

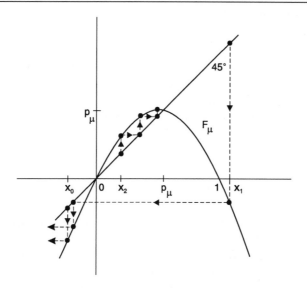

However, as μ increases beyond 3, F_μ undergoes various qualitative changes. Among these is a change that occurs as μ passes 4: the maximum value of F_μ (namely $F_\mu(1/2)$, which equals $\mu/4$) increases beyond 1, and some points in $[0,1]$ are thus mapped outside of $[0,1]$ by F_μ. For any such point x, we have $F_\mu(x) > 1$, and it follows from a previous remark that the orbit of $F_\mu(x)$,

$$F_\mu(x),\ F_\mu(F_\mu(x)),\ F_\mu^2(F_\mu(x)),\ ...,\ F_\mu^n(F_\mu(x)),\ ...,$$

that is,

$$F_\mu(x),\ F_\mu^2(x),\ F_\mu^3(x),\ ...,\ F_\mu^{n+1}(x),\ ...,$$

must diverge to $-\infty$. Hence, the orbit of x itself must diverge to $-\infty$. More generally, any orbit that originates in $[0,1]$ but does not remain in $[0,1]$ must diverge to $-\infty$.

Of particular interest is the parameter range $\mu > 2 + \sqrt{5}$. Although there are smaller values of μ for which chaotic dynamics appears, Devaney (6) has shown that, when $\mu > 2 + \sqrt{5}$, the demonstration of chaotic dynamics can be accomplished relatively simply. We assume, therefore, that $\mu > 2 +$

$\sqrt{5}$, and will eventually find that on the set of initial points in [0,1] whose orbits never leave [0,1], F_μ behaves chaotically.

Let Λ be this set. That is, let Λ be the set of all x in [0,1] for which each term of the orbit of x,

$$x, F_\mu(x), F_\mu^2(x), ..., F_\mu^n(x), ...,$$

is in [0,1]. The first task is determining the structure of Λ, which will be done by ascertaining the structure of the *complement* of Λ, the set of those points of [0,1] that are *not* in Λ.

For each n = 0, 1, 2, 3, ..., let A_n be the set of all x in [0,1] whose first n + 1 orbit terms,

$$x, ..., F_\mu^n(x),$$

are in [0,1] but whose next orbit term, $F_\mu^{n+1}(x)$, is not. Observe that Λ consists precisely of those points of [0,1] that lie in none of the A_n's. Moreover, the A_n's are pairwise disjoint. Thus, one can imagine constructing Λ through the following recursive process: from the interval [0,1], first remove the subset A_0; next, from what remains, remove A_1, and so on. In general, when $A_0, A_1, ..., A_n$ have been removed from [0,1], A_{n+1} must still (by disjointness) lie intact in the remaining subset of [0,1]. Remove A_n and continue this process *ad infinitum*. When all of the A_n's have been removed from [0,1], the subset of [0,1] that remains will be precisely Λ.

To picture what this process actually looks like, we rely on the fact that a point x lies in A_{n+1} if and only if $F_\mu(x)$ lies in A_n. (This property follows from the definition of the A_n's. In mathematical parlance, A_{n+1} is the pre-image of A_n relative to the function F_μ.) Now, A_0 is clearly an open interval of length less than 1 centered at 1/2. Thus, removing A_0 from [0,1] leaves two disjoint closed intervals, B_0^1 and B_0^2 (see Figure 1-5). To construct A_1, visualize a copy of A_0 on the y-axis by reflecting A_0 around the 45° line (see Figure 1-6). Then, determine from the graph of F_μ what points on the x-axis are mapped by F_μ into A_0. The set of all such points will be A_1 (see Figure 1-7). Note that, since the graph of F_μ rises continuously from 0 beyond 1 and then (farther to the right) descends continuously from beyond 1 back down to 0, A_1 consists of two disjoint open intervals, each lying inside of (and at a positive distance from the endpoints of) one of the closed intervals B_0^1, B_0^2. Thus, removing both A_0 and A_1 from [0,1] leaves behind *four* disjoint closed intervals.

A_2 is constructed similarly. Visualize a copy of A_1 on the y-axis and determine the set of all points on the x-axis that are mapped by F_μ into A_1; that set will be A_2, and it will consist of four disjoint open intervals, each

Figure 1-5

Removing the Interval A_0 from [0,1]

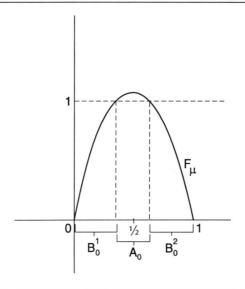

Figure 1-6

Copying the Interval A_0 onto the y-axis

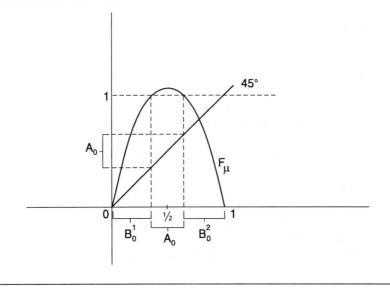

Figure 1-7

Constructing the Set A_1

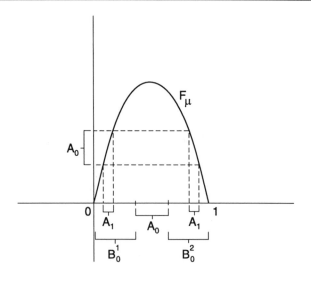

lying inside of (and at a positive distance from the endpoints of) one of the four closed intervals left behind after the removals of A_0 and A_1 from [0,1].

This process can be continued. In general, A_n will consist of 2^n disjoint open intervals, each lying inside of, and at a positive distance from the endpoints of, one of the 2^n closed intervals left behind after the removals of $A_0, ..., A_{n-1}$.

Thus, in brief, Λ is constructed by removing an open interval from the middle of the closed interval [0,1], then removing open intervals from the middles of the remaining closed intervals, and so on, *ad infinitum*. This construction bears a striking resemblance to the construction of a classic mathematical object called the *Cantor set*, a set defined by removing from [0,1] the open "middle third" interval $(1/3, 2/3)$, then removing the open middle third intervals $(1/9, 2/9)$, $(7/9, 8/9)$ from the two closed intervals remaining, and so on *ad infinitum*, always removing the open middle third interval of each closed interval remaining after the previous removals. The Cantor set has long been celebrated in mathematics for satisfying the following two conditions: (1) Its "length" is 0. (Indeed, by the formula for the sum of a geometric series, the total length of the disjoint intervals removed from [0,1] in constructing the Cantor set is:

$$1 \cdot (1/3) + 2 \cdot (1/9) + 4 \cdot (1/27) + \cdots = \sum_{n=1}^{\infty} 2^{n-1}/3^n$$

$$= (1/2)\sum_{n=1}^{\infty} (2/3)^n$$

$$= 1.$$

Modified forms of the Cantor set having positive length can be constructed by removing shorter intervals.) Yet, (2) the Cantor set contains as many points as all of [0,1]. (Specifically, it can be shown that there exists a one-to-one correspondence between the Cantor set and [0,1]. Since the elements of both sets can thus be paired off, the total number of points in each set must be the same. The fact that this number happens to be infinite should not be held against it. Infinite sets have sizes too.)

Λ is known to share property (2) with the Cantor set. However, it also shares two further properties having more direct empirical implications: first, Λ is *perfect*, whose significance here is that, as near as desired to any point of Λ, one can always find another point of Λ. That is, no point of Λ is isolated. Second, Λ is *totally disconnected* (it contains no open intervals),[6] from which it follows that, as near as desired to any point of Λ, one can always find a point of [0,1] that is *not* in Λ. As a consequence, whenever the dynamical system generated by F_μ is initialized on Λ, its long-run behavior is "infinitely sensitive" to errors in the initial condition, since within any interval (no matter how small) around an intended starting point in Λ, there exist both points in Λ (whose orbits, by definition, remain in [0,1]) and points not in Λ (whose orbits diverge to $-\infty$). Thus, if one attempted to study this dynamical system on a computer, inevitable rounding errors in determining the points of Λ would make accurate simulation over Λ impossible.

This sensitivity of orbits to the initial condition, while *suggestive* of true "sensitive dependence on initial conditions," must be carefully distinguished from it. The sensitivity just described compares orbits originating in Λ with orbits originating outside Λ. In contrast, true sensitive dependence refers to a kind of separating behavior between orbits originating nearby within the same set. A more formal definition will be provided later in this chapter.

Irregular sets such as Λ and the Cantor set have recently come to be referred to as "fractals" (from the Latin *fractus*, meaning "broken" and reflecting the disconnected character of such sets). Though the scientific community has not yet arrived at a consistent usage of this term, one often sees the following individual or joint criteria: exhibiting a high degree of jaggedness; self-similar (that is, defined by a recursive process in such a way that any part of the set, when magnified, looks the same as the entire set); and having noninteger dimension. (There are many ways to extend the usual concept of dimension (0 for a point, 1 for a curve, 2 for a surface, and so on) to more complicated sets. *Hausdorff* dimension (*13*), perhaps the most widely used, assigns to the Cantor set a dimension of ln 2/ln 3, or approximately 0.63. Some other notions of dimension suggested for application to fractal sets are *information* dimension, *correlation* dimension, and *Lyapunov* dimension. See (*17*).)

Until relatively recently, the Cantor-like sets now called fractals were considered exotic structures belonging solely to the world of pure mathematics. The discovery of their intimate connection with nonlinear dynamics has been striking. However, they are now understood to be a typical concomitant of nonlinear dynamical systems. (See, for example, (*9, 12, 17*) and the references contained therein.) They have been detected in the form of attractors (a fractal attractor is called a *strange* attractor) and in the form of the boundary between competing basins of attraction. (Consider an economic model that allows different initial conditions to generate different equilibria. Here, the boundary between basins of attraction corresponding to distinct equilibria may be a fractal exhibiting a type of sensitivity to the initial condition noted earlier: the slightest movement away from an initial point lying in one basin of attraction may move the system to a new basin of attraction and thus cause it to evolve toward a new attractor. The equilibrium generated by an initial condition lying on this boundary would be unpredictable.) In addition, fractals can appear in the form of the state space region on which chaotic behavior is manifested (see the next section).

Symbolic Dynamics

Having determined the structure of the set Λ of all points whose F_μ-orbits remain in [0,1], I now demonstrate the chaotic behavior of F_μ on this set.

It turns out that if one attempts to analyze the orbits of F_μ by direct computation the problem soon becomes prohibitively complex. Therefore, one constructs a *model* that abstracts from the phenomenon under study only its essential features. More specifically, I will construct a new dynamical system that is dynamically equivalent to the system determined by F_μ on Λ but far easier to analyze. This approach, used commonly in the theory of dynamical systems, is called the method of *symbolic dynamics*.

The state space of our model dynamical system will be the set Σ_2 of all sequences of 0's and 1's. We can represent a typical element of Σ_2 as an infinite vector,

$$(s_0, s_1, s_2, s_3, \ldots),$$

where s_i, either 0 or 1, is the ith term of the sequence. Note that we are starting our sequences with a "0th" term rather than a "1st" term. That is, our sequences are defined on the set of nonnegative integers rather than the set of positive integers. Later, this arrangement will enable us to associate the terms x, $F_\mu(x)$, $F_\mu^2(x)$, $F_\mu^3(x)$, ... of an orbit of F_μ with the terms $s_0, s_1, s_2, s_3, \ldots$ of a certain sequence in Σ_2.

An example of an element of Σ_2 is the vector:

$$(0, 1, 0, 1, 0, 1, \ldots),$$

(that is, $(s_0, s_1, s_2, s_3, \ldots)$, where $s_i = 0$ if i is even and $s_i = 1$ if i is odd). Again, *any* sequence of 0's and 1's is allowed as an element of Σ_2.

The system function in our model—the function whose dynamics on Σ_2 will parallel that of F_μ on Λ—will be the *shift operator*, σ, defined at any sequence $(s_0, s_1, s_2, s_3, \ldots)$ in Σ_2 by:

$$\sigma\left((s_0, s_1, s_2, s_3, \ldots)\right) = (s_1, s_2, s_3, s_4, \ldots).$$

Observe that σ maps a sequence to a new one whose ith term is the $(i+1)$st term of the original. (Note also that the initial term of the original sequence is ignored in forming the new one. Thus σ, like F_μ, is not invertible.) Symbolically, we may write:

$$(\sigma(s))_i = s_{i+1},$$

for any sequence s in Σ_2.

Next, we make precise the meaning of the dynamical equivalence of σ and F_μ. To do so, we generalize our earlier notion of dynamical equivalence, which relied on the concepts of homeomorphism and topological conjugacy. First, however, we must introduce a general definition of "continuous function."

Suppose f is a function mapping a set X into a set Y. Recall the intuitive meaning of continuity: as x approaches x', f(x) approaches f(x'). Suppose each of X and Y has been assigned some measure of the "distance" between its points. (Just as the sets X and Y can be quite different, these measures of distance can be quite different too.) Then, the intuitive meaning of continuity becomes: as the distance (in X) between x and x' approaches 0, the distance (in Y) between f(x) and f(x′) approaches 0. More formally, f is continuous at x′ if, for any ε > 0, there exists a δ > 0 such that, whenever the distance in X between x and x′ is less than δ, the distance in Y between f(x) and f(x′) is less than ε.

The set Λ comes equipped with a natural measure of distance: the absolute value of the difference between two points. As for Σ_2, we now define the distance between any of its sequences s and t to be:

$$d(s,t) = \sum_{i=0}^{\infty} \frac{|s_i - t_i|}{2^i}.$$

It is not difficult to prove that, with this distance measure, σ is continuous on Σ_2. We already know, of course, that F_μ is continuous on Λ.

We are now able to generalize our earlier notions of homeomorphism, topological conjugacy, and (thus) dynamical equivalence to apply to σ and F_μ. Suppose X and Y are any sets each of which has been assigned a distance measure. Then, by a *homeomorphism* between X and Y we mean an invertible function mapping X onto Y such that both the function and its inverse are continuous. Suppose f is a continuous function mapping X into itself and g is a continuous function mapping Y into itself. Then, we say f and g are *topologically conjugate* if there exists a homeomorphism h between X and Y such that, for each x in X,

$$h(f(x)) = g(h(x)).$$

As with our earlier definition, topologically conjugate functions map corresponding points to corresponding points, exhibit the same dynamical properties, and may be considered dynamically equivalent.

We now define a homeomorphism between Λ and Σ_2 by means of which F_μ and σ can be shown to be conjugate. Recall that, under our continuing assumption that $\mu > 2 + \sqrt{5}$, we earlier defined A_0 as the set of points in [0,1] whose F_μ-values lie outside [0,1], and we defined B_0^1 and B_0^2 as the disjoint closed intervals remaining when A_0 is removed from [0,1] (see Figure 1-5). To facilitate our defining a homeomorphism, we rename the intervals B_0^1 and B_0^2 as "I_0" and "I_1," respectively (see Figure 1-8).

We define a function, S, from Λ to Σ_2 as follows. Let x be an arbitrary point in Λ. By definition, the orbit of x never leaves [0,1]; thus, the orbit must remain within the sets I_0, I_1. We associate with x a sequence, S(x), of 0's and 1's whose ith term (i = 0, 1, 2, 3, ...) is defined by:

Figure 1-8

The Intervals I_0 and I_1

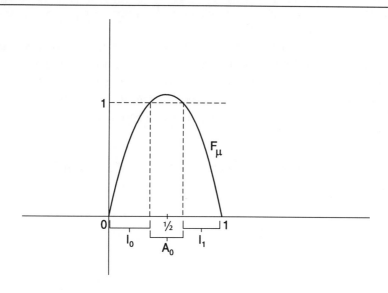

$$\left(S(x)\right)_i = \begin{cases} 0 & \text{if } F_\mu^i(x) \text{ lies in } I_0 \\ 1 & \text{if } F_\mu^i(x) \text{ lies in } I_1. \end{cases}$$

$S(x)$, called the *itinerary* of x, is obviously an element of Σ_2. Thus, S is a function mapping Λ to Σ_2. Rather amazingly, it turns out that S is, in fact, a homeomorphism between Λ and Σ_2. Moreover, by means of S, F_μ and σ can be shown to be topologically conjugate. The proofs of these facts go beyond the scope of this chapter [see (6)].

The conjugacy between F_μ and σ establishes their dynamical equivalence and permits information gleaned from σ to be applied to F_μ. To begin to exploit this feature, let us determine how many points of period n F_μ has. Now, by dynamical equivalence, σ must have exactly the same number of points of period n as F_μ. However, for a sequence s in Σ_2 to be of period n with respect to σ means that shifting s n times produces s again, that is, $s_{i+n} = s_i$ for each i. It follows that s must be a repeating sequence of the form:

$$(s_0, ..., s_{n-1}; s_0, ..., s_{n-1}; ...).$$

There are precisely 2^n ways of arranging 0's and 1's to form a finite string $s_0, ..., s_{n-1}$; hence, σ must have exactly 2^n periodic points of period n. The same holds, then, for F_μ. Using symbolic dynamics, we have thus established that, for example, F_μ has 64 periodic points of period 6, or 2^{117} periodic points of period 117.

A subset X' of a set X endowed with a distance measure is called *dense* in X if, for any point x in X, one can find some point from X' as close to x as desired. The set of all periodic points of σ is dense in Σ_2. In fact, given any sequence s in Σ_2 and any $\varepsilon > 0$ (no matter how small), choose n so that $1/2^n < \varepsilon$. Define a repeating, hence periodic, sequence s' in Σ_2 by:

$$s' = (s_0, ..., s_n; s_0, ..., s_n; ...).$$

(Note that s' merely repeats the first n + 1 terms of s.) From the definition of our distance measure $d(\cdot,\cdot)$ on Σ_2, it follows that:

$$d(s,s') = \sum_{i=0}^{n} 0 + \sum_{i=n+1}^{\infty} \frac{|s_i - s_i'|}{2^i}$$

$$\leq \sum_{i=n+1}^{\infty} 1/2^i$$

$$= 1/2^n$$

$$< \varepsilon.$$

Thus, the set of periodic points of σ is dense in Σ_2. Since dynamical equivalence is known to encompass denseness properties, we can conclude that the set of periodic points of F_μ is dense in Λ.

The preceding result tells us that cyclic orbits can be found originating arbitrarily near any point of Λ. We next show that erratic orbits can also be found originating arbitrarily near any point of Λ.

Define a sequence s^* in Σ_2 by concatenating all finite strings of 0's and 1's as follows. First list all strings of length 1 (there are only two of these, "0" and "1"), then list all strings of length 2 (there are four of these: "0,0", "0,1", "1,0", and "1,1"), then all strings of length 3, and so on. In general, after all of the 2^n strings of length n have been listed, continue with all strings of length n + 1 and beyond. Thus:

$$s^* = (0, 1; 0, 0, 0, 1, 1, 0, 1, 1; 0, 0, 0, 0, 0, 1, ...).$$

We shall show that the orbit of s^* with respect to σ is dense in Σ_2. In fact, given any sequence s in Σ_2 and any $\varepsilon > 0$, choose n so that $1/2^n < \varepsilon$, and observe that the string $s_0, ..., s_n$ consisting of the first $n + 1$ terms of s must appear somewhere in s^*. By the definition of σ, there must therefore exist a κ such that:

$$\sigma^\kappa(s^*) = (s_0, ..., s_n, ...),$$

that is, such that the first $n + 1$ terms of $\sigma^\kappa(s^*)$ and s agree. As before, the formula defining our distance measure then implies that:

$$d(\sigma^\kappa(s^*),s) \leq 1/2^n < \varepsilon.$$

It follows that the orbit of s^* is dense in Σ_2. By the dynamical equivalence between F_μ and σ, we can thus conclude that $S^{-1}(s^*)$, the point in Λ corresponding to s^* under the inverse of the itinerary homeomorphism S, has a dense F_μ–orbit in Λ. For brevity, put $x^* = S^{-1}(s^*)$.

The fact that the orbit of x^* is dense in Λ implies that, for any x in Λ and any $\varepsilon > 0$, there is an orbit point $F_\mu^m(x^*)$ lying in the interval $(x-\varepsilon,x+\varepsilon)$. However, a simple argument shows that the orbit of $F_\mu^m(x^*)$,

$$F_\mu^m(x^*), F_\mu^{m+1}(x^*), F_\mu^{m+2}(x^*), ...,$$

must also be dense in Λ. Thus, arbitrarily near any point of Λ there originates a dense orbit. Such an orbit would appear erratic and essentially random, for it would endlessly "dance" around Λ, visiting and revisiting the vicinity of each point of Λ infinitely many times.

Recent findings by both economists (4) and mathematicians (14) have shed additional light on this seemingly random character of chaotic orbits. There is now evidence that chaotic behavior is indeed often legitimately stochastic in the sense that chaotic orbits may be realizations of a stochastic process defined on the state space. In this situation, the long-run behavior of an economic variable may be described by an endogenously generated long-run probability distribution. Day and Shafer (4) proved the existence of such distributions in a standard dynamic macroeconomic model and calculated the distributions numerically. Their work suggests that, under some conditions, long-run point forecasting in a nonlinear economic model should be replaced by calculation of a long-run probability distribution over the entire state space (for further explanation, see (19)).

Finally, we define the hallmark of chaos—sensitive dependence on initial conditions—and verify that F_μ exhibits this property. Let X be any set endowed with a distance measure and f a function mapping X to itself. We say f exhibits *sensitive dependence on initial conditions* if there exists a $\delta > 0$ with the following property: for any x in X and any $\varepsilon > 0$, there is a point x′ in X within a distance of ε from x such that, for some n, the distance between $f^n(x)$ and $f^n(x')$ exceeds δ. Heuristically, sensitive dependence means that there is a constant $\delta > 0$ such that, arbitrarily close to any point of X, one can find another point of X whose orbit eventually diverges (even if only temporarily) from that of the given point by more than δ. (Lyapunov exponents are sometimes used as a pragmatic measure of this divergence (17).) Although this discrepancy in orbits is required only to exceed δ, not to be arbitrarily large in absolute terms, it should be noted that the *ratio* of this discrepancy to the distance between x and x' will become arbitrarily large when x' is chosen arbitrarily close to x. It is in this sense that sensitive dependence implies unpredictable long-run behavior for orbits originating arbitrarily near one another.

To show that F_μ exhibits sensitive dependence on initial conditions, let δ be any positive number less than the distance between the intervals I_0 and I_1, that is, less than the length of A_0 (see Figure 1-8). Choose any x in Λ and any $\varepsilon > 0$. Since, as noted earlier, no point of Λ is isolated, there must exist a point x' in Λ distinct from x whose distance from x is less than ε. However, since the itinerary mapping, S, is invertible, distinct points in Λ must have distinct itinerary sequences. Thus, for some n,

$$(S(x))_n \neq (S(x'))_n \, ,$$

that is, either $F_\mu^n(x)$ is in I_0 and $F_\mu^n(x')$ is in I_1 or vice versa. It follows at once that the distance between $F_\mu^n(x)$ and $F_\mu^n(x')$ exceeds δ , which proves the result.

While the examination of chaotic behavior over a fractal set such as Λ can reveal important aspects of the subject, chaos should not be viewed as a phenomenon that appears only on unusual sets. One can show, for example, that the function F_4 given by $F_4(x) = 4x(1-x)$ is chaotic on the entire interval [0,1]. Nor is the existence of chaos overly sensitive to functional form. The chaotic dynamics we have described for F_μ will also be exhibited by essentially any hill-shaped function with sufficiently large slope.

Conclusions

Recent findings in the field of nonlinear dynamical systems warrant a rethinking of traditional attitudes toward economic dynamics. It is now known that erratic long-run behavior and various forms of sensitivity to initial conditions can arise in even the simplest nonlinear models. Unless there are sound reasons in economic theory to believe that a given dynamic economic process is linear, the process must be viewed as at least potentially liable to the type of chaotic behavior described here.

Chaos theory suggests that the long-range prediction of nonlinear economic processes may be subject to the same basic mathematical limitations as long-range weather prediction. In both cases, future behavior may appear independent of the initial conditions that produced it.

It is difficult to study this subject without experiencing a certain humility concerning our ability to control nonlinear economic processes through policy intervention. Nonlinear systems can behave in a counterintuitive manner. The conditions under which we can properly use mathematical models to predict the long-run implications of policy actions need to be clarified.

The discoveries of recent years might seem to have revealed intrinsic mathematical limits to economic prediction. Yet, a deeper understanding of the limitations of long-run point prediction should ultimately enhance, not diminish, the accuracy and credibility of the information we provide. A further enhancement may derive from the replacement, in certain cases, of long-run point forecasts by forecasts based, in part, on endogenous long-run probability distributions.

We have attempted in this chapter to sketch some of the major themes of contemporary nonlinear dynamics. Many topics, however, had to be omitted. (For example, we have not discussed how the nonlinear dynamics literature might contribute to improvements in short-run forecasting models such as models of stock market behavior. An anonymous referee suggests that a small percentage reduction of short-run forecast errors may be possible. Such a reduction would be of particular interest to arbitrage traders.) Recommended further background reading would include (in order, 9, 6, 17, 12, 7, 15). For a sampling of the nascent economics literature on chaos, see (1, 2, 3, 4, 5, 8, 11, 16, 18).

Acknowledgments

The author thanks John McClelland and other participants in the ERS Chaos Theory Seminar for many stimulating discussions on chaotic dynamics. Carlos Arnade, Richard Heifner, and an anonymous referee furnished helpful review comments.

Notes

1   Italicized numbers in parentheses cite sources listed in the References section at the end of this chapter.

2   By convention, when r = 0, $f^{(r)}$ = f; that is, the 0th derivative of a function
is the function itself. Since C^0 is defined as the set of all functions with
continuous 0th derivative, C^0 is simply the set of all continuous functions.

3   The supremum of a set of numbers, denoted "sup," is the smallest
upper bound of the set. Thus, for example, the supremum of the open
interval (0,1) is 1. Supremum plays the role of maximum for sets that
may not have a largest element. The supremum of a set with no finite
upper bound is ∞.

4   From the Greek *homeo-* (similar) + *morphism* (form).

5   Topology is the study of those properties a mathematical object retains
when it is continuously transformed. The term "conjugate" originates
in the Latin *com-* (together) + *jugum* (yoke) and literally means "joined
or yoked together." Here, it is f and g that are "yoked together" by h.

6   This property should seem at least plausible in view of the method of
construction of Λ. It is in proving this property that the assumption that
$\mu > 2 + \sqrt{5}$ is first put to use. See (6). Interestingly, the property implies
that every point of Λ is on the boundary of Λ.

References

1. Benhabib, Jess, and Richard H. Day. "A Characterization of Erratic
Dynamics in the Overlapping Generations Model," *Journal of Economic
Dynamics and Control.* Vol. 4, 1982, pp. 37–55.

2. Brock, W. A., and A. G. Malliaris. *Differential Equations, Stability and
Chaos in Dynamic Economics.* Amsterdam: Elsevier Science Publishers
B.V., 1989.

3. Brock, W. A., and C. L. Sayers. "Is the Business Cycle Characterized by
Deterministic Chaos?" *Journal of Monetary Economics.* Vol. 22, 1988, pp.
71–90.

4. Day, Richard H., and Wayne Shafer. "Ergodic Fluctuations in Deterministic Economic Models," *Journal of Economic Behavior and Organization.*
Vol. 8, 1987, pp. 339–61.

5. Dendrinos, Dimitrios S., and Michael Sonis. *Chaos and Socio-Spatial
Dynamics.* New York: Springer-Verlag, 1990.

6. Devaney, Robert L. *An Introduction to Chaotic Dynamical Systems.* New
York: Addison-Wesley Publishing Co., 1987.

7. Edgar, Gerald A. *Measure, Topology, and Fractal Geometry.* New York: Springer-Verlag, 1990.

8. Frank, Murray, and Thanasis Stengos. "Chaotic Dynamics in Economic Time-Series," *Journal of Economic Surveys.* Vol. 2, No. 2, 1988, pp. 103–33.

9. Gleick, James. *Chaos.* New York: Penguin Books, 1987.

10. Li, Tien-Yien, and James A. Yorke. "Period Three Implies Chaos," *American Mathematical Monthly.* Vol. 82, Dec. 1975, pp. 985–92.

11. Mirowski, Philip. "From Mandelbrot to Chaos in Economic Theory," *Southern Economic Journal.* Vol. 57, No. 2, Oct. 1990, pp. 289–307.

12. Moon, Francis C. *Chaotic Vibrations.* New York: John Wiley and Sons, 1987.

13. Morgan, Frank. *Geometric Measure Theory.* San Diego: Academic Press, 1988.

14. Ornstein, D. S., and B. Weiss. "Statistical Properties of Chaotic Systems," *Bulletin of the American Mathematical Society.* Vol. 24, No. 1, Jan. 1991, pp. 11–116.

15. Parker, Thomas S., and Leon O. Chua. *Practical Numerical Algorithms for Chaotic Systems.* New York: Springer-Verlag, 1989.

16. Ramsey, James B., Chera L. Sayers, and Philip Rothman. "The Statistical Properties of Dimension Calculations Using Small Data Sets: Some Economic Applications," *International Economic Review.* Vol. 31, No. 4, Nov. 1990, pp. 991–1,020.

17. Rasband, S. Neil. *Chaotic Dynamics of Nonlinear Systems.* New York: John Wiley and Sons, 1990.

18. Savit, Robert. "When Random is Not Random: An Introduction to Chaos in Market Prices," *The Journal of Futures Markets.* Vol. 8, No. 3, 1988, pp. 271–89.

19. Weiss, Michael D. "Chaos, Economics, and Risk," *Quantifying Long Run Agricultural Risks and Evaluating Farmer Responses to Risk.* Proceedings of a seminar sponsored by Southern Regional Project S-232, San Antonio, Mar. 17–20, 1991. Department of Agricultural Economics and Rural Sociology, University of Arkansas, Fayetteville (1991), pp. 18–65.

2

WHEN RANDOM IS NOT RANDOM: AN INTRODUCTION TO CHAOS IN MARKET PRICES*

By Robert Savit

I. Introduction

When analyzing prices of commodities, securities, or financial instruments in a variety of markets, a commonly used assumption is that many of the fluctuations observed in the market prices are the result of purely stochastic (i.e., random) processes. One recognizes, of course, the effects on prices of external influences such as political developments, weather (especially important in the commodities markets), and a variety of macroeconomic factors. In addition, there are other well-understood, time-dependent influences, such as the time to delivery of a futures contract. But aside from these effects, the prevailing wisdom among analysts is that other price

Reprinted with permission from *The Journal of Futures Markets*, Vol. 8, No. 3 (June 1988): 271–89. © 1988 by John Wiley & Sons, Inc.

fluctuations are dominated by "noise" and can be represented by a stochastic process. One important goal of the analyst is then to understand the precise nature of the noise, and to develop tools for predicting its effect on market prices.

This is a very natural assumption. Once underlying trends (factors such as those described above) are subtracted out, the remaining price fluctuations often appear to be random. However, it may be that these remaining price movements are, to a great extent, the result of the inherent *nonlinearities* (a term that is explained below) in the marketplace.

To understand nonlinearities, feedback effects in price movements must be understood. An example of feedback: When the price of an item gets too high, self-regulating forces usually drive the price down, and vice versa. Feedback mechanisms can be either linear or nonlinear. If the feedback is linear, the market always responds to an out-of-kilter price by making price adjustments that are simply proportional to the amount by which the price varies from its "correct" value. By a sequence of such adjustments, the price is forced back in line. If this were the only feedback mechanism in the marketplace, it would be reasonable to describe most of the fluctuations in prices about their correct value as noise, because these simple linear feedback dynamics cannot generally produce the kinds of (random-looking) price fluctuations often observed in markets.

On the other hand, the feedback mechanisms may be nonlinear. In such a case, there will still be corrective effects for out-of-kilter prices, but the correction of the market will not always be simply proportional to the amount by which the price deviates from the item's real value. It is not unreasonable to expect these nonlinear corrections. An example of the kind of dynamics that might give rise to nonlinear effects comes from the study of market psychology, where it is understood that people (and markets) commonly overreact to bad news. There are many participants in a financial market with many complex sets of human relationships, motivations, and reactions. It would be a miracle if these complexities always averaged out to produce, in the aggregate, only simple linear feedback mechanisms. In the physical sciences there are many examples of systems—complex, but simpler than the financial markets—that clearly indicate that nonlinear responses do not generally average out. Turbulent fluid flow is perhaps the classic example. Once nonlinear feedback mechanisms are introduced into the description of the market, it is possible to explain many price fluctuations without recourse to stochastic effects. It may be possible to understand much of the market's price structure on the basis of completely deterministic market dynamics.

There are many simple mathematical examples of nonlinear feedback. The possible behaviors of such nonlinear systems may be extremely rich and complex. Of particular interest is the fact that for many kinds of nonlinear systems, the resulting functions (for example, market prices as a function of time) can look completely random when, in fact, there is no noise in the system. That is, a sequence of numbers is generated by a completely deterministic (and very simple) mathematical function. Those numbers betray no apparent pattern and seem to be random. Nevertheless, they are not random. They are determined by a single, simple nonlinear function. One might then suppose that since there is no noise in the system, it should be possible to predict the sequence with absolute certainty. This is both true and not true, and requires further explanation.

Section II of this chapter presents a simple pedagogical introduction to some of the main ideas associated with nonlinear systems. The varieties of behavior that such systems manifest will be demonstrated and the predictability of these behaviors will be explained. A simple mathematical example of a nonlinear system, called the logistic map, is described and its introduction as a paradigmatic description of price movements is motivated. The logistic map is not intended as a specific model of prices in some market. Rather, this mathematical function contains qualitative (nonlinear) features, analogues that can be expected in any dynamic market.

The behavior of the logistic map is controlled by a single parameter. Section III describes the behavior of the logistic map when this parameter is such that the map is in the chaotic regime. A chaotic price sequence is compared with a random one and it is shown that they look very similar. Nevertheless, the two sequences are fundamentally different, and those differences are discussed. Sections IV and V examine the logistic map for other values of its parameter, and describe kinds of behavior, besides chaos, that nonlinear systems can have. (The reader who is interested only in getting a general idea of chaotic behavior may wish to skip most of these two sections on a first reading. But the last two paragraphs of Section V are strongly recommended in any case.)

Section IV shows that for some values of its parameter the map has relatively simple, although still unexpected, behavior. It is shown how this simple behavior becomes increasingly complex as the parameter approaches the chaotic regime. Section V describes yet another kind of behavior called intermittency. The relevance of this behavior to the description of price movements is described. Section VI reexamines the chaotic regime and presents a brief discussion of the kind of hidden order that exists in chaos, which is not found in randomness. Some of the tools used to search for this hidden order are described, and it is suggested that these ideas can be used to improve short- or medium-term price predictability.[12] This chapter concludes with a summary, remarks, and a prospective of the applications and utility of nonlinear dynamics in the study of price movements.

II. The Logistic Map

Imagine a market that exhibits a sequence of prices of some item (futures contracts, securities, commodities, etc.) as a function of time. Let $p(t)$ be the price of the item in question at time t, where t is an integer, so that there is information of the prices at a series of discrete times. These could be, for example, daily prices of 90-day T-bills, or of stock index futures, or a sequence of intraday prices of some stock or some commodity contract. Notice that the real time represented by the difference between price observations at times t and $t + 1$ does not necessarily have to be a constant. If there is a sequence of daily or weekly prices, the time difference will be constant, but if there is a sequence of tick data, the time elapse represented by different pairs of successive integers $(t, t + 1)$, will not necessarily be the same.

Now, consider trading over a time period in which the macroeconomic environment as well as many of the other most important external influences on the market, is held constant. In such a situation, overall expectations and responses of traders and investors should be more or less constant, and so it may be possible to describe the dynamics of such a market by a mathematical function whose general form does not change with time. The same market in a different environment may be described by a different mathematical function.[1]

As a simple example of the kind of nonlinear function that might describe price movements in such a market, consider the function:

$$p(t + 1) = Ap(t)[1 - p(t)] = Ap(t) - Ap^2(t) \equiv F[p(t)] \tag{1}$$

where A is a positive constant. This simple quadratic function shows the price of the item of interest at time $t + 1$ in terms of the price at time t. Functions of this type fall into the category of objects called maps. In this case, Equation (1) "maps" the price at time t into the price at time $t + 1$. The particular map (1) has been the subject of much study in the mathematics and physics literature, and is called the logistic map. Notice that it has the kind of feature one might expect in a stable self-regulating market: The second term, proportional to p^2 is a negative feedback term that competes with the linear term and under many circumstances helps to stabilize the price fluctuations. For example, if $A > 1$, but not too large, and $p(0)$ is positive but less than one, then all subsequent $p(t)$ will be between zero and one. If, on the other hand, one discards the quadratic term in (1), it is found that $p(t) \approx A^t$ and so blows up exponentially. (It will be demonstrated that the effect of this quadratic term is actually much more complicated.)

It is also possible to construct a nonlinear map similar in form to Equation (1) as a model for price fluctuations. Suppose that over a given time period the average value of an item is more or less constant with a value $<p>$. (Alternatively, one can subtract out any obvious smooth, long-term price movements.) Let $g(t)$ be the deviations from this average so that:

$$p(t) = <p> + g(t). \tag{2}$$

Then, a model for the price fluctuations about the mean value $<p>$, which includes a simple nonlinear feedback term, could be constructed in terms of the variable $g(t)$.

In such a model, the variable, $g(t)$, naturally takes on a range of positive and negative values, while in (1), $p(t)$ takes on only positive values. Either case will present a nonlinear problem with a structure and range of variables analogous to what one finds in certain problems of price movements. It will be sufficient here to limit the discussion to Equation (1) with positive $p(t)$. Furthermore, most of the important properties one wishes to describe can be seen by studying this map for the case in which the variable is not only positive, but lies between zero and one. For pedagogical reasons, therefore, the focus will be mostly on Equation (1) with $0 \le p(t) \le 1$. Occasionally, reference may be made to a circumstance in which $p(t)$ lies outside this range. The reader should imagine that the discussion is of price movements of an item, the price of which always lies between zero and one.

Before proceeding, it should be emphasized that Equation (1) is *not* proposed as a realistic model of prices for any market. Rather, Equation (1) is a simple mathematical paradigm illustrating many of the effects one ought to expect in more realistic models of price movements. Indeed, many other simple nonlinear maps with competing terms and feedback effects have been studied by mathematicians and physicists, and it would be difficult to choose among them in constructing a basis for a model of price movements. However, using the ideas and the framework introduced, it should be possible to improve price predictability and to find general patterns in price movements that heretofore have been largely regarded as random.

III. Chaos in the Logistic Map

Despite its simplicity, the map (1) displays a remarkably rich variety of behavior as A varies. Of particular interest is the chaotic behavior manifested by the map. While the discussion here is directed toward the logistic map, the major concepts transcend this particular example and apply to other chaotic nonlinear systems.

As shown later, the price sequence generated by the map (1) is relatively simple for positive values of A less than about 3.5699. For values of A between 3.5699 and 4, the map displays a rich variety of behaviors. Fully developed chaos over the whole price range from zero to one first appears in the logistic map when $A = 4$.

A chaotic price sequence is illustrated in Figure 2-1. In this figure two price sequences are plotted. One is the sequence generated by the deterministic logistic map, Equation (1) with $A = 4$, and the other is a sequence of random numbers distributed with a simple probability weight to facilitate comparison with the logistic map. It is clear that the random and chaotic sequences appear qualitatively very similar. Nevertheless, the fundamental algorithms generating these two sequences are very different. Each price is determined independently for the random sequence and does not depend on the other prices in the sequence. The opposite is the case for the chaotic system. The price at time $t + 1$ is determined simply,[2] by Equation (1), from the price at time t. Despite these fundamental differences, the price sequences look remarkably similar. In fact, chaos can fool more than the naked eye into thinking it is random. It has been shown that even some standard statistical tests can fail to distinguish between certain chaotic maps and randomness.[3] (Although other, more sophisticated criteria can be used to discriminate between them. See Section VI.)

Despite their apparent similarity, there are important differences between chaotic and random sequences. There are three features a deterministic sequence should have if it is to be chaotic.[4] First, a chaotic sequence should typically sample all regions of its domain. In terms of Equation (1) this means that for most initial prices $p(0)$ the map (1) will eventually generate prices, $p(t)$, whose values range over the whole interval from near zero to near one. Thus, with the exception of certain special points such as $p(0) = 0$, one cannot generally have a situation in which a sequence of prices stays confined only to some small range of values.[5]

Second, a chaotic sequence is practically unpredictable over long time horizons in the following sense: Since Equation (1) is deterministic, it is true that if one had perfect knowledge of an initial price, and if one could compute $p(t)$ with absolute numerical precision, then perfect predictions of the price sequence could be made. But if there is any indeterminacy in one's knowledge or ability to compute, the situation is radically different. Consider, for example, two initial prices, $p_a(0)$ and $p_b(0)$. If these two initial prices are close to each other, then it might be expected that, since Equation (1) is deterministic, the price sequences generated by (1) from these initial

Figure 2-1(a)

A sequence of prices, *p(t)* generated by the logistic map, Equation (1) with *A* = 4.

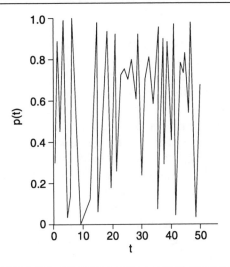

Figure 2-1(b)

A sequence of prices generated by a standard random number generator. These random prices are distributed according to a distribution function proportional to $[p(1 - p)]^{-1/2}$. This is the density distribution of prices generated by the logistic map (1). Other chaotic maps do generate prices that are uniformly distributed in interval (0,1).

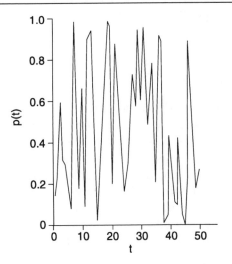

conditions would also be close to each other in the sense that $p_a(t)$ and $p_b(t)$ would be close to each other for all t. But this is not the case. For any initial price $p_a(0)$ one can find another initial price $p_b(0)$, as close to $p_a(0)$ as desired, such that after some time, t, the prices $p_a(t)$ and $p_b(t)$ will differ from each other by a large amount. (This statement can be made mathematically more precise.[6]) This means that any small indeterminacy in an initial price will generally lead, after some time, to very large errors in the predictions of the price sequence even though one is able to compute every ensuing price $p(t)$ deterministically and with absolute precision. Practically, the situation is even worse, since one cannot generally perform numerical computations to infinite precision because of round-off errors. For example, although the prices in the sequence shown in Figure 2-1 were calculated to 16 significant figures, it was possible to only reliably compute $p(t)$ for t up to about 50. In a chaotic system, round-off errors accumulate so rapidly that any long-term predictions of the usual type are impractical. This occurs even though the system is completely deterministic. Although these usual kinds of predictability are not practical, there are hidden patterns in chaotic sequences that are possible to discern.

Third, for a chaotic system one can find many initial prices $p(0)$ such that the sequence of prices generated by the chaotic map is periodic. In other words the sequence of prices $p(t)$ eventually repeats itself. Such initial prices are called periodic points. In a chaotic system, the majority of initial prices are not typically periodic points. However, in a sense that can be made mathematically precise,[6] there are a very large number of periodic points. In the case of the map (1) with $A = 4$, for example, the value $p(0) = (5 + \sqrt{5})/8$ is a periodic point with period 2. The existence of a large number of periodic points is just one example of the regularities hidden in a chaotic system.

IV. The Approach to Chaos

The previous section described the chaotic price sequence generated by the map (1) with $A = 4$. Now consider the nature of the price sequences obtained from (1) with $A < 4$. For most values of A less than 4, the behavior of the price sequence so generated is much simpler than in the region, $A \geq 4$; but is, nonetheless, surprising and interesting. Examining the region $A < 4$ will accomplish two things: First, studying the way in which a system with simple behavior becomes chaotic will lead to a deeper understanding of chaos. Second, intermittency, another kind of behavior of nonlinear systems, will be introduced, which may be important for the description of market prices. In this section we will consider the range of A between zero and 3.5699.

A. Fixed Points

To begin the discussion, refer to Figure 2-2(a), in which the vertical axis is $p(t + 1)$ and the horizontal axis is $p(t)$. The parabolic curve is just the right-hand side of Equation (1), with $A = 0.75$. On this same graph the line $p(t + 1) = p(t)$ is drawn. Suppose that at the beginning of a time sequence the price of an item is $p(0)$. The ensuing sequence of prices determined by the map (1) can be found graphically in the following way: Locate the value $p(0)$ on the horizontal axis and draw a vertical line to the parabolic curve. The y-coordinate at this point is just the value $p(1)$. From this point draw a horizontal line until it intersects the diagonal line defined by $p(t + 1) = p(t)$. The x-coordinate of this point is the value $p(1)$. From this point, draw a vertical line until it intersects the parabolic curve, and the value of the y-coordinate at this new intersection of the parabolic curve is just the value $p(2)$. Continuing in this way one can generate the entire sequence of prices $p(t)$, which are just the y-values of the successive intersections of the parabolic curve.[7] An example of this process for one value of $p(0)$ is shown in Figure 2-2(b).

Notice that in Figure 2-2(b), the sequence of prices $p(t)$ approaches zero as t gets larger. That is:

$$\lim_{t \to \infty} p(t) = 0 \tag{3}$$

Using the curves shown in Figure 2-2b, it can be seen that for any initial price, $p(0)$, between zero and one, this limit will be the same. If under the repeated action of a map, the variable approaches a definite limit, then the variable is said to approach a fixed point, and the limit which the variable approaches is the fixed point. Thus, the map shown in Figure 2-2a has a fixed point at zero. The basin of attraction of a fixed point is defined as the range of initial values such that the sequence of prices approaches that fixed point. In the case of Figure 2-2a, the basin of attraction is the entire x-axis between zero and one.

A qualitatively similar scenario occurs for the logistic map, Equation (1), for any positive value of A less than one. Of course, the precise sequence of prices $p(t)$ will depend on $p(0)$ and on A, but all of these sequences will inexorably march toward zero. This is not the kind of market environment in which most CEOs would be comfortable. Despite the fact that the parabola in Figure 2-2 is not linear, this simple fixed-point behavior does not really reflect any of the nonlinearity of Equation (1). The

Figure 2-2(a)

$p(t + 1)$ vs. $p(t)$ for the logistic map with $A = 0.75$. The line $p(t + 1) = p(t)$ is also plotted on this graph.

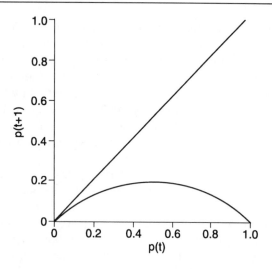

Figure 2-2(b)

The graphical construction of the price sequence, $p(t)$ for the logistic map with $A = 0.75$ as described in the text.

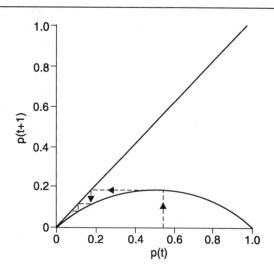

reason is that if $A < 1$, the parabolic curve is always below the diagonal line, and one could just as well have replaced the parabola by a straight line extrapolation of its tangent at $p(t) = 0$. One would still have had only one fixed point at zero whose basin of attraction was the entire x-axis between zero and one.

The first interesting effect of the nonlinearity occurs when $A > 1$. Examine Figure 2-3, which plots the logistic map, this time with $A = 2.25$ and the line $p(t + 1) = p(t)$. This figure also portrays the graphical construction described above, which gives the sequence of values $p(t)$ starting from some initial price $p(0)$. However, instead of the sequence converging to $p(t = \infty) = 0$, the sequence converges to a different fixed point, which is just the intersection of the parabola and the straight line at $p(t) = p^*$.

For this value of A, there are actually two fixed points, one at $p(t) = 0$, and one at $p(t) = p^*$. A fixed point will always be associated with an intersection of the curve and the line $p(t + 1) = p(t)$. A fixed point occurs at a value of p such that $p(t)$ gets "stuck" under the map, and doesn't change with t. The fixed points of (1) can be found by substituting $p(t)$ for $p(t + 1)$ on the left-hand side of Equation (1), and solving for $p(t)$. That is what is done graphically when the intersections of the parabola and the line $p(t + 1) = p(t)$ are plotted.

Figure 2-3

The graphical construction of the price sequence, $p(t)$ for the logistic map with $A = 2.25$.

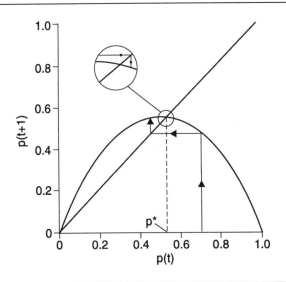

Although for A, somewhat greater than 1, there are two fixed points, only the fixed point at p^* has a finite basin of attraction, which is, in fact, the whole x-axis, not including the points $p(t) = 0$ and 1. The fixed point at zero has become repulsive; no sequence of prices will ever end up there unless $p(0) = 0$ to begin with.[8] This qualitative change in the long-time behavior of the price sequence first appears at $A = 1$. For this value of A, the fixed point at zero, which had been the attractive fixed point for $A < 1$, becomes unstable, and divides into two fixed points. One is attractive and moves away from zero continuously as A is increased and the other is repulsive and stays at zero. A fixed point will be attractive if the absolute value of the slope of the parabola at the fixed point is less than one, and repulsive if it is greater than one. (Compare, for example, Figures 2-4(a) and 2-4(b), which show an expanded view of the neighborhood of an intersection for these two cases.) This condition can be used to determine the values of A for which there is only one attractive fixed point at p^* in addition to the repulsive fixed point at $p(t) = 0$. With $p(t + 1) = y$ and $p(t) = x$, the equation for the parabola is:

$$y = Ax(1 - x),$$

and its derivative is:

$$\frac{dy}{dx} = A(1 - 2x). \tag{4}$$

On the other hand, p^* is determined by the simultaneous solution of:

$$p(t + 1) = p(t)$$

and

$$p(t + 1) = Ap(t)[1 - p(t)],$$

or,

$$p^* = Ap^*(1 - p^*)$$

the solution of which is $p^* = (A - 1)/A$. The condition that the absolute value of the derivative at the fixed point is less than one is therefore obtained by replacing x by $x = p^* = (A - 1)/A$ in the right-hand side of Equation (4), and requiring that the absolute value of Equation (4) is less than one. One finds the condition $|A - 2| < 1$, or $1 < A < 3$. Thus, this scenario of a single nonzero attractive fixed point whose basin of attraction is the entire x axis (with the exception of the points $x = 0$ and 1), persists for all values of A between 1 and 3.

Figure 2-4(a)

A detail of the region near the intersection of the logistic map with the line $p(t+1) = p(t)$ in the case in which the magnitude of the slope of the logistic map at the intersection point is less than one. Notice that the prices, $p(t)$, approach the fixed (intersection) point.

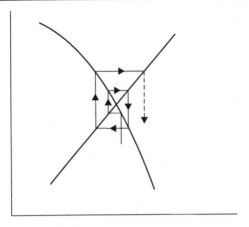

Figure 2-4(b)

A detail of the region near the intersection of the logistic map with the line $p(t+1) = p(t)$ in the case in which the magnitude of the slope of the logistic map at the intersection point is greater than one. In this case the price sequence does not approach the fixed (intersection point), but appears to move away from it. In the absence of the nonlinear term in the logistic map, the price sequence would just continue to diverge from this unstable fixed point.

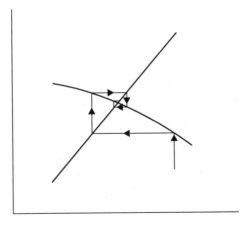

B. Limit Cycles

As A is increased the system still has two fixed points, one at zero and one at the intersection of the parabola and the straight line. However, neither of these is attractive, since the magnitude of the slope of the parabola is greater than one at each fixed point. If A is only slightly greater than 3, under the action of the logistic map, the sequence does not approach a single fixed point, but rather oscillates indefinitely between two values. Figure 2-5 shows the graphical construction for a sequence that starts at some value $p(0)$ for $A = 3.15$. As is apparent from this graph, the early part of the price sequence depends on the initial value $p(0)$; but, eventually, these initial transients go away and the price sequence simply oscillates indefinitely between two values, p_1 and p_2. This kind of behavior is called a limit cycle. In this case, since the prices oscillate indefinitely between only two values, our limit cycle can also be called a 2-cycle. Notice that there is no damping of these price oscillations and their final values do not depend on the initial price, $p(0)$.

Since there is a 2-cycle, then, for large enough times, one must have $p(t + 2) = p(t)$. But $p(t + 2)$ can be constructed from $p(t)$ simply by applying Equation (1) twice. That is:

$$p(t + 2) = F[p(t + 1)] = Ap(t + 1)[1 - p(t + 1)]$$

Figure 2-5

The graphical construction of the price sequence for the logistic map with $A = 3.15$. In this case the magnitude of the slope of the map at $p(t + 1) = p(t)$ is slightly larger than one, and the price sequence, $\{p(t)\}$ asymptotically approaches a 2-cycle.

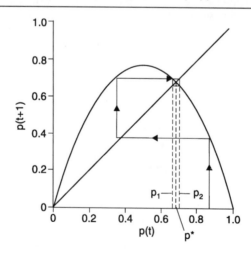

$$= AF[p(t)]\{1 - F[p(t)]\} = F(F[p(t)]) \equiv F^{[2]}[p(t)]. \tag{5}$$

Thus, if one focuses only on every other price, then, for that subsequence of prices evidently a kind of fixed-point behavior is established. The function that expresses that fixed-point structure is the function one gets when one composes F twice, i.e., it is the function defined as $F^{[2]}$ in Equation (5). (Note: $F^{[2]}$ does not mean "F-squared," it means F composed with itself twice.)

In Figure 2-6 $F^{[2]}$ is plotted along with the line $p(t + 2) = p(t)$ for $A = 3.15$. There are four fixed points, i.e., four intersections of the $F^{[2]}$ curve with the straight line. Two of them, the one at zero and the one at p^*, are the same as the fixed points of F. (It is easy to see that a fixed point of F is also a fixed point of $F^{[2]}$.) The magnitude of the slope of the $F^{[2]}$ curve is greater than one at zero and at p^* so that these fixed points are repulsive. However, there are also two new fixed points that appear in the $F^{[2]}$ curve. These are at the values p_1 and p_2 and represent the 2-cycle of the map F. Notice that the magnitude of the slope of the $F^{[2]}$ curve is less than one at p_1 and p_2 (the slopes at these two points are the same) so that these two fixed points of $F^{[2]}$ are attractive.

To review: The logistic map has a single attractive fixed point for $0 < A < 3$, so that all initial prices eventually settle down to that fixed-point

---

Figure 2-6

$p(t + 2)$ vs. $p(t)$ for $A = 3.15$. The function $F^{[2]}$, which is the once-iterated logistic map, is plotted along with the line $p(t + 2) = p(t)$, showing the unstable fixed point p^*, as well as p_1 and p_2, the stable fixed points of $F^{[2]}$, which are the 2-cycle values of F shown in Figure 2-5.

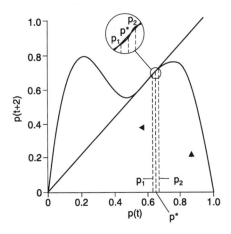

price after a long enough time. But for A somewhat larger than 3, there is no fixed point for the logistic map F. Rather, the price sequence approaches a state in which it oscillates indefinitely between two fixed values, p_1 and p_2. This 2-cycle of the map F which relates $p(t + 1)$ to $p(t)$, can be understood as fixed-point behavior of the map $F^{[2]}$, which relates $p(t + 2)$ to $p(t)$.

As A increases, the parabola, F, continues to steepen. In addition, the two humps of the curve, F^2 in Figure 2-6, also steepen; until at a value of $A \approx 3.449$ the magnitude of the slope of this curve at its fixed points, p_1 and p_2, becomes greater than one. These fixed points are now repulsive, and the function $F^{[2]}$ now shows limit cycle behavior. Not surprisingly, the limit cycle of $F^{[2]}$ is a 2-cycle. This means that the original map, F, which tells the price at time $t + 1$ in terms of the price at time t, now shows a new limit cycle, namely, a 4-cycle. That is, for A somewhat larger than 3.449 the price sequence for large times will oscillate among four values. As was the case with the 2-cycle behavior, these four values are independent of the initial price $p(0)$, although the values of the sequence $p(t)$ for t not too large will depend on the initial price.

As A continues to increase, this process, which is referred to as period doubling, continues. The 4-cycle behavior is stable for some range of values of A until a value is reached at which the 4-cycle bifurcates and becomes an 8-cycle. The 8-cycle is the stable long-time behavior for some range of A until a value of A is reached at which the 8-cycle bifurcates to a 16-cycle, etc. Call A_n the value of A at which the 2^n-cycle first appears. The range of A over which the 2^n-cycle describes the long-term price

Figure 2-7

Qualitative behavior of the logistic map for different values of A. Only the regions discussed in this chapter are shown. Other interesting behavior occurs for values of A between A_∞ and 4, as well as for values of $A > 4$.

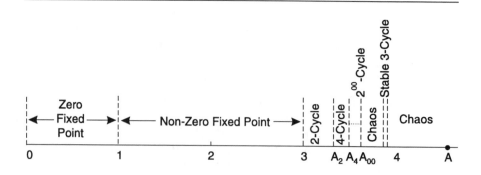

structure gets smaller and smaller as n increases. In fact, there is a finite value of A, $A \equiv A_\infty \approx 3.5699$, at which the limit cycle becomes infinitely long. At this value of A, the logistic map (1), starting from some initial price, will generate an infinite sequence of prices that never repeats itself. Figure 2-7 schematically indicates the values of A for which the map (1) has qualitatively different behavior.

Although the structure of the price sequence generated by (1) with $A = A_\infty$ is much less "regular" than a sequence of prices with a finite period of repetition, this structure is only a precursor of chaos and is not yet the fully developed chaotic behavior discussed in Section III. One very important difference between this 2^∞ limit cycle and true chaotic behavior is that the sequence of prices is still marginally predictable in the following sense: If the two initial prices chosen are close enough to each other, then, in general, the two price sequences generated by Equation (1) from these two initial prices will be very close to each other even after a very long time. The reason is that at $A = A_\infty$ the infinite limit cycle is stable. If two initial prices are both very close to one of the stop-over values of the infinite limit cycle, then each price sequence will pass close to the stop-over points of the infinite limit cycle in the same order, and so will always be close to each other. We can see a similar phenomenon in the simpler case of a 2-cycle, by referring to Figure 2-5 and constructing two price sequences starting from two nearby initial prices. This behavior is in marked contrast to the practical unpredictability of a fully chaotic system described in Section III.

V. From 2^∞ to Chaos

The logistic map holds still more surprises for values of A between A_∞ and 4. The behavior is easiest to describe if one imagines decreasing A from 4. When $A \approx 4$, the behavior of the price sequence is fully chaotic over the entire interval from 0 to 1, as we have described in Section III. As A decreases from 4, the sequence is still chaotic but the interval over which the chaos occurs decreases somewhat as A decreases. Regions near zero and near one are no longer visited by the $p(t)$. This behavior persists (an exception will be described below), until $A \approx 3.7$. At this point, the interval over which the prices are chaotic splits into two. A gap opens near $p(t) \approx 0.7$ and the $p(t)$ do not take on values in that gap. For values of A slightly less than 3.7 the prices, $p(t)$, generated by the logistic map alternate regularly between the two bands on either side of the gap; but within each band the prices are still chaotic. That is, the prices $p(t)$ bounce back and forth between the two bands like a 2-cycle; but within each band the subsequence, $p(t)$, $p(t + 2)$, $p(t + 4)$, ... is itself a chaotic sequence. As A is decreased the bands shrink, the empty space between the two bands increases, and the "chaotic 2-cycle" behavior continues until $A \approx 3.6$. At this point each of the two bands split into two. There are now four smaller bands and for values of A in this regime, the prices $p(t)$ execute a 4-cycle with respect to the four bands; so that $p(t + 4)$ and $p(t)$ are always in the same band, the behavior within each band is chaotic. This process of bifurcating chaotic bands continues until finally at $A = A_\infty$ there are 2^∞ "bands" each consisting of only one point. At this point, the behavior of the price sequence is that described in section IVB. The behavior of (1) for various values of A is indicated schematically in Figure 2-7.

This general behavior is correct for most values of A between A_∞ and 4. There are some exceptions, the most important of which is this: The chaotic behavior described above does not occur for a small range of values of A near 3.89. Instead, for almost any initial price $p(0)$, the price sequence $p(t)$ will, after a long enough time, oscillate among three values. Thus, for these values of A the sequence executes a 3-cycle. As shown in Figure 2-7 this 3-cycle behavior occurs only over a limited range of A, which is embedded in the midst of a larger range of A over which the sequence is chaotic. The question is, what happens when A has a value close to the boundary between the range over which the behavior is a 3-cycle and the chaotic regime? For values of A close to this boundary the system does not seem to be able to make up its mind between 3-cycles and chaos. As one moves close to the boundary from the chaotic region, one finds that the chaotic behavior is interrupted from time to time by behavior that looks very much like a nearly stable 3-cycle. That is, the price sequence will appear to be undergoing chaotic motion, and then, over a relatively short period of time, this chaotic motion will degenerate into 3-cycle behavior. After some time the 3-cycle behavior will cease and the price sequence will once again return to the chaotic pattern. As A gets closer and closer to the 3-cycle region, the system spends an increasingly larger fraction of its time executing 3-cycle behavior until finally, A enters the 3-cycle regime and the price sequence always executes periodic 3-cycle behavior.

This situation, in which the price sequence fluctuates between periods of regular motion (in this case, 3-cycle) and chaotic motion, is called intermittency. The potential application to the discussion of market prices is clear: It is not uncommon to see a price sequence that over different periods of time executes qualitatively different behavior. In trying to model such a situation, one supposes that these qualitatively different price histories require a description by qualitatively different models. For instance, one might seek an explanation in terms of a changing macroeconomic environment so that at the very least some parameter in the model would have assumed a new value and placed the system in a different regime. But this is not necessarily the case. As the example shows, it is quite natural for nonlinear systems to alternate between qualitatively different kinds of behavior, even if all their parameters are held fixed. In particular, if there are political, climatic, or macroeconomic indicators that send contradictory signals to the financial community, it is natural to expect that the markets will show alternating periods of qualitatively different behavior. Faced with a large change in market behavior, one does not necessarily have to seek a correspondingly large change in the fundamental environment. Small changes in the parameter A can induce qualitative changes in price sequences, and such qualitative changes can occur even with no changes in the external environment. The enormous price falls in the stock market in 1987 may be an example of this phenomenon, since there was apparently no dramatic change in major economic indicators or in the political environment on Black Monday.[9]

It is important to understand that in a nonlinear system, large qualitative changes in price behavior are not necessarily tied to large changes in the external environment. This insight should help construct better (and perhaps simpler) explanations for these kind of events, and ultimately improve our ability to anticipate, if not precisely predict, such large changes in market behavior.

VI. Order in Chaos

Although chaotic sequences appear random, and may even pass as random under certain simple statistical tests, there are important aspects of order hidden in chaotic systems. The existence of a large number of periodic points in a chaotic map is one indication of the hidden structure amid the chaos, but there are more. From a practical as well as a theoretical point of view, it is necessary to understand these structures; since one cannot hope to make any predictions about chaotic sequences without relying on this underlying, hidden order. In order to discern this structure, a chaotic price sequence must be viewed in a somewhat unusual way.

Rather than considering $p(t)$ as a sequence of single prices, one groups together d successive prices. Then, the set of d prices

$$\{p(t), p(t + 1), p(t + 2), \dots , p(t + d - 1)\}$$

can be represented by a point in a d-dimensional space whose Cartesian coordinates are just the values of these d prices. (Notice that the original sequence can just be considered to be the $d = 1$ case of this construction.) In this way, the original price sequence can be represented by a set of points in d-dimensions. If one considers a very long price sequence, then this set of points is called an attractor. Certain regions of the d-dimensional space may contain more points than other regions, and these are the regions to which the sequence of sets of d prices are "attracted."

Consider the nature of these attractors in d-dimensions. If the original price sequence is purely random, the d-dimensional set of points will show no interesting structure for any value of d, no matter how large. A completely random unweighted sequence of prices (which can vary between zero and one) will produce an attractor, a set of points in d-dimensions, which uniformly fills up the d-dimensional space between zero and one in each direction. (For example, in two dimensions, the random sequence fills up the square defined by $0 < x < 1$ and $0 < y < 1$.) On the other hand, if the sequence is chaotic, interesting structures may emerge for some value of d greater than one. It may happen, for example, that for some value of d, not all the space is filled. It may even happen that, unlike the random case, the dimension of the attractor in d-dimensions, is not d. That is, the attractor may be a fractal and have a noninteger dimension.[10] If this is the case, the attractor is sometimes called a strange attractor.

By studying the attractors for moderately low values of d, it is often possible to discern strong patterns in the otherwise apparently random-looking chaotic sequence. Understanding these patterns will lead to a better understanding of the dynamics of the market that produced the price sequence. A discussion of the methods used to characterize and study the attractors of chaotic systems is beyond the scope of this chapter. However, the following can be reported: First, these ideas suggest strategies for significant improvement of short-term price predictability in nonlinear systems. Second, a few studies of sequences of economic data have been carried out, and in some of these evidence has been found for the existence of nonlinear effects.[11] Such results are encouraging, and provide evidence for the relevance of the ideas of chaos and nonlinear dynamics to the study of price movements.

VII. Summary, Remarks, and a Prospective

This chapter has introduced some general ideas from the study of nonlinear dynamical systems and has shown how they are applicable to the problem of price movements in financial markets. A simple one-dimensional map, called the logistic map, was described, and it was shown how the price sequence generated by the map can be very simple or very complex, depending on the value of the parameter, A, contained in the map. The sequence of period doublings that occur in the map as A

approaches the chaotic regime was described along with the nature of the price sequence generated for values of A in the chaotic regime. It was demonstrated that a chaotic sequence and a random sequence look superficially the same, but that the sequences are very different. Unlike the random sequence, the chaotic sequence is completely deterministic, and contains a good deal of hidden order. The kinds of methods that can be used to discern that order, and so distinguish between chaos and randomness, were discussed. It was noted that the use of such methods can deepen the understanding of the dynamics of financial markets and may lead to improved short-term price predictability. Finally, the phenomenon of intermittency, which suggests ways of understanding major qualitative changes in price movements in the absence of significant changes in the macroeconomic environment, was explored.

This chapter raises a number of questions that require some additional remarks. First, although a particularly simple and well studied map was used to introduce the ideas, most of what was said applies more generally to a wide range of nonlinear systems. In particular, the general attributes of chaos go beyond the simple logistic map and apply, in ways that can be made precise, to chaotic behavior generally. On the other hand, it is true that there are other routes to chaos beside the period doubling one discussed here. However, the route to chaos is not completely specific to a particular map. In fact, it has been shown that very large classes of maps can share a variety of characteristics including a common route to chaos. This shared behavior is called "universality" and simplifies the task of analyzing nonlinear systems.

Second, it should be clear that there is a great deal of important information in the details of a chaotic sequence. This information will sometimes be crucial for discerning the hidden order in the sequence, and for understanding the nature of the sequence and using it advantageously. Many of the common techniques of statistical analysis that were developed to deal with "noisy" data involve various methods of smoothing the data. Many such methods are not generally appropriate to the study of chaotic systems, since too much useful information may be lost in the process of rendering the data smooth. Indeed, in some sense, the hallmark of chaos is precisely its jumpiness.

Third, the previous comment notwithstanding, it is probably true that a real price sequence generally involves some mixture of nonlinear effects and noise. (Notice that noise has not been carefully defined in this context. This is an important question, but one not addressed here.) Therefore, the most careful analysis of such a price sequence must take into account the important nonlinear effects as well as the influence of residual noise. The effects of stochasticity on nonlinear systems is a subject of much current research in physics, mathematics, and economics. The development of statistical methods appropriate to noisy nonlinear systems is clearly of great practical, as well as theoretical, significance.[12]

Fourth, in most of the discussion, the example of a nonlinear system that has been used was that of prices in a market subject to a more or less constant macroeconomic environment. But it may be that the macroeconomic environment itself, when viewed over a much longer time scale, shows evidence of nonlinear effects in appropriate quantities. The technical problems of analyzing such long-time-scale aggregate data are, of course, different from those encountered in a discussion of shorter-term price data in a specific market. Nevertheless, the ideas of nonlinear dynamics may well be appropriate to macroeconomic studies.

Finally, the analysis of market prices in terms of nonlinear dynamics presents a new twist not found in most macroscopic nonlinear systems that are studied in the natural sciences. In the marketplace, the study of the system disturbs the system itself. If many people trading in a market understand its nonlinear nature and use that knowledge to optimize return or reduce risk, then one can expect that the nature of the price movements will thereby be altered. Market prices in a nonlinear system can be very sensitive to small changes in the environment and it is not at all clear how such systems would respond to this additional kind of feedback. This interference by an observer on the phenomenon observed, while not usually important in macroscopic physical systems, is reminiscent of analogous considerations in quantum mechanics, which governs the microscopic physical world. Studying this process in a nonlinear market is certain to yield remarkable and interesting effects of great practical significance.

The application of the ideas of nonlinear dynamics and chaos to economics is still in its infancy. Nevertheless, it seems likely that these notions, in one form or another, will be important for a wide range of practical and theoretical problems in economic theory and market dynamics.

Acknowledgements

The author is grateful to David Hirschfeld for useful comments on the manuscript, and to him and Mark Powers for their encouragement. The author also wishes to thank William Brock for insightful comments on the general subject of nonlinear effects in economics.

Notes

1   To simplify the discussion, a clear distinction needs to be made between the time scale over which the macroeconomic environment changes, and the shorter time scale over which market prices fluctuate. (In reality, there are changes in the environment over many intermediate time scales that affect the market.) It may also be possible to use ideas of nonlinear dynamics to describe changes in price sequences observed over very long times or changes in the macroeconomic environment itself. See, for example, W. Brock, "Nonlinearity and Complex Dynamics in Economics and Finance," *The Economy as an Evolving Complex System*, D. Pines, ed. (New York: Addison-Wesley, 1988) and references therein, as well as the comments in Section VII of this chapter and the works cited in footnotes 11 and 12.

2   A stochastic model of price movements is tantamount to modeling the behavior of market participants in the aggregate as that of drunken sailors, whose decisions force market prices, at least on some time scale, to move randomly without regard to previous price values. A chaotic model without noise recognizes that each price movement is entirely dependent on its recent history. This point of view is preferable as a starting description of market dynamics because it more clearly reflects the fact that market participants make decisions motivated by a mix of rational and emotional considerations, which lead to nonlinear responses, but almost always with strong reference to information (albeit sometimes incomplete) about existing market prices. (However, even in a chaotic description there may be some noise. See Section VII for a discussion.)

3 See, for example, H. Sakai and K. Tokumaru, IEEE Trans. Acoust. Speech Signal Process. V.I. ASSP–28, 588, (1980).

4 There are a number of definitions of chaos, which differ primarily in technical ways. The one used here is topographical, and is most intuitive for our purposes. It is also the approach used in the excellent book quoted in reference 6.

5 It may happen, however, that the price sequence is chaotic over a smaller domain than the whole interval (0,1). In fact, this occurs for values of A between 3.5699 and 4. See Section V for a discussion.

6 A good mathematical introduction to chaos is contained in R. L. Devaney, *An Introduction to Chaotic Dynamical Systems* (Menlo Park, CA: Benjamin/Cummings, 1986).

7 This graphical construction has been used in economics in the context of linear maps, where it gives rise to the so-called "cobweb model." This model is Equation (1) without the quadratic term, and the cobweb is the graphical trajectory about a fixed point, similar to that shown in Figure 2-3. This linear model lacks the richness of the logistic map because of the absence of a stabilizing nonlinear term. See, for example, the discussion in A. Chiang, *Fundamental Methods of Mathematical Economics*, 2d ed. (New York: McGraw-Hill, 1974).

8 The initial price $p(0) = 1$ also ends up at the fixed point, $p(t) = 0$, but this is an unimportant exception.

9 The suggestion that events such as Black Monday may be understood as an example of intermittency should not be construed as a statement minimizing the importance of fundamental considerations in market behavior. Rather, it is suggested that the internal dynamics of the market are such that intermittent behavior may be a natural response to a certain set of external conditions, and a framework is presented for describing and quantifying that behavior.

10 A descriptive introduction to concepts useful in understanding fractals can be found in B. Mandelbrot, *The Fractal Geometry of Nature* (New York: W.H. Freeman, 1983).

11 J. Scheinkman and B. LeBaron, "Nonlinear Dynamics and Stock Returns," University of Chicago preprint: W. Brock and C. Sayers, University of Wisconsin SSRI preprint no. 8617, reprinted in the *Journal of Monetary Economics*; W. Brock, *Journal of Economic Theory*, 40, 168 (1986), and references therein.

12 R. Savit and M. Green, Physica D50, 95 and 521 (1991): K. Wu, R. Savit and W. Brock, Physica D69, 172 (1993); M. Casdagli and S. Eubank, eds. *Nonlinear Modeling and Forecasting*, Santa Fe Institute Studies in the Science of Complexity (Addison-Wesley, Redwood City, CA, 1992).

3

ADAPTIVE LEARNING
AND ROADS TO CHAOS:
THE CASE OF THE COBWEB

By Cars H. Hommes

Introduction

In economics there is a growing interest in the use of nonlinear deterministic models. The main reason is that a nonlinear deterministic model may
exhibit both stable periodic and chaotic behavior, and hence may provide
an endogenous explanation of the periodicity and irregularity observed in
economic time series. [For a survey on nonlinear economic models exhibiting chaos, see, e.g., Lorenz (1989).]

In this chapter, we investigate the dynamics of one of the simplest
nonlinear economic models: the cobweb model with adaptive expectations. The demand curve is linearly decreasing, while the supply curve is
nonlinear, S-shaped, and increasing. The dynamics of the expected prices
in the model is described by a one-dimensional nonlinear difference
equation $x_{n+1} = f(x_n)$. Chiarella (1988) approximated this model by the
well-known logistic map $x_{n+1} = \mu x_n(1 - x_n)$. Unfortunately, since the map

f is either increasing or has two critical points, the quadratic map (which has one critical point) is not a good approximation of the map f. In a related paper, Finkenstädt and Kuhbier (1992) present numerical evidence of the occurrence of chaos, in the case of linear supply and a nonlinear, decreasing demand curve.

In particular, we investigate how the dynamics of the model depend on the height of the demand curve and the expectations weight factor. In this chapter we present numerical results, and explain the validity of these results by means of theoretical results. The proofs of these theoretical results were presented in Hommes (1991, 1994).

The Cobweb Model with Adaptive Expectations

The well-known cobweb model is one of the simplest economic models. The model described the price behavior in a single market. We write p_t for the price, $\hat{p}_t$ for the expected price, q_t^d for the demand for goods, and q_t^s for the supply of goods, all at time t. The *cobweb model* is given by the following three equations:

$$q^{d_t} = D(p_t), \tag{1}$$

$$q_t^s = S(\hat{p}_t), \tag{2}$$

$$q_t^d = q_t^s. \tag{3}$$

In the traditional version of the cobweb model, the expected price equals the previous actual price, that is $\hat{p}_t = p_{t-1}$. It is well-known that if in the traditional cobweb model both the supply and demand curves are monotonic, then basically three types of price dynamics occur: convergence to an equilibrium price, convergence to period-two price oscillations, or unbounded, exploding price oscillations. It was shown by Artstein (1983) and Jensen and Urban (1984) that chaotic price behavior can occur if at least one of the supply and demand curves is nonmonotonic (see also Lichtenberg and Ujihara (1989)).

Nerlove (1958) introduced adaptive price expectations into the cobweb model, in the case of linear supply and demand curves. Adaptive expectations are described by the following equation:

$$\hat{p}_t = \hat{p}_{t-1} + w(p_{t-1} - \hat{p}_{t-1}), \ 0 \leq w \leq 1. \tag{4}$$

The parameter w is called the *expectations weight factor*, and for $w = 1$ the model reduces to the traditional cobweb model. In the case of linear supply and demand curves, the introduction of adaptive expectations in the cobweb model has a stabilizing effect on the price dynamics [see Nerlove (1958)]. However, the equilibrium price may still be unstable.

The question we address is *What can be said about the price behavior in the case of nonlinear, monotonic supply and demand curves?*

For simplicity we assume that the demand curve is linearly decreasing, and is given by

$$D(p_t) = a - bp_t, \quad b > 0. \tag{5}$$

Concerning the supply, we start off with the following two Economic Considerations:

(*EC1*) If prices are low, then supply increases slowly because of start-up costs and fixed production costs.

(*EC2*) If prices are high, then supply increases slowly because of supply and capacity constraints.

Based on these considerations we choose a nonlinear, increasing supply curve.

The simplest smooth curve satisfying (EC1) and (EC2) is an S-shaped curve S with the property that S has a unique inflection point $\bar{p}$, such that (1) the slope S' of S is maximal in $\bar{p}$, (2) S' is increasing for $p<\bar{p}$, and (3) S' is decreasing for $p>\bar{p}$. We change coordinates and choose the inflection point of the supply curve to be the new origin. Note that with respect to this new origin both "prices" and "quantities" can be negative. As an example of an S-shaped supply curve satisfying the above assumptions, we choose

$$S_\lambda (x) = \arctan (\lambda x), \quad \lambda > 0. \tag{6}$$

Observe that the parameter λ tunes the "steepness" of the S-shape.

Equations (1) through (5) yield a difference equation $x_{t+1} = f(x_t)$ describing the expected price dynamics, with f given by

$$f_{a,b,w,\lambda}(x) = - w S_\lambda(x)/b + (1 - w)x + aw/b. \tag{7}$$

We would like to point out that the price dynamics and the quantity dynamics are equivalent to the dynamics of the expected prices.

The map $f_{a,b,w\lambda}$ has a unique fixed point, which is the equilibrium price corresponding to the intersection point of the supply and demand curves. An important question is What can be said about the global dynamics of the model, when the equilibrium price is unstable?

Roads to Chaos

In this section we investigate how the dynamics of the model depends on the height of the demand curve (parameter a) and the expectations weight factor w. Figure 3-1 shows a bifurcation diagram with respect to the parameter a, with the other parameters fixed at $b = 0.25$, $w = 0.3$, and $\lambda = 4.8$. In fact a bifurcation diagram of a one-dimensional model shows an attractor of the model as a (multivalued) function of one parameter.

Figure 3-1 suggests the following bifurcation scenario. If a is small then there exists a stable equilibrium. If a is increased, then the equilibrium becomes unstable and period-doubling bifurcations occur. After infinitely many period-doubling bifurcations the price behavior becomes chaotic as a is increased. Next, after infinitely many period-halving bifurcations, the price behavior becomes more regular again. A stable period 2 orbit occurs for an interval of a-values, containing $a = 0$. When a is further increased, once more, after infinitely many period-doubling bifurcations, chaotic behavior arises. Finally, after infinitely many period-halving bifurcations, we have a stable equilibrium again, when a is sufficiently large.

Figure 3-1

Shifting the demand curve upwards, stable periodic and chaotic price behavior may interchange several times.

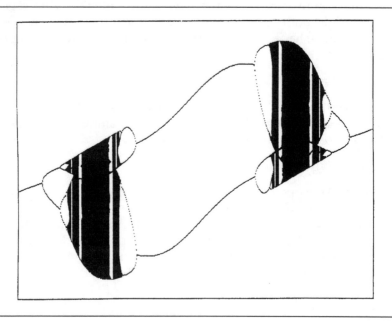

Concerning the dynamics of the model, for the particular supply curve in (6), the results in Hommes (1991, 1994) imply the following (we write f for $f_{a,b,w\lambda}$).

Given $b > 0$ and $0 < w < 1$, if λ is sufficiently large, then there exist $a_1 < a_2 < 0 < a_3 < a_4$ such that:

(1) f has a globally stable fixed point, if $a < a_1$.

(2) f has a period 3 orbit, for $a = a_2$.

(3) f has an unstable fixed point, a stable period 2 orbit, and no other periodic points, for $a = 0$.

(4) f has a period 3 orbit, for $a = a_3$.

(5) f has a globally stable fixed point, if $a > a_4$.

From a well-known result by Li and Yorke (1975) it follows that in the cases (2) and (4) the map $f_{a,b,w\lambda}$ is topological chaotic, that is: (i) there exist infinitely many periodic points with different period, and (ii) there exists an uncountable set of aperiodic points, for which there is sensitive dependence on initial conditions. Concerning the bifurcations scenario with respect to the parameter a, properties (1)–(5) imply the following:

(a) Infinitely many period-doubling bifurcations occur in the parameter intervals (a_1, a_2) and $(0, a_3)$.

(b) Infinitely many period-halving bifurcations occur in the parameter intervals $(a_2, 0)$ and (a_3, a_4).

Nusse and Yorke [1988] present a nice example $x_{n+1} = \mu F(x_n)$ (where F is a one-hump map with negative Schwarzian derivative and μ is a parameter) for which they showed that both infinitely many period-doubling and period-halving bifurcations do occur as μ is increased.

Recall that increasing the parameter a is just shifting the demand curve vertically upwards. Hence our theoretical results imply that, if the demand curve is shifted vertically upwards, then both infinitely many period-doubling and period-halving bifurcations occur and periodic and chaotic behavior interchange several times.

A bifurcation diagram with respect to the expectations weight factor w, with the other parameters fixed at $a = 0.8$, $b = 0.25$, and $\lambda = 4$, is shown in Figure 3-2. The diagram suggests that a stable equilibrium occurs for w close to 0. After infinitely many period-doubling bifurcations the price dynamics becomes chaotic, as w is increased. Next, after infinitely many period-halving bifurcations, the price behavior becomes more regular again, until a stable period 2 cycle occurs, for w close to 1.

The results in Hommes (1991, 1994) imply the following. Given $b > 0$, if λ is sufficiently large and for a suitable choice of the parameter a we have:

Figure 3-2

For *w* close to 0 a stable equilibrium occurs, while for *w* close to 1 stable period 2 oscillations with large amplitude occur; for intermediate values of *w* chaotic price oscillations with moderate amplitude arise.

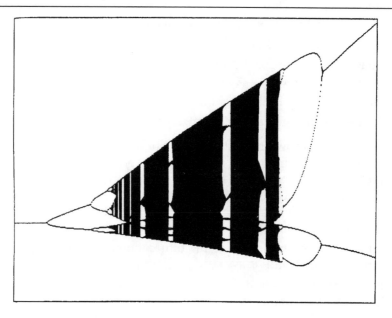

(1) f has a globally stable fixed point for w close to 0.

(2) f has a period 3 orbit for intermediate values of w.

(3) f has a stable period 2 orbit for w close to 1.

This result implies that both infinitely many period-doubling and period-halving bifurcations occur as w is increased from 0 to 1.

In the case of linear supply and demand curves, the introduction of adaptive expectations into the cobweb model has a stabilizing effect on the price dynamics; see Nerlove (1958). We present a corresponding result, in the case of nonlinear, monotonic supply and/or demand curves. Recall that $w = 1$ corresponds to the traditional cobweb model. As w is decreased from 1 to 0, then the amplitude of the price oscillations becomes smaller (see Figure 3-2). In the case of nonlinear, monotonic supply and/or demand curves the introduction of adaptive expectations into the cobweb model dampens the amplitude of the price cycles. Meanwhile a price cycle may become unstable and chaotic price oscillations may arise. Hence, from a quantitative point of view adaptive expectations have a stabilizing effect, but from a qualitative point of view adaptive expectations may have a destabilizing effect upon the price behavior.

Discussion

Expectations and learning behavior play an important role in economics. One of the fundamental differences between the physical and the social sciences is that in a physical system the laws of the system are often fixed, while in a social system individuals learn from the past and influence the laws of the system. It has been argued that, because of this fundamental difference, deterministic chaos, which plays an important role in the physical sciences nowadays, is of less interest to the economic and social sciences.

In the traditional cobweb model, there is no learning behavior: the suppliers believe that today's price will also hold tomorrow. Holmes and Manning (1988) showed that in a cobweb model with nonlinear, monotonic supply and demand, when the suppliers learn by arithmetic mean, that is, if they employ the mean of all past prices as their expectation of tomorrow's price, then prices always converge to a stable equilibrium. Holmes and Manning conclude that if agents use their memories, then chaos cannot occur; only when agents are forgetful, chaos may occur. Stated according to their aphorism, *"Those who do not learn from history are condemned to never repeat it."* [See Holmes and Manning (1988, p. 7) listed in the References to this chapter.]

Our results show that the conclusions of Holmes and Manning are not true in general. Whether or not chaotic behavior is possible when agents learn from the past, depends on both the model and the type of learning behavior. We have seen that in a cobweb model with adaptive learning and nonlinear, monotonic supply and demand, chaotic price behavior is possible, even in the long run. It is well known that adaptive price expectations means that the expected price is a weighted average, with geometrically declining weights, of all past observed prices. Hence, adaptive learning seems to be much more realistic than learning by arithmetic mean, since adaptive learning puts higher weights to the most recent prices. Unlike the aphorism of Holmes and Manning, one might say: *Even those who learn from the past, may never repeat it.*

In Hommes (1991, 1994) we analyzed the dynamics of the model, for a general class of S-shaped supply curves in more detail. Moreover, we presented a geometric explanation of the occurrence of chaotic price behavior in the cobweb model with adaptive expectations, for a large class of nonlinear, monotonic supply and demand curves.

Acknowledgments

This chapter was written during a visit to the Institute for Physical Science and Technology, University of Maryland, College Park. Financial support from the Netherlands Organization of Scientific Research (NWO) is gratefully acknowledged. I would like to thank Helena E. Nusse for several discussions and for helpful comments.

References

Artstein, Z., "Irregular Cobweb Dynamics," *Economics Letters* 11, 15–17 (1983).

Chiarella, C., "The Cobweb Model. Its Instability and the Onset of Chaos," *Economic Modelling*, 377–384 (1988).

Finkenstädt, B., and P. Kuhbier, "Chaotic Dynamics in Agricultural Markets," *Annals of Operations Research* 37 (1992).

Hommes, C. H., "Chaotic Dynamics in Economic Models. Some Simple Case-Studies," Groningen Theses in Economics, Management & Organization, Wolters-Noordhoff (1991).

Hommes, C.H., "Dynamics of the Cobweb Model with Adaptive Expectations and Nonlinear Supply and Demand," *Journal of Economic Behaviour and Organization* 24 (1994), 315–335.

Holmes, J. M., and R. Manning, "Memory and Market Stability. The Case of the Cobweb," *Economics Letters* 28, 1–7 (1988).

Jensen, R. V., and R. Urban, "Chaotic Price Behavior in a Nonlinear Cobweb Model," *Economics Letters* 15, 235–240 (1984).

Li, T. Y., and J. A. Yorke, "Period Three Implies Chaos," *American Mathematical Monthly* 82, 985–992 (1975).

Lichtenberg, A. J., and A. Ujihara, "Application of Non-linear Mapping Theory to Commodity Price Fluctuations," *Journal of Economic Dynamics and Control* 13, 225–246 (1989).

Lorenz, H.-W., *Non-linear Dynamical Economics and Chaotic Motion* (Springer-Verlag, Berlin, 1989).

Nerlove, M., "Adaptive Expectations and Cobweb Phenomena," *Quarterly Journal of Economics* 72, 227–240 (1958).

Nusse, H. E., and J. A. Yorke, "Period Halving for $x_{n+1} = mF(x_n)$ Where F has Negative Schwarzian Derivative," *Physics Letters* 127A, 328–334 (1988).

4

Chaos Models and Their Implications for Forecasting

By William J. Baumol and Richard E. Quandt

Introduction

Otto Eckstein's role as a master forecaster was beset by many perils, of which he was well aware. However, recent developments in the theory of dynamics, referred to as chaos theory, suggest that a profound and previously unsuspected pitfall threatens the work of the forecaster.

This chapter provides a brief introduction to the concept of chaos, offering an intuitive interpretation of the phenomenon that we believe to be somewhat novel. We will suggest that there is no reason to assume the phenomenon to be a mere curiosum, for it can apparently arise with very little provocation in nonlinear dynamic models relating to a wide variety of economic issues. And we will show that a chaotic regime is characterized by three attributes that can have extremely disturbing implications for the use of econometric forecasting procedures: (1) Even though a time series is generated entirely deterministically, its behavior is statistically very similar to that of a system subject to severe random shocks; (2) chaotic time series may proceed for substantial intervals of time manifesting patterns of behavior that seem extremely orderly, when a totally new pattern appears without warning, only to disappear just as unexpectedly; (3) the presence and location of such abrupt transitions are extremely sensitive to parameter values in the underlying model, appearing and disappearing with changes in the third or higher decimal places, which are beyond anything econometrics may be able to aspire to discover.

The "Chaos" Concept and Its Underlying Orderliness

Recently a number of mathematicians, ecologists, biologists, meteorologists, and economists have provided the new body of analysis that is the focus of this chapter. These writings have shown that dynamic difference or differential equation models, which are characterized by nonlinearity, can manifest chaotic properties over nontrivial ranges of values of their parameters, even in difference equation models of first order. Chaos is defined as a fully deterministic behavior pattern which is, in at least some respects, undistinguishable from a random process or, rather, a process perturbed by substantial random elements. It displays extreme sensitivity to changes in parameter values, and is characterized by an infinite number of equilibria, each approached by (superimposed) cycles of different periodicities, and whose simultaneous presence is what gives the appearance of randomness to a time series generated by a deterministic process.

"Chaos" is a persuasive term, romantic in its overtones, suggesting extreme disorder and absence of discernible patterns of behavior. Yet it turns out, for reasons that can only be suggested here, that what should be surprising about the performance of dynamic chaos models is not the disorder their performance manifests but the extreme regularity by which their structure is characterized. A simple economic model will be used to offer an intuitive explanation of what is going on and to suggest why chaotic time paths can give the appearance of randomness even though they are completely deterministic. Much harder to account for intuitively is the very elaborate structure that underlies such manifestations.[1]

It will be indicated that chaos represents an intermediate state in the transition from stability to instability in a basic nonlinear cycle, as the parameters of the model that generate the cycle leave their stable range. In this intermediate region oscillatory behavior underlying that basic cycle persists, but the time path fails to replicate itself perfectly in the period of oscillation of the basic cycle. That is (in the first-order case that we will consider), the time path, so to speak, then "misses its target" of perfect replication of its previous position two periods earlier. As a result, the basic cycle is perturbed, first (as the parameters move further from their stable range) by two four-period superimposed cycles, then by four eight-period superimposed cycles, etc., finally being disturbed in patterns so complicated as to merit the adjective "chaotic." Nevertheless, in the time path generated by the model the basic oscillatory process continues to manifest itself and, in fact, disguises the periodicity of the disturbances that prevent its perfect two-period replication.

A Simple Illustrative Model

Chaotic behavior in a first-order nonlinear difference equation

$$y_{t+1} = f(y_t) \tag{1}$$

arises when the graph of $f(\cdot)$ is hill-shaped and crosses the 45 degree ray (the locus of possible equilibria, $y_{t+1} = y_t$), at a point where $f'(\cdot) < 0$. As is well known, if at that point $-1 < f' < 0$ the resulting time path will be oscillatory and stable, approaching the equilibrium point with oscillation of ever declining amplitude.

Perhaps the most frequently used example of the chaos phenomenon is the equation

$$y_{t+1} = wy_t(1 - y_t) \tag{2}$$

which we will use throughout the discussion. Here the equilibrium point is given by $y_{t+1} = y_t = y_e$ or $1 = w - wy_e$, that is,

$$y_e = (w - 1)/w \tag{3}$$

and the slope at that point is given by

$$\frac{dy_{t+1}}{dy_t} = 2 - w. \tag{4}$$

Hence, stable oscillation requires $2 < w < 3$.

A simple economic example is provided by the relationship between a firm's profits and its advertising budget decision.[2] Suppose that without any expenditure on advertising the firm cannot sell anything. As advertising outlay rises, total net profits first increase, then gradually level off and finally begin to decline, yielding the traditional hill-shaped profit curve. If P_t represents total profit in period t and y_t is total advertising outlay, P_t can, for illustration, be taken to follow the expression

$$P_t = ay_t(1 - y_t). \tag{5a}$$

If, in addition, the firm devotes a fixed proportion, b, of its current profit to advertising outlays in the following period so that

$$y_{t+1} = bp_t \tag{5b}$$

it is clear that equation (5a) is immediately transformed into our basic equation (2), with w = ab.

Now, a moment's thought indicates why the time path of y_t can be expected to be oscillatory. For suppose the initial level of advertising, y_0, is an intermediate one that yields a high profit figure P_0. That will lead to a large (excessive) advertising outlay, y_1, in the next period, thereby bringing down the value of profit, P_1. That, in its turn, will reduce advertising again and raise profit and so on *ad infinitum*.

The thing to be noted about this process is that it gives us good reason to expect the time paths of profit and advertising expenditure to be oscillatory. *But it does not give us any reason to expect that these time paths need either be convergent or perfectly replicatory.* Exactly the same logical structure is consistent with "sloppiness" in the cycles, so that past behavior is reproduced only imperfectly in the future. This will turn out to be the key observation in the discussion that follows.

The Time Path as a Function of the Parameter Values

Taking off from the well-known qualitative changes in the time path generated in our model by changes in the values of the parameters—the w in our equation—we will examine the phase diagram of the model. A phase diagram for w < 3 would simply show a stable cobweb representing convergence toward the equilibrium point, y_e, the intersection between the curve $y_{t+1} = f(y_t)$ and the 45 degree ray.

It is just beyond w = 3 that there begin to occur the manifestations that were unanticipated before their revaluation by the chaos theorists. Just when w exceeds 3, so that y_e becomes unstable, there appear two new equilibrium points involving what may be described as every other period stationarity, at each of which

$$y_{t+2} = y_t = y^* \neq y_{t+1}. \tag{6}$$

Each of these is approached for values of w close to 3 by a stable cycle in y_{t+2}, y_t space. A similar result, which is well-known in the literature, holds for a wide class of hill-shaped functions[3] $y_{t+1} = f(y_t)$. However, for our difference equation (2) this can be shown directly in a manner that suggests what is going on. Here we have

$$y_{t+2} = f[f(y_t)] \quad = wy_{t+1}(1 - y_{t+1}) \tag{7}$$

$$= w[wy_t(1 - y_t)(1 - wy_t(1 - y_t))].$$

Every other period stationarity requires (6) so that the subscripts in the preceding equation can be suppressed, and (7) becomes an equation of fourth degree with four roots (equilibrium points). After some manipulation (7) can then be rewritten as

$$y^*(wy^* - w + 1)[w^2y^{*2} - (w^2 + w)y^* + w + 1] = 0 \qquad (8)$$

This obviously has the root $y^* = 0$, corresponding to the origin as a (trivial) equilibrium point. In addition, the first parenthetic expression tells us that a second root is given by

$$y^* = (w - 1)/w.$$

Thus, our initial equilibrium point, y_e—see (3)—while no longer stable, still continues to be a point of equilibrium. The last parentheses contain a quadratic expression that obviously offers us two roots. The usual formula for the roots of a quadratic expression, which we need hardly repeat here, show that as w goes from $3 - \delta$ to $3 + \delta$ for small $\delta > 0$, these roots change from complex (imaginary) values to real values, thus providing the two new (every-other-period) stationary points that have already been mentioned, along with the stable cyclical paths along which they are approached.

Figures 4-1 and 4-2 (in which $y_0 = 0.99$, $w = 3.45$) describe the situation. The first of these shows the first 14 periods, in which the time path begins to settle into its pattern. It is dominated by what looks like a limit cycle that has somehow gone a bit wrong. It follows a rectangular path but somehow fails to end up at its starting point. In Figure 4-2 this path is shown after 44 periods have passed.[4] We see that starting, say, from point A, the time path construction line assumes the familiar rectangular shape ABCD that one associates with a limit cycle. However, instead of returning to the initial point A, the path moves to neighboring point E and then goes along EFGH, *which intersects the earlier portion of the construction line along line segment CD*. After GH the construction line rejoins point A and then resumes its earlier path ABCD. We end up with what looks like two slightly displaced rectangles, because at point E the construction line "misses" the neighboring point A from which it had started off.

The corresponding time path is shown in Figure 4-3. What we see there, before anything else, is the persistence of a *two-period* oscillation with a high value of y succeeding each low value and vice versa. Where, then, are the two much-discussed oscillations that involve every other period and extend over four periods?

These, as we will see now, are cleverly concealed by the dominating large oscillations in Figure 4-3. These mysterious subcycles are revealed

Figure 4-1

Phase Diagram y(t+1)=wy(t)(1−y(t))   y0 = .999   w = 3.45

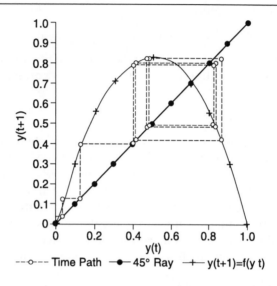

Figure 4-2

Phase Diagram y(t+1)=wy(t)(1-y(t))   y0 = .999   w = 3.5

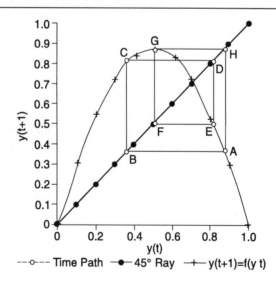

Figure 4-3

30-Period Time Path: y(t+1)=wy(t)(1-y(t))

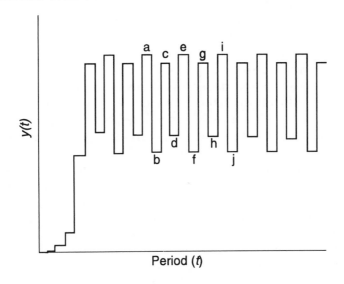

by looking first only at the upper horizontal segments a, c, e, g, and i in Figure 4-3, and then at the lower segments b, d, f, h, and j by themselves.

The upper segments give us the first of the hidden cycles—after an interval of a period there is a fall in y_t from the height of A to that of C. Thereafter, with another hiatus one period in length, it rises again to E, then falls again to G, etc. In exactly the same way, the lower horizontal segments reveal the second set of hidden oscillations of the every-other-period variety. It is easy to verify by calculating the roots of $y_{t+2} = f(y_t)$ (Equation (8)) or by following through its logic that these are indeed the cycles dealt with by chaos theory for the range of values of w considered so far.

Economic Interpretation of the Time Path

In our illustrative model, as has been noted, oscillation occurs because high profit periods are succeeded by overgenerous advertising budgets which, in their turn, cut into future profits, and hence into advertising expenditure. This basic alternation of high and low advertising outlays continues to show up very clearly in Figure 4-3—it is the two-period cycle that dominates the pattern traced by the time path.

However, there is nothing in our model antithetical, say, to a strong upward phase in the cycle being followed in the succeeding cycle by a much weaker recovery of advertising outlays. Indeed, one might expect that, in reality, a relationship between advertising and profits such as has been described would indeed be oscillatory but that the recoveries and declines might well vary markedly in their strengths. There is nothing in the basic story that calls for the cycles to be of constant amplitude—that is merely an artifact of the oversimplified difference equation model that has been used to describe (or, rather, to approximate) the process. What is, consequently, difficult to account for economically is not the difference between the amplitudes of succeeding cycles; but the fact that when the value of w lies in the range we are considering, larger and smaller amplitudes nevertheless succeed one another with perfect regularity.

Changes in the value of w, naturally, constitute variations in either the effect of advertising on profit or of the proportion of profit devoted to subsequent advertising. Specifically, by (2), (5a), and (5b), $w = ab$, where a is a parameter (multiplier) of dp_t/dy_t, the effect of increased advertising expenditure on current profitability, while $b = dy_{t+1}/dp_t$, is the change in the future advertising budget generated by a unit rise in current profit. A rise in w, then, must involve a rise in either a or b or both. Now it is obvious, intuitively, that if a and b are small, so that the same will be true of w, a given rise in advertising outlay can be expected to have a relatively small effect on profits, so that the next period's advertising budget will be affected only modestly, and so each cycle will take off on a smaller scale than its predecessor. Thus, with w small, economic intuition tells us that the cycle will be damped. The rate of dampening will obviously decline as a and b increase, and there will come a point (at $w = 3$) where the convergence of the cycle ceases altogether.

In a linear model, any larger value of w simply will lead to an explosion of the cycle, its amplitude expanding exponentially with time. When the advertising-profit relationship is hill-shaped, however, after a while the profit reward to diminished advertising falls off, and ultimately the other side of the hill is reached. There, further cuts in advertising actually reduce profit rather than continuing to raise it as in the linear case. At this point, the next cycle's upswing in advertising will decline and the cycle, instead of continuing on its explosive path, is brought to a halt, either temporarily or permanently.

It is clear why such a process *can* replicate itself every other go-round. If in some one period the declining profit payoff to cuts in advertising outlay leads to only a small reduction in advertising in the next go-round, this may keep matters to the right-hand side of the profit hill and in the next cycle it may thus yield a disproportionately large rise in profit with a correspondingly large effect on advertising, and so on. But there seems to be no *a priori* reason for events always to take such a simple path.

Attributes of the Chaotic Region

So far we have dealt primarily with the region of values of the pertinent parameter(s) in which a four-period cycle is superimposed upon the basic two-period cycle (w > 3 in our equation). But for reasons that are not difficult to describe, in the equation $y_{t+1} = wy_t(1-y_t)$, as w increases further (and a similar phenomenon occurs in other such equations), there comes a point at which eight-period cycles enter in a way exactly analogous to that of the earlier appearance of the four-period cycle, and then, at a higher value of w, 16-period cycles appear, etc. Finally, cycles whose periods are various uneven (odd) numbers make their appearance. When all of these have occurred, their superimposition brings us into the region of complete chaos. In our particular equation this occupies the set of values 3.83 (approx.) < w < 4. As May points out (*op. cit.*, p. 461) "It cannot be too strongly emphasized that the process is generic to most functions $y_{t+1} = f(y_t)$ with a hump of tuneable steepness" (i.e., to hill-shaped functions whose steepness is adjustable by modifications in the values of their parameters). Moreover, there are many functions whose chaotic ranges of parameter values are much larger than that in our example, and in some cases those ranges are infinite. The Li-Yorke theorem states, in effect, that if there exists some y_t value such that $y_{t+3} \leq y_t < y_{t+1} < y_{t+2}$, then chaotic behavior will occur.

We can now return to equation (2) to illustrate the behavior of its time path in the chaotic region. Figure 4-4 shows the sort of sequence of events that one can expect to encounter. Here we have $y_0 = 0.99$ and w = 3.94, with the initial value depicted by the position of the little square in the extreme upper left-hand corner of the diagra (Point A).

What is noteworthy about the picture is the relative homogeneity of the time path during its first 25 periods or so (the left half of the diagram) up to point B where, apparently out of nowhere, a time path that is qualitatively entirely different from its predecessor suddenly appears. How could any forecaster be expected to predict the extreme 10-period stability of path segment BC even from complete and completely accurate data for the preceding 25 periods?

This, then, illustrates and confirms the first attribute of chaotic time paths—the sudden breaks in their qualitative behavior.

Their second property, equally distressing for the work of the forecaster, is their extreme sensitivity to changes in parameter values. Mete-

Figure 4-4

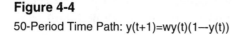

50-Period Time Path: y(t+1)=wy(t)(1—y(t))

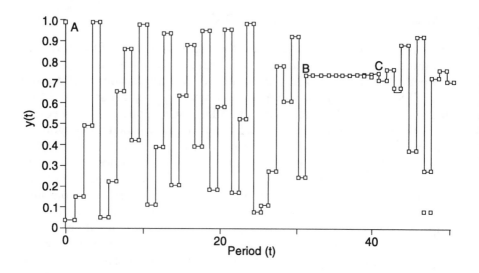

orologists have referred to this property as the butterfly's wing phenome-non, suggesting that under a chaotic regime the flap of the wing of a butterfly in Japan can have profound effects on weather in Kansas!

We illustrate this sensitivity in Figures 4-5 to 4-8, all of which involve tiny changes in the value of either w or y_0 from their magnitudes in Figure 4-4, which we have just examined. Yet in each of these graphs the myste-rious table region, BC, of Figure 4-4 vanishes completely. In Figures 4-5 and 4-6 y_0 is kept at its Figure 4-4 value, but in Figure 4-5 w is reduced from its 3.94 value in Figure 4-4 to w = 3.935. In Figure 4-6 it is raised to 3.945. Similarly, in Figures 4-7 and 4-8 y_0 is changed from the 0.99 value of Figure 4-4, respectively to 0.987 and 0.999. We see how little it takes to alter the character of the time path radically. The implications are clear for the reliability of forecasts based on an econometric model with statistically estimated parameter values, which can hardly be expected to be accurate to three decimal places.

This same point is brought out by an alternative calculation. The time path of (2) was first determined for 640 periods using computations accurate to seven digits, and then recalculated with computations accurate to 14 digits. For w = 3.5, that is, before the model entered the true chaotic region, the two calculations gave virtually the same figures. Specifically,

Figure 4-5

50-Period Time Path: y(t+1)=wy(t)(1-y(t))

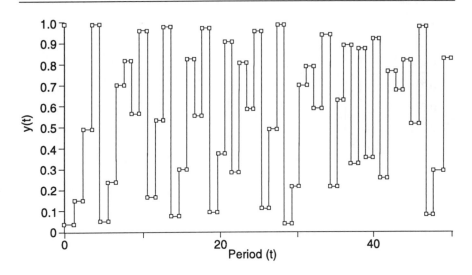

Figure 4-6

50-Period Time Path: y(t+1)=wy(t)(1-y(t))

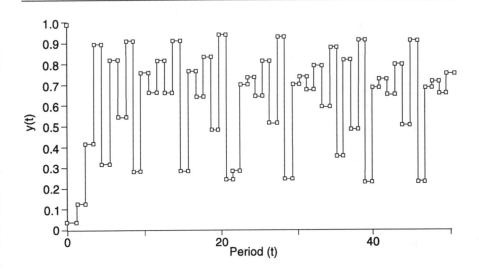

Figure 4-7

50-Period Time Path: y(t+1)=wy(t)(1−y(t))

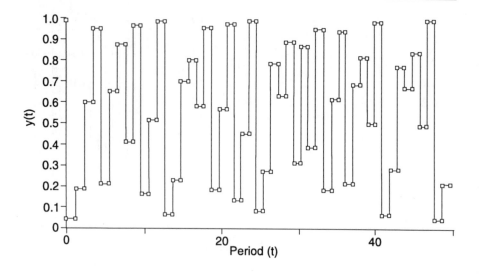

Figure 4-8

50-Period Time Path: y(t+1)=wy(t)(1−y(t))

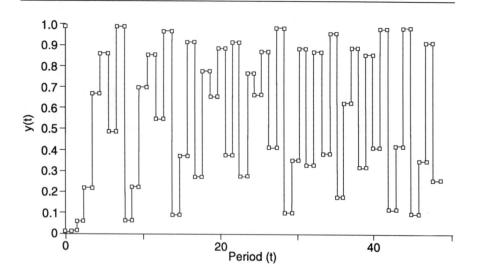

using $y(7)_{640}$ to represent the 640th observation with seven-digit accuracy in the calculations, etc., we obtained for w = 3.5.

$$y(14)_{640} = 0.3828196830, \quad y(7)_{640} = 0.3828207254.$$

But for w = 3.9, in the heart of the chaotic region, the two series lost all resemblance after only 30 periods, and gave us, for example

$$y(14)_{31} = 0.8823060155, \quad y(7)_{31} = 0.4794570208.$$

This clearly shows how sensitive the entire calculation becomes to very tiny cumulative errors, here all occurring after the seventh decimal place. The reason for this is, of course, that in the presence of stable limit cycles a rounding error acts as if it simply introduced a new starting value; however, from any starting value, convergence to the limit cycle is rapid. In the chaotic region, there is no such convergence and rounding error causes two series based on different numbers of decimal places to become less and less like the other. This illustrates another property of chaotic behavior: no matter how close to each other two sequences start, they will ultimately stray very far from one another. This is a particularly uncomfortable thought for those who view most relations as essentially continuous. With that viewpoint, one might expect that small perturbations in inputs will lead to small changes in outputs. In the chaotic case such expectations are guaranteed to be disappointed.

We come, finally, to the last property of the chaotic regime, its pseudorandomness.

First of all, it should be noted that chaotic behavior, while it effectively mimics some types of random behavior, is not to be interpreted as producing "random walks" or white noise. We have generated series of length 640, as noted before, and one of length 6400, and examined several of their features. (1) The autocorrelogram reveals fairly complicated behavior; for example, for w = 3.9, the first nine autocorrelation coefficients were –0.503, –0.013, 0.265, –0.215, 0.102, –0.010, –0.077, 0.111, after which the autocorrelations essentially die out. (2) If we classify a y_t value as A when it exceeds its predecessor and as B when it falls short of it, we can test for randomness by examining the number of runs of A and B. Using the usual approximation to the standardized number of runs (Siegel [1956]) we obtain a standard normal deviate of 55.52, rejecting the null hypothesis at all reasonable significance levels. (3) To test the hypothesis that all numbers produced by the process are equally likely, we use the Kolmogorov-Smirnov test to compare the sample cumulative frequency distribution with the uniform distribution on (0, 1). The null hypothesis of uniformity is overwhelmingly rejected. (4) Finally, we have computed the power spectrum of the series. It is most certainly not flat, but shows considerable power in the range of cycles of length 2.36 to 2.87 periods.

Finally, we note that it may be difficult to distinguish between deterministic chaotic processes and random processes superimposed on a nonchaotic process. If we take, for example, the deterministic process corresponding to w = 3.4 or 3.5, the power spectrum has (as one would expect) a very large spike at two-period cycles. If we now modify this process according to the specification described in the appendix, the power spectra become quite similar to those of chaotic regimes. The spike at the two-period cycle disappears and a considerable amount of power is found at the next three or four lower frequencies. It appears entirely possible that in such cases exploratory statistical procedures will tend to yield the wrong model.

Concluding Comment

The possibility of chaotic behavior is not confined to either the economic phenomena or the equations we have discussed. It arises in macroeconomic models as well as microeconomic ones. It arises for still broader ranges of parameter values in higher order equations. In short, it is not to be considered inherently unlikely and outre. Yet the very possibility suggests that substantial difficulties may threaten the work of the forecaster. Figure 4-4 and the succeeding graphs make that all too clear.

Acknowledgments

The authors appreciate deeply the support of the Division of Information Science and Technology and of the Economics Division of The National Science Foundation and the C.V. Starr Center for Applied Economics at New University.

Notes

1   For a beautifully lucid description of this structure and an explanation of its logic, see May [1976].

2   For other more interesting economic examples, see Benhabib and Day [1981], [1982] and Day [1983]. The example in the text is selected for its simplicity and transparency, not for realism or importance.

3   For an explanation that is far clearer and more general than that which follows, see May [1976]. A desire to save space and to avoid digression explains the avenue chosen for the exposition in the next few paragraphs.

4   Here the value of w has been changed from 3.45 to 3.5 because the latter yields a clearer picture.

References

Benhabib, J., and R. H. Day, "Rational Choice and Erratic Behavior," *Review of Economic Studies*, XLVIII (1981), 459–71.

_____. "A Characterization of Erratic Dynamics in the Overlapping Generations Model," *Journal of Economic Dynamics and Control*, IV (1982), 37–55.

Collet, P., and J-P. Eckmann, *Iterated Maps on the Interval as Dynamical Systems*. Boston: Birkhauser, 1980.

Day, R. H., "The Emergence of Chaos from Classical Economic Growth," *Quarterly Journal of Economics*, XCVII (1983), 201–213.

May, R. M., "Simple Mathematical Models with Very Complicated Dynamics," *Nature*, CCLXI (1976), 459–67.

Siegel, I., *Nonparametric Statistics*. New York: McGraw Hill, 1956.

Appendix: The Workings of the Artificial Stochastic Process

The stochastic process used to examine the random appearance of chaotic time paths was generated as follows: Set

A. $y_{t+1} = wy_t(1 - y_t)$ with probability 0.8;

B.   Define U to be a uniformly distributed number on the $(0,1)$ interval. Then set

$y_{t+1} = [0.8 + 0.2U]wy_t(1 - y_t)$ if $y_{t+1} < 1.0$,

$y_{t+1} = 0.99$ otherwise.

Let event B occur with probability 0.1;

C.   With the remaining probability of 0.1, set

$y_{t+1} = (0.9 + 0.099\ U)\ y_t$

$y_{t+2} = (0.9 + 0.099\ U)\ y_t$

$y_{t+3} = (0.9 + 0.099\ U)\ y_t,$

If event C occurs, we continue with the determination of y_{t+4}; if A or B occurs, we continue with the determination of y_{t+2}.

5

Structural Shifts and the Volatility of Chaotic Markets

By Sherrill Shaffer

1. Introduction

This chapter explores a theoretical connection between firm behavior, chaotic time paths, price volatility, and the 1987 stock market break. An attempt is made to construct a plausible explanation of an apparent increase in market volatility that may have contributed to the break. At the same time, the explanation suggests a basis for the excess volatility observed in stock prices by Shiller (1981), West (1988), and others.

The stock market break of October 1987 has drawn widespread attention and attempts at explanation. Most of the work surrounding the event has focused on possible causes of illiquidity in the market or, alternatively, on possible changes in the expected stock price levels (the question of "market fundamentals"). Reports by the Brady Commission (1988), the SEC (1988), and others maintain this emphasis.

A third direction of investigation has been explored by Leland (1987). He calculates the impact of an increase in long-run volatility on the equilibrium price level and concludes that a 20 percent drop in the stock market could have been brought about by a 25 percent increase in volatility. Volatility may thus have been a cause, not a result, of the break.

Empirical evidence suggests that an upward shift in volatility has indeed occurred. End-of-day prices in the months immediately following the break were about twice as volatile as before; much of this shift may be of a short-term nature, resulting from the break, as the market adjusts to the new price level. However, it is not unlikely that some of the shift may be of a more permanent character. Support for this idea is presented by Leland (1987) and also by Bhatt (1987), who identified a significant increase in volatility in the months immediately preceding the break. Thus, it appears that not all of the incremental volatility can be attributed to the break.

The following question then arises. If an upward shift in volatility did occur, and was at least partly responsible for the October market break, what caused this increase in volatility? Standard financial theory is of little help here, as it treats volatility as exogenous and, typically, fixed. A stochastic model that allows nonstationarity of stock prices would be consistent with time-varying volatility, but would be of no use in either forecasting changes in volatility or understanding structural relationships that may impinge on volatility.

Clearly, if an increase in volatility did play a causal role in the market break, then it becomes necessary to probe inside the "black box" of volatility and try to understand volatility as an endogenous variable. Any insight into the various factors that may underlie volatility will contribute to a better understanding of the market break and could lead to an improved policy response.

This chapter develops a model that provides a simple set of sufficient conditions for chaos to occur in the stock market. The conditions are based on the behavior of firms, not on trading strategies, thereby establishing that no regulatory policy aimed at trading strategies alone can ever guarantee freedom from chaos.

The chapter also uses computer simulations to examine the sort of price volatility that could be generated by a chaotic market and to explore the effect of small changes in structural parameters on the level of volatility. In a similar vein, Savit (1988, p. 287) has noted that small changes in the structural parameter of a chaotic system can qualitatively change the behavior of the system and could therefore have accounted for the stock market break. His remarks fall short of identifying a specific type of qualitative change that could have had the proposed result. This chapter fills that gap by demonstrating that small changes in the structural parameter can, within certain ranges, generate substantial increases in volatility sufficient to account for the market break.

The analysis of volatility associated with the chaotic time path also suggests an additional source of stock price volatility beyond those previously modeled. Such an additional component of volatility could be interpreted as partly explaining the empirical finding that stock prices are more volatile than can be accounted for by rational expectations of future dividends or interest rates [see Grossman and Shiller (1981), LeRoy and Porter (1981), Shiller (1981), Mankiw et al. (1985), and West (1988)].

2. The Stock Market and Deterministic Chaos

The traditional concept of stock market dynamics envisions a stream of stochastic "news" (information that cannot be anticipated) that may move prices in random directions. Nonlinearities in the process of disseminating and responding to such news could in principle generate a chaotic element that would result from the trading process. This chapter, by contrast, demonstrates that certain types of news (dividend announcements) may themselves follow a chaotic path and thus lead to chaotic prices, without any nonlinear or otherwise special trading process. The model is intended to be illustrative rather than an exact representation of the market.

The need for better models of stock market dynamics is further emphasized by the failure of purely stochastic models to account for the level of volatility that we observe in stock prices. The essence of empirical findings by Shiller (1981) and others is that movements in stock prices exceed those that could realistically be attributed to objective new information.

To begin with, it is formally incorrect to model the stock market as purely random. Each transaction, along with its price, is the result of conscious decisions by a buyer and a seller. Conventional microeconomic theory treats such decisions as the outcome of an optimization process and hence as deterministic [see also Kelsey (1988)]. Stochastic models have been applied to describe this process because of their tractability and because they closely approximate the observed pattern of price movements over time. However, when there is a question of causal factors, a deterministic model must be sought.

Previous work has explored the properties of deterministic systems that exhibit apparently random dynamic behavior, or chaos. Basic mathematical results due to May (1976), Feigenbaum (1978), and Collet and Eckmann (1980) have been applied to economic growth models [Stutzer (1980), Benhabib and Day (1980), and Day (1982, 1983)] as well as to cobweb market models [Jensen and Urban (1984)].

Most relevant to the work presented here, Scheinkman and LeBaron (1989) have found empirical evidence that the time path of stock market returns is consistent with nonlinear deterministic models (chaos) rather than purely stochastic behavior. However, they decline to suggest a model or explanation of the behavior they observe. Ramsey et al. (1990) challenge the chaotic interpretation of those results, citing nonstationarity in the time series and small-sample bias. After correcting for nonstationarity and bias, Ramsey et al. find no evidence of a chaotic attractor in stock returns.

Brock (1988) presents a conceptual argument suggesting that chaos in the stock market is "extremely unlikely," at least for hourly or daily stock price movements, as long as the markets are frictionless and prices are observed without error. However, stock price movements are discrete: there are lower bounds on the minimum observed nonzero price movement and indivisibilities in the observed price levels. Jensen (1987) has noted that such indivisibilities, like measurement error, can mask or substantially alter any underlying chaotic process. An underlying deterministic process may generate equilibrium prices that can only be approximated by the observed discrete prices. This result weakens Brock's argument against the possibility of an underlying chaotic process in the stock market. Likewise, transaction costs make it unprofitable to trade on the basis of price movements that are too small. This friction in the market, although slight, further weakens Brock's argument.

Moreover, Brock, like Scheinkman and LeBaron, found empirical evidence of a chaos-like intertemporal structure in weekly and monthly returns on aggregate stock price indices. He was able to rule out a January effect, linearly autoregressive conditional heteroscedasticity, and near-unit roots as possible explanations of that structure, strengthening the possibility that a truly chaotic process was being observed. Likewise, Ashley and Patterson (1989) find strong evidence of nonlinear stock market dynamics, which would be consistent with chaos but would not prove it. Other factors that might cause nonlinearity include price bounds and any trading based on asynchronous price data.

Section 3 shows that a simple and empirically supported decision rule for dividend payouts can lead to a chaotic time path in the stock market. In so doing, it provides one possible counterargument to Brock's reasoning that chaos would be unlikely in short-run stock prices. At the same time, it provides a possible theoretical basis for accepting the chaotic interpretation of previous empirical stock market analysis.

3. Dividends and Chaos

A heuristic definition of chaos is "behavior over time that appears to be random but is actually deterministic." Such behavior can be generated by certain types of nonlinear dynamic feedback loops, which can also be generalized to incorporate a stochastic component. Baumol and Benhabib (1989) and Devaney (1986) provide good introductions to the meaning and properties of chaos. Here we will present only as much of the theory as is necessary to convey the central point of the chapter.

In seeking a set of sufficient conditions to generate chaotic behavior in the stock market, one can choose to focus on trading and investment strategies (which practitioners refer to as "technical" aspects) or on the underlying technology, supply, and demand faced by the firms whose stock is traded (the so-called "fundamentals"). Both sets of factors are likely to be important. However, Roll (1988) presents evidence that computer-directed trading, including portfolio insurance and stock index arbitrage, did not contribute to the 1987 market break. Therefore, this section will focus exclusively on fundamentals and show how chaotic behavior can arise naturally from a simple policy of proportionate dividend payouts. This result establishes both that there is a plausible, rational basis for chaos in the stock market and that trading strategies theoretically need not be the cause. Perhaps more importantly, it demonstrates that institutional responses or regulatory policies aimed at the trading process alone can never guarantee freedom from chaos.

The two key assumptions in the model are:

A1 Firms pay dividends as a fixed proportion of realized profits.

A2 The remainder of profits is reinvested according to a marginal efficiency of investment (MEI) curve that declines linearly down to some minimum rate of return, such as the risk-free rate plus an appropriate risk premium.

It is further assumed for simplicity that the firm will always operate in the declining portion of the MEI schedule.

Support for the first assumption is found in Lintner (1956), who concluded from a survey that corporate managers tend to uphold the concept of a stable long-term payout ratio. Equivalently, we could entirely omit any consideration of dividends by assuming a payout ratio of zero, and the model would go through unchanged.

Support for the second assumption is found largely in the macroeconomic literature, where it has a pedigree extending back to before Keynes. In addition, reliance on external financing for some portion of investment could lead to a downward-sloping net MEI curve, if external financing is more costly and if it is used to an increasing extent for successively greater levels of investment. However, external financing is not explicitly modeled, and might be found to generate different dynamics.

Both assumptions are kept as simple as possible for clarity. An established property of chaotic models is that more complex linkages often generate the same sort of chaotic behavior that simpler conditions suffice to produce; see May (1976), Feigenbaum (1978), and Collet and Eckmann (1980). Lintner found that historical payout ratios did not entirely conform to managers' stated policy, but tended to exhibit some smoothing behavior, which could be expressed as a weighted average of past earnings over a number of years. There is little reason to suppose that such added complexity in the payout pattern would qualitatively alter the results. Likewise, the assumed linearity of the declining MEI schedule is not critical to the results.

Formally, we assume that the firm will pay out dividends of $(1 - \beta)\pi$ where π is profit and β is the retention rate with $0 < \beta < 1$. The firm's investment in period t is the remainder of the previous period's earnings,

$$I_t = \beta\pi_{t-1}. \tag{1}$$

Although the exact duration of the period t remains unspecified in the model, it is natural to assume that it corresponds to the frequency with which firms announce dividend payments. Alternatively, if $\beta = 1$ so that no dividends are ever declared, then any duration of t will be acceptable. The investment earns a marginal return according to

$$R(I_t) = a - bI_t, \tag{2}$$

subject to $a - \beta b\pi > R_{\min}$. One could imagine reasons why the marginal return could be positively correlated from one period to the next; for example, development of a new product could raise the MEI schedule for more than one period. Equation 4 below is capable of capturing a related effect for *total* earnings. Alternatively, one could argue that marginal returns might be negatively correlated over time; for instance, a stochastic component in the MEI schedule could introduce mean reversion such as has been empirically observed in some financial variables. On balance, rather than attempting to resolve the issue, it may be simpler to assume independence of marginal returns over time, as in Equation 2.

Total dollar earnings from this investment are just

$$E_t = \int_0^{I_t} R(i)\, di = aI_t - bI_t^2/2. \tag{3}$$

These earnings continue in subsequent periods (i.e., there is no depreciation), so

$$\pi_t = \pi_{t-1} + e_t, \tag{4}$$

from which

$$\pi_t = (1 + a\beta)\pi_{t-1} - b\beta^2\pi_{t-1}^2/2. \tag{5}$$

To transform Equation 5 into a form that is known to generate chaos, we seek a transformation of profits, $x_t(\pi_t)$, such that x_t satisfies

$$x_t = Ax_{t-1}(1 - x_{t-1}), \tag{6}$$

for some constant A and for $0 < x < 1$. Equation 6, the logistic equation, has been shown to be the basis of chaotic dynamic behavior in a wide variety of systems [May (1976), Feigenbaum (1978), Collet and Eckmann (1980)]. Many other functional forms can be transformed into the logistic equation, and indeed the chaotic dynamics exhibited by Equation 6 are also characteristic of other types of nonlinear difference equations (*ibid.*).

A linear transformation of π,

$$x_t = \gamma\pi_t, \tag{7}$$

will be shown to suffice. We solve for γ and A to satisfy Equations 6 and 7, where the restriction on the range of marginal returns in Equation 2 becomes $a - b/\gamma > R_{min}$. The solution is given by

$$A = 1 + a\beta \tag{8}$$

and

$$\gamma = b\beta^2/(2 + 2a\beta). \tag{9}$$

Positive profits can always be represented in units such that $0 < x < 1$, with a, b, I, and R also expressed according to those units. It is well known that many values of A between 3.57 and 4 will cause x to exhibit a chaotic time path in Equation 6 and hence cause π_t to exhibit a chaotic time path in Equation 5 [Baumol and Benhabib (1989), Jensen and Urban (1984)]. If the market adjusts its expectation of future earnings on the basis of current profits or a moving average of past profits, then chaotic profits also imply chaotic stock prices or returns. [Brock (1988) has also established that chaotic cash flows on assets can generate chaotic asset prices.] This result establishes that straightforward fundamental conditions may suffice to generate chaotic stock market behavior, depending on the parameter values.

Equation 8 states that the key structural parameter that determines whether profits are chaotic is positively related to the product of the intercept of the MEI schedule (i.e., the limiting marginal return as the amount invested approaches zero) and the profit retention rate. Equations 7 and 9 together state that the variable that actually follows the potentially chaotic time path is the firm's profit, times the slope of the MEI schedule, times a term that is inversely related to the intercept of the MEI schedule and positively but nonlinearly related to the profit retention rate. Thus, three parameters completely determine the dynamic behavior of the system: the intercept and slope of the MEI schedule, and the profit retention rate (or, equivalently, the dividend payout rate). Only two of these parameters affect the structural parameter A.

One property of Equation 6 is that, given a positive initial value of x, all subsequent values of x are also positive. That is, chaos as modeled here will never generate net losses. However, it is clearly possible to add an offset or intercept term to Equation 7 that would allow for losses in some states, so that a small but positive value of x could correspond to negative profits. Moreover, negative *marginal* returns in some periods would be consistent with the model as it stands.

An interesting feature of Equation 6 is that it yields a time path that, while satisfying certain formal tests for randomness, at the same time exhibits some apparent regularities to the casual observer. For example, low values of x can be followed by slowly monotonically increasing values of x for several periods until a sufficiently high value is reached to shift the system back to low values. Such apparent regularities also occur in the stock market and form the basis for so-called technical analysis, whereby traders attempt to predict future price movements by extrapolating certain patterns from recent historical prices [see, e.g., Weinstein (1988)]. Similar patterns may also be observed over longer time periods; see the graphs of the Standard and Poor's Composite Stock Price Index, 1871–1979, and the Dow Jones Industrial Average, 1928–1979, in Shiller (1981). While these apparent regularities do not prove that the market exhibits chaos, they at least demonstrate that chaotic models cannot be ruled out on the basis of such regularities.

Although the theoretical literature on chaos treats the structural parameter A as a constant in Equation 6, the model here establishes A as a function of the dividend retention rate and the marginal return on investment. Either or both of these variables may change over time, not necessarily from one period to the next, but at least over a sufficiently long set of periods.

In general, we may expect the firm-specific MEI curve shift over time, as a result of either firm-specific or macroeconomic factors. Equation 9 shows that changes in any of the three underlying parameters a, b, or β will rescale how profits are transformed into the variable x. Such rescaling will affect not only the level of x for a given π, but also the subsequent change in x, and hence the time path of both x and π. However, Equation 8 indicates that changes in the slope b will not affect the structural parameter A, which alone determines whether the system is chaotic; only changes in the intercept a (or in the retention rate β) are important for that purpose. In a growing economy, or where the firm invests in research and development, it is possible for a to increase over time, either stochastically or with a systematic component. By contrast, any factors that tend to exhaust the firm's temporary ability to earn above-market returns on a portion of investments will reduce a over time. Business cycle effects can go in either direction, depending on the phase of the cycle.

Since A is a function of a, any such changes will generate a shift in A. Thus, we have, perhaps for the first time in an economic application, a model of chaos where the key structural parameter can naturally be expected to vary over time, either up or down. Endogenous variations as a function of x could be expected to alter Equation 8 and hence the intertemporal linkage (Equation 6), while stochastic variation would superimpose a random component onto the deterministic linkage; however, previous work such as May (1976), Feigenbaum (1978), and Collet and Eckmann (1980) indicates that such changes would tend not to alter the chaotic behavior of the system. Therefore, we do not explicitly model changes in A. Instead, Section 4 builds on the basic theoretical result in Equations 6–9 by examining the sort of volatility generated by Equation 6. Of particular interest is whether small changes in the structural parameter A may lead to large changes in volatility.

4. Chaos and Volatility

Since the previous section established not only that a chaotic time path of returns can result from simple, fundamental behavioral factors, but also that the key structural parameter in the chaotic process is likely to exhibit some shifting or evolution over time, it becomes important to compare the properties of a chaotic time path for different values of the structural parameter A.

As explained in Leland (1987), the linkage between volatility and the stock price level can be straightforward. Historically, stocks have yielded an average annual return (including dividends and capital gains) of about six percentage points higher than corresponding Treasury bond rates. In other words, the market has tended to price stocks such that their yield equals the risk-free rate plus 6 percent. This differential or risk premium has been observed over a time period during which the annualized volatility or standard deviation of stock prices was about 20 percent, and suggests a market price of risk equal to 0.3 percent return per 1 percent of volatility (6 percent divided by 20 percent). If the volatility changes but expected future profits of the firm do not change, then the stock price must adjust so that the total yield on the stock incorporates the risk premium appropriate to the new volatility. For example, if volatility increases from 20 percent to 25 percent and the price of risk is constant, then the return on equity must increase to the risk-free rate plus 7.5 percent (0.3 percent times 25 percent). Leland has shown that such an increase in the risk premium would have required a fall in the stock price approximately equal to that observed in the October 1987 crash, given expectations of unchanged future profits.

Table 5-1 presents the standard deviation, or "volatility," of percentage changes in x resulting from different values of A according to Equation 6. These standard deviations were computed from simulations of 1,000 iterations of Equation 6, following 100 initializing iterations to eliminate any sensitivity of the time path to starting values of x, for each value of A from 3.58 to 3.99 (the relevant range for chaos). It is seen that the volatility of x ranges from 71 percent to 35 percent and varies nonmonotonically with A.

It is not possible to compare these figures directly with the levels of observed stock price volatility, since such a comparison would require exact knowledge of how the stock price varies with current profits. In addition, the duration of a time period in our model would have to be specified and related to annualized daily, weekly, or other stipulated volatility levels.

However, even though we cannot directly compare the *levels* of volatility, we know that a given percentage *change* in the volatility of x will correspond to a similar percentage change in the volatility of stock prices or returns. This result follows for stock returns from the proportionality of x to π given in Equation 7, while the corresponding linkage between returns and prices is established by Brock (1988).

Two regions of particular interest exist. As A increases from 3.73 to 3.74, the volatility of x rises by 18 percent. Also, as A goes from 3.82 to 3.83, the volatility of x increases by 25 percent. These figures suggest that indeed a small increase in A can lead to an increase in volatility of the magnitude estimated by Leland (1987) as sufficient to account for the 1987 market break.

Table 5-2 presents a more detailed breakdown of this latter region. It is apparent that sizable changes in volatility can result from smaller orders of magnitude of changes in the structural parameter A. Whereas an increment of A equal to 0.01 can change volatility by 25 percent, an increment of A equal to 0.001 can change volatility by 9 percent; even an increment of A equal to 0.000001 can change volatility by 6 percent.

Table 5-1

Structural Parameter and Volatility

A	σ_x	A	σ_x
3.58	0.7787	3.79	0.9198
3.59	0.7927	3.8	0.9519
3.6	0.7968	3.81	0.9686
3.61	0.7973	3.82	1.0088
3.62	0.7956	3.83	1.2566
3.63	0.7448	3.84	1.2760
3.64	0.7898	3.85	1.2826
3.65	0.7823	3.86	1.1524
3.66	0.7816	3.87	1.1622
3.67	0.7703	3.88	1.1122
3.68	0.7143	3.89	1.1533
3.69	0.7414	3.9	1.1635
3.7	0.7470	3.91	1.2382
3.71	0.7855	3.92	1.1493
3.72	0.8047	3.93	1.1532
3.73	0.7957	3.94	1.1973
3.74	0.9444	3.95	1.2231
3.75	0.8759	3.96	1.3046
3.76	0.8661	3.97	1.3294
3.77	0.9003	3.98	1.3423
3.78	0.9107	3.99	1.3478

It is possible to gain further insight into the dependence of volatility on the structural parameter A. For one-dimensional maps of the form $x_{n+1} = F(x_n)$, of which Equation 6 is a special case, the average Lyapunov exponent is defined as

$$\lambda = \lim_{N \to \infty} \frac{1}{N} \sum_{n=1}^{N} \ln\left(\left| dF(x_n)/dx \right| \right). \tag{10}$$

The average Lyapunov exponent may be interpreted as a measure of how quickly nearby trajectories of x diverge. Brock (1986) notes that the Lyapunov exponent may be viewed as an extension to general forward orbits of eigenvalues of the dynamical system at a fixed point. A necessary condition for a sample of time series data to be chaotic is that the largest

Table 5-2

Subregions of Table 5-1

Change in A			
Size	From	To	Percentage change in volatility of x
10^{-2}	3.82	− 3.83	24.6%
10^{-3}	3.827	− 3.828	8.6%
10^{-4}	3.827	− 3.8271	6.4%
10^{-5}	3.82709	− 3.8271	5.0%
10^{-6}	3.827099	− 3.8271	5.8%
10^{-7}	3.827099	− 3.8270991	3.4%

Lyapunov exponent for the sample must be positive (*ibid.*); negative values of the average Lyapunov exponent correspond to periodic cycles rather than chaos.

Jensen (1987) presents a graph of the average Lyapunov exponent as a function of *A*. The graph exhibits broadly monotonic behavior but with

Figure 5-1

Structural Parameter and Volatility

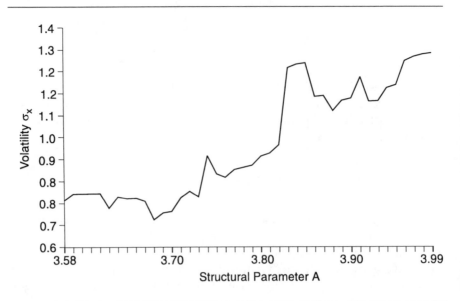

many small dips and peaks. In the range $3.58 < A < 3.99$, the two sharpest dips (both of which cross zero) occur between 3.73 and 3.74 and between 3.82 and 3.83, exactly where the sharpest increases in volatility are found in Table 5-1. This indicates that the sharp increases in volatility at these points arise from the transition between chaotic and periodic behavior (where the cycle in fact has period 3 at $A \approx 3.83$ and period 5 at $A \approx 3.74$).

Presumably, an even larger increase in volatility could occur as A is increased from $A < 3$ to $A \geq 3$, where x jumps from a steady state to a period-2 cycle; as the focus of this chapter is on chaotic behavior, such ranges of A were not explored. At any rate, it would appear that nonlinear dynamics can exhibit sharp volatility breaks, whether chaotic or not. A further consequence of this point is that a deterministic time path may exhibit a level of volatility that is quite sensitive to small changes in the values of the structural parameters, even if A lies outside the range of 3.57 to 4.

In general, we might expect significant changes in volatility to occur in regions where the average Lyapunov exponent changes abruptly with A. It is consistent with this expectation that sharp dips in the average Lyapunov exponent from positive values to near-zero or slightly negative values are observed to coincide with increases in volatility. As a result, we may be more confident that the results in Tables 5-1 and 5-2 are not merely flukes of the particular samples generated.

5. Concluding Remarks

To sum up, what has been shown is the following:

1. Chaotic time paths may be generated by fundamental causes, even apart from specific trading behavior; conditions as simple as a fixed dividend payout ratio, combined with a declining marginal efficiency of investment curve, can suffice to produce chaos, depending on the relevant parameter values.

2. A simple chaotic model can generate volatility of returns or prices in a pattern reasonably similar to that observed in the market.

3. Within certain regions, the level of volatility is quite sensitive to small changes in the value of the structural parameter.

4. The resulting change in volatility is of the order of magnitude estimated by Leland (1987) as capable of accounting for the market break of October 1987.

5. Finally, there are sound reasons to expect some shifting or evolution of the relevant structural parameter over time, although these were not explicitly modeled.

If this mechanism did contribute to the market break, there are two possible ways it could have happened. Either a one-time change in the structural parameter could have caused the apparent increase in volatility, or else a gradual upward trend in the structural parameter at some point encountered one of the regions where the volatility is particularly sensitive to that parameter.

The policy implications of these two scenarios are quite different. In the first case, attention would be best focused on controlling the structural parameter and its changes. In the second case, by contrast, a certain drift in the structural parameter would constitute a normal part of the market and would not need to be opposed. Instead, measuring the current value of the parameter and its drift would tell us whether we have reason to be concerned about a possible recurrence of a volatility-driven market break in the near future. Once the critical region is crossed, the market would be expected to behave normally until another critical region is encountered. Alternatively, if the structural parameter were to reverse its drift, the immediate impact would be a reduction of volatility and hence, by Leland's argument, an increase in stock prices.

Two facts stand out, however. First, chaos itself is not necessarily disastrous, as measured by the volatility of profits. Second, since fundamental causes suffice to produce chaos, no regulatory policy aimed solely at the trading process can ever guarantee freedom from chaos.

Clearly, more work would be needed to link both the functional form and the parameter values of the model to actual stock prices, and then to measure the current historical values of the critical structural parameter responsible for chaotic time paths. However, the results presented here suggest that such work could assist in the evaluation of alternative policy responses to the October market break.

Acknowledgments

The views expressed in this paper are those of the author and do not necessarily reflect the views of the Federal Reserve Bank of Philadelphia or the Federal Reserve System. The author is grateful for helpful comments from anonymous referees, Swati Bhatt, William Brock, Hasung Jang, Richard Lang, Mark Levonian, and Robert Savit.

References

Ashley, R. J., and D. M. Patterson, "Linear Versus Nonlinear Macroeconomics: A Statistical Test," *International Economic Review* 30, No. 3 (1989), 685–704.

Baumol, W. J., and J. Benhabib, "Chaos: Significance, Mechanism, and Economic Applications," *Journal of Economic Perspectives* 3, No. 1 (1989), 77–105.

Benhabib, J., and R. H. Day, "Erratic Accumulation," *Economics Letters* 6 (1980), 113–17.

Bhatt, S., "The Impact of Stock Index Arbitrage on Equity Markets: Theory and Evidence," Federal Reserve Bank of New York Research Paper No. 8707 (1987).

Brock, William A., "Distinguishing Random and Deterministic Systems: Abridged Version," *Journal of Economic Theory* 40 (1986), 168–195.

Brock, William A., "Nonlinearity and Complex Dynamics in Economics and Finance," SFI Studies in the Sciences of Complexity (Reading, MA: Addison-Wesley Publishing Company, 1988), 77–97.

Collet, P., and J. P. Eckmann, *Iterated Maps on the Unit Interval as Dynamical Systems* (Boston: Birkhauser, 1980).

Day, R. H., "Irregular Growth Cycles," *American Economic Review* 72 (1982), 406–414.

Day, R. H., "The Emergence of Chaos from Classical Economic Growth," *Quarterly Journal of Economics* 98 (1983), 201-213.

Devaney, R. L., *An Introduction to Chaotic Dynamical Systems* (Reading, MA: Addison-Wesley, 1986).

Feigenbaum, M. J., "Quantitative Universality for a Class of Nonlinear Transformations," *Journal of Statistical Physics* 19 (1978), 25–52.

Grossman, S. J., and R. J. Shiller, "The Determinants of the Variability of Stock Market Prices," *American Economic Review* 71, No. 2 (1981), 222–227.

Jensen, R. V., "Classical Chaos," *American Scientist* 75 (1987), 168–181.

Jensen, R. V., and R. Urban, "Chaotic Price Behavior in a Non-Linear Cobweb Model," *Economics Letters* 15 (1984), 235–240.

Kelsey, D., "The Economics of Chaos or the Chaos of Economics," *Oxford Economic Papers* 40 (1988), 1–31.

Leland, H. E., "On the Stock Market Crash and Portfolio Insurance," Mimeo (Berkeley, CA: University of California, 1987).

LeRoy, S., and R. Porter, "The Present-Value Relation: Tests Based on Implied Variance Bounds," *Econometrica* 49, No. 1 (1981), 97–113.

Lintner, J., "Distribution of Incomes of Corporations among Dividends, Retained Earnings, and Taxes," *American Economic Review* 46 (1956), 97–113.

Mankiw, N. G., D. Romer, and M. Shapiro, "An Unbiased Reexamination of Stock Market Volatility," *The Journal of Finance* 40 (1985), 677–687.

May, R. M., "Simple Mathematical Models with Very Complicated Dynamics," *Nature* 261 (1976), 459.

Ramsey, James B., Chera L. Sayers, and Philip Rothman, "The Statistical Properties of Dimension Calculations Using Small Data Sets: Some Economic Applications," *International Economic Review* 31, No. 4 (1990), 991–1020.

Report of the Presidential Task Force on Market Mechanisms. New York, 1988.

Roll, R., "The International Crash of October 1987," in *Black Monday and the Future of Financial Markets*, MAI Task Force (New York: Dow Jones-Irwin, 1988).

Savit, R., "When Random Is Not Random: An Introduction to Chaos in Market Prices," *The Journal of Futures Markets* 8, No. 3 (1988), 271–289.

Scheinkman, J. A., and B. LeBaron, "Nonlinear Dynamics and Stock Returns," *The Journal of Business* 62, No. 3 (1989), 311–338.

Shiller, R. J., "Do Stock Prices Move Too Much to Be Justified by Subsequent Changes in Dividends?" *American Economic Review* 71, No. 3 (1981), 421–436.

Stutzer, M., "Chaotic Dynamics and Bifurcation in a Macro Model," *Journal of Economic Dynamics and Control* 2 (1980), 353–376.

The October 1987 Market Break, U.S. Securities and Exchange Commission, 1988.

Weinstein, S., *Secrets for Profiting in Bull and Bear Markets* (Homewood, IL: Dow Jones-Irwin, 1988).

West, K., "Dividend Innovation and Stock Price Volatility," *Econometrica* 56, No. 1 (1988), 37–61.

PART II

STOCK MARKETS EVIDENCE

6

TESTING FOR NONLINEAR DEPENDENCE IN DAILY STOCK INDICES

By Thomas Willey

Introduction

Is the current market price of an asset the best estimate to the future price, making all attempts at forecasting price movements a useless exercise? Or is it possible to develop a model to fully explain day-to-day price fluctuations? The answer probably lies somewhere between these two extremes, in improving existing examples of short-term forecasting successes. Many empirical studies have shown that stock returns follow a white-noise model and are unable to be forecast successfully (Fama 1970), but new evidence has been presented that shows that these results may be supplemented, and perhaps replaced, by a new hypothesis of an underlying nonlinear process.

Nonlinear processes are the focus of research in many scientific areas. Although the beginnings of these new techniques have been in the natural sciences of physics and chemistry, they are now being applied to finance and economics. Interest in these techniques is based on the assumption that highly complex behavior that appears to be random is actually generated by an underlying nonlinear process. Typically, standard statistical tests, such as spectral analysis and autocorrelation functions, are used to test for randomness and may fail to detect this hidden order.

Empirical evidence of this phenomenon has been shown by various researchers. Brock and Sayers (1988) found nonlinearity in the U.S. labor market and investment. Barnett and Chen (1988) discovered low dimensionality in some U.S. monetary measures. Frank et al. (1988) indicated nonlinearities were present in Japan's quarterly real GNP. Strong nonlinear dependence was also found in daily price changes of five foreign-exchange rates by Hsieh (1989) and in financial and agricultural futures by Blank (1990). Scheinkman and LeBaron (1989) found that a significant part of the variation in weekly Center for Research in Security Prices (CRSP) stock index returns is due to nonlinearities instead of randomness. Other studies in this area include Frank and Stengos (1988), Hinich and Patterson (1985), and Savit (1988, 1989).

This nonlinear process, termed *deterministic chaos*, is the focus of this research. Specifically, the purpose of this article is to test for the presence of deterministic chaos in the daily prices of two time series: the Standard & Poor's 100 Stock Index (OEX) and the NASDAQ (NAS) 100 Stock Index.

Research Methodology

The methodology follows the lead of Brock (1986), Brock, Dechert, and Scheinkman (1987; hereafter BDS), Hsieh (1989), and Frank et al. (1988) by estimating the correlation dimension. The correlation dimension is used to differentiate between deterministic chaos and stochastic systems. Dimensionality is a measure of the complexity of an object. Brock and Sayers (1988) describe the dimension of an object as a rough indication of the number of nonlinear "factors" that describe the data. For example, a single point has zero dimension. A line has one dimension. A solid has three dimensions. A white-noise process is completely disorderly and has infinite dimension. Similarly, a purely random process has infinite dimension. A chaotic system has a positive but finite dimension (Frank et al. 1988).

One method to test for nonlinear dependence involves the "correlation integral," $C(e)$. For a time series $\{Y_t: t = 1, ..., T\}$ of D-dimensional vectors, the correlation integral measures the fraction of the pairs of points of $\{Y_t\}$ that are within a distance of e from each other. This value is:

$$C(e) = \lim_{T\to\infty} \frac{2}{T(T-1)} \sum_{i<j} I_e(Y_i, Y_j), \tag{1}$$

where $I_e(x, y)$ = indicator function that equals unity if $||x - y|| < e$, and zero otherwise; $||x - y||$ = the norm as measured by the Euclidian distance.

A form of the correlation integral is used by Grassberger and Procaccia (1983) and Swinney (1985) to define the "correlation dimension" of $\{Y_t\}$: Calculate this value by

$$C_m(e,T) = \#\left\{(t, s), 1 < t,s < T \mid \; |x_t^m - x_s^m| < e\right\}/T_m^2, \tag{2}$$

where

$\#S$ = the cardinality of set S;
$T_m = T - (m - 1)$ = the number of m-histories $x_t^m = (x_t, ..., x_{t+m-1})$
constructed from the sample of length T;
m = embedding dimension.

Theoretically, $T \to\infty$ but actually it is determined by the number of observations available for the analysis. This places limits on possible values for e and m. For a given m, e cannot be too small because $C_m(e, T)$ will contain too few observations. Also, e cannot be too large because $C_m(e, T)$ will contain too many observations. Barnett and Choi (1989) suggest selecting a small value for e, without allowing it to reach zero. This implementation of a lower limit guards against noise in the data. Hsieh (1989) defines e in terms of multiples of the series standard deviation. These multiples are 1.50, 1.25, 1.00, 0.75, and 0.50. For this study, e is defined by the same multiples of the standard deviation of the data. For small values of e it has been shown that $C_m(e, T) \sim e^D$ so that D is the system's dimensionality [Frank et al. (1988)]. The series dimension is estimated by

$$D^m = \lim_{e\to 0} [\log C_m(e,T)/\log e], \text{ if the limit exists.} \tag{3}$$

The correlation dimension is used to differentiate between deterministic chaos and stochastic systems. If chaos is present, as D^m is estimated for increasingly larger values of the embedding dimension, the dimension estimate will stabilize at some value. If this stabilization does not occur, the system is considered "high-dimensional" or stochastic.

Brock's Residual Test

The first procedure creates the data for use in Brock's Residual Test (Brock 1988). Baumol and Benhabib (1989) suggest, prior to analyzing a time series for nonlinear dynamics, that the series be transformed by ordinary least squares (OLS) and/or autoregressive techniques. The first task is to remove any linear structure in the data. This filtering, or *prewhitening*, is done by fitting an autoregressive model to the transformed series. This process allows for a nonlinear test for the presence of a deterministic system and, if accepted, enables the rejection of a linear generating process. The dimension of the residuals is estimated and compared with the dimension of the original data. If a nonlinear process is present, these values will be undisturbed. However, the results for this diagnostic must be interpreted with caution. A bias has been shown when the relatively smaller (100 to 2,000 observations) data sets available to economic researchers are used compared with the series in the natural sciences (10,000 to 30,000 observations). This bias results in estimation errors in the dimension estimates that lead to rejection of deterministic chaos, even when it is present (Brock 1988; Hsieh 1989; Ramsey et al. 1988).

Shuffling and Bootstrapping Procedure

Another diagnostic has been presented by Scheinkman and LeBaron (1989). They suggest taking the time series and randomly sampling from it with replacement. This "shuffled" series will be a new series of the same length as the original series. The estimated dimension of the shuffled residuals is compared with the estimated dimension of the original residuals. If the original series was chaotic, the underlying order would be upset. This would result in a higher value of estimated dimensionality for the shuffled series than for the original series. This procedure is repeated 50 times for each level of e, to carry out the bootstrapping aspect of the test.

BDS Test

BDS (1987) have presented a hypothesis test using the W statistic. This test is based on the correlation integral. The null hypothesis is that the data are independently and identically distributed (IID); this test is applied instead of an attempt to determine if the data are stochastic or chaotic. BDS have shown that tests based on the W statistic have a higher power for tests of stochastic or chaotic independence than other statistical techniques.

BDS show that under the null hypothesis (x_t) is IID with a nondegenerate density F (Hsieh, 1989),

$C_m(e, T) \rightarrow C_1(e)^m$ with probability equal to unity, as $T \rightarrow \infty$,

for any fixed m and e. Furthermore, they show that $T^{1/2}[C_m(e, T) - C_1(e, T)^m]$ has a normal limiting distribution with zero mean and variance equal to

$$\sigma_m^2(e) = 4\left[K^m + 2\sum_{j=1}^{m-1} K^{m-j}C^{2j} + (m-1)^2 C^{2m} - m^2 KC^{2m-2} \right], \quad (4.1)$$

where

$$C = C(e) = \int [F(z + e) - F(z - e)]\, dF(z), \quad (4.1a)$$

$$K = K(e) = \iint [F(z + e) - F(z - e)]^2\, dF(z).$$

Since $C_1(e, T)$ is a consistent estimate of $C(e)$, and

$$K(e,T) = \frac{6}{T_m(T_m - 1)\,(T_m - 2)} \sum_{t<s<r} I_e(x_t, x_s)\, I_e(x_s, X_r) \quad (4.2)$$

is a consistent estimate of $K(e)$. Therefore $\sigma_m(e)$ can be estimated by $\sigma_m(e, T)$, which uses $C_1(e, T)$ and $K(e, T)$ instead of $C(e)$ and $K(e)$. The W statistic has a standard normal limiting distribution and is calculated by

$$W_m(e,T) = T^{1/2}\left[C_m(e,T) - C_1(e,T)^m \right]/\sigma_m(e,T). \quad (4.3)$$

BDS show that, under the null of IID, $W_m \rightarrow N(0, 1)$, as $T \rightarrow \infty$. If the residuals from the estimated linear (or nonlinear) model are actually IID, the W statistics should be asymptotically $N(0, 1)$. Large values would indicate strong evidence for nonlinearity in the data.

Application to the Stock Indices

The data consist of the daily closing values of the respective stock indices. For the OEX, the observations begin on January 4, 1982, and end on December 30, 1988 ($n = 1,769$). For the NASDAQ series the period begins on October 7, 1985, and ends on June 20, 1989 ($n = 945$ observations). To ensure that the data are stationary, the first difference of the log of each series is taken. Let $x_t = [(\log$ of the OEX index on day $t) - (\log$ of the OEX index on day $t - 1)]$ and $y_t = [(\log$ of the NAS index on day $t) - (\log$ of the NAS index on day $t - 1)]$. Figures 6-1 and 6-2 contain the plots of x_t and y_t. Brock and Sayers (1988) have shown that the power of the BDS statistic

Figure 6-1

First Difference of Log (OEX).

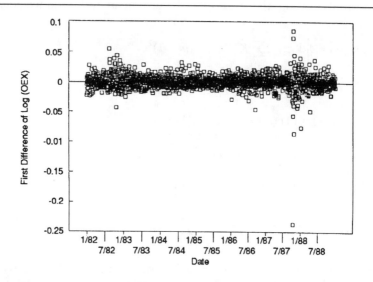

Figure 6-2

First Difference of Log (NAS)

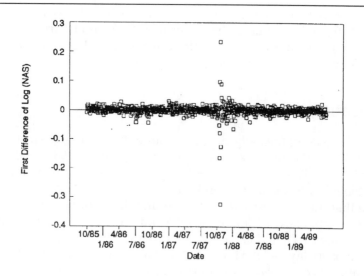

declines as higher-order AR(x) models are applied, leading to a need to set x as low as possible. An autoregressive model of order 3 [AR(3)] was fit to the OEX series and an AR(4) was fit to the NAS data to generate the white-noise residuals used in the analysis:

$$x_t = 0.13x_{t-1} - 0.08x_{t-2} - 0.02x_{t-3} + \delta x_t; \tag{5.1a}$$
$$\quad (5.6) \qquad (-3.5) \qquad (-0.8)$$

$$R^2 = 0.004,\ SSR = 0.281,\ SEE = 0.013,\ NOBS = 1764,\ DW = 1.99,$$

$$\sigma_x = 0.0126,\ \sigma_{\delta x} = 0.0126,\ \sigma_x/\sigma_{\delta x} = 1.00,$$

$$sk_x = -3.725,\ sk_{\delta x} = -4.022,$$

$$k_x = 74.266,\ k_{\delta x} = 78.279. \tag{5.1b}$$

$$y_t = -0.73y_{t-1} - 0.13y_{t-2} + 0.13y_{t-3} + 0.08y_{t-4} + \delta y_t; \tag{5.2a}$$
$$\quad (-22.53) \quad (-3.12) \qquad (3.11) \qquad (2.37)$$

$$R^2 = 0.142,\ SSR = 0.288,\ SEE = 0.018,\ NOBS = 939,\ DW = 1.99,$$

$$\sigma_y = 0.019,\ \sigma_{\delta y} = 0.017,\ \sigma_y/\sigma_{\delta y} = 1.08,$$

$$sk_y = -4.239,\ sk_{\delta y} = -3.458. \tag{5.2b}$$

$$k_y = 124.245,\ k_{\delta y} = 61.557$$

The numbers in parentheses are t statistics, SSR is the sum of squared residuals, SEE is the standard error of the estimate, $NOBS$ is the number of observations, and DW is the Durbin–Watson statistic. The symbols σ_z, sk_z, k_z represent the standard deviation of z, the skewness of z, and kurtosis of z.

Figures 6-3 and 6-4 contain plots for the residuals for both series. Table 6-1 contains the results of the autocorrelation tests for the unwhitened and whitened series. All linear structure has been removed by the AR(3) process for the OEX series. The AR(4) model fits the NAS series well, taking away all significant autocorrelations, except those at lags 7 and 26.

As a further test for structure in the residuals of both series, two diagnostics were applied. First, the series were tested for the presence of an autoregressive conditional heteroskedasticity (ARCH) process (Engle 1982). The test results for the OEX series were 32.71 (order = 1), 42.65 (order = 2), 45.91 (order = 3), and 45.89 (order = 4). The results for the NAS series were 215.93, 217.04, 285.33, and 306.20. The critical values follow a chi-square distribution with the chosen ARCH order as the degrees of freedom. In every case, the test statistic exceeded the critical value, indicating evidence of an ARCH process in the residuals.

Figure 6-3

OEX (AR3) Residuals

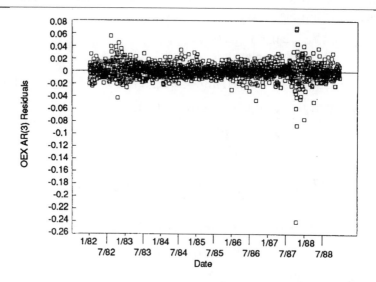

Figure 6-4

NAS AR(4) Residuals

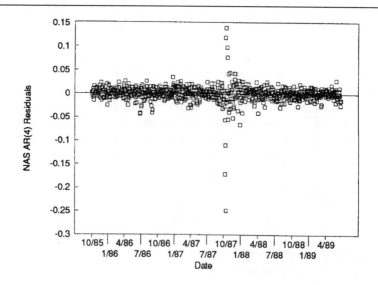

Table 6-1

Autocorrelations of the Unwhitened and Whitened Series

Lag	OEX(1)	NAS(1)	OEX(2)	NAS(2)
1	0.01	<u>−0.31</u>	−0.00	−0.00
2	−0.07	<u>0.24</u>	−0.00	−0.00
3	−0.02	0.03	0.01	0.00
4	−0.04	0.01	−0.05	0.01
5	0.04	−0.00	0.04	0.01
6	0.02	0.01	0.02	−0.04
7	−0.00	<u>−0.08</u>	−0.00	<u>−0.08</u>
8	−0.00	0.03	−0.00	0.02
9	−0.01	−0.01	−0.01	0.02
10	−0.02	−0.02	−0.03	−0.01
11	−0.01	−0.02	−0.02	−0.02
12	0.03	−0.00	0.02	−0.02
13	−0.04	−0.04	−0.04	−0.03
14	0.02	0.02	0.02	0.00
15	−0.01	−0.05	−0.01	−0.03
16	0.03	0.04	0.03	0.03
17	0.00	−0.03	0.00	−0.00
18	−0.02	0.03	−0.02	0.02
19	−0.04	−0.03	−0.04	−0.03
20	0.01	0.01	0.01	−0.00
21	0.01	−0.01	0.00	−0.01
22	−0.02	−0.02	−0.02	−0.02
23	0.01	0.01	0.01	−0.00
24	0.02	0.00	0.02	−0.01
25	−0.03	−0.01	−0.03	0.00
26	−0.02	0.06	−0.02	<u>0.07</u>
27	0.04	0.03	0.04	0.04
28	0.03	−0.00	0.03	−0.00
29	0.03	0.05	0.03	0.04
30	−0.00	0.02	0.01	0.02
Sample size	1768	944	1764	939
Critical values	0.05	0.06	0.05	0.06

Note: Index(1) = logged first difference of the closing value of stock index; index(2) = linear structure removed from index(1) using AR process as reported in equation (5.1) or (5.2); the lags are significant if the reported values are greater than or equal to the critical value. The underlined values are significant at 95 percent level.

Next, the Ljung-Box Q statistic for general serial correlation was employed (Ljung and Box 1978). Testing the OEX residuals for lags up to 126 days resulted in a Q statistic of 160.85 (p value = .014), indicating the series may have significant autocorrelations. The results for the NAS series supported randomness for lags up to 90 days (Q = 74.82, p value = .875).

Correlation Dimension Results

Figures 6-5 and 6-6 show the estimated correlation dimension (CD) for each series for embedding dimensions ranging from 2 to 6, given $e = 1.50$ times the series standard deviation. CD estimates for the log-first-differenced original series, Standard & Poor's Index [OEX(1)] and the NASDAQ [NAS(1)] 100 Stock Index, the AR(3) white-noise residuals for the OEX [OEX(2)], the AR(4) white-noise residuals for the NASDAQ[NAS(2)], and the 50 scrambled white-noise residuals [OEX(3) and NAS(3)] are contained in Table 6-2. The CDs for the OEX(1) range from 0.53 to 1.65, while the estimates for the NAS(1) series are from 0.17 to 0.95. Estimates for the CDs for the OEX(2) series range from 0.54 to 1.69, while the NAS(2) observations vary between 0.37 and 1.34. Both series of white-noise residuals have CDs that are similar to those of about 2 reported for Treasury bill returns by Brock (1988) and for the S&P 500 and the soybean nearby futures contract by Blank (1990), but are lower in terms of the absolute value than the previously reported CD of around 6 for another cash stock index (Scheinkman and LeBaron 1989).

At the present time, no statistical test has been developed to distinguish if two CD estimates are significantly different from each other. The OEX series passes Brock's Residual Test for low-dimension chaos, since there is no apparent difference between the CDs of the original series and the AR(3) white-noise residuals. The NASDAQ series fails this same test: A noticeable increase is present between the two estimates. Another indication that points to the lack of chaos in both series is that the estimated dimensions of both series continue to increase. CD estimates for chaotic systems stabilize at some value of the embedding dimension. In summary, these events imply that the two series are stochastic, not chaotic.

The CD estimates for the OEX(3) series range from 0.70 to 1.94 and for the NAS(3) data the values from 0.47 to 1.60. This increase in the dimensionality estimates of the shuffles, compared to the residuals of the whitened data, indicates that both series are chaotic. However, convergence of the dimension estimates occurs under this technique also, which indicates a nonchaotic series.

Figure 6-5

Standard & Poor's 100

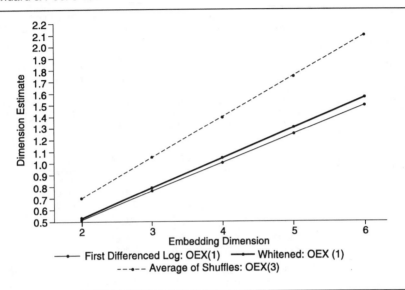

Figure 6-6

NASDAQ 100

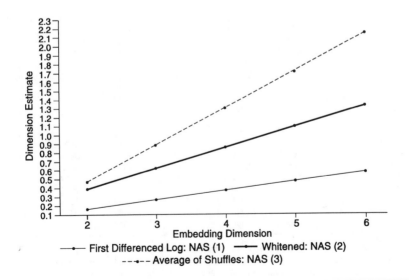

Table 6-2

Correlation Dimension Estimates

e	m	Standard & Poor's 100			NASDAQ 100		
		OEX(1)	OEX(2)	OEX(3)	NAS(1)	NAS(2)	NAS(3)
1.50	2	0.5257	0.5443	0.6977	0.1654	0.3651	0.4728
1.50	3	0.7858	0.8151	1.0471	0.2376	0.5159	0.7105
1.50	4	1.0419	1.0808	1.3963	0.3039	0.6633	0.9479
1.50	5	1.2934	1.3411	1.7468	0.3662	0.8075	1.1857
1.50	6	1.5443	1.5989	2.0947	0.4275	0.9487	1.4251
1.50	7	1.7889	1.8534	NA	0.4872	1.0873	1.6681
1.50	8	2.0312	2.1010	NA	0.5439	1.2229	1.9073
1.50	9	2.2759	2.3450	NA	0.6042	1.3552	2.1485
1.50	10	2.5353	2.6041	NA	0.6614	1.4807	NA
1.25	2	0.5834	0.6012	0.7494	0.2154	0.4271	0.5353
1.25	3	0.8726	0.9005	1.1246	0.3114	0.6069	0.8041
1.25	4	1.1571	1.1957	1.5004	0.4014	0.7822	1.0727
1.25	5	1.4370	1.4840	1.8755	0.4872	0.9550	1.3419
1.25	6	1.7143	1.7707	2.2594	0.5717	1.1249	1.1629
1.25	7	1.9770	2.0434	NA	0.6541	1.2929	1.8331
1.25	8	2.2317	2.3251	NA	0.7352	1.4599	2.1538
1.25	9	2.4790	2.5711	NA	0.8163	1.6236	NA
1.25	10	2.7391	2.8357	NA	0.8952	1.7840	NA
1.00	2	0.6520	0.6692	0.8105	0.2816	0.5008	0.6075
1.00	3	0.9765	1.0013	1.2158	0.4089	0.7159	0.9128
1.00	4	1.2944	1.3320	1.6222	0.5312	0.9277	1.2179
1.00	5	1.6060	1.6594	2.0337	0.6484	1.1401	1.5240
1.00	6	1.9135	1.9732	NA	0.7644	1.3495	1.8301
1.00	7	2.2202	2.2801	NA	0.8781	1.5538	2.1381
1.00	8	2.4968	2.5509	NA	0.9905	1.7521	NA
1.00	9	2.7561	2.8125	NA	1.1034	1.9465	NA
1.00	10	3.0070	3.0059	NA	1.2160	2.1510	NA
0.75	2	0.7298	0.7467	0.8799	0.3714	0.5908	0.6930
0.75	3	1.0944	1.1186	1.3189	0.5425	0.8503	1.0417
0.75	4	1.4646	1.4931	1.7575	0.7101	1.1040	1.3902
0.75	5	1.8354	1.8666	2.1994	0.8738	1.3614	1.7408
0.75	6	2.2049	2.2383	NA	1.0365	1.6231	NA
0.75	7	2.6147	2.7626	NA	1.1949	1.8805	NA
0.75	8	2.9122	NA	NA	1.3526	2.1391	NA
0.75	9	NA	NA	NA	1.5036	2.3286	NA
0.75	10	NA	NA	NA	1.6518	2.5153	NA
0.50	2	0.8304	0.8441	0.9684	0.4939	0.7035	0.7989
0.50	3	1.2441	1.2656	1.4515	0.7261	1.0196	1.2005
0.50	4	1.6538	1.6873	1.9380	0.9537	1.3416	1.6017
0.50	5	2.0623	2.1055	NA	1.1805	1.6572	NA
0.50	6	2.4293	2.5389	NA	1.3966	1.9327	NA
0.50	7	2.8131	2.8122	NA	1.6116	2.2543	NA
0.50	8	NA	NA	NA	1.8263	2.7399	NA
0.50	9	NA	NA	NA	2.0060	NA	NA
0.50	10	NA	NA	NA	2.1542	NA	NA

Note: e = multiples of index standard deviation; m = embedding dimension; index(1) = logged first difference of the closing value of stock index; index(2) = linear structure removed from index(1) using AR process as reported in equation (5.1) or (5.2); index(3) = average of 50 scrambles of index(2) series.

Table 6-3

BDS Statistics

		Standard & Poor's 100			NASDAQ 100		
e	*m*	OEX(1)	OEX(2)	OEX(3)	NAS(1)	NAS(2)	NAS(3)
1.50	2	0.0734	0.0665	−0.0055	0.5150	0.5909	0.0043
1.50	3	0.0588	0.0422	−0.0014	1.0559	0.9579	−0.0034
1.50	4	0.0430	0.0326	0.0000	1.5119	0.8928	−0.0039
1.50	5	0.0277	0.0217	0.0002	1.8091	0.7056	−0.0036
1.50	6	0.0145	0.0119	0.0002	1.9100	0.5157	−0.0034
1.50	7	0.0077	0.0060	0.0001	1.9020	0.3601	−0.0027
1.50	8	0.0038	0.0030	0.0001	1.8136	0.2456	−0.0017
1.50	9	0.0017	0.0014	0.0000	1.6751	0.1652	−0.0011
1.50	10	0.0006	0.0006	0.0000	1.5197	0.1121	−0.0006
1.25	2	0.0473	0.0422	−0.0028	0.4703	0.4833	0.0046
1.25	3	0.0323	0.0237	−0.0004	0.8798	0.6786	−0.0014
1.25	4	0.0218	0.0150	0.0000	1.1259	0.5517	−0.0016
1.25	5	0.0123	0.0092	0.0001	1.2075	0.3767	−0.0013
1.25	6	0.0058	0.0043	0.0000	1.1491	0.2378	−0.0010
1.25	7	0.0031	0.0022	0.0000	1.0342	0.1433	−0.0005
1.25	8	0.0015	0.0009	−0.0000	0.8939	0.0835	−0.0002
1.25	9	0.0007	0.0004	−0.0000	0.7456	0.0482	−0.0002
1.25	10	0.0003	0.0002	−0.0000	0.6154	0.0277	−0.0001
1.00	2	0.0271	0.0225	−0.0022	0.3900	0.3544	0.0041
1.00	3	0.0137	0.0133	0.0002	0.6457	0.4139	−0.0012
1.00	4	0.0091	0.0058	0.0002	0.6942	0.2748	−0.0012
1.00	5	0.0047	0.0024	0.0002	0.6394	0.1503	−0.0005
1.00	6	0.0019	0.0012	0.0001	0.5228	0.0770	−0.0003
1.00	7	0.0007	0.0005	0.0000	0.4049	0.0385	−0.0003
1.00	8	0.0003	0.0003	0.0000	0.3016	0.0191	−0.0001
1.00	9	0.0001	0.0001	0.0000	0.2159	0.0094	−0.0000
1.00	10	0.0001	0.0001	−0.0000	0.1512	0.0043	0.0000
0.75	2	0.0176	0.0113	−0.0014	0.2638	0.2233	0.0023
0.75	3	0.0051	0.0045	0.0004	0.3607	0.2017	−0.0014
0.75	4	0.0001	0.0008	0.0002	0.2999	0.1061	−0.0005
0.75	5	−0.0002	0.0002	0.0001	0.2138	0.0442	0.0000
0.75	6	−0.0001	0.0000	0.0000	0.1366	0.0165	0.0001
0.75	7	−0.0001	−0.0001	−0.0000	0.0849	0.0061	0.0000
0.75	8	0.0000	−0.0000	0.0000	0.0504	0.0021	−0.0000
0.75	9	−0.0000	−0.0000	−0.0000	0.0303	0.0011	−0.0000
0.75	10	−0.0000	−0.0000	−0.0000	0.0179	0.0005	0.0000
0.50	2	0.0085	0.0101	−0.0009	0.1393	0.1098	0.0020
0.50	3	0.0021	0.0020	0.0001	0.1346	0.0684	−0.0006
0.50	4	0.0006	0.0003	0.0000	0.0801	0.0216	−0.0002
0.50	5	0.0001	0.0001	0.0000	0.0386	0.0063	−0.0002
0.50	6	0.0001	0.0000	0.0000	0.0189	0.0022	0.0000
0.50	7	0.0000	0.0000	0.0000	0.0085	0.0005	0.0000
0.50	8	−0.0000	−0.0000	−0.0000	0.0036	0.0000	−0.0000
0.50	9	−0.0000	−0.0000	−0.0000	0.0019	−0.0000	−0.0000
0.50	10	−0.0000	−0.0000	−0.0000	0.0011	−0.0000	−0.0000

Note: e = multiples of index standard derivation; m = embedding dimension; index(1) = logged first difference of the closing value of stock index; index(2) = linear structure removed from index(1) using AR process as reported in Equation (5.1) or (5.2); index(3) = average of 50 scrambles of index(2) series.

The nonconvergence of the CD estimates may be attributed to the potential small sample size bias. Other researchers (Brock 1988; Hsieh 1989; Ramsey et al. 1988) have shown that CD estimates are lower and more stable as the number of observations increase. Evidence of this bias may be present in the mixed results of this study. On the one hand, the low CDs indicate the presence of nonlinearity; on the other hand, the lack of stability of the CDs leads to the conclusion of a stochastic process.

The added audit of the BDS Test for IID conditions in the data is applied to each of the six series and the results are presented in Table 6-3. The critical value for the test is 1.96, with a 5 percent level of significance. The values of the test statistic for the first-differenced NASDAQ series approach the critical value in 4 of a possible 45 cases. The conclusion is to reject the IID null hypothesis for this series. This is an indication that the series is generated by a nonlinear, as opposed to a linear, process. Applying the same test to the AR(3) and AR(4) residuals, as well as the two scrambled residual series, the null hypothesis is retained, because all BDS test values are less than the critical value. The significance of this test is that no underlying dependence, chaotic or otherwise, is present in the data.

Conclusion

This study presents three tests for the existence of deterministic chaos, or controlled randomness, in the daily prices of two cash stock indices. Also, the techniques and procedures used to implement these tests are discussed in relation to financial time series.

The results from an analysis of Standard & Poor's Index and the NASDAQ 100 Stock Index are used in the study. The results for both market indicators are very similar to each other, but they are lower than those found for a cash index in an earlier study. Both series have a correlation dimension of about 2. The existence of an underlying nonlinear relationship was indicated for the OEX by Brock's Residual Test and for both series by the Scrambled Residual Test. However, these results are not conclusive, because the estimated correlation dimension failed to stabilize at any single value. In an attempt to resolve this question, the results from another test using the BDS statistic led to the overall conclusion that changes in the price level of the two series were not deterministic, but are instead independent of past changes.

A primary purpose of this study was to apply current techniques to search for nonlinearities in a financial time series. While no strong nonlinear relationship was found in the data, perhaps the existence of such a condition in other assets may improve forecasting models by uncovering dependence in stock returns and aid in the unresolved debate about market efficiency.

Acknowledgments

The author would like to thank W. D. Dechert for providing access to his BDS computer program. Also, this chapter benefited from the comments of an anonymous reviewer. Any errors or misinterpretations are solely the author's.

References

Barnett, W., and P. Chen. "The Aggregation-Theoretic Monetary Aggregates Are Chaotic and Have Strange Attractors: An Econometric Application of Mathematical Chaos." In *Dynamic Econometric Modelling*, W. Barnett, E. Berndt, and H. White, eds. (Cambridge: Cambridge University Press, 1988), pp. 199–246.

Barnett, W., and S. Choi. "A Comparison between the Conventional Econometric Approach to Structural Inference and the Nonparametric Chaotic Attractor Approach." In *Economic Complexity: Chaos, Sunspots, Bubbles and Nonlinearity*, W. Barnett, J. Geweke, and K. Shell, eds. (Cambridge: Cambridge University Press, 1989), pp. 141–212.

Baumol, W., and J. Benhabib. "Chaos: Significance, Mechanism, and Economic Applications." *Journal of Economic Perspectives* (1989) 3:77–105.

Blank, S. "'Chaos' in Future Markets? A Nonlinear Dynamic Analysis." *Center for the Study of Futures Markets*, CSFM # 204, Columbia Business School, New York (1990).

Brock, W. A. "Distinguishing Random and Deterministic Systems: Abridged Version." *Journal of Economic Theory* (1986) 40:168–195.

Brock, W. A. "Nonlinearity and Complex Dynamics in Economics and Finance." In *The Economy as an Evolving Complex System*, P. Anderson, K. Arrow, and D. Pines, eds. (New York: Addison-Wesley, 1988), pp. 77-97.

Brock, W. A., W. D. Dechert, and J. Scheinkman. "A Test for Independence Based on the Correlation Dimension." *SSRI Working Paper*, No. 8702, Department of Economics, University of Wisconsin, Madison, Wisconsin (1987).

Brock, W. A., and C. Sayers. "Is the Business Cycle Characterized by Deterministic Chaos?" *Journal of Monetary Economics* (1988) 22:71–90.

Engle, R. F. "Autoregressive Conditional Heteroskedasticity With Estimates of the Variance of United Kingdom Inflation." *Econometrica* (1982) 50:987–1007.

Fama, E. "Efficient Capital Markets: A Review of Theory and Empirical Work." *Journal of Finance* (1970) 25:383–417.

Frank, M. Z., R. Gencay, and T. Stengos. "International Chaos?" *European Economic Review* (1988) 32:1569-1584.

Frank, M. Z., and T. Stengos. "Some Evidence Concerning Macroeconomic Chaos." *Journal of Monetary Economics* (1988) 22:423-438.

Grassberger, P., and I. Procaccia. "Measuring the Strangeness of Strange Attractors. *Physica* (1983) 9D:189-208.

Hinich, M., and D. Patterson. "Evidence of Nonlinearity in Daily Stock Returns." *Journal of Business and Economic Statistics* (1985) 3:69–77.

Hsieh, D. "Testing for Nonlinear Dependence in Daily Foreign Exchange Rates." *Journal of Business* (1989) 62:339–368.

Ljung, G. M. and G. E. P. Box. "On a Measure of Lack of Fit in Time Series Models." *Biometrica* (1978) 65:67–72.

Ramsey, J., C. Sayers, and P. Rothman. "The Statistical Properties of Dimension Calculations Using Small Data Sets: Some Economic Applications." C. V. Starr Center for Applied Economics, New York University, New York (1988).

Savit, R. "Nonlinearities and Chaotic Effects in Option Prices." *Journal of Futures Markets* (1989) 9:507–518.

Savit, R. "When Random Is Not Random: An Introduction to Chaos in Market Prices." *Journal of Futures Markets* (1988) 8:271–290.

Scheinkman, J., and B. LeBaron. "Nonlinear Dynamics and Stock Returns." *Journal of Business* (1989) 62:311–337.

Swinney, H. "Observations of Order and Chaos in Nonlinear Systems." *Physica* (1985) 5D:1–3, 3–15.

A CHAOTIC ATTRACTOR FOR THE S&P 500

By Edgar E. Peters

Introduction

The Efficient Market Hypothesis basically says that current prices reflect all known information. This implies that there is little or no correlation between returns; price changes occur in a random fashion, in reaction to new information. This assumption—which has never been conclusively proven—is the bedrock upon which standard statistical analysis of the markets has been built. The law of large numbers, for example, applies only if price changes are independent (i.e., "efficient"). And it is the law of large numbers that validates statistical calculus and other linear models.

Linear models will prove successful only to the extent that the system being analyzed is itself linear. If the system is not linear, the models will work, at best, only under "ideal" conditions and over short time periods. Thus the application of linear models to the market is questionable, in view of recent research suggesting that the capital markets, and the economy as a whole, may be governed in part by *nonlinear dynamics*.[1] When nonlinear dynamics are involved, a *deterministic system* can generate random-looking

Reprinted with permission from *Financial Analysts Journal*, Vol. 47, No. 2 (March–April 1991): 55–62, 81.

results that nevertheless exhibit persistent trends, cycles (both periodic and nonperiodic), and long-term correlations.

This chapter presents evidence that a *chaotic attractor* exists for the S&P 500. That is, an underlying, nonperiodic attractor explains most of the movements in the capital markets. These movements may appear random or chaotic, however, when analyzed using standard statistical analysis.

This evidence calls into question the Efficient Market Hypothesis, which underlies the linear mathematics used in most capital market theory. It also lends validity to a number of investment strategies that should not work if markets are efficient, including trend analysis, market timing, value investing, and tactical asset allocation. This finding is of particular importance for practitioners, because experience has shown that these strategies do work when properly applied, even though theory tells us they should not work in a random-walk environment. Conversely, strategies that depend on efficient markets and continuous pricing—such as portfolio insurance, Alexander filters, and stop/loss orders—become suspect because chaotic markets are neither efficient nor continuously priced. This calls into question the Capital Asset Pricing Model and most option-pricing theories, which are based on normal distributions and finite variances.

What Is an Attractor?

An attractor is a state that defines equilibrium for a specific system. As we shall see, *equilibrium* does not necessarily mean a "static" state, as econometric models define the term.

A simple attractor is a *point* attractor. A pendulum with friction is an example of a point attractor. If you were to plot the velocity of the pendulum versus its position, you would obtain a graph that spirals in toward the origin, where velocity and position are zero. At this point, the pendulum has stopped.

A graph of velocity versus position is called the *phase space* of a system. Each point on the graph defines the state of the system at that time. All paths in phase space lead to a point attractor, if one exists. No matter where the motion in phase space initiates, it must end up at the origin—the point attractor.

A pendulum that periodically receives energy goes back and forth with no variation in its path. Its phase-space plot becomes a closed circle, with the origin at its center. This is called a *limit cycle* attractor. The radius of the circle is determined by the amplitude of the pendulum's swing. As a time series, a limit cycle appears as a simple sine wave.

A third kind of attractor is a *chaotic,* or fractal, attractor. With a chaotic attractor, the trajectories plotted in phase space never intersect, although they wander around the same area of phase space. Orbits are always different, but remain within the same area; they are attracted to a space, but never converge to a specific point. Cycles, while they exist, are nonperiodic. With a chaotic attractor, equilibrium applies to a region, rather than a particular point or orbit; equilibrium becomes dynamic.

In economics, equilibrium is commonly defined as static. In other words, an economic system is commonly thought to tend to equilibrium (a point attractor) or to vary around equilibrium in a periodic fashion (a limit cycle). But there is no evidence that capital markets tend toward either type of equilibrium. If anything, the actual behavior of economic time series appears to be nonperiodic. That is, they have cycles without well-defined periods. If the markets are nonperiodic, then limit cycles and point attractors cannot define their dynamics.

Chaotic Attractors

Using a simple convection model, Edward Lorenz was able to define the first known chaotic attractor. The model is based on a fluid heated from below. At low temperature levels, heat transfer occurs by convection; the water molecules behave independently of one another. As the heat is turned up, a convection roll starts; the water molecules behave coherently and the warmer fluid on the bottom rises, cools as it reaches the top, and falls back to the bottom. The water molecules trace a limit cycle. If the heat is turned up further, turbulence sets in; the fluid churns chaotically. At this point, the water's phase space becomes a chaotic attractor.

Chaotic attractors have an interesting property. Because of the non-linearities in the underlying system, any errors in measuring current conditions eventually overwhelm any forecasting ability, even if the equations of motion are known. In other words, our ability to predict the future of a chaotic system is limited by our knowledge of current conditions. Errors in measurement grow exponentially in time, making any long-term forecast useless. This sensitive dependence on initial conditions made Lorenz conclude that any attempts at weather forecasting beyond a few days were doomed.

If the economic cycle is governed by a chaotic attractor, we can see why long-term econometric forecasts during the '70s and '80s were flawed.

How do we determine if a system has an underlying chaotic attractor? First, a phase space for the system must be constructed. (When the equations of motion are not known, this is not a simple task.) The resulting phase space must meet two criteria for a chaotic attractor—(1) a fractal dimension and (2) sensitive dependence on initial conditions. In the physical sciences, techniques have been developed to measure these items using experimental data. We can apply these to the S&P 500.

Constructing a Phase Space

A phase space consists of "m" dimensions, where each dimension is a variable involved in defining the motion of the system. In a system where the equations of motion are known, constructing a phase space is simple. However, we rarely know the dynamics of a real system.

By plotting one variable with different lags, one can reconstruct the original, unknown phase space with one dynamic, observable variable.[2] This reconstructed phase space has all the characteristics of the real phase space, provided the lag time and embedding dimension are properly specified. (We discuss below how these parameters are determined.)

Now the question becomes, what do we use as our single observable variable? Traditional analyses of the stock market use the percentage change in price (returns) or a logarithmic first difference. This removes the autocorrelations inherent in the original price series and makes the series suitable for linear statistical analysis. However, what standard statistical analysis considers undesirable may in fact be evidence of a nonlinear dynamic system. That is, the use of percentage changes in price may destroy any delicate nonlinear structure present in the data.[3]

In constructing attractors such as the Lorenz attractor, scientists use the actual value of the variables, not the rate of change. We apply this approach to our study of financial data. Economics, however, presents a problem that the physical sciences do not. As the economy grows, stock prices grow. Stock price data thus have to be detrended; in order to study the motion of stock prices, economic growth must be filtered out.

Ping Chen, in his study of monetary aggregates, filtered out the internal rate of growth over the period.[4] This method has the appeal of simplicity, but it assumes a constant rate of growth, which is unrealistic. As we know, economic growth is not constant, but varies over time.

We detrended the S&P 500 using inflation, in the following manner:

$$S_i = \log_e(P_i) - (a \cdot \log_e(CPI_i) + constant) \tag{1}$$

where

S_i = the detrended S&P 500 on month i,
P_i = the S&P 500 price on month i, and
CPI_i = the CPI on month i.

The values of a and the constant were derived by regressing the log of the S&P 500 against the log of the Consumer Price Index (CPI) from January 1950 through July 1989. By subtracting the relation between the S&P 500 and the CPI, we obtained the time series illustrated in Figure 7-1. Note the wavelike cycles, which appear to be nonperiodic.

Figure 7-2 shows a phase plot in two dimensions with a time lag of 15 months. The line moves in a clockwise manner similar to spiral chaos. Two basins of attraction can be seen in the second and fourth quadrants; these are connected by three "arms." The upper arms show the path from the lower "lobe" to the upper. The lower arm is the path from the upper lobe back to the lower. The two lobes are regions where the time series is consistently above or below the zero line in Figure 7-1.

This *log-linear* deflated S&P 500 time series is our dynamic observable. From this series, we can reconstruct a phase space to obtain a fractal dimension and to measure sensitive dependence on initial conditions.

Figure 7-1

S&P 500 Detrended Using CPI Inflation

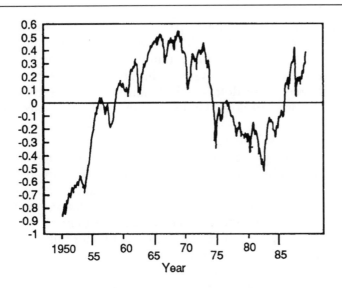

Figure 7-2

S&P 500 Detrended Using CPI Inflation with 15-Month Lag

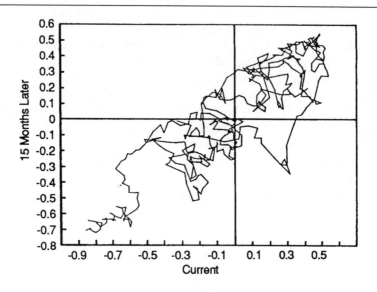

The Fractal Dimension

The fractal dimension of phase space gives us important information about the underlying attractor. More precisely, the next-higher integer above the fractal dimension is the minimum number of variables we need to model the dynamics of the system. This gives us a lower bound on the number of degrees of freedom in the whole system. It does not tell us what these variables are, but it can tell us something about the system's complexity. A low dimensional attractor of, say, three or four would suggest that the problem is solvable.

A pure random process, such as *white noise*, fills whatever space it is plotted in. In two dimensions it fills the plane. In three dimensions, it fills the three-dimensional space, and so on for higher dimensions. In fact, white noise assumes the dimension of whatever space you place it in because its elements are uncorrelated and independent.

The fractal dimension measures how an attractor fills its space. For a chaotic attractor, the dimension is fractional; that is, it is not an integer. Because a chaotic attractor is deterministic, not every point in its phase space is equally likely, as it is with white noise.

Grassberger and Procaccia estimate the fractal dimension as the cor-relation dimension, D.[5] D measures how densely the attractor fills its phase space by finding the probability that any one point will be a certain distance, R, from another point. The correlation integral, $Cm(R)$, is the number of pairs of points in an m-dimensional phase space whose dis-tances are less than R.[6]

For a chaotic attractor, Cm increases at a rate of R^D. This gives the following relation:

$$Cm = R^D,$$

or

$$\log(Cm) = D \cdot \log(R) + \text{constant}. \tag{2}$$

By calculating the correlation integral, Cm, for various embedding dimen-sions, m, we can estimate D as the slope of a log/log plot of Cm and R. Grassberger and Procaccia have shown that, as m is increased, D will eventually converge to its true value.[7]

We must determine which lag, t, is appropriate for our detrended S&P 500 time series in order to reconstruct the phase space. Wolf et al. have shown that a good estimate comes from the following relation:[8]

$$m \cdot t = Q \tag{3}$$

where

    m = the embedding dimension,
    t = the time lag, and
    Q = the mean orbital period.

The mean cycle of the S&P 500 has been shown to be 48 months by R/S analysis.[9] We can thus easily solve Equation 3 for t, given various m.

Figure 7-3 illustrates the log/log plot of Cm and R for embedding dimensions 2 through 7. (An eight-dimension calculation was also done; the points are similar to the seven-dimension points, with slightly lower values, as one would expect.) The figure shows the linear regions where the regressions can be performed.

Figure 7-4 shows the results of the estimates of D for various m. When m equals 6, D equals 2.31; when m equals 7 or 8, D equals 2.33. This analysis indicates that the fractal dimension of the detrended S&P 500 series is approximately 2.33. This means that the dynamics of this particular system can be defined with a minimum of three dynamic variables. Once these variables are defined, we can model the system.

Figure 7-3

Correlation Integrals (CPI-Detrended S&P 500)

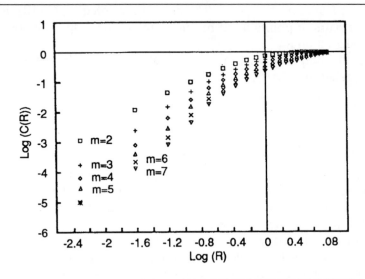

Figure 7-4

Convergence of the Fractal Dimension (CPI-Detrended S&P 500)

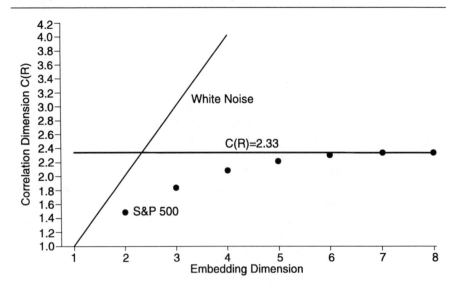

Of course, the fractal dimension does not tell us what the variables are, but only how many variables we need, at a minimum, to construct the model. Our estimate is low enough to suggest that the problem is solvable.

Sensitive Dependence on Initial Conditions

Chaotic attractors are characterized by sensitive dependence on initial conditions. An error in measuring initial conditions will grow exponentially, so that a small error could dramatically affect forecasting ability. The further out in time we look, the less certain we are about the validity of our forecasts.

Contrast this with the linear models used in econometric forecasts. A small change in measuring current conditions has little impact on the results of a forecast. Theoretically, linear models imply that, if we have enough variables, we can forecast an indefinite period into the future. While the certainty of linear models is desirable, the uncertainty inherent in nonlinear dynamics is closer to practical experience.

Lyapunov exponents measure the loss in predictive power experienced by nonlinear models over time. Lyapunov exponents measure how nearby trajectories in phase space diverge over time. Each dimension in phase space has its own Lyapunov exponent. A positive exponent measures expansion in phase space. A negative one measures contraction in phase space.

For a fixed point in three dimensions, the Lyapunov exponents are negative. For a limit cycle, two exponents are negative and one equals zero. For a chaotic attractor, one is positive, one negative, and one zero. A chaotic attractor is characterized by the largest Lyapunov exponent being greater than zero. It represents the divergence of points in phase space, or the sensitive dependence on the conditions represented by each point.

When the equations of motion are known, Lyapunov exponents can be calculated by measuring the divergence of nearby orbits in phase space. In a linear world, points that are close together in phase space would remain close together; this reflects the linear world, where a small error in measurement has little effect on the result. In a nonlinear world, things are different. Nearby points will diverge as the differences in initial conditions compound.

Consider how the volume of a ball with radius r expands over a time t. The full spectrum of the Lyapunov exponents (L_i) can be calculated by the following relationship:

$$L_i = \lim_{t \to \infty} \lim_{r(0) \to 0} \sum [(1/t) \cdot \log_2(r_i(t)/r_i(0))]. \tag{4}$$

The calculation is difficult when the equations of motion are not known, but there is a method for calculating the largest Lyapunov exponent, L_1, using experimental data.[10] An L_1 greater than zero would signify a chaotic attractor.

This method involves measuring the divergence of nearby points in the reconstructed phase space over fixed intervals of time. First, we choose two points that are at least one mean orbital period apart. The distance between the two points is measured after the fixed evolution period. If the distance is too long, one of the points is replaced. (This is necessary to ensure that we measure only the expansion of the points in phase space; if the points are too far apart, they will *fold* into one another.) In addition, the angle between the points is measured to keep the orientation of the points in phase space as close as possible to the original set.

Figure 7-5 provides an artist's sketch of the algorithm. The following is the formal equation:

$$L_1 = (1/t) \cdot \sum_{j=1}^{m} \log_2[L'(t_{j+1})/L(t_j)]. \tag{5}$$

In theory, with an infinite amount of noise-free data, Equation 5 is equivalent to Equation 4. However, the real world presents us with a finite amount of noisy data. This means that the embedding dimension, m, the time lag, t, and the maximum and minimum allowable distance must be chosen with care.

Wolf et al. give a number of "rules of thumb" for dealing with experimental data.[11] First, the embedding dimension should be larger than the phase space of the underlying attractor. (Often, a rough surface looks

---

Figure 7-5

Spectrum of Lyapunov Exponents (L_i)

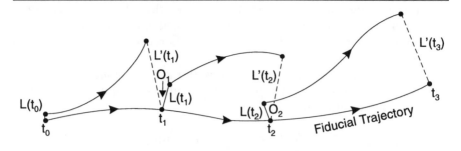

smoother when its dimensionality is raised.) We have already found D to be 2.33; the embedding dimension should thus be larger than three. The time lag used to reconstruct the phase space can be calculated from Equation 3; the maximum length of growth should be no greater than 10 percent of the length of the attractor in phase space. Finally, the evolution time should be long enough to determine stretching without including folds.

Once done, the calculation over a long time series should converge to a stable value of L_1. If stable convergence does not occur, it is possible that the parameters have not been well chosen, there are insufficient data for the analysis, or the system is not truly nonlinear.

I used the Wolf algorithm for the detrended S&P 500 data series (monthly data from January 1950 through December 1989), with an embedding dimension of four, a time lag of 12, and an evolution time of six months. This resulted in the stable convergence in Figure 7-6 to a Lyapunov exponent of 0.0241 bits per month.

This means that, even if we measure initial conditions to one bit of precision (one decimal place), all predictive power would be lost after $1/L_1$, or 42 months. This is roughly equal to the 48-month mean orbital period obtained from rescaled range analysis. This relation would not be true of white noise, or a random walk.

Figure 7-6

Convergence of the Largest Lyapunov Exponent

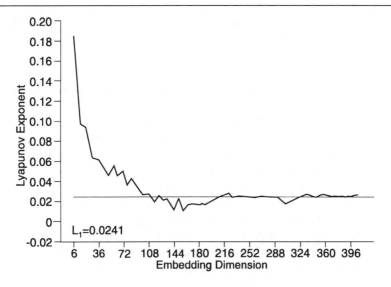

Implications

We have seen that the S&P 500 has an underlying low dimensional attractor. The fractal dimension of this attractor is approximately 2.33. The attractor is "chaotic," with a positive Lyapunov exponent.

All this indicates that there is an underlying, nonlinear mechanism to the S&P 500. The exact form of this mechanism is unknown at this time. A likely candidate, however, is a mixed feedback system coupling the various capital markets.

Earlier work has shown that the capital markets are nonlinear. Now we have additional evidence that the S&P 500 has an underlying chaotic attractor, which may involve the other capital markets. The next step is to develop a model that explains the nonlinear mechanism that generates the chaotic attractor. We leave that for further research.

Practical Considerations

The existence of a chaotic attractor and nonperiodic cycles vindicates a number of strategies that have been "disproved" using random-walk-based mathematics. Most studies of market timing and trend analysis, for example, make a Gaussian assumption about probability distributions. As we have noted, fractal distributions are infinite-variance distributions and require quite different analysis.

Strategies based on "mean reversion," including value-based stock selection and market-timing techniques, also need to be updated. Because equilibrium is dynamic, rather than static, mean-reversion models of value need to be dynamic as well. A "chaotic" market also means, however, that market timing, value investing, and tactical asset allocation may all have relevance, and if properly done, should be able to capitalize on the market cycle.

For the practitioner, this means that care should be taken when formulating an opinion about how the market works. For too long, we seem to have been divided between "technicians," who believe that the market follows a regular cycle, and "quants," who believe there is no cycle at all. The truth lies somewhere in between. There are cycles, but they are not regular, hence they may be invisible to standard statistical techniques. Investment professionals should begin relying on quantitative techniques that do not rely on random-walk assumptions but are more dynamic. These techniques are just beginning to be developed. Long-range market forecasting is impossible and should not be attempted, or even considered.

Final Considerations

On a broader scale, we can see why standard econometric methods have failed in the past. Attempts to "whiten" data in order to make it suitable for linear-based forecasting techniques cover up the conclusions nonlinear dynamics give us. Surprisingly, these conclusions tie in with experience:

1. The market has cycles and trends.
2. A small change in an indicator can have a major impact on the future.
3. The further out in time we go, the less reliable our forecasts are.

The last point is particularly important. It means that, as with the weather, accurate, long-range economic and market forecasting is not feasible from a practical standpoint. Even if we were able to determine the equations of motion underlying the S&P 500, we would still not be able to forecast beyond a short time frame because we are never able to measure current conditions with significant accuracy. The future in quantitative economic theory should thus revolve around estimating the current probability distribution, which is not normal, so that we can better analyze the risks. Once that is done, viable economic and investment decisions can be made.

Finally, the Efficient Market Hypothesis conforms to none of these observations. Neither does standard econometrics, which is based on static equilibrium assumptions. If the social sciences are to grow, consideration should be given to defining equilibrium in a more dynamic fashion. The next phase involves models that explain these dynamics and statistical techniques for estimating risk. There is still much work to be done.

Glossary

Linear Model: Standard statistical model of the form $y = a \cdot x + b$. Essentially, the value of y has a direct relation to the value of x, determined by the slope, a, and the intercept, b. In comparison to nonlinear dynamic models, the right-hand side of a linear model does not have an exponent greater than one, and there is no time element.

Nonlinear Dynamic System: A nonlinear system is one in which the right-hand side has one variable raised to a power higher than 1. It becomes a dynamic system if the current value of the system is a transformation of the past value. The following equation (called the *logistic equation*) is a simple nonlinear dynamic system:

$$X_{t+1} = a \cdot X_t \cdot (1 - X_t)$$

where

X = a variable between 0 and 1,
a = a constant, and
t = the time index.

Deterministic System: A system in which the outcome is determined by an equation or a system of equations. The result is the interaction of a small group of variables. A deterministic system has causality. The opposite of a deterministic system is a random system.

Attractor: The equilibrium level of a system. This should not be confused with econometric equilibrium, which is a narrow version of an attractor. An attractor is the level that a system reverts to after the effects of perturbation of the system die away.

Chaotic Attractor: A system that converges to a set of possible values. This set is infinite in possible number but limited in range. For example, a system that, out of possible values between 1 and 10, can be any fractional value between 2 and 3, without repetition, possesses a chaotic attractor. Chaotic attractors are nonperiodic.

Log-Linear: An equation in which the log (to any base) of the left-hand variable has a linear relation with the log of the right-hand variable. Because logarithms are exponential, an exponential relationship in real space will look linear in log/log space and will be solvable as such.

White Noise: Technically, white noise is the static we hear on the radio, or snow on television. It is another term for a random process that is invariant with respect to time or space because all the elements are uncorrelated.

Notes

1 See, for example, P. Chen, "Empirical and Theoretical Evidence of Economic Chaos," *System Dynamics Review* 4 (1988), pp. 81–108; W. A. Brock, "Distinguishing Random and Deterministic Systems," *Journal of Economic Theory* 40 (1986), pp. 168–195; and E. E. Peters, "Fractal Structure in the Capital Markets," *Financial Analysis Journal*, July/August 1989.

2 See Packard, N., P. Crutchfield, D. Farmer, and S. Shaw, "Geometry from a Time Series," *Physical Review Letters*, 45 (1980), pp. 712–716.

3 Chen, "Empirical and Theoretical Evidence of Economic Chaos," *op. cit.*

4 *Ibid.*

5 Grassberger and Procaccia, "Characterization of Strange Attractors," *Physical Review Letters,* January 1983.

6 The formal definition of a correlation integral is:

$$C_m(R) = (1/N^2) \sum_{\substack{i,j=1 \\ i \neq j}}^{N} z(R - |X_i - X_j|)$$

where

$z(x)$ $= 1$ if $R - |X_i - X_j|) > 0$, 0 otherwise;
N $=$ number of observations;
R $=$ radius; and
C_m $=$ correlation integral for dimension m.

7 Grassberger and Procaccia, "Characterization of Strange Attractors," *op. cit.*

8 Wolf, A., J. Swift, H. Swinney, and J. Vastano, "Determining Lyapunov Exponents from a Time Series," *Physica* 16D, July 1985.

9 E. E. Peters, "R/S Analysis Using Logarithmic Returns," *Financial Analysts Journal,* November/December 1992.

10 Wolf et al., "Determining Lyapunov Exponents," *op. cit.*

11 *Ibid.*

8

EVIDENCE OF CHAOS IN THE S&P 500 CASH INDEX

By Robert M. Eldridge, Christopher Bernhardt, and Irene Mulvey

I. Introduction

The past five years have seen a growing body of literature applying the concepts of nonlinear dynamics and chaos theory to the field of finance. Against a background of the Random Walk Hypothesis and the philosophies of "buy-and-hold" and "you can't beat the market over the long term," it is startling to read the first sentence in a recent paper by Fama and French (1988): "There is much evidence that stock returns are predictable." That predictability is increasingly thought to be a function of a chaotic characteristic of the generating process for stock prices. In this chapter we report the results of the first part of an ongoing study of the S&P 500 index covering a three-year period, 1982–1984. The study covers both the cash and futures values of the index. This chapter addresses only the cash market values.

We utilized a database provided by the Chicago Mercantile Exchange (CME), as well as one provided by the Center for the Study of Futures Markets (CSFM) at Columbia University. The CME database contains intraday values over several years, starting in 1982. The CSFM database contains, *inter alia*, a daily closing index value for both cash and futures markets. We focus here on the 1982–1984 period. Our objective is to examine the following issue: Do the cash index prices generated during the course of a trading day exhibit the correlation dimension/space characteristic that is a necessary, albeit not sufficient, condition to claim that they contain a chaotic component?

This chapter contains five sections: Section I, the introduction, outlines the scope of the chapter; Section II addresses some of the recent literature on the subject; Section III outlines the mathematical theory and structure of the study; Section IV reports on the results obtained; and Section V provides conclusions.

II. Recent Literature

We start with the attempts made to define chaos. Devaney (1989) defines chaos as a system that is (a) unpredictable, (b) indecomposable, and (c) having an element of regularity. Baumol and Benhabib (1989) define chaos as a condition "in which a dynamic mechanism that is very simple and deterministic yields a time path so complicated that it will pass most standard tests of randomness." Baumol and Quandt (1985) define chaos as "a fully deterministic behavior pattern which is, in at least some respects, indistinguishable from a random process." We suggest that bringing chaos theory to the analysis of security prices is not a paradigm shift in the theory of finance, but rather a broader way of viewing the basic problem of asset price determination. Gabisch (1987) recognizes this when, in discussing the applicability of nonlinear methodology to business cycles, he writes: "The irregular component of business cycles can systematically be analyzed within one [nonlinear, chaotic] model without changing to a different paradigm, as is usually done up to now by relying on stochastic explanations in this context." Savit (1988, 1989) provides an analytical framework for applications of chaos to asset prices and in particular to options prices. Poterba and Summers (1988), examining NYSE monthly returns and CRSP (Center for Research in Stock Prices [University of Chicago]) data find, *inter alia*, evidence of predictability in stock returns, even though they could not reject randomness in the data at normally accepted levels of significance. Scheinkman and LeBaron (1989), using the CRSP index of stock returns, reported the results of using newly developed statistical analytics to determine nonlinearities in the data and made the following observations: "[the results . . .] show the inadequacy of the 'random-walk' theory . . . The results suggest that nonlinearities may play an important role in explaining asset returns." Ashley and Patterson (1989) tested CRSP data in an attempt to distinguish between linear stochastic dynamic models and nonlinear dynamic models, both stochastic and chaotic. They report that the data showed strong evidence of a nonlinear mechanism as the generating model and were consistent with chaos. Hsieh (1989) also reports evidence of nonlinear dependence in daily foreign exchange rates but makes no specific claim that it is chaotic. Under the rubric of "Anomalies," De Bondt and Thaler (1989) provide, *inter alia*, a survey on studies of mean-reverting behavior in asset prices, during the course of which they quote from a paper of Fama and French (1986) as follows: "Whether predictability reflects market inefficiency or time-varying expected returns generated by rational investor behavior is, and will remain, an open issue." Merville and Pieptea (1989), examining the S&P 500 stock index futures contract as well as a basket of 25 stocks, find evidence of mean reversion in *ex ante* implied volatilities over a 10-year period. They state: "There is a long-term value toward which the instantaneous variance is pulled." The trend in the research today seems to assume market efficiency while looking at the underlying nature of returns as generated by rational investors. (This approach has a historic precedent in Cox and Ross (1976) who assumed that stock prices follow a deterministic path over which a random component is layered.) Within the concept of chaos, the existence of a "strange attractor," which, in some manner, constructs a pattern out of seeming disorder, is noted by Routh (1989) to have "some of the characteristics of a regression line to which the variable tends to return." In summary, there seems to be increasing evidence that:

1. The traditional random walk hypothesis of asset price generation is becoming increasingly suspect; and

2. The world of nonlinear dynamics and chaos may offer a promising framework for future work in this area.

III. Theory and Structure of Study

"In general, if $\{x(t)\}$ is generated by deterministic chaos, then the sequence of ordered m-tuples, $\{x(t), ..., x(t + m - 1)\}$, lies in an r dimensional space for all embedding dimensions m, big enough. Thus as a matter of pure theory, a test for deterministic chaos is simple: calculate the dimension of $\{x(t)\}$ and examine if it is small." Brock and Malliaris (1989, p. 303)

In this study, we consider the S&P 500 index from April 1982 through December 1984. Two treatments of the data were employed. In the first, we considered the daily closing prices of each of the days, and in the second treatment we considered all the transactions of a given day in each month of the study period. These days were selected based on a random number selection process using a uniform distribution. A total of 33 days was examined over the study period in addition to one day in 1987 that had been previously selected that happened to have approximately the same number of observations as the daily close segment. A list of the dates used is found in Appendix A to this chapter. In the daily closing price segment there were 744 observations; when examining daily trade-by-trade data, the number of observations per day ranged from the low two hundreds to a high of 383. To avoid the problem of the nominal nature of stock prices to rise over time, we conducted the examination on the first differences of the data rather than the raw data itself.

Using the detrended data, we consider the question of whether the data are smoothly deterministic as defined by Takens (1983). Roughly speaking, for each value of $m = 1, 2, ..., 12$, we construct a set of m-tuples from the set of data points. For example, when $m = 2$, we construct the set of ordered pairs (a1, a2), (a2, a3), (a3, a4), ... And, when $m = 5$, we construct the set of 5-tuples (a1, a2, a3, a4, a5), (a2, a3, a4, a5, a6), (a3, a4, a5, a6, a7), ... When the data points represent daily closing prices, one can think of this as looking at the information from the daily closing prices for five consecutive days. We do this for each value of $m = 1, 2, ..., 12$ and construct (for each such m) a set of m-tuples of consecutive data points called E[m]. Following the procedure set forth by Grassberger and Procaccia (1983), we compute the correlation dimension of E[m] in R^m (m-dimensional space). (Since in this first part of the study we are interested in a necessary, but not sufficient, condition for chaos, the concerns expressed in Ramsey, Sayers, and Rothman (1990) with respect to the application of correlation dimension analysis to small data sets, and the conclusion of Ramsey (1990) that correlation dimension results are not capable of discriminating between deterministic chaos and noisy, aperiodic shocks, are not considered applicable.) Precisely, the analysis proceeds in the following manner.

We represent the data as the finite sequence $\{a(i)\}^n_{i=1}$, where a(i) is the first difference of the (i + 1) and (i) daily index values, and n is the number of first difference observations. For each m, $m = 1, 2, ..., 12$, we construct a subset E[m] of R^m consisting of $n - m + 1$ m-tuples as follows:

$$E[m] = \{[a(1), a(2), ..., a(m)],$$

$$[a(2), a(3), ..., a(m + 1)], ..., \tag{1}$$

$$[a(n - m + 1), ..., a(n)]\}$$

or, in less cumbersome notation:

$$E[m] = \{a(1)[m], a(2)[m], ..., a(n - m + 1)[m]\} \qquad (1a)$$

where $a(i)[m]$ is the m-tuple beginning with the data value $a(i)$ obtained from the ordered set of data.

Let ε be a real number greater than zero. Now, define a set.

$$D(m)[\varepsilon] = \{(j,k): \mid a(j)[m] - a(k)[m] \mid <\varepsilon\}. \qquad (2)$$

It follows then that

$$D(m)[\varepsilon] = \{(j,k): [\{a(j) - a(k)\}^2 +$$

$$\{a(j+1) - a(k+1)\}^2 + ... + \{a(j+m-1) - \qquad (2a)$$

$$a(k+m - 1) \}^2]^{1/2} < \varepsilon\}$$

Let $\#D(m)[\varepsilon]$ be the number of elements in $D(m)[\varepsilon]$.
Let $\#E(m)$ denote the number of m-tuples in $E(m)$:

$$\#E(m) = n - m + 1 \qquad (3)$$

Define a variable $C(m)[\varepsilon]$ as follows:

$$C(m)[\varepsilon] = \#D(m)[\varepsilon] / \{(\#E(m))\}^2. \qquad (4)$$

This gives the fraction of elements in $E(m)$ that are close to (within ε of) each other. For an infinite set, the correlation dimension is defined to be

$$DIM = \lim_{\varepsilon \to 0} [ln \{C(m)[\varepsilon]\}/ln(\varepsilon)] \qquad (5)$$

For the finite set $E(m)$ we cannot take ε to be too large, or every pair of m-tuples will be within ε of each other and $C(m)[\varepsilon] = 1$. Conversely, we cannot take ε to be too small, as no distinct pair of m-tuples would be within ε of each other and $C(m)[\varepsilon] = 1/\#E(m)$. In this case of a finite set we plot $ln\{C(m)[\varepsilon]\}$ versus $ln[\varepsilon]$. The plot would begin horizontally (ε too small), increase in some linear fashion, and finally become horizontal again (ε too large). This is illustrated in Figure 8-1.

We compute the slope of the nonhorizontal portion of the plot by choosing "intermediate values" of ε and applying an ordinary least squares regression. The resulting slope is the correlation dimension of the finite set $E(m)$. This slope we denote by $d(m)$, for $m = 1, 2, ..., 12$. We note that the correlation dimension will in general not be an integer. Noninteger

Figure 8-1

Nonhorizontal Region of ln(Cm(ε))

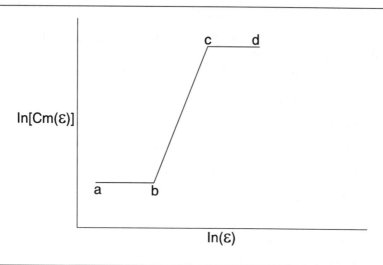

dimensions are often called fractal dimensions and the underlying sets are called fractals. In the terminology used by Mandelbrot (1983), $d(m)$ is the fractal dimension of the fractal $E(m)$. If the data being considered contain a detectable chaotic component, the correlation dimension $d(m)$ should initially increase with increasing values of m. However, at some point, it should level off and remain constant for all further values of m. If the data were from a purely random distribution, the correlation dimension would increase with increasing values of m. These relationships are illustrated in Figure 8-2.

Our focus of interest in this study is to examine the plot of $d(m)$ versus m for both the two sets of data under consideration, as well as a pseudo-randomly generated data set. The value of epsilon (ε) noted above was determined in the following manner. Let EP1 represent one one-hundredth (0.01) of the range of the data set: EP1 = (max − min)/100. Epsilon then is calculated as

$$\varepsilon = (EP1)[exp(ln\{300\})/100]^k \tag{6}$$

k ranges from 1 to 100.

The value of 300 in Equation 6 was chosen arbitrarily to provide a range of values of ε that would encompass the very small (1.0587 times the value of EP1), to the very large (300 times the value of EP1). In this manner,

Figure 8-2

d(m) for Random and Chaotic Processes

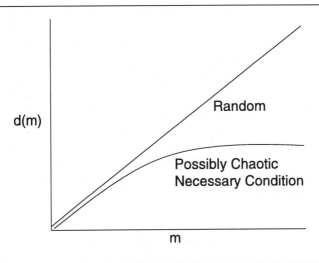

it was expected that a reverse Z-shaped function would be obtained similar to Figure 8-1. Since we are dealing with first differences of the S&P 500 index, the max and min values calculated to determine EP1 are themselves generally much less than 1. Of key importance to us was the necessity to generate an adequate number of points in the nonhorizontal region, between points b and c in Figure 8-1. Once we isolated that region, an adequate number of points was necessary for purposes of applying a least squares regression to calculate the slope.

In this study, we created a series of programs to calculate $d(m)$ over 12 embedding dimensions ($m = 1, 2, ..., 12$) and then compare the correlation dimensions against those of a computer-generated pseudo-random-number data set uniformly distributed over the interval [0,1] multiplied by 1,000, so as to generate data of the same order of magnitude as the index data being examined. In the next section, we report the results of that comparison.

IV. Empirical Results

Intraday Data

The plots of ln{ $C(m)[\varepsilon]$} versus ln[ε] were found to be essentially as expected: the reverse Z-shape discussed in Section III. Appendix B to this chapter provides a sample of the plots for a typical day in the study period, October 27, 1982.[1] Each plot represents a different value of m. For the first two embedding dimensions m, the plot is somewhat fuzzily defined and contains "hidden observations." (When using the plotting algorithm, multiple points with the same coordinates plot once, with the remaining points indicated as "hidden"). By the third embedding dimension the hidden observation characteristic has disappeared and all points are unique. Between the horizontal levels there are substantial gaps between the plotted points for the first three embedding dimensions. By the fourth embedding dimension there is a relatively smooth continuum between the horizontal layers that seems to be completed somewhere between dimensions 5 and 6. As the number of embedding dimensions increases, the lower horizontal line increases in length, indicative that as m increases it requires increasingly larger values of epsilon to increase the number of points captured within a given value of epsilon. Another way to view this result is that as m increases and more embedding dimensions are included in defining a point, the points tend to be farther apart in that dimension. At the same time, the upper horizontal line, which implies that above a certain value of epsilon there are no further points to be captured (the problem of epsilon being "too big" as discussed in Section III), is shrinking in length but at a slower rate than the lower line (the case of epsilon "too small") is growing. Hence, the connecting link shows an increasingly steeper slope. The critical issue is whether the slope stops increasing at a certain value of m. It is at this point that the problems of dealing with actual data as opposed to theoretical constructs are encountered. Whereas the theory would envision a specific inflection point at which the connecting link starts (point b in Figure 8-1) and ends (point c in Figure 8-1), when dealing with actual data, the inflection points are not well-defined and the connecting link is not totally linear. (Hence the rather fuzzily described selection of "intermediate points" in Section III.)

In our initial assessment of intraday data, that for November 5, 1987, we were quite successful in generating chaotic appearing results, as shown in Figure 8-3.

In this example, we estimate that the embedding dimension at which behavior consistent with chaos becomes evident is somewhere between 6 and 7. This result is consistent with that reported in Section 4.3 of Brock and Malliaris (1989). The evidence for the 1982–1984 period of study is less robust and considerably mixed. Samples of plots of $d(m)$ versus m for these dates are contained in Appendix C to this chapter. Five dates showed strong evidence of the necessary condition: June 7, 1982; December 10, 1982; January 19, 1983; January 18, 1984; and June 28, 1984. Four other dates showed a potential for a tapering off of the correlation dimension and thus

Figure 8-3

Slope of CM vs. M, and Random vs. M
S&P Intraday Data Using First Differences—Date 5 November 1987

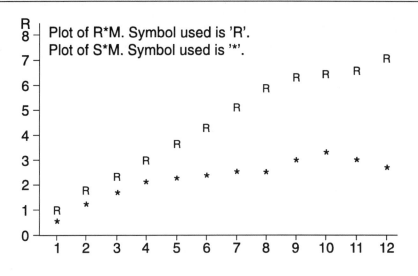

fall into a possible category. These dates are July 15, 1982; August 24, 1982; September 14, 1982; and July 7, 1983. All other dates displayed results that were essentially equivalent to the random number set. However, they are still being examined to ensure that the connecting link has been appropriately defined.

Daily Closing Data

Figure 8-4 provides the plot of $d(m)$ versus m for the daily closing prices against the same random number set results. It is evident that the daily close-to-close first differences are not distinguishable from a random set.

V. Conclusions

Of 34 days examined in this study where intraday data were used, six showed definite evidence consistent with the existence of a chaotic component in the pricing structure and an additional four are possible candidates. By contrast, the daily closing prices showed no evidence of a chaotic behavioral pattern. Although the evidence is not conclusive, it is sufficient

Figure 8-4

S&P Slope of CM vs. M and Random vs. M
Daily Closing Prices—First Differences

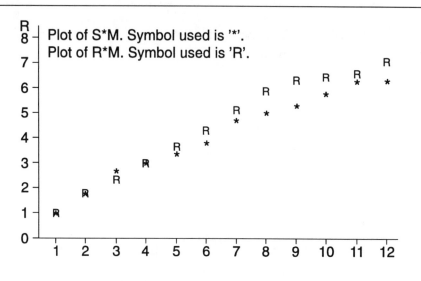

to cast additional doubt on the random walk hypothesis of security price generation. However, the admission that the price generation process may have a deterministic component raises troubling questions: If security prices are the present value of future cash flows, and changes to such prices arise only from the arrival of previously unexpected information, then how can they also be the result of a deterministic (and thus presumably predictable) pattern? (At this point we obviously overlook the difficulty of building a model that provides the prediction.) As the tools of analysis become more powerful, it becomes apparent that there will be a greater need to reconcile theory with the evidence of reality. We can relate the findings here to futures markets through the use of a standard arbitrage-type futures pricing model. Assuming a constant dividend rate, interest rate, and deterministic time, one can expect that the factors affecting the cash index also are going to affect the futures index value. Thus we would expect to find the same results in the futures prices.

Note

1   A complete set of the plots is available from the lead author.

References

Ashley, R. A., and D. M. Patterson. "Linear versus Nonlinear Macroeconomies: A Statistical Test." *International Economic Review* 30, No. 3 (August 1989), pp. 685–704.

Baumol, W. J., and J. Benhabib. "Chaos: Significance, Mechanism, and Economic Applications." *Journal of Economic Perspectives* 3 (Winter 1989), pp. 77–105.

Baumol, W. J., and R. E. Quandt. "Chaos Models and Their Implications for Forecasting." *Eastern Economic Journal* 11 (January–March 1985), pp. 3–15.

Brock, W. A., and A. G. Malliaris. *Differential Equations, Stability and Chaos in Dynamical Economics.* Amsterdam: Elsevier Science Publishers, 1989.

Cox, J. C., and S. A. Ross. "The Valuation of Options for Alternative Stochastic Processes." *Journal of Financial Economics* 3 (1976), pp. 145–166.

De Bondt, W. F. M., and R. H. Thaler. "A Mean-Reverting Walk Down Main Street." *Journal of Economic Perspectives* 3, No. 1 (Winter 1989), pp. 189–202.

Devaney, R. L. *An Introduction to Chaotic Dynamical Systems.* Redwood City, CA: Addison-Wesley, 1989.

Fama, E. F., and K. R. French. "Common Factors in the Serial Correlation of Stock Returns." Working Paper, Graduate School of Business, University of Chicago (October 1986).

_____. "Dividend Yields and Expected Stock Returns." *Journal of Financial Economics* 22 (1988), pp. 3–25.

Gabish, G. "Nonlinearities in Dynamic Economic Systems." *Atlantic Economic Journal* (December 1987), pp. 22–31.

Grassberger, P. and I. Procaccia. "Measuring the Strangeness of Strange Attractors." *Physica* 9D (1983), pp. 189–208.

Hsieh, D. "Testing for Nonlinear Dependence in Daily Foreign Exchange Rates." *Journal of Business* 62, No. 3 (1989), pp. 339–368.

Mandelbrot, B. B. *The Fractal Geometry of Nature.* New York: W.H. Freeman, 1983.

Merville, L. J., and D. R. Pieptea. "Stock-Price Volatility, Mean-Reverting Diffusion, and Noise." *Journal of Financial Economics* 24 (1989), pp. 193–214.

Poterba, J. M., and L. H. Summers. "Mean Reversion in Stock Prices." *Journal of Financial Economics* 22 (1988), pp. 27–59.

Ramsey, J. B. "Economic and Financial Data as Nonlinear Processes." In G. P. Dwyer, Jr., and R. W. Hafer, eds., *The Stock Market: Bubbles, Volatility and Chaos*. Proceedings of the Thirteenth Annual Economic Policy Conference of the Federal Reserve Bank of St. Louis, 1990.

Ramsey, J. B., C. L. Sayers, and P. Rothman. "The Statistical Properties of Dimensions Calculations Using Small Data Sets: Some Economic Applications." *International Economic Review* 31, No. 4 (November 1990), pp. 991–1020.

Routh, G. "Economics and Chaos." *Challenge* 1 (July–August 1989), pp. 47–52.

Scheinkman, J. A., and B. LeBaron. "Nonlinear Dynamics and Stock Returns." *Journal of Business* 62, No. 3 (July 1989). pp. 311–337.

Savit, R. "When Random Is Not Random: An Introduction to Chaos in Market Prices." *Journal of Futures Markets* 8, No. 3 (1988), pp. 271–289.

_____. "Nonlinearities and Chaotic Effects in Options Prices." *Journal of Futures Markets* 9, No. 6 (1989), pp. 507–518.

Takens, F. "Distinguishing Deterministic and Random Systems." In G.I. Barenblatt, G. Iooss, and D. D. Joseph, eds., *Non-Linear Dynamics and Turbulence*. Marshfield, MA: Pitman, 1983.

Appendix A: Dates Used in the Study

April 28, 1982	May 3, 1982	June 7, 1982
July 15, 1982	August 24, 1982	September 14, 1982
October 27, 1982	November 24, 1982	December 10, 1982
January 19, 1983	February 1, 1983	March 3, 1983
April 22, 1983	May 26, 1983	June 9, 1983
July 7, 1983	August 22, 1983	September 14, 1983
October 11, 1983	November 18, 1983	December 1, 1983
January 18, 1984	February 9, 1984	March 30, 1984
April 16, 1984	May 22, 1984	June 28, 1984
July 2, 1984	August 28, 1984	September 17, 1984
October 11, 1984	November 29, 1984	December 26, 1984
	November 5, 1987	

Appendix B

Figure B-1

LN(CME) = Y vs. LN(X) = X for M = 1 Dimensional Set
Epsilon Follows Path EP1*(exp(log(300)/100))**K   K = 1 – 100
S&P Intraday Data Using First Differences
Date: 27 October 1982

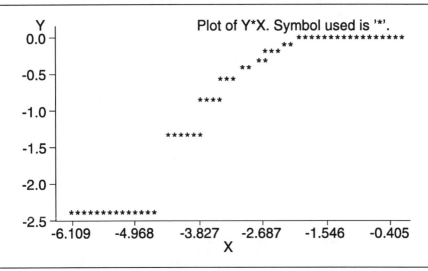

Plot of Y*X. Symbol used is '*'.

Note: 47 obs hidden

Figure B-2

LN(CME) = Y vs. LN(X) = X for M = 5 Dimensional Set
Epsilon Follows Path EP1* (exp (log(300)/100))**K   K = 1 – 100
S&P Intraday Data Using First Differences   Date: 27 October 1982

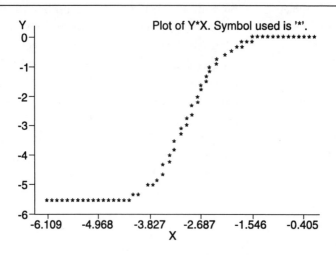

Figure B-3

LN(CME) = Y vs. LN(X) = X for M = 12 Dimensional Set
Epsilon Follows Path EP1* (exp(log(300)/100))**K   K = 1 – 100
S&P Intraday Data Using First Differences   Date: 27 October 1982

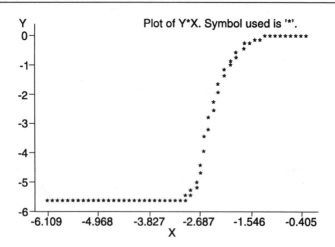

Appendix C

Figure C-1

Slope of CM vs. M, and Random vs. M
S&P Intraday Data Using First Differences
Date: 07 June 1982

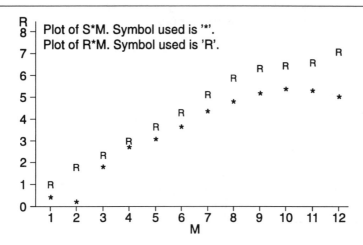

Figure C-2

Slope of CM vs. M, and Random vs. M
S&P Intraday Data Using First Differences
Date: 10 December 1982

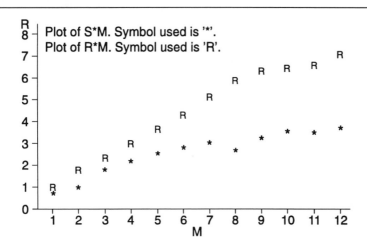

Figure C-3

Slope of CM vs. M, and Random vs. M
S&P Intraday Data Using First Differences
Date: 28 June 1984

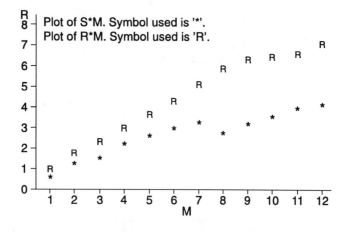

9

INVESTOR PREFERENCES AND THE CORRELATION DIMENSION

By Steve Satchell and Allan Timmermann

Introduction

The advent of nonlinear dynamics to economics has brought with it new models of dynamic behavior for asset returns. These models, such as long memory processes (Lo, 1991) and chaotic models (Brock, 1986) have in turn required the calculation of new attributes of the return process such as Lyapunov exponents, correlation dimensions, and Hurst exponents, to mention a few. However, although these measures have repeatedly been computed and reported in applied financial work,[1] it is not clear how to interpret such measures from an economic point of view. While we know that the utility function of a risk-averse investor is increasing in mean returns and decreasing in the volatility of returns, no similar results have yet been established for these new statistical measures.

This chapter explores a relationship between expected utility maximization and the correlation dimension. There are two sides to the relation between statistical measures characterizing the distribution of asset returns and the preferences of an investor. First, the statistical measures may enter directly as arguments in the utility function of an investor. On this point it is by no means obvious whether an expected utility maximizing investor prefers an asset with a high correlation dimension to one with a low correlation dimension. In fact, whether an asset with a high correlation dimension is preferred to an asset with a low correlation dimension seems to depend on how we measure the correlation dimension and on the data-generating process for the payoff of the asset. Whether it is sensible for expected utility maximizers to calculate expected utility on the basis of this measure, which may not be unique, is an interesting question that we do not attempt to answer here.

Secondly, the preferences of investors may be used to impose restrictions on the correlation dimension. For instance, in a mean-variance framework, if risk-averse investors only hold one of two assets with identical mean returns, we know that the preferred asset must have the smallest volatility. Along those lines we prove in this chapter a theorem on the relationship between the correlation dimension and a condition that implies first-order stochastic dominance, a concept that is frequently used in financial analysis. This theorem suggests a new way of constructing a bound on the correlation dimension of a process based on stochastic dominance and the empirical distribution function. Given the notorious difficulties associated with finite-sample estimation of the correlation dimension,[2] this may prove to be important in applied work. We provide an empirical example where the theorem turns out to be helpful in ranking the correlation dimensions of two stocks.

Financial Information in the Correlation Dimension

We will analyze the simple case where asset payoffs are identically and independently distributed (IID) and consider two random assets $\{X_i\}$ and $\{Y_k\}$, whose returns are mutually independent. Our starting point is to utilize the notion of stochastic dominance familiar from the finance literature. If X_i first order stochastically dominates Y_i, denoted by $X \geq_{fsd} Y$, then all individuals with utility functions that are increasing and continuous functions of final wealth do not prefer Y_i to X_i. It is well-known that this is equivalent to the condition that X is equal in distribution to Y plus α, where α is some nonnegative variable. First we present a result on the relationship between $(X_i - X_j)$ and $(Y_i - Y_j)$ in the case where X_i and X_j are two (independent) values of X and Y_i and Y_j are two independent values of Y. Let $\underline{d}$ denote distributional equivalence. Then we have

Lemma 1

Suppose that $X \stackrel{d}{=} Y + \alpha$, where α is a nonnegative variable and α and Y are independently distributed. Then $(X_i - X_j) \stackrel{d}{=} (Y_i - Y_j) + (\alpha_i - \alpha_j)$.

Proof

Since Y and α are independent, the characteristic function of X, $\varphi_x(t)$ is given by

$$\varphi_x(t) = \varphi_y(t)\varphi_\alpha(t),$$

where $\varphi_y(t)$ and $\varphi_\alpha(t)$ are the characteristic functions of Y and α. The characteristic function of $Z = X_i - X_j$, $\varphi_z(t)$ is given by

$$\varphi_z(t) = \varphi_x(t)\varphi_x(-t) = \varphi_y(t)\varphi_y(-t)\varphi_\alpha(t)\varphi_\alpha(-t),$$

which proves the result. QED.

Note that the condition in Lemma 1 implies $X \geq_{fsd} Y$.

We now move on to the notion of second-order stochastic dominance. By definition Y second order stochastically dominates X, $Y \geq_{ssd} X$, if all risk-averse individuals with utility functions whose derivatives are continuous prefer Y to X. We will show in Lemma 2 that if the conditions of Lemma 1 hold, then $(Y_i - Y_j) \geq_{ssd} (X_i - X_j)$.

Lemma 2

Assume that the conditions of Lemma 1 are satisfied. Then

$$Y_i - Y_j \geq_{ssd} X_i - X_j.$$

Proof

By lemma 1 $X_i - X_j \stackrel{d}{=} Y_i - Y_j + \alpha_i - \alpha_j$. Also, from the independence of Y and α,

$$E(\alpha_i - \alpha_j \mid Y_i - Y_j) = E(\alpha_i - \alpha_j) = E(\alpha_i) - E(\alpha_j) = 0,$$

where we have used the assumption that the α's are IID.

The last condition is proved by Rothschild and Stiglitz (Theorem 2, 1970) to be equivalent to $Y_i - Y_j \geq_{ssd} X_i - X_j$. QED.

Let $X_1, X_2, ..., X_T$ be a sample of observations of a variable X. Stack the observations in N-dimensional vectors to obtain a series $Z_i = (X_i, ..., X_{i+N-1})$, for $i = 1, ..., T-N+1$. Then for each value of the embedding dimension (N) the estimate of the correlation integral $C_T(r,N)$ is defined as the proportion of pairs of Z_i, Z_j that lie within a distance r of each other in the sample. Define the indicator variable

$$X_{ij} = 1 \text{ if } ||Z_i - Z_j|| < r, \tag{1}$$

$$= 0 \text{ if } ||Z_i - Z_j|| \geq r,$$

where $||.||$ is any metric. Then the correlation integral is defined as the limit of $C_T(r,N)$ as T goes to infinity, where

$$C_T(r,N) = \frac{2}{(t-N)(T-N+1)} \sum_{i=1}^{T-N} \sum_{j=i+1}^{T-N+1} X_{ij} \tag{2}$$

Consider the measure

$$d_x(r) = \frac{\ln\left(\text{Prob}\{ \max_{k=1,n} (|x_{ik} - x_{jk}|) < r\}\right)}{\ln(r)}, \tag{3}$$

where we shall take $r < 1$, so $\ln(r) < 0$. Intuitively $d_x(r)$ measures the elasticity of the probability that two points are "neighbors" in the sense that they lie within a distance r of each other, with respect to the distance r. Notice that the distance measure is calculated under the $L(\infty)$ norm, i.e., $||Z_i - Z_j|| = \max_{k=1,N} (|Z_{ik} - Z_{jk}|)$. It is not obvious how this measure relates to the correlation dimension. However, in the case of a fixed embedding dimension (N), which will always be the case in a finite sample, and under the assumption of an IID process, Satchell and Yoon (1992) show that, under the $L(\infty)$ norm, the empirical correlation dimension converges in probability to the quantity in Equation 1. Using this we get the following theorem (proved in the Appendix to this chapter).

Theorem

Suppose that $X \overset{d}{=} Y + \alpha$, where Y and α are independent, $\alpha \geq 0$, and the correlation dimension is defined by Equation 1 for two IID series X and Y. Let m be a nonnegative integer. Then

$$d_x(r) > d_y(r), \quad \text{for r near } 0,$$

if the number of crossings of the distribution functions of $(X_i - X_j)$ and $(Y_i - Y_j)$ is $4m + 1$, and

$d_x(r) < d_y(r)$,   for r near 0,

if the number of crossings of the distribution functions of $(X_i - X_j)$ and $(Y_i - Y_j)$ is 4m + 3.

The conclusion of Theorem 1 is very interesting. Consider the case where X and Y are IID. If Lemma 1 is satisfied, which implies that $X \geq_{fsd} Y$, then it follows that $d_x(r) > d_y(r)$ if the number of crossings of the distribution functions of the convolutions of $X_i - X_j$ and $Y_i - Y_j$ is 4m+1 for m = 0, 1, 2, ..., and where the correlation dimension is measured near 0 and is based on the $L(\infty)$ norm. This does not really allow us to say that asset markets with high (low) correlation dimensions are preferred by investors with increasing utility functions.

Suppose we know that the condition in Lemma 1 is satisfied, that $X \geq_{fsd} Y$ and we also know the probability laws of X and Y. We can then compute the distribution functions of the convolutions of the variables $X_i - X_j$ and $Y_i - Y_j$ and count the number of crossings, which will be either 4m+1 or 4m+3 (m = 0, ...) and then deduce whether the correlation dimension of X will be greater or less than the correlation dimension of Y. This is the converse of the Theorem: if the number of crossings of $(X_i - X_j)$ and $(Y_i - Y_j)$ is known and equal to 4m+1 and $d_x(r) > d_y(r)$ in the neighborhood between 0 and the first positive crossing and it is assumed that either $(X_i - X_j) \geq_{ssd} (Y_i - Y_j)$ or $(Y_i - Y_j) \geq_{ssd} (X_i - X_j)$, then in fact $(Y_i - Y_j) \geq_{ssd} (X_i - X_j)$.

We have not been able to treat the correlation dimension as a parameter entering into investors' expected utility functions in the same way as the mean and variance. However, this seems to be an interesting avenue for further research. Insofar as returns in markets with a low correlation dimension are easier to predict, at least over short horizons, than returns in markets with a high correlation dimension, it seems intuitively right to expect investors to prefer markets with low correlation dimensions.

An Empirical Example

To illustrate how the theorem can be used to rank the correlation dimension of two assets, we considered daily data on two British stocks, Allied-Lyons (X) and ASDA Group (Y) over the period 1/1/1980 to 12/31/1992. This gave us a sample of 3,287 observations. In percentages the average daily return on Allied-Lyons was .064 while that of ASDA was .0123. Their standard deviations (in percent) were 1.57 and 2.31, respectively. In Figure 9-1 we plot the cumulative distribution functions of $F(X_i - X_j)$ and $F(Y_i - Y_j)$ as well as their difference. The first diagram suggests that $(Y_i - Y_j) \geq_{ssd}$

Figure 9-1

Cumulative Density Functions for First-Differenced Daily Returns on Allied-Lyons and ASDA Group, 1980–1992

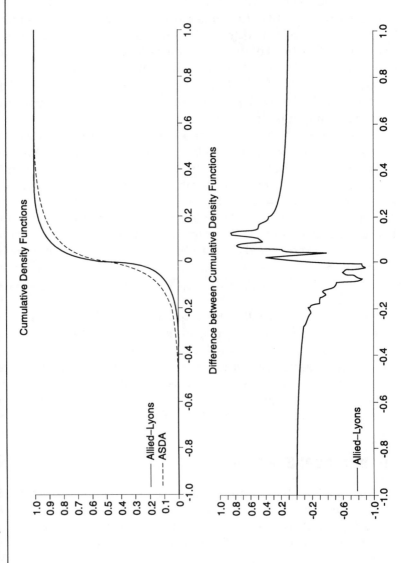

$(X_i - X_j)$. There appear to be three crossings between the cumulative distribution functions suggesting that $d_x < d_y$ under the assumption that $X \geq_{fsd} Y$. It is, however, important to recognize the difficulty that the empirical distribution function is only an estimate of the true distribution function.

We also estimated the value of the two correlation dimensions. For Allied Lyons (X) we obtained an estimate of $4.523 \pm .099$, while the value for ASDA (Y) was $4.344 \pm .295$. These values are very similar and, in the light of the size of the standard errors, one cannot determine which of the two values is the larger one. It is exactly in a situation like this that the Theorem seems useful: It provides support for the conclusion that, in fact, the correlation dimension of ASDA is the largest one.

Notes

1   See, for instance, Brock et al. (1991) and Frank and Stengos (1988).

2   A nonexhaustive list of such difficulties includes: the estimate of the correlation dimension may be very sensitive to the choice of distance (Brock et al., 1991), Grassberger and Proccacia (1983)]; serial correlation in the data may bias the correlation estimate (Wolff, 1990); lack of sufficient observations may lead to inaccurate measurement (Ramsey et al., 1990); the assumption that distances are independently distributed is likely to be violated (Theiler, 1990).

References

Brock, W. "Distinguishing Random and Deterministic Systems: Abridged Version." *Journal of Economic Theory* 40 (1986), 168–95.

Brock, W., D. A. Hsieh, and B. LeBaron. *Nonlinear Dynamics, Chaos and Instability: Statistical Theory and Economic Evidence*. Cambridge, MA: MIT Press, 1991.

Frank, M. Z., and T. Stengos. "Some Evidence Concerning Macroeconomic Chaos." *Journal of Monetary Economics* 22 (1988), 423–38.

Grassberger, P., and F. Procaccia. "Measuring the Strangeness of Strange Attractors." *Physica* D9 (1983), 189–208.

Lo, A. "Long Term Memory in Stock Market Prices." *Econometrica*,59 (1991), 1 279–1314.

Lukacs, E. *Characteristic Functions*, 2d ed. London: Griffin, 1970.

Ramsey, J. B., C. L. Sayers, and P. Rothman. "The Statistical Properties of Dimension Calculations Using Small Data Sets: Some Economic Applications." *International Economic Review* 31 (1990), 991–1020.

Rothschild, M., and J. Stiglitz. "Increasing Risk I: A Definition." *Journal of Economic Theory* 2 (1970), 225–43.

Satchell, S. E., and Y. Yoon. "Misspecification in Measurement of the Correlation Dimension." Unpublished manuscript, University of Cambridge (1992).

Theiler, J. "Statistical Precision of Dimension Estimators." *Physical Review* 41 (1990), 3038–51.

Wolff, R. "A Note on the Behaviour of the Correlation Integral in the Presence of a Time Series." *Biometrica* 77 (1990), 689–697.

Appendix

Proof of the Theorem

Let P_x be the number of neighbor points that lie within a distance (r) of each other. Under the assumption that distances are independently distributed, we obtain

$$P_x = \text{Prob}\left(\max_{k=1,n} \left(|x_{ik} - x_{jk}|\right) < r\right) = \left(\text{Prob}\left(|x_{ik} - x_{jk}|\right) < r\right)^n$$

$$= \left(\text{Prob}\left(-r < x_{ik} - x_{jk} < r\right)\right)^n.$$

We will denote by $F_x(.)$ the distribution function of $X_{ik} - X_{jk}$, and by $F_y(.)$ the distribution function of $Y_{ik} - Y_{jk}$. It follows from Theorem (3.4.2) of Lukacs (1970) that $F_x()$ and $F_y()$ are both symmetric so that $F_x(r) = 1 - F_x(-r)$,

and $\quad P_x = \left(2F_x(r) - 1\right)^n, \quad$ for $0 < r < 1$.

Also, $\quad d_x > d_y \Leftrightarrow \dfrac{\ln(P_x)}{\ln(r)} > \dfrac{\ln(P_y)}{\ln(r)} \Leftrightarrow \ln(P_x) < \ln(P_y) \Leftrightarrow F_x(r) < F_y(r)$.

By Lemma 2 $(Y_i - Y_j) \geq {}_{ssd} (X_i - X_j)$. It follows from the symmetry of $F_x(r)$ and $F_y(r)$ that the number of crossing points of $F_x(r)$ and $F_y(r)$ are odd, and that the number of crossings is at least one, since the two distribution functions cross at 0, $F_x(0) = F_y(0) = \frac{1}{2}$. Define n as the number of crossings between 0 and 1, not counting 0 or 1; n can be odd or even (0, 1, 2, ...). Let n = 2m in the even case

2m+1 in the odd case

Then the total number of crossings (including 0) is by symmetry equal to (4m+1) in the even case and (4m+3) in the odd case. If the number of crossings is 4m+1, then for r near 0, i.e., in the interval between 0 and the next crossing, it must be the case that $F_y(r) < F_x(r)$ from the conditions for second-order stochastic dominance. This implies that $d_x > d_y$. If the number of crossings is 4n+3, we get the reverse implication by an identical argument. QED.

10

Modeling Structured Nonlinear Knowledge to Predict Stock Market Returns

By Ypke Hiemstra

1. Introduction

Finance literature suggests that fundamental linear models can predict part of the variation in stock market returns at the monthly and quarterly frequency. On the other hand, portfolio managers respond to the complexities of stock market prediction by applying imprecise, qualitative knowledge of a structured rulelike format that relates input variables in a much more complex—i.e., nonlinear—way to stock market behavior.

This chapter presents a fuzzy expert system (FES) to predict quarterly stock market excess returns. A fuzzy expert system represents expert knowledge of a particular domain using fuzzy logic. Fuzzy logic, founded by Zadeh (1965), is a formalism for reasoning with vague knowledge. As portfolio managers apply imprecise concepts and imprecise reasoning, fuzzy logic is a natural choice for knowledge representation. The system handles nonlinearities, captures expert knowledge, and is open for inspection to explain its conclusions. Since the risk-free rate of return is known, it makes sense to focus on the excess return—the market return minus the risk-free rate of return.

This chapter presents, in Section 2, a general approach to predicting the stock market that forms the basis for the FES design. Section 3 discusses fuzzy logic; and in Section 4 the chapter presents the FES. Section 5 evaluates the model's predictive power, and presents the results of a tactical asset allocation policy exploiting the predictions. Section 6 discusses tuning of the system, and Section 7 contains the conclusions.

2. Forecasting the Stock Market

Finance studies have produced evidence that a significant part of the variation in monthly and quarterly excess returns can be predicted using information known at the time of prediction, e.g., Campbell (1987); Chen, Roll, and Ross (1986); Fama and French (1989); Ferson and Harvey (1991); Pesaran and Timmermann (1994); and Solnik (1993). These studies apply linear models and adopt a fundamental approach to stock market prediction that captures the forces that drive the stock market, as opposed to technical approaches, which focus on market dynamics. In particular evidence has been accumulated that ex ante information on inflation, interest rates, the business cycle, and valuation measures like the dividend yield can be used to predict monthly and quarterly excess returns.

Chaos, Nonlinearities, and Functional Mapping

The technical approach views the stock market as a nonlinear dynamic system that can produce chaotic behavior. There are two types of dynamic systems: continuous systems, described by differential equations, and discrete systems [see, for example, Strogatz (1994)]. A discrete nonlinear dynamic system can mathematically be represented as:

$$x_{n+1} = f(x_n) \tag{1}$$

where f is a nonlinear function f: $R_m \to R_m$, m being the number of variables describing the system's state. The role of feedback is crucial: the system's previous state determines its next state, generating a sequence of states x_1, x_2, ..., x_n. The system is a chaotic one when the sequence never repeats itself. An example of a discrete chaotic system is the Henon Mapping [see, for example, Welstead (1994)].

The fundamental approach views the stock market as an information processing system. The information set changes continuously, and the market's information processing adjusts prices to produce the expected excess return that the market considers appropriate. If the return generating process is nonstationary (i.e., the expected excess return varies), the market forms an expectation of the next period's excess return conditional on presently available information. Mathematically:

$$E(R_{t+1} \mid \theta_t) = f(\theta_t) \tag{2}$$

where R is the excess return, and θ the information set.

Both views involve complex nonlinear functions. Peters (1991) claims that the stock market has the properties of a nonlinear dynamic system that produces chaotic behavior. Hiemstra (1994c) presents evidence that neural networks capture nonlinearity present in Equation 2. The motivation to apply intelligent, adaptive systems like neural networks and fuzzy logic is that these technologies can capture the complexities of the functional mapping, and that the form of the function that applies to the stock market is unknown. Neural networks and fuzzy logic are parameter-free methods that do not require the functional specification of the function to approximate.

A General Fundamental Model to Predict the Stock Market

This chapter adopts a general fundamental approach to predicting the stock market return that corresponds to the way experts work, and that serves as the basis for designing an FES. Portfolio managers use individual approaches to predict the stock market, but any portfolio manager adopting the fundamental approach will confirm that business cycle, inflation, interest rates, and valuation measures play an important role in predicting the stock market. The model relates fundamental information about macroeconomic and market conditions to the market excess return. Figure 10-1 shows the general model.

The stock market excess return is predicted on the basis of market valuation and macroeconomic investment conditions. The basic idea is to compare investment conditions to the market valuation. The better investment conditions, given a particular market valuation, the higher the expected excess return; if investment conditions are poor and market valuation is high, the expected excess return is low. Three factors—the business cycle, interest rates, and inflation—determine investment conditions.

Often market efficiency, the instantaneous and perfect processing of all available information, is claimed to generate unpredictability of returns. However, Equation 2 claims a relation between the information available at time t and R_{t+1} if the return generating process is nonstationary. When the market is efficient, this relation exists as market risk and the price of risk fluctuate, and the market rationally updates prices to produce an appropriate expected return. If θ includes information on investment conditions and market valuation as in Figure 10-1, Equation 2 can detect situations of overvaluation or undervaluation and also capture predictability caused by market inefficiency.

The Motivation to Use Fuzzy Logic

The prediction model provides structured knowledge, knowledge that explicitly relates variables. The knowledge has an imprecise or vague character because of the use of qualitative concepts like low, medium, and high. Several considerations motivate to apply fuzzy logic:

- ❖ Modeling of (imprecise) structured knowledge
- ❖ Parameter-free, universal approximation
- ❖ Open for inspection
- ❖ Tuning instead of training

The knowledge of portfolio managers has an intrinsically vague character. Experts make statements of the type, "It seems likely that inflation in the G7 group will ease somewhat further" [Goldman Sachs (1992), p. 1.01]. The description of the expected inflation has vague boundaries, and

---

Figure 10-1

A General Fundamental Model to Predict Stock Market Returns

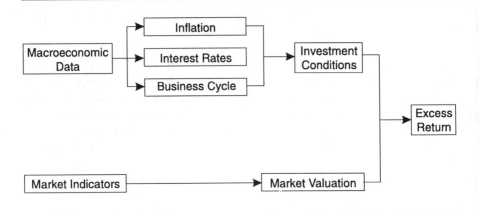

does not refer to particular quantitative values. Fuzzy logic is directed at modeling vague knowledge. Secondly, fuzzy systems are parameter-free approximators of input-output functions, which do not require a mathematical specification of how outputs depend on inputs [Kosko (1991)]. To build a fuzzy logic model, there is no need for a functional specification of the relationship between inputs and output. In addition, fuzzy systems are universal approximators, which can model complex, nonlinear dependencies of any kind. Fuzzy logic employs a rulelike knowledge representation, providing a transparent knowledge representation. This supports interactive use of the model, and portfolio managers will feel comfortable relying on conclusions they can trace back to model inputs. Welstead (1994) notes that the pattern of rule activation can be used to estimate predictive power. If the system uses the rules in a way similar to some reference set of predictions, the predictive performance will be comparable. Finally, if structured knowledge is available, it is advantageous to encode this knowledge directly, and use data for fine-tuning the knowledge instead of training a model from scratch.

3. Fuzzy Logic

Fuzzy logic treats vague concepts as linguistic variables: variables that have words as values instead of numbers. The meaning of each word is defined by a fuzzy set, represented by a membership function, which expresses the degree to which an element of the universe of discourse belongs to the fuzzy set. This degree is viewed to be the truth value of the statement that the vague concept applies to the element. If X is a linguistic variable in a universe of discourse, and L is an adjective defined by a fuzzy set, the membership function $f_L(X)$ specifies the degree to which X belongs to the fuzzy set denoted by L. This degree is the truth value of the fuzzy proposition p: X = L, which states that L applies to X.

Usually the membership functions have a trapezoidal or triangular shape. As an example, consider the linguistic variable market valuation, and suppose the set of possible values is {Low, Medium, High}. If we express market valuation by an index ranging from −2.5 to 2.5, its universe of discourse is {−2.5, 2.5}. Figure 10-2 shows three membership functions that could define each of the vague concepts. The figure shows that a value of −0.5 belongs to a degree of slightly more than 0.2 to the fuzzy set Low, and to a degree of slightly less than 0.8 to the fuzzy set Medium.

Figure 10-2

Membership Functions

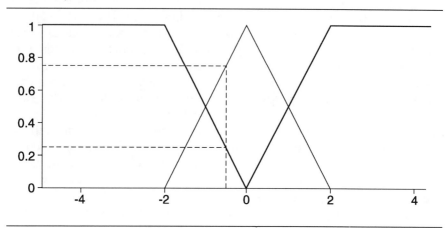

To relate fuzzy propositions, fuzzy inference applies fuzzy rules, conditional statements of the form:

If P_1 and/or P_2 ... and/or P_n then C

where P_i and C are fuzzy propositions. The rule's condition expresses one or more conditions in terms of a fuzzy proposition. Connectives (e.g., *and* and *or*) compute the truth value of a compound condition.

In its simplest form, fuzzy inference assigns to the conclusion the truth value of the condition. One inference rule is the max-prod inference rule, which creates a fuzzy set by multiplying the membership function of the fuzzy set referred to in the rule's conclusion with the truth value of the rule's condition. Application of the rules in the knowledge base creates a collection of fuzzy sets. Summation of the fuzzy sets yields a fuzzy set representing the conclusion. Figure 10-3 shows how two fuzzy sets, multiplied by the truth values of the rule x and rule y, respectively, form the fuzzy set that represents the conclusion. Approximate reasoning, a more advanced type of fuzzy inference, takes the reliability of rules into account [see, for example, Yager and Zadeh (1992)]. Defuzzification transforms the fuzzy conclusion into a concrete statement. A popular method is the centroid method, which calculates the center of gravity of the output fuzzy set, the point at which the fuzzy set is in balance (indicated by the arrowhead in Figure 10-3).

Figure 10-4 shows the basic structure of a fuzzy inference unit. A fuzzy inference unit fuzzifies inputs by calculating degrees of membership. Rule

Figure 10-3

Fuzzy Inference

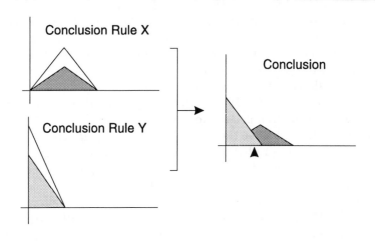

Figure 10-4

Fuzzy Inference Unit

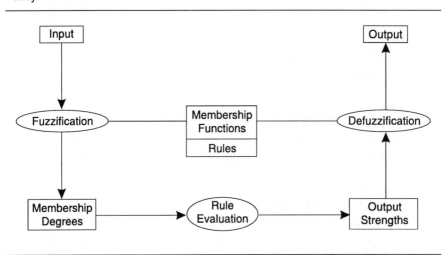

evaluation takes place by assigning compound truth values of the rules'
conditions as strengths to fuzzy outputs. Defuzzification of the fuzzy
conclusion yields a concrete solution.

4. A Fuzzy Expert System to Forecast the Stock Market

The prediction model outlined in Section 2 indicates the relevant variables and relations to predict the stock market. By adopting this model, the FES is certain to have a general character that experts can tune to match their individual beliefs. The design of the FES concentrates on formulating the rules. To formulate the rules and test the system, we use as inputs dividend yield (YSP), short-term interest rate (SIR), inflation rate based on the consumer price index (CPI), and the change in the 12-month moving average of the industrial production index (DIP). YSP and SIR are instantaneously available, and so the latest observations prior to the forecasted period were used to predict, e.g., the values at the end of the preceding month. Macroeconomic information is available typically on a monthly basis with a lag of some 20 days, and so DIP and CPI were used with a two-month lag. The data set consists of 93 quarterly observations covering the period 1970–1993, of YSP_{t-1}, DIP_{t-2}, SIR_{t-1}, and CPI_{t-2}. The desired output is the S&P 500 quarterly excess return, defined as total return (price movement plus dividends related to the initial investment) minus the risk-free rate of return, the three-month T-bill rate.

There are two types of rules: the rules that conclude on the investment conditions, and the rules that use that conclusion plus the market valuation to predict the excess return. For both types of rules, we distinguished the three input adjectives {Low, Medium, High}, and the five output adjectives {VeryLow, Low, Medium, High, VeryHigh}. To actually generate the rules, we performed a linear regression using the data from 1970 to 1977 to estimate the qualitative effect of a particular input on the excess return by the signs of the regression coefficients. Weights were assigned to each of the three rule input adjectives, and the sum of the weights of a rule condition selected the appropriate rule conclusion. To facilitate the definition of membership functions, all variables are expected to be normalized, with membership functions specified as in Figure 10-2.

Two fuzzy inference units are the building blocks of the FES. The FES applies a two-step fuzzy inference. The first fuzzy inference evaluates macroeconomic investment conditions. The second fuzzy inference calculates the excess return on the basis of the macroeconomic investment conditions and market valuation. Using a two-step process simplifies the rules, as each rule processes only a few variables. Rules relating the four inputs directly to the excess return are more complex, and with three values for each input, the rule set would total 3^4 rules. A small rule set, consisting of simple rules, simplifies the process of tuning the model. Figure 10-5 shows a partial listing of the rule base. The number in front of

Figure 10-5

Three Rules from the Rule Base

(1.0) If Market Valuation is Low and Investment Index is Low then
Excess Return = Medium @ Rule D1;
(1.0) If Market Valuation is Low and Investment Index is Medium then
Excess Return = High @ Rule D2;
(1.0) If Market Valuation is Low and Investment Index is High then
Excess Return = Very High @ Rule D3.

each rule is the rule's reliability. The rule reliabilities of the basic FES are all equal to 1. The ampersand precedes the rule's name.

5. Performance of the Fuzzy Expert System

The FES processes and produces normalized values. Means and standard deviations of the variables to preprocess inputs and postprocess the predictions were estimated using the same data that were set aside to generate the fuzzy rules, so the predictions for the period 1978–1993 can be considered true out-of-sample predictions. Figure 10-6 shows actual quarterly excess returns versus predictions. Table 10-1 shows the correlation among predictions and realizations and the error rate, the ratio of predictions with the wrong sign to all predictions. At the quarterly frequency, an out-of-sample correlation of 0.34 is a very good result [cf. DuBois (1992)].

To evaluate the FES's added value, we simulated a tactical asset allocation policy. Asset allocation refers to the diversification of a portfolio across asset classes. Asset allocation typically involves selecting a strategic portfolio and applying a tactical policy that adjusts the strategic portfolio to respond to short-term market characteristics [Sharpe (1987)]. Figure 10-7 shows the performance of the FES when applying a straightforward tactical asset allocation policy. The top panel of Figure 10-7 shows two policy efficient frontiers (PEF). A PEF [Hiemstra (1994b)] represents the annualized ex post risk-return properties of a particular tactical investment policy for those strategic portfolios that produced the highest return for the respective risk exposures. The tactical policies shown operate on a strategic portfolio consisting of stocks and bonds. The black line represents the results of a simple buy-and-hold policy, a 100 percent bonds portfolio located at the lower end, a 100 percent stocks portfolio located at the higher end. The gray line shows the results by applying a policy that exits the

Figure 10-6

Predictions (the Gray Line) versus Actual Quarterly Excess Returns (the Black Line), 1978–1993

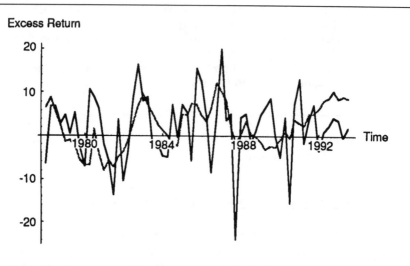

Table 10-1

Correlation and Error Rate of Out-of-Sample Forecasts

Correlation	0.34
Error rate	0.37

stock market when the FES predicts a negative excess return. The policies were tested on data covering the period 1978–1993, the Shearson-Lehman Bond Index representing bond returns (net of trading cost).

Figure 10-7 shows that active management based on the FES produces a dramatic payoff. For a particular risk exposure (i.e., a particular strategic portfolio), the FES can add up to nearly 4 percent return annually. The bottom panel shows the relative value of an initial 1978 investment when adopting a strategic portfolio fully invested in stocks, the gray line representing active management, the black line a buy-and-hold policy.

Figure 10-7

The top panel shows two policy efficient frontiers, the bottom panel the relative value of a 1978 investment when adopting a strategic portfolio of 100 percent stocks. In both cases, buy-and-hold is the bottom line, and the upper lines represent the FES results.

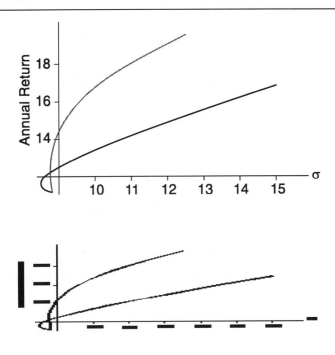

6. Tuning the Expert System

The FES produces excellent results on the basis of a general model. Tuning may further improve the system's performance. Tuning can be automated in various ways. Kosko (1991) combines fuzzy systems with neural networks. Another option is to apply genetic algorithms [see, for example, Goldberg (1989)]. Welstead (1993) discusses a genetic fuzzy system to predict interest rates. This system manipulates the rules to generate a good fit. Alternatively, the tuning may focus on other model elements, in particular rule weights. Figure 10-8 presents a hierarchical view of the FES elements.

Figure 10-8

A Hierarchical View of the FES Elements

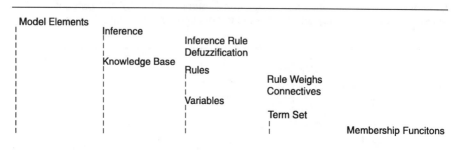

7. Conclusion

A stock market FES can capture the complex nonlinear relationship between fundamental information and the excess return, and is in addition to that open for inspection. The FES shows excellent performance, and produces a dramatic payoff when applying a straightforward tactical asset allocation policy. Tuning should improve performance even further. Tuning may be automated, and one way to do so is to apply genetic algorithms. Portfolio managers can understand the system and trace its conclusions back to model inputs.

References

Campbell, J.Y. "Stock Returns and the Term Structure." *Journal of Financial Economics*. 18 (1987), 373–399.

Chen, N-F., R. Roll, and S. A. Ross. "Economic Forces and the Stock Market." *The Journal of Business*, Vol. 59, No. 3 (1986), pp. 383–403.

DuBois, C. H. "Tactical Asset Allocation: A Review of Current Techniques," in *Active Asset Allocation*, R. D. Arnott and F. J. Fabozzi, eds. London: McGraw-Hill, 1992.

Fama, E., and K. French. "Business Conditions and Expected Stock Returns." *Journal of Financial Economics*, Vol. 25 (1989), pp. 23–50.

Ferson, W. E., and C. R. Harvey. "Sources of Predictability in Portfolio Returns." *Financial Analysts Journal*, May–June 1991, pp. 49–56.

Goldberg, D. E. *Genetic Algorithms in Search, Optimization & Machine Learning*. Reading, MA: Addison-Wesley, 1989.

Goldman Sachs. *The International Economic Analyst,* Vol. 7, Issue No. 11 (1992).

Hiemstra, Y. "A Stock Market Forecasting Support System Based on Fuzzy Logic," The 27th Annual Hawaii International Conference on System Sciences, IEEE Computer Society Press (1994a).

Hiemstra, Y. "Applying Intelligent Systems to Tactical Asset Allocation." Workshop AI in Finance and Business, 11th European Conference on AI, Amsterdam (1994b).

Hiemstra, Y. "Linear Regression versus Backpropagation Networks to Predict Quarterly Excess Returns," The Second International Workshop on Neural Networks in the Capital Markets, CalTech, Pasadena (1994c).

Kosko, B. *Neural Networks and Fuzzy Systems.* Englewood Cliffs, NJ: Prentice-Hall, 1991.

Pesaran, M. H., and A. Timmermann. "Forecasting Stock Returns." *Journal of Forecasting,* Vol. 13 (1994), 335–367.

Peters, E. E. *Chaos and Order in the Capital Markets.* New York: Wiley, 1991.

Sharpe, W. F. "Integrated Asset Allocation," *Financial Analysts Journal,* 43 (September–October, 1987), pp. 25–32

Solnik, B. "The Performance of International Asset Allocation Strategies Using Conditioning Information." *Journal of Empirical Finance,* 1 (1993), pp. 33–55.

Strogatz, S. H. *Nonlinear Dynamics and Chaos.* Reading, MA: Addison-Wesley, 1994.

Welstead, S. "Financial Data Modeling with Genetically Optimized Fuzzy Systems." *Proceedings of the Second International Conference on Artificial Intelligence Applications on Wall Street,* Roy S. Freedman, ed. Gaithersburg, MD: Software Engineering Press, 1993, pp. 280–285.

Welstead, S. *Neural Network and Fuzzy Logic Applications in C/C++.* New York: Wiley, 1994.

Yager, R. R., and L. A. Zadeh, eds. *An Introduction to Fuzzy Logic Applications in Intelligent Systems.* Dordrecht: Kluwer Academic Publishers, 1992.

Zadeh, L. A. "Fuzzy Sets." *Information and Control,* 8 (1965), pp. 338–353.

PART III

COMMODITY MARKETS EVIDENCE

11

Evidence of Chaos in Commodity Futures Prices

By Gregory P. DeCoster, Walter C. Labys, and Douglas W. Mitchell

Introduction

The analysis and modeling of commodity futures price behavior continues to be an important issue. Much of this research centers on the following issues (Kamara, 1982):

1. Forecasting performance—is the futures price an unbiased predictor of the spot price at maturity, or are there explainable systematic biases?

2. Stochastic or structural character of futures prices—can they be explained by some linear or nonlinear model, or some form of random walk?

3. Distribution of futures prices—do they follow a normal distribution, and if not, what other form?

4. Equilibrium pricing of futures contracts within the capital market—how are they related to the prices of other risky assets?

Reprinted with permission from *The Journal of Futures Markets*, Vol. 12, No. 3 (June 1992): 291–305. ©1992 by John Wiley & Sons, Inc.

This chapter is concerned with the second issue; specifically, whether there exists nonlinear dynamic structure and, in particular, chaotic structure in the behavior of futures prices.[1] Chaotic dynamic systems are capable of generating a rich variety of time series patterns, and such time series are often random-appearing. Yet, if such structure can be shown to exist, the implication would be that the empirical validity of simple, early versions of the efficient markets hypothesis [e.g., Fama (1970)], which imply a random walk for asset prices, is called into question.[2] This would indicate that future research should be directed toward the difficult task of identifying the specific form of the underlying price structure. When that is accomplished, a better understanding of the economic behavior underlying the markets, and the potential for improved short-term (though not long-term) predictions will result.[3]

The search for nonlinear structure in financial and economic time series has become widespread in the past few years. Of particular note in the context of commodity prices are the works of Frank and Stengos (1989), who find evidence of nonlinear structure in gold and silver rates of return, and of Blank (1990), who finds nonlinear structure in soybean futures prices. Other examples include Scheinkman and LeBaron (1989a) and Hinich and Patterson (1985) on stock returns; Blank (1990) on stock futures prices; Barnett and Chen (1988) and DeCoster and Mitchell (1991b) on monetary aggregates and components; Hsieh (1989) on exchange rates; and Frank and Stengos (1988b), Frank, Gencay, and Stengos (1988), Brock and Sayers (1988), and Scheinkman and LeBaron (1989b) on macroeconomic data. These studies collectively suggest that chaotic dynamics may be of considerable importance in financial and economic data.

A technique commonly used in these articles is the correlation dimension technique of Grassberger and Procaccia (1983). The purpose of this chapter is to use the correlation dimension technique to search for chaotic structure in daily futures price data for each of four commodities: sugar, coffee, silver, and copper. This study finds that, for all four futures price series, there is strong evidence of nonlinear structure, and possibly chaos. The results are not explained by the alternative hypothesis of an ARCH model. As pointed out by Barnett and Hinich (1993), this evidence can be interpreted as a failure to reject the null hypothesis of chaos in the data. It should be noted that all the data series contain in excess of 4,000 observations (far more than in most previous correlation dimension studies in economics). Thus, while there is some question as to the effectiveness of this technique in very small samples [Ramsey, Sayers, and Rothman (1988)], the use of the technique is strongly justified by the sizes of this study's data sets. The concern in DeCoster and Mitchell (1991a) about possible insufficient ability to detect chaos in samples of the present size is not important in the present context.

Modeling Futures Prices

The idea that futures prices might follow a random walk is initially found in Working (1958), who postulates that the continuous flow of many different kinds of information into the market causes frequent price changes, which might be nearly random. Still this model allows for some gradualness of price changes, and thus, for some degree of a very short-term predictability. Samuelson (1965) further developed this model by postulating that futures prices follow a Martingale process. That is, futures prices, insofar as they constitute unbiased estimates of future spot prices, can be described by a stochastic process in which the expected price in the next period equals the current price.

Most of the empirical tests of the random walk and Martingale processes search for the existence of serial correlation and trends, since both processes require price changes to be independent. In practice, even when systematic dependencies in price changes are detected, it is very difficult to determine whether their magnitude and frequency are sufficient to violate the random walk model. Previous findings in this regard are well known and need not be mentioned except briefly. Trend deviations from random walk were first discovered for wheat and corn by Houthakker (1961), and for soybeans by Smidt (1965). Their results, based on filter or trading rules, are questioned by Cargill and Rausser (1975). Rocca (1969), Labys and Granger (1970), and Cargill and Rausser (1972), in performing spectral analysis of more than 20 futures price series, find some evidence for a modified random walk process, mostly resembling the Martingale process. Such studies test for the existence of a linear model; yet it is possible that some form of nonlinear model might underlie the price fluctuations in question. Stevenson and Bear (1970) and Leuthold (1972) employing filter rules confirm positive and negative price dependence to cast doubt on the validity of the random walk model.

Another approach of interest deals with the testing of the weak form and semistrong form efficient market models. Even though the Martingale model may be rejected in empirical tests of futures price behavior, this does not constitute a rejection of the efficient market model underlying that behavior. A market can be said to use information efficiently if no way exists to use available information to increase expected wealth by frequent trading. This implies that trading rules are worthless and price information cannot indicate the best opportunities to buy and sell. Regarding the efficient market hypothesis, it can be said to be true if the risk-adjusted return net of all costs from the best trading rule is not more than the comparable figure, when assets are traded infrequently [Jensen (1978), Taylor (1986)]. The interpretation of this hypothesis in a commodity futures price context is sometimes confusing: (1) trading rules do not replicate real trading possibilities; (2) it is difficult to find benchmarks for return comparisons; (3) insufficient information is available about the distribution of filter returns to confirm the significance of a distribution; and (4) retrospective optimization of the parameters or structure of a filter is dubious [see Taylor (1986)]. Danthine (1977) finds confusion in linking Martingale processes and efficiency in commodity markets for other reasons. In particular, the possibility of shortages may lead to above-normal expected profits, and a diminishing marginal rate of transformation over time may cause a severe correlation of price changes, even in an efficient market.

Guimaraes, Kingsman, and Taylor (1989) attempt to reappraise the efficiency hypothesis. Taylor's (1980) approach evaluates a futures price model, which resembles a random walk yet includes a price-trend for which formal stochastic processes are conjectural. This model, used on tests of ten commodity futures contracts traded in London, identifies a "price drift," which can be associated with the weak form of the efficient market model. Gross (1988) is concerned also about whether futures prices fully incorporate all publicly available information at the time of contracting. Based on a study of LME futures prices for copper and aluminum, he finds that the efficiency hypothesis cannot be rejected for these metals. Gupta and Mayer (1981), in performing efficiency tests for sugar, cocoa, and coffee prices as well as tin prices, also confirm the efficiency hypothesis. Both tests involve the more rigorous semistrong form of the hypothesis. Among studies that have difficulty in confirming the hypothesis, MacDonald and Taylor (1988), also employing LME futures prices, confirm the hypothesis for copper and lead but not for zinc. They employ a more rigorous vector autoregressive methodology using appropriate stationarity-inducing transformations. Brorsen et al. (1984) cannot confirm the hypothesis for cotton futures prices representing contract funding in New York.

While most of the above studies are based on linear models, a more recent approach to futures price modeling considers the possibility that other deviations from random processes may exist. That approach involves the use of nonlinear equations generating chaotic behavior. Interestingly, the application of the concept of chaos to commodity futures price behavior can be found in an earlier work by Mandelbrot.

Drawing upon Houthakker's (1961) analysis of cotton prices, Mandel-brot (1963a and b) developed a model of price behavior by replacing Gaussian probability laws with those termed "stable Paretian." His approach represented an attempt to discover orderly behavior within what appeared to be a random series of price fluctuations. It is in this context that Frank and Stengos (1989) investigated the Martingale hypothesis using an approach of Sims (1984) as well as a chaos-based approach. Although Frank and Stengos were not able to reject the Martingale hypothesis in a series of standard econometric tests involving daily and weekly silver and gold prices, they did provide correlation dimension-based evidence of the presence of nonlinear structure. Note that such structure can be consistent with efficient markets. This chapter follows Frank and Stengos in investigating whether nonlinear structure exists in futures price data for four commodities.

The Correlation Dimension Technique

The correlation dimension technique was originally developed by the physicists Grassberger and Procaccia (1983).[4] The technique is intended to detect the presence of chaotic structure in data by embedding overlapping subsequences of the data in m-space for various embedding dimensions, m. Purely random data are infinite-dimensional, and thus will "fill" a region of m-space for any finite m. On the other hand, data generated by a deterministic system will have a finite dimension, which will be no greater than the number of independent state variables in the system and which may be a noninteger. Thus, for sufficiently large m, one will be able to detect structure in deterministic data.

Specifically, suppose a deterministic system $y_t = f(y_{t-1})$ where y is an n-dimensional vector of (possibly unobserved) state variables. Suppose further a time series of a scalar variable, x, generated by $x_t = g(y_t)$ for some observer function, g. Then Takens' (1980) embedding theorem states that $m \geq 2n + 1$ is a sufficiently large embedding dimension to detect the structure. Since n is not known, an increasing sequence of m values must be tried.

For any value of m, one computes the correlation dimension of a stationary series $\{x_t\}$ by first computing the correlation integral $C(\varepsilon, m)$ for various values of a critical distance, ε. $C(\varepsilon, m)$ is defined to be the fraction of pairs of m-dimensional points $(x_i x_{i+1} \ldots x_{i+m-1})$, $(x_j x_{j+1} \ldots x_{j+m-1})$ whose distance from each other is no greater than ε. The distance is measured according to the commonly used sup norm, defined as:

$$\| (x_i x_{i+1} \dots x_{i+m-1}), (x_j x_{j+1} \dots x_{j+m-1}) \| \equiv \max_{k \in [0,m-1]} \{ x_{i+k} - x_{j+k} \}$$

One computes the correlation integral for a variety of ε equally spaced on a log scale, so that $C(\varepsilon, m)$ ranges from near zero to unity.

The correlation dimension for given m is the elasticity of $C(\varepsilon, m)$ with respect to ε. Thus, one needs to run a linear regression of log $C(\varepsilon, m)$ on log ε with an intercept. To prepare for this regression, one first plots log $C(\varepsilon, m)$ against log ε, and visually inspects the plot. While, in principle, the plot should be linear throughout, in practice, the presence of noise in the data is likely to result in a separate and relatively steep region at low values of ε; and finiteness of the data set may cause a choppy appearance in the plot as well as curvature at high values of ε. Therefore, one must judgmentally determine the linear range over which to run the regression. The slope estimate from this regression is the correlation dimension estimate for this value of m.

This procedure is repeated for a sequence of increasing values of m. If the data are purely random, then in infinite samples, the correlation dimension will equal m for all m. In practice, with a finite data set, the correlation dimension estimate may be substantially below m and may rise with m at less than a one-for-one rate [Frank and Stengos (1988b, 1989); Ramsey and Yuan (1987)]. If the data are deterministic, the slope estimates should "saturate" at some m, not rising any more as m is further increased; this saturation value of the slope is the correlation dimension estimate for the unobserved structure that generates the data. In practice, the slope estimates may never completely stop rising. Thus, the process of determining whether saturation has occurred and structure has been detected, can, in general, be rather judgmental.[5] However, in all the cases reported in this study, the evidence that structure is detected is strong. The slope estimates are usually well under one-third of the respective m values used to generate them, and they rise only slowly with m.

The data for which this procedure is conducted must be stationary. Since the raw data, as described below, are futures prices, the data are rendered stationary by taking the first difference of the logs of the price data. Thus, the transformed data are rates of return.

To make sure that the detected structure is nonlinear rather than linear, Brock's (1986) residual test is employed. The stationary data are delinearized by replacing the data with residuals from an autoregression of the data. If nonlinear structure is present, this procedure should, in principle, make no difference for the estimated correlation dimensions. However, in practice [Brock and Sayers (1988, p. 84)] the correlation dimension estimates rise with the number of terms in the autoregression. Therefore, this procedure should be used cautiously. The following procedure is utilized.

Simple autocorrelations of rates of return are computed for lags 1–24. Then, an autoregression is run for the rate of return, including any lags for which the simple autocorrelation is significant at the 1 percent level. The residuals from this autoregression serve as the AR-transformed data. Thus, the correlation dimension technique is performed for each commodity price series on both the rate of return data and on the AR-transformed data.

The shuffle test is also appropriate, given the tendency of finite sets of both noise and structured data to depart from idealized behavior in their correlation dimension estimates. The shuffle test of Scheinkman and Le-Baron (1989a) tests the hypothesis that a given correlation dimension estimate can come from a data series of noise with the same data distribution as that exhibited by the actual data. For the AR residuals of each of the four rate of return series, 20 artificial noise series with the same length and distribution as the AR residuals are created by sampling with replacement from those residuals. Then the correlation dimension is estimated for each artificial series, at the previously determined saturation embedding dimension and also at the highest embedding dimension (40). If at least 95 percent of these correlation dimension estimates for noise are above the corresponding estimates for the unshuffled data, the hypothesis that the unshuffled data are noise is rejected and the alternative hypothesis of nonlinear structure is accepted.

Finally, financial market data frequently appear to have a time-varying variance, which could produce correlation dimension estimates suggestive of deterministic nonlinear structure even if there are no deterministic components in the data. A time-varying variance could be generated by either a (stochastic) ARCH process or a deterministic process. Therefore, an ARCH filter is used to see if it is possible to rule out an ARCH process as an alternative explanation of the data. The same AR structure is used as before, and an ARCH(10) test is employed. Correlation dimension estimates are calculated for the standardized ARCH residuals, and shuffle tests are conducted for each series at the saturation embedding dimension and at the highest embedding dimension.

Data and Results

Daily data series of near futures prices for sugar, silver, copper, and coffee are used. These series have, respectively, 4462, 5297, 5308, and 4087 observations beginning between January 1968 and October 1972 and ending in March 1989. Further details appear in the Appendix to this chapter.

As previously indicated, the data are transformed into first differences of logs of futures prices. The AR-transformed data, derived as described above, involve AR regressions with lags at 1 and 21 for sugar; at 3 and 15 for silver; at 2, 3, and 6 for copper; and at 1, 16, and 17 for coffee.

The correlation integral graphs, computed for embedding dimension values 4–40 by increments of 4, all look very similar to each other. For the non–AR-transformed data, a typical correlation integral graph, that of copper, is shown in Figure 11-1 for embedding dimensions 28–40 by increments of 4. Figure 11-2 shows a blow-up of the nearly linear region for ε values 0.020258 through 0.027296. The curves appear close to parallel, suggesting saturation.

Table 11-1 shows the correlation dimension estimates for the four rate-of-return series for embedding dimensions 4–40 by increments of 4. The correlation dimensions are always far below the corresponding embedding dimensions, and never rise above 11. The most striking results are for coffee. The correlation dimension is always below 6, strongly suggesting nonlinear structure with a relatively low state dimension. The other three series show strong evidence of structure as well.

The information provided by the level of the correlation dimension estimates is confirmed by the data in Table 11-2, which shows how fast these estimates rise with the embedding dimension. This rate of rise is measured by $H \equiv \Delta$ (correlation dimension)$/\Delta m$, where the increment Δm

Figure 11-1

Correlation Integral, Copper

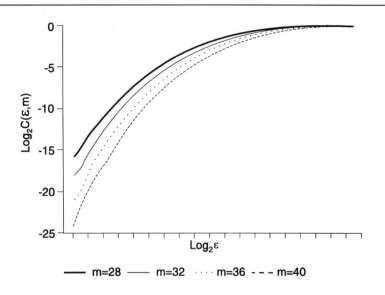

— m=28 —— m=32 ···· m=36 - - - m=40

Figure 11-2

Linear Region, Correlation Integral, Copper

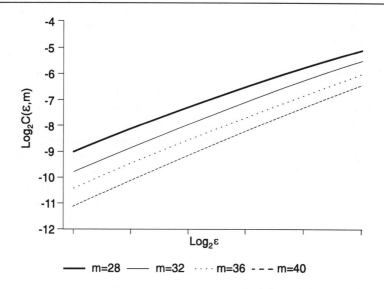

— m=28 —— m=32 ···· m=36 - - - m=40

Table 11-1

Correlation Dimension Estimates for Daily Rate of Return Data

	Correlation Dimension			
m	Silver (N = 5297)	Copper (N = 5308)	Sugar (N = 4462)	Coffee (N = 4087)
4	1.65	2.16	1.80	1.51
8	2.73	3.84	3.14	2.46
12	3.58	5.23	4.18	3.23
16	4.28	6.39	5.06	3.84
20	4.90	7.37	5.89	4.34
24	5.46	8.26	6.71	4.75
28	6.03	8.96	7.52	5.06
32	6.61	9.64	8.39	5.35
36	7.18	10.33	9.36	5.62
40	7.76	10.99	10.29	5.88

is always 4. By the time an embedding dimension of 20 is reached, the H values for the four series are 0.16, 0.25, 0.21, and 0.13, and for higher embedding dimensions they drop even lower. In each case, these are much closer to the theoretical value of zero for pure structured, noiseless data than to the theoretical value of unity for structureless noise; thus, these results effectively approximate saturation, implying the presence of noisy structure. So the results for both the level and the saturation of the correlation dimension support a hypothesis of structure in the data. Note again that any inference of the specific saturation embedding dimension would necessarily be very imprecise; the point is simply that there is strong evidence for saturation and thus for the presence of structure.

To make sure that this structure is not linear, the residual test as described above is performed. Correlation dimension estimates computed for the autoregressive residuals are reported in Table 11-3. The results in Table 11-3 are very close to those in Table 11-1 for the non–AR-transformed data, thereby supporting the notion that the structure detected is nonlinear rather than linear. H values for Table 11-3 estimates are presented in Table 11-4.

While these results strongly suggest the presence of nonlinear structure, it is prudent to check further the possibility that pure noise data could have generated these results in samples of these sizes. As discussed above, the shuffle test for the AR-transformed data for each commodity is performed using 20 shuffles at each of $m = 40$ and the m value for which H

Table 11-2

H Values for Daily Rate of Return Data: [H ≡ (Correlation Dimension for This Embedding Dimension Minus That for the Next Lower Embedding Dimension) Divided by 4]

m	Silver	Copper	Sugar	Coffee
4	—	—	—	—
8	0.27	0.42	0.34	0.24
12	0.21	0.35	0.26	0.19
16	0.18	0.29	0.22	0.15
20	0.16	0.25	0.21	0.13
24	0.14	0.22	0.21	0.10
28	0.14	0.18	0.20	0.08
32	0.15	0.17	0.22	0.07
36	0.14	0.17	0.24	0.07
40	0.15	0.17	0.23	0.07

Table 11-3

Correlation Dimension Estimates for AR Residuals

	Correlation Dimension			
m	Silver (N = 5282)	Copper (N = 5302)	Sugar (N = 4441)	Coffee (N = 4070)
4	1.75	2.18	1.90	1.77
8	2.90	3.89	3.30	2.92
12	3.80	5.31	4.38	3.80
16	4.55	6.50	5.30	4.50
20	5.22	7.51	6.16	5.06
24	5.83	8.41	7.01	5.51
28	6.46	9.12	7.85	5.92
32	7.10	9.80	8.81	6.33
36	7.73	10.48	9.94	6.75
40	8.36	11.16	11.07	7.16

Table 11-4

H Values for AR Residuals: [H ≡ (Correlation Dimension for This Embedding Dimension Minus That for the Next Lower Embedding Dimension) Divided by 4]

m	Silver	Copper	Sugar	Coffee
4	—	—	—	—
8	0.29	0.43	0.35	0.29
12	0.23	0.36	0.27	0.22
16	0.19	0.30	0.23	0.18
20	0.17	0.25	0.22	0.14
24	0.15	0.23	0.21	0.11
28	0.16	0.18	0.21	0.10
32	0.16	0.17	0.24	0.10
36	0.16	0.17	0.28	0.11
40	0.16	0.17	0.28	0.10

(taken out to three decimal places) is minimized (thus showing the strongest saturation). For each set of 20 shuffles Table 11-5 gives the mean, the high, and the low values of the estimated correlation dimension, and compares them to that of the corresponding unshuffled series.

Table 11-5 shows that, out of a total of 160 shuffle correlation dimension estimates computed, not a single one is as low as the corresponding nonshuffle estimate. Thus one can reject, with high confidence, the possibility that the data reflect simply structureless noise masquerading as structured data.

Finally, to test for an ARCH explanation of the data, an ARCH(10) test is run on the above AR specifications, standardizing the ARCH residuals to remove the time-varying aspect of their variance, estimating the correlation dimensions of the standardized residuals, and conducting shuffle tests. The correlation dimension estimates, H values, and shuffle results appear in Tables 11-6, 11-7, and 11-8, respectively (note that for three commodities the lowest H value occurs at the highest embedding dimension—40—so for those commodities only one shuffle test is needed).

A comparison of Table 11-6 with Table 11-3 shows that the ARCH filtering process increases the estimated correlation dimensions, as would be expected of any filtering process with finite data. However, the in-

---

Table 11-5

Shuffle Results, AR Residuals: Mean, High, and Low Values of Correlation Dimension Estimates over 20 Shuffles

	Silver			Sugar	
$m = 24$	Mean = 7.42		$m = 28$	Mean = 9.27	
	Low = 5.97			Low = 8.08	
	High = 10.43			High = 10.69	
	Unshuffled = 5.83			Unshuffled = 7.85	
$m = 40$	Mean = 12.42		$m = 40$	Mean = 13.32	
	Low = 10.02			Low = 11.72	
	High = 17.54			High = 15.72	
	Unshuffled = 8.36			Unshuffled = 11.07	
	Copper			**Coffee**	
$m = 32$	Mean = 12.74		$m = 28$	Mean = 8.42	
	Low = 11.75			Low = 7.46	
	High = 14.75			High = 10.62	
	Unshuffled = 9.80			Unshuffled = 5.92	
$m = 40$	Mean = 16.01		$m = 40$	Mean = 12.20	
	Low = 14.77			Low = 10.78	
	High = 18.36			High = 15.83	
	Unshuffled = 11.16			Unshuffled = 7.16	

Table 11-6

Correlation Dimension Estimates for Standardized ARCH Residuals

	Correlation Dimension			
m	Silver (N = 5262)	Copper (N = 5282)	Sugar (N = 4421)	Coffee (N = 4050)
4	1.57	1.59	1.56	1.57
8	3.15	3.23	3.10	3.01
12	4.64	4.93	4.61	4.45
16	5.99	6.55	6.00	5.83
20	7.22	8.08	7.28	7.07
24	8.36	9.53	8.55	8.09
28	9.46	10.84	9.70	9.00
32	10.54	12.04	10.85	9.87
36	10.55	13.23	12.07	10.63
40	12.55	14.40	13.34	11.32

Table 11-7

H Values for Standardized ARCH Residuals

m	Silver	Copper	Sugar	Coffee
4	—	—	—	—
8	0.40	0.41	0.39	0.36
12	0.37	0.43	0.38	0.36
16	0.34	0.41	0.35	0.35
20	0.31	0.38	0.32	0.31
24	0.29	0.36	0.32	0.26
28	0.28	0.33	0.29	0.23
32	0.27	0.30	0.29	0.22
36	0.26	0.30	0.31	0.19
40	0.24	0.29	0.32	0.17

creases are not very large. The H values are also increased, as shown by Table 11-7 in comparison with Table 11-4, but they still reach minima much closer to the theoretical deterministic value of zero than to the theoretical noise value of 1. The shuffle tests on the ARCH residuals uniformly

Table 11-8

Shuffle Results, Standardized ARCH Residuals: Mean, High, and Low Values of
Correlation Dimension Estimates over 20 Shuffles

Silver		Sugar	
$m = 40$	Mean = 16.04	$m = 28$	Mean = 10.79
	Low = 13.10		Low = 9.85
	High = 19.95		High = 13.84
	Unshuffled = 12.55		Unshuffled = 9.70
		$m = 40$	Mean = 15.28
			Low = 14.09
			High = 18.09
			Unshuffled = 13.34
Copper		Coffee	
$m = 40$	Mean = 16.32	$m = 40$	Mean = 13.97
	Low = 14.64		Low = 12.46
	High = 19.31		High = 17.05
	Unshuffled = 14.40		Unshuffled = 11.32

confirm the earlier shuffle results. All 100 correlation dimension estimates
for shuffled series of ARCH residuals are higher than the corresponding
unshuffled correlation dimension estimate. This result is striking in light
of the substantial filtering the data undergo, and it provides strong evidence for the proposition that there is some nonlinear process with a
deterministic component underlying these data series.

Conclusions

This study applies the correlation dimension technique, along with the
associated AR and ARCH residual tests and shuffle test, to rate-of-return
series for the futures prices of four commodities. The results for the
rate-of-return data and for their autoregressive and ARCH residuals, both
in regard to the level and saturation of the correlation dimension estimates,
strongly suggest the presence of structure in the data. The fact that the
results are relatively unchanged by the use of AR residuals implies that
this structure is nonlinear in nature, and the fact that the results hold up
under ARCH filtering shows that the apparent structure does not simply
reflect heteroskedasticity. Further, the fact that the shuffle tests are passed
with "flying colors" implies that the results are not a fluke, which could

have been achieved misleadingly with unstructured data. It is worth noting that, since the data series had in excess of 4,000 observations, the procedures employed are stronger than they would be with the much smaller data series commonly used with these procedures by economists.

A noise explanation of the data as well as a linear-structure-plus-noise explanation are rejected. Thus, the hypothesis of nonlinear structure is accepted. As Barnett and Hinich (1989) point out, this acceptance is necessary but not sufficient for the presence of chaos in the data. If chaos is viewed as the null hypothesis, this study fails to reject it. Evidence for the presence of chaos is provided, but, as Barnett and Hinich say, "further research is needed before we can confirm or reject the discovery of chaos." In any event, if chaos is present, it is probably accompanied by noise, so even if the chaos is exactly identified, an incentive for risk-averse agents to engage in hedging behavior still exists.

The evidence of structure in futures prices raises further questions about the efficient markets hypothesis, since it creates the possibility that profitable, nonlinearity-based trading rules may exist. Clearly then, an important area for future research is to identify more precisely the nature of the nonlinearity in the data. Only then can it be established what, if any, profitable trading rules exist. Moreover, identification of the structure would establish whether prediction beyond some horizon is precluded, due to the sensitive dependence on initial conditions inherent in chaotic systems. Another important area for future research is to further develop equilibrium models of financial markets, which can give rise to dynamic structure in rates of return. Previous work in this vein includes van der Ploeg (1986) and Lucas (1978). Perhaps this substrand of literature could further clarify the relation between market efficiency and nonlinear dynamics.

Acknowledgments

The authors are grateful to Curt Taylor for his excellent and extensive programming assistance, and to Rachel Connelly, Dan Gijsbers, and John Georgellis for their generous help.

Notes

1   *Chaos* refers to deterministic dynamic behavior that is bounded and neither periodic not asymptotically periodic. Some nonlinear dynamic equations generate chaos, while some generate periodic behavior (re-

peating sequences). Accessible introductions to the mathematics of chaos are to be found in Savit (1988), Gabisch (1987), Kelsey (1988), Baumol and Quandt (1985), Baumol and Benhabib (1989), and Frank and Stengos (1988a).

2   Van der Ploeg (1986) presents a model in which asset prices can evolve according to the logistic equation, which admits chaos, implying that rates of return would not be white noise. Lucas (1978) gives another model with structure in rates of return.

3   Long-term prediction of a chaotic system is impossible even if the form and parameterization of the system are perfectly known. This is because chaotic systems have sensitive dependence on initial conditions, meaning that minute errors in the observation of the state of the system when predictions are made get translated into increasingly large errors in the predicted state of the system as the predictions go farther into the future. However, short-term prediction remains feasible.

4   See also Brock (1986) and Barnett and Chen (1988) for descriptions of this technique.

5   Note that the slope estimate for given m can be quite sensitive to the choice of the linear range over which to run the regression. Thus numerical estimates of the correlation dimension must be regarded with caution. However, the judgment of whether saturation has occurred tends to be insensitive to the choice of linear range.

References

Barnett, W. A., and P. Chen. "The Aggregation-Theoretic Monetary Aggregates Are Chaotic and Have Strange Attractors," in *Dynamic Econometric Modeling*, W. Barnett, E. Berndt, and H. White, eds. Cambridge, UK: Cambridge University Press, 1988, 254–263.

Barnett, W. A., and M. J. Hinich. "Has Chaos Been Discovered with Economic Data?" *Evolutionary Dynamics and Nonlinear Economics*, P. Chen and R. Day, eds. Oxford: Oxford University Press, 1993, 254–263.

Baumol, W., and J. Benhabib. "Chaos: Significance, Mechanism, and Economic Applications." *Journal of Economic Perspectives* (1989) 3:77–105.

Baumol, W., and R. Quandt. "Chaos Models and Their Implications for Forecasting." *Eastern Economic Journal* (1985) 11:3–15.

Blank, S. "'Chaos' in Futures Markets? A Nonlinear Dynamical Analysis." Columbia Business School Center for the Study of Futures Markets, Working Paper #204. Columbia University, New York (January 1990).

Brock, W. "Distinguishing Random and Deterministic Systems: Abridged Version." *Journal of Economic Theory* (1986) 40:168–195.

Brock, W., and C. Sayers. "Is the Business Cycle Characterized by Deterministic Chaos?" *Journal of Monetary Economics* (1988) 22:71–90.

Brorsen, B. W., D. Von Bailey, and J. W. Richardson. "Investigation of Price Discovery and Efficiency for Cash and Futures Cotton Prices." *Western Journal of Agricultural Economics* (1984) 9:170–176.

Cargill, T. F., and G. C. Rausser. "Time and Frequency Domain Representation of Futures Prices as a Stochastic Process." *Journal of the American Statistical Association* (1972) 67:23–30.

Cargill, T. F., and G. C. Rausser. "Temporal Price Behavior in Commodity Futures Markets." *Journal of Finance* (1975) 30:1043–1053.

Danthine, J. P. "Martingale, Market Efficiency and Commodity Prices." *European Economic Review* (1977) 10:1–17.

DeCoster, G. P., and D. W. Mitchell. "The Efficacy of the Correlation Dimension Technique in Detecting Determinism in Small Samples." *Journal of Statistical Computation and Simulation* (1991a) 39:221–229.

DeCoster, G. P., and D. W. Mitchell. "Nonlinear Monetary Dynamics." *Journal of Business and Economic Statistics* (1991b) 9:455–461.

Fama, E. "Efficient Capital Markets: Review of Theory and Empirical Work." *Journal of Finance* (1970) 25:383–417.

Frank, M., R. Gencay, and T. Stengos. "International Chaos?" *European Economic Review* (1988) 32:1569–1584.

Frank, M., and T. Stengos. "Chaotic Dynamics in Economic Time-Series." *Journal of Economic Surveys* (1988a) 2:103–133.

Frank, M., and T. Stengos. "Some Evidence Concerning Macroeconomic Chaos." *Journal of Monetary Economics* (1988b) 22:423–438.

Frank, M., and T. Stengos. "Measuring the Strangeness of Gold and Silver Rates of Return." *Review of Economic Studies* (1989) 56:553–567.

Gabisch, G. "Nonlinearities in Dynamic Economic Systems." *Atlantic Economic Journal* (1987) 15:22–31.

Grassberger, P., and I. Procaccia. "Measuring the Strangeness of Strange Attractors." *Physica* (1983) 9D:189–208.

Gross, M. "A Semi-Strong Test of the Efficiency of the Aluminum and Copper Markets at the LME." *Journal of Futures Markets* (1988) 8:67–77.

Guimaraes, R. M., B. G. Kingsman, and S. J. Taylor. *A Reappraisal of the Efficiency of Financial Markets.* Berlin: Springer-Verlag, 1989.

Gupta, S., and T. Mayer. "A Test of the Efficiency of Futures Markets in Commodities." *Weltwirtschaftliches Archives* (1981) 117:661–671.

Hinich, M. J., and D. M. Patterson. "Evidence of Nonlinearity in Daily Stock Returns." *Journal of Business and Economic Statistics* (1985) 3:69–77.

Houthakker, H. "Systematic and Random Elements in Short-Term Price Movements." *American Economic Review* (1961) 51:164–172.

Hsieh, D. A. "Testing for Nonlinear Dependence in Daily Foreign Exchange Rates." *Journal of Business* (1989) 62:339–368.

Jensen, M. C. "Some Anomalous Evidence Regarding Market Efficiency: An Editorial Introduction." *Journal of Financial Economics* (1978) 6:95–101.

Kamara, A. "Issues in Futures Markets: A Survey." Working Paper CSFM-30, Center for the Study of Futures Markets, Columbia University. New York (1982).

Kelsey, D. "The Economics of Chaos or the Chaos of Economics," *Oxford Economic Papers* (1988) 40:1–31.

Labys, W. C., and C. W. J. Granger. *Speculation, Hedging and Commodity Price Forecasts.* Lexington, MA: Heath Lexington Books, 1970.

Leuthold, R. M. "Random Walk and Price Trends: The Live Cattle Futures Market." *Journal of Finance* (1972) 27:879–889.

Lucas, R. E. "Asset Prices in an Exchange Economy." *Econometrica* (1978):46:1429–1445.

MacDonald, R., and M. P. Taylor. "Testing Rational Expectations and Efficiency in the London Metal Exchange," *Oxford Bulletin of Economics and Statistics* (1988) 50:41–52.

Mandelbrot, B. "New Methods in Statistical Economics." *Journal of Political Economy.* (1963a) 41:421–443.

Mandelbrot, B. "The Variation of Certain Speculative Prices," *Journal of Business.* (1963b) 36:394–429.

Ploeg, F. van der "Rational Expectations, Risk and Chaos in Financial Markets." *Economic Journal* 96 (suppl.) (1986) 151–162.

Ramsey, J. B., C. L. Sayers, and P. Rothman. "The Statistical Properties of Dimension Calculations Using Small Data Sets: Some Economic Applications." Research Report #88-10, C. V. Starr Center, New York University (1988).

Ramsey, J. B., and H.-J. Yuan. "The Statistical Properties of Dimension Calculations Using Small Data Sets." Research Report #87-20, C. V. Starr Center, New York University (1987).

Rocca, L. H. "Time Series Analysis of Commodity Futures Prices." Ph.D. dissertation, University of California, Berkeley (1969).

Samuelson, P. "Proof That Properly Anticipated Prices Fluctuate Randomly." *Industrial Management Review* (1965) 6:41–49.

Savit, R. "When Random Is Not Random: An Introduction to Chaos in Market Prices." *Journal of Futures Markets* (1988) 8:271–289.

Scheinkman, J. A., and B. LeBaron. "Nonlinear Dynamics and Stock Returns." *Journal of Business* (1989a) 62:311–337.

Scheinkman, J. A., and B. LeBaron. "Nonlinear Dynamics and GNP Data," in *Economic Complexity*, W. Barnett, J. Geweke, and K. Shell, eds. Cambridge, UK: Cambridge University Press (1989b).

Sims, C. A. "Martingale-Like Behavior of Prices and Interest Rates." Discussion Paper No. 205, Department of Economics, University of Minnesota, Minneapolis (1984).

Smidt, S. "A Test of the Serial Independence of Price Changes in Soybean Futures," as reprinted in *Selected Writings on Futures Markets*, A. Peck, ed. Chicago: Chicago Board of Trade 1965/1977, pp. 257–277.

Stevenson, R. A., and R. M. Bear. "Commodity Futures: Trends or Random Walk?" as reprinted in *Selected Writings on Futures Markets*, A. Peck, ed. Chicago Board of Trade 1970/1977, pp. 279–294.

Takens, F. "Detecting Strange Attractors in Turbulence," in *Dynamical Systems and Turbulence: Lecture Notes in Mathematics* #898. D. Rand, and I. Young, eds. Berlin: Springer-Verlag 1980, pp. 366–382.

Taylor, S. J. "Conjectured Models for Trends in Financial Prices: Tests and Forecasts." *Journal of the Royal Statistical Society A* (1980) 143:338–362.

Taylor, S. J. *Modeling Financial Time Series*. Chichester, UK: Wiley, 1986.

Working, H. "A Theory of Anticipatory Prices," as reprinted in *Selected Writings of Holbrook Working*. Chicago: Chicago Board of Trade 1958/1977.

Appendix

Daily futures price data are gathered for four major commodities traded on exchanges in New York: (1) The Coffee "C" contract at the Cocoa, Sugar, and Coffee Exchange, Inc., in ¢/100 lbs.; (2) The Sugar No. 11 contract at the Cocoa, Sugar, and Coffee Exchange, Inc., in ¢/100 lbs.; (3) The Silver .999 Fine contract at the Commodity Exchange, Inc., in ¢/10 troy oz.; and (4) The Refined copper contract, at the Commodity Exchange, Inc., in

¢/100 lbs. The data are in the form of settlement prices and are from the Center for the Study of Futures Markets, Graduate Business School, Columbia University, New York.

The typical structure of commodity futures price series is that they are quoted for selected months of the year for which contracts are traded. The terms of these contracts are spaced from the near months to the more distant months. The accepted practice [Labys and Granger (1970); Taylor (1986)] is followed to compile the near future prices series. These series adopt prices from the contract nearest to the present or spot data; a jump is made to the prices of the successive contract at the beginning of the month in which the near contract comes to maturity. The series for silver and copper begin in January 1968; the series for sugar begins in January 1971; and the series for coffee begins October 1972. All series end in March 1989.

12

"Chaos" in Futures Markets? A Nonlinear Dynamical Analysis

By Steven C. Blank

Introduction and Objectives

Commodity market analysts constantly seek better explanations of price behavior in the form of economic models. Such models are used for many types of forecasting. However, the various linear models developed to date do not always work very well [Just and Rausser (1981)]. Some cases of short-term forecasting success of time series and econometric models imply that futures and spot prices are not always generated by a "random" process, but the long-term failure of these models to explain price behavior indicates they have not captured the true nature of the underlying generating process. For example, residuals in commodity price models may not be random, as assumed, but the result of a nonlinear process. It may be time to change existing theoretical assumptions and/or empirical approaches.

Reprinted with permission from *The Journal of Futures Markets*, Vol. 11, No. 6 (December 1991): 711–728.

A new methodology, called nonlinear dynamics (or "chaos"), evolving recently in physics and other natural sciences, may offer an alternative explanation for behavior of economic phenomena [Brock (1988a)]. Based on the assumption that at least part of the underlying process is nonlinear, chaos analysis evaluates whether that process is a deterministic system [Jensen (1987)].[1] Deterministic processes that look random under statistical tests such as spectral analysis and the autocovariance function are called "deterministic chaos" in nonlinear science. In practice, some economists argue that separating deterministic and stochastic processes may be very difficult due to the "noisy" nature of economic data [Mirowski (1990)]. Although applications of chaos analysis in economics are still very rare [examples include Baumol and Benhabib (1989); Brock (1986); Brock and Sayers (1988); Candela and Gardini (1986); Day (1983); Goodwin (1990); Lorenz (1987); Melese and Transue (1986)], there may be potential for its use in some markets.

In markets for undifferentiated commodities, intuition leads to expectations of multiple sources for chaos or nonlinear feedback [Savit (1988)]. Cyclical and seasonal patterns are often visible in charts of both prices and trade volumes. The futures price-setting process is similar to that in many financial spot markets where evidence of chaos has been found [see Brock (1988b); Frank and Stengos (1989); Hinich and Patterson (1985); Scheinkman and LeBaron (1989); van der Ploeg (1986)]. Also, there are a number of marketing strategies based, at least implicitly, on behavioral and structural aspects of commodity markets. In sum, futures markets appear to be a logical place to expand the analysis of chaos hypothesis.

Applying a new methodology to any problem raises many questions. The first question is usually "why bother?" It is sometimes claimed that if a model gives a "reasonable approximation" of reality, it is good enough. This implies that the cost of developing a more complex model may not be well spent. Considering the adequate performance of some linear economic models, some analysts may be satisfied to continue using them. But are those models "good enough" only because methods are not yet advanced enough to know that the world is round (nonlinear), not flat (linear)? It may be that BLUE (Best Linear Unbiased Estimate) is not always the relevant "color" for economic models. If the real structure of prices is nonlinear, using linear models may give noisy results; however, a completely deterministic nonlinear function may explain prices with no noise, meaning that forecasting may be possible. While the goal of improving forecasting models through the use of chaotic parameters may seem out of reach at present, the possibility makes studies such as this necessary.

The general objectives of this study are to (1) evaluate commodity futures markets using the methodology of nonlinear dynamics to detect whether there are any signs of a deterministic system underlying prices over time; and (2) while doing so, to illustrate the empirical procedures and their limitations. Specific objectives of this study are to determine whether (a) there is a difference between chaotic analysis results for cash and futures markets of financials/ (b) there is a difference between results for futures markets of financials and agricultural products; and (c) chaos is detectable over a period lengthy enough to justify development of forecasting models. The presentation begins with a summary of related studies. That is followed by a section introducing the basic concepts in chaos analysis. Empirical procedures are outlined then and the results from analyses of two heavily traded futures markets, the S&P 500 index and soybeans, are presented as examples.

Summary of Previous Work

Applying chaos analysis methods to commodity futures prices raises questions ranging from behavioral to structural issues.[2] One motivation for considering chaos as a possible explanation for commodity spot and futures price behavior is the poor results produced by studies using traditional methods. For example, using regression analysis, Roll (1984) explains only 1 to 3 percent of the daily variation in orange juice futures prices. If deterministic models can be developed with the assistance of chaos methods, forecasting of futures prices could be improved.

Empirical applications of nonlinear dynamical analysis techniques in economics are few in number. They are concentrated in two areas: assessments of the business cycle [Brock and Sayers (1988), Day (1983), Lorenz (1987)] and financial markets [Hinich and Patterson (1985), Savit (1989), Scheinkman and LeBaron (1989), van der Ploeg (1986)]. The results are somewhat mixed, possibly due to the nature of data used. Studies of macroeconomic variables, such as the business cycle, do not generate results as strong as microlevel analyses of some specific markets [Barnett and Chen (1988)]. Therefore, evaluating data characteristics should be an early stage of any empirical study.

The first indication that relying on traditional analysis methods alone may be inadequate comes from studies evaluating the characteristics of futures market data. Cornew et al. (1984) find that futures prices are not normally distributed, creating error in traditional trading performance measures, all of which are based on the normality assumption. Helms and Martell (1985) also reject the normality assumption concerning the distribution of futures price changes. However, they find that the normal distribution fit their data better than other members of the stable Paretian class of distribution. They note that the underlying generating process does not appear to be stationary, possibly being a subordinated stochastic or compound process requiring a more sophisticated approach to determine its exact nature. Garcia et al. use nonparametric tests and find more "nonrandomness" in livestock futures prices than are found using traditional tests. They suggest that the nonrandomness may be nonlinear in nature. These conclusions are similar to those reached by Hinich and Patterson (1985) regarding stock market returns.

These results are significant because traditional, linear models assume the data are normally distributed [Stevenson and Bear (1970); Kenyon et al. (1987)], while nonlinear dynamics makes no a priori assumptions concerning data distributions. In fact, distributions are hypothesized to change across nonlinear systems of differing degrees of chaotic behavior.

The usual way of looking for order in a time series entails spectral analysis. [Economic applications are illustrated by Shumway (1988) and Talpaz (1974).] The process involves transforming a series into a number of independent components associated with different frequencies. If the series includes periodic motion, the resulting power spectrum corresponds to the fundamental frequency. At the opposite extreme is white noise; all frequencies contribute equally. Unfortunately, the presence of sharp spectral peaks in a time series does not necessarily indicate a periodic attractor, nor does the absence of such peaks exclude the possibility of deterministic dynamics [Barnett and Hinich (1991)]. Therefore, other methods of analysis must be used to identify chaos in economic time series data.

An intermediate step is illustrated by Ashley and Patterson's (1989) use of the bispectral nonlinearity test. They test for a linear generating mechanism for both an aggregate stock market index and an aggregate industrial production index, rejecting the hypothesis in both cases. They conclude that their results strongly suggest that nonlinear dynamics should be an important feature of any macroeconomic model. The general state-dependent models outlined by Priestly (1988) could be one of the practical ways of pursuing nonlinear modeling in the future.

In microeconomic analysis, one method used to test the speculative efficiency hypothesis is called rescaled range analysis, which is capable of identifying persistent or irregular cyclic dependence in time series data. The hypothesis that respective price changes are independent of previous price changes is rejected in applications of rescaled range analysis to the foreign exchange market [Booth et al. (1982a)], the gold market [Booth et al. (1982b)], and the stock market [Greene and Fielitz (1977)]. Long-term persistent dependence is found in each study. A similar study of soybean futures markets finds nonperiodic cycles (persistent dependence) in both daily and intraday futures prices [Helms et al. (1984)].

Mandelbrot (1977) evaluates cotton prices and finds patterns that match across *scales* of time (daily, monthly). This raises the question, "Is scaling a problem or an answer?" [Feigenbaum (1983)]. Economists use different data aggregations in their analyses (annual, quarterly, monthly, weekly, daily, and for futures—intraday). In particular, futures and spot price data for commodities give the appearance of having what Mandelbrot (1977) called *fractal dimensions*. Empirical studies for gold and silver [Frank and Stengos (1989); Scheinkman and LeBaron (1989)] and T-bills [Brock (1988b)] consider only the spot market, but the fact that each undifferentiated product tested produces positive results indicates that further investigation is warranted.

Concepts in Chaos Analysis

As explained by Brock and Sayers (1988), a data time series (a_t) can be characterized as deterministically chaotic if there exists a system, (h, F, x_0), such that h maps R^n to R, F maps R^n to R^n, $a_t = h(x_t)$, $x_{t+1} = F(x_t)$, and x_0 is the initial condition at time $t = 0$. In this case, the map F is deterministic, the state space is n-dimensional, all trajectories (x_t) lie on an attractor A, and two nearby trajectories on A locally diverge. The variable h is a general function of the unknown state vector x, and F is an unknown dynamic that governs the evolution of the state. Also, x_0 is, in general, unknown. The goal of analysis is to discover information about the system (h, F, x_t) from observations (a_t).

An *attractor*, A, is a subset of the n-dimensional phase space, R^n. Attractors—i.e., collections of points to which initial conditions tend—can be loosely defined as having the following property. Solutions (trajectories) originating at points on the attractor remain there forever; solutions based at points *not* on the attractor, but within a region called the attractor's "basin of attraction," approach the attractor to an arbitrary degree of closeness. In the case of price data, an attractor might be particular (equilibrium?) price levels or patterns.

Chaos theory deals with deterministic processes that appear to be random (stochastic), but whose dimension is finite. Specifically, a "random process" is defined to have a "high" dimension, while a "deterministic process" has a "low" dimension. The object of analysis is to distinguish between the two. To do so, "dimension" must be defined and measured. In chaos analysis, the focus is on *fractal dimensions:* similar patterns across different (time) scalings.

One of the three types of probabilistic fractal dimension[3] is the "correlation dimension" (hereafter CD). It and the Lyapunov exponent (LE) (defined below) have become the most popular measures of nonlinear systems [Abraham et al. (1984); Grassberger and Procaccia (1983); Lorenz (1987)]. It is a measure of the minimal number of nonlinear "factors" needed to describe the data [Brock and Sayers (1988)]. To estimate the correlation dimension it is first necessary to compute the distances between all the points of a time series and then to determine what fraction of those distances is less than a series of predetermined length scales. This gives a measure called the "correlation integral," which is defined for different scale lengths, g, by the equation

$$C(g) = \lim_{N \to \infty} \left[\frac{1}{N(N-1)} \right] \sum_{i \neq j}^{N} (g, X_i, X_j) \tag{1}$$

where N is the sample size, X_i and X_j are (vector-valued) observations in the time series, and

$$(g, X_i, X_j) = \begin{cases} 1 \text{ if } |X_i - X_j| < g \\ 0 \text{ if } |X_i - X_j| > g \end{cases}$$

Grassberger and Procaccia (1983) argue that for small g

$$C(g) = Constant \cdot g^n \tag{2}$$

where the exponent n is the CD. Empirical procedures used to estimate the CD are discussed in the methodology section later in this chapter.

Low-dimensional chaos involves instability and "overshooting," while stochastic processes are infinite dimensional [Brock and Dechert (1991); van der Ploeg (1986)]. The few economic applications of this measure involve a stock returns index and gold and silver spot prices, all of which have CD estimates of about 6 (considered to be low) using weekly data [Frank and Stengos (1989); Scheinkman and LeBaron (1989)], and Treasury bill returns, which have a dimension around 2 [Brock (1988b)].

Lyapunov exponents are simply generalized eigenvalues averaged over the entire attractor. They measure the average rate of contraction (when negative) or expansion (when positive) on an entire attractor. They can be positive or negative, but at least one must be positive for an attractor to be classified as chaotic or "strange" [Wolf (1986)]. In the one-dimensional case, where $x_{i+1} = F(x_i)$, the Lyapunov exponent, λ, is defined as

$$\lambda = \lim_{N \to \infty} \left(\frac{1}{N} \right) \sum \log_2 \left| \frac{dF}{dx} \right| \tag{3}$$

where the derivative is evaluated at each point on the trajectory and logarithms are taken to the base 2. Usually, LEs are reported in units of bits per observation. Positive exponents can be viewed as measuring the rate at which new information is created; specifically, the rate at which unmeasurable (because they are too small) variations are magnified to the point where they can be observed.

In summary, Savit (1988) lists three features a deterministic sequence should have to be chaotic:

1. It should sample all regions of its domain (eventually).

2. It is practically unpredictable in the long term (if there is any indeterminacy in one's knowledge or ability to compute).[4]

3. There are many initial prices, P_0, called periodic points,[5] and the sequence of prices generated by the chaotic map is periodic, i.e., over time the sequence of prices P_t eventually repeats itself.

This list makes it clear that chaos analysis must begin with a detailed description of the data involving a set of statistics new to most market analysts.

General Methodology

Empirical methods derived from those applied in previous economic studies of chaotic systems [Brock (1986); Deneckere and Pelikan (1986)] are used here. To accomplish this study's first general objective, this three-step process of dynamical analysis is followed:

1. Calculate the Grassberger-Procaccia correlation dimension for various embedding dimensions [Abraham et al. (1984); Swinney (1983)].

2. Apply a residual test for the presence of deterministic chaos as an alternative for the best-fitting linear model of prices [Brock and Sayers (1988)].

3. Estimate the largest Lyapunov exponent for various embedding dimensions [Abraham et al. (1984); Swinney (1983); Wolf (1986); Wolf and Swift (1984); Wolf et al. (1985)].

Operationally, the correlation dimension [n in Equation 2] is the slope, k, of the regression: log $C(g)$ versus log g for small values of g. To estimate the CD from a single variable time series, the procedure is as follows:

1. The data are embedded in successively higher dimensions as prescribed by Takens (1985).

2. For each embedding, $C(g)$ is computed and the scaling factor, k, is estimated.

3. The procedure is repeated until the estimates of k converge.

The correlation dimension is therefore expected to equal whatever value at which k remains stable over a number of embedding dimensions.

Lyapunov exponents are local quantities that are averaged over the attractor. To compute the largest LE from a time series, the program by Wolf et al. (1985) is used, which suggests choosing a so-called "fiducial" trajectory and estimating the rate at which it and a nearby test trajectory diverge. When the distance between the two points becomes large, a new point is chosen near the fiducial trajectory and the procedure is repeated. The entire time series is stepped through in this way and the stretchings and contractions are averaged.

In practice, estimating Lyapunov exponents in this way requires experimentation on the part of an analyst. Wolf's algorithm requires that the following information be provided:

❖ An embedding dimension and time lag for the reconstruction of the attractor;

❖ The time interval over which the two pieces of the trajectory are followed (called the "evolution");

❖ The minimum acceptable separation between points that are to be followed; and

❖ The maximum acceptable separation.

As a result of this flexibility in inputs, an analyst must simply experiment. The goal of the experimentation is to find a region in parameter space over which the estimate is approximately constant. Clearly, this portion of the analysis is rough, hence the reluctance of previous authors to report exact LE values for economic data series.

The data used in this study are futures prices for the S&P 500 index and soybeans. These products are selected as examples to represent, respectively, financial and agricultural futures markets because they are traded heavily and each market has been studied previously by analysts using a variety of methods, which provides a base for comparison. The S&P index, in particular, is selected because it is the product traded on futures markets that is closest to the variables studied in earlier chaotic analyses of the cash stock market. This enables direct comparison between results from previous studies of the cash stock market and the results produced here for the futures index. For each product, daily closing price data for recent individual futures contracts and nearby contracts are evaluated. For soybeans, the November 1986 and November 1987 contracts are used. The data for each contract begins during July of the previous calendar year, giving 337 and 335 observations, respectively. The nearby futures price series, constructed from the closing prices of the futures contract closest to its maturity date at each point in time, covers the period from March 1966 through June 1988, with 5,823 observations. The December 1986 and December 1987 S&P 500 contracts are used. Each contract has 250 observations covering the previous calendar year. The S&P 500 nearby series begins in May 1982, ends in December 1987, and has 1,420 observations.

Before conducting nonlinear dynamical analysis, the data are detrended using ordinary least squares and autoregressive methods, deseasonalized and transformed (if necessary) as described by Baumol and Benhabib (1989). If a time series has a deterministic explanation, fitting a smooth time series model with a finite number of leads and lags will generate a residual series with the same CD and largest LE as the original series. The key is to first make the residuals as close to "white noise" as possible with traditional linear methods. In this way, if nonlinear models find significant traces of a deterministic system in the residuals, the hypothesis of a linear generating system can be rejected.

Brock and Sayers (1988) evaluate the H_0: whiteness tests and diagnostics do not alter chaotic systems and can be used to test residuals from the best linear model. They use a new "W" statistic to test for independence. Based on the correlation integral, the W statistic for embedding dimension m is defined as

$$W_m(g,N) \equiv \sqrt{N}\left(\frac{D_m(g,N)}{b_m(g,N)}\right) \tag{4}$$

where $D_m = C_m - (C_1)^m$, and b_m is an estimate of the standard deviation

$$b_m = (1,-mC_{m-1})' \sum (1,-mC_{m-1}) \tag{5}$$

as discussed by Brock (1988a). The W test detects misspecification caused by a linear model fit to nonlinear data and indicates such by giving a nonzero value. Brock and Dechert (1991) show that $D_m(g, N)$ converges to a nonzero number if evaluated using the residuals from a misspecified model, while the residuals from a correctly fitted linear model are independent and identically distributed and are characterized by $D_m(g, \infty) \equiv D_m(g) = 0$ for all m and all $g > 0$. This means that a W value of 0 indicates a stochastic process and a large W is evidence of a misspecified (nonlinear) model. Statistically significant nonlinearity appears to exist at the 5 percent level when the W value is greater than 1.96 [Brock and Dechert (1991)]. W statistics are reported below for the data series evaluated.

Due to the weakness of the standard CD empirical processes in some cases, it is desirable to calculate the correlation dimension for "random" numbers generated to provide a basis for comparison and to report the W statistic for those values [Brock (1986)]. The random numbers used are the residuals "scrambled" as described by Scheinkman and LeBaron (1989). If the data are stochastic, the CD estimates for the residuals and the "scrambled" residuals will be identical; if the scrambled data generate higher CD estimates, this is evidence of hidden (nonlinear) structure in the residuals. The scrambled residuals test is conducted in this study.

Also, the small sample distribution of the CD and LE statistics is illustrated here by presenting values calculated from 100 series of random numbers. The series are drawn using random number generators based on the following distributions: normal, log, chi-square, exponential, double exponential, geometric, poisson, F-distribution, T-distribution, and beta. Ten series are drawn from each distribution, since no a priori assumption is made concerning which distribution is "best." Each series includes 250 observations. The 100 CD values estimated are averaged to provide a benchmark representing stochastic processes. As in the scrambled residual test, deterministic CD values must be below those estimated from the random numbers. For LEs, two sets of estimates are reported: average values for the 100 series and the highest of the 100 LEs observed for each group of experiments. The average values for the random series can be compared against the values estimated from the actual futures price data to establish the general case for evidence of deterministic processes in the LE values. A qualitative assessment of the degree of significance of actual LE values can be made by a second comparison involving the highest of the 100 random estimates. This means that an LE for futures price data must be both positive and greater than the average LE from the random data to be considered evidence of a chaotic process; but, in addition, it must be greater than the highest of the 100 random LE values to be convincing evidence.

Empirical Results and Implications

Estimates of correlation dimensions and Lyapunov exponents are both given below, along with a discussion of the results. First, measures used to "prewhiten" the data are noted.

A generalized autoregressive conditional heteroskedasticity (GARCH) model is used to generate the residuals used in the analysis. The

GARCH procedure, developed by Bollerslev (1986), is applied in studies of exchange rates [Hsieh (1989)] and stock market returns using spot market data [Baillie and DeGennaro (1990); Scheinkman and LeBaron (1989)] and futures market data [Cheung and Ng (1990)] as well as in studies of commodity markets [Aradhyula and Holt (1988)]. GARCH methods are found to be useful in detecting nonlinear patterns in variance while not destroying any signs of deterministic structural shifts in a model [Lamoureux and Lastrapes (1990)]. Therefore, it serves as a good filter for studies of chaos.

Brock and Sayers (1988) demonstrate that the power of the W statistic is weak if an autoregressive [AR(q)] model is applied with a high order (q) and, therefore, q should be set as low as possible in GARCH whitening processes. In this study, if conventional criteria finds that a GARCH(1, 1) model produces white noise residuals, it is used. If a GARCH(1, 1) model fails this test, a GARCH(2, 2) model would be fitted next, and so forth until white noise is found.

The data for the two S&P 500 contracts cover years during which prices generally trended. Prices of the December 1986 S&P 500 contract fluctuate around an upward-sloping trendline. As a result, the GARCH(1, 1) model for the December 1986 S&P 500 contract price at time t is

$$x_t = 0.207 - 0.024 x_{t-1} + 0.013 x_{t-2} + \delta_t \qquad (6a)$$
$$(0.192) \quad (0.011) \qquad (0.011)$$

$$h_t = 6.592 + 0.633 \delta_{t-1}^2 + 0.566 h_{t-1} \qquad (6b)$$
$$(0.847) \quad (0.459) \qquad (0.490)$$

where the x_t's are first differences, δ is a residual, h is the conditional variance of the residuals, and the standard errors are in parentheses. Stock prices are lower during 1987 due to the "crash" in October. The uptrend-ending jolt gives the December 1987 S&P 500 contract a model of

$$x_t = 0.008 - 0.252 x_{t-2} - 0.120 x_{t-4} + 1.109 x_{t-5} + \delta_t \qquad (7a)$$
$$(0.455) \quad (0.064) \qquad (0.064) \qquad (0.062)$$

$$h_t = 49.072 + 0.696 \delta_{t-1}^2 + 0.752 h_{t-1} \qquad (7b)$$
$$(33.831) \quad (0.391) \qquad (0.359)$$

using the same notation.

The data for the two soybean contracts cover the same two years, but display trends for those years with slopes opposite to those in the S&P 500 data. Whereas stock prices rise during 1986, soybean prices trend downward that year. The GARCH(2, 2) model of the November 1986 soybean contract price at time t is

$$x_t = -0.143 - 0.108x_{t-2} + 0.065x_{t-3} + \delta_t \tag{8a}$$
$$(0.258)\quad (0.055)\qquad (0.055)$$

$$h_t = 21.793 + 0.143\delta^2_{t-1} - 0.541\delta^2_{t-2} + 0.365h_{t-1} + 0.507h_{1-t} \tag{8b}$$
$$(2.883)\quad (0.343)\qquad (0.166)\qquad (0.343)\qquad (0.182)$$

On the other hand, during 1987 stock prices are lower on the year, while soybean prices rise. The price of the November 1987 soybean contract at time t is

$$x_t = 0.197 - 0.093x_{t-1} - 0.086x_{t-5} + \delta_t \tag{9a}$$
$$(0.349)\quad (0.055)\qquad (0.055)$$

$$h_t = 39.964 - 0.738\delta^2_{t-1} - 0.853\delta^2_{t-2} - 0.703h_{t-1} - 0.515 \tag{9b}$$
$$(6.867)\quad (0.050)\qquad (0.049)\qquad (0.080)\qquad (0.079)h_{t-2}$$

The fact that both soybean models have GARCH(2, 2) processes while both S&P 500 series have GARCH(1, 1) processes may indicate a difference in time series properties of commodity and financial futures.

The two nearby futures contract price series produce models more similar to each other. The price of the nearby S&P 500 contract at time t is

$$x_t = 0.075 + 0.451x_{t-1} - 0.220x_{t-2} - 0.094x_{t-4} + 0.095x_{t-5} + \delta_t \tag{10a}$$
$$(0.240)\quad (0.044)\qquad (0.045)\qquad (0.045)\qquad (0.044)$$

$$h_t = 28.011 + 0.701\delta^2_{t-1} + 0.773h_{t-1} \tag{10b}$$
$$(18.136)\quad (0.181)\qquad (0.159)$$

Stock prices steadily rise during the period covered by the S&P 500 index futures contract data, despite some "corrections." The nearby soybean contract price data have a spiky pattern in which numerous periods of trending prices are evident. As a whole, the GARCH(1, 1) model for the data is

$$x_t = 0.831 - 0.154x_{t-2} + 0.168x_{t-3} + 0.191x_{t-4} - 0.141x_{t-5} + \delta_t \tag{11a}$$
$$(0.415)\quad (0.048)\qquad (0.053)\qquad (0.054)\qquad (0.054)$$

$$h_t = 45.168 + 0.849\delta^2_{t-1} + 1.107h_{t-1} \tag{11b}$$
$$(13.266)\quad (0.027)\qquad (0.013)$$

Correlation Dimension Results

Correlation dimension estimates made from the residuals, δ, of Equations 6–11 are presented in Table 12-1. Observations that can be made from the results in the table include:

1. Both the S&P index and soybeans have "low" CDs in absolute terms and in comparison to CDs reported in earlier cash stock market studies.

2. Both nearby series have lower CDs than the contract series.

3. All series pass both the "scrambled residuals" and random number tests: their CDs are lower than those of the scrambled and random data.

Table 12-1

Correlation Dimension Estimates for S&P 500 and Soybean Futures Prices

	Embedding Dimension									
	1	2	3	4	5	6	7	8	9	10
Contract Series										
S&P 12/86	1.0	1.5	2.1	2.2	2.4	2.5	2.3	2.7	2.4	2.3
S&P 12/86[a]	1.1	1.9	2.8	3.2	4.1	4.2	4.5	5.3	6.1	5.8
S&P 12/87	1.0	1.6	2.1	2.1	2.3	2.0	2.0	2.3	2.7	2.8
S&P 12/87[a]	1.0	2.0	2.9	3.6	4.3	4.4	4.4	5.1	4.8	4.9
Soybean 11/86	0.9	1.4	1.7	1.9	1.9	2.0	1.6	1.7	1.4	1.4
Soybean 11/86[a]	0.9	1.8	2.8	3.0	3.4	3.7	4.5	4.8	5.3	5.8
Soybean 11/87	0.9	1.3	1.6	1.9	2.0	2.2	1.9	2.1	2.2	2.1
Soybean 11/87[a]	0.9	2.0	2.7	4.0	4.4	4.8	5.1	5.5	5.6	6.2
Nearby Series										
S&P nearby	0.9	1.3	1.4	1.6	1.6	1.7	1.5	1.6	1.5	1.4
S&P nearby[a]	1.0	2.1	3.2	3.8	4.1	5.2	6.0	7.2	7.9	8.3
Soybean nearby	0.9	1.0	1.2	1.2	1.3	1.3	1.3	1.3	1.3	1.3
Soybean nearby[a]	0.9	2.2	3.4	3.9	4.4	5.8	6.4	7.1	8.0	9.2
Random Series[b]	0.9	2.1	3.6	4.5	5.1	6.3	7.8	8.9	9.6	10.3

[a] Results from a "scrambled" series created for comparison.

[b] Average results from 100 series of random numbers generated from various distributions for comparison.

The general implication of these results is that both the S&P index and soybeans appear to have nonlinearities in their underlying generating processes. More-detailed observations are made below before presenting the W statistic results from tests of the nonlinear hypothesis.

Table 12-1 presents results for the first 10 embedding dimensions to enable the reader to see how the CDs stabilize. The CD estimates are rounded to one decimal point from the regression output for each embedding dimension. Despite this imprecision, it appears that the estimates converge after the fourth or fifth embedding dimension in the case of each data series. Convergence does not occur in most of the scrambled series, nor in the random series.

It appears that the CDs in Table 12-1 are lower for soybeans than for the S&P index and that both futures markets evaluated have CDs lower than those Scheinkman and LeBaron (1989) report for cash stock market returns, although no statistic is available to aid in determining whether one CD estimate is significantly different from another. The difference between stock and soybean futures results is more apparent for the contract price series than for the nearby series. The general CDs for the November 1986 and 1987 soybean contracts, respectively, seem to be 1.7–2.0 and 1.9–2.2. The CDs for both S&P contracts are 2.3–2.7. The nearby soybean series has a CD of 1.3, while the S&P nearby data have a CD of 1.5–1.7. These values may not be significantly different from each other, but it is expected that they are significantly lower than the CDs of 6–7 which Scheinkman and LeBaron (1989) report.

The level and stability of the CD estimates in Table 12-1 give rise to the question of sample size effects. Ramsey and Yuan (1987) show that CDs may be underestimated from small data sets. In this case, estimates are lower and more stable for larger samples. For example, the nearby soybean series is the largest with 5,823 observations and it has the lowest, most stable CD estimates across embedding dimensions. This indicates that no conclusions can be reached concerning the relative differences in CDs between the two markets noted above. Nevertheless, the fact that even the smallest data sets (the S&P contract series) generated CDs that are "low," compared to the CDs for the scrambled and random series, supports the hypothesis that nonlinearity exists in all six series. To resolve the question of significance, W statistics are calculated.

Table 12-2 presents W statistics for each of the six series, their respective scrambled counterparts, and the random series. For each price series the statistic exceeds the 1.96 value needed (at the 95 percent confidence level) to reject the null hypothesis of a linear process. For the soybean nearby series, in particular, the results are strong. This indicates that nonlinearities are present in the data. However, although the W statistic

Table 12-2

W Statistics for S&P 500 and Soybean Futures Price Series

		Embedding Dimension		
	Observations (*n*)	4	5	6
Contract Series				
S&P 12/86	250	4.21	5.81	5.95
S&P 12/86[a]	250	1.27	1.55	1.80
S&P 12/87	250	6.99	7.76	8.12
S&P 12/87[a]	250	3.03	3.62	4.15
Soybean 11/86	335	5.86	6.07	7.23
Soybean 11/86[a]	335	1.17	1.31	1.43
Soybean 11/87	337	4.66	5.40	6.92
Soybean 11/87[a]	337	1.05	1.11	1.31
Nearby Series				
S&P nearby	1420	6.61	7.22	8.10
S&P nearby[a]	1420	0.75	0.99	1.31
Soybean nearby	5823	12.32	13.00	14.26
Soybean nearby[a]	5823	1.27	1.37	1.52
Random Series[b]	250	0.92	1.06	1.15

[a] Results from a "scrambled" series created for comparison.
[b] Average results from 100 series of random numbers.

can distinguish between a linear and nonlinear generating process, it cannot detect whether that process is stochastic of deterministic. Therefore, additional evidence, such as LE estimates, is needed to make this distinction.

Lyapunov Exponent Results

Lyapunov exponent estimates for soybean and S&P 500 prices are presented, respectively, in Tables 12-3 and 12-4. In the absence of statistics for use in determining the significance level of these estimates, only qualitative observations can be made, using the random number results presented in Table 12-5, including:

1. Both the S&P 500 index and soybeans have positive, stable, LEs across embedding dimensions, implying the presence of chaos.

2. LEs for the S&P nearby series appear to be of similar magnitude to those for S&P contract series and are higher than the random number

Table 12-3

Lyapunov Exponents for Soybean Futures Price Series

Price Series	Evolution[a]	Embedding Dimension		
		3	5	9
November 1986 Contract	5	0.0430	0.0613	0.0484
	10	0.0401	0.0525	0.0401
	21	0.0308	0.0337	0.0180
	42	0.0112[b]	0.0136	0.0172
	63	0.0109[b]	0.0129[b]	0.0067[b]
November 1987 Contract	5	0.0382[b]	0.0517	0.0410
	10	0.0285	0.0431	0.0402
	21	0.0240	0.0366	0.0180
	42	0.0233	0.0137	0.0126
	63	0.0263	0.0128[b]	0.0122
Nearby Contract	5	0.0002[b]	0.0051[b]	0.0067[b]
	10	0.0001[b]	0.0050[b]	0.0057[b]
	21	0.0000[b]	0.0031[b]	0.0045[b]
	42	−0.0011[b]	0.0039[b]	0.0037[b]
	63	−0.0012[b]	0.0042[b]	0.0035[b]

[a] Number of observations over which the two pieces of the trajectory are followed.

[b] Values fall between the average and highest estimates for the relevant entry in Table 12-5.

Note: The minimum and maximum scale lengths used here are 1 and 45 cents per bushel, respectively.

LEs in many cases, while the LEs for the soybean nearby series are consistently lower than both the soybean contract series' LEs and the highest of the random number LEs.

3. For all series, LE values decline as evolution lengths increase, as expected.

The general conclusion is that these results support those of the correlation dimension analysis: both the S&P index and soybeans appear to have chaotic nonlinearities in their underlying generating processes. More detailed observations are made below.

Tables 12-3 and 12-4 present estimates of the largest Lyapunov exponent calculated for different embedding dimensions using different evolution lengths. Dimensions 3, 5, and 9 are selected to illustrate results across the range that has stable CDs. For each of those dimensions, LEs are calculated for evolution lengths equaling one week (five observations),

Table 12-4

Lyapunov Exponents for S&P 500 Futures Price Series

Price Series	Evolution[a]	Embedding Dimension		
		3	5	9
December 1986 Contract	5	0.0334	0.0316[b]	0.0339
	10	0.0316	0.0261[b]	0.0317
	21	0.0245	0.0232	0.0168
	42	0.0149	0.0195	0.0097[b]
	63	0.0081[b]	0.0058[b]	0.0183
December 1987 Contract	5	0.0960	0.0978	0.0695
	10	0.0623	0.0930	0.0550
	21	0.0708	0.0647	0.0216
	42	0.0012[b]	−0.0018[b]	0.0100[b]
	63	−0.0027[b]	0.0009[b]	0.0065[b]
Nearby Contract	5	0.0216[b]	0.0465	0.0423
	10	0.0211[b]	0.0336	0.0280
	21	0.0199[b]	0.0120[b]	0.0202
	42	0.0066[b]	0.0077[b]	0.0149
	63	0.0071[b]	0.0129[b]	0.0138

[a] Number of observations over which the two pieces of the trajectory are followed.

[b] Values fall between the average and highest estimates for the relevant entry in Table 12-5.

Note: The minimum and maximum scale lengths used here are 1 and 25 index points, respectively.

two weeks (10 observations), one month (21 observations), two months (42 observations), and three months (63 observations).

This cross section of LEs is estimated in a "bootstrapping" effort to add robustness to any conclusions reached concerning the presence of chaos and to provide for a preliminary test of the hypothesis that futures prices are detectably deterministic over a long enough time period to make (short-term) price forecasting models possible. As noted by Frank and Stengos (1989, p. 555), "A chaotic system will be quite predictable over very short time horizons. If however the initial conditions are only known with finite precision, then over long intervals the ability to predict the time path will be lost." This means that if chaos can be detected at an evolution interval, the deterministic system generating prices has not been overwhelmed by stochastic noise and the development of forecasting models may be possible. If the largest LE is never positive in experiments across evolution lengths, the system is stochastic. However, if LEs are positive for short evolutions and turn negative at some longer length, the implication is that at that time interval stochastic noise becomes dominant and deterministic forecasting models are not empirically viable, even though the underlying system may be completely deterministic in nature. In summary, experimenting with evolution lengths provides a way in which analysts can assess the potential for developing forecasting models.

Table 12-5 provides results for the random numbers for the same cross section of LE experiments. These results illustrate the small sample distribution of the LE statistic and provide a basis for assessing the effects of noise on the estimates. The "Average Estimates" reported in Table 12-5 are the main estimates of the LE from the 100 series of random numbers. The fact that all but two of the values reported are negative indicates that Wolf et al.'s (1985) procedure for calculating LEs does a good job of detecting stochastic processes in general. However, in any particular case there is some chance of mislabeling a stochastic process as being deterministic due to the effects of noise in the small sample (of 250 observations). This is evident in Table 12-5 as the "Highest Estimates" are positive for each experiment. In other words, at least one of the 100 random series produces a positive LE for each combination of evolution length and embedding dimension. Therefore, actual data that produce LE estimates falling between the average and highest value reported for the relevant experiment in Table 12-5 may or may not have a deterministic generating process.

Table 12-5

Lyapunov Exponents for 100 Series of Random Numbers

Price Series	Evolution[a]	Embedding Dimension		
		3	5	9
Average Estimates	5	−0.0123	0.0032	−0.0037
	10	−0.0191	0.0006	−0.0112
	21	−0.0265	−0.0069	−0.0131
	42	−0.0281	−0.0080	−0.0143
	63	−0.0254	−0.0101	−0.0162
Highest Estimates	5	0.0238	0.0456	0.0070
	10	0.0223	0.0286	0.0141
	21	0.0185	0.0160	0.0117
	42	0.0140	0.0108	0.0105
	63	0.0152	0.0182	0.0102

[a] Number of observations over which the two pieces of the trajectory are followed.

In Table 12-3 all but two LEs are positive, strongly supporting the conclusion that soybean futures prices have a chaotic nonlinear generating process. Also, that process may be predictable over periods as long as the three-month evolutions evaluated here. However, a closer look leads to some interesting issues for future research. For example, the LEs for the two contract price series are very similar across embedding dimensions and evolution lengths, but they differ from LEs for the nearby series. LEs for nearby prices are approximately zero at dimension 3 and, although they stabilize at higher dimensions, no actual estimate exceeds the relevant "Highest Estimate" from Table 12-5. One hypothesis is that the two types of series will have different generating systems because contract series have less noise (possibly indicated by a lower coefficient of variation) and fewer trends, compared to more volatile nearby series, which contain multiple trends.

One explanation for this hypothesis comes from expectations concerning the two types of data series. Futures contract price series reflect increasing amounts of information about the relatively few factors known to influence prices expected at one point in time (the contract maturity date). Over the life of a particular contract, trade volume tends to rise as information changes become easier to interpret, making the market more liquid and, hence, more efficient in its reaction to information flows. On the other hand, nearby futures contract prices reflect a liquid market's interpretation of information concerning many supply and demand factors for different points in time. Trading volume in whatever contract is "nearby" at the moment tends to remain high and be closely correlated with spot prices of the commodity [Blank et al. (1991)].

The results in Table 12-3 indicate that compared to contract series, nearby soybean futures prices have a more complex generating system requiring analysis at a higher embedding dimension before the effects of chaos (if any) can be captured. The differences in LEs between dimensions may also mean that more complex models will be required for forecasting, making successful specification of those models less likely.

Table 12-4 presents LE estimates for S&P 500 futures prices which, in general, are surprisingly similar to those for soybeans, but which have two subtle differences raising additional issues for future research. First, the LEs for the December 1986 contract and the nearby series are similar to the soybean contracts' LEs. One hypothesis for this phenomenon is that the S&P nearby series is like many contract series in that the data have a single trend around which prices demonstrate relatively low levels of noise (at least at higher embedding dimensions). If multiple trends are present, the S&P nearby series might produce a more complex set of results, as in the case of soybeans.

Second, the LE results for the December 1987 S&P contract are unique compared to the other three contract series studied, drawing attention to the effects of the sharp market correction in October 1987. The LE values for all embedding dimensions are noticeably higher than those of any other series at evolution lengths of 5-21 days, yet for evolutions of 42 and 63 days the LEs are low and occasionally negative. It is hypothesized that the strong uptrend in S&P prices prior to the "crash" had so little noise in it that forecasting was quite possible for periods of up to one month (21 trading days), but longer forecasts necessitate more-complex models to account for the effects of "Black Monday," which are interpreted as noise by simple models. This illustrates the frustration that will no doubt continue to face modelers: even if a system such as that underlying stock prices is deterministic, forecasting models cannot be expected to detect every trend or turning point. As long as initial conditions are not perfectly identified, analysts will not know whether a model is correctly specified until it fails. In other words, no matter how complex a deterministic model is, additional complexity may be required to avoid forecasting errors so large as to question the modeling effort's value.

Summary and Concluding Comments

This chapter provides results of nonlinear dynamical analysis of two commodity futures markets. It illustrates what type of methodological and empirical procedures must be used to evaluate these markets. It also raises and attempts to address issues concerning identification and measurement of nonlinear generating systems in economic data, providing a guide for research in the future. Although chaos analyses in economics are still very rare, the results presented here and elsewhere give reason for expecting use of these methods to expand, but with difficulty.

Results from analyses of a financial, the S&P 500 index, and an agricultural product, soybeans, are presented as examples. All empirical results in this study are consistent with those of markets with underlying generating systems characterized by deterministic chaos. Comparing results for the stock index and soybean futures reveals surprising similarity, yet the CDs for the index are noticeably different than those reported in earlier stock market studies that use cash price data. Both futures markets are shown to have a "low" correlation dimension of about two, while CDs are slightly lower for soybeans and for nearby series compared to contract series. The statistical significance of this difference in CDs between product types is unclear, but statistical tests do indicate the presence of nonlinearities in both markets. Estimates of Lyapunov exponents indicate that these nonlinearities are (at least partially) deterministic, rather than stochastic in nature. However, the absence of any tests for the statistical significance of estimated LEs makes the results of this study necessary but not sufficient conditions to prove the existence of deterministic chaos.

Although providing just an introduction to the study of nonlinear dynamics in future markets, the results of this analysis may be useful for commodity market analysts in industry, academia, and government. The fact that futures prices appear to have a nonlinear generating process of a type not recognized previously raises the possibility that short-term forecasting models may be improved by incorporating these new factors. This, in turn, has significant implications for resource allocation and marketing strategies for firms trading in these product markets. Ultimately, the discovery of a nonlinear, nonrandom process in commodity futures markets could raise the level of debate in the economic literature concerning "random walk" hypotheses and definitions of pricing efficiency. However, from a practical viewpoint, chaos analysis procedures provide another test for (deterministic) nonlinearity, but do not easily lend themselves to direct applications in forecasting model construction.

Acknowledgment

This study was partially funded by a grant from the Center for the Study of Futures Markets, Columbia University. This is Giannini Foundation Research Paper No. 976.

Notes

1 Compared to linear methods, nonlinear dynamics may be a less restrictive approach to modeling economic systems simply because of the assumption it does *not* make, concerning the distribution, for example, as discussed later.

2 For example, "Can nonlinear dynamics explain speculative bubbles?" or "Do trading rules, such as those imposed on futures markets, create price patterns similar to patterns generated by "strange attractors" (defined in the next section)?" Intuitively, there is reason to believe chaos may contribute to the debate over "bubbles," and structural aspects of commodity trading may provide some of the explanation.

3 Probabilistic dimensions explicitly consider the frequency distribution with which points on the attractor are visited.

4   For example, rounding errors accumulate rapidly in the calculations involved in estimating fractal dimensions, thus reducing precision in distant forecasts.

5   The existence of a large number of periodic points is just one example of hidden regularities in a chaotic system.

References

Abraham, N., J. Gollub, and H. Swinney. "Testing Nonlinear Dynamics." *Physica* (1984) IID:252–264.

Aradhyula, S., and M. Holt. "GARCH Time-Series Models: An Application to Retail Livestock Prices." *Western Journal of Agricultural Economics* (1988) 13:365–374.

Ashley, R., and D. Patterson. "Linear versus Nonlinear Macroeconomics: A Statistical Test." *International Economic Review* (1989) 30:685–704.

Baillie, R., and R. DeGennaro. "Stock Returns and Volatility." *Journal of Financial and Quantitative Analysis* (1990) 25:203–214.

Barnett, W., and P. Chen. "The Aggregation-Theoretic Monetary Aggregates Are Chaotic and Have Strange Attractors: An Econometric Application of Mathematical Chaos," in *Dynamical Econometric Modeling*, Barnett, Berndt, and White, eds. Cambridge: Cambridge University Press, 1988, pp. 199–246.

Barnett, W., and M. Hinich. "Has Chaos Been Discovered with Economic Data?" in *Evolutionary Dynamics and Nonlinear Economics*, Chen and Day, eds. Oxford University Press, 1991.

Baumol, W., and J. Benhabib. "Chaos: Significance, Mechanism, and Economic Applications." *The Journal of Economic Perspectives* (1989) 3:77–105.

Blank, S., C. Carter, and B. Schmiesing. *Futures and Options Markets: Trading Commodities and Financials.* Englewood Cliffs, NJ: Prentice-Hall, 1991, Chapter 3.

Bollerslev, T. "Generalized Autoregressive Conditional Heteroscedasticity." *Journal of Econometrics* (1986) 31:307–327.

Booth, G., F. Kaen, and P. Koveos. "R/S Analysis of Foreign Exchange Rates Under Two International Monetary Regimes." *Journal of Monetary Economics* (1982a) 10:407–415.

Booth, G., F. Kaen, and P. Koveos. "Persistent Dependence in Gold Prices." *Journal of Financial Research* (1982b) 85–93.

Brock, W. A. "Distinguishing Random and Deterministic Systems: Abridged Version." *Journal of Economic Theory* (1986) 40:168–195.

Brock, W. A. "Introduction to Chaos and Other Aspects of Nonlinearity," in *Differential Equations, Stability, and Chaos in Dynamic Economics*, W. Brock and A. Malliaris, eds. New York: North Holland (1988a).

Brock, W. A. "Nonlinearity and Complex Dynamics in Economics and Finance," in *The Economy as an Evolving Complex System*. New York: Addison-Wesley Publishing Company (1988b).

Brock, W., and W. Dechert. "Theorems on Distinguishing Deterministic from Random Systems," in *Dynamic Econometric Modeling*, Barnett, Berndt, and White, eds. Cambridge: Cambridge University Press, 1991.

Brock, W., and C. Sayers. "Is the Business Cycle Characterized by Deterministic Chaos?" *Journal of Monetary Economics* (1988) 22:71–90.

Candela, G., and A. Gardini. "Estimation of a Non-Linear Discrete-Time Macro Model." *Journal of Economic Dynamics & Control* (1986) 10:249–255.

Cheung, Y., and L. Ng. "The Dynamics of S&P 500 Index and S&P 500 Futures Intraday Price Volatilities." *The Review of Futures Markets* (1990) Vol. 9: 458–486

Cornew, R., D. Town, and L. Crowson. "Stable Distributions, Futures Prices, and the Measurement of Trading Performance." *The Journal of Futures Markets* (1984) 4:531–557.

Day, R. H. "The Emergence of Chaos from Classical Economic Growth." *The Quarterly Journal of Economics* (1983) 98:201–213.

Deneckere, R., and S. Pelikan. "Competitive Chaos." *Journal of Economic Theory* (1986) 40:13–25.

Feigenbaum, M. J. "Universal Behavior in Nonlinear Systems." *Physica* (1983) 7D:16–39.

Frank, M., and T. Stengos. "Measuring the Strangeness of Gold and Silver Rates of Return." *Review of Economic Studies* (1989) 56:553–567.

Garcia, P., M. Hudson, and M. Waller. "The Pricing Efficiency of Agricultural Futures Markets: An Analysis of Previous Research Results." *Southern Journal of Agricultural Economics* (1988) 20:119–130.

Goodwin, R. *Chaotic Economic Dynamics*. Oxford: Oxford University Press, 1990.

Grassberger, P., and I. Procaccia. "Measuring the Strangeness of Strange Attractors." *Physica* (1983) 9D:189–208.

Greene, M., and B. Fielitz. "Long Term Dependence in Common Stock Returns." *Journal of Financial Economics* (1977) 4:339–349.

Helms, B., and T. Martell. "An Examination of the Distribution of Futures Price Changes." *The Journal of Futures Markets* (1985) 5:259–272.

Helms, B., F. Kaen, and R. Rosenman. "Memory in Commodity Futures Contracts." *The Journal of Futures Markets* (1984) 4:559–567.

Hinich, M., and D. Patterson. "Evidence of Nonlinearity in Daily Stock Returns." *Journal of Business and Economic Statistics* (1985) 3:69–77.

Hsieh, D. "Testing for Nonlinear Dependence in Daily Foreign Exchange Rate Changes." *Journal of Business* (1989) 62:339–368.

Jensen, R. V. "Classical Chaos." *American Scientist* (1987) 75:168–181.

Just, R., and G. Rausser. "Commodity Price Forecasting with Large Scale Econometric Models and the Futures Market." *American Journal of Agricultural Economics* (1981) 63:197–208.

Kenyon, D., K. Kling, J. Jordan, W. Seale, and N. McCabe. "Factors Affecting Agricultural Futures Price Variance." *The Journal of Futures Markets* (1987) 7:73–91.

Lamoureux, C., and W. Lastrapes. "Persistence in Variance, Structural Change, and the GARCH Model." *Journal of Business and Economic Statistics* (1990) 8:225–234.

Lorenz, H.-W. "Strange Attractors in a Multisector Business Cycle Model." *Journal of Economic Behavior & Organization* (1987) 8:397–411.

Mandelbrot, B. *The Fractal Geometry of Nature.* New York: Freeman, 1977.

Melese, F., and W. Transue. "Unscrambling Chaos through Thick and Thin." *The Quarterly Journal of Economics* (1986) 101:419–423.

Mirowski, P. "From Mandelbrot to Chaos in Economic Theory." *Southern Economic Journal* (1990) 57:289–307.

Priestly, M. B. *Non-Linear and Non-Stationary Time Series Analysis.* San Diego: Academic Press, 1988.

Ramsey, J., and H. Yuan. "The Statistical Properties of Dimension Calculations Using Small Data Sets." New York: C. V. Starr Center for Applied Economics, New York University (1987).

Roll, R. "Orange Juice and Weather." *American Economic Review* (1984) 74:861–880.

Savit, R. "When Random Is Not Random: An Introduction to Chaos in Market Prices." *The Journal of Futures Markets* (1988) 8:271–289.

Savit, R. "Nonlinearities and Chaotic Effects in Options Prices." *The Journal of Futures Markets* (1989) 9:507–518.

Scheinkman, J., and B. LeBaron. "Nonlinear Dynamics and Stock Returns." *Journal of Business* (1989) 62:311–337.

Shumway, R. H. *Applied Statistical Time Series Analysis.* Englewood Cliffs, NJ: Prentice-Hall, 1988.

Stevenson, R., and R. Bear. "Commodity Futures: Trends or Random Walks?" *Journal of Finance* (1970) 25:65–81.

Swinney, H. L. "Observations of Order and Chaos in Nonlinear Systems." *Physica* (1983) 7D:3–15.

Takens, F. "On the Numerical Determination of the Dimension of an Attractor," in *Dynamical Systems and Bifurcations*, N. Braaksma, H. Broer, and F. Takens, eds. Berlin: Springer-Verlag, 1985, pp. 99–106.

Talpaz, H. "Multi-Frequency Cobweb Model: Decomposition of the Hog Cycle." *American Journal of Agricultural Economics* (1974) 56:38–49.

van der Ploeg, F. "Rational Expectations, Risk and Chaos in Financial Markets." *Economic Journal* (1986) 96:151–161.

Wolf, A. "Quantifying Chaos with Lyapunov Exponents," in *Nonlinear Science: Theory and Applications*, A. Holden, ed. Manchester: Manchester University Press, 1986.

Wolf, A., and J. Swift. "Progress in Computing Lyapunov Exponents from Experimental Data," in *Statistical Physics and Chaos in Fusion Plasmas*, C. Horton and L. Reichl, eds. New York: John Wiley & Sons, 1984.

Wolf, A., J. Swift, H. Swinney, and J. Vastano. "Determining Lyapunov Exponents from a Time Series." *Physica* (1985) 16D:285–317.

13

Nonlinear Dynamics of Daily Futures Prices: Conditional Heteroskedasticity or Chaos?

By Seung-Ryong Yang and B. Wade Brorsen

Introduction

Research on futures prices [Hudson et al. (1987); Cornew et al. (1984); Gordon (1985); Hall et al. (1988)] has found that the distribution of futures prices is not normal but leptokurtic. Specifically, the empirical distributions of daily price changes have more observations around the means and in the extreme tails than does a normal distribution. Leptokurtosis also appears in stock returns [Fama (1965); Brock et al. (1991)] and exchange rate changes [Hsieh (1988); Friedman and Vandersteel (1982)]. Further, nonlinear dependence has been found in futures price changes [Taylor (1985); Blank (1990); Fujihara and Park (1990)]. Yet, empirical research on market anomalies has either ignored the nonnormality and dependence or resorted to nonparametric tests, which generally are less powerful than parametric tests.

Reprinted with permission from *The Journal of Futures Markets*, Vol. 13, No. 2 (April 1993): 175–91. © 1993 by John Wiley & Sons, Inc.

Past research suggests distributions such as the stable Paretian [Mandelbrot (1963); Fama (1965)] and more recently a diffusion-jump process [Akgiray and Booth (1988)] as models of speculative prices. These distributions partly explain leptokurtosis, but since they assume that successive observations are independent, these distributions are inconsistent with empirical work that has found linear and nonlinear dependence. The generalized autoregressive conditional heteroskedasticity (GARCH) model, however, can explain both nonlinear dependence and leptokurtosis.

Various time varying variance models have been considered by several authors [Friedman and Vandersteel (1982); McCulloch (1985); Taylor (1986); Akgiray (1989); Brorsen and Yang (1989); Fujihara and Park (1990); Randolph and Najand (1991); Baldauf and Santoni (1991)]. Results suggest such an approach looks promising. While a GARCH or similar time varying model looks promising, the adequacy of such models has not been tested rigorously.

Savit (1988, 1989) suggests that asset returns may not follow a stochastic process. Rather, they might be generated by deterministic chaos in which the forecasting error grows exponentially so that the process appears stochastic. Savit (1989) shows the effect of chaos on pricing options. Frank and Stengos (1986) find evidence of nonlinear structure for gold and silver markets. Scheinkman and LeBaron (1989) find some support for the hypothesis that stock returns follow a nonlinear dynamic system. Blank (1990) finds results consistent with deterministic chaos in futures prices.

The objective of this research is to test both the GARCH and deterministic chaos processes for a large sample of daily futures price changes. No past model successfully explains nonnormality and dependence in speculative price changes. This study considers market anomalies, including seasonality, day-of-the-week, and maturity effects. Previous studies using simple ARCH or GARCH models [Bollerslev et al. (1990)] do not fully describe the underlying return generating process.

This study extends previous work in several ways. It provides a more appropriate test of market anomalies because the estimates of the GARCH models are heteroskedasticity and autocorrelation-adjusted. Numerous studies have tested a single market anomaly. This work considers seasonality, day-of-the-week, and maturity effects at the same time. This study uses goodness-of-fit tests to determine the adequacy of the GARCH model. It does not simply select a model that is more descriptive among alternatives, but tests whether the model can generate the sample data.[1] In addition, the hypothesis that futures returns are generated by a nonlinear deterministic process is tested using standardized residuals. Since conditional heteroskedasticity is a type of nonlinear dynamics, adjusting for conditional heteroskedasticity could lead to very different conclusions about deterministic chaos than when no adjustment is made.

Statistical Models and Estimation Procedures

The GARCH Process

The GARCH model [Bollerslev (1986)] generates data with fatter tails than the normal distribution. The GARCH process implies serial dependence in the second moment. The GARCH process can model factors that violate the identically independently distributed (IID) assumption other than conditional heteroskedasticity. The GARCH model of this study includes the well-documented market anomalies of day-of-the-week effects [Chiang and Tapley (1983); Junkus (1986)], seasonality in variance [Anderson (1985); Kenyon et al. (1987)] and maturity effects [Milonas (1986)]. Ten lagged dependent variables are included in the model to allow for autocorrelation in the mean [Taylor (1986)]. Finally, to test for the risk-return relationship, the GARCH model includes the conditional standard deviation in the mean equation.

Bollerslev (1986) suggested that the simplest but often very useful GARCH model is the GARCH(1, 1) process. This study follows Bollerslev's proposition. By specifying the model, a priori, and not using the data to select the model, in-sample hypothesis tests remain valid. The specific GARCH models to be estimated are

$$y_t = a_0 + \sum_{s=1}^{10} a_s y_{t-s} + a_{11}D_M + a_{12}D_T + a_{13}D_W + a_{14}D_H + a_{15}h_t + e_t,$$

$$h_t^2 = b_0 + \alpha e_{t-1} + \beta h_{t-1}^2 + b_1 D_M + b_2 D_T + b_3 D_W + b_4 D_H + b_5 D_{hol}$$

$$+ b_6 M_t + b_7 \cos(2\pi I/126) + b_8 \cos(2\pi I/252) + b_9 \sin(2\pi I/126)$$

$$+ b_{10} \sin(2\pi I/252),$$

$$e_t \mid \psi_{t-1} \sim N(0, h_t^2) \quad (1)$$

When y_{t-s} denotes the lagged dependent variable, the dummy variables for each day-of-the-week are $D_M = 1$ if Monday, $D_T = 1$ if Tuesday, D_W if Wednesday, D_H if Thursday. They are 0 otherwise. M_t indicates remaining days to contract maturity. I in the sine and cosine functions is the number of trading days after Jan. 1 of the particular year. This avoids any bias from different numbers of trading days in different years. Denominators in the sine and cosine functions are the specified cycle length in days, so 126 indicates a 6-month cycle and 252 a 1-year cycle.

The GARCH models are estimated by maximum likelihood using the algorithm developed by Berndt, Hall, Hall, and Hausman (1974) with a numerical gradient method. Hypothesis tests are conducted with Wald tests, using the cross product of the gradients as the estimate of the information matrix.

If the GARCH models are well-calibrated models of the data, the residuals from the models should be IID normal. To test for normality, the hypothesis that the standardized residuals, $\hat{e}_t / \hat{h}_t$, are normal is tested with the Kolmogorov–Smirnov D-statistic. The estimated kurtosis and skewness are calculated also and compared to those of the original data.

Deterministic Chaos

It is widely assumed that certain characteristics of the economy such as taste, productivity, and technology are random. However, there is an alternative to the stochastic assumption to explain economic fluctuations. Many early economists tried to identify the internal mechanisms that could explain the observed variations in price movements [Hayek (1933)]. Deterministic chaos allows for a nonlinear dynamic model that is deterministic with respect to initial conditions, but errors made in estimating parameters and initial conditions can accumulate into forecasting errors [Brock (1986)]. This makes the process look random. Deterministic processes that look stochastic are referred to as *deterministic chaos*. The deterministic process cannot be distinguished from the stochastic process by statistical tests based on spectral densities or autocovariances [Brock and Dechert (1986)].

Consider a time series, $\{x_t\}$ and a sequence of m-histories, $X_t^m = (x_t, x_{t+1}, \ldots, x_{t+m-1})$ that is, the m-dimensional vectors obtained by putting m consecutive observations together. The embedding theorem [Takens (1980)] says that the behavior of an m-history will mimic that of the underlying unknown dynamic process if m is large enough. To illustrate, a good random number generator for IID uniform [0, 1] should fill the closed interval [0, 1]. If the numbers clump together on a few points, then the series is said to be low dimensional. If the 2-dimensional vectors $[(X_t^m, X_{t+1}^m)]$ fill out the unit square of $[0, 1]^2$, the series $\{x_t\}$ has correlation dimension ≥ 2. Likewise, a good random number generator provides a random series that fills m-cubes for any embedding dimension, m. If a series is generated by a deterministic process, m-dimensional vectors may not fill m-cubes but clump onto a low-dimensional subset or a few points. Consequently, the objective is to determine whether m-histories of $\{x_t\}$ fail to fill m-cubes for large embedding dimensions, or, equivalently, whether the estimated dimension is well below the embedding dimension.

The correlation dimension is estimated using the correlation integral $[C_m(\varepsilon)]$:

$$C_m(\varepsilon) = \lim_{T \to \infty} \left\{ \# \text{ of } (i, j) \text{ for which } || X_i^m - X_j^m || < \varepsilon, i \neq j \right\} / T^* \qquad (2)$$

where m is an embedding dimension, and ε is a sufficiently small number. $T^* = (T^2 - T)/2$, where T is the number of m-histories that can be made out of a series of length N. From the sample size N, $T = N - (m + 1)$ m-histories can be made. The norm $(|| \cdot ||)$ used in the computer program is the sup norm. The correlation integral measures the asymptotic probability that the distance between any two m-histories is less than ε. If the data are generated by a deterministic process, the correlation integral in Equation 2 will be independent of m but will increase with ε. The correlation dimension (SC_m) is defined as:

$$SC_m = [\ln C_m(\varepsilon_i) - \ln C_m(\varepsilon_{i-1})]/[\ln \varepsilon_i - \ln \varepsilon_{i-1}] \qquad (3)$$

Eleven values of ε are used: $0.9^1, 0.9^2, ..., 0.9^{11}$. Four embedding dimensions are used: 2, 4, 6, and 8. The median of the 10 estimates of SC_m for each m is employed as the estimate of the correlation dimension, since the distribution of estimates of SC_m for each embedding dimension has great dispersion and skewness.

One test of deterministic chaos is the residual test suggested by Brock (1986). He shows that if time series data are chaotic, the estimated dimension of residuals from the best fitting time series model is the same as that of the original data. If the data are stochastic, the dimension of the residuals will increase, since they have less structure than the original data. Brock's residual test is easy to apply and especially useful for this study since the GARCH processes provide residuals that are adjusted for possible linear and quadratic dependence. The drawback of Brock's residual test is that no formal hypothesis testing is possible. Therefore, the stronger test of Brock, Dechert, and Scheinkman (1986), which is called the BDS test, is used as well.

The BDS statistic is used to test the null hypothesis of an independent identical distribution [Brock et al. (1991)]. The BDS test has power against chaotic alternatives, unlike conventional tests. The statistic is based on the correlation integral. Under the null hypothesis that $\{x_t\}$ is IID, the BDS statistic is,

$$W_m(\varepsilon,T) = T^{\frac{1}{2}}[C_m(\varepsilon,T)^m - C_1(\varepsilon,T)^m]/\sigma_m(\varepsilon) \qquad (4)$$

This statistic converges in distribution to a standard normal random variable under the null hypothesis. Based on Monte Carlo results by Hsieh and LeBaron (1988), the epsilon chosen is $\varepsilon = \sigma$ with embedding dimensions, $m = 3, 6$, and 9, where σ is the standard deviation of the data series. A rejection of the null hypothesis may be due to linear or nonlinear dependence or to chaotic structure.

The BDS statistic converges in distribution to a standard normal random variable under the null hypothesis. But Brock et al. (1991) show that the distribution of the statistic changes when applied with GARCH residuals. They use Monte Carlo methods to obtain the distribution of the BDS statistic applied with GARCH(1, 1) standardized residuals and 2,500 observations. The hypothesis tests for raw data are based on the asymptotic distribution; but for the GARCH residuals, the table in Brock et al. (1991) is used.

Sample Data

The data are the first differences of the natural logarithms of daily closing futures prices. Changes in the logarithms of the prices can be interpreted as percentage changes in continuous time. Daily returns are multiplied by 100 to avoid possible scaling problems in estimation and to express them in percentage terms. The data set is composed of 15 contracts actively traded in U.S. futures markets. The list of data and sample periods of each commodity are shown in Table 13-1. The data are for the 10 years from January 1979 to December 1988, except for contracts that began trading after January 1979. Only the three stock indexes began trading after January 1979. For these contracts, data is included for the first full year of trading through December 1988 (when the data are available). The more than 2,500 observations for each commodity (except for the stock indexes) provide enough degrees of freedom that it seems reasonable to use tests that are only asymptotically valid.

A continuous series of data is constructed. The data consist of changes in the log of daily closing of the futures contract closest to delivery until the third Tuesday of the month prior to delivery, after which the log changes in the next nearest delivery month are used. A few low-volume contracts such as September corn are not included in the data set. Since all data are close to maturity, the maturity effect should be less important in this data. The data are from the Dunn & Hargitt Commodity Data Bank.

Table 13-2 provides summary statistics of the data. All means are not statistically different from zero. Sample sizes vary slightly by commodity because the various exchanges observe different holidays and because markets are closed occasionally when exchanges fear traders may panic in

Table 13-1

Sample Period and Contract Months for Futures Commodities

Commodity	Sample Period	Contract Months	Price Limit[a]
Corn	1/79–12/88	Mar May Jul Dec	yes
Coffee	1/79–12/88	Mar May Jul Sep Dec	yes
Oats	1/79–12/88	Mar May Jul Sep Dec	yes
Soybean	1/79–12/88	Jan Mar May Jul Nov	yes
Soybean meal	1/79–12/88	Mar May Jul Dec	yes
Wheat (Chicago)	1/79–12/88	Mar Jul Dec	yes
Wheat (Kansas City)	2/79–12/88	Mar Jul Dec	yes
Copper	1/79–12/88	Mar May Jul Sep Dec	yes
Gold (NY)	1/79–12/88	Feb Apr Jun Aug Sep	yes
Palladium	1/79–12/88	Mar Jun Sep Dec	yes
Platinum	1/79–12/88	Jan Apr Jul Oct	yes
Silver	1/79–12/88	Mar May Jul Sep Dec	yes
NYSE	1/84–12/88	Mar Jun Sep Dec	no
S&P 500	1/83–12/88	Mar Jun Sep Dec	no
Value Line	1/84–12/88	Mar Jun Sep Dec	no

[a] Source: Commodity Trading Manual.

response to some new announcement. Estimated variances are very different from commodity to commodity even though the data are unitless due to using log changes. Twelve of 15 contracts are skewed. The skewness is mostly negative, but sometimes positive. All are leptokurtic at conventional levels of significance. Three stock index futures, NYSE, S&P 500, and Value Line, have exceptionally large kurtosis. These extremes result from the stock market crash of 1987. Kurtosis can be greatly affected by a single outlier, even in a sample of 2,500.

Results

Brock's Residual Test

Table 13-3 shows the estimated correlation dimensions for the raw and rescaled data (standardized residuals). If time series data are stochastic, the estimated dimensions should have full dimension; that is, equal or very close to the embedding dimensions. Only silver has an estimated dimen-

Table 13-2

Summary Statistics of Daily Futures Returns

Commodity	Sample Size	Mean	Variance	Skewness	Relative Kurtosis
Corn	2524	−0.015	1.433	0.038	1.899[a]
Coffee	2510	0.018	3.104	−0.279[a]	3.771[a]
Oats	2522	−0.002	2.673	0.103[a]	1.093[a]
Soybean	2523	−0.024	1.943	−0.131[a]	1.317[a]
Soybean meal	2524	−0.017	2.190	0.005	1.740[a]
Wheat (Chi)	2524	−0.011	1.874	0.722[a]	13.289[a]
Wheat (KC)	2494	−0.000	1.580	0.615[a]	29.084[a]
Copper	2519	0.017	3.207	−0.260[a]	2.994[a]
Gold (NY)	2521	−0.016	1.350	−0.016	3.469[a]
Palladium	2496	0.017	4.532	−0.093[a]	1.742[a]
Platinum	2508	−0.011	4.528	−0.112[a]	0.947[a]
Silver	2514	−0.041	4.893	−0.193[a]	1.485[a]
NYSE	1353	0.021	2.286	−6.280[a]	170.806[a]
S&P 500	1669	0.038	2.316	−5.720[a]	156.713[a]
Value Line	1350	0.003	1.623	−4.819[a]	72.804[a]

[a] Denotes rejection of the null hypothesis of a normal distribution.

sion distinctly lower than the embedding dimension. This can be evidence of a deterministic structure. However, silver does not pass Brock's residual test. The estimates for the rescaled data for silver are larger.

Estimated dimensions detect some contracts that seem to pass the residual test. However, they tend to have full dimensions; that is, those estimated dimensions are close to the embedding dimensions, implying no evidence of deterministic structure. To confirm deterministic chaos, diagnostics should meet the saturation condition as well as Brock's residual test. That is, beyond some embedding dimension, estimated correlation dimensions for both raw and residual data should be the same and be stable with embedding dimension. None of the series that pass the residual test also satisfy the saturation condition.[2] Correlation dimensions and embedding dimensions increase together.

Brock's residual test shows no evidence of low-dimension deterministic chaos for the futures data. However, formal hypothesis tests are not

Table 13-3

Correlation Dimension Estimates[a]

Commodity	Original Data			Rescaled Data		
	m = 4	m = 6	*m = 8*	*m = 4*	*m = 6*	*m = 8*
Corn	3.48	4.93	6.11	3.78	5.52	7.19
Coffee	3.68	5.49	7.13	3.68	5.43	7.39
Oats	3.53	5.09	6.80	3.77	5.72	7.39
Soybean	3.63	5.33	6.90	3.74	5.42	7.12
Soybean meal	3.57	5.18	6.52	3.64	5.44	6.88
Wheat (Chi)	3.73	5.45	7.02	3.72	5.44	7.02
Wheat (KC)	3.49	4.94	6.52	3.59	5.31	6.79
Copper	3.63	5.22	5.92	3.71	5.62	7.88
Gold (NY)	3.52	5.35	6.90	3.58	5.44	7.01
Palladium	3.69	5.45	7.02	3.62	5.20	6.91
Platinum	3.78	5.59	7.13	3.73	5.36	6.86
Silver	3.69	4.63	2.19	3.69	5.01	5.84
NYSE	3.63	5.44	7.16	3.58	5.53	7.41
S&P 500	3.60	5.62	7.09	3.66	5.44	6.89
Value Line	3.68	5.44	7.29	3.71	5.52	7.60

[a] For each embedding dimension, 11 adjacent values of epsilon. 0.9^n, $n = 1, 2, ..., 11$ are used. The median is reported as the estimate of the correlation dimension.

possible with Brock's residual test. Also, higher dimensions might be needed to find the saturation point.

Estimated Results of the GARCH Process

Table 13-4 reports estimates and test results of the GARCH model. First, estimated coefficients for the ARCH term, α and the GARCH term, β are positive and significant at the 5 percent level for all commodities. The conditional standard deviation is not significant in the means equation of any commodity. This may mean that traders are risk neutral or that the conditional standard deviation is a poor measure of risk.

The null hypothesis of no linear dependence is rejected only for silver and platinum. This is less autocorrelation than was found in past studies such as Taylor (1986). Mean returns differ from day to day only for coffee.

Table 13-4

Estimated Parameters and Statistics of the GARCH(1, 1) Process

	Wheat (Chi)	Wheat (KC)	Soybean	Soybean meal	Oats
Mean					
Intercept	−0.025	−0.116	−0.057	−0.055	−0.043
	(−0.26)	(−1.77)	(−0.64)	(−0.58)	(−0.40)
D (Monday)	−0.041	−0.058	−0.064	−0.170[a]	−0.121
	(−0.54)	(−0.93)	(−0.84)	(−2.04)	(−1.40)
D (Tuesday)	−0.028	0.024	0.037	−0.060	−0.096
	(−0.40)	(0.43)	(0.53)	(−0.75)	(−1.11)
D (Wednesday)	0.118	0.172	0.138[a]	0.095	−0.004
	(1.71)	(2.82)	(2.00)	(1.28)	(−0.05)
D (Thursday)	−0.120	−0.043	0.012	0.005	−0.184[a]
	(−1.75)	(−0.73)	(0.18)	(0.07)	(−2.11)
Std. dev.	0.021	0.102	−0.007	0.035	0.080
	(0.26)	(1.88)	(−0.10)	(0.50)	(1.24)
Variance					
Intercept	0.133	0.228[a]	−0.075	0.003	0.175
	(1.78)	(5.97)	(−0.99)	(0.03)	(1.79)
Alpha	0.084[a]	0.157[a]	0.063[a]	0.067[a]	0.067[a]
	(10.26)	(15.46)	(7.48)	(8.46)	(8.17)
Beta	0.881[a]	0.810[a]	0.916[a]	0.912[a]	0.928[a]
	(73.28)	(80.97)	(90.91)	(94.33)	(109.7)
D (Monday)	0.270[a]	−0.074	0.464[a]	0.435[a]	−0.205
	(2.18)	(−1.06)	(3.60)	(3.23)	(−1.24)
D (Tuesday)	−0.449[a]	−0.437[a]	−0.368[a]	−0.352[a]	−0.141
	(−3.72)	(−9.14)	(−3.20)	(−2.95)	(−0.97)
D (Wednesday)	−0.127	−0.117[a]	0.085	0.010	−0.162
	(−1.19)	(−2.50)	(0.85)	(−0.08)	(−1.19)
D (Thursday)	−0.121	−0.239[a]	0.215	−0.040	−0.214
	(−0.91)	(−3.87)	(1.71)	(−0.297)	(−1.42)
D (holiday)	0.594[a]	0.231[a]	0.356[a]	0.399[a]	0.150[a]
	(5.42)	(4.91)	(3.73)	(4.13)	(1.33)
Maturity	−0.001	0.000	0.008[a]	0.006[a]	−0.007
	(−0.39)	(0.23)	(2.85)	(2.61)	(−1.90)
Autocorrelation(10)[b]	1.31	1.27	1.17	0.92	0.99
M (day-of-the-week)[b]	4.56	3.54	1.17	2.66	0.95

Table continues

Table 13-4 (Continued)

	Wheat (Chi)	Wheat (KC)	Soybean	Soybean meal	Oats
V (day-of-the-week)[b]	15.96[a]	72.26[a]	54.79[a]	13.59[a]	0.81[a]
V (seasonality)[b]	15.72[a]	78.18[a]	15.40[a]	22.32[a]	3.26
Ljung–Box(15)[c]					
$\hat{e}(t)/\hat{h}(t)$	4.80	13.06	7.57	10.01	9.36
$\hat{e}(t)^2/\hat{h}(t)^2$	16.25	2.62	15.90	12.60	8.05
BDS tests ($\varepsilon = \sigma$)					
Raw data					
dimensions = 3	2.02[a]	3.14[a]	3.24[a]	3.55[a]	3.33[a]
dimensions = 6	7.92[a]	12.69[a]	14.23[a]	14.70[a]	15.79[a]
dimensions = 9	18.20[a]	29.53[a]	36.86[a]	36.35[a]	47.44[a]
Standardized residuals					
dimensions = 3	−0.09	0.18	−0.23	0.33	0.27
dimensions = 6	−0.78	−0.20	−0.44	0.58	0.77
dimensions = 9	−1.33	0.19	−0.09	1.28	1.04

	Corn	Coffee	Copper	Gold	Silver
Mean					
Intercept	−0.005	0.165	−0.031	−0.055	−0.148
	(−0.08)	(1.95)	(−0.31)	(−0.58)	(−0.89)
D (Monday)	0.019	−0.151	−0.284[a]	−0.102	−0.392[a]
	(0.30)	(−1.90)	(−3.19)	(−1.21)	(−3.13)
D (Tuesday)	−0.026	−0.119	−0.096	0.003	−0.135
	(−0.43)	(−1.50)	(−1.01)	(0.04)	(−1.13)
D (Wednesday)	0.090	−0.065	0.114	0.060	0.038
	(1.52)	(−0.87)	(1.29)	(0.73)	(0.32)
D (Thursday)	−0.076	0.006	0.046	−0.043	−0.138
	(−1.31)	(0.08)	(0.08)	(−0.54)	(−1.18)
Std. dev.	−0.013	−0.048	0.037	0.014	0.142
	(−0.20)	(−0.81)	(0.66)	(0.25)	(1.81)
Variance					
Intercept	0.093[a]	0.034	0.193[a]	0.384[a]	0.254
	(2.22)	(0.45)	(2.32)	(5.13)	(1.12)
Alpha	0.088[a]	0.119[a]	0.043[a]	0.077[a]	0.101[a]
	(7.94)	(12.42)	(8.28)	(11.28)	(9.99)
Beta	0.883[a]	0.864[a]	0.952[a]	0.900	0.855[a]
	(62.00)	(84.86)	(172.6)	(117.0)	(66.67)

Table continues

Table 13-4 (Continued)

	Corn	Coffee	Copper	Gold	Silver
D (Monday)	0.186^a	0.250	−0.096	−0.141	1.107^a
	(2.33)	(1.91)	(−0.76)	(−1.02)	(2.92)
D (Tuesday)	-0.292^a	−0.046	−0.168	−0.992	-1.208^a
	(−4.06)	(−0.36)	(−1.11)	(−8.51)	(−3.65)
D (Wednesday)	−0.084	−0.031	-0.572^a	-0.202^a	−0.106
	(−1.39)	(−0.26)	(−4.89)	(−2.43)	(−0.38)
D (Thursday)	−0.140	−0.116	−0.176	-0.484^a	−0.091
	(−1.77)	(−0.80)	(−1.19)	(−4.41)	(0.29)
D (holiday)	0.283^a	0.390^a	0.556^a	0.946^a	2.139^a
	(4.14)	(3.00)	(5.05)	(9.37)	(6.13)
Maturity	0.001	−0.002	0.001	0.002	-0.018^a
	(0.72)	(−0.56)	(0.53)	(0.95)	(−2.11)
Autocorrelation(10)[b]	1.20	1.27	1.81	1.63	3.78
M (day-of-the-week)[b]	2.15	19.00^a	3.60	0.82	3.57
V (day-of-the-week)[b]	20.12^a	3.08	8.51	26.35^a	25.53^a
V (seasonality)[b]	16.58^a	10.88^a	21.91^a	4.98	14.49^a
Ljung–Box(15)[c]					
$\hat{e}(t)/\hat{h}(t)$	6.14	9.31	2.69	15.82	21.13
$\hat{e}(t)^2/\hat{h}(t)^2$	9.57	31.68^a	11.86	13.39	12.03
BDS tests ($\varepsilon = \sigma$)					
Raw data					
dimensions = 3	3.99^a	5.44^a	3.83^a	4.13^a	3.99^a
dimensions = 6	18.97^a	24.37^a	16.74^a	16.29^a	16.32^a
dimensions = 9	52.67^a	66.00^a	41.42^a	39.05^a	40.73^a
Standardized residuals					
dimensions = 3	0.08	0.40	0.26	0.60	0.56
dimensions = 6	1.32^a	0.89	0.73	1.47^a	1.04
dimensions = 9	2.65^a	1.02	0.80	2.06^a	1.63^a

	Pall.	Plat.	NYSE	S&P 500	Value Line
Mean					
Intercept	0.073	−0.105	0.019	−0.085	0.163
	(0.57)	(−0.55)	(0.16)	(−0.87)	(1.81)
D (Monday)	−0.084	−0.146	−0.009	0.007	−0.015
	(−0.75)	(−1.13)	(−0.11)	(0.09)	(−0.17)

Table continues

Table 13-4 (Continued)

	Pall.	Plat.	NYSE	S&P 500	Value Line
D (Tuesday)	0.075	−0.01	0.027	0.018	0.019
	(0.74)	(−0.01)	(0.32)	(0.24)	(0.24)
D (Wednesday)	0.146	0.007	−0.003	−0.003	−0.037
	(1.44)	(0.05)	(−0.04)	(−0.04)	(−0.51)
D (Thursday)	−0.076	−0.125	−0.029	−0.023	0.089
	(−0.073)	(−1.01)	(−0.34)	(−0.30)	(1.09)
Std. dev.	−0.038	0.067	0.050	0.155	−0.148
	(−0.61)	(0.78)	(0.45)	(1.75)	(−1.52)
Variance Intercept	0.093	0.650[a]	−0.053	−0.084	−0.108
	(0.56)	(3.05)	(−0.70)	(−1.31)	(−1.62)
Alpha	0.141[a]	0.064[a]	0.200[a]	0.148[a]	0.146[a]
	(11.25)	(6.65)	(13.89)	(18.31)	(16.61)
Beta	0.821[a]	0.909[a]	0.712[a]	0.822[a]	0.774[a]
	(68.47)	(66.61)	(24.16)	(57.90)	(36.67)
D (Monday)	0.786[a]	−0.044	0.304[a]	0.266[a]	0.468[a]
	(2.58)	(−0.12)	(2.38)	(2.36)	(4.08)
D (Tuesday)	−1.02[a]	−1.885[a]	0.222	0.251[a]	0.183
	(−4.03)	(−5.36)	(1.92)	(2.28)	(1.87)
D (Wednesday)	0.210	−0.385	0.070	−0.001	0.090
	(1.06)	(−1.39)	(0.65)	(−0.09)	(0.87)
D (Thursday)	0.180	−0.405	0.430[a]	0.277[a]	0.428[a]
	(0.77)	(−1.10)	(3.12)	(2.20)	(3.19)
D (holiday)	1.267[a]	1.200[a]	0.688[a]	0.442[a]	0.764[a]
	(4.29)	(3.93)	(3.62)	(3.37)	(4.67)
Maturity	0.006	−0.009	−0.011[a]	−0.007[a]	−0.013[a]
	(0.99)	(−1.23)	(−2.21)	(−2.25)	(−4.06)
Autocorrelation(10)[b]	0.44	1.85[a]	0.40	0.76	0.27
M (day-of-the-week)[b]	0.04	0.36	0.04	0.39	0.70
V (day-of-the-week)[b]	55.97[a]	43.72[a]	32.78[a]	22.83[a]	45.84[a]
V (seasonality)[b]	11.10[a]	6.20	5.52	5.61	10.37
Ljung–Box(15)[b]					
$\hat{e}(t)/\hat{h}(t)$	12.95	8.80	11.40	8.89	8.39
$\hat{e}(t)^2/\hat{h}(t)^2$	26.44	19.87	8.27	5.58	17.63

Table continues

Table 13-4 (Continued)

	Pall.	Plat.	NYSE	S&P 500	Value Line
BDS tests ($\epsilon = \sigma$)					
Raw data					
dimensions = 3	5.54[a]	3.39[a]	0.76	1.34	0.29
dimensions = 6	23.54[a]	12.94[a]	2.82[a]	5.55[a]	1.11
dimensions = 9	59.63[a]	29.11[a]	5.80[a]	12.67[a]	2.19[a]
Standardized residuals					
dimensions = 3	1.49[a]	0.72	−1.07	−1.00	0.46
dimensions = 6	3.80[a]	1.66[a]	−3.06[a]	−2.99[a]	2.56a
dimensions = 9	4.70[a]	2.63[a]	−4.17[a]	−4.25[a]	8.20[a]

[a] The null hypothesis of a normal distribution is rejected.

[b] The test statistics are Wald F-statistics.

[c] Test statistics are asymptotically distributed as chi–squared. Significance is based on five degrees of freedom for $\hat{e}(t)/\hat{h}(t)$ and 13 degrees of freedom for $\hat{e}(t)^2/\hat{h}(t)^2$ under the null hypothesis of no autocorrellation.

The results, however, show volatility does differ by day of the week. Including the holiday effect, only three series have no significant differences in variances. Thus, different variability of returns for each day of the week seems to be a general phenomenon in futures markets. Specifically, most Mondays and all holidays have significantly higher variances, and most Wednesdays have lower variances.

The type of day of the week effects found is not truly an anomaly. The fact that variances are higher on Monday and following holidays favors the calendar time hypothesis over the trading time hypothesis.

The maturity effect is significant in six cases. Moreover, the effect is less than 1 percent of the variance. This implies that studies that use nearby price series do not need to be concerned about differences in maturity. The maturity effect might be more important when differences in maturity are greater.

Nine cases reveal significant seasonal patterns in price volatility. The results agree with Kenyon et al. (1987), who found that the price volatility of corn, soybeans, and wheat is affected by the season of the year.

Model Validation

This study assumes that the standardized residuals of the GARCH model are Gaussian white noise. Second-order dependence in standardized residuals, $\hat{e}_t / \hat{h}_t$, is detected only for coffee. The results imply that the lag structure of the conditional variance is correctly identified in most cases.

In every case, the BDS test for the raw data (Table 13-4) rejects the null hypothesis of IID. Such a finding is consistent with deterministic chaos. The GARCH model, however, removes considerable serial dependence in the raw data. The BDS test statistics for the rescaled data indicate significant dependence for eight contracts. In two of these cases, the BDS statistic is negative, which is not consistent with deterministic chaos. Results for about half of the commodities are consistent with deterministic chaos.[3] Neither the Ljung–Box nor the BDS test for the rescaled data reject the null hypothesis of independence for six cases. A higher-order GARCH process may be appropriate when the Ljung–Box test is rejected.

Table 13-5 contains Kolmogorov-Smirnov tests of normality and goodness-of-fit tests for the rescaled data from the GARCH model. Estimated skewness for the rescaled data from the GARCH model is significant in 10 of 15 cases compared to 12 of 15 for the raw data. One explanation for skewness is asymmetry in price movements. Traders generally believe that prices fall faster than they rise, which would result in negative skewness. However, soybean meal and the two wheat futures have positive skewness, so asymmetry does not seem to be a complete explanation of the skewness. The GARCH model's inability to remove skewness is no surprise, because the model can capture skewness only through the exogenous factors. In contrast, the GARCH model reduces leptokurtosis considerably. The most dramatic reduction in kurtosis is for the NYSE index futures from 170.8 to 10.1. The other two stock indices, S&P 500 and Value Line, show similar reductions. Only oats passes the Kolmogorov–Smirnov test of fit.

Thus, the GARCH models do not model precisely the distributions of daily futures price changes under consideration in this study. However, the models do remove most of the dependence and reduce the observed leptokurtosis considerably. The hypothesis tests in Table 13-4 are asymptotically valid via the central limit theorem if the variance is finite, even though the residuals are still leptokurtic, but are not asymptotically valid if unexplained heteroskedasticity or other nonlinearity remains.

Conclusions

The daily price changes considered in this study are largely linearly independent, but nonlinearly dependent. All of the estimated GARCH terms are significant at the 1 percent level, which implies that variances of price changes are autocorrelated. The BDS test supports serial dependence

Table 13-5

Normality and Goodness-of-Fit Tests with Standardized GARCH Residuals

	Skewness	Kurtosis	D_{max}
Corn	0.065	0.888	0.018[a]
Coffee	−0.120[a]	1.003[a]	0.033[a]
Oats	−0.059	0.473[a]	0.016
Soybean	−0.017	0.496[a]	0.021[a]
Soybean meal	0.162[a]	1.038[a]	0.034[a]
Wheat (Chi)	0.141[a]	1.032[a]	0.029[a]
Wheat (KC)	1.838[a]	27.349[a]	0.056[a]
Copper	−0.297[a]	1.885[a]	0.030[a]
Gold (NY)	0.026	2.093[a]	0.056[a]
Palladium	0.026	1.071[a]	0.037[a]
Platinum	−0.155[a]	0.386[a]	0.024[a]
Silver	0.113[a]	1.352[a]	0.031[a]
NYSE	−1.082[a]	10.132[a]	0.064[a]
S&P 500	−1.058[a]	11.329[a]	0.057[a]
Value Line	−0.748[a]	4.427[a]	0.057[a]

[a] The null hypothesis of a normal distribution is rejected.

in daily price changes. The BDS test rejects the null hypothesis of IID for all the original data. Moreover, no distribution is normal. They are slightly skewed and have fat tails.

The hypothesis of low-dimension deterministic chaos is not supported by Brock's residual test. Estimated dimensions for rescaled data are either larger than those for the raw data, or estimates for both series are increasing with embedding dimensions. This result favors the stochastic approach when determining the return generating process. But, the results using the preferred BDS test statistic are mixed. The GARCH residuals are not IID for about half of the commodities, which is consistent with deterministic chaos.

The GARCH(1, 1) process is not a perfect model of the data. Kolmogorov-Smirnov test of fit rejects the GARCH(1, 1) process for all cases. Results suggest a higher order GARCH process may be appropriate for some price series. However, the model provides great improvements. Nonlinear dependence in the raw data and leptokurtosis are reduced. For the price series for which the GARCH model is able to remove dependence, the hypothesis tests for market anomalies are asymptotically valid even though the distribution is not normal, provided the variance of the error term is finite and the model is specified correctly.

The most prominent market anomaly is day-of-the-week effects on variance. The variance is larger on Mondays and after holidays. This offers some partial support for the calendar-time hypothesis. Several commodities, especially agricultural commodities, exhibit seasonality in variance. A few commodities show significant autocorrelation, day-of-the-week in mean, or maturity effects on variance. In no case is the variance of the futures prices significant in the mean equation.

The results provide strong support for the existence of conditional heteroskedasticity, but they also show the GARCH model is not totally adequate. The results do not provide strong support for or against deterministic chaos. Results for about half of the commodities examined are consistent with deterministic chaos.

Acknowledgments

The authors wish to thank Blake LeBaron for providing computer programs used in this study. Helpful comments from Jean-Paul Chavas are gratefully acknowledged.

Notes

1 These are tests of whether the model is "well-calibrated." Bunn defines a model as well-calibrated if, over the long run, for all propositions assigned a given probability, the proportion that is true equals the probability assigned.

2 Higher levels of embedding dimensions have been considered in past research. The data might meet the saturation condition at higher embedding dimensions. Thus, the results only provide a test of low-dimension deterministic chaos.

3 In his study of stock prices, Hsieh (1991) argues that remaining nonlinearity is in the variance and not in the mean. This may not be true for futures prices. Past research [Irwin and Brorsen (1985); Lukac and Brorsen (1989)] shows that trend-following technical trailing systems yield positive gross returns (research is not conclusive about whether returns net of transaction costs are positive). Little linear correlation is

found in the mean here. Thus, technical analysis yielding positive gross returns suggests possible nonlinear dynamics in the mean.

References

Akgiray, V. "Conditional Heteroskedasticity in Time Series of Stock Returns: Evidence and Forecasts." *Journal of Business* (1989) 62:55–80.

Akgiray, V., and G. Booth. "Mixed Diffusion-Jump Process Modeling of Exchange Rate Movements." *Review of Economics and Statistics* (1988) 70:631–637.

Anderson, R. W. "Some Determinants of the Volatility of Futures Prices." *The Journal of Futures Markets* (1985) 5:332–348.

Baldauf, B., and G. J. Santoni. "Stock Price Volatility: Some Evidence from an ARCH Model." *The Journal of Futures Markets* (April 1991) 11:191–200.

Berndt, E. K., B. H. Hall, R. E. Hall, and J. A. Hausman. "Estimation and Inference in Nonlinear Structural Models." *Annals of Economic and Social Measurement* (1974) 3/4:653–665.

Blank, S. C. "'Chaos' in Futures Markets? A Nonlinear Dynamical Analysis." Center for the Study of Futures Markets Working Paper #204, Columbia Business School (February 1990).

Bollerslev, T. "Generalized Autoregressive Conditional Heteroskedasticity." *Journal of Econometrics* (1986) 31:307–327.

Bollerslev, T., R. Y. Chou, and K. F. Kroner. "ARCH Modeling in Finance: A Review of the Theory and Empirical Evidence." Working Paper No. 97, Department of Finance, Northwestern University (November 1990).

Brock, W. A. "Distinguishing Random and Deterministic Systems: Abridged Version." *Journal of Economic Theory* (1986) 40:168–195.

Brock, W., and W. D. Dechert. "Theorems on Distinguishing Deterministic from Random Systems." *Dynamic Economic Modelling.* Cambridge: Cambridge University Press, 1988.

Brock, W., W. D. Dechert, and J. Scheinkman. "A Test for Independence Based in the Correlation Dimension." Unpublished Manuscript, University of Wisconsin, and Chicago (1986).

Brock, W. A., D. A. Hsieh, and B. LeBaron. *Nonlinear Dynamics, Chaos, and Instability: Statistical Theory and Economic Evidence.* Cambridge, MA: The MIT Press, 1991.

Brorsen, B. W., and S. R. Yang. "Generalized Autoregressive Conditional Heteroskedasticity as a Model of the Distribution of Futures Returns."

Applied Commodity Price Analysis, Forecasting, and Market Risk Management, M. Hayenga, ed. Ames, IA: Iowa State University, 1989.

Bunn, D. W. *Applied Decision Analysis*. New York: McGraw-Hill, 1984.

Chiang, R. C., and T. C. Tapley. "Day of the Week Effects and the Futures Market." *Review of Research in Futures Markets* (1983) 2:356–410.

Chicago Board of Trade. *Commodity Trading Manual*. Chicago: Chicago Board of Trade, 1985.

Cornew, R. W., D. E. Town, and L. D. Crowson. "Stable Distributions, Futures Prices, and the Measurement of Trading Performance." *The Journal of Futures Markets* (1984) 4:531–557.

Fama, E. "The Behavior of Stock Market Prices." *Journal of Business* (January 1965) 38:34–105.

Frank, M. Z., and T. Stengos. "Measuring the Strangeness of Gold and Silver Rates of Return." Discussion Paper No. 1986–13, Dept. of Economics, University of Guelph (1986).

Friedman, D., and S. Vandersteel. "Short-run Fluctuations in Foreign Exchange Rates." *Journal of International Economics* (August 1982) 13:171–186.

Fujihara, R., and K. Park. "The Probability Distribution of Futures Prices in the Foreign Exchange Market: A Comparison of Candidate Processes." *The Journal of Futures Markets* (December 1990) 10:623–641.

Gordon, J. D. "The Distribution of Daily Changes in Commodity Futures Prices." Technical Bulletin No. 1702, ERS, USDA (July 1985).

Hall, J. A., B. W. Brorsen, and S. H. Irwin. "The Distribution of Futures Prices: A Test of the Stable Paretian and Mixture of Normals Hypotheses." *Journal of Financial and Quantitative Analysis* (March 1989) 24:105–116.

Hayek, F. A. *Monetary Theory of the Trade Cycle*. New York: Harcourt, 1933.

Hsieh, D. "The Statistical Properties of Daily Foreign Exchange Rates: 1974–1983." *Journal of International Economics* (1988) 24:129–145.

Hsieh, D. A. "Chaos and Nonlinear Dynamics: Application to Financial Markets." *Journal of Finance* (1991) 46:1839–1877.

Hsieh, D., and B. LeBaron. "Finite Sample Properties of the BDS Statistic." Unpublished Manuscript, University of Chicago (1988).

Hudson, M. A., R. M. Leuthold, and G. F. Sarassoro. "Commodity Futures Price Changes: Recent Evidence for Wheat, Soybean and Live Cattle." *The Journal of Futures Markets* (June 1987) 7:287–301.

Irwin, S. H., and B. W. Brorsen. "Public Futures Funds." *The Journal of Futures Markets* (1985) 5:149–171.

Junkus, J. C. "Weekend and Day of the Week Effects in Returns on Stock Index Futures." *The Journal of Futures Markets* (1986) 3:397–407.

Kenyon, D., K. Kling, J. Jordan, W. Seale, and N. McCabe. "Factors Affecting Agricultural Futures Price Variance." *The Journal of Futures Markets* (1987) 7:73–91.

Lukac, L. P., and B. W. Brorsen. "A Comprehensive Test of Futures Market Disequilibrium." *The Financial Review* (1990) 25:593–622.

Mandelbrot, B. "The Variation of Certain Speculative Prices." *Journal of Business* (October 1963) 36:394–419.

McCulloch, J. H. "Interest-Risk Sensitive Deposit Insurance Premia: Stable ACH Estimates." *Journal of Banking and Finance* (March 1985) 9:137–156.

Milonas, N. "Price Variability and the Maturity Effect in Futures Markets." *The Journal of Futures Markets* (1986) 6:443–460.

Randolph, W. L., and M. Najand. "A Test of Two Models in Forecasting Stock Index Futures Price Volatility." *The Journal of Futures Markets* (April 1991) 11:179–190.

Savit, R. "When Random Is Not Random: An Introduction to Chaos in Market Prices." *The Journal of Futures Markets* (June 1988) 8:271–289.

Savit, R. "Nonlinearities and Chaotic Effects in Options Prices." *The Journal of Futures Markets* (December 1989) 6:507–518.

Scheinkman, J. A., and B. LeBaron. "Nonlinear Dynamics and Stock Returns." *Journal of Business* (June 1989) 62:311–337.

Takens, F. "Detecting Strange Attractors in Turbulence," in *Dynamical Systems and Turbulence*, D. Rand and L. Young, eds., Lecture Notes in Mathematics. Berlin: Springer-Verlag, 1980, 898:366–382.

Taylor, S. "The Behavior of Futures Prices over Time." *Applied Economics* (1985) 17:713–734.

Taylor, S. *Modelling Financial Time Series*. New York: Wiley, 1986.

14

MEASURING THE STRANGENESS OF GOLD AND SILVER RATES OF RETURN

By Murray Frank and Thanasis Stengos

1. Introduction

The purpose of this chapter is to examine the predictability of asset price changes. In well-functioning markets it is often held that asset price changes should be unpredictable. Otherwise speculators will take advantage of the predictable price change,thereby forcing the change to happen immediately. Any subsequent changes are then left unpredictable. This intuition was formalized by Samuelson (1965) and has been incorporated in standard textbooks such as Brealey and Myers (1984). This intuition is often taken to be synonymous with the efficient market hypothesis. Analysis of intertemporal general equilibrium models indicates that this intuition is only rigorously justified under fairly stringent conditions, see Lucas (1978) and Brock (1982). Despite being a rather special case theoretically, considerable empirical support has been reported for the "martingale hypothesis," see Fama (1970).

Sims (1984) has provided an interesting rationalization of the empirical success of the martingale hypothesis. Our focus is on the extent to which the views of Sims, or "chaos" in the sense of Brock (1986), might be responsible for the empirical success of the martingale hypothesis. These two approaches are quite different. Scheinkman and LeBaron (1986) tested for chaos using weekly returns on stocks taken from the Center for Research in Security Prices (CRSP) at the University of Chicago. They devoted most attention to an index of stocks but also considered a number of individual stocks. Their results are seemingly consistent with chaos.[1]

This chapter is organized as follows. Section 2 is concerned with some theoretical background. First we give an indication of the restrictions needed to generate the martingale hypothesis in a standard economic setup. Then we discuss the approach of Sims (1984). That approach was developed in reaction to the restrictiveness of the assumptions required to generate the martingale hypothesis in a standard setup. Next a definition of chaos is offered in order to illustrate the sense in which chaos provides an alternative to Sims (1984).

Section 3 is concerned with the testing methods. Our work is based on the correlation dimension and the Kolmogorov entropy. Since these are not yet standard tools in empirical economic research, we attempt to motivate their use. As the correlation dimension has already been analyzed by Brock (1986) and Brock and Dechert (1988), we focus more attention on the Kolmogorov entropy. The empirical results are set out in Section 4, and a brief conclusion is offered in Section 5.

2. Theoretical Underpinnings

A. Traditional Efficient Markets Hypothesis

A standard context in which to consider asset pricing issues is the intertemporal models of Lucas (1978) and Brock (1982). In the Lucas model one derives a Euler equation for the representative agent relating the marginal utility of consumption at date t to expected marginal utility of consumption at date $t + 1$. In order to obtain the martingale hypothesis in asset prices, added structure is required. One needs to correct for dividends and discounting and then either assume risk-neutrality or else assume that there is no aggregate risk.

Let p_t be the price of an asset at date t and let E_t be the expectations operator conditioned on the information available at date t. A process $\{p_t\}$ is said to be a martingale if $E_t P_{t+s} = p_t$ for all $s > 0$. The claim that asset prices constitute a martingale is frequently identified in textbooks as the essence of the "efficient markets hypothesis." For theoretical analysis of such economies, see the general equilibrium models of Lucas (1978) and Brock (1982). Hansen and Singleton (1983) have an important special case of the Lucas-Brock approach for which there is a closed-form solution.[2] Hansen and Singleton (1983) empirically test their solution.

B. Sims's Approach

To obtain the martingale hypothesis in a Lucas-Brock setup requires very restrictive assumptions. This led Sims to question whether the apparent empirical success of the martingale hypothesis is little more than a robust fluke. In place of the Lucas-Brock framework Sims (1984) provides an analysis in which the martingale hypothesis is obtained for very short time intervals. Lengthy time intervals need not satisfy the martingale property.

Definition 2.1. A process $\{p_t\}$ is said to be instantaneously unpredictable (I.U.) if

$$\lim_{v \to 0} \frac{E_t[p_{t+v} - E_t(p_{t+v})^2]}{E_t[p_{t+v} - (p_t)^2]} \to 1 \text{ a.s.}$$

If asset prices satisfy Definition 2.1 and there are stationary increments, then a regression of $(p_{t+s} - p_t)$ on any variable known at date t will have an R^2 that approaches zero as s approaches zero. Changes over long time periods may be forecastable, but short-term price changes should be unpredictable. In modern financial theory diffusion processes are often assumed. Diffusion processes satisfy the I.U. property. Any process with well-behaved derivatives will not satisfy the I.U. property.

Sims (1984) provides a detailed discussion of the I.U. property and a very strong argument for it as the basis of the empirical success of the martingale hypothesis. He concludes that "except for the easily identified exceptional cases, neither the real world nor an analytically manageable economic model is likely to generate security prices which fail to be instantaneously unpredictable."

C. Chaos

In some respects "chaos" or "strangeness" is the polar opposite to a process that is instantaneously unpredictable. There are a number of different definitions of chaos in current use. Not all of the definitions are equally practical for empirical research.

Definition 2.2. Let Ω be a space with metric d and let $f: \Omega \to \Omega$ be a continuous mapping defined on Ω. A discrete dynamical system (Ω, f) is said to be chaotic (or strange) if there exists a $\delta > 0$ such that for all $\omega \in \Omega$ and all $\varepsilon > 0$ there is $\omega' \in \Omega$ and k such that $d(\omega, \omega') < \varepsilon$ but $d(f^k \omega, f^k \omega') \geq \delta$.

In this definition $f^k \omega$ denotes the k-fold iteration of point ω by the map f. Definition 2.2 contains less than is frequently included in definitions of chaos. Devaney (1986) for example includes the requirement that there exist dense orbits and that periodic points are dense. We do not take such a definition since the additional conditions do not seem to be verifiable nor refutable for empirical systems. There seems little point to including conditions that one cannot check. In practice the existence of dense orbits must be assumed in any case in order to characterize the system. Our definition follows the usage of Eckmann and Ruelle (1985) who take "chaos" to be synonymous with "sensitive dependence on initial conditions." Brock (1986) defines chaos in terms of the largest Lyapunov exponent being positive. The Lyapunov exponent definition is related to the Kolmogorov entropy. The Kolmogorov entropy is a lower bound on the sum of the positive Lyapunov exponents, see Eckmann and Ruelle (1985). The Kolmogorov entropy is discussed in Section 3B.

A chaotic system will be quite predictable over very short time horizons. If however the initial conditions are only known with finite precision, then over long intervals the ability to predict the time path will be lost. This is despite the process being deterministically generated. Typically for chaotic systems nearby trajectories locally separate exponentially fast.

The mathematical theory of chaos is currently an active research area, see Lasota and Mackey (1985), Devaney (1986), and Guckenheimer and Holmes (1986). There are a great many ways in which chaos might enter an economic system. Our work is not tied to any particular entry mechanism. If evidence of chaos is found then it becomes a natural topic for further research to attempt to identify its source or sources.[3]

We have three alternative possible interpretations of the observed irregularity of asset prices. The Lucas (1978) framework considered in Section A does not tie the martingale hypothesis to the size of the time intervals being employed empirically. Sims generates unpredictability explicitly for short time intervals. For lengthy time intervals Sims's theory permits the asset price changes to be predictable. The chaos interpretation leaves unspecified the economic mechanism that generated the data. It is consistent with many possible theories including versions of the Lucas-Brock setup. Chaos is not consistent with Sims's approach. If chaos is present, then asset price changes will (at least in principle) be predictable over short time intervals, but not over long time intervals. Over long time intervals, due to the sensitive dependence on initial conditions, the asset prices will not be predictable.

It is worth emphasizing that these three approaches by no means exhaust the set of conceivable theories of the observed irregularity of asset prices. These three approaches are considered together, since each has been suggested previously as a possible interpretation. In rejecting one or more of these possible views, we do not establish that a particular alternative is true. This familiar methodological point is particularly pertinent with respect to any suggestion of *deterministic* chaos.

3. Testing Methodology

In this section we describe the two measures on which our empirical work is based. The theoretical underpinning is an assumption of ergodicity. Such an assumption is required if we are to use time averages as representative of the system's behavior. The first invariant of the system is the correlation dimension. The second invariant of interest is the Kolmogorov entropy. We take these in turn.

A. Correlation Dimension

The correlation dimension is originally due to Grassberger and Procaccia (1983) and Takens (1983). For more detail than we provide see Brock and Dechert (1988) and Eckmann and Ruelle (1985).

Start by assuming that the system is on an "attractor." An attractor is a closed compact set S with a neighborhood such that almost all initial conditions in the neighborhood have S itself as their forward-limit set. In other words, these initial conditions are "attracted" to S as time progresses. The neighborhood is termed the "basis of attraction" for the attractor. An attractor satisfying Definition 2.2 is then called a strange attractor or else a chaotic attractor.

Consider a time-series of rates of return r_t, $t = 1, 2, 3, ..., T$. We suppose that these were generated by an orbit or trajectory that is dense on the attractor. Use the time-series to create an embedding. In other words create "M-histories" as $r = r_t^M = (r_t, ..., r_{t+M-1})$. This converts the series of scalars into a series of vectors with overlapping entries. If the true system which generated the time-series is n-dimensional,[4] then provided $M \geq 2\, n+1$ generically the M-histories recreate the dynamics of the underlying system (there a is diffeomorphism between the M-histories and the underlying data generating system. This extremely useful mapping between the underlying system and the M-histories was established by Takens (1980). It is this result that permits the empirical work. Broomhead and King (1986) discuss certain practical limitations on the use of Takens' theorem.

Next one measures the spatial correlations among the points (M-histories) on the attractor by calculating the correlation integral, $C^M(\varepsilon)$. For a particular embedding dimension M, the correlation integral is defined to be

$$C^M (\varepsilon) = \{\text{the number of pairs } (i,j)$$
$$\text{whose distance } ||\, r_i^M - r_j^M \,|| \leq \varepsilon \}/T^2. \tag{3.1}$$

Here $|| \cdot ||$ denotes the distance induced by the selected norm. We use the Euclidean distance. The other distance function that is sometimes employed is the sup-norm. By Theorem 2.4 of Brock (1986) the correlation dimension is independent of the choice of norm. In principle T should go to infinity, but in practice T is limited by the length of the available time series. This will in turn place limitations on the choice of ε.

To obtain the correlation dimension, D^M take

$$D^M = \lim\nolimits_{\varepsilon \to 0} \{\ln C^M(\varepsilon)/\ln \varepsilon\}. \tag{3.2}$$

As a practical matter one searches to see if the values of D^M stabilize at some value D as M increases. If so, then D is the correlation dimension estimate. If, however, as M increases the D^M continues to increase at the same rate, then the system is taken to be "high dimensional," or in other words stochastic. If a low value for D^M is found, then the system is substantially deterministic even if complicated. In principle an independently and identically distributed stochastic system is infinite dimensional. Each time one increases the available degrees of freedom, the system utilizes that extra freedom. With finite data sets, high dimensionality will be indistinguishable from infinite dimensionality empirically, see Ramsey and Yuan (1987) concerning small data sets.

Two practical problems concerning ε should be noted. If ε is too large, then $C^M(\varepsilon) = 1$ and no information about the system is obtained. It is also possible for ε to be too small. With finite data sets there is a limit to the degree of detail that one may discern. This limitation on the ability to get a detailed focus means that even in principle one can never exclude the possibility of the system containing some degree of additive noise. However, the test still can find out if there are substantial nonlinearities moving the system. Empirically finding an appropriate range of values for ε is not difficult for these series.

There are several papers in economics that use the correlation integral. Barnett and Chen (1988) used it to examine monetary aggregates, a low correlation dimension estimate was obtained. Brock and Sayers (1988) investigated American macroeconomic time-series. They reject chaos but find some evidence of nonlinear structures. As previously indicated Scheinkman and LeBaron (1986) examined American stock market data and obtained results strikingly similar to those that we obtain. Since the number of related papers is large and rapidly growing, we do not carry out a full survey here. For an overview of the literature see Frank and Stengos (1988).

B. Kolmogorov Entropy

Dimension measures the degree of complexity of a system. Entropy is a measure of time dependence. The Kolmogorov[5] entropy, K, quantifies the concept of "sensitive dependence on initial conditions." It is frequently described as measuring the rate at which information is created. This is due to the following argument. Consider two trajectories that are so close initially as to be indistinguishable to an observer. As time passes, the trajectories may separate and become distinguishable. The entropy measures how rapidly this happens.

For an ordered system, that is to say quasi-periodic or less erratic still, $K = 0$, while for an independent and identically distributed stochastic system $K = +\infty$. For a deterministic chaotic system $0 < K < \infty$ and K may be thought of as a measure of predictability of the system. Let T be the average length of time for which knowledge of the current state of the system (at specified accuracy) can be used to predict the future evolution, then $K \sim T^{-1}$.

Since the Kolmogorov entropy is not yet a standard tool in the economics literature, we provide a formal definition to help clarify matters. Let (Ω, F, μ) be a probability space, with Ω the space of states of nature, F a sigma-algebra, and μ a measure. We are interested in partitions of (Ω, F, μ) into disjoint collections of the elements of F whose union is Ω. Let $A = \{A_1, A_2, ..., A_n\}$ represent such a finite partition. There is a one-to-one correspondence between finite partitions and finite sub-sigma-algebras. We can define the entropy of the partition A by

$$K(A) = -\sum_{i=1}^{n} \mu(A_i)\ln \mu(A_i) \tag{3.3}$$

and $a \ln a = 0$ when $a = 0$. Hess (1983) provides an economic interpretation of $K(A)$ where the particular partition is directly into the states of nature.

Next let $f: \Omega \to \Omega$ and $f^{-k}A_i$ is the set of points mapped by f^k into A_i. If $B = \{B_1, B_2, ..., B_k\}$ is another finite partition of (Ω, F, μ) then the "join" of A and B is

$$A \vee B = \{A_i \cap {}^{\circ} B_j \mid i = 1,2,3, ... , n; j = 1,2,3, ..., k\}. \tag{3.4}$$

Now take $A^m = A \vee f^{-1}A \vee f^{-2}A \vee \ldots \vee f^{-m+1}A$ which is a partition composed of pieces $A_i \cap f^{-1} A_i \cap \ldots \cap f^{-m+1} A_{i_n}$ with $i_1 \in \{1, 2, 3, \ldots, n\}$. A^m is the "least common refinement" of the partitions A through $f^{-m+1}A$. A partition f^kA is derived from A by iteration of the map f backwards in time k steps. The partition A^m is the partition generated by A over a time interval of length m.

We can now distinguish the entropy of a particular partition from the entropy of the source $K(A, f)$:

$$K(A, f) = \lim_{m \to \infty} K(A^m) / m. \tag{3.5}$$

Petersen (1983) gives conditions under which this limit exists. Now $K(A, f)$ measures the average uncertainty per unit time about which part of the partition A, a trajectory will enter next given the past history of that trajectory. $K(A, f)$ is the entropy of the mapping f with respect to the partition A.

So far not much has been asserted about the nature of the partition A. In a general setup the choices of partitions could themselves be economic issues. A poorly selected partition could induce poor decisions. For present purposes we simply take the entropy of the mapping f to be

$$K(f) = \text{supremum}_A K(A, f), \tag{3.6}$$

where A is from some feasible set of possible partitions. In $K(f)$ we have a measurement of the average uncertainty concerning where f sends the various points of Ω. The magnitude of $K(f)$ is a measure of chaos, since it measures the extent to which f creates disorder. For a derivation of some properties of $K(f)$ see Petersen (1983).

Between 1979 and 1981 there were several attempts to directly implement $K(f)$. As discussed by Eckmann and Ruelle (1985) these efforts proved problematic in part due to the difficulty in implementation of the supremum. An empirical approximation of $K(f)$ has been suggested by Grassberger and Procaccia (1983b) which is much more readily implemented. This approximation, denoted K_2, is based on their correlation integral $C^M(\varepsilon)$. First define:

$$K_2(A) = -\ln \sum_{i=1}^{n} \mu (A_i)^2. \tag{3.7}$$

Letting ε represent the size of the partitions in A we then have

$$K_2(\mu) = \lim_{\varepsilon \to 0} \lim_{m \to \infty} K_2(A^m)/m. \tag{3.8}$$

How does K_2 relate to $K(f)$?

$$0 \le K_2(\mu) \le K(f). \tag{3.9}$$

For an i.i.d. system K_2 will be infinite, while for a chaotic system it will be positive but finite.

Grassberger and Procaccia (1983b) suggest that K_2 is preferable to K. Typically K_2 and K are numerically close. The implementation of K_2 is simply to find

$$K_2 = \lim_{\varepsilon \to 0} \lim_{M \to \infty} \lim_{N \to \infty} \ln \left(\frac{C^M(\varepsilon)}{C^{M+1}(\varepsilon)} \right). \tag{3.10}$$

The practical limitations on the implementation of K_2 are much the same as for implementation of the correlation dimension. The fact that the length of the time-series is finite is perhaps the most serious difficulty. Due to the finiteness of the time-series, as M increases, the correlation integral will be reduced to counting only the points themselves. Accordingly, $C^M(\varepsilon)$ and $C^{M+1}(\varepsilon)$ will each converge to the same value, and then $\ln 1 = 0$. Thus if one examines too large an embedding dimension then the estimated value of K_2 will be biased toward zero. For further background concerning entropy, see Cohen and Procaccia (1985) as well as Eckmann and Ruelle (1985).

How is one to determine whether one is using "too large" an embedding dimension? Since there is no strong a priori theory to appeal to, we took the following approach. We used iterations of the "tent map" to create series with various degrees of complexity and with the same length of time series as our data sets. Using this generated data we then check to see at what level of M the bias toward zero starts to take effect. We then limit attention to values of M below those at which the bias appears to become important.

The "tent map" is given by $x_{t+1} = f(x_t)$ where

$$f(x) = 2x, \quad x \in \left[0, \frac{1}{2}\right], \quad f(x) = 2(1-x), \quad x \in \left[\frac{1}{2}, 1\right]. \tag{3.11}$$

The tent map is a one-dimensional map. If one uses a series of tent maps with the output of one map fed into the next, then one can create systematically more complex maps. Such iterations are sometimes termed as the "extrapolation time." From Figure 14-1 we see that as expected the bias toward zero takes effect earlier for greater extrapolation times. Also observe that K_2 does distinguish simpler from more complex objects as theory suggests.

4. Empirical Results

The data that we used are the daily prices for gold and silver. For gold we used the closing price in London, England, measured in U.S. dollars per fine ounce. The series starts at the beginning of 1975 and runs through June

Figure 14-1

Simulation Results for the Kolmogorov Entropy Approximation (K_2)

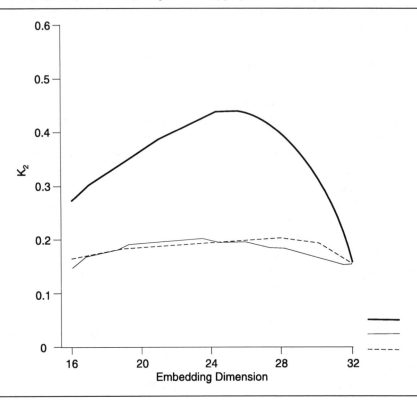

1986. The data were obtained from I. P. Sharp commodities database, identified as comdaily series EAUD. For silver we also used the closing price in London, but starting at the beginning of 1974 through June 1986. Silver is measured in British pence per troy ounce. The silver data also come from I. P. Sharp commodities database and are identified as comdaily series EAGDSPB.

Following Sims (1984) the null hypothesis being tested has short time interval data series possessing the martingale property (I.U.). However, longer time interval series are allowed to be more predictable and consequently less likely to follow a martingale process.

To test this hypothesis we considered daily, weekly, and biweekly series of gold and silver rates of return. Consideration of weekly data series is useful as a check on whether results in the daily data might be due to a weekend effect. The null hypothesis is that the daily series should be more random than the weekly series, while the biweekly data should possess the most (if any) structure. This theory also allows for the possibility that there will be no structure in any of these series. The traditional martingale hypothesis, as in Section 2, implies that none of these series should have low dimensionality.

We first estimated the following equation for both the gold and silver series rates of return and for each of the daily, weekly, and biweekly time intervals

$$r_t = \beta_0 + \beta_1 r_{t-1} + u_t. \tag{4.1}$$

In Equation 4.1 we have $r_t = (p_t - p_{t-1})/p_{t-1}$, where p_t is the price of the asset at date t. According to the martingale hypothesis $\beta_0 = \beta_1 = 0$. According to Sims (1984) for short time intervals these regressions ought to have R^2 values near zero.

Table 14-1 reports the results of the estimations of Equation 4.1 for the various series.[6] We also examined the error structure of Equation 4.1 and tested for the possible presence of ARCH (Autoregressive Conditional Heteroskedastic) effects. The ARCH model is a nonlinear stochastic specification due to Engle (1982). It is often fitted to economic time-series when these series are observed to be quite volatile, see Engle and Bollerslev (1986). We tested for the presence of a general ARCH (p) process by obtaining the residuals from the AR (1) specification reported in Table 14-1, and running a regression of the squared residuals on a constant and the squared residuals lagged p times. Then nR^2 is the test statistic distributed as chi-square with p degrees of freedom, where n is the number of observations.

For the daily series p was found to be 12 for both gold and silver, since any additional lags did not noticeably improve the test statistic, they only affected the degrees of freedom. Similarly, p was found to be 6 for both weekly and biweekly series. Table 14-1 reports the results of these tests. In the Appendix to this chapter, Tables 14-A1 and 14-A2 present the maximum likelihood estimates of the ARCH models for the relevant series.

As expected, the results in Table 14-1 appear supportive of the martingale hypothesis. The finding of ARCH effects is also fairly common in financial time-series, see Engle and Bollerslev (1986). These results suggest that the returns on both gold and silver are fairly typical of financial data.

A. Correlation Dimension Estimates—Daily Data

We have already indicated that a certain amount of judgment is required to measure the correlation dimension. One must choose reasonable values

Table 14-1

AR(1) Results for Gold and Silver

r_t	β_0	β_1	R^2	A(6)	A(12)
Gold (D)	0.0004	−0.0606	0.0003	–	88.43
(S.E.)	(0.3199)	(0.0866)			
Silver (D)	0.0284	−0.0609	0.0008	–	51.43
(S.E.)	(0.1419)	(0.0793)			
Gold (W)	0.0026	0.0668	0.0035	50.24	–
(S.E.)	(0.0253)	(0.0045)			
Silver (W)	0.0046	−0.0284	0.0057	46.89	–
(S.E.)	(0.0264)	(0.0398)			
Gold (BW)	0.0029	0.1093	0.0053	39.06	–
(S.E.)	(0.0208)	(0.5843)			
Silver (BW)	0.0051	−0.0192	0.0084	51.34	–
(S.E.)	(0.0370)	(0.0567)			

Notes. In this table D = daily series, W = weekly series, BW = biweekly series. The columns beneath A(6) and A(12) give the results of ARCH tests for an ARCH (6) and an ARCH (12) process. These were computed as nR^2 from regressing the squared residuals of the AR (1) regressions given above on their own 6 lags or 12 lags, respectively. And n is the number of observations. The critical values of χ^2 with 6 and 12 degrees of freedom at the 5 percent level are 12.59 and 21.03, respectively.

for ε and M. For our data the relevant range[7] for values of ε was between $(0.9)^{20}$ and $(0.9)^{33}$.

For each embedding dimension one plots $\ln C^M(\varepsilon)$ against $\ln \varepsilon$. Over the relevant range of values of ε one calculates the slopes by ordinary least squares. In Table 14-2 the results of these calculations are reported for embedding dimensions $M = 5, 10, 15, 20, 25$. We stop at an embedding dimension of 25, since the system did not seem to use the extra freedom available to it when higher embedding dimensions were tried. It should also be noted that an embedding dimension of 25 is also the highest embedding dimension before the Kolmogorov entropy estimates started to be biased toward zero for the tent map with an extrapolation time of 10. At an embedding dimension of 25 both the gold and the silver series have a correlation dimension between 6 and 7. Column R of Table 14-2 reports the results for estimates from a computer-generated series of length 3,000 observations with the same mean and variance as the gold series. The computer-generated random numbers are higher dimensional than the actual asset rates of return.

We next carried out Brock's (1986) Residual Test. If a series is generated by deterministic chaos, then the residuals from a linear, or smooth non-linear transformation of the data, should yield the same correlation dimension as the original series. To implement this test we took the residuals from the ARCH (12) specification for both gold and silver series and calculated their correlation dimensions. As reported in Table 14-2, at an embedding dimension of 25 the correlation dimension estimates again turn out to be between 6 and 7. The daily series appears to pass Brock's Residual Test.

Scheinkman and LeBaron (1986) have proposed a "shuffle diagnostic" for chaos. One recreates the data series by sampling randomly with replacement from the data until you have a shuffled series of the same length as the original. The shuffled series should be considerably more random than the original data if the original data is strange. If the original data is not strange but rather is independently and identically distributed, then the shuffling will leave the correlation dimension unchanged since there was no structure present to be destroyed by shuffling.

To carry out the shuffle diagnostic we resampled from the ARCH residuals using a uniform pseudo-random number generator. If the ARCH procedure picked up the relevant structure, then the reshuffled data will have the same correlation dimension. In Table 14-2 estimates are reported for the typical reshuffled series. The dimension estimates are raised substantially.

Motivated by the methodology of "bootstrapping"[8] we attempted to generate an empirical distribution for the shuffle diagnostic. We performed repeated shuffling of the original series as well as for the ARCH

Table 14-2

Correlation Dimensions for Daily Data

M	G	S	R	ARCHG	ARCHS	SHG	SHS
5	1.11	2.01	3.15	1.25	1.13	2.85	3.01
10	2.45	3.91	5.42	2.23	3.58	5.12	5.25
15	3.83	5.32	8.91	4.51	4.91	7.01	6.77
20	5.41	6.31	11.52	5.82	6.22	9.51	9.81
25	6.31	6.34	13.48	6.65	6.71	11.27	10.59

Notes. M = embedding dimension, G = daily gold series, S = daily silver series, R = computer-generated (pseudo-) random numbers, ARCHG = residuals from ARCH (12) of the gold series, ARCHS = residuals from ARCH (12) of the silver series, SHG = reshuffled ARCHG series, SHS = reshuffled ARCHS series.

residuals. At an embedding dimension of 25 we performed 30 replications of each shuffle. For each of these 30 replications for both the original and the ARCH residuals, we calculated the correlation dimensions. The range of estimates thereby obtained is reported in Table 14-3. Evidently, at $M = 25$ all of the original estimates are below the estimates from the shuffled series. Since the intent of the bootstrap method is to permit confidence interval type statements, these results are strong. It seems that there is considerable structure remaining in the data even after use of the ARCH procedure.

B. Correlation Dimension Estimates— Weekly and Biweekly Data

To create the weekly and the biweekly time-series we took data from Wednesdays and from alternate Wednesdays, respectively. The results of the AR(1) regressions are reported in Table 14-1. As with the daily data these results appear to be consistent with the martingale hypothesis and with Sims's (1984) approach. It would appear from the results in Table 14-1 that even biweekly data might represent a "short" time interval in the sense of Sims (1984).

Table 14-4 presents the various correlation dimension estimates for both weekly and biweekly data. The results again indicate dimensionality between 6 and 7 and that such dimensionality is not accounted for by an ARCH structure. These series again seem to pass Brock's Residual Test. In Table 14-3 the outcomes of 30 replications for each series of the shuffle diagnostic are reported. For all cases the shuffled series were of higher dimensionality than the unshuffled series.[9]

The results of this analysis offers quite a clear pattern. Weekend effects are not responsible for the structures detected in the daily data. The data possess a structure that is somewhere between 6 and 7 dimensional. This structure is not accounted for by the ARCH procedure. The structure is as evident in the weekly and biweekly data as it was in the daily.

C. Kolmogorov Entropy Estimates

As previously indicated, we calculate the Grassberger and Procaccia (1983b) approximation to the Kolmogorov entropy, denoted K_2. Recall the interpretation of K_2. It measures how strange a time-series is. If a time-series is completely random then $K_2 = \infty$. If a time-series is completely smooth then $K_2 = 0$. Entropy measures the rate at which indistinguishable paths become distinguishable when the system is observed with only some finite level of accuracy. The lower the value of K_2 the more predictable the system is, at least in principle.

Table 14-3

Correlation Dimension (D) Estimates at M = 25

Series Name	Unshuffled D	Maximum Shuffled D	Minimum Shuffled D
		Daily Data	
G	6.31	11.44	9.23
S	6.34	11.71	9.12
ARCHG	6.65	12.01	9.45
ARCHS	6.71	11.35	9.43
		Weekly Data	
G	6.47	11.62	8.98
S	6.49	11.50	8.38
ARCHG	6.59	11.18	8.15
ARCHS	6.79	11.38	8.44
		Biweekly Data	
G	6.62	10.27	8.32
S	6.38	10.55	8.11
ARCHG	6.66	10.71	8.44
ARCHS	6.73	10.44	8.30

Notes. For each series we report the unshuffled dimension estimate as well as the maximum and minimum values obtained from 30 reshufflings of the data. G = gold series. S = Silver series. ARCHG = residuals from the ARCH (12) gold series for the daily data and from ARCH (6) gold series for the weekly and biweekly data. ARCHS = residuals from the ARCH (12) silver series for the daily data and from ARCH (6) silver series for the weekly and biweekly data.

Empirically, for daily data, for gold our estimate of K_2 is 0.15 ± 0.07. For daily silver data the value of K_2 is 0.19 ± 0.09. These values are not too different from each other and their ranges overlap. For weekly data we get that K_2 is 0.20 ± 0.04 for gold and 0.22 ± 0.05 for silver. The corresponding estimates for the biweekly data were 0.24 ± 0.03 for gold and 0.24 ± 0.05 for silver.

A variety of comparison series were examined for K_2. Comparison with Figure 14-1 shows that at an embedding dimension of 25 the empirical findings are similar to a tent map at an extrapolation time ranging from 3 to 6. They are lower than the tent map iterated tenfold. We also examined iterated versions of the Hénon map and the logistic map. Their behavior was similar to the iterated tent map in two respects. Higher numbers of iterations led to higher estimates for K_2. With 3,000 observations the bias toward zero starts to take effect at an embedding dimension of about 25.

Table 14-4

Correlation Dimensions for Weekly and Biweekly Data

M	G	S	R	ARCHG	ARCHS	SHG	SHS
			Weekly				
5	1.43	1.56	3.12	1.14	1.07	2.71	2.63
10	3.49	3.83	5.70	2.28	2.30	5.03	4.95
15	3.99	4.55	9.50	4.27	3.81	7.12	6.91
20	5.41	5.95	12.11	5.78	5.51	9.11	9.23
25	6.47	6.49	14.01	6.59	6.79	10.80	11.01
			Biweekly				
5	1.01	1.64	3.01	1.21	1.71	2.65	3.01
10	2.72	3.08	6.25	2.81	3.01	4.93	5.01
15	4.31	4.92	10.01	4.71	5.31	6.91	6.83
20	5.82	5.37	12.45	5.61	5.85	8.12	8.32
25	6.62	6.38	13.75	6.66	6.73	9.48	10.31

Notes. M = embedding dimension, G = gold series, S = silver series, R = computer-generated (pseudo-) random numbers, ARCHG = residuals from ARCH (6) of gold series, ARCHS = residuals from ARCH (6) of silver series, SHG = reshuffled ARCHG series, SHS = reshuffled ARCHS series.

In consideration of the dimension, shuffling provided a useful diagnostic. Shuffling did not work so well for the Kolmogorov entropy estimates. It led to numerically sensitive results. Small changes in ε and the embedding dimension produced fairly large changes in the estimates for K_2.

The K_2 estimates bolster the results of the correlation dimension estimates. Once again the patterns are consistent with the chaos interpretation of these time-series. These findings may also be consistent with some nonlinear stochastic processes.

5. Conclusion

In this study we examined certain properties of the rates of return on gold and silver from the mid-1970s to the mid-1980s. Using familiar econometric techniques it was shown that, as expected, neither series caused one to reject the martingale hypothesis. We examined daily, weekly, and biweekly series.

While the martingale hypothesis is not rejected by the standard techniques, this result was shown to be misleading. By estimation of the correlation dimension and the Kolmogorov entropy, evidence of structures not captured in the usual approach was found. This evidence calls into question Sims's (1984) rationalization of the empirical success of the martingale hypothesis.[10] Our evidence is consistent with certain of the earliest tests of the efficient markets hypothesis.[11] Overall there appears to be some sort of nonlinear process of between 6 and 7 dimensions, which generated the observed gold and silver rates of return. Such a structure might be rationalizable within the Lucas-Brock framework, but not in the currently available versions.[12] The findings seem to be robust. They require a satisfactory theoretical explanation.

Acknowledgment

We would like to thank Richard Arnott, William Brock, Roger Farmer, David Fowler, Clive Granger, and Jose Scheinkman for valuable discussions. Lars Hansen's criticisms of an earlier draft were extremely helpful. The comments by the referees are appreciated. This research was partly supported by a grant from the Research Excellence Program of the University of Guelph. We are grateful to all of these individuals, but none of them are responsible for any remaining deficiencies in our work.

Notes

1 "The behavior . . . seems to leave no doubt that past weekly returns help predict future ones . . . Further it seems that most of the variation on weekly returns is coming from nonlinearities as opposed to randomness. Or more moderately, the data is not incompatible with a theory where most of the variation would come from nonlinearities as opposed to randomness and is *not* compatible with a theory that predicts that the returns are generated by independent random variables." Scheinkman and LeBaron (1986).

2 The consumer has constant relative risk-aversion and the joint distribution of consumption and returns is lognormal.

3 A particularly simple ad hoc example is as follows: Let $X_{t+1} = 4 X_t(1 - X_t)$ and let $P_{t+1} = P_t + (X_t - 0.5)$. Simulate this two-equation system starting with $X_1 \in (0, 1)$ and $P_1 = 100$. On the simulated data test $(P_{t+1} - P_t) = \alpha_0 + \alpha_1(P_t - P_{t-1}) + \varepsilon_t$. One will be unable to reject $\alpha_0 = \alpha_1 = 0$ and the R^2 will be very close to zero. However this example is anything but unpredictable. This example is discussed more fully in Frank and Stengos (1988). Also consider endnote 12.

4 For an intuitive discussion of the meaning of "dimension" see Frank and Stengos (1988). Familiar smooth examples include: a point is zero-dimensional, a line is one-dimensional, a plane is two-dimensional. These objects retain their dimensionality even when embedded in less restricted spaces, say R^5.

5 It is also termed "Kolmogorov-Sinai invariant," "measure theoretic entropy," or sometimes simply "entropy."

6 We also looked at longer AR specifications. All had R^2 values very close to zero.

7 A more detailed presentation of our calculations can be found in an earlier version of this chapter, which circulated as Discussion Paper # 1986-13, Economics Department, University of Guelph.

8 See for example Bickel and Friedman (1981).

9 Sims (1984) notes that in moving to longer time intervals one is also typically moving to fewer observations. One does not want the number of observations to be responsible for one's empirical results. We therefore also conducted the analysis for shorter daily series consisting of the last 600 observations for both gold and silver series. This length of series agrees with the actual length of the weekly data series. The correlation dimension estimates obtained from these shorter daily series were not noticeably different from the original daily series. The number of observations is not responsible for our findings.

10 In his discussion Sims (1984) takes one week as an illustrative example of a small time interval. Our results show that if Sims's theory works it must be on a scale in which a small time interval is less than one day. Over large time intervals Sims (1984) neither predicts nor precludes the presence of structure. Sims takes a year as an illustrative example of a large time interval.

11 "... it is possible to devise trading schemes based on very short-term (preferably intra-day but at most daily) price swings that will on average outperform buy-and-hold," Fama (1970). Fama's discussion is concerned with linear dependence and he argues that trading costs make such schemes unprofitable due to frequent trading costs. Present analysis indicates that nonlinear dependence may be more to the point.

12 Take the model in Brock (1982) and replace the stochastic shock process that affects the production functions by a chaotic deterministic process. Agents knowing this would be unable to obtain excess utility of profits despite the advance knowledge of the changes. Such an approach focuses attention on the question of what economic forces induce the chaotic process in the first place.

References

Barnett, W., and P. Chen. "The Aggregation-Theoretic Monetary Aggregates Are Chaotic and Have Strange Attractors," in W. Barnett, E. Berndt, and H. White, eds., *Dynamic Econometric Modelling*. Cambridge: Cambridge University Press, 1988.

Bickel, P., and D. Friedman. "Some Asymptotic Theory for the Bootstrap." *Annals of Statistics* (1981) 9:1296–1317.

Brealey, R., and S. Myers. *Principles of Corporate Finance*, 2d ed. New York: McGraw-Hill Inc., 1984.

Brock, W. "Asset Prices in a Production Economy," in J. J. McCall, ed., *The Economics of Information and Uncertainty*. Chicago: The University of Chicago Press, 1982.

Brock, W. "Distinguishing Random and Deterministic Systems: Abridged Version." *Journal of Economic Theory* (1986) 40:68–195.

Brock, W., and W. D. Dechert. "Theorems on Distinguishing Deterministic and Random Systems," in W. Barnett, E. Berndt, and H. White, eds., *Dynamic Econometric Modelling*. Cambridge: Cambridge University Press, 1988.

Brock, W., and C. Sayers. "Is the Business Cycle Characterized by Deterministic Chaos?" *Journal of Monetary Economics* (1988) 22:71–90.

Broomhead, D. S., and G. P. King. "Extracting Qualitative Dynamics from Experimental Data." *Physica D* (1986) 20:217–236.

Cohen, A., and I. Procaccia. "Computing the Kolmogorov Entropy from Time Signals of Dissipative and Conservative Dynamical Systems." *Physical Review A* (1985) 31:1872–1882.

Devaney, R. L. *An Introduction to Chaotic Dynamical Systems*. Menlo Park, CA: Benjamin/Cummings Publishing, 1986.

Eckmann, J. P., and D. Ruelle. "Ergodic Theory of Chaos and Strange Attractors." *Reviews of Modern Physics* (1985) 57:617–656.

Engle, R. F. "Autoregressive Conditional Heteroscedasticity with Estimates of the Variance of U.K. Inflation." *Econometrica* (1982) 50:987–1008.

Engle, R. F., and T. Bollerslev. "Modelling the Persistence of Conditional Variances." *Econometric Reviews* (1986) 5:1–50.

Fama, E. "Efficient Capital Markets: A Review of Theory and Empirical Work." *Journal of Finance* (1970) 25:383–417.

Frank, M., and T. Stengos. "Chaotic Dynamics in Economic Time-Series." *Journal of Economic Surveys* (1988) 2:103–133.

Grassberger, P., and I. Procaccia. "Measuring the Strangeness of Strange Attractors." *Physica D* (1983a) 9:189–208.

Grassberger, P., and I. Procaccia. "Estimation of the Kolmogorov Entropy from a Chaotic Signal." *Physical Review A*, (1983b) 28: 2591–2593.

Guckenheimer, J., and P. Holmes. *Nonlinear Oscillations, Dynamical Systems, and Bifurcations of Vector Fields* (Second Printing, Revised and Corrected.) (New York: Springer-Verlag, 1986.

Hansen, L. P., and K. Singleton. "Stochastic Consumption, Risk Aversion, and the Temporal Behavior of Asset Returns." *Journal of Political Economy* (1983) 91:249–265.

Hess, J. D. *The Economics of Organization*. Amsterdam: North-Holland, 1983.

Lasota, A., and M. C. Mackey. *Probabilistic Properties of Deterministic Systems*. Cambridge: Cambridge University Press, 1985.

Lucas, R. E., Jr. "Asset Prices in an Exchange Economy." *Econometrica* (1978) 64:1426–1445.

Petersen, K. *Ergodic Theory*. Cambridge: Cambridge University Press, 1983.

Ramsey, J., and H. Yuan. "The Statistical Properties of Dimension Calculations Using Small Data Sets." R. R. #87-20, C. V. Starr Center for Applied Economics, New York University, 1987.

Samuelson, P. A. "Proof That Properly Anticipated Prices Fluctuate Randomly." *Industrial Management Review* (1965) 6:41–49.

Scheinkman, J. A., and B. LeBaron. "Nonlinear Dynamics and Stock Returns." Manuscript, Department of Economics, University of Chicago, 1986.

Sims, C. A. "martingale-Like Behavior of Prices and Interest Rates." Discussion Paper No. 205, Department of Economics, University of Minnesota, Minneapolis, 1984.

Takens, F. "Detecting Strange Attractors in Turbulence," in D. Rand and L. Young, eds., *Dynamical Systems and Turbulence, Warwick 1980*. Berlin: Springer-Verlag, 1980.

Takens, F. "Invariants Related to Dimension and Entropy." *Proceedings of the Thirteenth Coloquio Brasileino de Matematica*, 1983.

Appendix

Table 14-A1
ARCH Results from the Table 14-1 Estimation for Gold

	Gold (D)	Standard Error	Gold (W)	Standard Error	Gold (BW)	Standard Error
β_0	0.0002	(0.0004)	0.0016	(0.0014)	0.0019	(0.0021)
β_1	−0.0473	(0.0513)	0.0568	(0.0413)	0.1093	(0.5736)
α_0	0.0447	(0.0320)	0.1344	(0.0420)	0.2732	(0.0586)
α_1	0.0788	(0.0331)	0.1677	(0.0430)	0.0	—
α_2	0.0621	(0.0342)	0.0446	(0.0473)	0.0036	(0.0064)
α_3	0.0741	(0.0574)	0.0	—	0.1180	(0.0606)
α_4	0.0198	(0.0318)	0.1250	(0.0356)	0.0828	(0.0668)
α_5	0.0	—	0.0101	(0.0431)	0.2577	(0.0589)
α_6	0.0214	(0.3281)	0.0320	(0.0444)	0.0132	(0.0523)
α_7	0.0248	(0.4443)				
α_8	0.1632	(0.0317)				
α_9	0.0004	(0.0321)				
α_{10}	0.0581	(0.0255)				
α_{11}	0.0247	(0.0322)				
α_{12}	0.0345	(0.0333)				
log L	2790.08		1265.64		563.81	

Note. The α terms represent the coefficients of the ARCH covariance structure. Lower bounds of zero are used. A zero entry means that the model included the corresponding variable but the coefficient reached its lower bound of zero. The ARCH model following Engle (1982) is given below. Let X_i be the vector of explanatory variables for the dependent variable and let the error term $\varepsilon_i \sim N(0, h_t)$. Then $y_t = X_t^T \gamma + \varepsilon_t$ and $h_i = \alpha_0 +$

$$\sum_{j=1}^{12} \alpha_j \varepsilon_{t-j}^2.$$

Table 14-A2

ARCH Results from the Table 14-1 Estimation for Silver

	Silver (D)	Standard Error	Silver (W)	Standard Error	Silver (BW)	Standard Error
β_0	0.002	(0.0007)	0.0036	(0.0026)	0.0041	(0.0041)
β_1	−0.1109	(0.3148)	−0.0284	(0.0398)	−0.0172	(0.0567)
α_0	0.0026	(0.0005)	0.2420	(0.0447)	0.2356	(0.0582)
α_1	0.1833	(0.0333)	0.0774	(0.0416)	0.1049	(0.0432)
α_2	0.0145	(0.0345)	0.0169	(0.0423)	0.0034	(0.0578)
α_3	0.0866	(0.0415)	0.0394	(0.0514)	0.0152	(0.0073)
α_4	0.0221	(0.0367)	0.0179	(0.0053)	0.2805	(0.0573)
α_5	0.0317	(0.0327)	0.0097	(0.0035)	0.0	—
α_6	0.0	—	0.0073	(0.0041)	0.0053	(0.0054)
α_7	0.0671	(0.0324)				
α_8	0.0413	(0.0334)				
α_9	0.0729	(0.0354)				
α_{10}	0.0368	(0.0388)				
α_{11}	0.0801	(0.0324)				
α_{12}	0.0	—				
log L	5124.98		3253.41		1121.21	

PART IV

MONEY MARKETS EVIDENCE

15

A LOW-DIMENSIONAL FRACTAL ATTRACTOR IN THE FOREIGN-EXCHANGE MARKETS?

By Dominique M. Guillaume

1. Introduction

Recently, nonlinear dynamic systems known as deterministic chaos attracted new interest among economists [see Boldrin and Woodford (1990), Brock and Dechert (1991), Grandmont (1992), De Grauwe and Dewachter (1993)]. With only a few degrees of freedom—i.e., a low-dimensional[1] fractal attractor—such systems can indeed mimic a stochastic behavior and thus reconcile the classical deterministic view with the apparent unpredictability and randomness observed in real-world data [Mirowski (1990)]. These theoretical developments are promising as they provide a natural extension to traditional low-dimensional macroeconomic models but have so far been limited to the analysis of the conditions of emergence of multiple and unstable equilibria.[2] Ultimately, their empirical relevance rests on findings that detect chaotic behavior in real world data.

A second and parallel source of interest for the investigation of chaos in economic time series comes from the empirical literature on financial markets. It is by now widely accepted that financial markets are nonlinear [see, e.g., Hsieh (1989)] and do not follow a simple random walk although they seem rather unpredictable with global models [see, e.g., Diebold and Nason (1990)]. On the other hand, the more sophisticated ARCH-like processes are not satisfactory, as illustrated by the recent effort by Ding, Granger, and Engle (1993) to adapt the ARCH-model to better fit the data. The algorithms developed in the chaos literature to compute global statistics or invariants—such as the fractal dimension, the spectrum of Lyapunov exponents, and the Kolmogorov-Sinaï entropy[3]—provide an interesting alternative characterization of the financial markets. Yet again, a breakthrough of chaos in the time-series literature requires convincing evidence of chaotic behavior in the data.

A number of studies[4] have been aimed at detecting the presence of chaos in several economic time series. Regrettably, the direct application of techniques originally developed in physics presents a number of problems such as the fact they deal with relatively short and noisy data sets, as is rightly put forward by Ramsey et al. (1989, 1990, 1992). More specifically, the studies referred to above usually share the following problems: spurious short-term autocorrelation is taken into account when the proper time delay is not computed; the number of data points is too small to infer the presence of a low-dimensional attractor even if the estimated dimension seemed to be lower than a random permutation of the data; the plots of the dimension estimates in function of the size of the radii are not displayed, so the saturation of the dimension estimates found in tables are often misleading; empirical evidence of chaos is not checked by the simultaneous use of different techniques; and no stochastic component is taken into account.

This chapter extends on the existing literature in that the methodology deals with these problems. In particular, the presence of noise is explicitly taken into account and the methodology is applied to a very large data set consisting of both foreign-exchange returns and their absolute values. We compute the fractal dimension of the foreign-exchange markets, which gives a lower bound to the number of degrees of freedom of the system.[5] This can thus be considered as a very general test of adequacy of (low-dimensional) macroeconomic modeling. Furthermore, it is the first step in the empirical investigation of chaos as it provides necessary information for the computation of the spectrum of Lyapunov exponents.[6] The methodology presented is suited to cope with reasonably small stochastic noise. In order to tackle the small sample problem, we used intradaily returns over a long period of time.[7] We also applied the algorithms on the absolute values of the exchange-rate returns as a measure of the volatility to find whether the nonlinearities present in the second moment could be due to the presence of a deterministic attractor. Our main thrust of findings is the absence of a low-dimensional attractor both for the foreign-exchange returns and their absolute values. This questions both the practical adequacy of economic modeling based on chaos theory and the empirical relevance of the chaotic algorithms for the characterization of the dynamics of the foreign-exchange markets.

The chapter is organized as follows: In the next section, we discuss our methodology. We first present the time-delay and the singular value decomposition methods of reconstruction of the embedding phase space. We then discuss the implementation of the Grassberger-Procaccia algorithm to compute the correlation dimension. Then Section 3 presents our data set and results. Section 4 concludes the chapter.

2. Methodology

Reconstruction of the Embedding Phase Space

Assume that the foreign-exchange markets are described by m variables $x_0, x_1, ..., x_{m-1}$. Each variable x_k generates over time an n-vector $x_k(1), ..., x_k(n)$. Assume that the dynamics is described by the following ergodic[8] system of first-order-difference equations:

$$Y(t) = F(Y(t-1)) \qquad t=2, ..., n \tag{1}$$

where $Y(t)$ is the set $\{x_0(t), x_1(t), ..., x_{m-1}(t)\}$ and F is a smoothly differentiable nonlinear function. These m vectors span a space called phase space. Assume further that the trajectory of the system converges to an invariant subset of the phase space called attractor.

The embedding theorem [Sauer et al. (1991), Packard et al. (1980), Takens (1981)] proves that the attractor can be reconstructed without a priori knowledge of the nature of the variables or the functional form of the difference equations. The measurement in time of a single variable, say x, suffices for the characterization of the dynamics of the system evolving in a multivariable space.

Using the time delay method [Takens (1981)], a set of m variables can be constructed from a single time series. These variables are obtained by shifting the original time series by a fixed time lag τ, $\tau \in N$. We thus have the following matrix:

$$X = \{x(t), x(t+\tau), ..., x(t+\tau(m-1))\} \quad t=1, ..., n-(m-1)\tau \tag{2}$$

Takens proved that for $m \geq 2D + 1$ (where D is the dimension of the attractor) the phase space spanned by this set of m variables will be an embedding, i.e., it will be topologically equivalent to the original one and therefore have the same dimension and Lyapunov exponents. Unfortunately, the theorem does not specify how to determine the different parameters in Equation 2. First, we do not know a priori what is the dimension of the system under study. Besides, a much-overlooked problem[9] is that Takens does not give any indication regarding the choice of the proper time delay τ). In practice, to avoid any spurious observation of correlation, this time delay should correspond to the first zero of the autocorrelation function or, better, to the first zero of the mutual information function [Fraser and Swinney (1986)]. This respectively guarantees the linear and general independence of the subsequent elements of the matrix X but can drastically reduce the number of observations.

Another empirical problem is that for a more realistic description of the dynamics of the foreign-exchange markets, Equation 1 should replaced by

$$Y(t) = F(Y(t-1)) + \varepsilon(t) \tag{3}$$

where ε is a stochastic term relatively small with respect to the size of the attractor and $E(\varepsilon(t)/Y(t-1))=0$. According to Equation 3, the seemingly random behavior of the foreign-exchange markets is mainly due to the nonlinear self-interaction of different types of agents whose reactions can rapidly amplify the effect of any external shock or news.[10] In the case of intradaily foreign-exchange rates, empirical evidence indeed shows that much of the dynamics of the markets cannot be directly attributed to the presence of news (Goodhart, 1989). Another interpretation of Equation 3 is that, contrary to previous works like the seminal paper of Meese and Rogoff (1983), it provides a very general test for the adequacy of (low-dimensional) macroeconomic models, as it does not rely on any functional form. Finally, besides economic intuition, another motivation for the use of the formulation given in Equation 3 is that a small noise component can result in misleading negative conclusions about the presence of a low-dimensional attractor.[11]

We are, however, only interested in the underlying deterministic system whose dimension gives us an indication of the number of degrees of freedom of the attractor. In order to reduce the effect of small stochastic shocks without affecting the true dynamics of the system, different filters have recently been proposed.

A first very efficient method was suggested by Schreiber and Grassberger (1991, 1993). The phase space is first reconstructed using g delay and k advance coordinates. Each measurement $x(t)$ is then replaced by the average value of this coordinate over points in its neighborhood in this phase space. Formally, we have

$$W = (x(t-k), ..., x(t+g)) \quad t=k+1, ..., n-g \tag{4}$$

Let W_t be the t-th row $(x(t-k), ..., x(t+g))$ of the matrix W. For each W_t, let $S(W_t,\varepsilon)$ be the sphere with center W_t and radius ε, i.e.

$$S(W_t,\varepsilon) = \{W_j \mid d(W_t, W_j) \le \varepsilon\} \tag{5}$$

where W_j is the j-th row $(x(j-k), ..., x(j+g))$ of the matrix W and the distance d is defined as follows:

$$d(W_t, W_j) = max\{\mid x(j-k) - x(t-k)\mid, ..., \mid x(j+g) - x(t+g)\mid\} \tag{6}$$

We then replace the present coordinate $x(t)$ by its mean value in $S(W_t,\varepsilon)$,

$$x(t)^{corr} = \frac{1}{\mid S(W_t,\varepsilon)\mid} \sum_{W_j \in S(W_t,\varepsilon)} x(j) \tag{7}$$

where $x(j)$ is the $k+1$'th coordinate of the vector W_j.

This nonlinear filter is optimal in the sense that it integrates both past and future information, i.e., along the stable and unstable directions. The phase space is then reconstructed using the time-delay method with the corrected time series, as in Equation 2.

An alternative way to both filter out the noise and reconstruct the attractor is based on the singular value decomposition (SVD) introduced in nonlinear dynamics by Broomhead and King (1986a, 1986b). The main idea of the SVD is to transform the embedding space into an equivalent space whose coordinates are linearly independent (orthogonal). Let C be the covariance matrix of the matrix X defined in Equation 2 [see Broomhead and King (1986a)]:

$$C = X^T . X \quad \in \Re^{mxm} \tag{8}$$

C is real symmetric, positive-definite and can be transformed into a diagonal matrix Λ by a series of rotations that can be expressed as:

$$\Lambda^2 = E^t (.C.E = (X.E)^T (X.E) \tag{9}$$

where $\Lambda^2 = \{\delta_{ij}.\lambda_i^2; i,j=1, ..., m\}$ and $E \in \Re^{mxm}$. The elements λ_i^2 on the diagonal of Λ^2, usually ordered by magnitude, are called eigenvalues. The vectors e_i forming the columns of the matrix E are the corresponding eigenvectors. The matrix $X.E$ represents the trajectory matrix projected onto the basis $\{e_i\}$. The choice of $\{e_i\}$ as a basis for the projection is optimal in the sense that it makes the columns of the trajectory matrix independent. This absence of correlation between the components of the trajectory matrix allows us to take a time delay $\tau = 1$ in Equation 2 for the construction of $X(t)$.

Λ and E can be directly obtained from the singular value decomposition of the trajectory matrix:

$$X = Z.\Lambda.E^T \tag{10}$$

where $Z \in \Re^{nxm}$ and $E \in \Re^{mxm}$ are referred to as the left and right singular vectors of X, while the elements of the diagonal matrix $\Lambda \in \Re^{mxm}$ are called the associated singular values.

To filter out the noise, Broomhead and King (1986a) suggest to divide the embedding space into a deterministic subspace where the orbits would stay in the absence of noise, and a stochastic subspace, in which the motion is due only to noise. They claim that from the spectrum of eigenvalues the dimension of the deterministic subspace d can be determined by identifying the eigenvalues situated above a "noise level" corresponding to a flat tail in the spectrum of eigenvalues.

Assuming that the d significant directions have been more or less correctly identified, we can split the matrix Λ as follows:

$$\Lambda = \Lambda^* + \Lambda^\circ \tag{11}$$

where Λ^* is obtained from Λ by putting the $m - d$ eigenvalues belonging to the noise floor equal to zero, and Λ° is also obtained from Λ by putting the d significant eigenvalues equal to zero. Replacing Λ by Λ^* or Λ° in Equation 10, we obtain, respectively, the deterministic and stochastic components of the trajectory matrix, namely:

$$X^* = Z.\Lambda^*.E^T \qquad \in \Re^{nxm} \tag{12}$$

$$X^\circ = Z.\Lambda^\circ.E^T \qquad \in \Re^{nxm} \tag{13}$$

Adding Equations 12 and 13, we can verify that

$$X = X^* + X^\circ \tag{14}$$

Since we are interested in the d deterministic directions, we can project the trajectory matrix onto the deterministic subspace spanned by the eigenvectors corresponding to the eigenvalues above the noise floor as follows:

$$\underline{X} = X^*.E \qquad \in \Re^{nxd} \tag{15}$$

The columns of $\underline{X}$ are often called principal components. As mentioned by Albano et al. (1988), the major drawbacks of the SVD are the arbitrariness of the choice of both the so-called window length m in Equation 2 and the number of deterministic directions d. Recently, Fraedrich and Wang (1993) showed how to bypass these problems by simply "reembedding" the projected trajectory matrix $\underline{X}$ with the time-delay method. The reembedding space is thus obtained as follows:

$$K = \{\underline{X}(t), \underline{X}(t+\tau), ..., \underline{X}(t+\tau(M-1))\} \qquad K \in \mathfrak{R}^{nx(Mxd)} \qquad (16)$$

The topological characteristics of the reembedding space are independent of the choice of the window-length m in Equation 2, the number d of deterministic directions in Equation 12, the reembedding dimension M and the time-lag τ in Equation 16.

Computation of the Fractal Dimension

On the basis of the reconstructed (re)embedding phase space, we then compute the fractal dimension of the attractor by means of the correlation dimension algorithm proposed by Grassberger and Procaccia (1983a, b). The correlation integral is defined in the M-dimensional reconstructed space as the probability of finding a pair of vectors whose distance is not larger than r:

$$C(M, r) = \frac{1}{n(n-l)} \times \sum_{i} \sum_{j} I(r - |Y(i) - Y(j)|) \qquad (17)$$
$$|i-j| \geq \tau^{\circ}$$

where $I(x)$ is the Indicator Function and is valued at 1 if the distance between the two points $Y(i)$ and $Y(j)$ in the M-dimensional space is less than r, and at 0 if the distance is greater; τ° is the correlation time due to the dynamics [Theiler (1986)]. According to Grassberger and Proccacia (1983a), the correlation dimension D_2 is derived from

$$D_2 = \lim_{r \to 0} D_2(M,r) \qquad (18)$$

for sufficiently large M, where $D_2(M,r)$ is the slope of $C(M, r)$:

$$D_2(M,r) = \frac{d \ln C(M,r)}{d \ln(r)} \qquad (19)$$

In other words, for r sufficiently small and for M sufficiently large, the slope of the correlation integral will saturate to the correlation dimension. In practice, one should observe a "plateau" on the plot of the correlation dimension in function of the radius r for values of M greater than m, m being an embedding in the above-defined sense. Note that this is a stronger requirement than having lower dimension estimates than those obtained by a random permutation of the data [see, for example, Frank and Stengos (1989)]. We use the sup-norm as in the above nonlinear filter to compute the distance between points in Equation 17 and the fast box-counting algorithm proposed by Grassberger (1990). To avoid any spurious correlation estimate, the correlation time τ° was set equal to the time-lag τ in the case of the time-delay reconstruction and to the embedding dimension m in the case of the SVD method.

A largely discussed practical problem[12] of the Grassberger-Procaccia algorithm is the minimum number of data points n_{min} needed for estimating the dimension of an attractor of dimension D. Without going into the details of the arguments, Eckmann and Ruelle (1992) suggest that

$$n_{min} > 10^{(D/2)(log(1/e))} \tag{20}$$

where $\rho = r/d \ll 1$, with r defined as above and d being the diameter of the reconstructed attractor. ρ is usually taken to equal 0.1 but can be small as 0.001 in our case. Therefore, using decimal logarithms, one easily notices that no dimension estimates higher than 2–6 can be obtained with daily data that corresponds to the estimates usually obtained.[13] This relativizes previous findings of a low-dimensional attractor [see, for example, Peters (1989, 1991), Scheinkman and LeBaron (1989), Blank (1991), DeCoster and Mitchell (1991), Frank and Stengos (1989)] and clearly points out the need for a sufficiently large data set.

3. Results

Data

In order to detect the presence of a low-dimensional fractal attractor, a time series should have the following properties: (1) it should be sampled at fixed time intervals; (2) to capture fine structure, the sampling frequency should be as large as possible though not too large, to avoid the problem of noise as detailed below; (3) to be representative of the structure of the system, it should cover a sufficiently long time period; (4) the time series should be stationary; (5) finally, it should have a sufficient number of data points as derived in the above section.

Our data set is composed of intradaily foreign-exchange-rate returns obtained from Olsen & Associates at constant time intervals for the USD/DEM, USD/BPD, USD/JPY, USD/FRF.[14] The main source of this data set is the interbank spot prices published by Reuters in a multiple contributors page (the FXFX page). This covers the market worldwide and 24 hours a day. However, those prices are quotations of bid and ask prices and not actual trading prices. Furthermore, they are irregularly sampled and therefore termed as tick-by-tick prices.

In order to meet the conditions outlined above, we took equally time-spaced changes of the average of bid/ask quoted prices for a period of six years from the 1/1/1987 to 12/31/1992.[15] The sampling frequency chosen is equal to 15, 30, and 60 minutes, yielding respectively approximately 294,000, 147,000, and 73,500 data points. The data set of other studies using intradaily data such as Tata and Vassilicos (1991) usually present the shortcoming that the time-span of their data is very short (one week) although they have a large data set. We use the linear interpolation method to obtain price values within a data hole or any interval between ticks as in Müller et al. (1990). Alternative methods such as taking the previous ticks do not yield significantly different results. Outliers such as 100 times the normal price were filtered out using the low-pass filter described in the appendix of Dacorogna et al. (1993b).

We took 15 minutes as the minimum sampling interval to avoid the different possible sources of noise such as the transmission delays or different trading habits as described in Müller et al. (1990). This problem of noise is most obvious from the spurious negative first-order correlation one observes for the smaller time intervals [Goodhart and Figliuoli (1991); Dacorogna et al. (1993b); Bollerslev and Domowitz (1993)]. Besides irregular spacing, this is another reason for not using tick-by-tick data, as very short-term correlation would make the results spurious. Finally, at higher frequencies, the size of the spread becomes significant relative to the size of the price changes so that the uncertainty about the real value of the transaction prices rises significantly. Indeed, banks frequently skew the spread toward a more favorable price, to offset their position. In that context, the bid (or the ask) price acts as a pure dummy. Therefore, on average the best approximation of the transaction price will be the average of the bid and ask price rather than the bid or the ask series. This skewness of the spread is also probably the reason behind the discreteness of quoted spreads (5, 7, 10, or 15 basis points) [Bollerslev and Melvin (1993)].

Formally, the intradaily returns are defined as

$$R_{id}(t) = 100(X(t) - X(t-1)) \tag{21}$$

where $X(t)$ is the average of the bid and ask log prices $(logP_{bid}(t) + logP_{ask}(t))/2$ and 100 is a scaling constant so that $R_{id}(t)$ is expressed in percentage.

In order to avoid a too large amount of linear interpolations, we exclude the weekends (from Friday 20:30 GMT to Sunday 22:30 GMT) and certain holidays when all the big markets are closed. The time scale can therefore be considered as a business time scale. We argue that the choice of this time scale rather than the physical time scale does not negatively affect our results. Indeed, the omitted data points cannot be the source of the structure of the system. However, one could consider taking alternative time scales such as the deseasonalized time (θ) proposed in Dacorogna et al. (1993).

We took the absolute values of the intradaily returns as a measure of the volatility. A justification for the separate analysis of the volatility comes from the fact that they have different empirical distributions [see, e.g., Dacorogna et al. (1993)]. Although similar results can be obtained with the squared returns, it follows from Ding et al. (1993) that the absolute values of the returns is a more accurate measure of the volatility process.

Results

Three different methods were used for the reconstruction of the attractor. First, we used the time-delay method described in Equation 2 with a time-lag τ equal to the first zero of the autocorrelation function. The same time-delay method was then applied on the filtered time series using Equations 4 and 7. As suggested by Schreiber (1993), we took a value of 3, 4, and 5 for the time-delay k and set it equal to time-advance g in Equation 4. In Equation 7, the size of the neighborhood was fixed to 10 or 20 neighbors. Finally, we applied the SVD and the reembedding technique described by Equations 12, 15, and 16. A window size m of 50 was taken as in Broomhead and King (1986a). Figures 15-1 and 15-2 show the spectrum of eigenvalues for the USD/DEM intradaily returns and their absolute values. The frequency is one hour. Although we do not present them here to save space, similar figures were obtained for other frequencies and for the other currencies. It is interesting to note that the spectrum is almost flat so that no distinct noise floor can be observed on either of the two figures, with the exception of the first eigenvalue for the absolute values of the returns. This is due to the high autocorrelation observed in the volatility [see, e.g., Dacorogna et al. (1993)]. Those figures already suggest that no deterministic subspace can be distinguished. This is further confirmed by the spectrum of the first eigenvectors (Figures 15-3 and 15-4), which clearly correspond to a decomposition of the different modes of the system analog to a Fourier decomposition. Indeed, the spectra of eigenvectors of higher order correspond to modes of higher order, whereas for a chaotic process with some small stochastic noise one would notice that from some higher order on, the spectrum has a noisy shape. On the basis of those graphics, we chose a number of deterministic directions d in Equation 12 equal to 1 or 5 and then reembedded the obtained manifold.

Figure 15-1

Spectrum of Eigenvalues for the USD/DEM Intradaily Returns

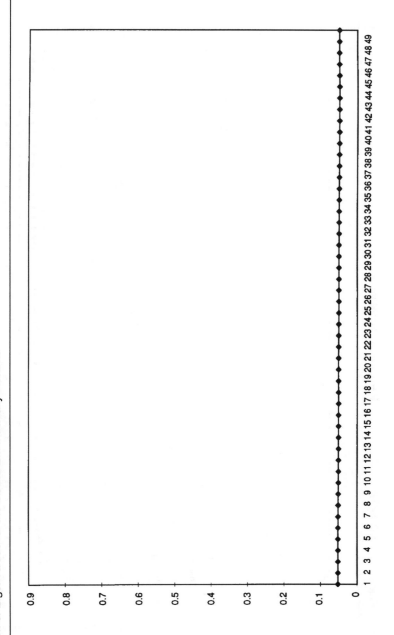

Figure 15-2

Spectrum of Eigenvalues for the USD/DEM Intradaily Returns in Absolute Value

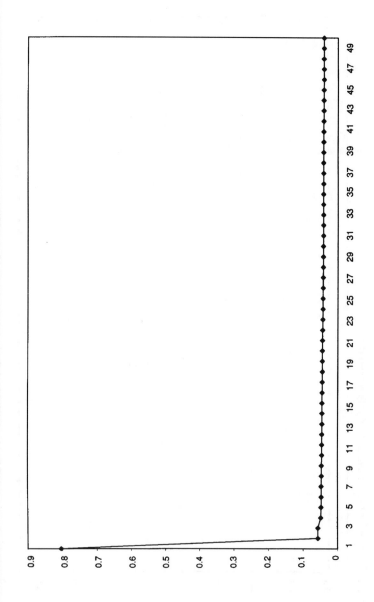

Figure 15-3

Spectrum of the First Eigenvectors for the USD/DEM Intradaily Returns

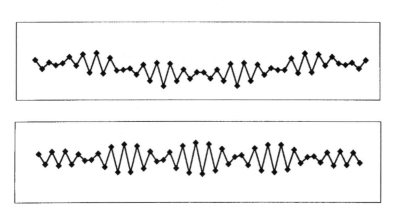

On the basis of the reconstructed attractors, we then computed the correlation integral defined in Equation 17 and the correlation dimension defined in Equation 18 as shown in Figures 15-5 and 15-6 for the intradaily returns, and Figures 15-7 and 15-8 for the absolute value of the intradaily returns for the USD/DEM at the one hour frequency. The reconstruction method used was the SVD and reembedding technique. To spare spaces, we do not present graphics of the results using the first two reconstruction methods that yield similar results quite consistently [Destexhe et al. (1988)]. Similar results were also obtained for the other currencies at all frequencies. Contrary to a clearly chaotic system, no distinguishable plateau or saturation of the correlation dimension can be observed on the figures for any value of the radius r. One has therefore to conclude that there is no clearly distinguishable low-dimensional fractal attractor in the foreign-exchange markets.

4. Concluding Remarks

In this chapter, we computed the fractal dimension of intradaily returns and of their absolute values for the main foreign-exchange rates w.r.t. to the USD using several methods for the reconstruction of the embedding

Figure 15-4

Spectrum of the First Eigenvectors for the USD/DEM Intradaily Returns
in Absolute Value

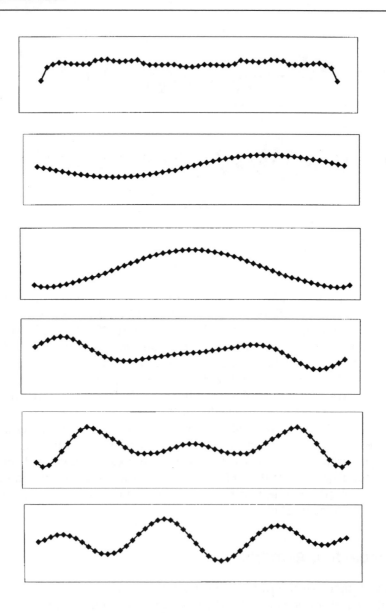

Figure 15-5

Correlation Integral for the USD/DEM Intradaily Returns (S.V.D.)

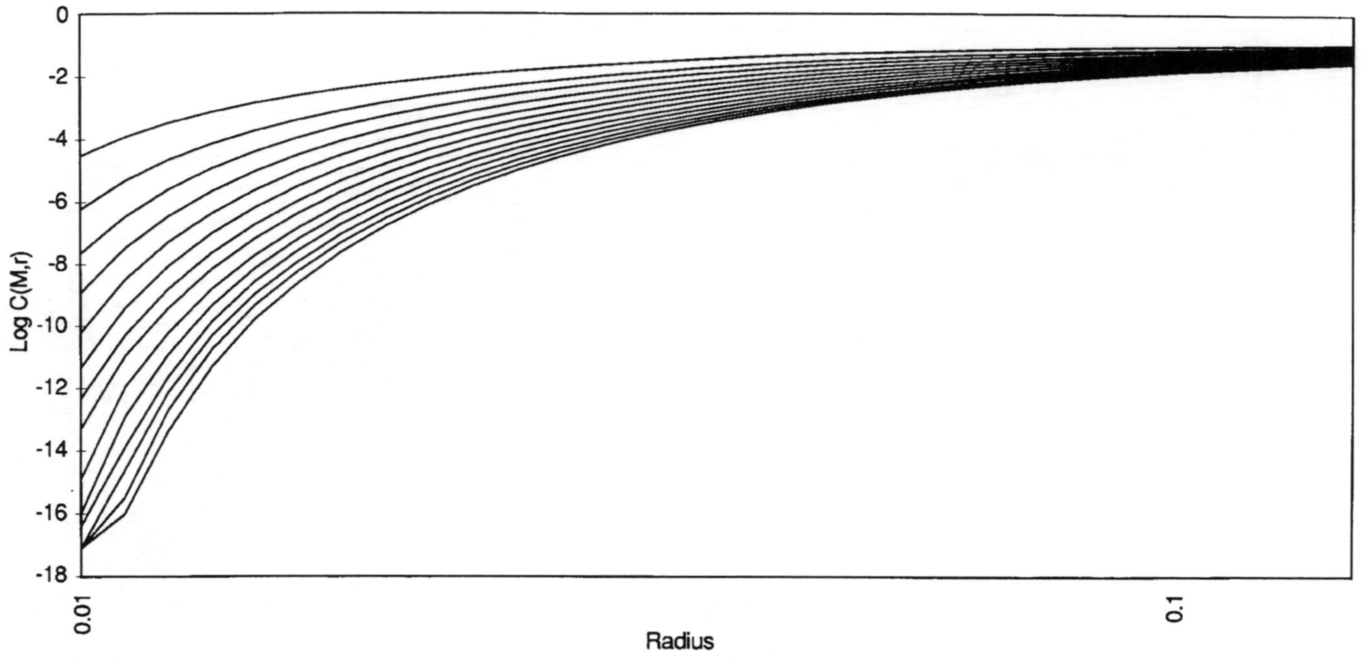

Figure 15-6

Correlation Dimension for the USD/DEM Intradaily Returns (S.V.D.)

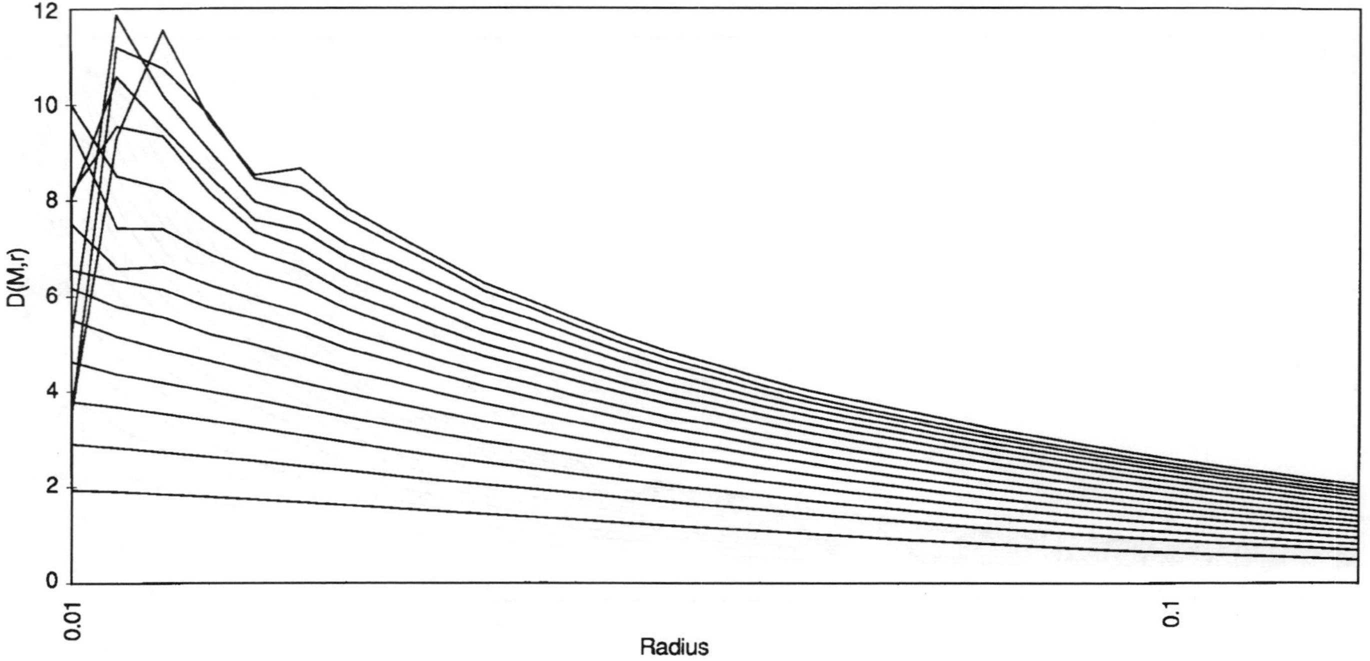

Figure 15-7

Correlation Integral for the USD/DEM Intradaily Returns in Absolute Value (S.V.D.)

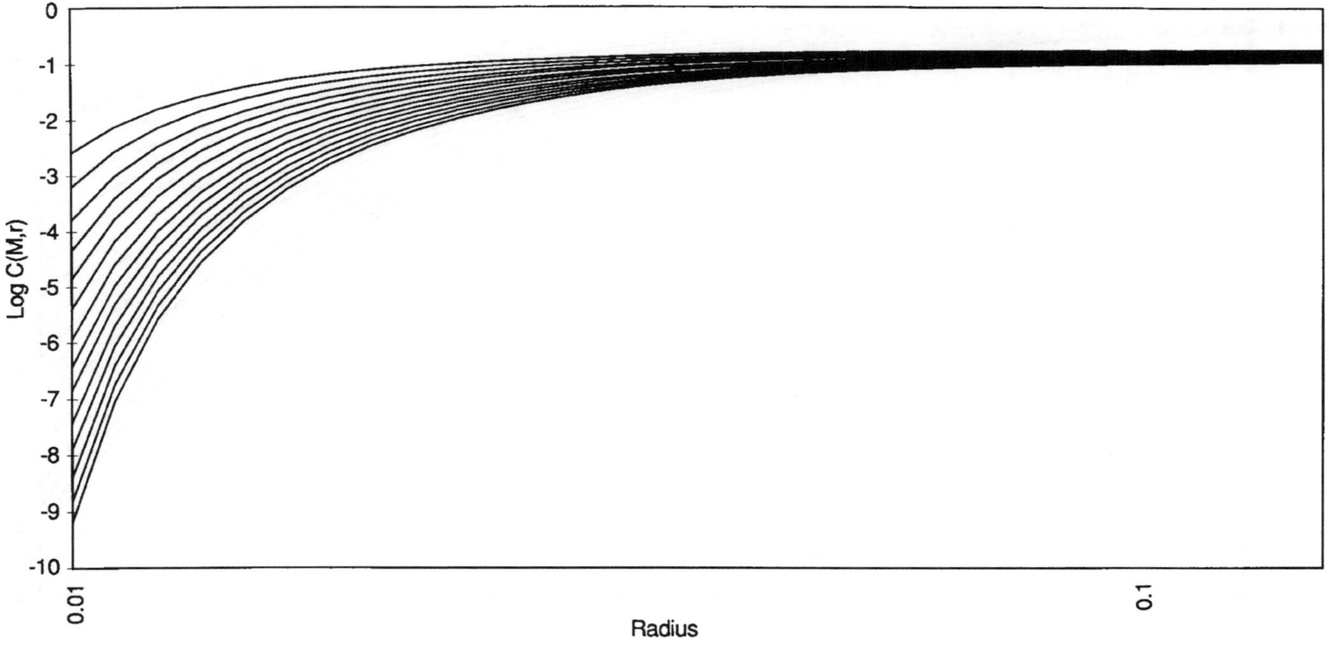

Figure 15-8

Correlation Dimension for the USD/DEM Intradaily Returns in Absolute Value (S.V.D.)

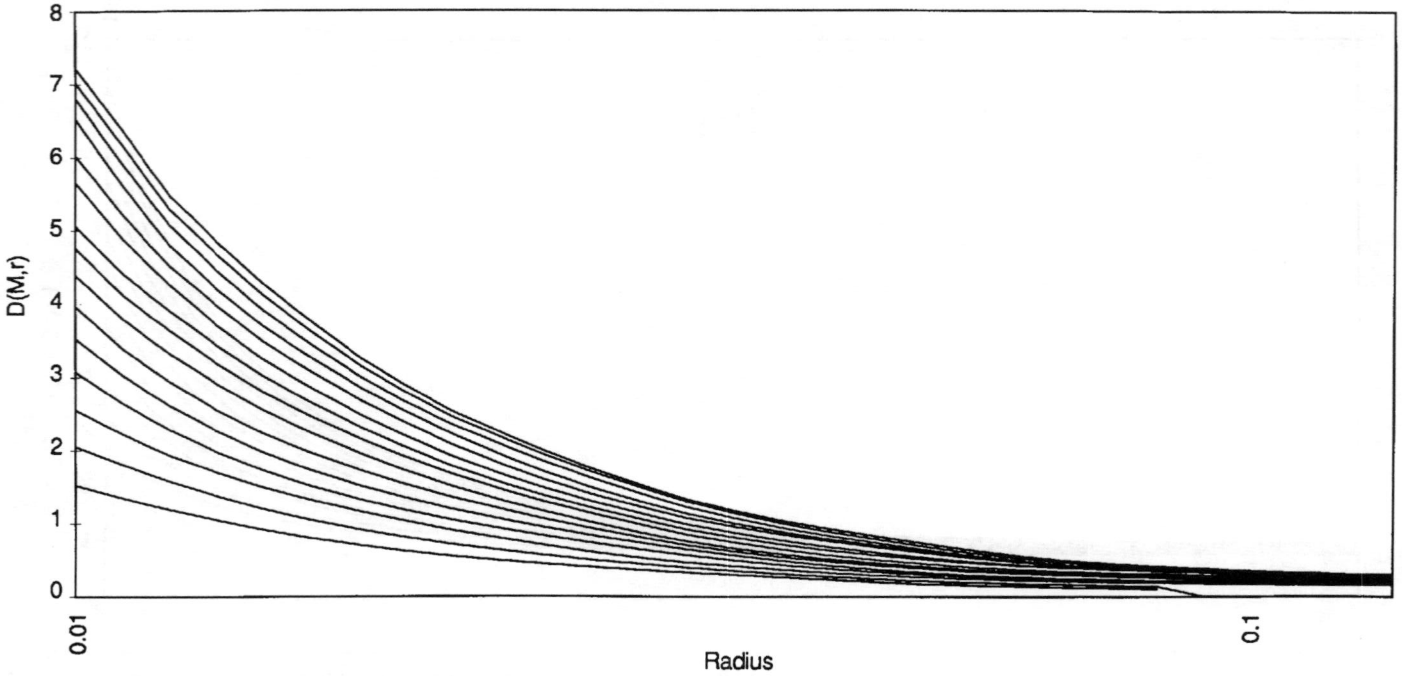

phase space. A detailed implementation of the Grassberger-Proccacia algorithm for noisy data sets was presented. However, neither the application of nonlinear filters nor the singular value decomposition could demonstrate the presence of a low-dimensional attractor. This is consistent with the absence of any distinguishable noise floor in the spectrum of eigenvalues.

This is further corroborated by results of dimension estimates for daily exchange-rate returns for the USD/DEM, USD/BPD, USD/JPY, for the period 1973–1990, which display only mixed evidence in favor of a low-dimensional fractal attractor [Dewachter and Guillaume (1992)]. Indeed, on the one hand, those results are not completely robust to the Ramsey and Yuan (1989) procedure of correction for the small sample bias; on the other hand, the period 1973–1981, not covered by our intradaily sample, seems to be responsible for the relatively robust evidence in favor of a low-dimensional fractal attractor in the case of USD/BPD. Finally, Mayfield and Mizrach (1992) found that the predictability horizon of high-frequency stock index was smaller than 15 minutes, which corresponds to our minimum time interval.

In order to explain the absence of a low-dimensional attractor, two reasons can be put forward. First, the basic assumption underlying the application of chaos algorithms, i.e., the hypothesis of ergodicity, might not be satisfied.

A second reason might be that the time series are indeed of high, if not infinite dimension, which is not surprising both in the case of the returns and the volatility. On the one hand, the more efficient and liquid are the markets, the higher should be their dimension. On the other hand, the estimated values of GARCH parameters are often compatible with an infinite variance.[16]

The above results lead us to be very cautious with respect to results arguing the presence of a low-dimensional attractor in economic data. Before considering dimension estimates as valid, we first recommend that the ergodicity of the time series be tested. Second, one should check that the number of available data points is sufficient to satisfy at least the minimum number of data points required in Eckmann and Ruelle (1992). Third, one should avoid (spurious) short-term autocorrelation of the data when reconstructing the phase space. Fourth, plots of correlation integral and correlation dimension estimates in function of the radius size should always be displayed. Then, a clear plateau should be seen on the figures of correlation dimension estimates. It is indeed not sufficient that the dimension estimates are lower than for those obtained from a random permutation of the data. Finally, these dimension estimates should be confirmed by the estimation of the dimension based on the spectrum of Lyapunov exponents, as conjectured by Kaplan and Yorke (1979).

More fundamentally, our results question the validity of the corner-stone of low-dimensional models in economics, in particular of chaotic models. Future research will have to analyze in more detail the nature of the stochasticity present in the data. This is the basis of the appropriate modeling of the foreign-exchange markets.

Acknowledgments

I am indebted to Olsen & Associates, who kindly provided the intradaily data set. I owe also much to valuable comments from F. Abraham, M. Dacorogna, P. De Grauwe, D. Gallez, G. Gielens, L. Lauwers, M. Vuylsteke, participants at the PASE '93 Workshop, the '94 Symposium on Nonlinear Econometrics and Theory in Boston, the '94 KNIE-workshop in Amsterdam, and the International Economics Workshop at the University of Leuven. L. Van Rentegem provided useful computer assistance. J-M. Grandmont, Th. Schreiber, and H. Tong are acknowledged for communicating their work. The usual disclaimer of course applies.

Notes

1 By number of degrees of freedom ($d°$), we imply the number of first-order difference (or differentiable) equations of the system. A low-dimensional system is a system for which $d° \leq 10$.

2 In contrast to the one-dimensional problem usually studied in theoretical models, the hereafter proposed methodology deals with the multi-dimensional case.

3 For good surveys of these concepts, see, e.g., Eckmann and Ruelle (1985), Ruelle (1989), Grassberger et al. (1991).

4 Barnett and Chen (1988), Frank and Stengos (1988, 1989), Eckmann et al. (1988), Peters (1989, 1991), Scheinkman and LeBaron (1989), Vassilicos (1990), Ramsey et al. (1990), Blank (1991), DeCoster and Mitchell (1991), Hsieh (1991), Tata and Vassilicos (1991), Dechert and Gencay (1992), Bajo-Rubio et al. (1992), Mayfield and Mizrach (1992), Jaditz and Sayers (1993).

5 We have that $d° \in [D, 2D+1]$, where D is the next integer to the fractal dimension.

6 It indicates the minimum number of "true" exponents to be computed. Note that, strictly speaking, a low-dimensional fractal attractor is not

necessarily strange or chaotic and conversely [see Eckmann and Ruelle (1985), p. 625, for a counter-example].

7 We are grateful to B. Mizrach and C. Goodhart who respectively brought to our knowledge the existence of the paper of Mayfield and Mizrach (1992) and those of Vassilicos (1990) and Tata and Vassilicos (1991). Although those papers differ in their methodology and make use of a more restrictive data set, they come to similar conclusions.

8 A system is said to be ergodic when averages in time are equal to averages in space. Therefore, an ergodic system should be autonomous or strongly stationary [for further details, see Eckmann and Ruelle (1985)].

9 With the exception of the paper of Mayfield and Mizrach (1992).

10 A similar approach to the definition of noisy chaos has been formulated by Chan and Tong (1994).

11 Schreiber (1993) gives the example of the Mackey-Glass system with 5 percent Gaussian noise added.

12 Ramsey and Yuan (1989), Smith (1988), Nerenberg and Essex (1990), Eckmann and Ruelle (1992).

13 As discussed in Grassberger et al. (1991) and references therein, dimensions inferior to 2 should not be mistaken as small attractor dimensions; they rather correspond to stochastic processes.

14 Standard abbreviations of the International Organization for Standardization (ISO, code 4217).

15 See Müller et al. (1990) for a complete description of the data.

16 A necessary condition for an infinite variance is that the coefficients α_1 and β_i sum to one in the following GARCH(p,q) model: $E_{t-1}(\varepsilon_t) = 0$

$$E_{t-1}(\varepsilon_t^2) = h_t + \omega + \sum_{i=1}^{q} \alpha_i \varepsilon_{t-i}^2 + \sum_{j=1}^{p} \beta_j h_{t-j}$$

which is approximately verified in Engle and Bollerslev (1986), and Bollerslev (1987).

References

Albano, A., J. Muench, and C. Schwartz. "Singular-Value Decomposition and the Grassberger-Procaccia Algorithm." *Physical Review A* 38 (1988), 3017.

Bajo-Rubio, O., F. Fernandez-Rodriguez, and S. Sosvilla-Rivera. "Chaotic Behaviour in Exchange-Rate Series." *Economics Letters* 39 (1992), 207–211.

Barnett, W., and P. Chen. "The Aggregation-Theoretic Monetary Aggregates Are Chaotic and Have Strange Attractors," in W. Barnett, E. Berndt, and H. White, eds., *Dynamic Econometric Modelling* (1988), 199–245.

Blank, S. "Chaos in Futures Markets? A Nonlinear Dynamical Analysis." *Journal of Futures Markets* 11 (1991), 711–728.

Boldrin, M., and M. Woodford. "Equilibrium Models Displaying Endogenous Fluctuations and Chaos, a Survey." *Journal of Monetary Economics* 25 (1990), 189–222.

Bollerslev, T. "A Conditionally Heteroskedastic Time Series Model for Speculative Prices and Rates of Return." *Review of Economics and Statistics* (1987), 542–547.

Bollerslev, T., and I. Domowitz. "Trading Patterns and Prices in the Interbank Foreign Exchange Market." *The Journal of Finance* 48 (1993), 1421–1443.

Bollerslev, T., and M. Melvin. "Bid-Ask Spreads and Volatility in the Foreign Exchange Market: an Empirical Analysis." Working paper, Department of Finance, Kellogg Graduate School of Management, Northwestern University (1993), 134.

Brock, W., and W. D. Dechert. "Non-linear Dynamical Systems: Instability and Chaos in Economics," in W. Hildenbrand and H. Sonnenschein, eds., *Handbook of Mathematical Economics IV* (1991), 2209–2235.

Broomhead, D., and G. King. "Extracting Qualitative Dynamics from Experimental Data." *Physica D*, 20 (1986a), 217–236.

Broomhead, D., and G. King. "On the Qualitative Analysis of Experimental Dynamical Systems," in S. Sarkar, ed., *Nonlinear Phenomena and Chaos* (1986b), 113–144.

Chan, K., and H. Tong. "A Note on Noisy Chaos." *Journal of Royal Statistical Society* 56 (1994), 301–312.

Dacorogna, M., C. Gauvreau, U. Müller, R. Olsen, and O. Pictet. "Changing Time Scale for Short-Term Forecasting in Financial Markets." Presentation given at the International Conference on "Financial Markets Dynamics and Forecasting" held in Paris on September 2–4, 1993. MMD. 1993-08-09, Olsen & Associates, Seefeldstrasse 233 8008 Zürich, Switzerland (1993a).

Dacorogna, M., U. Müller, R. Nagler, R. Olsen, and O. Pictet. "A Geographical Model for the Daily and Weekly Seasonal Volatility in the FX Market." *Journal of International Money and Finance* 12 (1993b), 413–438.

Dechert, W., and R. Gencay. "Lyapunov Exponents as a Nonparametric Diagnostic for Stability Analysis." *Journal of Applied Econometrics* 7 (1992), S41–S60.

DeCoster, G., and D. Mitchell. "Nonlinear Monetary Dynamics." *Journal of Business and Economic Statistics* 9 (1991), 455–461.

De Grauwe, P., and H. Dewachter. "A Chaotic Model of the Exchange Rate: The Role of Fundamentalists and Chartists." *Open Economies Review* 4 (1993), 351–379.

Destexhe, A., J. A. Sepulchre, and A. Babloyantz. "A Comparative Study of the Experimental Quantification of Deterministic Chaos." *Physical Letters A* 132 (1988), 101–106.

Dewachter, H., and D. Guillaume. "Is There Deterministic Chaos in the Foreign Exchange Markets?" Catholic University of Leuven, mimeo (1992).

Diebold, F., and J. Nason. "Nonparametric Exchange Rate Prediction?" *Journal of International Economics* 28 (1990), 315–332.

Ding, Z., C. Granger, and R. Engle. "A Long Memory Property of Stock Market Returns and a New Model." *Journal of Empirical Finance* 1 (1993), 83–106.

Eckmann, J., and D. Ruelle. "Ergodic Theory of Chaos and Strange Attractors." *Review of Modern Physics* 57 (1985), 617–656.

Eckmann, J., S. Kamphorst, D. Ruelle, and J. Scheinkman. "Lyapunov Exponents for Stock Returns," in P. Anderson, K. Arrow, and D. Pines, eds., *The Economy as an Evolving Complex System*, Santa Fe Institute Studies in the Sciences of Complexity, Addison-Wesley (1988).

Eckmann, J., and D. Ruelle. "Fundamental Limitations for Estimating Dimensions and Lyapunov Exponents in Dynamical Systems." *Physica D* 56 (1992), 185–187.

Engle, R., and T. Bollerslev. "Modelling the Persistence of Conditional Variances." *Econometric Reviews* 5 (1986), 1–50.

Fraedrich, K., and R. Wang. "Estimating the Correlation Dimension of an Attractor from Noisy and Small Datasets Based on Re-embedding." *Physica D* 65 (1993), 373–398.

Frank, M., and T. Stengos. "Some Evidence Concerning Macroeconomic Chaos." *Journal of Monetary Economics* 22 (1988), 423–438.

Frank, M., and T. Stengos. "Measuring the Strangeness of Gold and Silver Rates of Return." *Review of Economic Studies* 56 (1989), 553–567.

Fraser, A., and H. Swinney. "Independent Coordinates for Strange Attractors from Mutual Information." *Physical Review A* 33 (1986), 1134–1140.

Goodhart, C. "'News' and the Foreign Exchange Market." *Proceedings of the Manchester Statistical Society* (1989), 1–79.

Goodhart, C., and L. Figliuoli. "Every Minute Counts in Financial Markets." *Journal of International Money and Finance* 10 (1991), 23–52.

Grandmont, J-M. "Expectations Driven Nonlinear Business Cycles," *Proceedings of the Stockholm Conference* (FIEF papers) (1992).

Grassberger, P. "An Optimized Box-Assisted Algorithm for Fractal Dimensions." *Physics Letters A* 148 (1990), 63–68.

Grassberger, P., and I. Procaccia. "Characterization of Strange Attractors." *Physical Review Letters* 50 (1983a), 346–349.

Grassberger, P., and I. Procaccia. "Measuring the Strangeness of Strange Attractors." *Physica D* 9 (1983b), 189–208.

Grassberger, P., T. Schreiber, and C. Schaffrath. "Nonlinear Time Sequence Analysis." *International Journal of Bifurcation and Chaos* 1 (1991), 521–547.

Hsieh, D. "Testing for Non-linear Dependence in Daily Foreign Exchange Rates." *Journal of Business* 62 (1989), 339–368.

Hsieh, D. "Chaos and Nonlinear Dynamics: Application to Financial Markets." *Journal of Finance* 46 (1991), 1839–1877.

Kaplan, J., and J. Yorke. "Chaotic Behavior of Multi-dimensional Difference Equations," in H. Peitgen and H. Walther, eds., *Functional Differential Equations and Approximation of Fixed Points, Lecture Notes in Mathematics*, Springer (1979), 204–227.

Jaditz, T., and C. Sayers. "Is Chaos Generic in Economic Data?" *International Journal of Bifurcation and Chaos* 3 (1993), 745–755.

Mayfield, E., and B. Mizrach. "On Determining the Dimension of Real-Time Stock-Price Data." *Journal of Business and Economic Statistics* 10 (1992), 367–374.

Mirowski, P. "From Mandelbrot to Chaos in Economic Theory." *Southern Economic Journal* (1990), 289–307.

Müller, U., M. Dacorogna, R. Olsen, O. Pictet, M. Schwarz, and C. Morgenegg. "Statistical Study of Foreign Exchange Rates, Empirical Evidence of a Price Change Scaling Law, and Intraday Analysis." *Journal of Banking and Finance* 14 (1990), 1189–1208.

Nerenberg, M., and C. Essex. "Correlation Dimension and Systematic Geometric Effects." *Physical Review A* 42 (1990), 7065–7074.

Packard, N., J. Crutchfield, D. Farmer, and S. Shaw. "Geometry from a Time Series." *Physical Review Letters* 45 (1980), 712–716.

Peters, E. "Fractal Structure in the Capital Markets." *Financial Analysts Journal* (1989), 32–37.

Peters, E. *Chaos and Order in Capital Markets.* New York: John Wiley & Sons, 1991.

Ramsey, J., and H. Yuan. "Bias and Error Bars in Dimension Calculations and Their Evaluation in Some Simple Models." *Physical Letters A* 134 (1989), 287–297.

Ramsey, J., C. Sayers, and P. Rothman. "The Statistical Properties of Dimension Calculations Using Small Data Sets: Some Economic Applications." *International Economic Review* 31 (1990), 991–1020.

Ramsey, J., and P. Rothman. "A Reassessment of Dimension Calculations Using Some Monetary Data," Technical Report 92-28, C.V. Starr Center for Applied Economics, New York University (1992).

Ruelle, D. *Chaotic Evolution and Strange Attractors.* Cambridge University Press 1989, 96 pp.

Sauer, T., J. Yorke, and M. Casdagli. "Embedology." *Journal of Statistical Physical* 65 (1991), 579–616.

Scheinkman, J., and B. LeBaron. "Nonlinear Dynamics and Stock Returns." *Journal of Business* 62 (1989), 311–337.

Schreiber, T., and P. Grassberger. "A Simple Noise-Reduction Method for Real Data." *Physical Letters A* 160 (1991), 411–422.

Schreiber, T. "Extremely Simple Nonlinear Noise-Reduction Method." *Physical Review E* 47 (1993), 2401–2404.

Schreiber, T. Personal communication (1993).

Smith, L. "Intrinsic Limits on Dimension Calculations." *Physical Letters A* 133 (1988), 283–288.

Takens, F. "Detecting Strange Attractors in Turbulence," in D. Rand and L. Young, eds., *Lecture Notes in Mathematics.* Berlin-Heidelberg-New York: Springer (1981), 898, 366–381.

Tata, F., and C. Vassilicos. "Is There Chaos in Economic Time Series? A Study of the Stock and the Foreign Exchange Markets." *London School of Economics Financial Markets Group Discussion Paper* 120 (1991).

Theiler, J. "Spurious Dimension from Correlation Algorithms Applied to Limited Time-Series Data." *Physical Review A* 34 (1986), 2427–2432.

Vassilicos, J. "Are Financial Markets Chaotic? A Preliminary Study of the Foreign Exchange Market." *London School of Economics Financial Markets Group Discussion Paper* 86 (1990).

16

IMPLICATIONS OF NONLINEAR DYNAMICS FOR FINANCIAL RISK MANAGEMENT

By David A. Hsieh[*]

I. Introduction

A number of recent papers in the economics and finance literature have found strong evidence of nonlinear dynamics in short-term movements of asset returns.[1] The next logical question is: What is the relevance of this finding? In the presence of any dynamics (whether linear or nonlinear), conditional densities can provide a better description of short-term asset price movements than can unconditional densities. This may be important for financial risk management, especially when highly leveraged instruments, such as futures contracts, are involved. For example, hedge ratios and the amount of capital needed to cover possible losses during the time a futures position is held depend critically on the probability distribution of changes in futures prices.

Reprinted with permission from *Journal of Financial & Quantitative Analysis*, Vol. 28, No. 1 (March 1993): 41–64.

Traditional methods of estimating a probability density use a smoothed histogram of past price changes. This corresponds to the unconditional density. A conditional density can provide a more accurate assessment of price changes, since it uses more information. If the dynamics of asset prices were linear in nature, their conditional densities could be obtained in a straightforward manner. The empirical finding that the dynamics of asset prices are nonlinear, however, substantially complicates the estimation of their conditional densities. This chapter illustrates how the conditional density can be estimated in a computationally efficient manner, and then it is applied to foreign currency futures.

The outline of this chapter is as follows: Section II discusses the difference between conditional and unconditional densities. If price changes are independent and identically distributed (IID), then the two densities are the same. It is, therefore, important to test for independence and identical distribution. Section III introduces the Brock, Dechert, and Scheinkman (1987) test for independence and identical distribution, which is applied to four currency futures contracts traded on the Chicago Mercantile Exchange. It finds that price changes are not IID. In particular, there is strong evidence of conditional heteroskedasticity. Section IV describes a simple two-step seminonparametric method for approximating the conditional densities. Step one extracts the predictable parts of price changes parametrically. For the futures data, the conditional mean is approximately zero, but the conditional variance can be modeled by an autoregressive process. Step two describes the remaining unpredictable movements of price changes nonparametrically. Applications to futures trading are then provided in Section V. The section shows how to determine the capital needed to cover a given probability of losses over the next trading day. Using the estimated conditional density, the capital requirement changes with the conditional variance of futures price changes, while that based on the unconditional density is constant over time. Section V also shows how to use simulation to determine the capital needed to cover a given probability of cumulative losses over a longer horizon. The section finds that the unconditional density can give time-varying capital requirements, which may be more accurate than those from the unconditional density. Concluding remarks are offered in Section VI.

II. Conditional and Unconditional Densities

This section describes the difference between conditional and unconditional densities. To facilitate discussion, let P_t be the price of an asset at time t. Define $x_t = \text{Log}(P_t/P_{t-1})$ as its continuously compounded rate of change. The unconditional density of x_t is obtained by fitting a density to the histogram of x_t, using either parametric or nonparametric methods. The conditional density of x_t, given its own past values, is obtained by postulating and estimating a complete probability model for the law of motion of x_t over time.[2] Usually the unconditional density is much simpler to estimate, particularly in the case of the parametric method, which explains its popularity in finance.[3] There are situations, however, when the conditional density gives a more accurate probability model of the short-term behavior of x_t.

To highlight the differences between conditional and unconditional densities, consider the following example: Let x_t be a first order autoregressive process,

$$x_t = \alpha + \beta x_{t-1} + u_t,$$

where u_t is IID, normal, with mean 0 and variance σ_u^2, and $|\beta| < 1$. The conditional distribution of x_t is normal, with mean $(\alpha/(1-\beta))$ and variance $\sigma_u^2/(1-\beta^2)$, while the distribution of x_t conditional on x_{t-1} is normal, with mean $(\alpha + \beta x_{t-1})$ and variance σ_u^2. The conditional and unconditional distributions are the same whenever $\beta = 0$, i.e., x_t is IID. They are different whenever $\beta \neq 0$, i.e., x_t is not IID.

The two distributions are related as follows: Suppose only x_{t-2} is observed. Then, the conditional distribution of x_t given x_{t-2} is normal, with mean $(\alpha(1 + \beta) + \beta^2 x_{t-2})$ and variance $\sigma_u^2(1 + \beta^2)$. By repeated substitution, it can be shown that the conditional distribution of x_t, given x_{t-k}, converges to the unconditional distribution as $k \to \infty$. In other words, the unconditional distribution describes the long-run behavior of x_t, while the conditional distribution describes its short-run behavior. In the first-order autoregression, the conditional variance is always smaller than the unconditional variance. In general, however, the conditional variance can be larger or smaller than the unconditional variance.[4]

III. Test of Independence and Identical Distribution

The Brock, Dechert, and Scheinkman (1987) (BDS) test for independence and identical distribution is used. This test is chosen because it can detect many types of departures from independence and identical distribution, such as nonstationarity, nonlinearity, and deterministic chaos. Any of these departures from the IID case imply that the conditional distribution is different from the unconditional distribution. Furthermore, the BDS test can serve as a general model specification test, especially in the presence of nonlinear dynamics.[5]

The BDS test has been discussed in detail elsewhere.[6] Only a brief review is provided here. Let $\{x_t, t = 1, ..., T\}$ be a time series, and denote $x_t^m = (x_t, x_{t-1}, ..., x_{t-m+1})$ a point in the m-dimensional Euclidean space. Define the correlation integral $C_m(\delta)$ to be the fraction of pairs of points, x_t^m and x_s^m, that are within a distance δ of each other,

$$C_m(\delta) = \operatorname{plim}_{T \to \infty} \# \left\{ (t,s), \ 0 < t < T, \right.$$

$$\left. 0 < s < T : \max_{i=0,...,m-1} \ |x_{t-i} - x_{s-i}| < \delta \right\} / T^2.$$

For the purposes here, the maximum norm will be used, although the standard Euclidean norm is perfectly acceptable. If $\{x_t\}$ were IID, then $C_m(\delta) = (C_1(\delta))^m$. Brock, Dechert, and Scheinkman (1987) construct a statistic for testing the null hypothesis that $C_m(\delta) = (C_1(\delta))^m$.[7] They show that the test statistic is asymptotically a standard normal distribution. Brock, Hsieh, and LeBaron (1991) and Hsieh and LeBaron (1988) report extensive simulations and show that the asymptotic distribution is a good approximation of the finite sample distribution when there are more than 500 observations. They recommend using δ between one-half to two times the standard deviation of the raw data. Also, the accuracy of the asymptotic distribution deteriorates for high embedding dimensions, particularly when m is 10 or above.

The data consist of daily settlement prices for four currency futures contracts traded on the Chicago Mercantile Exchange (CME): the British pound (BP), Deutsche mark (DM), Japanese yen (JY), and Swiss franc (SF), from February 22, 1985, to March 9, 1990, totaling 1,275 observations per contract. The starting date corresponds to the time when daily price limits were removed. Currency futures expire four times per year. In order to obtain a continuous time series, the contracts were rolled over to the next expiration cycle one week prior to expiration.

It is appropriate to discuss why currency futures prices were chosen for analysis instead of forward exchange rates, even though the forward exchange market is many times the size of the currency futures markets. The reason is that financial risk management is generally concerned with the market value of a futures or forward contract over its entire life. Unfortunately, daily forward exchange rates are typically given in fixed maturities of one month, three months, . . . etc., which do not provide sufficient information. For this reason, currency futures are turned to, because futures exchanges provide information on daily movements of the futures price throughout the life of a futures contract. Cornell and

Reinganum (1981) find that there is practically no difference between forwards and futures in the foreign-exchange market. Therefore, futures prices can be used to construct a probability model, which can be applied to forward contracts as well.

Table 16-1 provides a statistical description of log price changes. The means are not statistically different from zero. The annualized standard deviations are 12.96 percent, 12.47 percent, 11.26 percent, and 13.82 percent, respectively, for the BP, DM, JY, and SF, assuming that each calendar year consists of 253 trading days. All four series have strong departures from normality, as the coefficients of skewness and kurtosis are statistically different from those of a normal distribution. The BDS statistics for testing independence and identical distribution are provided in Table 16-1, for embedding dimensions (m) 2 through 5, and distances (δ) 0.5, 1.0, 1.5, and 2.0 times the standard deviation of the raw data. If the 1 percent marginal significance level is used, independence and identical distribution will be rejected in all 16 statistics for the BP and the JY, 11 of the 16 for the DM, and four of the 16 for the SF. Even though the BDS statistics for each of the currency futures are not independent, they show strong evidence of departure of independence and identical distribution for at least three currency futures. This is consistent with similar findings in the spot currency markets, as in Hsieh (1989).

As the BDS test is sensitive to any departure from independence and identical distribution, it is useful to know the cause of the rejection. Table 16-2 provides some information. It shows that the autocorrelation coefficients of log price changes are not statistically different from zero, either individually or jointly (using the Box-Pierce statistic for the first 15 lags).[8] On the other hand, the autocorrelation coefficients of the absolute values of log price changes are much larger. More than half of them are statistically different from zero, and the joint test using the Box-Pierce statistic rejects the hypothesis that the first 15 lags are zero. This evidence is consistent with the hypothesis that the rejection of independence and identical distribution is not due to linear, but rather nonlinear, dependence in exchange rates.[9]

The rejection of independence and identical distribution implies that the conditional density differs from the unconditional density in describing short-term dynamics of futures prices. Furthermore, the presence of nonlinear dependence implies that linear (e.g., Box-Jenkins) methods cannot be used to model the conditional density. This motivates the goal in the rest of this chapter, namely, to obtain a useable form of the conditional density that takes into account the nonlinear dependence, and to provide some interesting applications.

Table 16-1

Statistical Description of Daily Log Price Changes
February 22, 1985–March 9, 1990 (1,275 observations)

	BP	DM	JY	SF
Mean	0.00045	0.00043	0.00032	0.00037
Median	0.00036	0.00000	0.00000	0.00016
Std. Dev.	0.00815	0.00784	0.00708	0.00869
Skewness	0.36	0.28	0.34	0.18
Kurtosis	6.25	5.32	7.81	4.94
Maximum	0.04553	0.04832	0.05333	0.04967
Minimum	−0.02899	−0.03264	−0.04133	−0.03692

BDS Statistics

m	δ	BP	DM	JY	SF
2	0.5	2.39*	1.68	4.15*	1.01
3	0.5	2.76*	2.23	4.95*	1.08
4	0.5	3.58*	3.16*	6.39*	1.77
5	0.5	4.40*	3.91*	7.88*	2.57
2	1.0	3.34*	1.48	4.06*	0.46
3	1.0	4.00*	2.10	4.49*	0.85
4	1.0	4.86*	3.11*	5.69*	1.59
5	1.0	5.73*	3.85*	6.52*	2.40
2	1.5	3.96*	1.99	3.68*	0.81
3	1.5	4.84*	2.97*	4.29*	1.62
4	1.5	5.75*	3.95*	5.61*	2.57
5	1.5	6.54*	4.69*	6.32*	3.38*
2	2.0	3.88*	2.51*	3.16*	1.35
3	2.0	4.86*	3.79*	3.84*	2.37
4	2.0	5.77*	4.75*	5.14*	3.30*
5	2.0	6.54*	5.53*	5.73*	4.02*

* Significant at the 1 percent level using a two-tailed test.

m is the embedding dimension.

δ is the distance between points, measured in terms of number of standard deviations of the raw data.

The critical values (marginal significance level) of the statistics for a two-tailed test are: 1.645 (10 percent), 1.960 (5 percent), 2.326 (2 percent), and 2.576 (1 percent).

Table 16-2

Autocorrelations of Price Changes and Their Absolute Values

	BP	DM	JY	SF
Panel A. Autocorrelation Coefficients				
$p(1)$	0.032	−0.019	0.024	−0.006
$p(2)$	−0.016	−0.009	0.000	−0.013
$p(3)$	−0.017	0.042	0.057	0.029
$p(4)$	−0.019	−0.043	−0.004	−0.032
$p(5)$	−0.005	0.014	0.012	0.009
$p(6)$	0.054	0.033	0.021	0.007
$p(7)$	−0.045	−0.021	−0.026	−0.017
$p(8)$	0.029	0.047	0.051	0.021
$p(9)$	−0.016	0.005	0.022	0.008
$p(10)$	−0.020	−0.037	−0.005	−0.033
$p(11)$	−0.039	−0.009	0.014	−0.011
$p(12)$	−0.015	−0.022	0.025	−0.008
$p(13)$	0.056	0.018	−0.002	0.034
$p(14)$	0.005	0.015	0.042	0.002
$p(15)$	0.052	0.056	0.022	0.066
$Q(15)$	20.09	17.12	14.25	12.26
Panel B. Autocorrelation Coefficients of Absolute Values				
$r(1)$	0.107[*]	0.059	0.118[*]	0.027
$r(2)$	0.094[*]	0.038	0.058	0.025
$r(3)$	0.108[*]	0.079[*]	0.101[*]	0.052
$r(4)$	0.112[*]	0.055	0.041	0.040
$r(5)$	0.081[*]	0.088[*]	0.084[*]	0.084[*]
$r(6)$	0.096[*]	0.107[*]	0.087[*]	0.097[*]
$r(7)$	0.088[*]	0.099[*]	0.010	0.096[*]
$r(8)$	0.101[*]	0.087[*]	0.088[*]	0.061
$r(9)$	0.088[*]	0.063	0.069	0.054
$r(10)$	0.129[*]	0.128[*]	0.023	0.113[*]
$r(11)$	0.047	0.020	0.041	0.038
$r(12)$	0.078[*]	0.068	−0.005	0.075[*]
$r(13)$	0.092[*]	0.086[*]	0.023	0.088*
$r(14)$	0.116[*]	0.073[*]	0.055	0.048
$r(15)$	0.108[*]	0.115[*]	0.028	0.103[*]
$Q(15)$	182.41[**]	128.85[**]	79.50[**]	98.69[**]

[*] Significant at the 1 percent level using a two-tailed test.

[**] Significant at the 1 percent level using a one-tailed test.

$Q(15)$ is the Box-Pierce statistic testing for the first 15 lags to be different from zero. The critical values (marginal significance levels) are: 22.31 (10 percent), 25.00 (5 percent), and 27.49 (1 percent).

IV. A Two-Step Method for Estimating Conditional Densities

In theory, the conditional density can be estimated nonparametrically, for example, using kernels, splines, neural networks, or series expansions. In practice, nonparametric methods have two drawbacks. They require substantial computational time, and little is known about the sample sizes required for accurate estimation. This chapter tries a different approach.

The approach to estimating conditional density is essentially a two-step seminonparametric approach. Step one estimates the predictable part of the data parametrically. Step two estimates the remaining unpredictable part nonparametrically. Speed of computation is the primary motivation for doing this in two steps, rather than jointly estimating the parametric and nonparametric parts.[10]

The parametric part in step one deals with the conditional mean and conditional variance of x_t, defined as,

$$\mu_t = E(x_t \mid x_{t-1}, x_{t-2}, \dots),$$

$$\sigma_t = V(x_t \mid x_{t-1}, x_{t-2}, \dots)^{\frac{1}{2}}.$$

For the four currency futures, it will be shown, below, that the conditional mean is zero and that the conditional variance is time-varying and depends nonlinearly on past realizations of x_t. In addition, it is demonstrated that the conditional variance captures most of the predictability of price changes, using the BDS statistic. Therefore, the unpredictable part is modeled as IID,

$$z_t = (x_t - \mu_t)/\sigma_t.$$

The nonparametric part in step two deals with the density of z_t.

It is important to note that not all nonlinear dependence can be modeled in this way. This method is not appropriate when, for example, there is dependence in higher order moments. Careful diagnostics are therefore needed.

A. Estimating the Conditional Mean Function

The chapter now proceeds to characterize the conditional mean function of price changes given its own past, which is defined as,

$$\mu_t = E(x_t \mid x_{t-1}, x_{t-2}, \dots) = f(x_{t-1}, x_{t-2}, \dots).$$

Operationally, this means that

$E(x_t - f(x_{t-1}, x_{t-2}, \dots)) \mid x_{t-1}, x_{t-2}, \dots) = 0.$

Based on the findings on spot currencies that the conditional mean is zero, it is argued that the same is true for currency futures.

Hsieh (1989) proposes a test of the null hypothesis that the conditional mean function is zero. The test makes use of the fact that, if the conditional mean of x_t is zero, then its bicorrelation coefficients, $E(x_t x_{t-i} x_{t-j})/V(x_t)^{3/2}$, are zero for $i,j \geq 1$.[11] Table 16-3 provides the estimated bicorrelation coefficients up to the fifth lag. None of them, either individually or jointly, are statistically different from zero. While the bicorrelation test results are consistent with the null hypothesis of a zero conditional mean function, Pemberton and Tong (1981) point out that there exist nonlinear models with zero bicorrelation coefficients and nonzero conditional means. To deal with these types of models, a second approach is turned to using nonparametric methods to directly estimate the conditional mean function.

Table 16-3

Bicorrelation Coefficients

Lags					
i	*j*	**BP**	**DM**	**JY**	**SF**
1	1	−0.119	−0.059	−0.072	−0.037
1	2	−0.041	−0.011	−0.030	−0.013
2	2	0.232	0.156	0.103	0.185
1	3	−0.024	0.009	0.073	−0.001
2	3	0.125	0.076	−0.003	0.060
3	3	−0.006	−0.097	0.231	−0.035
1	4	0.006	0.000	0.039	−0.012
2	4	−0.012	−0.013	0.034	−0.015
3	4	−0.030	0.021	0.068	0.027
4	4	0.008	−0.016	0.149	0.018
1	5	0.028	−0.020	0.039	−0.005
2	5	−0.007	−0.065	−0.023	−0.045
3	5	0.037	0.037	−0.033	−0.010
4	5	−0.097	−0.027	0.021	−0.005
5	5	0.026	0.015	0.051	0.061
$\chi^2(15)$		15.58	12.42	11.35	12.01

Suppose x_t is generated by the following model.

$$x_t = g\left(x_{t-1}, x_{t-2}, \ldots \right) + \varepsilon_t,$$

where ε_t is IID.[12] If $g(\ )$ is sufficiently well behaved, Stone (1977) shows that nonparametric regression methods can be used to estimate $g(\ )$ consistently. There are many ways to implement nonparametric regressions. Diebold and Nason (1990) and Meese and Rose (1990) use the method of locally weighted regression (LWR) in Cleveland and Devlin (1988).[13] Briefly, LWR can be illustrated in the following way. Suppose it is believed that the conditional mean function $g(\ )$ includes only x_{t-1}.[14] LWR looks at the history of x_t, finds those instances when x_{t-i-1} is close to x_{t-i} by choosing the nearest k neighbors of x_{t-1}, and runs a weighted regression of x_{t-i} on x_{t-i-1} by giving more weights to closer neighbors. This gives a local estimate of $g(\ )$ around the point x_{t-1}. This local estimate can be used to forecast x_t by evaluating it at x_{t-1}.

There are a number of choices to make in this forecasting exercise. The first is the number of nearest neighbors k. Ten percent of all available history, up to 90 percent, is tried in steps of 10 percent. The second is the number of lags of x_{t-1} to include as arguments of $g(\ )$. Lags 1 through 5 are used. The third is the weighting scheme of the local regression. The tricubic weights proposed in Cleveland and Devlin (1988) are used. The length of the out-of-sample forecast is the fourth choice. The last third of this chapter's sample is chosen.

Table 16-4 provides the ratio of the root mean squared errors (RMSE) of the LWR forecasts to that of a random walk model of futures prices (where the predicted x_t is zero). For each currency, there are 45 different RMSEs, corresponding to the five choices of lag lengths and nine sizes of nearest neighborhoods. A ratio larger than 1 indicates that the RMSE of the LWR is higher than that of the random walk model. In the BP, JY, and SF, LWR performed worse than the random walk model. In the DM, three of the 45 LWR forecasts beat the random walk, but the improvement is less than half a percent. These results are consistent with those in Diebold and Nason (1990) and Meese and Rose (1990), and indicate that there is little evidence of a nonzero conditional mean in price changes in currency futures.[15]

B. Estimating the Conditional Variance Function

While the conditional mean is statistically not different from zero, the large autocorrelations of the absolute values of price changes suggest that the conditional variance is time varying. The difficulty in modeling the con-

Table 16-4

Ratio of Root Mean Squared Forecast Errors

No. of Lags	Fraction of Sample	BP	DM	JY	SF
1	0.1	1.0209	1.0081	1.0547	1.0285
1	0.2	1.0254	0.9953	1.0371	1.0325
1	0.3	1.0260	0.9971	1.0323	1.0250
1	0.4	1.0221	0.9996	1.0301	1.0214
1	0.5	1.0188	1.0020	1.0278	1.0196
1	0.6	1.0170	1.0037	1.0263	1.0186
1	0.7	1.0155	1.0051	1.0256	1.0172
1	0.8	1.0141	1.0064	1.0260	1.0154
1	0.9	1.0133	1.0068	1.0260	1.0135
2	0.1	1.0605	1.0312	1.1094	1.0342
2	0.2	1.0548	1.0211	1.0935	1.0121
2	0.3	1.0491	1.0162	1.0831	1.0080
2	0.4	1.0431	1.0102	1.0742	1.0044
2	0.5	1.0370	1.0067	1.0664	1.0019
2	0.6	1.0315	1.0048	1.0593	0.9997
2	0.7	1.0268	1.0041	1.0540	0.9982
2	0.8	1.0232	1.0038	1.0496	0.9973
2	0.9	1.0204	1.0040	1.0459	0.9976
3	0.1	1.1473	1.0777	1.2062	1.0744
3	0.2	1.1019	1.0655	1.1572	1.0305
3	0.3	1.0810	1.0567	1.1323	1.0190
3	0.4	1.0678	1.0477	1.1140	1.0148
3	0.5	1.0582	1.0404	1.0990	1.0112
3	0.6	1.0508	1.0347	1.0855	1.0089
3	0.7	1.0435	1.0303	1.0750	1.0067
3	0.8	1.0375	1.0252	1.0656	1.0048
3	0.9	1.0315	1.0196	1.0590	1.0038
4	0.1	1.3497	1.1755	1.3802	1.1763
4	0.2	1.2435	1.0841	1.2608	1.0698
4	0.3	1.1892	1.0587	1.2091	1.0373
4	0.4	1.1548	1.0472	1.1764	1.0208
4	0.5	1.1302	1.0402	1.1536	1.0125
4	0.6	1.1095	1.0348	1.1362	1.0081
4	0.7	1.0914	1.0291	1.1216	1.0053
4	0.8	1.0742	1.0241	1.1080	1.0049
4	0.9	1.0596	1.0194	1.0958	1.0056
5	0.1	1.4288	1.4386	1.7291	1.3289
5	0.2	1.2553	1.2397	1.4582	1.1802
5	0.3	1.1847	1.1638	1.3585	1.1271
5	0.4	1.1448	1.1182	1.2929	1.0958
5	0.5	1.1162	1.0875	1.2401	1.0739
5	0.6	1.0954	1.0661	1.1983	1.0583
5	0.7	1.0799	1.0507	1.1619	1.0468
5	0.8	1.0673	1.0404	1.1316	1.0382
5	0.9	1.0546	1.0338	1.1077	1.0314

Underlined value represents the lowest ratio in a given currency.

ditional variance is that it is never observed directly. In this chapter, two different approaches are taken.

The first approach is motivated by the popularity of the autoregressive conditional heteroskedasticity models of Engle (1982), Bollerslev (1986), and Nelson (1991). See Bollerslev, Chow, and Kroner (1990) for a survey. Nelson's (1991) EGARCH model was selected and is given by

$$X_t = \mu + h_t^{1/2} \eta_t,$$

$$\eta_t \mid \Omega_{t-1} \sim N(0,1),$$

$$\text{Log } h_t = \alpha + \beta \text{ Log } h_{t-1} + \varnothing \left(\mid \eta_{t-1} \mid - (2/\pi)^{1/2} \right) + \gamma \eta_{t-1},$$

where Ω_{t-1} is the information set at time $t - 1$.[16] Since h_t is known at $t - 1$, it is included in Ω_{t-1}. The EGARCH model is chosen over Engle's (1982) ARCH or Bollerslev's (1986) GARCH models for two reasons: (1) EGARCH allows the conditional variance to respond differently to a decline versus an advance (by allowing γ to be different from zero), while ARCH and GARCH impose a symmetric response; and (2) unlike ARCH and GARCH, EGARCH does not need to impose any constraints on the coefficients of the variance equation to enforce nonnegativity of the variance. This makes estimation much simpler.

The Berndt, Hall, Hall, and Hausman (1974) estimation procedure is used, and the results are given in Table 16-5. First, the estimates of β are all statistically greater than zero. In fact, those for the BP, DM, and SF are very close to one, which indicates that volatility is highly persistent in currency futures. The much smaller value of β for the JY indicates that its volatility is less persistent. However, the estimates of β for all four currency futures are smaller than one, which means that the distribution is strictly stationary. Secondly, there appears to be no asymmetry in the variance equation, since the estimates of γ are not statistically different from zero. These results are similar to those found in spot exchange rates.

While the EGARCH model can be justified on the grounds that it can approximate variance changes,[17] this chapter's main interest is to see if it can capture all the nonlinear dependence in price changes. If it does, the second step of this chapter's seminonparametric procedure can be taken. This can be tested as follows. Let $\hat{h}_t$ and $\hat{\mu}$ denote the fitted values of h_t and μ in the EGARCH model. The chapter wants to test whether the remaining movements in price changes, called standardized residuals,

$$\hat{\eta} = (x_t - \hat{\mu}) / \hat{h}_t^{1/2},$$

Table 16-5

EGARCH Estimates

$$x_t = \mu + h_t^{1/2}\eta_t$$

$$\eta_t \sim N(0,1)$$

$$\text{Log}h_t = \alpha + \beta\text{Log}h_{t-1} + \varphi\left(|\eta_{t-1}| - (2/\pi)^{1/2}\right) + \gamma\eta_{t-1}$$

	BP	DM	JY	SF
μ	0.000319	0.000377	0.000232	0.000239
	(0.000208)	(0.000214)	(0.000189)	(0.000235)
α	−0.688127	−1.072229	−4.438289	−0.993241
	(0.030088)	(0.041828)	(0.756704)	(0.032479)
β	0.928780	0.889511	0.550707	0.895527
	(0.002995)	(0.004386)	(0.075851)	(0.003508)
ϕ	0.135854	0.187005	0.282167	0.157669
	(0.019961)	(0.028388)	(0.093357)	(0.024013)
γ	−0.110718	0.084173	0.313274	0.129035
	(0.177458)	(0.147279)	(0.201531)	(0.166507)

Bollerslev-Woolridge robust standard errors are in parentheses.

are IID. This can be done by running the BDS tests on the standardized residuals.

The results are reported in Table 16-6. There is one important caveat here. The asymptotic distribution of the BDS test cannot be used, as Brock, Hsieh, and LeBaron (1991) show that the BDS test is biased in favor of the null hypothesis of independence and identical distribution when applied to standardized residuals of EGARCH models. Therefore, simulated critical values of the BDS test that are provided in Table 16-6 are used. They indicate that the standardized residuals still reject independence and identical distribution for the DM and the SF, which means that the EGARCH model cannot capture all the nonlinear dependence in those two currency futures.

The second approach to modeling volatility is now turned to. The idea is to construct a daily measure of volatility using intraday futures data, which then allows the fitting of a time-series model of volatility. As in Kupiec (1990), this chapter's daily measure of volatility is the Parkinson (1980) range estimator of the standard deviation,

Table 16-6

EGARCH Standardized Residuals BDS Test for IID

m	δ	BP	DM	JY	SF
2	0.5	−0.61	−1.10	0.12	−1.34
3	0.5	−0.78	−1.35	0.17	−1.88*
4	0.5	−0.52	−1.08	0.95	−1.71*
5	0.5	−0.09	−0.99	1.90	−1.67
2	1.0	−0.50	−1.65	−0.62	−2.23*
3	1.0	−0.59	−1.77*	−0.69	−2.55*
4	1.0	−0.40	−1.45*	0.32	−2.35*
5	1.0	−0.14	−1.33*	0.89	−2.04*
2	1.5	−0.42	−1.54	−1.03	−2.41*
3	1.5	−0.56	−1.51*	−1.09	−2.59*
4	1.5	−0.50	−1.25*	0.16	2.29*
5	1.5	−0.31	−1.19*	0.77	−2.08*
2	2.0	−0.42	−1.24	−1.01	−2.05*
3	2.0	−0.54	−1.18	−0.89	−2.07*
4	2.0	−0.41	−0.97	0.33	−1.72*
5	2.0	−0.28	−0.98	0.85	−1.58*

* Statistically significant at the 5 percent two-tailed test based on the simulated critical values of an EGARCH model for 1,275 observations with 2,000 replications:

m	δ			
	0.50	1.00	1.50	2.00
2.5 Percent Critical Values				
2	−2.04	−1.95	−1.77	−1.62
3	−1.63	−1.39	−1.30	−1.31
4	−1.66	−1.22	−1.14	−1.15
5	−1.66	−1.22	−1.14	−1.15
97.5 Percent Critical Values				
2	1.73	1.58	1.57	1.56
3	1.70	1.45	1.49	1.83
4	1.85	1.47	1.49	2.22
5	1.85	1.47	1.49	2.22

$$\sigma_{P,t} = (0.361 \times 1{,}440/M)^{\frac{1}{2}} \operatorname{Log}\left(\text{High}_t/\text{Low}_t\right).$$

where $High_t$ and Low_t are the high and low transaction prices during each trading day, and M is the number of minutes during a trading day.[18] It should be pointed out that the standard deviation of the trading day in the CME, which is approximately 400 minutes at the end of the sample, is scaled up to a trading day of 24 hours (i.e., 1,440 minutes). While this particular scaling is motivated by the fact that the foreign-exchange market is open around-the-clock, any scaling factor is innocuous, as the second step of the chapter's seminonparametric method will provide the appropriate scaling factor.

It is important to stress here that $\sigma_{P,t}$ is the ex post measure of volatility, while this chapter is mainly interested in the ex ante, i.e., conditional, forecast of volatility. To obtain a conditional forecast of volatility, the following model for log price changes, x_t, is posited,

$$x_t = \sigma_{P,t}\, u_t,$$

$$\text{Log } \sigma_{P,t} = \alpha + \sum \beta_i \text{ Log } \sigma_{P,t-i} + v_t$$

where v_t is IID. This model is called the autoregressive volatility model. It is motivated by the fact that $\sigma_{P,t}$ is autocorrelated.[19] The ex ante volatility can be recovered, as follows. Regress Log $\sigma_{P,t}$ on its own lags and a constant term using ordinary least squares. For simplicity, this is called the "autoregressive volatility" model. The number of lags of Log $\sigma_{P,t}$ is determined by the Schwarz (1978) criterion: eight for the BP, eight for the DM, five for the JY, and eight for the SF. The estimates are given in Table 16-7. The persistence of volatility is measured by the sum of the β coefficients, which are 0.782 for the BP, 0.760 for the DM, 0.624 for the JY, and 0.736 for the SF. They are statistically less than 1 in all four cases, indicating that log volatility is strictly stationary. When compared to the EGARCH model, the autoregressive volatility model has much less persistence for the BP, DM, and SF. This will have an impact on the simulations in Section V.

As the issue of volatility persistence is important in the distinction between the autoregressive volatility and the EGARCH model, several tests of sensitivity and misspecification of the autoregressive volatility model are performed. First, the lagged values of log volatility up until the 20th lag are included. This does not change the results substantially. In particular, the sums of the β parameters increase slightly, to 0.844 (BP), 0.793 (DM), 0.675 (JY), and 0.779 (SF). But they are still statistically less than 1, as the $F(1,1234)$ statistics are 15.36 (BP), 21.69 (DM), 38.27 (JY), and 27.43 (SF).

Table 16-7

Estimates of the Autoregressive Volatility Model Using Parkinson's Standard Deviations

$$\text{Log } \sigma_{P,t} = \alpha + \Sigma \, \beta_i \text{Log } \sigma_{P,t\text{-}i} + v_t$$

	BP	DM	JY	SF
α	−1.037	−1.139	−1.874	−1.219
	(0.171)	(0.187)	(0.199)	(0.193)
$\text{Log}\sigma_{P,t\text{-}1}$	0.192	0.153	0.208	0.115
	(0.028)	(0.028)	(0.028)	(0.028)
$\text{Log}\alpha_{P,t\text{-}2}$	0.134	0.111	0.137	0.106
	(0.029)	(0.028)	(0.028)	(0.028)
$\text{Log}\alpha_{P,t\text{-}3}$	0.062	0.052	0.058	0.068
	(0.029)	(0.028)	(0.029)	(0.028)
$\text{Log}\alpha_{P,t\text{-}4}$	0.069	0.092	0.109	0.091
	(0.029)	(0.028)	(0.028)	(0.028)
$\text{Log}\alpha_{P,t\text{-}5}$	0.137	0.091	0.112	0.118
	(0.028)	(0.028)	(0.028)	(0.028)
$\text{Log}\alpha_{P,t\text{-}6}$	0.027	0.072		0.074
	(0.029)	(0.028)		(0.028)
$\text{Log}\alpha_{P,t\text{-}7}$	0.073	0.110		0.086
	(0.028)	(0.028)		(0.028)
$\text{Log}\alpha_{P,t\text{-}8}$	0.088	0.079		0.078
	(0.028)	(0.028)		(0.028)
$\bar{R}^2$	0.274	0.227	0.170	0.193
$\Sigma\beta_i$	0.782	0.760	0.624	0.736
	(0.129)	(0.124)	(0.165)	(0.099)
Test of				
$\Sigma\beta_i = 1$	36.59	37.27	91.73	55.71
$F(n_1, n_2)$	1,1258	1,1258	1,1264	1,1260
	[0.0000]	[0.0000]	[0.0000]	[0.0000]

Standard errors in parentheses, p-values in square brackets.

The standard errors and test of $\Sigma\beta_i = 1$ do not change when using a heteroskedasticity-consistent covariance matrix.

Second, the day-of-the-week dummy variables are added to the model, since the literature has found them to be statistically important in variance changes.[20] While most of the day-of-the-week dummies are statistically different from zero, they add little to the explanatory power. The $\bar{R}^2s$ improve only marginally, rising to 0.284 (from 0.274), 0.242 (from 0.227), 0.181 (from 0.170), and 0.208 (from 0.193) in the BP, DM, JY, and SF, respectively. In addition, the Schwarz criterion worsens in three of the four currencies. These dummies also did not change the amount of volatility persistence. The sums of the β coefficients are 0.785 (BP), 0.765 (DM), 0.627 (JY), and 0.740 (SF), which are essentially the same as those without the dummies and remain statistically different from unity in all four cases. Thus, day-of-the-week dummies are excluded from the final model. Third, lags of the log volatilities of the other currencies are included. They did not appear to be statistically significant, and the Schwarz criterion worsens in all cases. Hence, the specification as reported in Table 16-7 has been kept.

To ensure that the autoregressive volatility model can capture all the predictability in currency futures, the BDS test is run on the standardized residuals,

$$z_t = x_t / \hat{\sigma}_{P,t},$$

where $\hat{\sigma}_{P,t}$ is the fitted value from the autoregressive volatility model. The results are reported in Table 16-8. Critical values of the BDS statistics are obtained through simulation, as done in Table 16-6. Little evidence has been found against the hypothesis that the standardized residuals are IID. For the BP, DM, and JY, there are no rejections of the null, while for the SF, three of the 16 statistics reject the null. Note that this rate of rejection is much lower than that of the EGARCH model in Table 16-6.

C. Estimating the Density of the Unpredictable Part of Futures Price Changes

The tests indicate that the autoregressive volatility model is appropriately specified and appears to have captured the predictable movements in exchange rates. The second step of the seminonparametric method, which involves modeling $z_t = x_t / \hat{\sigma}_{P,t}$, the unpredictable part of log price changes, is now considered.

Table 16-8 provides some information about z_t. The mean is close to zero. The standard deviation is close to unity. There is little evidence of skewness, but strong evidence of leptokurtosis. Using the BDS test, it has already been shown that z_t is IID, so its unconditional density can be estimated using standard methods. For example, a parametric density function, such as the Student-t, or a nonparametric density, using kernels or series expansions, can be fitted.

For the purposes of the applications in Section V, the density of z_t does not actually need to be estimated at all. Section V.A requires only the quantiles of z_t, which are provided in Table 16-8. In Section V.B, future values of x_t are simulated by "bootstrapping" from z_t, as per Efron (1982). These applications are now turned to.

Table 16-8

Statistical Description of Standardized Residuals of the
Autoregressive Volatility Model

	BP	DM	JY	SF
Mean	0.042	0.036	0.037	0.024
Median	0.051	0.000	0.000	0.019
Std. Dev.	0.880	0.853	1.031	0.842
Skewness	−0.035	0.053	0.196	0.025
Kurtosis	5.249	4.360	7.485	4.426
Maximum	5.078	3.389	6.897	3.513
Minimum	−3.560	−3.626	−5.205	−4.000
Quantiles				
0.50 percent	−3.017	−2.399	−3.623	−2.306
1.00 percent	−2.474	−2.245	−2.821	−2.080
5.00 percent	−1.411	−1.319	−1.557	−1.322
10.00 percent	−0.970	−0.937	−1.046	−0.985
90.00 percent	1.067	1.135	1.228	1.096
95.00 percent	1.504	1.487	1.697	1.422
99.00 percent	2.304	2.220	2.611	2.137
99.50 percent	2.590	2.418	3.271	2.572
BDS Statistics				
m $\quad$ δ				
2 $\quad$ 0.5	−0.61	−0.45	1.69	−1.27
3 $\quad$ 0.5	−0.96	−1.09	1.45	−1.64
4 $\quad$ 0.5	−0.97	−1.24	1.65	−1.20
5 $\quad$ 0.5	−1.01	−1.36	2.04	−1.20
2 $\quad$ 1.0	−0.24	−0.91	1.77	−1.80
3 $\quad$ 1.0	−0.86	−1.28	1.33	−2.23*
4 $\quad$ 1.0	−0.94	−1.17	1.69	−2.07*
5 $\quad$ 1.0	−1.02	−1.25	1.77	−1.88
2 $\quad$ 1.5	0.42	−0.68	1.48	−1.80
3 $\quad$ 1.5	−0.23	−0.83	1.17	−2.04*
4 $\quad$ 1.5	−0.32	−0.66	1.91	−1.82
5 $\quad$ 1.5	−0.44	−0.73	1.99	−1.73
2 $\quad$ 2.0	0.75	−0.40	0.84	−1.42
3 $\quad$ 2.0	0.41	−0.32	0.88	−1.52
4 $\quad$ 2.0	0.38	−0.11	1.60	−1.31
5 $\quad$ 2.0	0.26	−0.20	1.66	−1.34

* Statistically significant at the 5 percent two–tailed test, based on the simulated critical values of an autoregressive volatility model for 1,275 observations with 2,000 replications:

			δ	
m	0.50	1.00	1.50	2.00
2.5 Percent Critical Values				
2	−1.84	−1.86	−1.86	−1.96
3	−1.86	−1.88	−1.85	−1.96
4	−1.86	−1.87	−1.93	−1.96
5	−1.77	−1.89	−1.91	−1.96
97.5 Percent Critical Values				
2	1.90	1.94	1.92	1.96
3	2.01	1.94	2.00	1.96
4	2.01	1.95	2.12	1.96
5	2.04	2.06	2.05	1.96

V. Application to Risk Management: Minimum Capital Requirements

There are many uses of the conditional density of price changes. In this section, the minimum capital requirement of a futures position is calculated. First, it is shown that there is a direct method to obtain daily minimum capital requirements and, second, that longer-term minimum capital requirements can be obtained via simulation.

A. Daily Minimum Capital Requirements

Suppose a firm holds a long position of L_t units of a foreign currency futures contract. An important question in risk management is: What is the minimum capital K needed to cover losses of this long position with a 99.5 percent probability?

The minimum capital is the sum of prearranged lines of credit and short-term liquid instruments that can be converted to cash almost instantaneously, e.g., Treasury bills, negotiable certificates of deposit, money market funds, interest-bearing checking accounts, etc. Note that 99.5 percent has been selected as the "coverage probability" purely for illustrative purposes.[21]

The capital requirement, K_t, is determined as follows. Let P_{t+1} be the settlement price in the following trading day. The losses of the long position are given by $(P_t - P_{t+1})L_t$. Thus, K_t is wanted to solve the following equation,

$$\Pr\{(P_t - P_{t+1})L_t > K_t\} = 0.005.$$

The left-hand side can be rewritten as follows:

$$\Pr\left\{\text{Log}(1 - \kappa_t)/\sigma_{t+1|t} > z_{t+1}\right\} = 0.005,$$

where $\kappa_t = K_t/(P_t L_t)$, $z_{t+1} = x_{t+1}/\sigma_{t+1|t}$, $x_{t+1} = \text{Log}(P_{t+1}/P_t)$, and $\sigma_{t+1|t}$ denotes $\exp\{E_t(\text{Log}\,\sigma_{t+1})\}$. In particular, a rolling regression method can be used to sequentially generate $\sigma_{t+1|t}$. The minimum capital is now expressed as a fraction of $P_t L_t$.

To solve for κ_t, the quantiles of the distribution of z_{t+1}, which are provided in Table 16-8, only need to be known. The quantile z_l is the point where

$$\Pr\left\{z_l > z_{t+1}\right\} = 0.005.$$

In particular, z_l is -3.017 for the BP, -2.399 for the DM, -3.623 for the JY, and -2.306 for the SF. For each currency, then, the minimum capital as a fraction of the market value of the long position is

$$\kappa_t = 1 - \exp (\sigma_{t+1|t} z_l) .$$

Since z_l is a negative number, an increase in $\sigma_{t+1|t}$ will increase the capital requirement.

As $\sigma_{t+1|t}$ is time varying, so is κ_t. In contrast, the capital requirement using the unconditional density is constant over time. When the conditional variance is larger (smaller) than the unconditional variance, the capital requirement using the conditional density is higher (lower) than that of the unconditional density.

In the second example, suppose the firm is holding a short position of S_t units of currencies in futures contracts. (Shorts are represented by *negative* quantities, i.e., $S_t < 0$.) The capital requirement, K_t, which can cover the losses of the short position with a 99.5-percent probability, is found in an analogous manner. Let $\zeta_t = K_t / (-P_t S_t)$ be the capital requirement as a fraction of $(-P_t S_t)$. Then ζ_t is given by the equation,

$$\zeta_t = \exp (\sigma_{t+1|t} z_h) - 1,$$

where z_h is the quantile of z_t such that,

$$\Pr \{z_h > z_t\} = 0.995.$$

Based on Table 16-8, z_h equals 2.590 for the BP, 2.418 for the DM, 3.271 for the JY, and 2.572 for the SF. As z_h is positive, an increase in $\sigma_{t+1|t}$ will raise the capital requirement. In contrast, the capital requirement using the unconditional density is constant over time.

In the third example, a futures exchange setting futures margin requirements to protect the capital of its clearing members from defaults by futures traders is considered. There are two types of futures margins: initial margins and maintenance margins. For illustrative purposes, the maintenance margin is concentrated on. Suppose the futures exchange desires to set the maintenance margin to ensure that it is sufficient to cover possible losses of either long or short positions at least 99.5 percent of the time. In other words, the maintenance margin as a percent of the price times the size of the futures contract should be the maximum of the capital requirements for the long and the short sides, i.e., max $\{k_t, \zeta_t\}$. While there is a 0.5 percent chance that the maintenance margin cannot cover the losses of the futures contract, this should be interpreted as an upper bound of the default probability for a futures contract, since a trader can add funds to his or her account to cover losses exceeding the maintenance margin.

B. Application to Risk Management: Longer-Term Minimum Capital Requirements

So far, the capital requirements for holding a futures position for one trading day have been considered. It would be reasonable to ask how much capital is needed for holding a futures position for longer periods.

This consideration can arise in many contexts. For example, a firm is planning to use a currency futures contract to hedge the exchange-rate risk of inflows of British pounds three months from now. The goal of the hedge is to balance gains (losses) in the cash inflow with losses (gains) in the futures position as the exchange rate fluctuates. The problem facing the firm, however, is that a futures position is marked to market, so that gains and losses are settled at the end of each trading day, while the cash position is settled in entirety three months from now. If the exchange rate moves in such a way that the cash position is making profits while the futures position is sustaining losses, the firm may need additional funds to meet margin requirements on the futures position because it cannot use the gains in the cash position to offset these losses. If the firm is unable to meet margin requirements, it will be forced to liquidate the futures position prematurely, which defeats the purpose of hedging. Before the firm commits to the hedging strategy using futures, it must know how much capital (e.g., additional funds) may be needed to maintain this futures position for the next three months.

The answer to this question can be obtained via a simulation study. Start with the conditional density of price changes at the time when the firm initially opens the futures position. For the sake of illustration, take this to be the end of the data sample, March 9, 1990. Simulate the path of the futures price over the course of the next three months. At the end of each trading day, track the value of the futures position, and record its lowest value during the three-month period. This is the maximum "drawdown" for this simulated path, which represents the maximum loss sustained by the firm while holding the futures position. If the firm's additional funds are less than this maximum drawdown, it would not be able to maintain its futures position. By repeating this for 10,000 simulated paths, an empirical distribution of the maximum drawdown is generated. The capital requirement can then be set to the amount that is able to cover a given percentage of the simulated maximum drawdowns. The 90 percent coverage probability is used, because 10,000 replications is not accurate enough to measure the extreme tails of a distribution.

The simulation can be done as follows. Recall that the seminonparametric model of futures price changes is given by

$$x_t = \sigma_{P,t}\, u_t,$$

$$\text{Log } \sigma_{P,t} = \alpha + \sum\beta_i \text{ Log } \sigma_{P,t-i} + v_t,$$

where $x_t = \text{Log}(P_t/P_{t-1})$. A simulated path of future x_ts is generated recursively using the estimates of α and βs from the sample, and the values of $\sigma_{P,t}$ at the end of the sample. The u_t and v_t are drawn randomly, with replacement, from the residuals in a "bootstrap" fashion, per Efron (1982).

Table 16-9 reports the results of the simulation experiment for the capital requirement needed to hold a futures position with 90 percent probability. The holding period of the futures position is varied over 1, 5, 10, 15, 20, 25, 30, 60, 90, and 180 trading days. The 95 percent central confidence intervals for these capital requirements are given in Table 16-10.[22] For comparison, the simulations using the unconditional density and the EGARCH model are also reported. In the case of the unconditional density, the x_ts are drawn randomly, with replacement, from the 1,275 observed price changes. In the case of the EGARCH model, the simulated x_ts use the estimated values of α, β, ϕ, and λ, and the value of h_t at the end of the sample. The η_ts are drawn randomly, with replacement, from the standardized residuals, in a way analogous to the autoregressive volatility model.

To understand the results, keep in mind that the simulation was started on March 9, 1990, when the volatility was below the sample average.[23] Thus, the autoregressive volatility model predicts a lower volatility in the near future than the unconditional density.

Consider holding a long futures position in the BP. For a one-day holding period, the capital requirement is 0.73 percent of the initial face value of the contract according to the autoregressive volatility model and 0.91 percent according to the unconditional density. (If the simulation had started on a day that had a higher volatility than the sample average, the capital requirement based on the autoregressive volatility model would have been higher than that based on the unconditional density.) For a five-day holding period, the capital requirements are, respectively, 1.9 percent and 2.3 percent.

These differences in capital requirements are both statistically and economically significant. In the case of the one-day holding period for the BP, there is a 95 percent probability that the correct capital requirement using the autoregressive model is higher than 0.70 percent and lower than 0.74 percent of the initial face value of the contract. At the same time, there is a 95 percent probability that the correct capital requirement using the unconditional density is higher than 0.85 percent and lower than 0.95 percent. Furthermore, the difference between capital requirements of 0.73

Table 16-9

Capital Requirement for 90 Percent Coverage Probability
as a Percent of the Initial Value

	No. of Days	Long Position			Short Position		
		AR	Uncond.	EGARCH	AR	Uncond.	EGARCH
BP	1	0.73	0.91	0.93	0.80	0.98	1.05
	5	1.90	2.30	2.61	2.18	2.76	3.00
	10	2.83	3.27	4.19	3.38	4.22	4.88
	15	3.54	3.94	5.72	4.45	5.48	6.67
	20	4.10	4.61	6.96	5.24	6.33	8.43
	25	4.59	5.15	8.25	6.20	7.36	10.46
	30	5.02	5.58	9.08	7.11	8.33	12.06
	60	7.24	7.44	14.50	11.64	12.87	20.71
	90	8.74	8.70	17.91	15.45	16.90	28.03
	180	11.38	10.67	24.25	25.81	27.36	48.02
DM	1	0.72	0.87	0.83	0.89	1.00	0.95
	5	1.89	2.18	2.34	2.23	2.70	2.91
	10	2.77	3.14	3.93	3.40	4.12	5.03
	15	3.52	3.86	5.37	4.36	5.30	6.92
	20	4.05	4.45	6.54	5.19	6.14	8.91
	25	4.55	4.90	7.86	6.14	7.21	10.69
	30	4.93	5.37	8.75	7.02	7.88	12.36
	60	7.16	7.24	13.14	11.36	12.38	20.86
	90	8.87	8.39	16.06	14.68	16.16	27.75
	180	11.38	10.35	21.69	24.25	26.25	45.68
JY	1	0.56	0.74	0.72	0.68	0.87	0.86
	5	1.61	1.99	2.22	1.92	2.36	2.73
	10	2.59	2.82	3.46	3.06	3.53	4.41
	15	3.30	3.46	4.37	4.11	4.60	5.79
	20	3.95	4.10	5.09	5.13	5.45	6.77
	25	4.42	4.58	5.78	5.91	6.30	7.98
	30	4.95	4.92	6.34	6.58	6.85	8.81
	60	6.99	6.84	8.72	10.53	10.74	13.58
	90	8.43	8.00	10.51	13.61	14.00	17.63
	180	10.97	10.27	13.99	21.86	22.21	27.39
SF	1	0.82	0.97	0.89	0.93	1.12	0.98
	5	1.99	2.51	2.48	2.23	2.93	2.98
	10	2.87	3.60	4.12	3.37	4.53	5.09
	15	3.67	4.35	5.60	4.22	5.67	7.03
	20	4.24	5.10	6.82	5.09	6.69	8.86
	25	4.81	5.65	8.12	5.90	7.77	10.93
	30	5.23	6.20	9.12	6.70	8.47	12.50
	60	7.69	8.41	13.73	10.55	13.10	21.27
	90	9.23	9.93	16.89	13.60	17.06	27.80
	180	12.18	12.57	22.92	21.72	27.45	45.47

percent versus 0.91 percent is economically significant, when transactions have face values of several hundred million dollars, such as the case when highly leveraged instruments are involved.

Tables 16-9 and 16-10 also provide some information on the convergence behavior of the autoregressive volatility model to the unconditional density. First, it is observed that the capital requirements (and their associated confidence intervals) of the former approach those of the latter as the holding period lengthens. For the BP, this occurs in 90 (trading) days. The DM takes 60 trading days, while the JY takes only 30 days. But the SF takes more than 180 days.[24] However, the convergence is likely to be oscillatory rather than monotonic, as the autoregressive model of volatility has several lags.

In comparison, the EGARCH model produced dramatically different results. Over a one-day holding period, the capital requirements based on the EGARCH model are similar to those based on the unconditional density. However, when simulating into the future, the EGARCH model produces much larger capital requirements than both the autoregressive volatility model and the unconditional density. This phenomenon is due to the high degree of volatility persistence in the EGARCH model. During the simulation period, a large price change (either positive or negative) will cause the conditional variance of the EGARCH model to increase and to remain high for a long period of time.[25] In contrast, there is much less volatility persistence in the autoregressive volatility model and none in the unconditional model. This persistence in volatility also means that the convergence of the EGARCH model to the unconditional density is extremely slow. As many as 500 trading days into the future have been simulated. For the BP, DM, and SF, the capital requirements from the EGARCH model are still twice as high as those from the unconditional density. The exception is the JY. Its capital requirements from the EGARCH model are roughly 50 percent higher than those from the unconditional density. This demonstrates that, while the EGARCH model may produce satisfactory one-day-ahead volatility forecasts, it may not be appropriate for multistep-ahead volatility forecasts.

Another interesting feature in Table 16-9 is that a short position requires more capital than a corresponding long position at any given coverage probability. This is due to the fact that the futures price is bounded below by zero, but unbounded above. Even when the logarithmic rate of change of the futures price is symmetric, the change in the futures price itself is asymmetric. Thus, the probability of a one-dollar decrease in futures price is less than that of a one-dollar increase. This accounts for the difference in the capital requirements between a long and a short position.

Table 16-10

Approximate 95 Percent Central Confidence Intervals for Capital Requirement for 90 Percent Coverage Probability as a Percent of the Initial Value

	No. of Days	Long Position			Short Position		
		AR	Uncond.	EGARCH	AR	Uncond.	EGARCH
BP	1	[0.70, 0.74]	[0.86, 0.95]	[0.90, 0.96]	[0.78, 0.82]	[0.96, 0.99]	[1.01, 1.07]
	5	[1.87, 1.95]	[2.26, 2.37]	[2.54, 2.67]	[2.14, 2.25]	[2.70, 2.83]	[2.95, 3.06]
	10	[2.76, 2.91]	[3.19, 3.34]	[4.08, 4.30]	[3.30, 3.48]	[4.15, 4.30]	[4.77, 4.99]
	15	[3.47, 3.61]	[3.87, 4.02]	[5.57, 5.90]	[4.36, 4.53]	[5.38, 5.59]	[6.54, 6.84]
	20	[4.02, 4.20]	[4.52, 4.72]	[6.82, 7.17]	[5.12, 5.34]	[6.22, 6.44]	[8.31, 8.62]
	25	[4.49, 4.70]	[5.03, 5.29]	[8.06, 8.43]	[6.08, 6.33]	[7.22, 7.51]	[10.26,10.64]
	30	[4.94, 5.14]	[5.44, 5.72]	[8.87, 9.32]	[7.00, 7.25]	[8.15, 8.48]	[11.83,12.30]
	60	[7.10, 7.45]	[7.31, 7.58]	[14.21,14.78]	[11.37,11.89]	[12.66,13.08]	[20.41,21.11]
	90	[8.55, 8.94]	[8.57, 8.92]	[17.51,18.25]	[15.22,15.73]	[16.56,17.23]	[27.50,28.62]
	180	[11.15,11.66]	[10.45,10.92]	[23.93,24.74]	[25.33,26.29]	[27.00,27.76]	[47.00,49.05]
DM	1	[0.68, 0.75]	[0.81, 0.90]	[0.78, 0.85]	[0.85, 0.91]	[0.96, 1.08]	[0.93, 0.99]
	5	[1.85, 1.94]	[2.15, 2.23]	[2.28, 2.40]	[2.19, 2.28]	[2.64, 2.75]	[2.86, 2.97]
	10	[2.70, 2.84]	[3.08, 3.22]	[3.86, 4.02]	[3.34, 3.47]	[4.04, 4.22]	[4.92, 5.16]
	15	[3.44, 3.58]	[3.77, 3.93]	[5.28, 5.51]	[4.28, 4.44]	[5.21, 5.40]	[6.80, 7.08]
	20	[3.96, 4.14]	[4.35, 4.55]	[6.41, 6.69]	[5.10, 5.28]	[6.02, 6.26]	[8.70, 9.07]
	25	[4.47, 4.65]	[4.80, 5.00]	[7.71, 8.00]	[6.00, 6.26]	[7.07, 7.38]	[10.47,10.90]
	30	[4.84, 5.06]	[5.24, 5.47]	[8.57, 8.95]	[6.91, 7.16]	[7.73, 8.02]	[12.10,12.65]
	60	[7.03, 7.33]	[7.12, 7.42]	[12.94,13.43]	[11.15,11.59]	[12.18,12.57]	[20.58,21.32]
	90	[8.66, 9.06]	[8.22, 8.60]	[15.77,16.44]	[14.48,15.03]	[15.89,16.46]	[27.17,28.27]
	180	[11.13,11.63]	[10.11,10.59]	[21.31,22.14]	[23.88,24.61]	[25.83,26.64]	[44.81,46.62]
JY	1	[0.56, 0.60]	[0.72, 0.76]	[0.70, 0.75]	[0.68, 0.72]	[0.86, 0.92]	[0.81, 0.89]
	5	[1.60, 1.67]	[1.94, 2.04]	[2.16, 2.28]	[1.89, 1.98]	[2.33, 2.41]	[2.67, 2.81]
	10	[2.45, 2.58]	[2.77, 2.88]	[3.38, 3.53]	[3.06, 3.20]	[3.46, 3.61]	[4.30, 4.51]
	15	[3.23, 3.39]	[3.41, 3.54]	[4.26, 4.46]	[4.03, 4.21]	[4.50, 4.69]	[5.65, 5.93]
	20	[3.84, 4.01]	[4.02, 4.19]	[4.99, 5.18]	[4.93, 5.15]	[5.36, 5.58]	[6.65, 6.93]
	25	[4.33, 4.52]	[4.47, 4.67]	[5.66, 5.91]	[5.75, 6.00]	[6.17, 6.41]	[7.81, 8.13]
	30	[4.79, 4.97]	[4.84, 5.03]	[6.24, 6.46]	[6.50, 6.77]	[6.74, 6.99]	[8.61, 9.05]
	60	[6.90, 7.19]	[6.69, 6.97]	[8.61, 8.92]	[10.33,10.70]	[10.57,10.95]	[13.35,13.87]
	90	[8.29, 8.63]	[7.87, 8.16]	[10.32,10.69]	[13.36,13.91]	[13.81,14.28]	[17.31,17.93]
	180	[10.76,11.23]	[10.09,10.49]	[13.74,14.25]	[21.47,22.26]	[21.79,22.47]	[26.97,27.93]
SF	1	[0.79, 0.84]	[0.95, 1.01]	[0.86, 0.92]	[0.89, 0.96]	[1.10, 1.16]	[0.95, 1.02]
	5	[1.94, 2.04]	[2.45, 2.57]	[2.44, 2.54]	[2.19, 2.29]	[2.86, 3.00]	[2.91, 3.04]
	10	[2.80, 2.94]	[3.51, 3.67]	[4.06, 4.18]	[3.30, 3.45]	[4.43, 4.62]	[4.98, 5.21]
	15	[3.59, 3.75]	[4.28, 4.45]	[5.46, 5.74]	[4.16, 4.32]	[5.57, 5.75]	[6.91, 7.17]
	20	[4.15, 4.33]	[4.99, 5.20]	[6.68, 6.97]	[4.98, 5.18]	[6.57, 6.83]	[8.68, 9.06]
	25	[4.71, 4.93]	[5.54, 5.77]	[7.96, 8.27]	[5.80, 6.02]	[7.60, 7.93]	[10.63,11.12]
	30	[5.11, 5.34]	[6.11, 6.31]	[8.97, 9.29]	[6.58, 6.84]	[8.33, 8.65]	[12.16,12.80]
	60	[7.55, 7.80]	[8.23, 8.57]	[13.48,14.00]	[10.37,10.80]	[12.92,13.37]	[20.88,21.64]
	90	[9.06, 9.42]	[9.72,10.17]	[16.69,17.17]	[13.32,13.89]	[16.83,17.34]	[27.36,28.37]
	180	[11.98,12.43]	[12.27,12.87]	[22.62,23.29]	[21.34,22.09]	[27.01,27.88]	[44.72,46.46]

The first number in the square bracket is the left side of the confidence interval. The second number is the right side of the confidence interval.

VI. Conclusions

This chapter demonstrates that when log price changes are not IID, their conditional density may be more accurate than their unconditional density for describing short-term behavior. Using the BDS test of independence and identical distribution, it is shown that daily log price changes in four currency futures contracts are not IID. While there appear to be no predictable conditional mean changes, conditional variances are predictable, and can be described by an autoregressive volatility model. Furthermore, this autoregressive volatility model seems to capture all the departures from independence and identical distribution.

Based on this model, daily log price changes can be decomposed into a predictable part and an unpredictable part. The predictable part is described parametrically by the autoregressive volatility model. The unpredictable part can be modeled by an empirical density, either parametrically or nonparametrically. This two-step seminonparametric method yields a conditional density for daily log price changes, which has a number of uses in financial risk management.

In particular, the chapter shows how to directly calculate the capital requirement needed to cover losses of a futures position over one trading day, and how to use simulation to obtain the capital requirement over longer holding periods. The chapter finds that the conditional density can provide different, and probably more accurate, capital requirements than the unconditional density.

Acknowledgments

The author acknowledges the help of Cathy McCrae and Richard McDonald of the Chicago Mercantile Exchange in providing the data used in the analysis. He is grateful for comments from Francis Diebold and JFQA Referee Wayne Ferson, as well as participants at the November 1991 Conference on Volatility at the Amsterdam Institute of Finance and the April 1992 Conference on Global Risk Management of Interest Rate and Exchange Rate Risk at the Berkeley Program in Finance.

Endnotes

1   See LeBaron (1988), Scheinkman and LeBaron (1989), and Hsieh (1991) for stock returns and Hsieh (1989) for exchange rates.

2   This is more restrictive than the general notion, which allows conditioning on other information. The univariate approach in this paper is much simpler computationally than the multivariate approach. When conditioning on other information, such as trading volume, these additional variables will need to be modeled.

3   Parametric unconditional densities have been estimated by Fama (1965) and Blattberg and Gonedes (1974) for stock returns, and Westerfield (1977), Rogalski and Vinso (1978), and Boothe and Glassman (1987) for exchange rates.

4   Suppose x_t is given by the following process,

$$x_t = \sigma_t u_t,$$

$$\text{Log } \sigma_t = \alpha + \beta \text{ Log } \sigma_{t-1} + v_t,$$

where u_t is IID, normal, with mean 0 and variance 1, and v_t is IID, normal, with mean 0 and variance σ_v^2. Furthermore, u_t and v_s are independent for all t and s, and $|\beta| < 1$. It is easy to verify that the conditional and unconditional distribution of x_t is different, and that the conditional variance of x_t can be either larger or smaller than the unconditional variance.

5   See Brock, Hsieh, and LeBaron (1991) for a discussion of this point.

6   See Scheinkman and LeBaron (1989) and Hsieh (1989).

7   Note that IID implies that $C_m(\delta) = (C_1(\delta))^m$, but the converse is not true. Dechert (1988) gives some pathological examples of non-IID data for which $C_m(\delta) - (C_1(\delta))^m$.

8   This finding contradicts those of Hodrick and Srivastava (1987) and McCurdy and Morgan (1987), who find strong autocorrelation in log price changes in currency futures prices using data for which daily price limits were in effect but were not taken into account. Kodres (1988) uses a limited dependent variable method, but fails to take account of the conditional heteroskedasticity, as pointed out by Harvey (1988).

9   The reader may be concerned with the role of maturity drift in these results using futures data. It is possible that a fixed maturity futures price change is IID, but the distribution of an n-period maturity futures price change is different from that of an $n-1$ period maturity futures price change. This may induce "spurious" rejection of IID. To check that this is not the case, Appendix A and B (available from the author) provide the BDS statistics and autocorrelation coefficients of the abso-

lute values of daily log price changes of spot currencies, collected by the Board of Governors of the Federal Reserve System, for the same time period. The spot exchange rates (on a two-day forward contract) have essentially the same statistical behavior as the currency futures.

10 The two-step procedure may suffer from some efficiency loss. However, with the sample size here, the longer computation time of joint estimation is a greater cost than any gain in efficiency.

11 The proof relies on the law of iterated expectations, $E(x_t x_{t-i} x_{t-j}) = E(E[Ex_t | x_{t-1}, \ldots] x_{t-i} x_{t-j}) = 0$.

12 Note the restriction that ε_t is IID is needed to prove consistency of nonparametric methods to estimate the function $g(\ )$.

13 Diebold and Nason (1990) and Meese and Rose (1990) found that LWR does not outperform a random walk model in forecasting spot exchange rates in terms of mean squared error or mean absolute error. It is possible that LWR has low power in detecting conditional mean changes. But the simulations in Hsieh (1991) show that LWR can detect all the nonlinear dynamics models most often cited in the time-series literature.

14 The extension to the case with multiple lags is straightforward.

15 The significance of day-of-the-week dummies, which turn out not to be a factor in the conditional mean, has also been tested for.

16 The $(2/\pi)^{1/2}$ is used to center the mean of $|\eta_{t-1}|$ at 0.

17 See Nelson (1990) for a discussion.

18 For the BP, the trading hours are 7:30 a.m. to 1:24 p.m. from 2/22/85 until 10/14/85, and 7:20 a.m. to 1:24 p.m. from 10/15/85 to 10/04/88. For the DM, the corresponding trading hours are 7:30 a.m. to 1:20 p.m. and 7:20 a.m. to 1:20 p.m. For the JY, they are 7:30 a.m. to 1:22 p.m. and 7:20 a.m. to 1:22 p.m. For the SF, the corresponding trading hours are 7:30 a.m. to 1:16 p.m. and 7:20 a.m. to 1:16 p.m. Since 10/05/88, the trading hours for all currency futures are 7:20 a.m. to 2:00 p.m.

19 A similar model was identified for the Standard & Poor's 500 cash index in Hsieh (1991).

20 See Hsieh (1988) for a discussion of day-of-the-week effects in spot currencies.

21 A theory of hedging is needed to determine whether "coverage probability" is the appropriate amount for hedging and what the optimal "coverage probability" should be.

22 Efron (1982) provides a nonparametric method to estimate the confidence interval for a quantile. Let X be a random variable with distribution F. θ, defined as $\text{Prob}\{X < \theta\} = q$, needs to be estimated. Let $x(1)$, ..., $x(n)$ be the ordered data from a sample of size n. A confidence interval for θ, $(x(j), x(k))$, can be found as follows. Observe that $\text{Prob}\{x(j) < \theta \leq x(k)\} = \text{Prob}\{j < Z \leq k\}$, where $Z = \#\{x(i) < \theta\}$ is a binomial distribution. Suppose a 90 percent confidence interval for θ is wanted. j and k can be determined such that $\text{Prob}\{j < Z \leq k\} = 0.95$. If n is small, the exact binomial distribution of Z can be used. Since n is large in this case (i.e., 10,000) the binomial distribution is approximated with a normal distribution.

23 On that day, the Parkinson volatilities are 12.48 percent, 9.51 percent, 7.90 percent, and 8.90 percent, respectively, for the BP, DM, JY, and SF. Over the entire sample, the averages of the Parkinson volatilities are 16.13 percent, 16.06 percent, 12.68 percent, and 18.01 percent, respectively.

24 The SF actually takes about 250 trading days, according to the simulations, which are not reported in Tables 16-9 and 16-10.

25 This explanation is confirmed by the following experiment. The EGARCH model is estimated subject to the constraint that $\beta = 0$ in the variance equation. This allows much less volatility persistence. In the case of the BP, the restricted EGARCH model produced capital requirements of 12.26 percent at the 180-day holding period for long positions, and 31.00 percent for short positions. These are much closer to the capital requirements in Table 16-9 for the autoregressive volatility model and the unconditional density, and very different from those produced by the unrestricted EGARCH model.

References

Berndt, E. K., B. H. Hall, R. E. Hall, and J. A. Hausman. "Estimation and Inference in Nonlinear Structural Models." *Annals of Economic and Social Measurement*, 4 (1974), 653–665.

Blattberg, R. C., and N. Gonedes. "A Comparison of the Stable Paretian and Student Distribution as Statistical Model for Prices." *Journal of Business*, 47 (1974), 244–280.

Bollerslev, T. "Generalized Autoregressive Conditional Heteroskedasticity." *Journal of Econometrics*, 31 (1986), 307–327.

Bollerslev, T., R. Chow, and K. Kroner. "ARCH Modeling in Finance: A Review of the Theory and Empirical Evidence." Working Paper No. 97, Dept. of Finance, Kellogg Graduate School of Management, Northwestern University (1990).

Bollerslev, T., and J. Wooldridge. "Quasi Maximum Likelihood Estimation of Dynamic Models with Time Varying Covariances." Unpubished Manuscript, Dept. of Economics, MIT (1989).

Boothe, P., and D. Glassman. "The Statistical Distribution of Exchange Rates: Empirical Evidence and Economic Implications." *Journal of International Economics*, 22 (1987), 297–319.

Brock, W., W. Dechert, and J. Scheinkman. "A Test for Independence Based on the Correlation Dimension." Working Paper, University of Wisconsin at Madison, University of Houston, and University of Chicago (1987).

Brock, W., D. Hsieh, and B. LeBaron. *Nonlinear Dynamics, Chaos, and Instability, Statistical Theory and Economic Evidence.* Cambridge, MA: MIT Press, 1991.

Clark, P. K. "A Subordinated Stochastic Process Model with Finite Variance for Speculative Prices." *Econometrica*, 41 (1973), 135–155.

Cleveland, W. S., and S. J. Devlin. "Locally Weighted Regression. An Approach to Regression Analysis by Local Fitting." *Journal of the American Statistical Association*, 83 (1988), 596–610.

Cornell, B., and M. Reinganum. "Forward and Futures Prices: Evidence from the Foreign Exchange Markets." *Journal of Finance*, 36 (1981), 1035–1046.

Cox, J., and S. Ross. "A Valuation of Options for Alternative Stochastic Processes." *Journal of Financial Economics*, 3 (1976), 145–166.

Dechert, W. "A Characterization of Independence for a Gaussian Process in Terms of the Correlation Dimension." SSRI Working Paper 8812, University of Wisconsin at Madison (1988).

Diebold, F., and J. Nason. "Nonparametric Exchange Rate Prediction?" *Journal of International Economics*, 28 (1990), 315–332.

Efron, B. *The Jackknife, the Bootstrap, and Other Resampling Plans.* Philadelphia, PA: Society for Industrial and Applied Mathematics, 1982.

Engle, R. "Autoregressive Conditional Heteroscedasticity with Estimates of the Variance of U.K. Inflations." *Econometrica*, 50 (1982), 987–1007.

Fama, E. "The Behavior of Stock Market Prices." *Journal of Business*, 38 (1965), 34–105.

Gallant, R., D. Hsieh, and G. Tauchen. "On Fitting a Recalcitrant Series: The Pound/Dollar Exchange Rate, 1974–83." In *Nonparametric and Semiparametric Methods in Econometrics and Statistics, Proceedings of the Fifth International Symposium in Economic Theory and Econometrics.* W. A. Barnett, J. Powell, and G. Tauchen, eds. Cambridge, England: Cambridge University Press, 1991.

Harvey, C. "Commentary on Tests of Unbiasedness in the Foreign Exchange Futures Markets: The Effects of Price Limits." *Review of Futures Markets,* 7 (1988), 167–171.

Hodrick, R., and S. Srivastava. "Foreign Currency Futures." *Journal of International Economics,* 22 (1987), 1–24.

Hsieh, D. "Statistical Properties of Daily Exchange Rates." *Journal of International Economics,* 24 (1988), 129–145.

———. "Testing for Nonlinearity in Daily Foreign Exchange Rate Changes." *Journal of Business,* 62 (1989), 339–368.

———. "Chaos and Nonlinear Dynamics: Application to Financial Markets." *Journal of Finance,* 46 (1991), 1839–1877.

Hsieh, D., and B. LeBaron. "Finite Sample Properties of the BDS Statistic." Unpublished Manuscript, University of Chicago and University of Wisconsin at Madison, 1988.

Kodres, L. "Tests of Unbiasedness in the Foreign Exchange Futures Markets: The Effects of Price Limits." *Review of Futures Markets,* 7 (1988), 139–166.

Kupiec, P. "Futures Margins and Stock Price Volatility: Is There Any Link?" Board of Governors of the Federal Reserve System, Finance and Economics Discussion Paper No. 104 (1990).

LeBaron, B. "The Changing Structure of Stock Returns." Working Paper, University of Wisconsin (1988).

McCurdy, T. H., and I. G. Morgan. "Tests of the Martingale Hypothesis for Foreign Currency Futures." *International Journal of Forecasting,* 3 (1987), 131–148.

Meese, R., and A. Rose. "Nonlinear, Nonparametric, Nonessential Exchange Rate Estimation." *American Economic Review,* 80 (1990), 192–196.

Nelson, D. "ARCH Models as Diffusion Approximations." *Journal of Econometrics,* 45 (1990), 7–38.

———. "Conditional Heteroskedasticity in Asset Returns: A New Approach." *Econometrica,* 59 (1991), 347–370.

Parkinson, M. "The Extreme Value Method of Estimating the Variance of the Rate of Return." *Journal of Business*, 53 (1980), 61–65.

Pemberton, J., and H. Tong. "A Note on the Distribution of Non-Linear Autoregressive Stochastic Models." *Journal of Time Series Analysis*, 2 (1981), 49–52.

Rogalski, R., and J. Vinso. "Empirical Properties of Foreign Exchange Rates." *Journal of International Business Studies*, 9 (1978), 69–79.

Schwarz, G. "Estimating the Dimension of a Model." *Annals of Statistics*, 6 (1978), 461–464.

Scheinkman, J., and B. LeBaron. "Nonlinear Dynamics and Stock Returns." *Journal of Business*, 62 (1989), 311–337.

Stone, C. J. "Consistent Nonparametric Regressions." *Annals of Statistics*, 5 (1977), 595–620.

Westerfield, J. "An Examination of Foreign Exchange Risk under Fixed and Floating Rate Regimes." *Journal of International Economics*, 7 (1977), 181–200.

17

Chaotic Behavior in Exchange-Rate Series: First Results for the Peseta-U.S. Dollar Case

By Oscar Bajo-Rubio, Fernando Fernández-Rodríguez,
and Simón Sosvilla-Rivero

1. Introduction

Since the adoption of floating exchange rates in the early 1970s, economic literature has witnessed a remarkable effort to model exchange rates in terms of other macroeconomic variables.

The dominant model has been for a long time the so-called asset market approach, which emphasized the role of the capital account of the balance of payments, as opposed to the current-account emphasis of the traditional flow model. However, the empirical performance of these models has been very poor and, as shown in the now classic paper by Meese and Rogoff (1983), their predictive ability has proved even worse than the one provided by a simple random walk.

Given these results, an alternative line of research has taken as its starting point the empirical regularities in the behavior of exchange rates [Mussa (1979)], stressing the role of the new information available to the agents, or "news." Such "news" would explain the observed deviations of exchange rates from the random walk.

Even though this line of research has proved to be a useful tool for helping us to understand exchange-rate movements, some problems remain. So, since "news" is not observable, these models would imply the impossibility of forecasting exchange rates. In addition, one might think that the extreme exchange-rate volatility experienced in the last years would be very difficult to explain only in terms of unanticipated information.

On the other hand, there has recently been a growing interest among economists for a new field of study that could offer an alternative explanation to the apparently random behavior of some economic variables. We are talking about *deterministic chaos*.

According to these new theories, a variable is said to show a chaotic behavior when its evolution seems to be apparently random, but is really deterministic. Then, a chaotic variable is a particular case of a nonlinear variable of which its future values, unlike the case of a random variable, can be predicted from some initial conditions. Frank and Stengos (1988) provide a survey on the economic applications of chaos theory.

Empirical tests on the existence of deterministic chaos in economic series have proliferated in recent years [see Sayers (1991) for a survey]. In general, it has been stressed that an accurate empirical testing of chaos requires the availability of high-quality, high-frequency data, which makes financial time series a good candidate for analyzing chaotic behavior.

Regarding exchange rates, De Grauwe and Vansanten (1990) have developed a formal model in which the introduction of nonlinearities results in chaotic behavior of the exchange rate. However, as far as we know, there are no available tests for the presence of deterministic chaos in exchange rates. Nevertheless, the existence of nonlinearities has been studied, with ambiguous results: even though Hsieh (1989) and Kugler and Lenz (1993) detect nonlinearities for several exchange rates (which can be explained by means of GARCH models), other papers by Diebold and Nason (1990) and Meese and Rose (1990, 1991) carry out nonparametric estimations of nonlinear models, without reaching significant improvements with respect to the linear models of exchange rates, and in particular the random walk model.

The purpose of this chapter, which presents the first results from a wider project in process [see, e.g., Sosvilla-Rivero et al. (1994)], is to test for the presence of deterministic chaos in the Spanish peseta–U.S. dollar spot and one- and three-month forward exchange rate series, with daily data for the January 1985–May 1991 period. The finding of a chaotic behavior in the series will allow us, as a derivation of the previous analysis, to make short-run forecasts.

In Section 2 we briefly describe the tests and introduce a forecasting procedure in chaotic systems. In Section 3 we present the results from these tests as well as the predictions for different horizons. Section 4 concludes the chapter.

2. Deterministic Chaos in Time Series: Detection and Prediction

The two more extensively used procedures for detecting chaos are the correlation dimension and the Lyapunov exponents [see, e.g., Frank and Stengos (1988) for a detailed description of both procedures].

Both tests are based on the Takens (1981) embedding theorem: given a time series X_t ($t = 1, 2, ..., T$) in a n-dimensional phase space, the M-histories

$$X_t^M = (X_t, X_{t+1}, ..., X_{t+M-1})$$

can, if $M \geq 2n + 1$, mimic the dynamics of the data generation process.

The correlation dimension test, proposed by Grassberger and Procaccia (1983), is based on the integral correlation

$$C^M(\varepsilon) = \#\left\{(i,j),\ 1 \leq i,\ j \leq T,\ i \neq j:\ ||\ X_i^M - X_j^M\ || < \varepsilon\right\} / T_M^2,$$

where $\#A$, $||\cdot||$, M, T, and T_M denote, respectively, the cardinality of the set A, the Euclidean distance, the embedding dimension, the sample size, and the number of M-histories. Then, the correlation dimension is given by

$$D^M = \min_{\varepsilon \to 0}\ \lim_{T \to \infty}\ \left\{\ln C^M(\varepsilon)/\ln \varepsilon\right\}.$$

If the system is chaotic, then D^M will stabilize at some value D.

On the other hand, the fact that D^M stabilizes is only a necessary condition for detecting chaotic systems. Since one of the features defining chaotic systems is their strong dependence on initial conditions, an additional test for the existence of deterministic chaos in a time series would be given by a measure of the degree of divergence of the trajectories from two initial situations. This can be measured by the Lyapunov exponents.

Consider a very small ball with a radius $p(0)$ at time $t = 0$. The ball may distort into an ellipsoid as the dynamic system evolves. Denoting the length of the i-th principal axis of this ellipsoid at time t by $p_i(t)$, the i-th Lyapunov exponent would be given by

$$\lambda_i = \lim_{t \to \infty} \frac{1}{t} \ln \frac{p_i(t)}{p_i(0)} \, .$$

The presence of at least one positive exponent is taken generally as a definition of chaos. The Wolf algorithm allows us to compute the maximum Lyapunov exponent in empirical applications.

Under certain technical conditions, the inverse of the sum of the positive Lyapunov exponents provides the system's forecasting deterministic horizon [see Schuster (1984)].

The presence of deterministic chaos in a time series opens the possibility of short-term forecasting. Following Farmer and Sidorowich (1987), we can consider the last M-history:

$$X_N^M = (X_N, X_{N-1}, X_{N-2}, ..., X_{N-M+1}),$$

and then construct a local predictor by looking for the closest k points in the phase space $\mathfrak{R}^M$, where $k \geq M + 1$. In addition, we have also used two other local predictors, which take the k points most similar to the final M-history of the series (X_N^M) in two alternative ways: (1) by looking for the M-histories with the highest correlation with X_N^M, and (2) by looking for the M-histories with the lowest angle (i.e., the maximum cosine) with X_N^M. In what follows, these local predictors will be called, respectively, predictors by distance, by correlation, and by cosine.

3. Results

Given the presence of a unit root in the series, they were first differenced in order to obtain stationary series. In addition, and given the rather heterogeneous nature of the period under study, we divided the sample into three parts, the breaking points being January 1988 (when a reform in the Bank of Spain's intervention system took place) and June 1989 (when the peseta entered into the exchange rate mechanism of the European Monetary System [EMS]).

Table 17-1 presents the correlation dimensions obtained for different embedding dimensions. As shown in that table, the correlation dimensions stabilize from some embedding dimension (denoted by an asterisk) that indicates the presence of deterministic chaos. This result is further reinforced by the maximum Lyapunov exponents given in Table 17-2.

Table 17-1

Correlation Dimensions

					Embedding dimension							
	1	2	3	4	5	6	7	8	9	10	11	12
(A) Spot exchange rate												
Period I	0.6	1.1	1.6	2.1	2.7	3.1*	3.2	3.2	3.2	3.1	3.1	3.0
Period II	0.7	1.2	1.8	2.4	2.8*	2.8	2.7	2.5	2.4	2.4	2.4	2.4
Period III	0.8	1.1	1.8	2.3	2.6	2.7*	2.7	2.7	2.8	2.7	2.7	2.7
(B) One-month forward exchange rate												
Period I	0.8	1.7	2.3	2.7	2.9*	2.8	2.5	2.4	2.4	2.5	2.6	2.8
Period II	0.3	0.8	1.4	2.2	2.9*	3.1	3.0	2.9	2.6	2.4	2.3	2.2
Period III	0.5	0.9	1.8	2.0	2.4	2.7*	2.7	2.6	2.5	2.5	2.4	2.4
(C) Three-month forward exchange rate												
Period I	0.7	1.2	1.8	2.5	3.0	3.3*	3.4	3.3	3.2	3.1	3.0	3.0
Period II	0.7	0.9	1.1	1.4	1.6	1.7	1.9	2.0*	2.0	2.0	2.0	2.0
Period III	0.8	1.1	1.5	1.8*	1.9	1.8	1.8	1.9	1.9	1.9	1.9	1.9

Note: The asterisks are explained in the text.

Table 17-2

Maximum Lyapunov Exponents

	Period I	Period II	Period III
Spot	0.0856	0.0541	0.0631
1-month forward	0.0991	0.0813	0.0696
3-month forward	0.1365	0.0454	0.0643

Table 17-3 presents the inverse values of the maximum Lyapunov exponents shown in Table 17-2, providing the forecasting deterministic horizon in days.

Table 17-3

Forecasting Deterministic Horizons (in Days)

	Period I	Period II	Period III
Spot	11	18	15
1-month forward	10	12	14
3-month forward	7	22	15

Once we found chaotic behavior in the series under study as well as their forecasting deterministic horizons, we could apply our local predictors. Table 17-4 shows the root mean square errors (RMSEs) computed from both our predictors and the forecasts derived from a random walk.

As can be seen in this table, our local predictors provide lower RMSEs than those from the random walk in all cases for the one- and three-month forward exchange rates. As for the spot rate, the RMSEs from the local predictors are lower than that of the random walk only in the first period, and for the predictor by distance in period III.

4. Conclusions

In this chapter we have presented the first results from testing for the presence of deterministic chaos on daily data from the Spanish peseta–U.S. dollar, spot and one- and three-month forward exchange rates, for the period January 1985–May 1991.

Both the Grassberger-Procaccia test and the Lyapunov exponents seemed to suggest the presence of chaotic behavior for the three series under study. Next, several local predictors were proposed and computed,

Table 17-4

Root Mean Square Forecasting Errors

Predictor	Period I	Period II	Period III
(A) Spot exchange rate			
By correlation	0.0054	0.0194	0.0622
By cosine	0.0054	0.0193	0.0645
By distance	0.0093	0.0112	0.0196
Random walk	0.0383	0.0099	0.0254
(B) 1-month forward exchange rate			
By correlation	0.0037	0.0197	0.0059
By cosine	0.0042	0.0188	0.0062
By distance	0.0063	0.0196	0.0029
Random walk	0.0366	0.0322	0.0265
(C) 3-month forward exchange rate			
By correlation	0.0170	0.0276	0.0115
By cosine	0.0207	0.0254	0.0195
By distance	0.0248	0.0220	0.0169
Random walk	0.0549	0.0368	0.0376

which outperformed the random walk in all cases for the forward rates, whereas for the spot rate this only occurred in four out of nine cases.

References

De Grauwe, P., and K. Vansanten. "Deterministic Chaos in the Foreign Exchange Market." Discussion paper 370 (CEPR, London, 1990).

Diebold, F., and J. Nason. "Nonparametric Exchange Rate Prediction?" *Journal of International Economics* 28 (1990), 315–332.

Farmer, D., and J. Sidorowich. "Predicting Chaotic Time Series." *Physical Review Letters* 59 (1987), 845–848.

Frank, M., and T. Stengos. "Chaotic Dynamics in Economic Time-Series." *Journal of Economic Surveys* 2 (1988), 103–133.

Grassberger, P., and I. Procaccia. "Characterization of Strange Attractors." *Physical Review Letters* 50 (1983), 346–349.

Hsieh, D. "Testing for Nonlinear Dependence in Daily Foreign Exchange Rates." *Journal of Business* 62 (1989), 339–368.

Kugler, P., and C. Lenz. "Chaos, ARCH and the Foreign Exchange Market: Empirical Results from Weekly Data." *Rivista Internazionale di Scienze Economiche e Commerciali* 40 (1993), 127–140.

Meese, R., and K. Rogoff. "Empirical Exchange Rate Models of the Seventies: Do They Fit Out of Sample?" *Journal of International Economics* 14 (1983), 3–24.

Meese, R., and A. Rose. "Nonlinear, Nonparametric, Nonessential Exchange Rate Estimation." *American Economic Review* 80 (1990), 192–196.

Meese, R., and A. Rose. "An Empirical Assessment of Non-linearities in Models of Exchange Rate Determination." *Review of Economic Studies* 58 (1991), 603–619.

Mussa, M. "Empirical Regularities in the Behavior of Exchange Rates and Theories of the Foreign Exchange Market." *Carnegie-Rochester Conference Series on Public Policy* 11 (1979), 9–57.

Sayers, C. "Statistical Inference Based upon Non-linear Science." *European Economic Review* 35 (1991), 306–312.

Schuster, H. *Deterministic Chaos: An Introduction.* Weinheim: Physik-Verlag, 1984.

Sosvilla-Rivero, S., F. Fernández-Rodríguez, O. Bajo-Rubio, and J. Martín-González. "Exchange Rate Volatility in the EMS Before and After the Fall." Documento de Trabajo 94–16 (FEDEA, Madrid, 1994).

Takens, F. "Detecting Strange Attractors in Turbulence," in: D. Rand and L. Young, eds., *Dynamical Systems and Turbulence* Berlin: Springer-Verlag, 1981, 366–381.

18

NONLINEARITY IN THE INTEREST RATE RISK PREMIUM

By Ted Jaditz
and Chera L. Sayers

1. Introduction

In this chapter, we use nonlinear time-series methods to predict movements in the interest rate risk premium—the difference between interest rates on six-month commercial paper and six-month Treasury bills. It is well known that this risk premium is highly variable over time; see Lauterbach (1989) and references therein. Several authors have identified it as a variable that is useful in forecasting the future state of the economy. Yet modeling the spread presents certain problems. If one tries to model the spread using standard linear time-series techniques, diagnostic tests indicate significant dependence in the model residuals.

This chapter examines whether nearest-neighbor prediction methods can exploit this nonlinear dependence to improve out-of-sample forecasting. Our purpose is to determine whether near-neighbor forecasts are significantly better than global linear predictors. To model the spread, we use a nearest-neighbor algorithm (Casdagli, 1992) that utilizes local information to form a piecewise linear approximation to an unknown nonlinear function. Models with nonlinear level equations have offered remarkable improvements in out-of-sample forecasting in a number of economic and financial data sets. Some examples include Hamilton (1989) and Potter (1992) for GNP and Engle and Hamilton (1990) for exchange rates. In this chapter, we show how one can use the near-neighbor methodology as a diagnostic to help identify whether general nonlinearities are present in a time series.

Our evaluation is not based on model goodness of fit, as it is commonly known that in-sample fit is not necessarily linked to accurate out-of-sample forecasts. Rather, evaluation of our nonparametric method is based on out-of-sample forecast improvement. Our study contains similarities to the work of Diebold and Nason (1990), which investigates the predictability of exchange rates by utilizing locally weighted regression prediction techniques as proposed by Cleveland (1979). This chapter advances the previous work in several important respects. First, we apply a number of recently developed tests from nonlinear science to demonstrate that the data exhibit substantial nonlinear dependence. Second, we use a test of forecast performance due to Mizrach (1992a) in order to evaluate whether forecasts generated by the near-neighbor methodology are significantly better than forecasts generated by alternative null models. Third, we conduct a far more exhaustive search of near-neighbor specifications in order to identify the best near-neighbor model. We show how summary plots of the forecast performance of the near-neighbor models can be useful in identifying the presence of deterministic and stochastic nonlinearities in mean.

The six-month paper-bill spread has been identified by researchers such as Bernanke (1990), Friedman and Kuttner (1989, 1993), and Stock and Watson (1989) as a financial variable that contains significant information about the future course of the economy. The power of the paper-bill spread as a predictor of real macroeconomic variables is attributed to a number of factors that serve to make commercial paper and Treasury bills imperfect substitutes. First, interest income on commercial paper is subject to greater taxability, in general, than interest income from Treasury bills. Second, the market for Treasury bills tends to be more liquid than the market for commercial paper. Third, the paper-bill spread, as the difference between a risky asset versus a safe return, incorporates information on default risk and investor expectations of the likelihood of future economic downturns. The return to holding commercial paper must compensate investors for holding additional risk, compared to the relatively risk-free Treasury bill. Historically, the paper-bill spread has typically widened prior to and during recessions.

In addition, the spread changes in response to factors that affect the relative supply of the two instruments. First, as monetary policy tightens and bank reserves grow at smaller rates, borrowers shift out of the bank loan market and into the commercial paper market. Second, in the final stages of a business expansion, firms' credit requirements increase, implying an increase in the supply of commercial paper. Finally, Fed open-market operations affect the supply of Treasury bills. Thus, monetary policy, through its influence on relative supplies of the assets, may affect the spread.

There are several reasons why one might be interested in forecasting the risk premium. First, empirical evidence seems to identify the paper-bill spread as a variable that contains important forecasting potential for the real macroeconomy. If one could forecast movements in the risk premium, one might be able to forecast movements in other macro aggregates more accurately. Second, accurate forecasts of the risk premium may be useful to traders dealing in Treasury bills and corporate commercial paper. The third reason is related to certain claims regarding the characteristics of the underlying economic data-generating processes. Barnett and Chen (1988) and DeCoster and Mitchell (1991) claim to find evidence of nonlinear determinism in monetary aggregates. Given that the risk premium is closely related to monetary variables, our ability to predict the premium may have important implications for these claims. The techniques used here are known to be extremely useful in predicting simple nonlinear deterministic processes; see Casdagli (1992). While systems characterized by a deterministic data-generating process should contain a high degree of forecasting potential, systems characterized by primarily stochastic data-generating processes should yield considerably less favorable prediction results.

This chapter is organized as follows: Section 2 contains a description of the nonlinear forecasting methodology utilized, and Section 3 presents results on the algorithm's forecasting performance on time series generated by various nonlinear deterministic and nonlinear stochastic processes. Section 4 discusses the data series and its characteristics. Here we present results of the nonlinear forecasting methodology as applied to the weekly six-month paper-bill spread, and a comparison of the forecasting performance of the nonlinear method versus the Martingale predictor, the unconditional mean predictor, and the global linear predictor. Section 5 concludes with a summary and discusses implications of our empirical results for the probable characteristics of the underlying data-generating process for the paper-bill spread.

To summarize, we illustrate how nonlinear methods are very successful at forecasting nonlinear deterministic processes and nonlinear deterministic processes infected with observer noise. The nearest-neighbor method is moderately successful at forecasting nonlinear stochastic processes, and the method may serve as a useful diagnostic to identify processes that exhibit nonlinear structure in mean. In application to the interest rate risk premium, the nearest-neighbor method offers statistically significant improvement in root mean square error forecast over Martingale and unconditional mean predictors. In contrast, the method offers slight but statistically insignificant improvements in forecasting performance over global linear methods for the risk premium series. As local approximation does not help to predict the level of the spread, this provides an indication that the majority of the nonlinear structure inherent in the spread is present in the higher-order moments. Thus it is unlikely that the data generator for the interest rate risk premium is, for example, a simple nonlinear deterministic process with additive noise.

2. Methodology

Nearest-neighbor methods are beginning to find use in economics and finance. Recent efforts include Diebold and Nason (1990), LeBaron (1992), Meese and Rose (1990), and Mizrach (1992b). To motivate the method, suppose that we observe a time series from an unknown data generator that we suspect is highly nonlinear. Suppose only that the data generator is a smooth function of the form

$$x_t = f(x_{t-1}, x_{t-2}, ..., x_{t-d}) + \varepsilon_t, \ \varepsilon_t \text{ "white noise,"} \tag{1}$$

where the number of arguments of f is unknown. If the data-generating function $f(.)$ is fixed over time, and given enough observations, we may be able to deduce aspects of the local structure of the function. If the signal-to-noise ratio is "high," then when ($x_{t-1}, x_{t-2} ..., x_{t-d})$ is "close" to $(x_{s-1}, x_{s-2}, ..., x_{s-d})$, we expect that x_t will be "close" to x_s. Linear models estimated from points that are "close" to $(x_{t-1}, x_{t-2} ..., x_{t-d})$ may have forecast errors that have a lower component of bias or (functional) specification error, compared to a global linear model. Thus, forecast errors may be lowered even though we reduce estimator efficiency by in effect discarding some of our data.

Our implementation follows the scheme suggested by Casdagli (1992). We start with observations on a time series $\{x_t\}_{t=1,T}$ which we partition into a fitting set F and a prediction set P, for example:

$$F = \{ x_t: m +1 < t \le N_f \} \tag{2}$$

$$P = \{ x_t: N_f < t \le T \}$$

for some $N_f < T$. The aim is to use the information in F to predict observations in P.

For a given lag length m, construct for each observation $\{ x_t \}_{t=m+1,T}$ an m history x_{t-1}^m,

$$x_{t-1}^m = (x_{t-1}, x_{t-2}, ..., x_{t-m}). \tag{3}$$

Thus we have a set of ordered pairs $\{ (x_t, x_{t-1}^m) \}_{t=m+1,T}$. For each x_t in the prediction set, we calculate the distance between x_{t-1}^m and x_{s-1}^x $\forall$ s $\in$ F. We then select the k nearest pairs (x_s, x_{s-1}^m) to estimate the parameters in the local regression

$$x_s = \alpha_{0,k} + x_{s-1}^m {}'\alpha_k + \varepsilon_s. \tag{4}$$

The estimated parameters $\hat{\alpha}_{0,k}$ and $\hat{\alpha}_k$ are used to calculate the prediction

$$\hat{x}_t = \hat{\alpha}_{0,k} + x_{t-1}^m {}'\hat{\alpha}_k. \tag{5}$$

The prediction is then used to calculate the prediction error $x_t - \hat{x}_t = e_{t,k}$.

Our approach to nearest-neighbor estimation differs from other approaches only in certain technical details. Casdagli suggests using the sup norm to calculate distances,

$$|| x || = \max_i | x_i |. \tag{6}$$

Others [Cleveland and Devlin (1988), Yakowitz (1987)] advocate the Euclidean norm:

$$|| x || = (\sum_i x_i^2)^{0.5} . \tag{7}$$

We choose the sup norm, primarily because the computation burden is significantly less than that of the Euclidean norm.

Other implementations of nearest-neighbor estimation (notably Cleveland and Devlin) advocate local weighting schemes that place greater weights on near observations in estimating the local linear regression. While such weighting schemes have certain theoretical attractions, there are practical difficulties in their implementation. Wayland et al. (1992) show that in the presence of noise, unweighted algorithms tend to yield superior results. With noise, a problem arises with "false" near neighbors that is analogous to the problem of not taking a long enough lag length.

Further, our own numerical experiments indicate that weighted algorithms may be numerically less stable than the unweighted algorithms. To explain the problem, note that when we calculate the parameters of the local regression, we must invert an $X'X$ matrix where the constituent observations are highly colinear. (The rows of the data matrix are, after all, selected because they are very similar to a given x_t^m.) For small numbers of near neighbors, these matrices tend to be highly ill-conditioned. When the $X'X$ matrix is close to singular, the parameter estimates are numerically highly unstable. In numerical experiments, for a given number of near neighbors, the weighted $X'X$ matrix can be much closer to singular (have a much poorer condition number) than the unweighted matrix. Hence forecasts based on these parameters can be more erratic in the weighted case than the forecasts based on the unweighted algorithm. We therefore focus only on the results for the unweighted algorithm.

Rather than adopt a model based on goodness of fit, we evaluate our model solely on the basis of prediction efficiency. One measure of forecast efficiency is the normalized root mean square error (RMSE) of the forecast,

$$R_k(m) = (\sum_{t \in P} e_{t,k}^2)^{0.5} / \sigma_P . \tag{8}$$

where σ_P is the sample standard deviation of the $x_t \in P$. We use plots of $R_k(m)$ to help identify specifications that are particularly successful at forecasting the series. We then use a test due to Mizrach (1992a) to evaluate whether the forecast improvement is statistically significant.

The test is a refinement of an approach due to Granger and Newbold (1986) and Meese and Rogoff (1988). To review the test, let $\{\varepsilon_{1,t}\}$ be the forecast residuals from method 1, and let $\{\varepsilon_{2,t}\}$ be the forecast residuals from method 2. Granger and Newbold test whether $\mathrm{var}(\varepsilon_{1,t}) = \varepsilon_1^2$ is significantly less than $\mathrm{var}(\varepsilon_{2,t}) = \sigma_2^2$ by looking at the orthogonalized residuals $u_t = \varepsilon_{1,t} - \varepsilon_{2,t}, v_t = \varepsilon_{1,t} + \varepsilon_{2,t}$. The correlation between u_t and v_t is just $\sigma_1^2 - \sigma_2^2$. Thus if the correlation between u_t and v_t is significantly greater (less) than zero, then σ_1^2 is significantly greater (less) than σ_2^2.

Mizrach's refinement is to generalize the test to biased, heteroskedastic forecast residuals, using Newey-West (1987) hardware. Mizrach shows that given that the two sequences are a mixing, the statistic

$$R = \sqrt{T} \left(\frac{\frac{1}{T} \sum_{i=1}^{T} u_i v_i}{\left[\sum_{i=k}^{k} w(i) S_{uvuv}(i) \right]^{1/2}} \right) \sim N(0,1) \tag{9}$$

asymptotically, where

$$w(i) = 1 - \frac{|i|}{k+1}$$

$$S_{uvuv}(j) = \frac{1}{T} \sum_{j=1}^{T} u_j v_j u_{j-i} v_{j-i} \quad j \geq 0$$

$$\frac{1}{T} \sum_{j=t+1}^{T} u_{j+t} v_{j+t} u_j v_j \quad j < 0$$

$$k = k(T), \text{ with } \lim_{n \to \infty} \frac{K(T)}{T^{1/2}} = 0.$$

$$= \text{int}(T^{1/3}) + 1, \text{ for example.}$$

Mizrach's Monte Carlo analysis indicates that the statistic is properly sized in samples greater than n = 100.

We estimate our nearest-neighbor forecasts at embedding dimensions 5, 10, 15, and 20. We try three different strategies for estimating the nearest-neighbor regressions. First, we estimate under what we call a "fixed window": in this case, the fitting set is fixed throughout the exercise to be the first N_f observations of the time series, $F = \{x_s: 1 < s < N_f, \supset t \in P \}$. Second, we try a "sliding window": the fitting set is given as the N_f observations immediately prior to the observation that we are trying to forecast. That is, given $x_t \in P$, $F = \{x_s: t - N_f < s < t\}$. Thus, early observations in the time series are continually being dropped from the fitting set while more recent observations are being added. Third, we try an "expanding window," where every observation prior to t is used to attempt to predict x_t. Formally, given $x_t \in P$, $F = \{x_s: 1 < s < t\}$.

The choice of window may be of some importance, depending on the data-generating mechanism. One might expect that the sliding window would outperform the fixed window if the data generator is stochastic and nonstationary. With a nonstationary data generator, the sliding window may well outperform the expanding window. The expanding window ought to outperform both alternatives if the data generator is stochastic and stationary, or alternatively if the data generator is deterministic.

3. Does Near-Neighbor Forecasting Work?

Numerical experiments in Casdagli (1992) show that for large data sets from nonlinear deterministic data generators, $R_k(m)$ plots achieve a very distinctive shape. The typical plot achieves a global minimum for a relatively small number of near neighbors and is more or less continuously upward sloping as more near neighbors are added, out to the limit where we are essentially replicating the global linear predictor. This distinctive shape is easily seen in the first two examples below, where we apply the method to the Hénon system, a deterministic nonlinear data generator. In subsequent examples, we apply the nearest-neighbor method to see how well we can forecast some popular stochastic models that have significant nonlinearities in mean. We consider Potter's (1992) Self Exciting Threshold Autoregressive (SETAR) model of GNP, Hamilton's (1989) Markov trend model, and the Time Varying Parameter (TVP) GARCH-M model estimated by Chou et al. (1992).

In order to obtain results that are comparable to the results we obtain later for interest rates, for each example we construct a time series of 1,711 observations and use a model estimated on the first 1,411 observations to forecast the last 300. For all of our examples, we select a lag length m = 5 for computational convenience.

The Hénon system [Hénon (1976)] is an example of a nonlinear, chaotic deterministic dynamical system. This system evolves perfectly deterministically from a given initial condition, in a pattern that appears highly erratic to the eye. It is given by the pair of equations

$$x_t = y_{t-1} + 1 - 1.4\, x_{t-1}^2 \tag{10}$$

$$y_t = 0.3\, x_{t-1}.$$

The time paths of this system evolve on a fractal attractor that is known to have a dimension of 1.3. Figure 18-1 gives a plot of $R_k(m)$ as a function of the number of nearest neighbors, k, for an embedding dimension of 5. Root mean square error is minimized at k = 7. Note that at this embedding dimension, the Hénon map is virtually perfectly forecastable. Local regressions based on seven near neighbors have a RMSE of 0.015; about 98.5 percent of the total variation of the process can be correctly forecast. In this sample, an AR(5) model predicts only 12.4 percent of the variation of the process.

Perhaps more realistic is the case of "noisy chaos." Again, we have an underlying system that evolves deterministically. However, observations on the state of the system are polluted by IID observer noise. Given a time series of observations on the Hénon map { x_t }, we analyze the series z_t,

$$z_t = x_t + \varepsilon_t,\ E[\,\varepsilon_t\,] = 0,\ \text{Std}(\,\varepsilon_t\,) = 0.5\,\sigma \tag{11}$$

where σ is the standard deviation of the raw Hénon data. This corresponds to a noise-to-signal ratio of 50 percent. The plot for this exercise is also given in Figure 18-1. Here, the optimal forecast is for k = 40, where the root

Figure 18-1

RMSE Plot for Hénon Map Examples

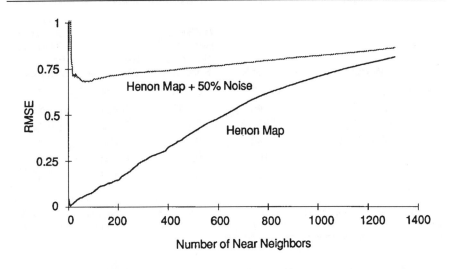

mean square error is 0.683, compared to an RMSE of 0.921 for the global AR(5) forecast.

These examples illustrate two points. First, it is possible that the near-neighbor forecasting algorithm can yield large improvements in forecast accuracy over global linear methods. The robust test of forecast efficiency indicates that the decline in mean square error is highly significant in both cases. (See Table 18-1 for a summary of the forecast results for all of our examples.) Second, these examples illustrate the upward sloping $R_k(m)$ plot that is characteristic of forecastable nonlinearities. In both cases, prediction performance degrades smoothly as more and more near neighbors are added to the local regression. Casdagli gives numerous additional examples calculated on deterministic data generators, further illustrating this point.

It is useful to compare these results to the results obtained by applying the method to pseudorandom numbers. Figure 18-2 gives an $R_k(m)$ plot calculated on the output of a normal pseudorandom number generator. Note that the plot is basically flat. The plot is minimized at $k = 874$ where RMSE is equal to 0.996. RMSE for the AR(5) forecast is 0.998. The reduction in RMSE is not statistically significant.

The common stochastic models based on nonlinear level equations are seldom as predictable as the deterministic systems. For our first example,

Table 18-1

Summary of Forecasting Examples

Model	Best k	RMSE for Best Near Neighbor Forecast	RMSE for AR5 Model	Test Statistic: Test of Forecast Efficiency
Hénon Map	7	0.015	0.886	5.75
Henon Map + 50% Noise	40	0.683	0.921	4.89
Pseudorandom Numbers	874	0.996	0.998	0.12
Potter SETAR Model	140	0.658	0.736	2.49
Hamilton Model	153	0.919	0.943	1.02
TVP-GARCH(1,1)-M Model	267	0.410	0.432	2.38

Mizrach's test statistic is distributed as a standard normal random variable under the hypothesis that the mean squared error is the same in both samples. A positive value indicates that the variance of the AR forecast is greater than the variance of the near neighbor forecast.

Figure 18-2

RMSE Plot for Pseudorandom Numbers

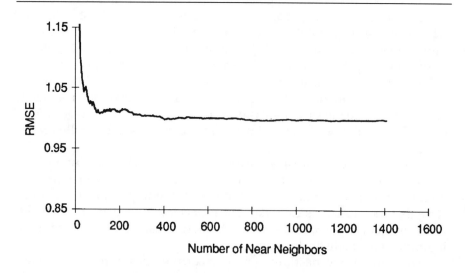

Potter (1992) estimates the following SETAR model to GNP growth rate data for the period 3Q 1948 to 4Q 1990:

if $y_{t-2} < 0$ then   (12)

$y_t = -0.705 + 0.510\ y_{t-1} - 0.849\ y_{t-2} - 0.048\ y_{t-3} - 0.123\ y_{t-4} + 0.398\ y_{t-5} + e_{1t}$,

$E[\ e_{1t}\ ] = 0,\ \sigma_1^2 = 1.59$

if $y_{t-2} \geq 0$ then

$y_t = -0.545 + 0.312\ y_{t-1} + 0.245\ y_{t-2} - 0.104\ y_{t-3} - 0.057\ y_{t-4} - 0.094 y_{t-5} + e_{2t}$,

$E[\ e_{2t}\ ] = 0,\ \sigma_2^2 = 0.758.$

We simulate this model using normal errors to obtain the requisite 1,711 observations. The $R_k(m)$ plot in Figure 18-3 shows the upward-sloping shape that is characteristic of nonlinearity in the data generator. The best RMSE forecast occurs at k = 140, where RMSE is 12 percent lower than the RMSE for the simple AR(5) forecast. The robust test of forecast efficiency indicates that the improvement in forecast performance is highly significant.

Next, we simulate the Hamilton (1989) Markov Trend model of GNP. Hamilton estimates the following model on GNP growth rates, 2Q 1952 to 4Q 1984:

Figure 18-3
RMSE Plot for the Potter SETAR Model

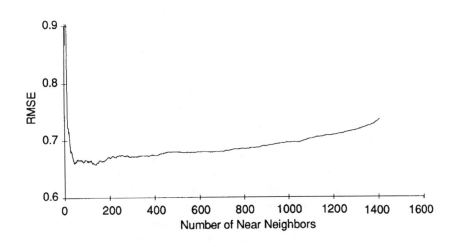

$$y_t = -0.3577 + 1.522\, s_t + z_t \tag{13}$$

if $s_{t-1} = 1$ $s_t \sim$ Bernoulli(p), p = 0.9049

if $s_{t-1} = 0$, $s_t \sim$ Bernoulli(q), q = 0.7550

$z_t = 0.014\, z_{t-1} - 0.058\, z_{t-2} - 0.247\, z_{t-3} - 0.213\, z_{t-4} + \varepsilon_t$

$E[\, \varepsilon_t \,] = 0$, $\sigma_\varepsilon = 0.7690$

Again, we simulated the model with normal errors. The $R_k(m)$ plot shows a noticeable global minimum at k = 154, and a slight upward slope as k increases. Near-neighbor methods yield a forecast improvement of about 3 percent, as compared to linear models. The test of forecast efficiency indicates that the improvement in RMSE is not statistically significant.

Finally, we examine the Chou, Engle, and Kane (1992) Time Varying Parameter GARCH(1,1)-M model:

$$r_t = b_t h_t + \varepsilon_t \tag{14}$$

$\varepsilon_t \sim N(0, h_t)$

$b_t = b_{t-1} + v_t$, $E[v_t] = 0$, $\mathrm{Var}(v_t) = 0.032$

$h_t = 0.989 + 0.127\, \varepsilon_{t-1}^2 + 0.836\, h_{t-1}.$

To simulate the model, we set ε_t and v_t as normally distributed. In this case, the $R_k(m)$ plot is fairly flat. The minimum occurs at 267 near neighbors. There, the RMSE is about 5 percent lower than the RMSE for the global AR(5) forecast. Our robust test of forecast efficiency indicates that the improvement is in fact statistically significant.

These results illustrate how the nearest-neighbor methodology may be useful in identifying whether nonlinearities are present in the level equation of an unknown data generator. An unambiguous signal of non-linearity is if the nearest-neighbor algorithm generates forecasts that are significantly superior to the forecasts generated by a linear model.

As we see in the examples, the near-neighbor approach does very well at forecasting deterministic nonlinearities. We cannot always guarantee a significant forecast improvement for stochastic nonlinear models. Even so, the $R_k(m)$ plots themselves may be useful as an informal diagnostic. The single most striking feature of these plots is that when there are nonlineari-ties present, the plot appears to have a distinctive upward slope. If the data generator is deterministic, possibly with a low level of noise, the slope may be quite striking. For stochastic data generators, the slope is typically much more shallow. Even when we are unable to generate forecast improve-ments, we still observe that the $R_k(m)$ plot has a noticeable upward slope, and the global minimum RMSE occurs at a relatively small number of near neighbors. While this is not a statistical test, it may still prove useful as a signal to consider alternative nonlinear specifications.

4. Results

Our data is a time series of 1,711 weekly observations on the spread between six-month Treasury bills and six-month commercial paper, from January 8, 1960, to October 16, 1992. The Treasury bill rate used to compute the spread is the average issuing price for the weekly Monday Treasury auction of six-month bills. The commercial paper rate is the average dealer issuing rate for six-month prime commercial paper, as of the Monday of the Treasury auction. Thus, our data series represents an ex ante risk premium, rather than an ex post realized difference in returns.

The raw data exhibit highly significant autocorrelation and significant volatility clustering. Next, we consider whether the empirical distribution of the data is constant over time. The data marginally pass a unit root test.[1] However, the estimated coefficient on lagged values of the interest-rate spread is very small. Even though the low standard error allows us to formally reject the hypothesis of a unit root, the data have the charac-

Figure 18-4

First Difference of the Interest-Rate Spread

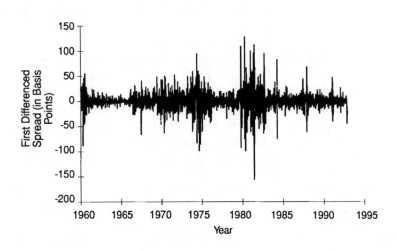

teristics of a highly persistent process. There is evidence of strong persistence in the autocorrelation plot and a rapid falloff in the partial correlation plot. This suggests differencing is not out of order. Figure 18-4 displays the first difference of the interest-rate premium.

To apply the forecasting procedure to our interest-rate data, we need to select an appropriate lag length, m, for our data. In applications involving prediction of chaotic deterministic nonlinear systems, Casdagli suggests setting the embedding dimension equal to twice the estimated dimension of the process, plus 1. In a chaotic physical system, the dimension of the process is a description of the degrees of freedom driving a process. In stochastic systems, the dimension is a measure of the complexity of the process. In either case, the dimension number gives a lower bound on the number of variables necessary to model a process. [See Hsieh (1991) for a brief introduction into the application of these concepts to finance and economics.]

For the interest-rate spread, we estimate the dimension using the procedures of Brock and Baek (1991). The test statistics are calculated relative to the null hypothesis of independent and identically distributed (IID) underlying data. Under the IID hypothesis, dimension estimates should be space-filling. Thus, the expected value of the dimension estimate is equal to the embedding dimension.

Our estimates of the dimension of the process are given in Table 18-2. The Brock-Baek procedure gives an estimate of the dimension of the process of between 4 and 5. As a check on the results, we apply the tests to the AR filtered residuals of the differenced data. (Table 18-3 describes the filter, and Table 18-4 the dimension results.) Again, we obtain an estimated dimension in the range of 4 to 5. Regardless of linear filtering, the test results consistently suggest significant deviation from the IID null. Since the AR filtered data have been bleached of linear structure, this suggests there is significant nonlinear structure in our risk premium data. The issue now is one of whether this apparent nonlinear structure can be exploited to yield significant gains in forecast performance.

The dimension estimates suggest that the risk premium is a moderately complex process. Consequently, we may wish to have a relatively large fitting set to use to train the forecast algorithm. Thus we attempt to forecast the last 300 observations in the series, using the first 1,411 observations for the fitting set.

Applying the method to the interest-rate data, out-of-sample forecast performance is very poor regardless of the embedding dimension or the window selection method, in spite of apparent nonlinear structure in the data. Figure 18-5 is an $R_k(m)$ plot for the fixed-window fitting set specification. Figure 18-6 is an $R_k(m)$ plot that compares the various fitting set

Table 18-2

General Structure in the Differenced Data

Embed. Dim.	Estimated Dimension	Test Statistic
2	1.436	−11.22
3	1.994	−12.66
4	2.471	−13.65
5	2.895	−14.19
6	3.269	−14.49
7	3.617	−14.51
8	3.937	−14.37
9	4.236	−14.11
10	4.513	−13.77
11	4.765	−13.39
12	4.994	−12.98
13	5.210	−12.53
14	5.411	−12.06

Notes: The dimension of the process is estimated as the elasticity of the correlation integral with respect to the link scale e. Under the null of independent and identically distributed data (IID), the expected value of this statistic is equal to the embedding dimension. The test statistic should be distributed as a standard normal random variable under the null of IID.

Table 18-3

AR Filter Summary

AR(p) Filtered Residuals: p = 54

		Test Statistic	D.F.	Prob.
Diagnostic Tests	Ljung Box Q Test	53.49	40	0.075
	McLeod Li Test	1,485.65	40	0.000
	c 2 Test	35.34	28	0.160

specifications at a given (representative) embedding dimension. Several features of the plots deserve mention. First, changes in the embedding dimension make little difference. The plots for m = 5 are virtually indistinguishable from the plots for m = 10, or m = 15. (The curve for m = 20 is virtually identical to m = 15, and is left off of the plot to improve legibility.)

Table 18-4

Nonlinear Structure in the AR Residuals

Embed. Dim.	Estimated Dimension	Test Statistic
2	1.306	−13.92
3	1.824	−14.90
4	2.261	−15.62
5	2.648	−15.95
6	3.028	−15.83
7	3.366	−15.63
8	3.675	−15.33
9	3.987	−14.86
10	4.277	−14.36
11	4.550	−13.83
12	4.795	−13.30
13	5.019	−12.78
14	5.232	−12.23

See notes to Table 18-2.

Figure 18-5

Fixed-Window Results

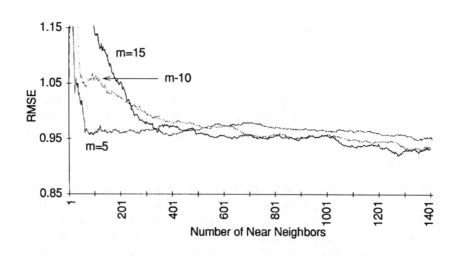

Figure 18-6

Various Windows, Embedding Dimension = 10

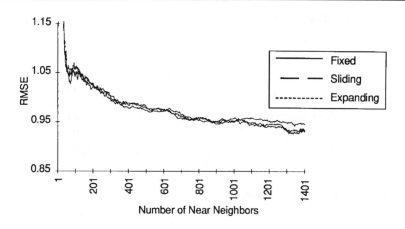

Second, no one fitting set specification seems to perform any better than any other. As Figure 18-6 shows, at m = 10, the various plots lie virtually on top of one another. Third, the shape of the plots is not consistent with the hypothesis that there are significant nonlinear effects in the level of the process. In most cases, the minimum standardized root mean square error occurs near the maximum number of near neighbors.

Table 18-5 summarizes the prediction results. Sliding-window forecasts generally outperform fixed-window forecasts. The expanding-window forecast does not appear to offer appreciably improved forecasts over the sliding-window or the fixed-window methods. Overall, the nonlinear methods generate a slight but noticeable improvement in forecast performance.

The obvious question is, Are these improvements in forecast performance significant? Selecting the best results from Table 18-5, we assess whether the nonlinear method is significantly better than either guessing the unconditional mean or an AR alternative. The single best nonlinear alternative is the fixed window at embedding dimension 20. In Table 18-6, we show the results when we compare these forecast errors to the errors for an AR(15) model and the errors for the unconditional mean forecast. As we see in Table 18-6, the nearest-neighbor forecast is significantly better than the unconditional mean forecast. However, the nonparametric forecast is not significantly better than the forecast obtained using the AR(15) model coefficients estimated on the fixed fitting set. Thus, our methods are

Table 18-5

Summary of Out-of-Sample Prediction Results

Prediction Method	m	Best k	$R_k(m)$
Fixed Window Near Neighbor	5	1352	0.948
	10	1319	0.948
	15	1276	0.920
	20	1247	0.918
Sliding Window Near Neighbor	5	1361	0.946
	10	1336	0.926
	15	1283	0.919
	20	1259	0.919
Expanding Window Nearest Neighbor	5	1387	0.954
	10	1343	0.942
	15	1263	0.933
	20	1141	0.933
AR Model, Fixed Fitting Set	5		0.950
	10		0.933
	15		0.933
	20		0.934
AR Model, Sliding Fitting Set	5		0.949
	10		0.933
	15		0.931
	20		0.935
Martingale Prediction			1.646
Unconditional Mean			1.026

Notes:

m   =   Embedding dimension

Best k =   Number of near neighbors that minimizes $R_k(m)$

$R_k(m)$ =   Relative efficiency of forecast, equal to the normalized root mean square error

unable to exploit the apparent nonlinear dependence in the series to significantly improve the forecast of the level. The nonlinear, local information prediction method does not appear to offer significantly improved forecast performance over the global approximation linear predictors.

Table 18-6

Mizrach's Robust Forecast Comparison

Data Set 1	Data Set 2	Test Statistic
Unconditional Mean Forecast	Fixed Window, Embedding Dimension 20	2.29
Unconditional Mean Forecast	AR(15), Fixed Fitting Set	2.07
AR(15), Fixed Fitting Set	Fixed Window, Embedding Dimension 20	1.61

Under null of equal forecast accuracy, the test statistic should be distributed as a standard normal random variable.

5. Conclusions

In this chapter, we explored the use of near-neighbor forecasting methods as a diagnostic for identifying important nonlinearity in mean in a data set. We apply the method to simulated data from popular nonlinear stochastic and deterministic models. In the simulated data, the nearest-neighbor prediction algorithm can often generate out-of-sample forecasts that are significantly better than forecasts based on a global linear model. For nonlinear deterministic processes, the improvement can be quite striking.

Even when the forecasts are not statistically better than the linear forecasts, the shape of the $R_k(m)$ plot may give a clue that important nonlinearities are present. For deterministic processes, the nearest-neighbor prediction plots have a characteristic upward slope, which may be quite steep. The shapes of the nearest-neighbor prediction plots for nonlinear stochastic processes that contain significant structure in mean also appear to have the characteristic upward slope.

We apply the method to data on the interest rate risk premium. We find that the out-of-sample near-neighbor forecasts are not significantly more accurate than forecasts from simple AR models with the same number of lags, although the forecasts are more accurate than either the Martingale predictor or the unconditional mean predictor. Further, the $R_k(m)$ plots for the interest-rate data are not upward sloping. By this diagnostic, the risk premium series exhibits little evidence of nonlinearity in level.

These results do not support claims of determinism in macroeconomic data. The degree of forecast improvement is not consistent with the hypothesis of a low-dimensional attractor underlying the risk premium data.

Apart from claims of nonlinear determinism, one might expect non-linear stochastic models of some type to fit the data. Regime shifting models are a natural alternative, in light of the many changes in the economy over the 22 years covered in our sample. Fiscal policies have varied from regimes of nearly balanced budgets to regimes of large deficits. Monetary policies have varied over regimes of interest-rate targets and money supply targets. Finally, there have been significant changes in the institutional characteristics of financial markets. Comparing the results for simulated data from common regime shifting models, we conclude that the signatures of regime shift nonlinearity do not appear to be present in the risk premium data. Thus our results offer little support for the view that regime effects are significant in this data set.

Thus, we conclude that the paper-bill spread series appears to have a predominantly stochastic data-generating process, with little structure in mean. Given evidence of significant nonlinear dependence in the residuals of global linear models, this nonlinear structure is likely contained in the higher order moments of the process.

Acknowledgment

We wish to thank but not otherwise implicate Rochelle Antoniewicz, Ralph Bradley, Jerry Dwyer, Jesus Gonzalo, Bruce Mizrach, Jack Praschnik, Leigh Riddick, and participants in seminars at the BLS, the University of Maryland Applied Dynamics Seminar, Clemson, Rutgers Business School, and the 1993 Winter Meetings of the Econometric Society. The views expressed here do not necessarily reflect the policy or views of the Bureau of Labor Statistics or the views of other BLS staff members.

Note

1   We test the hypothesis of a unit root in our time series with an augmented Dickey–Fuller test. Given a time series $\{x_t\}$, we construct $dx_t = x_t - x_{t-1}$ and perform the regression

$$dx_t = a + b\, x_{t-1} + c\, t + \Sigma\, dx_{t-1} + \varepsilon_t.$$

We then test the hypothesis that the estimated parameter b is significantly different from zero. If not, then we cannot reject the hypothesis that the original series $\{x_t\}$ exhibits a unit root. In our case, the estimated coefficient was -0.045, compared to the null hypothesis of zero. The value of the test statistic on the coefficient b is −4.07, which is close to the 1 percent critical value of −3.96.

Note that the results for the raw data are qualitatively quite similar to the results for the differenced data.

References

Barnett, W. A., and P. Chen. "The Aggregation-Theoretic Monetary Aggregates Are Chaotic and Have Strange Attractors: An Econometric Application of Mathematical Chaos." In *Dynamic Econometric Modeling, Proceedings of the Third International Symposium on Economic Theory and Econometrics*, W. A. Barnett, E. R. Berndt, and H. White, eds. Cambridge, MA: Cambridge University Press, 1988, 199–245.

Bernanke, B. S. "On the Predictive Power of Interest Rates and Interest Rate Spreads." *New England Economic Review* (November/December 1990), 51–68.

Brock, W. A., and E. G. Baek. "Some Theory of Statistical Inference for Nonlinear Science." *Review of Economic Studies* 58 (1991), 697–716.

Brock, W. A., W. D. Dechert, and J. A. Scheinkman. "A Test for Independence Based on the Correlation Dimension." Social Systems Research Institute, University of Wisconsin-Madison, Working Paper 8702 (1987).

Casdagli, M. "Chaos and Deterministic versus Stochastic Nonlinear Modeling." *Journal of the Royal Statistical Society* Series B 54 (1992), 303–328.

Chou, R., R. F. Engle, and A. Kane. "Measuring Risk Aversion from Excess Returns on a Stock Index." *Journal of Econometrics* 52 (1992), 201–224.

Cleveland, W. S. "Robust Locally Weighted Regression and Smoothing Scatter Plots." *Journal of the American Statistical Association* 74 (1979), 829–836.

Cleveland, W. S., and S. J. Devlin. "Locally Weighted Regression: An Approach to Regression Analysis by Local Fitting." *Journal of the American Statistical Association* 83 (1988), 596–610.

DeCoster, G. P., and D. W. Mitchell. "Nonlinear Monetary Dynamics." *Journal of Business and Economic Statistics* 9 (1991), 455–461.

Diebold, F., and J. A. Nason. "Nonparametric Exchange Rate Prediction?" *Journal of International Economics* 28 (1990), 315–322.

Engle, C., and J. D. Hamilton. "Long Swings in the Dollar: Are They in the Data and Do the Markets Know It?" *American Economic Review* 80 (1990), 689–713.

Friedman, B., and K. N. Kuttner. "Money, Income and Prices after the 1980's." NBER Working Paper 2852 (1989).

Friedman, B., and K. N. Kuttner. "Why Does the Paper-Bill Spread Predict Real Economic Activity?" In *Business Cycles, Indicators, and Forecasting, NBER Studies in Business Cycles*, Vol. 28, J. Stock and M. Watson, eds. Chicago: University of Chicago Press, 1993.

Granger, C. W. J., and P. Newbold. *Forecasting in Business and Economic Time Series*. San Diego: Academic Press, 1986.

Hamilton, J. D. "A New Approach to the Economic Analysis of Non-Stationary Time Series and the Business Cycle." *Econometrica* 57 (1989), 357–384.

Hénon, M. "A Two Dimensional Mapping with a Strange Attractor." *Communications in Mathematical Physics* 50 (1976), 69–77.

Hsieh, D. A. "Chaos and Nonlinear Dynamics: Application to Financial Markets." *Journal of Finance* 46 (1991), 1839–1877.

Lauterbach, B. "Consumption Volatility, Prediction Volatility, Spot-Rate Volatility, and the Returns on Treasury Bills and Bonds." *Journal of Financial Economics* 24 (1989), 155–179.

LeBaron, B. "Forecast Improvements Using a Volatility Index." *Journal of Applied Econometrics* 7 (1992), S137–S149.

Meese, R., and K. Rogoff. "Was It Real? The Exchange Rate Differential Relation over the Modern Floating Rate Period." *Journal of Finance* 43 (1988), 933–948.

Meese, R. A., and A. K. Rose. "Nonlinear, Nonparametric, Nonessential Exchange Rate Estimation." *American Economic Review* 80 (1990), 192–196.

Mizrach, B. "Forecast Comparisons in L^2." Federal Reserve Bank of New York, Research Function, April (1992a).

Mizrach, B. "Multivariate Nearest Neighbor Forecasts of EMS Exchange Rates." *Journal of Applied Econometrics* 7 (1992b), S151–S163.

Newey, W., and K. West. "A Simple Positive Semi-Definite Heteroscedasticity and Autocorrelation Consistent Covariance Matrix." *Econometrica* 55 (1987), 703–708.

Potter, S. M. "A Nonlinear Approach to GNP." Mimeo, UCLA (1992).

Stock, J. H., and M. K. Watson. "New Indexes of Coincident and Leading Economic Indicators." In *NBER Macroeconomics Annual*, O. J. Blanchard and S. Fischer, eds. Cambridge, MA: The M.I.T. Press, 1989, 351–394.

Wayland, R., D. Pickett, D. Bromley, and A. Passamante. "Measuring the Predictability of Noisy Recurrent Time Series." Naval Air Warfare Center, Aircraft Division, August (1992).

Yakowitz, S. J. "Nearest Neighbor Methods for Time Series Analysis." *Journal of Time Series Analysis* 8 (1987), 235–247.

PART V

METHODOLOGICAL ISSUES

19

USING THE CORRELATION
EXPONENT TO DECIDE WHETHER
AN ECONOMIC SERIES IS CHAOTIC

By T. Liu, Clive W. J. Granger, and Walter P. Heller

Introduction

Econometricians and applied economists often take the viewpoint that
unforecastable shocks and innovations continually bombard the actual
economy. In other words, the economy is essentially stochastic in nature.
By contrast, some models in the economic theory literature (e.g. Grandmont, 1985) suggest that an essential nonlinearity in real economic forces
permits deterministic time series to have the appearance of chaos. It is our
purpose here to examine some of the tests that have been proposed to
resolve the issue. The choice is whether the economy is better modeled as
(1) essentially linear in structure with significant stochastic elements, or
(2) having a nonlinear structure with insignificant stochastic forces, or (3)
having a clear nonlinear structure but with significant stochastic shocks.
Much of the chaos literature discusses only the first two of these three

Reprinted with permission from *Journal of Applied Econometrics*, Vol. 7 (December 1992):
S25–S39. © 1992 by John Wiley & Sons, Ltd.

possibilities. Our results cast doubt on the hope that stochastic shocks can be reduced to insignificance in nonlinear models when doing empirical work.

In applied economic models it is common practice for the unforecastable shocks to an economy to be equated to the residuals of a specification. Assume that the shocks are independent and identically distributed (or i.i.d., for short). Further, assume the existence of second moments. Necessary conditions for a series x_t to be i.i.d. are: (1) that the mean and variance of x_t are constant, and (2) autocovariances $\text{cov}(x_t, x_{t-k})$ are all zero for all $k \neq 0$. These are called the "white noise conditions," and a series that has them is called white noise. Clearly an i.i.d. series is a white noise but not necessarily vice versa, although a Gaussian white noise is i.i.d.. It is well known that non-i.i.d. processes can have the white noise properties; see the examples in Granger (1983).

Some deterministic processes can also have white noise properties. Many find this observation interesting, and even surprising. A chaotic deterministic process is often characterized by its nonperiodic trajectory. In particular, some chaos has first and second moment properties (means, variances, and covariances) that are the same as a stochastic process. If these properties are the same as white noise, the process will be called here "white chaos." An example of such a process is the tent map, where it is generated by:

$$x^t = a^{-1}x_{t-1}, \qquad \text{if } 0 \leq x_{t-1} < a$$
$$= (1-a)^{-1}(1-x_{t-1}), \qquad \text{if } a \leq x_{t-1} \leq 1. \tag{1}$$

Sakai and Tokumaru (1980) show that the autocorrelations for the tent map are the same as that of some first-order autoregressive process. Especially when the constant a is near to 0.5, the autocorrelations for tent map are close to that of an i.i.d. process.

Time-series data from the "logistic map" have similar properties. The logistic map is given by:

$$x_t = 4x_{t-1}(1 - x_{t-1}) \tag{2}$$

with some suitable starting value x_0 in the range (0, 1). Table 19-1 shows the estimated autocorrelations and partial autocorrelations for a tent map and logistic map. The autocorrelations for x_t are all small and insignificantly different from zero, indicating that these series have at least the dynamic part of the white noise properties. However, x_t is clearly not i.i.d., as x_t is generated from a nonlinear deterministic process. Surveys of the relevance of chaos in economics can be found in Frank and Stengos (1988) and Brock and Sayers (1988).

Table 19-1

Autocorrelation and Partial Autocorrelation Function
for the Tent Map and Logistic Map

| | The original series | | | | The squares of observations | | | |
| | Tent map estimated | | Logistic map estimated | | Tent map estimated | | Logistic map estimated+ | |
Lag	ACF	PACF	ACF	PACF	ACF	PACF	ACF	PACF
1	0.001	0.001	0.016	0.016	−0.215*	−0.215*	−0.221*	−0.221*
2	−0.006	−0.006	0.006	0.006	−0.058*	−0.110*	0.001	−0.050*
3	−0.012	−0.012	0.004	0.004	−0.024	−0.066*	0.001	−0.009
4	0.001	0.001	0.006	0.006	−0.000	−0.030*	0.005	0.004
5	0.004	0.003	−0.001	−0.001	0.005	−0.008	0.004	0.007
6	−0.008	−0.008	−0.025	−0.025	−0.008	−0.013	−0.026*	−0.025
7	−0.003	−0.003	0.003	0.004	−0.003	−0.009	0.010	−0.000
8	0.006	0.006	−0.003	−0.002	0.009	0.004	−0.003	−0.002
9	−0.006	−0.007	−0.002	−0.002	−0.008	−0.007	−0.004	−0.005
10	0.003	0.003	0.012	0.012	0.006	0.004	0.014	0.012

Note: The initial value is 0.1, and 6,000 observations are generated. The first 100 observations are truncated. For the tent map, the constant a in (1) is 0.49999. Asterisks indicate significant lags.

Correlation Exponent Tables

The existence of deterministic white chaos raises the question of how one can distinguish between it and a true stochastic white noise, such as an i.i.d. series. One possibility is to use a statistic known as the "correlation exponent." Let $[x_t]$ be a univariate time series. Define first the "correlation integral" as

$$C(\varepsilon) = \lim_{N \to \infty} \frac{1}{N^2} \{\text{number of pairs } (i,j) \text{ such that } |\, x_i - x_j\,| < \varepsilon \} \quad (3)$$

Thus, all pairs of values of the series are compared and those within ε of each other are counted; they are then normalized by the number of all possible pairs N^2. The limit is taken as N grows large.

Intuitively, $C(\varepsilon)$ measures the probability that any particular pair in the time series is close. Suppose that for small values of ε, $C(\varepsilon)$ grows exponentially at the rate υ:

$$C(\varepsilon) \approx \varepsilon^{\upsilon} \quad (4)$$

The symbol υ is the above-mentioned correlation exponent: it is also called the "correlation dimension." Grassberger and Procaccia (1983) show that the correlation exponent is bounded above by the Hausdorff dimension and information dimension.

These dimensions are measures of the local structure of fractal attractors. For some chaotic process the dimension of the attractors is fractional. Notice that the correlation exponent is used not only for distinguishing white chaos from stochastic white noise, but also for distinguishing the low-dimensional chaos from high-dimensional stochastic process.

A generalization is needed to obtain a useful set of statistics. Let $X_{t,m}$ be the vector of m consecutive terms $(x_t, x_{t+1}, ..., x_{t+m-1})$. Define the correlation integral as:

$$C_m(\varepsilon) = \lim_{N \to \infty} N^{-2} \text{ \{number of pairs } (i,j) \text{ such that each corresponding } \quad (5)$$
$$\text{component of } X_{i,m} \text{ and } X_{j,m} \text{ is less than } \varepsilon \text{ apart}\}.$$

Thus, for each $X_{i,m}$ all other lengths of m of the series are compared to it. If $X_{i,m}$ and $X_{j,m}$ are ε close to each other, then they are counted. Similarly, for small values of ε, $C_m(\varepsilon)$ grows exponentially at the rate υ_m:

$$C_m(\upsilon) = \varepsilon^{\upsilon_m} \tag{6}$$

The length m is called the "embedding dimension." By properly choosing m, the correlation exponent υ of a deterministic white chaotic process can be numerically measured by υ_m, provided $m > \upsilon$. Grassberger and Procaccia (1983) give some numeral values of υ_m with different m values for logistic map and Hénon map.

However, it is easily seen that, for stochastic white noise, $\upsilon_m = m$ for all m. If the correlation exponent υ is very large (so that one has a high-dimensional chaotic process), then it will be very difficult to estimate υ without an enormous amount of data. It is also true that it is difficult to distinguish high-dimensional chaos from stochastic white noise by just looking at estimates of υ_m. The length of economic time series is usually short by comparison with the physical sciences, and this fact diminishes the usefulness for macroeconomics of statistics based on the correlation exponent. For choosing the proper sample size, refer to the paper by Smith (1992a). The correlation exponent, υ_m can be approximated by

$$\hat{\upsilon}_m = \lim_{\varepsilon \to 0} \frac{d \log(C_m(\varepsilon))}{d \log(\varepsilon)}. \tag{7}$$

There are several empirical ways of estimating the correlation exponent. For example, ordinary linear regression is used by Denker and Keller (1986) and by Scheinkman and LeBaron (1989); generalized least-square is used by Cutler (1991); and the random coefficient regression is used by Ramsey and Yuan (1989). In the regression method a set of log $C_m(\varepsilon)$ and log ε are obtained from the data series by "properly" choosing some values of ε. It is obvious that the choice of the range of ε is arbitrary and subjective. Brock and Beck (1991) also note this point.

The other type of estimation of the correlation exponent is the regression-free method. The typical examples are the point estimator presented in this paper and the binomial estimator used by Smith (1992a, b). Because of the similarity between these two estimators a comparison will be made in the following. More extensive references for these estimations of correlation exponent can be found in papers listed above.

The point estimator is defined by

$$\upsilon_{m,j} = \frac{\log(C_m(\varepsilon_j)) - \log(C_m(\varepsilon_{j-1}))}{\log(\varepsilon_j) - \log(\varepsilon_{j+1})} \tag{8}$$

where ε_j and ε_{j+1} are constants greater than zero and less than 1. That is $\varepsilon_j = \phi^j$ with $0 < \phi < 1$, $j \geq 1$, and $C_m(\varepsilon_j)$ is the correlation integral defined by Equation 5. Notice that υ_{mj} is the point elasticity of $C_m(\varepsilon)$ on ε. In the following empirical work the minimum of the sample will be subtracted from each observation and then divided by the sample range. Hence, the transformed observations will take a value between zero and 1. This ensures that the distance between any two points of $\{x_t\}$ is less than 1. Thus the constant ε_j can also be restricted within the range of zero and 1, and the possible range of ε is objectively given. As shown in Equations 4 and 6, the correlation exponent can be observed only when ε is small enough. Let $\varepsilon_j = \phi^j$, for $0 < \phi < 1$ and $j \geq 1$. Then the correlation exponent is related to the value of υ_m, j for sufficiently large j.

The point estimator is also used by Brock and Beck (1991). They derived the statistical property of this estimator under the assumption that x_t is i.i.d.. However, this statistical property cannot apply to low-dimensional chaos. When statistical inference for chaos is conducted, the statistic should be based on an assumption of low information dimension. Also, hypothesis testing based on the x_t being i.i.d. cannot be used for testing the difference between deterministic chaos and a stochastic process. This is because the rejection of the null is caused by dependence among the x_t. Our section on the BDS test will give details of this argument.

The assumptions on x_t can be relaxed from i.i.d. toward some degree of mixing [as in Denker and Keller (1986) and Hiemstra (1992)]. But the derived statistics are still not appropriate for statistical inference and hypothesis testing for chaos. Any statistic based on the null of stochastic

x_t, instead of more general assumptions, will give the estimate $\upsilon_m = m$. If the statistic is used for low-dimensional chaos, which has $\upsilon_m = \upsilon$ and $\upsilon < m$, the statistical inference will be incorrect and the conclusion from the hypothesis testing is ambiguous. Furthermore, the correlation exponent is only approximated for ε close to zero. Any statistic based on the correlation exponent needs to consider this point.

Smith (1992b) defines his binomial estimator with this in mind. He uses the independence assumption in a different way. In his estimator for correlation exponent, independence is applied to the interpoint distance. If there are N data points for x_t, then there are $N(N - 1)/2$ interpoint distances. The "independent distance hypothesis" (IDH) implies that these interpoint distances are independent when $\varepsilon \to 0$ (Theiler, 1990). This IDH is different from an independence assumption on x_t, and it avoids the problem of $\upsilon_m = m$ if x_t is assumed to be stochastic. Let N_j be the number of interpoint distances less than ε_j, where $\varepsilon_j = \varepsilon_0 \phi^j$ for $j \geq 0$ and $0 < \phi < 1$. Based on IDH, Smith's binomial estimator is

$$\tilde{\upsilon}_m = \frac{\log\left(\sum_{j=0}^{K} N_{j+1}\right) - \log\left(\sum_{j=0}^{K-1} N_j\right)}{\log \phi} \tag{9}$$

For sufficiently large N, Equation 5 implies that

$$C(\varepsilon_j) = \frac{N_j}{[N(N-1)/2]}$$

and

$$\tilde{\upsilon}_m = \frac{\log\left(\sum_{j=0}^{K} C(\varepsilon_{j+1})\right) - \log\left(\sum_{j=0}^{K-1} C(\varepsilon_j)\right)}{\log \varepsilon_{j+1} - \log \varepsilon_j} \tag{10}$$

An alternative estimator for the correlation exponent used by Smith (1992a) is

$$\tilde{\upsilon}_m = \frac{\dfrac{1}{K} \sum_{j=1}^{K} (\log N_j - \log N_{j-1})}{\log \phi} \tag{11}$$

It is equivalent to

$$\tilde{\upsilon}_m = \frac{1}{K} \sum_{j-1}^{K} \left(\frac{\log C(\varepsilon_j) - (\log C(\varepsilon_{j-1})}{\log \varepsilon_j - \log \varepsilon_{j-1}} \right) \tag{12}$$

which is the average of the point estimator in Equation 8 for some range values of ε_j. The following simulation shows the properties of the point estimator and consequentially it also provides some of the properties of the binomial estimator $\tilde{\upsilon}_m$.

Table 19-2 shows the point estimates of the correlation exponent, υ_{mj}, for six values of the embedding dimension m and 25 epsilon values. The table uses data from the logistic map with sample sizes of 500 and 5,900. For most macroeconomic series, 500 is a large but plausible sample size (approximately 40 years of monthly data). A sample of 5,900 observations is large compared to most economic time series. However, financial data are often of this size (20 years of weekday daily price data). The data are chaotic and known to have a true correlation dimension of one. Thus, for $m \geq 2$ and small ε_j (or large j), where $\varepsilon_j = 0.9^j$, the figures in the table should all equal 1 if the sample size is large enough. Using the larger sample of 5,900 observations, the values are indeed near 1 for $2 \leq m \leq 5$ and small epsilon, or $j > 20$. There does appear to be a slight downward bias, with most values under 1.0.

The estimate is less reliable for $m = 10$. Using a much smaller sample of 500 observations, this general pattern is the same but with higher variability. Looking at the table for $m > 1$ and small enough epsilon (or large j) gives ample visual evidence that the quantity being estimated is close to unity. It is stable as m goes from 2 to 5. This result is consistent with those of Grassberger and Procaccia (1983). In particular, they also found that υ_m is underestimated when $m = 1$.

These results are thus encouraging, as tables such as these do give the correct pattern if the data are truly chaotic. The same results were found with data from the Hénon map, but these are not shown. Table 19-3 shows the same results for "stochastic" Gaussian white noise series, of sample sizes 500 and 5,900, respectively. Theory suggests that these estimates should equal m and thus should take the value 1, 2, 3, 4, 5, and 10 in the columns. The pattern in these tables is as predicted by the theory for small enough epsilon, say $j > 25$. Note that there is a fairly consistent downward bias in the calculated dimension. The results from the correlation exponent tables are rather similar to those from the regression approach, such as Ramsey and Yuan (1990).

Interpretation of this type of "ocular econometrics" is not easy. One has to be selective as to which parts of the table are emphasized. Statistical inference is needed for more accurate conclusions. Brock and Beck (1991) and Smith (1991a, b) give statistical properties for the correlation exponent. The simulations as shown in Tables 19-2 and 19-3 reveal an important message on the empirical use of the correlation exponent. The choice of epsilon is important. Different ranges of epsilon may give different conclusions. Further, distinguishing stochastic white noise from white chaos based on the correlation exponent is valid only for small epsilon. Brock

Table 19-2

Correlation Exponents for Logistic Map

	Sample size = 500 m						Sample size = 5900 m					
j	1	2	3	4	5	10	1	2	3	4	5	10
16	0.78	0.96	1.05	1.00	0.95	0.80	0.76	0.89	0.97	1.02	1.14	2.16
17	0.66	0.82	0.84	0.88	0.96	1.27	0.77	0.90	0.97	1.01	1.11	1.41
18	0.66	0.80	0.78	0.84	0.91	0.80	0.77	0.90	0.97	1.00	1.08	1.32
19	0.74	0.86	0.85	0.87	0.98	2.17	0.79	0.90	0.96	0.99	1.05	1.39
20	0.77	0.90	0.92	1.02	1.12	0.76	0.78	0.90	0.96	0.98	1.02	1.19
21	0.82	0.88	0.95	0.92	0.92	0.73	0.78	0.89	0.94	0.97	0.99	1.18
22	0.77	0.89	0.90	0.94	0.96	0.79	0.78	0.89	0.95	0.98	1.02	1.33
23	0.73	0.84	0.87	0.88	0.82	0.53	0.77	0.89	0.94	0.97	1.00	1.38
24	0.86	0.89	0.93	0.92	0.90	1.04	0.78	0.88	0.93	0.97	0.99	1.22
25	0.81	0.89	0.94	0.93	0.86	0.50	0.80	0.91	0.97	1.00	1.03	1.15
26	0.81	0.95	0.99	1.01	0.93	0.39	0.81	0.91	0.96	0.99	1.02	1.05
27	0.77	0.83	0.90	0.91	0.87	0.84	0.80	0.89	0.95	0.98	1.00	1.12
28	0.79	0.81	0.86	0.87	0.83	0.45	0.80	0.88	0.94	0.96	0.99	1.14
29	0.81	0.81	0.87	0.88	0.88	0.97	0.80	0.88	0.94	0.97	0.97	1.22
30	0.74	0.88	1.00	0.98	0.97	1.08	0.81	0.89	0.95	0.98	0.98	1.11
31	0.84	0.85	0.93	1.02	1.16	0.79	0.82	0.90	0.95	0.98	0.99	0.98
32	0.68	0.79	0.83	0.80	0.82	0.86	0.82	0.90	0.95	0.97	0.98	0.98
33	0.83	0.89	1.02	1.06	0.88	0.23	0.83	0.91	0.96	0.97	0.98	1.10
34	0.83	0.93	0.99	1.06	0.81	0.00	0.82	0.90	0.95	0.98	0.96	0.95
35	0.81	0.85	0.84	0.86	0.97	0.47	0.83	0.90	0.94	0.97	0.95	1.01
36	0.77	0.86	0.84	0.71	0.87	1.59	0.82	0.89	0.93	0.95	0.94	0.94
37	0.88	0.83	0.82	0.93	0.97	0.90	0.82	0.89	0.94	0.96	0.94	1.01
38	0.88	0.95	0.93	0.89	0.78	0.00	0.85	0.92	0.96	0.98	0.99	1.02
39	0.87	0.90	0.96	0.94	0.82	1.00	0.86	0.91	0.96	0.96	0.98	1.08
40	0.74	0.80	0.81	0.78	0.90	1.94	0.83	0.91	0.97	0.99	1.05	1.20

Note: Each column represents different embedding dimension m and each row shows different value of j such that $\varepsilon_j = 0.9^j$. Each cell is the point estimate of the correlation exponent, $v_{m,j}$, as defined in Equation 8.

Table 19-3

Correlation Exponents for Gaussian White Noise

| | Sample size = 500 | | | | | | Sample size = 5900 | | | | | |
| | m | | | | | | m | | | | | |
j	1	2	3	4	5	10	1	2	3	4	5	10
16	0.78	1.56	2.34	3.13	3.91	7.49	0.66	1.32	1.97	2.63	3.30	6.61
17	0.83	1.67	2.47	3.25	4.01	9.95	0.72	1.43	2.15	2.86	3.58	7.21
18	0.88	1.80	2.76	3.74	4.73	9.79	0.76	1.52	2.28	3.04	3.81	7.61
19	0.89	1.82	2.75	3.61	4.26	5.79	0.80	1.61	2.41	3.22	4.03	8.15
20	0.88	1.75	2.62	3.46	4.39	9.70	0.84	1.68	2.52	3.35	4.20	8.43
21	0.90	1.83	2.68	3.38	3.89	10.43	0.87	1.73	2.60	3.46	4.33	8.51
22	0.95	1.86	2.87	3.87	5.17	3.85	0.89	1.78	2.67	3.55	4.43	8.46
23	0.96	1.91	2.93	4.01	4.96	—	0.91	1.83	2.75	3.67	4.60	9.43
24	0.96	1.90	2.90	3.64	4.33	—	0.93	1.86	2.79	3.73	4.69	9.24
25	0.99	1.95	2.91	3.71	4.55	—	0.94	1.88	2.81	3.76	4.69	10.61
26	0.99	2.01	2.81	4.19	5.22	—	0.95	1.90	2.85	3.79	4.75	7.14
27	0.99	2.06	3.12	3.88	4.59	—	0.96	1.92	2.87	3.79	4.67	8.84
28	0.99	1.89	2.64	3.56	2.99	—	0.97	1.94	2.91	3.85	4.86	5.88
29	0.99	2.05	3.08	5.06	8.52	—	0.97	1.95	2.93	3.93	4.94	11.89
30	0.99	1.99	3.04	4.33	5.75	—	0.98	1.97	2.95	3.92	4.98	—
31	0.99	2.13	2.88	4.17	1.73	—	0.98	1.97	2.95	3.90	4.88	—
32	0.94	1.82	2.73	4.01	4.85	—	0.99	1.98	2.97	4.00	5.23	—
33	1.00	2.07	3.14	6.09	3.85	—	0.99	1.98	3.01	4.11	5.32	—
34	0.99	1.94	2.73	3.39	6.58	—	0.99	1.99	2.92	3.88	4.95	—
35	0.96	1.83	2.46	0.00	—	—	0.99	1.97	2.93	4.00	5.53	—
36	0.96	1.82	2.69	8.04	—	—	0.99	1.98	2.98	4.00	5.62	—
37	0.96	1.97	2.08	3.85	—	—	0.99	1.98	2.93	3.87	4.81	—
38	0.97	1.84	2.67	0.00	—	—	1.00	1.97	2.94	4.00	5.37	—
39	0.95	2.26	2.99	6.58	—	—	0.99	1.98	2.91	3.85	2.86	—
40	1.00	1.71	1.94	0.00	—	—	1.00	2.02	3.03	4.15	5.38	—

Note: See footnote in Table 19-2.

and Beck (1991) have similar and intensive simulations on point estimates for Gaussian white noise. It should be noticed that their statistic is for all epsilon and not only for small epsilon, as is required for the definition of the correlation exponent.

Smith (1992b) has a simulation for the binomial estimates of low-dimension chaos. It is clear from Table 19-2 that the quality of binomial estimates is related to the range of epsilon chosen. In addition, the reliability in estimating the correlation exponent varies with the sample size and the embedding dimension. Ramsey and Yuan (1989) and Ramsey, Sayers, and Rothman (1990) also recognize this point.

It follows that a chaotic series can be distinguished if it has a fairly low correlation dimension, say 5 or less. Random number generators on computers typically have at least this dimension. Brock (1986) reports a dimension of approximately 11 for the Gauss random number generator. It is also true that it is difficult to distinguish high-dimensional chaos from stochastic white noise just by looking at estimates of υ_m. For more on choosing the proper sample sizes and embedding dimensions, refer to the papers by Smith (1992a, b), Sugihara and May (1990), and Cheng and Tong (1992).

Statistical inference on chaos is a difficult task, and it is not easy to solve all the issues at the same time. When using statistics based on the correlation exponent for chaos, one must bear in mind their limitations. The point estimate tables indicate that it may be possible to distinguish a low-dimensional chaotic process from a truly stochastic i.i.d. process. Operationally, a "stochastic process" here is a high-dimensional chaotic process, such as the random number generators used in this experiment.

To be useful with economic data these techniques must cope with added, independent "measurement error." With this in mind, data were formed

$$z_t = x_t + \sigma\,\varepsilon_t \tag{13}$$

where x_t is white chaos generated by the logistic map as in Equation 2, ε_t is i.i.d. Gaussian white noise, and σ^2 is varied to produce four alternative "signal to noise ratios" (S). We show the results in Table 19-4 for various signal to noise ratios.

The point estimates for the correlation exponent are shown only for m = 1, 3, 5 and for a reduced set of epsilon. Note that if the data were pure white chaos, the numbers should be approximately equal (to 1) for each m value. For the majority of the table the estimates increase approximately proportionally to m, suggesting that the data are stochastic. Only for the largest S values and for a narrow range of epsilon values ($10 \le j \le 20$, say) does the estimate seem to be approximately constant. Smith (1992b) also gives estimators of the correlation exponent and variance of noise for the chaos with additive noise. From Table 19-4 it is found that his estimators are sensitive to the range of epsilon chosen.

In a sense the correlation technique is working too well, since the true data-generating mechanism does contain a stochastic (or high-dimensional) element, ε_t. This is what is "seen" by the point estimates. The low-dimensional deterministic chaos component, x_t, is totally missed, even when it has a much larger variance than the noise. It may well be that when deterministic chaos is present in economic data, it can be found only

Table 19-4

Correlation Exponents for Logistic Map with Additive White Noise
(Sample Size = 5,900)

	m			m			m			m		
	1	3	5	1	3	5	1	3	5	1	3	5
j	$\sigma^2 = 0.3, S = 0.4$			$\sigma^2 = 0.1, S = 1.2$			$\sigma^2 = 0.01, S = 12$			$\sigma^2 = 0.001, S = 120$		
4	0.01	0.02	0.03	0.01	0.03	0.06	0.21	0.64	1.07	0.65	2.27	3.59
8	0.13	0.40	0.66	0.21	0.64	1.08	0.67	2.02	3.46	0.69	1.40	1.83
12	0.45	1.34	2.24	0.56	1.66	2.76	0.73	1.38	1.99	0.71	1.03	1.43
16	0.72	2.15	3.57	0.79	2.30	3.80	0.80	1.49	2.10	0.76	1.01	1.18
20	0.87	2.61	4.33	0.90	2.65	4.39	0.88	2.01	3.12	0.79	1.07	1.21
24	0.94	2.83	4.74	0.96	2.85	4.72	0.94	2.50	4.03	0.84	1.39	1.78
28	0.98	2.89	4.75	0.98	2.92	4.83	0.97	2.75	4.74	0.90	1.96	2.94
32	0.99	2.98	5.03	0.99	3.00	4.90	0.98	2.85	4.72	0.95	2.45	3.95
36	0.99	3.00	5.04	1.00	2.95	4.91	1.00	2.96	5.00	0.98	2.76	4.62
40	1.00	3.11	9.16	1.00	2.92	5.31	1.00	3.02	5.46	0.99	2.82	5.39

Note: The variance of the logistic map is about 0.12 and σ^2 is the variance of the white noise. S = (variance of logistic map/variance of noise), i.e., "signal/noise ratio." See also footnote in Table 19-2. Only partials of j are shown in this table.

if it contains very little measurement error. Further, the generating process must be of low correlation dimension for detection to take place.

A possible source of such data is stock market prices. Two series were used: daily rates of returns for IBM and the Standard & Poor's 500 stock index, for the period 2 July 1962 to 31 December 1985, giving 5,903 observations. The autocorrelations for both series were uniformly very small and generally insignificant, as predicted by efficient market theory. Table 19-5 shows the point estimates for the IBM returns and S&P 500 returns. The patterns of the estimates for these two returns are extremely similar. Values were small for larger epsilon. Further, for small enough epsilon, the estimates are seen to increase approximately with m, but again with a downward bias. The pattern is consistent either with these returns being a stochastic white noise or being chaotic with a true correlation dimension of around 6. To distinguish between these alternatives higher m values would have to be used. This would require a much larger sample size. These stock price series are not low-dimensional chaos, according to this technique. Other studies involving aggregate and individual stock market time series confirm this experience (Scheinkman and LeBaron, 1989).

Table 19-5

Correlation Exponents for Daily IBM and S&P 500 Rate of Returns
(from 2 July 1962 to 31 December 1985, with 5,903 Observations)

	IBM daily returns m						S&P 500 daily returns m					
j	1	2	3	4	5	10	1	2	3	4	5	10
16	0.20	0.38	0.55	0.72	0.87	1.56	0.33	0.63	0.89	1.14	1.36	2.27
17	0.26	0.50	0.72	0.94	1.14	2.04	0.40	0.75	1.07	1.37	1.64	2.71
18	0.33	0.63	0.91	1.18	1.43	2.56	0.46	0.87	1.24	1.59	1.90	3.13
19	0.39	0.76	1.10	1.43	1.73	3.09	0.52	0.99	1.42	1.81	2.17	3.54
20	0.46	0.90	1.31	1.68	2.05	3.63	0.58	1.10	1.58	2.03	2.43	3.93
21	0.53	1.03	1.49	1.93	2.35	4.17	0.63	1.21	1.74	2.23	2.68	4.30
22	0.59	1.15	1.68	2.18	2.65	4.75	0.69	1.32	1.90	2.43	2.91	4.63
23	0.65	1.27	1.85	2.40	2.93	5.26	0.73	1.41	2.03	2.61	3.13	4.97
24	0.70	1.37	2.00	2.60	3.18	5.79	0.77	1.49	2.16	2.77	3.33	5.32
25	0.74	1.46	2.14	2.78	3.41	6.27	0.81	1.57	2.27	2.92	3.51	5.65
26	0.79	1.55	2.28	2.98	3.66	6.77	0.84	1.63	2.37	3.07	3.69	5.94
27	0.83	1.63	2.40	3.14	3.86	7.22	0.87	1.69	2.45	3.16	3.82	6.44
28	0.85	1.69	2.49	3.26	4.02	7.68	0.89	1.74	2.53	3.28	3.96	6.59
29	0.88	1.74	2.58	3.39	4.19	8.08	0.91	1.78	2.60	3.39	4.12	7.00
30	0.89	1.76	2.61	3.44	4.27	8.44	0.93	1.82	2.67	3.49	4.25	6.93
31	0.92	1.82	2.70	3.56	4.42	8.81	0.94	1.86	2.72	3.56	4.35	7.81
32	0.93	1.85	2.76	3.65	4.52	8.56	0.95	1.88	2.77	3.63	4.47	8.37
33	0.95	1.89	2.83	3.74	4.62	9.54	0.96	1.89	2.80	3.69	4.56	7.67
34	0.96	1.91	2.86	3.82	4.82	9.10	0.97	1.92	2.84	3.74	4.60	7.60
35	0.97	1.93	2.88	3.82	4.79	9.84	0.98	1.94	2.88	3.79	4.75	11.00
36	0.96	1.90	2.84	3.79	4.78	14.62	0.98	1.95	2.90	3.82	4.71	7.75
37	0.99	1.98	2.97	3.98	5.04	10.43	0.98	1.94	2.90	3.84	4.75	7.09
38	0.96	1.92	2.87	3.77	4.85	—	0.99	1.96	2.91	3.81	4.74	10.43
39	0.98	1.96	2.90	3.89	4.89	—	0.99	1.98	2.93	3.95	4.79	—
40	0.98	1.96	2.94	3.86	4.94	—	0.99	1.98	2.92	3.84	4.81	—

Note: See footnote in Table 19-2.

The BDS Test

Looking for patterns in tables may be useful, but as different people may reach different conclusions, it is preferable to have a formal test with no subjectivity. Brock and Beck (1991) describe the statistical properties of the point estimator for the correlation exponent under the i.i.d. assumption for x_t. We are interested in how well it detects the presence of chaos. Since the point estimator for the correlation exponent is equal to the point elasticity of the correlation integral, Brock and Beck's statistic is derived from a statistic using the correlation integral. Such a statistic was developed by Brock, Dechert, and Scheinkman (1987) (henceforth BDS). We examine the properties of the BDS statistic here, yielding some insight into the statistic proposed by Brock and Beck. A good discussion of a BDS application can be found in Brock and Sayers (1988).

Using the correlation integral $C_m(\varepsilon)$ (defined in Equation 5), the BDS test statistic is

$$S(m, \varepsilon) = C_m(\varepsilon) - [C_1(\varepsilon)]^m \qquad (14)$$

The null hypothesis is

$$H_0 : x_t \text{ is i.i.d.} \qquad (15)$$

and it is shown that for large samples under the null, $S(m,\varepsilon)$ is asymptotically distributed as normal, i.e.

$$S(m,\varepsilon) \sim N(o,q) \qquad (16)$$

where q is a complicated expression depending on m, ε, and sample size.

If a series is linear but has autocorrelation, then the test should reject the null. In practice the BDS test statistic is applied to the residuals of a fitted linear model. The model specification is constructed first and then tested to see if the fitted model gives i.i.d. residuals. BDS (1987) show that asymptotically, Equation 16 still applies when residuals are used, so that there is no "nuisance parameter" problem. However, it was pointed out by Brock *et al.* (1991a) that the BDS test is not free of the nuisance parameter problem if heteroskedastic errors are involved. Since BDS is being used here as a test for stochastic or deterministic nonlinearity, it is necessary to remove linear components of the series before applying the test. To do this in practice, an AR(p) model is built for x_t, using some criteria such as AIC or BIC[1] to select the order p of the model. The test is then applied to the residuals of this linear fitting procedure.

Recall that the test is constructed using a null of i.i.d., and that rejection of the null does not imply chaos. The test may well have good power against other alternatives, such as stochastic nonlinear processes. Nevertheless, if the linear component has been properly removed, rejection of the null does correspond to presence of "nonlinearity" in the data, however defined.

Lee, White, and Granger (1990) have compared the BDS with several other tests of nonlinearity for a variety of univariate nonlinear processes. They find that it often has good power, but does less well than some of the other tests. However, the test used there had an embedding dimension of $m = 2$ and just a single epsilon value. Other simulations, such as Hsieh and

LeBaron (1991) and Hsieh (1991), also show the size and power of BDS test for some nonlinear models. We study here how the BDS test is affected by other values of m and how sensitive it is to the choice of epsilon. Also, it is essential to look at the BDS test properties when epsilon values are small, where it is the only relevant range for the testing of chaos. Then it can also be applied to the statistical properties of the point estimator used by Brock and Beck (1991).

The following experiment was conducted. A series of length 200 is generated by some mechanism. As the BDS test is not affected by the norm used in calculating the correlation integral, each observation can be transformed within the range (0, 1) as above. The BDS test is then applied and the null rejected or not, and this procedure repeated 1,000 times. The tables show the percentage of rejections with given significance levels for m = 2, 3, and 4, and for epsilon values $\varepsilon_j = 0.8^j$, with $j = 1, 2, 4, 6, 8$, and 10. Small j values correspond to large epsilons, and this is a range of no relevance for testing chaos.

To check if the critical values used in the test (which are based on the asymptotic theorem) are unbiased, the experiment was first run in the case where the null hypothesis was correct. Machine-generated random numbers from a Gaussian distribution were used. These numbers were random shuffled to reduce any hidden nonrandomness in the data. Both sets of data produced similar results, and just those for the shuffled data are shown. Table 19-6 shows the size of the BDS test for various significance levels.

Table 19-6

Size of BDS Test for Shuffled Pseudorandom Numbers

	$\alpha = 1\%$ m			$\alpha = 2.5\%$ m			$\alpha = 5\%$ m			$\alpha = 10\%$ m		
j	2	3	4	2	3	4	2	3	4	2	3	4
1	0.878	0.821	0.819	0.893	0.848	0.832	0.910	0.868	0.849	0.931	0.884	0.867
2	0.157	0.207	0.268	0.225	0.284	0.331	0.315	0.374	0.430	0.421	0.480	0.514
4	0.033	0.033	0.034	0.056	0.059	0.060	0.085	0.094	0.105	0.154	0.166	0.181
6	0.016	0.018	0.015	0.041	0.033	0.034	0.067	0.059	0.067	0.118	0.116	0.112
8	0.017	0.019	0.016	0.045	0.032	0.050	0.072	0.072	0.075	0.126	0.128	0.131
10	0.041	0.059	0.078	0.070	0.086	0.124	0.111	0.139	0.169	0.184	0.207	0.240

Note: Four significance levels (α), 0.01, 0.25, 0.05, and 0.10, are used for the BDS statistic, $S(m, \varepsilon_j)$, with different embedding dimension m and different epsilons, $\varepsilon_j = 0.8^j$ The pseudorandom numbers are generated from Fortran subroutine, IMSL. Each observation in the replication is randomly chosen from an array of 100 dimension. The numbers in this array are randomly generated from pseudonormal numbers and the position of the array being chosen is randomly decided by pseudouniform random numbers.

For columns with significance level $\alpha = 0.05$, for example, if the asymptotic critical values were correct, the proportion of times the null hypothesis is rejected should be 5 percent of the time. The approximate 95 percent region is 0.037–0.063. The values are seen consistently biased toward too frequent rejection of H_0 with a sample size of 200.[2]

However, in most cases, with $j = 6$ and $j = 8$, the values are not badly biased. With the other values of j the critical values are so biased that they are unusable. This is not surprising. When low j values (i.e., larger epsilon values) are considered, most of the pairwise distances in Equation 5 will be smaller than epsilon. Clearly, when epsilon is small (e.g., $j = 10$), few pairs are within an epsilon distance. In either case it is not easy to find the independence based on the relationship of $C_m(\varepsilon) = C_1(\varepsilon)^m$. It will be more likely that $C_m(\varepsilon)$ is close to $C_1(\varepsilon)$ instead of $C_1(\varepsilon)^m$. Hence $S\,(m,\varepsilon)$ should not have mean zero and the null hypothesis is easily rejected. The results are seen to vary little as m goes from 2 to 4. Although values are shown for all j with the other experiments, only for $j = 6$ and 8 are sensible interpretations and comments about power possible.

Further experiments are conducted for the testing i.i.d. of the fitted residuals. Table 19-7 shows the size and power of the BDS test based on fitted residuals using 5 percent significance level. Applying the BDS test to the residuals from a linear fitted model of autoregressive order 1 and 2, gives the size of the test. As shown in the upper part of Table 19-7, the size is similar to the random numbers case. The power of the test is examined by applying the test to (1) a moving average model, (2) two white chaos series, and (3) seven nonlinear stochastic processes. In the white chaos case, no linear regression is needed before applying the BDS test.

The test works very well for a fairly small sample size with true chaotic series, in that the null is rejected uniformly for smaller epsilon values. Using data from the logistic map, which is chaos data, the BDS test rejected the null with a probability of 1.0 for all j values, $j \geq 4$. Similar results were found with chaotic data generated by the tent map.

The experiments for nonlinear stochastic process are divided into two groups. For the first group the BDS test has very good power. The BDS test rejects the null hypothesis of i.i.d. more than 90 percent of replications. The results are shown in the center part of Table 19-7 along with the results on white chaos. The models in this group are bilinear (BL) and bilinear moving average (BLMA) models, which are

(BL) $x_t = 0.7 x_{t-1} \varepsilon_{t-2} + \varepsilon_t$ (17)

(BLMA) $x_t = 0.4 x_{t-1} - 0.3 x_{t-2} + 0.5 x_{t-1} \varepsilon_{t-1} + 0.8 \varepsilon_{t-1} + \varepsilon_t$ (18)

Table 19-7

Size and Power of BDS Test for Residuals

j	m 1	m 2	m 3	m 1	m 2	m 3	m 1	m 2	m 3	m 1	m 2	m 3
	AR(1)			AR(2)			MA(2)			NLSIGN		
1	0.931	0.885	0.885	0.916	0.892	0.877	0.909	0.860	0.864	0.886	0.845	0.840
2	0.350	0.413	0.439	0.338	0.405	0.442	0.344	0.436	0.448	0.310	0.374	0.394
4	0.086	0.092	0.099	0.098	0.106	0.107	0.100	0.126	0.130	0.102	0.119	0.108
6	0.061	0.058	0.057	0.061	0.068	0.079	0.073	0.094	0.089	0.059	0.073	0.075
8	0.070	0.064	0.078	0.063	0.079	0.100	0.092	0.095	0.116	0.070	0.123	0.162
10	0.107	0.124	0.157	0.102	0.124	0.155	0.132	0.158	0.226	0.113	0.205	0.311
j	Logistic map			Tent map			Bilinear			BLMA		
1	1.000	0.985	0.887	0.776	0.872	0.847	0.969	0.907	0.911	0.975	0.931	0.934
2	0.955	0.961	0.978	0.999	0.802	0.592	0.546	0.584	0.579	0.393	0.391	0.400
4	1.000	1.000	1.000	1.000	1.000	0.985	0.878	0.920	0.917	0.675	0.725	0.717
6	1.000	1.000	1.000	1.000	1.000	1.000	0.988	0.996	0.995	0.971	0.988	0.990
8	1.000	1.000	1.000	1.000	1.000	1.000	0.987	0.997	0.996	0.992	0.996	0.996
10	1.000	1.000	1.000	1.000	1.000	1.000	0.981	0.993	0.991	0.986	0.997	0.996
j	NLMA1			NLAR			TAR			NLMA2		
1	0.969	0.925	0.902	0.942	0.910	0.906	0.896	0.853	0.861	0.894	0.824	0.832
2	0.405	0.480	0.518	0.381	0.486	0.516	0.325	0.408	0.453	0.375	0.426	0.442
4	0.080	0.120	0.150	0.082	0.100	0.103	0.187	0.185	0.182	0.371	0.464	0.455
6	0.081	0.165	0.194	0.126	0.171	0.209	0.145	0.134	0.132	0.328	0.435	0.436
8	0.075	0.170	0.234	0.242	0.372	0.489	0.195	0.168	0.168	0.285	0.402	0.414
10	0.065	0.182	0.245	0.417	0.711	0.914	0.464	0.443	0.391	0.273	0.400	0.420

Note: The residuals from first-order autoregressive regression for AR(1), NLSIGN, Bilinear, NLAR, and TAR models are derived for the BDS statistic $S(m, \varepsilon_j)$, $\varepsilon_j = 0.8^j$. For AR(2), MA(2), BLMA, NLMA1, and NLMA2 models, the residuals are derived from the second-order autoregressive regression. In case of chaos, the BDS test is applied to the original series. The numbers show the percentage rejections in 1,000 replications with 5 percent significance level.

For the second group the BDS test has power smaller than 50 percent. This means that the BDS test does not easily detect these types of nonlinearity. The models are the nonlinear sign model (NLSIGN), two nonlinear moving average models (NLMA1 and NLMA2), rational nonlinear autoregressive model (NLAR), and threshold autoregressive model (TAR), which have the following forms:

(NLSIGN) $x_t = \text{SIGN}(x_{t-1}) + \varepsilon_t$, $\text{SIGN}(x) = 1, 0$, or -1, if $x < 0, = 0, > 0$ (19)

(NLMA1) $x_t = \varepsilon_t - 0.4\varepsilon_{t-1} + 0.3\varepsilon_{t-2} + 0.5\varepsilon_t\varepsilon_{t-2}$ (20)

(NLAR) $x_t = \dfrac{0.7 \mid x_{t-1} \mid}{2 + \mid x_{t-1} \mid} + \varepsilon_t$ (21)

(TAR) $x_t = 0.9x_{t-1} + \varepsilon_t$ if $\mid x_{t-1} \mid \leq 1$ (22)
$\quad\quad\quad = -0.3x_{t-1} + \varepsilon_t$ if $\mid x_{t-1} \mid > 1$

(NLMA2) $x_t = \varepsilon_t - 0.3\varepsilon_{t-1} + 0.2\varepsilon_{t-2} + 0.4\varepsilon_{t-1}\varepsilon_{t-2} - 0.25\varepsilon_{t-2}^2$ (23)

Table 19-7 shows that the BDS test has the greatest power on the bilinear model. It rejects the null hypothesis of i.i.d. more than 90 percent replications. But the BDS test has the least power on the nonlinear sign model. Actually, the residuals are seen to be i.i.d. by the BDS test. For the other four models the power for the NLMA1 model is slightly higher than nonlinear sign model, and the highest power is found for the NLMA2 model. The power of these four models is shown in the lower part of Table 19-7. The low power of NLMA1 and NLMA2 may be because of the heteroskedastic errors.

As noted before, the figures for $j = 1, 2,$ and 10 are based on a biased significance level and so should be discounted. The power is seen to vary widely with the type of nonlinearity that is present, as is found to occur with other tests of nonlinearity. There is a general pattern of increasing power as j increases and as m increases, but this does not happen in all cases. It does seem that the choice of epsilon is critical in obtaining a satisfactory test, and that this is more important than the choice of the embedding dimension. Furthermore, the "correct" range of epsilon for BDS test may or may not coincide with the range of small epsilon required for the definition of low-dimensional chaos. Other simulations, such as Hsieh and LeBaron (1988); Hsieh (1991); Brock et al. (1991a); and Brock, Hsieh, and LeBaron (1991b) also show the size and power of BDS test for some nonlinear models. Those results are rather similar to what has been found here. The BDS test may be useful in distinguishing linear stochastic process from nonlinear stochastic process. It cannot be used alone for distinguishing between deterministic chaos and stochastic process. In addition to the problem of choosing proper epsilon, rejection of the i.i.d. null hypothesis may be caused by dependence among x_t or stochastic nonlinearity in x_t.

Conclusions

Our specific results include the following:

1. Some deterministic systems behave like white noise (Table 19-1).

2. The correlation exponent technique can be used to distinguish these systems (Table 19-2) from stochastic white noise (Table 19-3).

3. The correlation exponent does not work very well in uncovering even a low-dimensional deterministic process when stochastic noise is present (Table 19-4).

4. Real economic data fail to exhibit low-dimensional chaos (e.g., Table 19-5).

5. A BDS test for stochastic white noise correctly rejects a null of white noise when the series is deterministically generated, but rejected the null too often in cases where the data came from essentially stochastic sources (Table 19-6).

6. The BDS test has power to reject the stochastic nonlinearity, but its power varies as models differ (Table 19-7). BDS correctly rejected the i.i.d. null if the data came from bilinear processes, but had less power when series came from threshold autoregressive or nonlinear, moving-average processes. It had no power for the nonlinear sign model or the NLAR.

7. For empirical work, both the correlation exponent and the BDS test require a great deal of care in choosing epsilon, see Tables 19-2 to 19-5 and Table 19-7.

Our results are consistent with current practice in the economic literature. Any economy is in theory essentially nonlinear in nature, with complex interactions among many variables of economic significance. However, at the current state of the art there is no good way to capture the richness of these models in testable form. At the level of applied works the models are linearized and the corresponding error terms modeled as residuals. The question remains: Do we live in an essentially linear economic world with unforecastable events exogenous to the model? Pragmatism dictates that we continue to develop better estimation methods for a world having both nonlinear interactions and unforecastable shocks.

Some general speculative remarks can be made about the difficulties of distinguishing between chaotic and stochastic processes. There are several tests, such as BDS, with stochastic white noise as the null. If the null is rejected with prewhitened data, then nonlinearity can be accepted. However, the theory is still lacking for making the choice between stochastic and deterministic. This lacuna follows from our observation that, so far as we are aware, there is no statistical test with deterministic chaos as its null hypothesis.

A common fallacy in many fields using time-series data is that "the data-generating process G has property P; if our data has property P it is because they are generated by process G." Naturally, this is logically correct only if P characterizes G. That the data are consistent with G does not rule out other models of the universe. It is vital for researchers working with time series to have a statistic that completely characterizes chaotic processes.

One can certainly argue that statistical tests are not the proper way to detect deterministic processes. In this view, evidence of "strange attractors," say, is convincing enough. However, the sample sizes available from economic time-series data are not large enough to provide such evidence. New techniques that could cope with small sample sizes are needed here as well. We are led to the conclusion that probabilistic methods are for the time being the most appropriate technique for analyzing economic time-series data. We suspect that this conclusion also applies to much data where chaos has been "found" in the behavioral sciences, biology, health sciences, and education.

Acknowledgment

The work of C. W. J. Granger was partially supported by NFS Grant SES 89-02950.

Notes

1 I.e., Akaike's Information Criterion and the Bayesian Information Criterion, respectively.

2 Hsieh and LeBaron (1988) and Brock, Hsieh, and LeBaron (1991b) find that the BDS test does not have good finite sample properties. The size of the test can be improved by increasing the sample size.

References

Brock, W. A. "Distinguishing Random and Deterministic Systems." *Journal of Economic Theory*, 40 (1986), 168–195.

Brock, W. A., and E. G. Beck. "Some Theory of Statistical Inference for Nonlinear Science." *Review of Economic Studies*, 58 (1991), 697–716.

Brock, W. A., and C. L. Sayers. "Is the Business Cycle Characterized by Deterministic Chaos?" *Journal of Monetary Economics*, 22 (1988), 71–90.

Brock, W. A., W. D. Dechert, and J. A. Scheinkman. "A Test of Independence Based on the Correlation Dimension." SSRI Working Paper No. 8702, Department of Economics, University of Wisconsin, Madison (1987).

Brock, W. A., W. D. Dechert, J. A. Scheinkman, and B. LeBaron. "A Test of Independence Based on the Correlation Dimension." Department of Economics, University of Wisconsin, Madison (1991a).

Brock, W., D. Hsieh, and B. LeBaron. *Nonlinear Dynamics, Chaos and Instability,* Cambridge, MA: MIT Press (1991b).

Cheng, B., and H. Tong. "Consistent Nonparametric Order Determination and Chaos." *Journal of Royal Statistical Society B,* 54 , (1992).

Cutler, C. "Some Results on the Behavior and Estimation of the Fractal Dimensions of Distributions on Attractors." *Journal of Statistical Physics,* 62 (1991), 651–708.

Denker, G., and G. Keller. "Rigorous Statistical Procedures for Data from Dynamical Systems." *Journal of Statistical Physics,* 44 (1986), 67–93.

Frank, M., and T. Stengos. "Chaotic Dynamics in Economic Time Systems." *Journal of Economic Surveys,* 2 (1988), 103–134.

Grandmont, J. "On Endogenous Competitive Business Cycles." *Econometrica,* 53 (1985), 995–1045.

Granger, C. W. J. "Forecasting White Noise." In A. Zellner, ed., *Applied Time Series Analysis of Economic Data.* Washington, DC: U.S. Department of Commerce, Bureau of the Census, (1983).

Grassberger, P., and I. Procaccia. "Measuring the Strangeness of Strange Attractors." *Physica,* 9D (1983), 189–208.

Hiemstra, C. "Detection and Description of Nonlinear Dynamics: Using Correlation Integral Based Estimators." Department of Economics, Loyola College, Baltimore, January 1992.

Hsieh, D. A. "Chaos and Nonlinear Dynamics: Application to Financial Markets." *Journal of Finance,* 46(5) (1991), 1839–1877.

Hsieh, D. A., and B. LeBaron. "Finite Sample Properties of the BDS Statistic." University of Chicago and University of Wisconsin, Madison (1988).

Lee, T. W., H. White, and C. W. J. Granger. "Testing for Neglected Nonlinearity in Time Series: A Comparison of Neural Network Methods and Alternative Tests." Working Paper, Economics Department, University of California, San Diego (1990).

Ramsey, J., and H. Yuan. "Bias and Error Bias in Dimension Calculation and Their Evaluation in Some Simple Models." *Physical Letters A*, 134 (1989), 287–297.

Ramsey, J., and H. Yuan. "The Statistical Properties of Dimension Calculations Using Small Data Sets." *Nonlinearity*, 3 (1990), 155–176.

Ramsey, J. B., C. L. Sayers, and P. Rothman. "The Statistical Properties of Dimension Calculations Using Small Data Sets: Some Economic Applications." *International Economic Review*, 31(4) (1990), 991–1020.

Sakai, H., and H. Tokumaru. "Autocorrelations of a Certain Chaos." *IEEE Transactions on Acoustics, Speech, and Signal Processing*, ASSP-28(5) (1980), 588–590.

Scheinkman, J., and B. LeBaron. "Nonlinear Dynamics and Stock Returns." *Journal of Business*, 62 (1989), 311–337.

Smith, R. L. "Optimal Estimation of Fractal Dimension." In M. Casdagli and S. Eubank, eds., *Nonlinear Modeling and Forecasting*, SFI Studies in the Science of Complexity, Proceeding, Vol. 12. Reading, MA: Addison-Wesley, (1992a).

Smith, R. "Estimating Dimension in Noisy Chaotic Time Series." *Journal of Royal Statistical Society B*, 54 (1992b), 329–352.

Sugihara, G., and R. M. May. "Nonlinear Forecasting as a Way of Distinguishing Chaos from Measurement Error in Time Series." *Nature*, 344 (1990), 734–741.

Theiler, J. "Statistical Precision of Dimension Estimators." *Physical Review A*, 41 (1990), 3038–3051.

20

A NEW TEST FOR CHAOS

By Claire G. Gilmore

1. Introduction

Recent work on nonlinear dynamics, particularly chaotic systems, in the natural sciences has provoked interest in the potential applicability of the theory of chaos to other fields. While the persistent irregularity of such variables as GNP, employment, interest rates, and exchange rates has generally been attributed to random shocks, the ability of even simple deterministic chaotic models to produce complex time paths that appear to be random has attracted attention as a possible alternative explanation. Several useful introductory discussions are now available in the literature, including Baumol and Benhabib (1989). Theoretical applications have been made in such areas as growth models [Stutzer (1980), Day (1982, 1983)], rational decision making [Benhabib and Day (1981)], business cycles [Grandmont (1985), H.-W. Lorenz (1987b)], international trade [H. W. Lorenz (1987a)], and stock returns [Shaffer (1990)].

Empirical research on detection of chaotic behavior has expanded rapidly, but the results have tended to be inconclusive, due to lack of appropriate testing methods. Standard techniques, such as spectral analysis or the autocorrelation function, cannot distinguish whether a time series was generated by a deterministic or a stochastic mechanism [Sakai and Tokumaru (1980)]. The correlation dimension test, a metric approach developed by Grassberger and Procaccia (1983a,b), has been widely used in the natural sciences, generally in conjunction with related procedures such as the calculation of Lyapunov exponents. Application of these tests to relatively small, noisy data sets, which are common in economics and finance, is of dubious validity, and the reliability of the methodology has also come into question, even in the natural sciences, where large, fairly clean data sets are often available [Mindlin et al. (1990)]. Possible evidence of chaotic behavior has been produced by the metric approach for U.S. business cycle data [Brock and Sayers (1988)], work stoppage data [Sayers (1986, 1987)], weekly stock returns [Scheinkman and LeBaron (1986, 1989)], Treasury bill returns [Brock and Malliaris (1989)], gold and silver returns [Frank and Stengos (1989)], and several demand Divisia monetary aggregates [Barnett and Chen (1989)]. Frank and Stengos (1988) found no chaotic behavior in the Canadian counterparts of U.S. business cycle data, nor was there any indication of chaos in the GNP series for Italy, Japan, the U.K., or West Germany [Frank, Gençay, and Stengos (1988)]. The Scheinkman and LeBaron (1989), Sayers (1987), and Barnett and Chen (1988) work was reexamined by Ramsey, Sayers, and Rothman (1990), who applied a procedure by Ramsey and Yuan (1989, 1990) to reduce the small sample size bias in dimension calculations. They concluded that there was no evidence of chaos in any of these series, except possibly in the work stoppage data.

Recently, a promising new approach to testing for low-dimensional deterministic chaos, based on the topological properties of chaotic processes, has been developed in the physics literature [Mindlin et al. (1990), Tufillaro et al. (1990), Mindlin et al. (1991)]. This method includes a "close returns" test for detecting chaos that is of particular interest for researchers in fields such as finance and economics, since it works well on relatively small, noisy data sets. Further, the topological approach is potentially far more useful than metric methods, since it is capable of providing additional information about the underlying system generating chaotic behavior, once evidence of chaos is detected. The present study will demonstrate this new method, using a data set generated from a chaotic model, and will then adapt it to test for the presence of deterministic chaos in selected financial and economic time series data, comparing the results to those reported in earlier studies.

The metric and the topological approaches to testing for chaotic behavior will be explained and compared in Section 2. In Section 3 the close returns method is applied to chaotic data; a forecasting technique suggested by this test is also discussed. Results of the close returns test on economic and financial time series data are given in Section 4. Conclusions are presented in Section 5.

2. Metric and Topological Methodologies

At present there are two broad approaches to the analysis of data generated by a process exhibiting chaos: the metric and the topological. The metric approach is characterized by the study of distances between points on a strange attractor. The topological approach is characterized by the study of the organization of the strange attractor. A strange attractor is the set of points toward which a chaotic dynamical path will converge.[1]

The description of many systems is facilitated by the use of a phase space. Here the state of a system is described by a point $y = (y_1, y_2, ..., y_n)$, and R^n is some n-dimensional phase space. The point describing the system, $y_t = (y_{1t}, y_{2t}, ..., y_{nt})$ evolves with time. If the system is in a steady state, the point y_t does not move. If the system behaves cyclically, the orbit y_t, is closed and periodic. If the system is governed by a set of nonlinear ordinary differential equations and the behavior is bounded but neither static nor periodic, then this deterministic nonperiodic behavior may be chaotic. The phase space trajectory that describes the behavior of the system lies on a strange attractor.

Two mechanisms are responsible for the existence of a strange attractor. These are "stretching" and "compressing." The first mechanism, stretching, is responsible for "sensitive dependence on initial conditions." This means that two nearby points in phase space, representing slightly different initial states of the system, will evolve along divergent trajectories and exhibit dramatically different states of the system after some finite time. This mechanism is responsible for the long-term unpredictability generally attributed to systems exhibiting chaos. The second mechanism, compressing, is responsible for the recurrent behavior exhibited by all chaotic (as opposed to stochastic) systems. If initial conditions were to be stretched apart indefinitely, the trajectories would not be confined to a bounded region of phase space. To ensure that trajectories do not run off to infinity, the flow must somehow be returned to a bounded region of phase space. The compressing mechanism is responsible for patterns that almost repeat themselves throughout a chaotic data set. This mechanism is at the heart of both the metric and the topological approaches to the analysis of chaotic data sets.

Typically, time series data for a *single* variable are available for the analysis of some process. The metric and the topological methods each depend on the recurrent nature of the time series flow to test for the existence of a strange attractor. However, they differ on how the time series data are prepared for analysis.

Metric Method

In the metric approach the time series data $\{x_t\}$, where $i = (1, 2, ..., N)$, are first used to construct a series of m-tuples $\{x_i^m\} = \{x_i, x_{i+1\tau}, x_{i+(m-1)\tau}\}$, where τ is a time-delay parameter. Each m-tuple represents a point in an m-dimensional Euclidean space. This mapping of a time series into an m-dimensional space, $\{x_i\} \rightarrow \{x_i^m\}$, is called an ($m$-dimensional) *embedding* of the data. The embedding is done for successively larger values of m. For each embedding dimension a series of calculations is carried out to estimate the recurrence properties of the trajectory. The idea is as follows. If the motion occurs on a strange attractor, then the trajectory will return to the ε-neighborhood of any point after some time. The smaller the neighborhood, the longer the time.

The correlation between points is computed by use of the correlation integral

$$C_m(\varepsilon) = \{ \, \# \, (i,j): \; \| x_i^m - x_j^m \| < \varepsilon \}/N_m^2, \; |i - j| > 1, \tag{1}$$

where x_i^m and x_j^m are the ith and jth m-tuples, respectively, N is the sample size $N_m = N - (m - 1)\tau$ is the number of m-tuples that can be produced from the sample, and ε measures the size of the sphere around each point. Theoretically, N should be infinite. The correlation integral is then used to compute metric properties such as the correlation dimension [Grassberger and Procaccia (1983a,b)]. The correlation is defined as

$$D_m = \lim_{N \to \infty} \lim_{\varepsilon \to 0} \ln C_m(\varepsilon)/\ln\varepsilon. \tag{2}$$

The limit as the embedding dimension goes to infinity gives the correlation dimension of the strange attractor:

$$D = \lim_{m \to \infty} D_m. \tag{3}$$

Correlation dimension is estimated by a linear regression of $\ln C_m(\varepsilon)$ on $\ln(\varepsilon)$ over an appropriate subinterval of the range of ε. Variations of this counting procedure are used to compute other metric properties, such as the Lyapunov exponent, which measures the rate at which two nearby trajectories converge or diverge.[2] For detailed discussions of metric methods see Cvitanovic (1984). The reliability of these metric computations as a means of detecting low-dimensional chaos has been called into question, as there are a number of problems associated with its implementation:

1. The estimate of the correlation dimension converges to the dimension of the chaotic attractor as N, the number of observations, goes to infinity. With small data sets the number of observations may be insufficient for convergence to occur.[3]

2. Noise in the time series may render dimension calculations useless [Brock (1986)].

3. Estimation of the scaling region, (symbol), to be used in the calculation requires the exercise of judgment and is subjective [Brock (1986)].

4. Lack of formal statistical distribution theory for the correlation dimension has made clear-cut conclusions difficult, although see the recent advances by Brock and Baek (1991).

5. There is substantial bias in dimension correlations with small data sets [Ramsey and Yuan (1989, 1990)].

6. Dimension calculations provide little information on how to "model the dynamics" of the underlying system [Gunaratne et al. (1989)]. The procedure throws away time-ordering information, so even a positive result, indicating chaos, cannot possibly lead to information about the dynamics of the process responsible for generating chaotic behavior;

7. The procedure must be implemented carefully to capture only geometric correlation in the time series and eliminate dynamic correlation [Grassberger (1990)]. Dynamic correlation contributes to the count simply because of the fact that in a smooth flow two points, x_i^m and x_{i+1}^m, which are nearby in time, will be nearby in phase space. For geometric correlation, the m-vectors x_i and x_j, where $|i-j|$ is large, can be nearby due to the recurrent nature of the flow, which the compressing mechanism causes; the counting procedure attempts to measure this proximity to capture some properties of the strange attractor. Therefore, the sum in Equation 1 must be restricted by the condition $|i-j| > fT$, where T is some characteristic period of the data, measured in terms of the sample rate, and f is some fraction of 1 (e.g., f = ¼), the larger the better [Grassberger (1990)]. This is a different issue from determination of the delay parameter τ. Failure to implement this precaution has rendered many previously reported dimension calculations "obsolete" [Grassberger (1990)].

Topological Method

The topological approach analyzes the way in which the mechanisms responsible for stretching and compressing the strange attractor act on the unstable periodic orbits, intertwining them in a very specific way. Mingled with the strange attractor are periodic orbits that are unstable. Each attractor contains a large number of unstable orbits of many periodicities; they are "dense." For example, a time series moving in phase space around an unstable period-1 orbit will return close to its original starting point, x_i, after cycling once through phase space; for a period-2 orbit it cycles twice through phase space before returning close to x_i, and so forth for higher-period orbits.

The first stage in the topological analysis is the close returns test, which searches for the unstable periodic orbits embedded in a strange attractor. It is a qualitative method that detects whether a time series exhibits chaotic behavior by searching for evidence of the unstable periodic orbits embedded in a chaotic system's strange attractor. This test is explained below.[4] Once a positive finding of chaos is made in a time series, the topological method enables the researcher to proceed to characterize the underlying process in a quantitative way. This is possible because the topological method preserves the time ordering of the data, which the metric method does not. The mathematical description of the way these periodic orbits are linked allows one to reconstruct completely the stretching and compressing mechanisms responsible for generating the strange attractor.[5] This process is not (yet) capable of identifying the equation system that has generated the time series. However, it does make possible the rejection of models that are proposed as the source of an observed time series if they are incompatible with the computed reconstruction of the strange attractor for that series. The mathematical procedures involved in reconstruction of the strange attractor are beyond the scope of this chapter; the reader is referred to Mindlin et al. (1990) for a detailed theoretical discussion and to Mindlin et al. (1991) for the first successful application to experimental data, in which the underlying dynamic mechanism was reconstructed.[6]

The starting point for implementing the topological algorithm is the time series $\{x_i\}$ without an embedding. If one of the observations x_i occurs near a periodic orbit, then subsequent observations will evolve near that orbit for a while before being repelled away from it. If the observations evolve near the periodic orbit for a sufficiently long time, they will return to the neighborhood of x_i after some interval, T, where T indicates the length of the orbit, measured in units of the sampling rate (e.g., if the data cycle every 30 days and sampling is daily, then the length of the orbit is

30). This means that $|x_i - x_{i+T}|$ will be small. Further, x_{i+1} will be near x_{i+1+T}, x_{i+2} will be near x_{i+2+T}, and so on. Thus it makes sense to look for a series of consecutive data elements for which $|x_i - x_{i+T}|$ is small.[7]

To detect these regions of "close returns" in a data set, a color-coded graph can be constructed. All differences $|x_i - x_{i+t}|$ are computed. If a difference is less than ε, it is coded black; if larger than ε, it is coded white. The horizontal axis of the graph indicates the observation number, i, where $i = (1, 2, ..., N)$, and the vertical axis is designated as t, where $t = (1, 2, ..., N-i)$. Close returns in the data set are indicated by horizontal line segments. For example, for a horizontal segment between i_a and i_b the beginning of the segment, observation x_{ia}, indicates where the chaotic time series begins to follow an unstable periodic orbit; the final observation in the segment is x_{ib+T}, where T is the length of the orbit in terms of the sampling rate. If the data set is chaotic, a number of horizontal line segments will be seen in this plot. However, if the data set is stochastic, a generally uniform array of black dots will appear. A periodic signal can be identified by solid black lines running horizontally across the entire graph at intervals determined by the period measured in units of the sampling time. A quasi-periodic orbit (consisting of two frequencies) produces a pattern resembling a contour map.

The determination of the appropriate size of ε for a given data set can be accomplished as follows. First, compute the maximum difference between any two observations in the set. Next, set ε at some small fraction of that difference—e.g., between 0.01 and 0.1—and construct the close returns plot. If ε is set too small, there will be an insufficient number of black points to identify a pattern that characterizes the data; as ε is reduced below the standard deviation of additive noise, the pattern degrades gracefully. If ε is too large, the pattern will be hidden. Once an appropriate range for ε is identified, there will be a sufficient array of points to allow determination of the type of pattern generated by the data. The level of ε can be varied within that range without altering the qualitative nature of the pattern. The exact specification of ε is *not* critical to the interpretation of the behavior of the data. Examples of these plots, together with descriptions of the data sets used in their construction, are given in Section 3.

The topological method of identifying and analyzing low-dimensional chaos has several important advantages over the metric approach:

1. The topological method is applicable to relatively small data sets, such as are typical in economics and finance.

2. It is robust against noise.

3. Since the topological analysis maintains the time-ordering of the data, it is able to provide additional information about the underlying system generating chaotic behavior.

4. Falsifiability is possible, as verification can be made of the reconstruction of the strange attractor [Mindlin et al. (1991)].

The ability of the close returns test to detect low-dimensional chaos in relatively small, noisy data sets will be demonstrated in the next section. Quantitative reconstruction of a chaotic strange attractor and the method of verification are discussed in Mindlin et al. (1990, 1991).

3. Application to Simulated Chaotic Time Series

Data

A simulated discrete time series data set generated by the Roessler model [Roessler (1976)] is used to demonstrate the close returns test. This model is a system composed of three ordinary differential equations:

$$dx/dt = -y - z,$$

$$dy/dt = x + ay, \tag{4}$$

$$dz/dt = b + z(x-c).$$

The equations of the model were integrated for 500 seconds and the results recorded at equal time intervals (0.1 second), giving a length of 5,000 for the data set. The parameter values used for the Roessler equations are: $a = 0.448$, $b = 2.0$, $c = 4.0$.

Procedure

Figure 20-1 presents a plot of a 1,000 (horizontal) × 960 (vertical)-observation section of the complete graph of the 5,000-point Roessler time series. The evidence of chaotic behavior in the data is revealed by the series of nearly horizontal line segments of close returns, which indicate the presence of unstable periodic orbits. The continuous horizontal line at the top of the graph represents $|x_i - x_{i+0}| = 0$. The pattern of the plot may be interpreted as follows. The horizontal segment in the upper left area, at T_x on the vertical axis, locates the first and second cycles of the time series trajectory around an unstable periodic orbit, probably a period-1 orbit. The first cycle consists of the i_a through i_b observations and the second of the i_{a+T} through i_{b+T} observations. The next horizontal segment below it, at T_y, identifies the third cycle of the trajectory around that unstable orbit. Traces

Figure 20-1

Close returns plot of chaotic time series, generated from Roessler model. If difference $|x_i - x_{i+T}|$ is less than ε, the difference is coded black, otherwise white. Horizontal line segments indicate the presence of unstable periodic orbits.

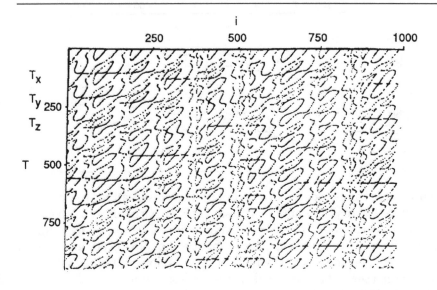

of subsequent cycles around this orbit will gradually disappear, due to the fact that the trajectory is being "repelled" further and further away from the unstable period orbit. Near the center of the graph, at T_x on the vertical axis, the horizontal segment likely indicates the initial cycles around an unstable period-2 or period-3 orbit. Explicit identification of each of these segments as belonging to a period-1, period-2, etc., orbit can easily be made by isolating and plotting each segment of close returns in phase space.

It should be noted that the evidence of chaotic behavior pervades the entire close returns plot of the Roessler series. Consequently, although this plot used the first 1,960 (1,000 + 960) points from the 5,000-observation set, a much smaller subset would also reveal the chaotic pattern. Other chaotic systems will also generate a similar structure of horizontal lines in a close returns plot. For example, Figure 20-2 is a smaller, 500 × 50-observation plot from a time series produced from the logistic map, $x_{t+1} = ax_t(1 - x_t)$, with $a = 3.75$.

A useful device to summarize the occurrence of close returns in a data set is a histogram of the incidence of close returns "hits," $H(t)$, summing at each value of t, with $H(t) = \Sigma\theta(\varepsilon - |x_i - x_{i+t}|)$, where θ is the Heaviside

Figure 20-2

Close returns plot for logistic map. The parameter $a = 3.75$.

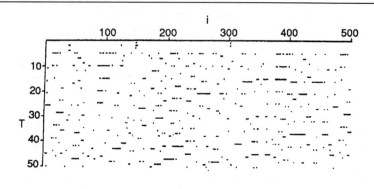

function. This can be done for the set of plotted observations but can also be computed across the entire data set. This is particularly convenient when the data set under study is too large to fit easily onto a single graph. Figure 20-3 presents such a histogram for the full 5,000-observation Roessler set, over the first 300 values of t. For chaotic data the histogram will contain a series of sharp peaks, more or less evenly spaced.

To establish a benchmark for comparison, a series of pseudorandom numbers, uniformly distributed on the interval 0 to 1, was constructed, and a $1,000 \times 960$ close returns plot was made. In contrast to the distinctive pattern produced by a chaotic time series, this close returns plot, Figure 20-4, consists of a scattering of dots without discernible pattern where the difference $|x_i - x_{i+t}|$ is small. A histogram for a random time series will exhibit a scattering around a uniform distribution (see Figure 20-5).

It can be demonstrated that the close returns procedure is quite robust against noise. A subset of 2,000 points of the Roessler data set was used to illustrate this property of the close returns method. A second 2,000-observation data set of additive Gaussian noise was created and normalized to the Roessler series.[8] Increasing percentages of noise were then added to the Roessler subset. With a 15 percent addition of noise ($f = 0.15$) evidence of the unstable periodic orbits is still clearly visible (Figure 20-6). As the noise level is increased, the pattern becomes less distinct, and it is thoroughly obscured by a 100 percent addition of noise. However, even at high noise levels, the chaotic signal may still be retrieved under this test by means of noise averaging. Using the chaotic data with a 200 percent addition of noise, each x_i value was plotted as an average of itself plus the

Figure 20-3

Close returns histogram of Roessler chaotic series. *H(T)* records the number of times the differential $|x_i - x_{i+T}|$ is less than the threshold e.

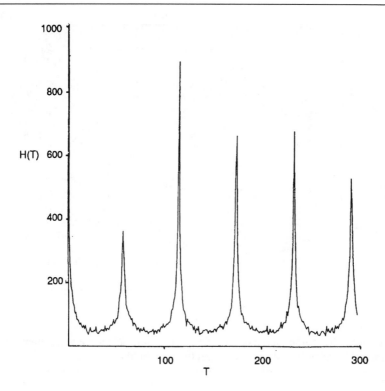

$$x_i = \sum_{j=0}^{9} x_{i+j}/10$$

next 9 points ($x_i = \sum_{j=0}^{9} x_{i+j}/10$). This procedure averages out some of the noise, but the chaotic behavior of the original time series is not lost, as it has a longer time scale. The differences $|x_i - x_{i+t}|$ were then replotted, and the chaotic signal reemerged (compare Figures 20-7a and 20-7b).

The ability of the close returns test to distinguish between a chaotic and a near unit root autoregressive process was also examined, as the dimension estimate procedure has been shown to have a poor ability to discriminate between the two [Brock and Sayers (1988)]. The near unit root process can confuse the dimension test because the number of near neighbors at any point can behave with a power law dependence on the box size,

Figure 20-4

Close returns plot of pseudorandom time series.

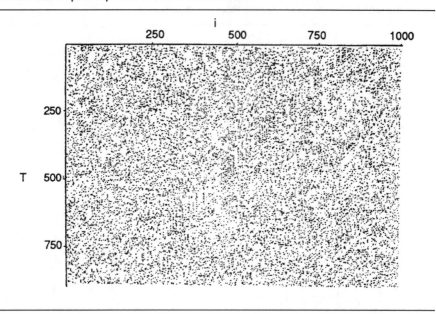

Figure 20-5

Close returns histogram of a pseudorandom data set. $H(T)$ records the number of times the difference $|x_i - x_{i+T}|$ is less than the threshold ε.

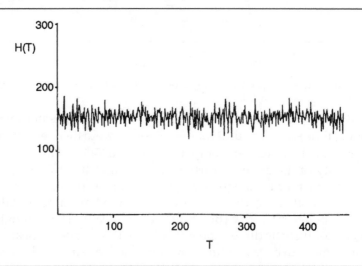

Figure 20-6

Close returns plot of Roessler chaotic series with 15 percent addition of noise. Chaotic pattern remains easily visible.

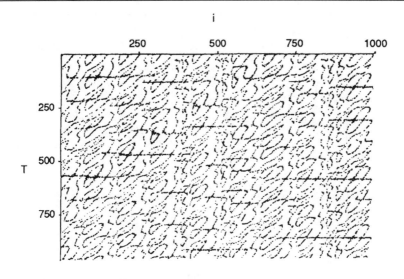

as is also the case with a chaotic process. To determine how well the close returns test can distinguish between the two processes, close returns plots for a number of data sets generated by near-unit root processes were examined. In no case did the close returns plot resemble the plots generated by chaotic processes. There was a relatively high density of black points near and parallel to the x axis, indicating dynamical correlation. The results are not reproduced here but are available on request. The apparently superior ability of the close returns test to discriminate between chaotic and near-unit root processes probably arises from the fact that these plots maintain temporal correlation, while the metric test does not.

At the present time there is not a statistical theory of standard error bands for the close returns plot. Research in this area is in an early stage. It should be pointed out that the close returns plots are themselves only the first part of a multistage procedure whose objective is to produce a quantitative description of the chaotic strange attractor. This process yields falsifiable results; consequently, if a close returns plot erroneously indicates a chaotic time series, the chaotic explanation can ultimately be rejected in the subsequent steps. Given the results of the close returns plots

Figure 20-7

In 20-7(a) chaotic signal is completely obscured by 200 percent addition of noise to Roessler series. Smoothing of data with a 10-point moving average allows recovery of chaotic signal, 20-7(b).

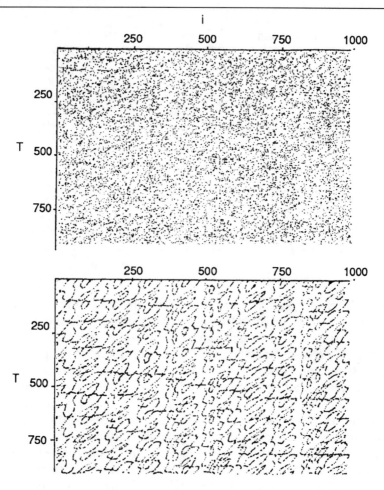

for the economic and financial data tested in Section 4, the quantitative steps, which are complex, are not developed here.

Short-Term Forecasting

One potential benefit of the method of close returns is in applications to forecasting of financial and economic time series. There is order hidden in chaotic systems. Since chaotic systems are deterministic, they are in principle predictable, although the prediction degrades rapidly with the "prediction horizon." Good long-run forecasting is unlikely because of the divergence of nearby trajectories that characterizes chaos. However, the fact that nearby initial conditions evolve very similarly under a deterministic model for a short time before diverging may be used for short-term forecasting. Thus it is potentially possible, for example, to forecast future sequences of daily financial data based on selected subsets of data that closely match the immediately preceding sequence, provided the underlying process is chaotic rather than random.

To apply this procedure on the 5,000-point set of data generated from the Roessler model, an initial 20-point segment of x_i values was selected for which the following 10 values were to be predicted. A search was then made across the entire series for closely matching sequences. All such sequences were identified and the next ten values following each set were extracted. A weighted average value was then calculated for each of the 10 x_i values to be predicted, using the corresponding values in each of the extracted sequences. The weighting procedure assigned different weights, depending on how closely the respective 20-point segments tracked the test segment. These averaged values then were used as the predicted values for the forecasting interval. This was done for 2,000 different 20-point sequences in the data set. R^2 statistics were computed for each prediction and were plotted on a histogram (Figure 20-8). It can be seen that the values of the R^2 statistics are very high, clustering above 0.90.

While this procedure is not valid for long-term forecasting, the short-term forecast can be updated as desired. The composition of the subsets of data used for prediction will then change as the projection path of the time series moves through different regions of the attractor.

4. Application to Economic and Financial Data

Empirical studies, using the now-standard metric procedures of estimating correlation dimensions and Lyapunov exponents, have focused on two areas—the behavior of business cycles and of financial markets. The

Figure 20-8

Histogram of R^2 values for 2,000 short-term predictions for chaotic time series. The test segment is compared with previous segments, and the most similar previous segments are used in the prediction. Over 90 percent of the R^2 are in excess of 0.9.

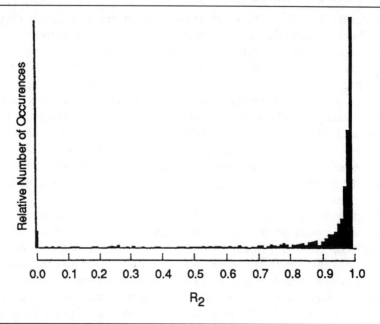

question of interest for business cycles is to determine whether they may be produced endogenously from the internal dynamics of the economic system. With respect to financial data the usual assumption is that in well-functioning markets changes in asset prices will be unpredictable. A chaotic explanation of asset price behavior would present significant theoretical implications.

Several economic series which have been tested for chaotic behavior using metric methods were selected for application of the topological approach. U.S. postwar macroeconomic data have been analyzed by Brock and Sayers (1988). Their series included the unemployment rate, employment, real GNP, gross private domestic investment, and industrial production. Man-days idle due to work stoppages, monthly for the period 1928 to 1981, published by the Bureau of Labor Statistics, were examined by Sayers (1986, 1987). Since financial series tend to be larger and more disaggregated than economic data, chaotic behavior, if it exists, may be easier to establish in these cases. Scheinkman and LeBaron (1989) used daily stock returns (including dividend) on the value-weighted portfolio of the Center for Research in Security Prices to construct a weekly returns series by simple compounding. Brock and Malliaris (1989) examined a Treasury-bill series taken from Ibbotson and Sinquefield (1977). We have also included several series of daily exchange rates.

Brock and Sayers (1988) reported that correlation dimension estimates and calculation of Lyapunov exponents on their detrended series produced positive evidence of chaos in all cases. However, this evidence could not be accepted as conclusive, since many economic time series are near unit root processes, and the ability of metric tests to distinguish between such processes and low-dimensional chaos is poor [Brock and Sayers (1988)]. Application of metric tests in such situations may give a misleading impression that the series is chaotic. Therefore, Brock and Sayers fit each series to a suitable $AR(q)$ model and ran the tests again on the residuals.[9] The rationale for the residual test is the argument that if a series is chaotic, the estimate of the correlation dimension will not be altered by the linear transformation. A unit root process, however, will yield dramatically different results. The residual test rejected the null hypothesis of chaos for all the series. This was also not conclusive, however, since the residual test may reject the null hypothesis too often when it is true [Brock (1986)]. It proved impossible to reject the null hypothesis of linear AR processes for any of the macroeconomic series, but this result may have been driven by limitations in the test applied and by the shortness of the series [Brock and Sayers (1988)]. Ramsey, Sayers, and Rothman (1990) applied the Ramsey and Yuan (1989a,b) correction for small-sample-size bias in the correlation dimension estimate to work stoppage data studied by Sayers (1986, 1987). The conclusion was that there was a probability at least of a low dimension for the series, although there was no strong evidence of a strange attractor.

The results of close returns tests are presented in Figures 20-9a through 20-9e for the macroeconomic series. The U.S. unemployment rate data covers the period 1949:I–1982:I, providing 133 observations; employment is for 1950:I–1983:IV, for 136 observations; real gross national product and gross private domestic investment are for 1947:I–1985:I, 153 observations; and industrial production covers 1948:1–1983:12, giving 432 observations. All series are deseasonalized and are quarterly, except industrial production, which is monthly. All series were detrended as in the original research: linear detrending for all series except employment, to which a quadratic detrending was applied. The close returns plots have a triangular rather than a rectangular shape here, since each of the series was small enough to fit completely onto one graph. In these and the later plots in this

Figure 20-9

Close returns plots of U.S. postwar macroeconomic series

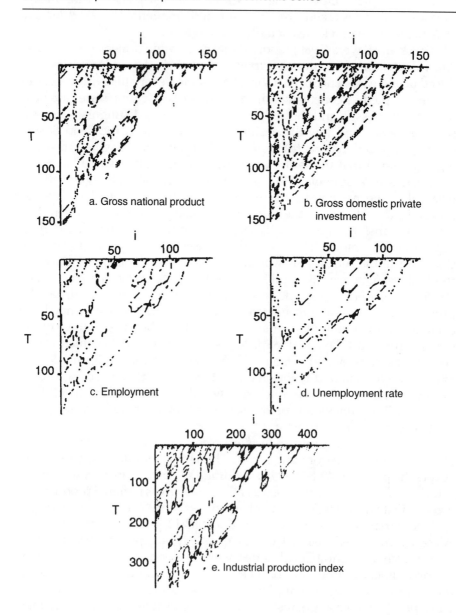

a. Gross national product

b. Gross domestic private investment

c. Employment

d. Unemployment rate

e. Industrial production index

section an epsilon value in the range of 0.02 to 0.05 of the maximum difference $|x_i - x_{i+t}|$ was used.

In each case the plots did not produce the evidence for the presence of unstable periodic orbits which is characteristic of a strange attractor, that is, there is no pattern of horizontal lines. Thus, this test does not provide any support for the positive indications of chaos from the metric tests on the detrended data. The correlation dimension procedure was unable to distinguish between chaotic and near unit root processes, but the close returns test did so. The close returns test does support the negative findings that resulted from application of the metric tests to the residuals of linear models for each series.

Beyond showing a lack of chaotic behavior in the macroeconomic series, do the close returns plots provide any further information? This test has been developed specifically as a means to distinguish chaotic from a range of alternative types of behavior, both linear and nonlinear, deterministic and stochastic. Its ability to discriminate within this range of alternatives is a subject of further research, but some tentative comments may be made. The fluctuations of the various series around their trend, while not chaotic, are also clearly not random and are not strictly periodic. Each of the plots indicates the presence of some type of structure in the data. Areas within each plot exhibit connected curves (contour-like structure) that may be evidence of quasi-periodic behavior, of either a linear or a nonlinear origin. This possible alternative was explored by examining the Fourier spectrum of each series. For a quasi-periodic series composed of two frequencies, the spectrum should be discrete with two strong peaks. If these peaks are not observed, the hypothesis of a quasi-periodic behavior can be rejected. The spectra for these series showed a pattern of a large number of strong peaks. Therefore, the null hypothesis that the data are quasi-periodic (two-period) was rejected.

For the work stoppage series, monthly data from 1935:1 through 1981:12, not deseasonalized, were used, producing 564 observations. The series was detrended by filtering out the low frequencies, using a fast Fourier transform. This close returns plot (Figure 20-10) also does not indicate chaotic behavior and thus does not sustain the tentative conclusion of Ramsey, Sayers, and Rothman (1990) that there is some probability of an underlying chaotic attractor, although again there is structure evident in the series. In addition to the information contained in the close returns plot, the corresponding histogram may be able to reveal further information about the data set under study. The histogram for the work stoppage data (Figure 20-11) shows sharp peaks, spaced at approximately annual intervals over much of the series, revealing a strongly cyclical

Figure 20-10

Close returns plot of work stoppage data

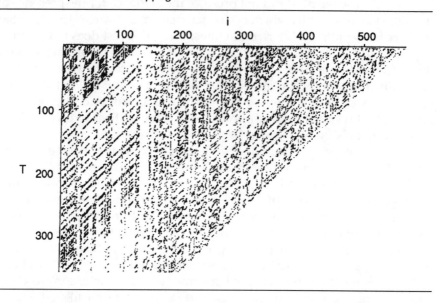

Figure 20-11

Close returns histogram of work stoppage data. Note prevalence of regularly spaced sharp peaks

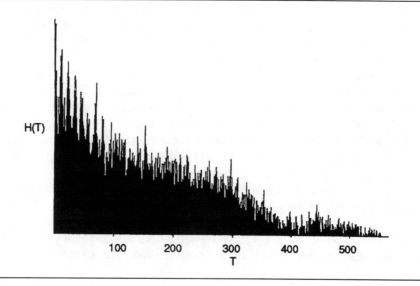

behavior. As indicated above, further development of the close returns procedures is needed to allow us to extract additional information about the nature of the time series when it is not generated by a chaotic process.

When the topological method is applied to financial data, it again demonstrates the necessity to be cautious in drawing any conclusion, based on metric tests, that any of these series has been generated by a chaotic process. Scheinkman and LeBaron (1989) obtained dimension estimates of about six for their original stock return data and for the residuals from a fitted model. They also applied a shuffle diagnostic, which involved recreating the data series with the same stationary distribution as the original series is obtained. If the original series is chaotic, the shuffled series should be more random, and the dimension estimate for the latter should be higher than for the original series. If the original series is stochastic, the dimension estimate should not change as a result of the shuffling. For the stock returns the shuffled series produced a higher dimension estimate than did the original series. Brock and Malliaris (1989) calculated a dimension estimate of about two for Treasury-bill returns and also for the residuals from an $AR(8)$ model fit to the data. While this evidence was consistent with a chaotic solution, they also cautioned that the analysis had not been carried far enough to reach a conclusion.

Daily stock returns (including dividends) on the value-weighted CRSP portfolio were used, covering the period July 2, 1962, through December 29, 1989, to obtain a weekly returns series by means of simple compounding. The weekly series contained 1,439 observations. As in the original study by Scheinkman and LeBaron (1989), the series was not detrended. The Treasury-bill series contained 780 monthly observations covering the period January 1926 through December 1990. Log first differences of these returns were used in the Brock and Malliaris (1989) study for estimating a correlation dimension, and the same processing was used in the close returns test. The close returns plots for the weekly stock returns (Figure 20-12) and for the Treasury-bill returns (Figure 20-13) contains no positive indication of unstable periodic orbits in the data, although some structure is again present in each case. The reservations expressed in Ramsey, Sayers, and Rothman (1990) about a possible chaotic explanation for the stock data are reinforced by these close returns results.

With respect to exchange rate data, some evidence has been found by Hsieh (1989) for nonlinear structure in five daily series, although he did not test specifically for chaotic behavior. We initially carried out the correlation dimension calculations on four daily series, according to the procedure as specified in Grassberger (1990). The series were the Canadian dollar, the Deutsche mark, the French franc, and the Japanese yen against the U.S. dollar, for the period 1986–1989 (935 observations in each series).

Figure 20-12

Close returns plot of weekly stock returns

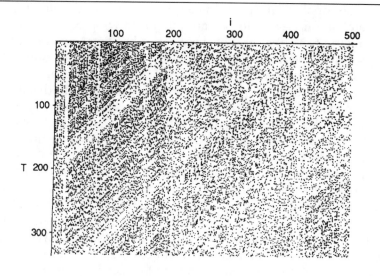

Figure 20-13

Close returns plot of Treasury-bill returns

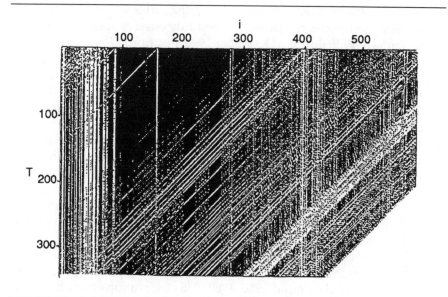

Table 20-1

Slopes of $C_m(\varepsilon)$ vs. ln ε. Log-Differenced Exchange Rates

Exchange rate series	Embedding dimension					
	3	4	5	6	7	8
U.S.–U.K.	2.58	3.71	4.52	6.01	6.44	6.64
U.S.–Japan	3.03	3.54	4.16	5.42	6.63	6.37
U.S.–Canada	2.91	3.91	4.73	5.24	5.67	6.82
U.S.–W. Germany	2.85	3.76	4.41	5.22	5.58	6.36

The series were first made stationary by taking log first differences. Table 20-1 presents the results of the calculations for embedding dimensions 3 through 8.[10] Within this range of embeddings the slopes continue to increase for all four currencies. This lack of convergence suggests that the signal is stochastic rather than chaotic, but, taken alone, the evidence is not persuasive. Since it is not the purpose here to elaborate on metric methods, we will not apply further procedures of that type but will instead turn to the evidence provided by the close returns test. The plots for each series provide no support for an interpretation of chaotic behavior in exchange rates, thus confirming the tentative evidence from the correlation dimension calculations. Since all four series yielded qualitatively similar results, only the plot for the Deutsche mark is shown (Figure 20-14). Horizontal line segments of any length are virtually nonexistent.

Given the very different results produced by the metric and the topological tests, how do we assess their relative reliability?

First, as pointed out above, Grassberger (1990) has recently clarified the necessity of calculating the dimension estimates so as to reflect only the geometrical correlation and not the dynamic correlation in the time series data. If a correction for this problem is not incorporated into the procedure, it will distort the results, possibly creating spurious evidence of low dimension. Consequently, many of the earlier dimension estimates that have been reported in the literature must be viewed skeptically. Ruelle (1990) has emphasized another precaution that should be observed in calculating the correlation dimensions. One should measure the slope of $\log_{10} C_m(\varepsilon)$ versus $\log_{10}(\varepsilon)$ over at least one decade of ε in order to produce a reliable result. If this is done, the dimension estimate will saturate out at a limit of $2\log_{10} N$. Because of this, "one should not believe dimension estimates that are not well below $2\log_{10} N$" [Ruelle (1990)]. Ruelle reviewed several studies, including the Scheinkman and LeBaron (1989) analysis of

Figure 20-14

Close returns plot of log first-differenced German–U.S. exchange rate, daily January 1986–August 1989

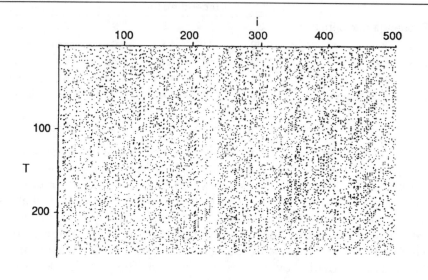

stock returns (where $N \approx 10^3$ and correlation dimensions of approximately 6 were estimated), and stated that "the 'proof' that one has low-dimensional dynamics is therefore inconclusive, and the suspicion is that the time series evolutions under discussion do not correspond to low-dimensional dynamics."

Second, the relatively small size of the economic and financial data sets examined above, several of which have fewer than 200 observations, is a serious obstacle for application of metric methods. Consequently, great care should be exercised in interpretation of the results, a point made in several of the studies reviewed. In the theoretical construction the correlation dimension estimate converges to its correct values as N, the sample size, approaches infinity. Wolf et al. (1985) estimated the minimal appropriate number of observations needed to permit estimation of an attractor's dimension at $N = a^D$, where D is the attractor dimension and a is on the order of 10. Thus, the size required increases with the attractor dimension and can quickly outstrip the data set size that may be available.

The close returns test, on the other hand, does not present such large sample size requirements. The pattern of repeated cycling of the item series trajectory around the attractor's unstable periodic orbits will emerge more clearly with a large data set, but as demonstrated in Section 3, small data sets can also produce a clear chaotic signal. Nevertheless, in analyzing very limited data sets it is possible that ambiguous results could be produced by the close returns test. This could occur, for example, if an unpredictable external influence (such as a policy shift or political event) were to disturb a chaotic system, altering the values of the variables or of the parameters of the model. Following such a disturbance the dynamical path of the data would either return to the old attractor or relax to a new one. The larger the data set available, the more likely would be the detection of chaotic behavior under such circumstances.

Unlike the relatively clean data and stationary processes that are common in the natural sciences, economic and financial data may contain considerable measurement noise and are typically nonstationary. Noise and nonstationarity are problems that can affect both the metric and the topological tests. These problems are more severe in metric tests than in close returns tests. Dimension estimates degrade rapidly with additive noise [Brock (1986)]. However, we have seen in Figure 20-7 that noise averaging can allow the close returns test to retrieve a chaotic signal. Nonstationarity presents a different set of problems. The Grassberger-Procaccia box counting cannot be applied to nonstationarity data [Grassberger (1990)]. The reason is that in that algorithm all nearest neighbors of any particular point are counted, no matter how distant in the time series. If the series is nonstationary, these nearest neighbors will drift away, affecting the average count. This problem is much less severe in the close returns test, in which temporal ordering of the data is maintained. This comes about because the close returns test typically searches over relatively nearby points in the time series and can produce evidence of the tracking of nearby segments even if a trend obscures that evidence for widely separated segments.

To handle noise and nonstationarity several different procedures were explored, including Fourier transforms and centered moving averages, as a means to check whether the close returns results reported above would be altered.[11] In particular there was concern that the common practice of taking logarithmic first differences, used on several of the series, would distort the results, since that process emphasizes the noise component relative to any signal that may be present in the data, possibly obscuring the latter. In the first procedure the data were transformed using either a Fourier transform or a fast Fourier transform. The low and high frequency terms were removed, reducing the drift and noise, respectively. The inverse transform then gave a processed data set, which was detrended and had reduced noise. In the second procedure moving averages were computed using a small number of neighbors and a much larger number of neighbors. The former moving average smoothed out some of the noise and the latter estimated trend. The difference between these two averages was a signal with reduced noise and trend. The appropriate widths of the moving averages can be determined by inspecting the Fourier transform spectrum. In general, these procedures produce essentially indistinguishable data sets. Close returns tests were then run on these filtered series. Table 20-2 lists the procedures applied to each series to produce stationarity. In each case the resulting plots did not differ qualitatively from the results reported above. The evidence produced by the close returns test, therefore, appears to be fairly robust with respect to the problems of stationarity and noise when applied to economic and financial data.

It should be pointed out that while the results of the topological tests conflict with the positive evidence found in some cases by the metric methods, our findings do not exclude the presence of other forms of nonlinear behavior in these data. The metric approach has given rise to new ways to test for the adequacy of linear models. In particular the BDS family of statistics is a test for general dependence, which has power against both linear and nonlinear alternatives [Brock, Dechert, and Scheinkman (1987)]. Using the BDS statistics and additional techniques, evidence of nonlinear behavior has been found in U.S. employment, unemployment, and industrial production series [Brock and Sayers (1988)], although not for similar Canadian series [Frank and Stengos (1988)], in Japanese GNP [Frank, Gençay, and Stengos (1988)], in work stoppage data [Sayers (1986, 1987)], in stock returns [LeBaron (1988), Brock (1988), Sche-

Table 20-2

Detrending Methods

	Detrending method			
Series	Polynomial detrending	Log first differencing	Moving average	Low frequency filtering
Unemployment rate	x	x		x
Employment	x	x		x
Real GNP	x	x		x
GPDI	x	x		x
Industrial production	x	x	x	x
Work stoppages		x	x	x
Stock returns				x
Treasury-bill returns		x	x	x
Exchange rates		x	x	x

inkman and LeBaron (1989)], as well as in exchange rates [Hsieh (1989)]. Analysis of these series using the close returns test is not incompatible with a nonlinear, but nonchaotic, generating mechanism.

5. Conclusions

Metric tests have become a standard procedure to test for chaotic behavior in time series data. While these methods may produce credible results for very extensive, stationary, clean data sets, they are not well adapted to the types of data generally encountered in the study of economic and financial phenomena. Some modifications have been introduced to increase the reliability of these methods, but it may be more useful in the long run to apply the newer techniques associated with a topological approach to chaos, which are currently in early stages of development. This approach provides a robust qualitative way to detect chaos, as illustrated in this chapter. It also creates a means to quantitatively describe chaotic behavior when it is found to exist in a time series. The capacity to provide a quantitative description of the underlying chaotic process is beyond the ability of metric methods.

Using the close returns test, we examined a number of economic and financial series that had been analyzed for low-dimensional deterministic chaos using the metric approach. The limitations of the latter method, particularly when applied to small, noisy data sets, produced inconclusive results. It was shown that the close returns test is capable of detecting chaotic behavior in relatively small data sets, even with fairly high noise levels. The results using this more powerful method indicate that claims to find chaotic behavior in economic and financial data need to be viewed skeptically. Some type of (nonchaotic) nonlinear model may underlie some of the processes reviewed here, and reliance on linear models with stochastic disturbances may well be inappropriate to describe the behavior. Further development of techniques to identify and analyze nonlinear behavior is warranted. However, the case for a generating mechanism of low-dimensional deterministic chaos in economic and financial time series remains to be made.

Acknowledgment

The author would like to thank G. B. Mindlin and X.-J Hou for useful discussions about new topological methods, Professor James B. Ramsey for insights on nonlinear modeling, as well as the editor and anonymous referees for helpful suggestions on earlier versions of this manuscript. This work was begun at Drexel University, as part of the author's doctoral research, under the direction of Professor Thomas C. Chiang.

Notes

1 For a discussion of strange attractors see Brock (1986).

2 For a mathematical definition see Brock (1986).

3 There is a limited range of ε over which $C_m(\varepsilon)$ goes from 0 to 1. In this range the curve of $C_m(\varepsilon)$ is not likely to have a well-defined linear segment from which a slope could be estimated when the data set is small. See Caputo (1989).

4 The close returns method, although independently developed, is similar in spirit to the recurrence plots published somewhat earlier by Eckmann, Kamphorst, and Ruelle (1987). In contrast to metric tests, both the recurrence plots and the close returns plots make use of time-ordering information. The recurrence plots are constructed from a d-dimensional embedding of the time series data and a coding procedure to identify near neighbors of plotted points that use a sphere of variable radius. The close returns method uses the scalar time series (although an embedding can also be used), specifies a fixed ε value for measuring close returns, and is organized in a more easily readable horizontal form rather than the diagonal orientation of the recurrence plots. As constructed, the recurrence plots were used to measure the "time consistency" [Eckmann, Kamphorst, and Ruelle (1987)] of a dynamical system. The authors also observed the prevalence of short straight-line segments in their plots using chaotic data and correctly pointed out that these would not occur in a random data set. However, the implications of this observation were not further developed. The close returns method uses the plot initially as a means to distinguish chaotic from other types of time series behavior. If chaotic behavior is identified, the next steps in the close returns method involve a mathematical reconstruction of the strange attractor.

5 Unlike the correlation dimension calculation, the topological method does not determine the strange attractor's dimension. Metric properties, such as correlation dimension and Lyapunov exponents, are independent of coordinate system but depend on control parameter values. That is, a small change in parameter values can produce large changes in the correlation dimension and Lyapunov exponent. The topological method aims to compute the structure of the strange attractor, for

example, to distinguish the Roessler from the Lorenz attractor. This quantitative classification is independent of both coordinate system changes *and* changes in control parameter values.

6 See, in particular, Eq. (12) in Mindlin et al. (1991) and Fig. 1 in Mindlin (1990).

7 Comparing observations separated by a fixed time interval t, ($|x_i - x_{i+t}|$), is reminiscent of the standard autocorrelation function. However, the autocorrelation is an average over the entire sample and is not designed to identify specific, highly correlated segments of data within the sample. The close returns test is specifically constructed to do this.

8 A signal $S_i = R_i + f\sigma G(0,1)$ was created, where R_i is the Roessler time series with standard deviation σ, G is a Gaussian independent and identically distributed random variable with zero mean and standard deviation = 1, and f is some fraction.

9 For a discussion of the residual test see Brock (1986); a critique of this test is in Day and Chen (1993).

10 Given the level of precision of the data (four places) higher-dimension embeddings are not advisable. See Mitschke et al. (1988) and Lange and Moller (1989).

11 An anonymous referee pointed out a potential problem in detrending data with a low-frequency filter and then looking for evidence of chaotic behavior. In theory, removing the lower frequencies will eliminate some evidence of chaos (the very high period orbits). In practice, however, this does not appear to be a problem. This detrending technique has been applied to empirical data and chaos was successfully detected [see Mindlin et al. (1991)]. This author also tested the procedure by adding a trend to simulated chaotic data. A low-frequency filter was then applied and the chaotic pattern emerged strongly in the close returns plot of the filtered data.

References

Barnett, W., and P. Chen. "The Aggregation-Theoretic Monetary Aggregates Are Chaotic and Have Strange Attractors: An Economic Application of Mathematical Chaos," in *Dynamic Economic Modeling, Proceedings of the Third International Symposium on Economic Theory and Econometrics*, W. Barnett, E. Berndt, and H. White, eds. Cambridge: Cambridge University Press, 1988, ch. 11.

Baumol, W. J., and J. Benhabib. "Chaos: Significance, Mechanism, and Economic Applications." *Journal of Economic Perspectives,* 3 (1989), 77–105.

Benhabib, J., and R. H. Day. "Rational Choice and Erratic Behavior." *Review of Economic Studies,* 48 (1981), 459–472.

Brock, W. A. "Distinguishing Random and Deterministic Systems: Abridged Version." *Journal of Economic Theory,* 40 (1986), 168–195.

Brock, W. A. "Nonlinearity and Complex Dynamics in Economics and Finance," in *The Economy as an Evolving Complex System, SFI Studies in the Sciences of Complexity,* P. Anderson, K. Arrow, and D. Pines, eds. Reading, MA: Addison-Wesley, 1988.

Brock, W. A., and E. G. Baek. "Some Theory of Statistical Inference for Nonlinear Science." *Review of Economic Studies,* 58 (1991), 697–716.

Brock, W. A., and W. D. Dechert. "Theorems on Distinguishing Deterministic from Random Systems," in *Dynamic Economic Modeling, Proceedings of the Third International Symposium on Economic Theory and Econometrics,* W. Barnett, E. Berndt, and H. White, eds. Cambridge: Cambridge University Press, 1988.

Brock, W. A., W. D. Dechert, and J. A. Scheinkman. "A Test for Independence Based on the Correlation Dimension." Department of Economics, University of Wisconsin, Madison, 1987.

Brock, W. A., and A. G. Malliaris. *Differential Equations, Stability and Chaos in Dynamic Economics.* Amsterdam: Elsevier, 1989.

Brock, W. A., and C. L. Sayers. "Is the Business Cycle Characterized by Deterministic Chaos?" *Journal of Monetary Economics,* 22 (1988), 71–90.

Caputo, J. G. "Practical Remarks on the Estimation of Dimension and Entropy from Experimental Data," in *Measures of Complexity and Chaos,* N. B. Abraham et al., eds. New York: Plenum Press, 1989.

Cvitanovic, P. *Universality in Chaos.* Bristol, U.K.: Adam Helger, 1984.

Day, R. "Irregular Growth Cycles." *American Economic Review,* 72 (1982), 406–414.

Day, R. "The Emergence of Chaos from Classical Economic Growth." *Quarterly Journal of Economics,* 54 (1983), 201–213.

Day, R., and P. Chen, eds. *Evolutionary Dynamics and Nonlinear Economics.* Oxford: Oxford University Press, 1993.

Eckmann, J.-P., S. O. Kamphorst, and D. Ruelle. "Recurrence Plots of Dynamical Systems." *Europhysics Letters,* 4 (1987), 973–977.

Frank, M. Z., R. Gençay, and T. Stengos. "International Chaos?" *European Economic Review*, 32 (1988), 1569–1584.

Frank, M. Z., and T. Stengos. "Some Evidence Concerning Macroeconomic Chaos." *Journal of Monetary Economics*, 22 (1988), 423–438.

Frank, M. Z., and T. Stengos. "Measuring the Strangeness of Gold and Silver Rates of Return." *Review of Economic Studies*, 56 (1989), 553–567.

Grandmont, J. M. "On Endogenous Competitive Business Cycles." *Econometrica*, 53 (1985), 995–1045.

Grassberger, P. "An Optimized Box-Assisted Algorithm for Fractal Dimensions." *Physics Letters A*, 148 (1990), 63–68.

Grassberger, P., and I. Procaccia. "Measuring the Strangeness of Strange Attractors." *Physica*, 90 (1983a), 189–208.

Grassberger, P., and I. Procaccia. "Characterization of Strange Attractors." *Physical Review Letters*, 50 (1983), 346–349.

Gunaratne, G. H., P. S. Linsay, and M. J. Vinson. "Chaos beyond Onset: A Comparison of Theory and Experiment." *Physics Review Letters A*, 63 (1989), 1–4.

Hinich, M., and D. Patterson. "Evidence of Nonlinearity in Daily Stock Returns." *Journal of Business and Economic Statistics*, 3 (1985), 69–77.

Hsieh, D. "Testing for Nonlinear Dependence in Daily Foreign Exchange Rates." *Journal of Business*, 62 (1989), 339–368.

Ibbotson, R., and R. Sinquefield. *Stocks, Bonds, Bills and Inflation: The Past (1926–1976) and the Future (1977–2000)* Financial Analysis Research Foundation, University of Virginia, Charlottesville, VA, 1977.

Lange, W., and M. Moller. "Systematic Errors in Estimating Dimensions from Experimental Data," in *Measures of Complexity and Chaos (Proceedings of a NATO Advanced Research Workshop on Quantitative Measures of Dynamical Complexity in Nonlinear Systems)*, N. Abraham, ed. Bryn Mawr College, Bryn Mawr, PA, June 22–24, 1989. New York: Plenum Press, 1989, 137–146.

LeBaron, B. "Stock Return Nonlinearities: Comparing Test and Finding Structure." Mimeo. Department of Economics, University of Wisconsin—Madison, 1988.

Lorenz, E. N. "Deterministic Nonperiodic Flow." *Journal of the Atmospheric Sciences* 20 (1963), 120–141.

Lorenz, H.-W. "International Trade and the Possible Occurrence of Chaos." *Economics Letters* 23 (1987a), 135–138.

Lorenz, H.-W. "Strange Attractors in a Multisector Business Cycle Model." *Journal of Economic Behavior and Organization*, 8 (1987b), 397–411.

Mindlin, G. B., et al. "Classification of Strange Attractors by Integers." *Physical Review Letters*, 64 (1990), 2350–2353.

Mindlin, G. B., et al. "Topological Analysis of Chaotic Time Series Data from the Belousov-Zhabotinskii Reaction." *Journal of Nonlinear Science*, 1 (1991), 147–173.

Mitschke, F., et al. "On Systematic Errors in Characterizing Chaos, Optical Bistability IV," in W. Firth et al., eds., *Editions Physique*, Paris, p. C2-397 [reprinted from *Journal of Physics Colloquia* 49 (1988), suppl. 6: C2–397].

Ramsey, J. B., and H. J. Yuan. "Bias and Error Bars in Dimension Calculations and Their Evaluation in Some Simple Models." *Physics Letters A–134* (1989), 287–297.

Ramsey, J. B., and H. J. Yuan. The Statistical Properties of Dimension Calculations Using Small Data Sets." *Nonlinearity*, 3 (1990), 155–175.

Ramsey, J. B., C. L. Sayers, and P. Rothman. "The Statistical Properties of Dimensions Calculations Using Small Data Sets: Some Economic Applications." *International Economic Review*, 31 (1990), 991–1020.

Roessler, O. E. "An Equation for Continuous Chaos." *Physics Letters A*, 57 (1976), 397–398.

Ruelle, D. "Deterministic Chaos: The Science and the Fiction." *Proceedings of the Royal Society of London*, A427 (1990), 241–248.

Sakai, H., and H. Tokumaru. "Autocorrelations of a Certain Chaos." *IEEE Transactions on Acoustics, Speech and Signal Processing*, V. I. ASSP-28 (1980), 588–590.

Sayers, C. L. "Work Stoppages: Exploring the Nonlinear Dynamics." Department of Economics, University of North Carolina, Chapel Hill, 1986.

Sayers, C. L. "Diagnostic Tests for Nonlinearity in Time Series Data: An Application to the Work Stoppage Series." Department of Economics, University of North Carolina, Chapel Hill, 1987.

Sayers, C. L. "Chaos and the Business Cycle," in *The Ubiquity of Chaos*, Saul Kramer, ed. Washington, DC: American Association for the Advancement of Science, 1989.

Scheinkman, J. A., and B. LeBaron. "Nonlinear Dynamics And GNP Data." Department of Economics, University of Chicago, Chicago, IL, 1987.

Scheinkman, J. A., and B. LeBaron. "Nonlinear Dynamics and Stock Returns," *Journal of Business*, 62 (1989), 311–337.

Shaffer, S. "Structural Shifts and the Volatility of Chaotic Markets." *Journal of Economic Behavior and Organization*, 15 (1990), 201–214.

Solari, H. G., et al. "Relative Rotation Rates for Driven Dynamical Systems." *Physical Review A*, 37 (1988), 8.

Stutzer, M. "Chaotic Dynamics and Bifurcations in a Macro Model." *Journal of Economic Dynamics and Control*, 2 (1980), 353–376.

Tufillaro, N. B. "Chaotic Themes from Strings." Unpublished Ph.D. thesis, Department of Physics, Bryn Mawr, 1990.

Tufillaro, N. B., et al. "Relative Rotation Rates: Fingerprints for Strange Attractors." *Physical Review A*, 41 (1990), 5717–5720.

Wolf, A., A. Brandstater, and J. Swift. "Comment on Recent Calculations of Fractional Dimension of Attractors." University of Texas at Austin, TX, preprint, 1985.

21

MEASURING COMPLEXITY OF NONLINEARITY BY A RELATIVE INDEX WITH APPLICATION TO FINANCIAL TIME SERIES

By M. A. Kaboudan

Introduction

Determining the fundamental dynamic behavior of stock returns is an enduring controversy that will continue to receive attention as long as stock returns remain unpredictable. Theoretical dissension endures because different studies provide contradicting evidence. While Fama (1965) and Malkiel (1981), for example, support the hypothesis that dynamic movements of stock returns follow a random walk, more recent studies prove otherwise. Here are some examples of such recent investigations: Jensen (1978) and Lo and MacKinlay (1988) present anomalous evidence against market efficiency. Jegadeesh (1990) finds evidence of predictable behavior in monthly stock returns. Scheinkman and LeBaron (1989), Hsieh (1991), and Willey (1992), among others, provide evidence of nonlinear and possibly chaotic structure in weekly and daily returns. Hinich and Paterson (1985) find nonlinear randomness in 15 common stocks, using a test that can detect nonconstant skewness in the bispectrum. Akgiray (1989) and Brock et al. (1990) identify nonlinear stochastic behavior in returns using GARCH-in-mean type models. White (1988) applies a neural network model and finds evidence against the efficient market hypothesis.

A new test, developed and presented below, probes the efficient market hypothesis once more. This new one is an index that measures complexity of any discrete time series relative to the complexity of a random series. The proposed measure permits classifying and ranking series according to the complexity of their data-generating process and helps distinguish between linear, nonlinear, and stochastic structures. Data belonging to systems known to be purely deterministic, nonlinear stochastic, and pseudorandom are generated and employed to develop the index. Such an index should help identify the underlying dynamical process of a sequence prior to specifying a hypothetical model to predict the series' movements over time. Its advantage over other tests for non-linearity is in, at least hypothetically, "quantifying" complexity, thus discriminating between processes that are mostly noise and those that are mostly or purely signal. Basically, the relative index compares an estimate of a series' noise-to-signal ratio as a measure of its complexity with that of a stochastic process. To estimate a series' unknown noise-to-signal ratio, the notion of correlation integral introduced during the eighties to char-acterize chaotic behavior is used. The relative complexity index (Γ) is constructed such that $0 \leq \Gamma \leq 1$, where $\Gamma = 1$ if the process investigated is purely random, and $\Gamma \to 0$ if it is a signal free from noise. Since there is no known measure of complexity available, we propose using a hypothetical approximation of the noise-to-signal ratio to estimate it. (Noise-to-signal rather than a series' signal-to-noise ratio is used because it conveniently forces $\Gamma \leq 1$, otherwise $\Gamma \to \infty$.) For real-world data, the signal-to-noise ratio is unknown and is measured here as a function of a coefficient θ that captures the effect of shuffling a sequence. If the observed series is already random or pure noise, shuffling its sequence will not increase its complex-ity, and the ratio of pre-to-post shuffling effect measure (θ) will be approxi-mately equal to 1. If the observed series is the result of a (at least partially) deterministic process, its complexity will increase by shuffling and $\theta < 1$. Using signal-to-noise in studies of complexity is not new [see Liu et al. (1991), Albano et al. (1992), Wayland et al. (1993), Kaboudan (1993)], but using it in developing an index to measure complexity is.

A forecaster's success in detecting the dynamical structure underlying a series' data-generating process may help formulate or hypothesize a model that closely represents the true one. Dynamical structures (or data-generating processes) of time series may be characterized within the general framework of linear signals, nonlinear signals, or white noise/stochastic processes. Observed series may also be signals tainted with noise that yield processes like linear stochastic (e.g., ARIMA) or nonlinear stochastic (e.g., GARCH, bilinear, and TAR). The correct characterization of a process or a dominant signal is a persistent problem even though more than a dozen statistical tests are already available. Perhaps the problem persists because classification methods test the null hypothesis that a series has a single structure with power against everything else. Thus, and for example, tests for linearity in frequency and time domains [see Tong (1990), pp. 221–251, for a review] fail to distinguish between possible presence of nonlinear and random structures. Similarly, tests for nonlinearity [such as Keenan (1985), Tsay (1986), and White (1987), reviewed in Lee et al. (1993)] fail to distinguish between nonlinear stochastic and pure white-noise processes. Also methods that test if a series is IID random [see Hinich (1982) and Brock et al. (1987)] fail to distinguish between nonlinear, nonlinear stochastic, and linear stochastic structures.

Difficulties with characterizing data-generating processes were aggravated by recent advances in chaos theory, which introduced a few measures to identify nonlinearity [for a summary, see Grabec (1992), pp. 477–482]. Although the ideas introduced added a new dimension that may ultimately enhance our ability to model and predict time series, resulting tests to isolate nonlinear deterministic processes are not successful. The theory's main contribution was bringing to recognition the existence of series that appear random when their underlying data-generating process is nonlinear deterministic but sensitive to initial conditions. By the early eighties, chaos-related terminology invaded many disciplines, and researchers were soon calculating correlation dimensions, correlation entropy, and Lyapunov exponents to isolate chaotic behavior. However, by the early nineties, it was clear that none of these measures succeeds in unambiguously detecting chaotic signals. They provide inconclusive and conflicting results. Discussions of the problems with those measures are in Ramsey and Yuan (1990), Provenzale et al. (1992), Theiler et al. (1992), and Wayland et al. (1993). Generally, the measures fail in two ways: (1) their estimates may be statistically unreliable and (2) they are not unique to chaotic signals. Statistical estimation problems occur because key parameters, such as the minimum number of data points (T) and the embedding dimension (m), must be selected. Small sample size or low embedding dimension can generate biased statistics. Arbitrariness still influences the selection of T and m, although advancements are slowly emerging. For example, Ruelle (1990) and Eckmann and Ruelle (1992) provide guidelines on minimum T required for estimating the measures, while Aleksic (1991) proposes a method for estimating the proper embedding dimension. Even if it is possible to optimally select these parameters, the measures still fail to detect chaotic signals because they provide indicators that are typical of but not unique to chaotic signals [e.g., discussion in Theiler et al. (1992), p. 77].

In this chapter, a relative complexity index (Γ) is introduced. It appears to provide some new hints about the dynamic structure of a series' data-generating process. When applied to measure the complexity of a few financial series (Abbott Labs, Du Pont, and IBM and the S&P 500), the index revealed that daily stock returns are not purely random. Our results indicate that Du Pont stock returns are the least complex (only one-fourth the complexity of a random series), Abbott Labs and IBM returns are almost twice the complexity of Du Pont's returns, while the S&P 500 is most complex and about 82 percent the complexity of a random series. Their complexities resemble nonlinear stochastic processes and their underlying dynamic processes are not the same. Noticeable in these preliminary results is the higher complexity the S&P 500 has relative to those individual stocks, possibly due to averaging. Each series' signal-to-noise ratio λ is the foundation upon which Γ is calculated. Stock returns evaluated were found to have signal-to-noise ratios between 1 and 2, and the S&P 500 had a ratio of less than 1. Several other series with known structures are developed and their complexities are measured as well.

Before presenting and discussing the results, we plan to review the development of that algorithm that helps approximate a relative complexity index Γ. In the next section, the methodological foundation, including an introduction of a method to estimate a series unknown λ used to construct Γ is described. Before concluding this chapter, a section is devoted to applying the methodology to quantify the complexities of selected processes.

Methodological Foundation

Consider the general time series process $Y_t = f(X_t, \varepsilon_t)$, where $t = 1, ..., T$, ε_t are independent stochastic disturbances with the usual normality assumptions, i.e., $\varepsilon_t \sim N(0, \sigma^2)$, f is a real-valued linear or nonlinear function, and $X_t = f(Y_{t-1}, ..., Y_{t-h})$ with integer $h < T$. If ε_t is zero, Y_t is either a deterministic linear or a nonlinear signal and its complexity index should be relatively low, i.e., $\Gamma_Y \to 0$. Conversely, if the deterministic signal (X_t) is nonexistent and the process is white noise, Y_t is maximally complex with $\Gamma_Y \to 1$. By construction, the index should manifest that $\Gamma_{linear} < \Gamma_{linearstochastic} < 1$ and $\Gamma_{nonlinear} < \Gamma_{nonlinearstochastic} < 1$. To compute Γ, signal-to-noise ratios of the subject series and a random series are estimated first. Signal-to-noise ratio is generally defined as λ, where

$$\lambda = \sigma_{signal}^2 / \sigma_{noise}^2 , \tag{1}$$

or the ratio of signal variance to that of noise. Conventionally, this measure is converted to decibels (dB), which we define as ω, and where

$$\omega = 10 \, Log \, \lambda. \tag{2}$$

(Although λ is easier to interpret, ω plays a useful role in estimating relative complexity, as shown later.) Theoretically, a series that is IID Gaussian white noise with a constant variance σ_{noise}^2 has no signal and its $\lambda = 0$. Conversely, a deterministic process is strictly signal and its λ is undefined or infinite. Practically and especially for testing purposes, it is helpful to assume that IID Gaussian white noise can be reasonably represented by pseudorandom series generated by the computer using some highly complex deterministic process with $\lambda \to 0$. Further, since a strictly deterministic process has $\lambda = \infty$, the maximum finite measure of λ empirically found in this study is assumed infinite.

As mentioned earlier, Γ is a measure of the ratio of two complexity measures, that of the observed series $= 1/\lambda_Y$ and that of a random series $= 1/\lambda_r$. Thus, $\Gamma_Y = \lambda_r/\lambda_Y$, where Y labels an observed sequence with a structure to be classified and r labels a pseudorandom data set generated using any computer program. When analyzing real-world data, λ_Y is unknown a priori, and a model to estimate a series' λ is essential. Two ingredients are needed to construct such a model: one is a large number of series with different signal-to-noise ratios that fairly represent the spectrum of values λ may take, and the other is at least one variable that can be measured from the created series capable of explaining the variation in λ. (This variable must also be measurable for any series to be classified later.) It is shown below that a θ statistic [Kaboudan (1993)] is a logical and reliable variable to use. Although the simple specification $\lambda_n = f(\theta_n)$ to estimate λ using n different ratios is inherent, $\omega = f(\theta_n)$ provided statistically preferred results. θ is reproduced below after illustrating the construction of series with deliberately controlled λs.

Generating Data with Desired λ

It is feasible to generate noise-corrupted signals with desirable λs by manipulating the variance σ_ε^2 (or altering the noise added to each signal). Each point in ε_t is multiplied by a constant α to alter the variance. To calculate α, first one decides on λ (the desired signal-to-noise ratio), computes the respective variances, then uses them to calculate the constant. Formally, let s^2_{signal} = sample variance of a signal X_t, s^2_{noise} = sample variance of the added noise ε_t, then

$$\alpha = \left[s^2_{signal} / (\lambda * s^2_{noise}) \right].$$ (3)

Here is how series with different λs were generated and used to estimate the needed model to compute ω. Two nonlinear functions (known to be chaotic and often cited in the literature on nonlinearity) were used to generate many series with different λ values. They are the logistic map [May (1976)]:

$$Y_t = 4 Y_{t-1} (1 - Y_{t-1}),$$ (4)

and the Hénon map [in Grassberger and Procaccia (1983)]:

$$H_t = A_{t-1} + 1 - 1.4 H_{t-1}^2,$$ (5)

$$A_t = 0.3 H_{t-1}.$$

Equations 4 and 5 were used to produce

$$X_t = Y_t + \alpha \varepsilon_t$$ (6)

and

$$Z_t = H_t + \alpha \varepsilon_t.$$ (7)

X_t and Z_t are noise-corrupted series with the desired λs. In Equations 4 and 5, initial values for right-hand-side lagged variables are set equal to 0.1. In Equations 6 and 7, $\varepsilon_t \sim N(0,\sigma^2)$, and the simulated values X_t and Z_t are normalized to the positive unit interval. Normalizing series neutralizes the effect of a series' unit of measurement on estimating λ and provides for consistent comparison between this test and others that also test normalized series. Using these series to estimate λ will follow a brief review of the derivation of θ.

Calculating θ

Kaboudan (1993) proposed a θ statistic to test for complexity. Fundamentally, the theta test is based on the notion that the correlation dimension of a random series should not change (at least statistically) when its sequence is shuffled or randomized. In its final form however, θ measures the change in the correlation integral after shuffling a series. Randomizing or shuffling a series is an old idea that was recently applied in tests for nonlinear chaos [e.g., Frank and Stengos (1988), Scheinkman and LeBaron (1989), Theiler et al. (1992)]. Randomizing may be with or without replacement, depending on the length of the data set available. Efron's (1982) well-known bootstrap method, which randomly samples series with replacement, was used to generate the shuffles for this study. To calculate the correlation integral we follow Grassberger and Procaccia's (1983) definition. Specifically:

$$C\,(m,e) = \frac{1}{T^2} \sum_{\substack{i,j=1 \\ i \neq j}}^{T} I_e\,(X_i{}^m, X_j{}^m), \tag{8}$$

where e is a separation scale in a fractal set, $I(.)$ is the indicator kernel that takes the value of 1 if $||X_i - X_j|| < e$ and zero otherwise, $||.||$ designates the sup-norm, $1 \leq i \leq T$, and $1 \leq j \leq T$. Four parameters must be selected prior to calculating Equation 8: T, m, e, and τ, where τ is an inter-observation lag length upon which m depends, and T and m are as defined earlier. First, according to Ruelle (1990), the minimum number of observations needed to estimate the correlation dimension v is $T_{min} > 10^{0.5v}$, and since for all practical purposes a data-generating process with $v \geq 6$ generates complex data that are almost random, $T_{min} = 1,000$ will be used below to estimate $C(m,e)$ which is needed to estimate θ. Second, according to Takens (1980), the embedding dimension should be selected such that $m > 2\,v$. It suffices to estimate the correlation integral for m = 2, ..., 10 only because often $C(m, e) = 0$ when the embedding dimension exceeds 10 and e is sufficiently low. Proper calculation of $C(m,e)$ demands minimizing e, and following Hsieh (1989) it should be selected such that $0.5\sigma \leq e \leq 2\sigma$, where σ is the standard deviation of the tested series. Finally, Zeng et al. (1992) proposed two methods to estimate τ, space-filling and autocorrelation. To simplify the discussion below, τ is set equal to 1, as it is usually set when analyzing discrete series.

Theta is the ratio of two correlation integral estimates, those of the subject series and its shuffled counterpart. This ratio of integral values is the same as the ratio of correlation dimension if the same e values are used when calculating the integral for both. For a series Y_t,

$$v_Y(m) = \Delta \ln C_Y(e) / \Delta \ln e \tag{9}$$

is correlation dimension at each m. In Equation 9, ln is the natural logarithm and Δ is the change between two levels of e. Several tests suggested that when $T \geq 1,000$, $e_{Y1} \geq \sigma$ and $e_{Y2} \geq 0.75\sigma$ work well. Using the same e_{Y1} and e_{Y2}, the random data have a dimension of:

$$v_r(m) = \Delta \ln C_r(e) / \Delta \ln e. \tag{10}$$

If Equation 9 is divided by Equation 10, and if the same $\Delta \ln e$ is used to estimate both $\Delta \ln C_Y(e)$ and $\Delta \ln C_r(e)$, the division produces the reduced form:

$$\theta_m = \Delta \ln C_Y(e) / \Delta \ln C_r(e), \tag{11}$$

a ratio of changes in the logarithmic correlation integral estimates. Equation 11 provides a meaningful ratio so long as every $C_Y(e) > 0$ and $C_r(e) > 0$ at the maximum embedding dimension M.

Figure 21-1 presents a magnification of the effect of shuffling on the correlation integral estimates at selected m levels and e values using 1,000 consecutive points of logistic map [May (1976)] data. It shows plots that compare five shuffles with the original for selected embedding values, m = 2, 4, ..., 10. Clearly, the intercepts and slopes of the plots at each m belonging to the original logistic data are distinctively different from those that belong to their shuffled counterparts. These plots also show that the shuffles produce different sets of curves. Appropriately, the result of every shuffle at every embedding dimension should be included when calculating θ, i.e., calculating an average $\theta = \Sigma \theta_m / M - 1$. Further, to secure a reasonable and unbiased approximation of the true θ, it is imperative to average several θ estimates from different generated series for each map with identical λ. Using $k = 1, ..., K$ shuffles (where $K \geq 30$ is statistically large enough), the coefficient θ is

$$\theta = \frac{1}{K} \sum_{k=1}^{K} \left[\frac{1}{M-1} \sum_{m=2}^{M} \left(\frac{\Delta \ln C_Y(e)}{\Delta \ln C_{rk}(e)} \right) \right]. \tag{12}$$

θ as calculated is inversely related to λ's behavior. If a variable is pure white noise, its $\theta \to 1$ and $\lambda \to 0$, and when it has little or no noise the variable's $\theta \to 0$ and $\lambda \to 1$. We now use such a relationship to estimate a series' signal-to-noise ratio and then quantify complexity.

Estimating λ

To estimate λ, series with known and deliberately controlled λ are used. First, Equations 6 and 7 were employed to produce several series with different λs. It is reasonable to start with $\lambda = 1$ and continue to increase it

Figure 21-1

Plots of ln c(e) versus e for m = 2,4,6,8, and 10 using 1,000 consecutive data points generated by the logistic map and five random shuffles of the generated data set.

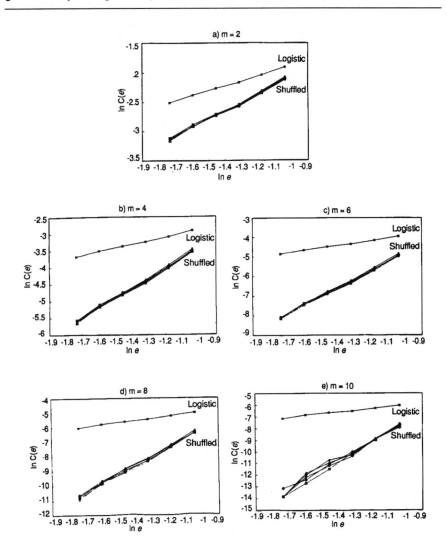

Figure previously appeared in *Physics Letters A,* Vol. 181 (1993), p. 382. Reprinted by permission from Elsevier Science Publishers.

until the calculated θ stabilizes or changes insignificantly. Accordingly, series with λ= 1, 2, ..., 10, 20, 30, 40, and 50 for each map were produced. (The difference between θ estimates at λ = 50 and λ = 60 was insignificant.) To measure the relationship between the signal-to-noise ratio and θ, 30 θ estimates (each using L = 30 shuffles) were generated for every one of the 14 λ values from the two maps using different and independently generated ε_t. A total of 840 sets were generated. In addition, θ estimates were also obtained for 28 pseudorandom series. All 868 θs were used to develop a model to estimate λ.

Prior to specifying the model, a graphical examination of 28 averages of λ–θ relations was evaluated. As shown in Figure 21-2, it is clear that a nonlinear θ–λ relationship exists. $\omega = f(\theta_n)$ becomes the logical specification alternative. After testing several specifications, a reasonable model to reproduce ω was only possible by including dummy variables in the equation. Dummy variables conveniently accommodate intercept shifting. Figure 21-2 suggests that the intercept shifted when λ > 20 and, although not as clear, when λ < 4. Seven dummy variables with observa-

Figure 21-2

Signal-to-Noise Ratio versus Theta

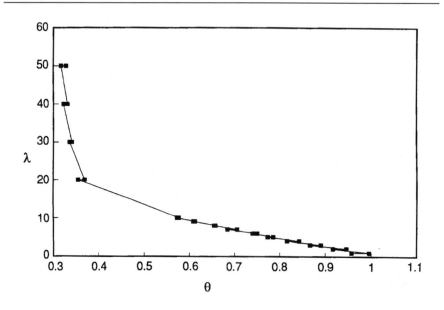

tions taking one of two values, 0 or 1, were developed and used. DV0 was designed such that it is equal to 1 only when $\lambda < 1$ or θ estimate belongs to pseudorandom data, and is equal to 0 otherwise. Similarly, DV1 = 1 if the series has $\lambda \approx 1$ and 0 otherwise. DV2 = 1 if the series $\lambda \approx 2$ and 0 otherwise. The other four dummy variables (DV3, DV30, DV40, and DV50) are similarly designed. Using 868 actual ω values, their associated θ estimates, and the seven dummy variables, the final equation was estimated and is presented in Table 21-1. Clearly, the estimated coefficients are all statistically significantly different from zero, and the equation seems to be free from estimation problems.

Here is how the results in Table 21-1 can be used. Assume a series X_t with t = 1, ..., 1,000 to test. First one would normalize the series to the positive unit interval, generate 30 shuffles, estimate the correlation integral at each m for the normalized X_t and for each of the 30 shuffles, then compute the average θ as described in Equation 12. Once obtained, that average θ is used in two ways. First it is used to determine the dummy variable to activate, if any; then it is used as input into the estimated

Table 21-1

Regression to Estimate Omega

Dependent Variable:		Omega	
Estimation Method:		Least Squares	
R Bar **2:		0.99	
Regression F Statistic:		16528	
Durbin–Watson Statistic:		1.76	
Q Statistic:		249.52	

Variable	Coeffic.	Std. Error	t–Stat.
Constant	17.746	0.089	199.86
Theta	–13.546	0.132	–102.45
DV0	–6.200	0.089	–69.97
DV1	–4.524	0.070	–64.33
DV2	–2.120	0.067	–31.68
DV3	–1.077	0.063	–16.99
DV30	1.608	0.070	22.90
DV40	2.705	0.071	38.04
DV50	3.613	0.071	50.54

equation to calculate ω. To determine the dummy variable to activate, Table 21-2 is useful. It was constructed by evaluating the 868 θ values obtained with known λ. According to Table 21-2, if the estimated θ is within a specific range, the dummy variable relating to that range takes the value of 1, and all other dummy variables are set equal to zero. If the θ estimate is outside all ranges, all dummy variables values are set equal to zero. In summary, to estimate a series' unknown λ, the computed θ average is substituted in the regression equation in Table 21-1 and the dummy variable to activate is determined according to the range within which θ falls. If any is activated, it takes the value of 1, and the solution for ω is calculated. Once an ω value is produced it is converted to λ following (2), or $\lambda_Y = 10^{\omega/10}$.

Calculating Γ

Before estimating Γ, a series must be identified as being linear in structure or not. The Γ measure as proposed does not discriminate between linear stochastic and nonlinear stochastic processes. To discriminate between linearity and nonlinearity, the original series is first linearly filtered. Any linear model can be used [see Lee et al. (1989)], but estimating the simple model $Y_t = \alpha + \beta Y_{t-1}$ is usually sufficient to detect the presence or absence

---

Table 21-2

Dummy Variable "Theta" Activation Range

| IF | THEN | | | | | | |
| | Value of each dummy variable is: | | | | | | |
Theta Range	DV0	DV1	DV2	DV3	DV30	DV40	DV50
$0.99 =$ or $<$ Theta	1	0	0	0	0	0	0
$0.95 =$ or $<$ Theta < 0.99	0	1	0	0	0	0	0
$0.90 =$ or $<$ Theta < 0.95	0	0	1	0	0	0	0
$0.85 =$ or $<$ Theta < 0.90	0	0	0	1	0	0	0
$0.33 =$ or $<$ Theta < 0.34	0	0	0	0	1	0	0
$0.32 =$ or $<$ Theta < 0.33	0	0	0	0	0	1	0
Theta < 0.32	0	0	0	0	0	0	1
All other values	0	0	0	0	0	0	0

of any form of linear structure. If the resulting estimated β is significantly different from zero, the series has some form of linear structure (and not necessarily the one specified here). If β is not significantly different from zero, the data-generating process is free from any linear structure. If the data-generating process is linear in structure, two Γ values need to be estimated. If not, Γ calculation proceeds by estimating λ_Y, λ_r, θ, and ω. λ_r can be estimated using pseudorandom sets independently generated. Alternatively, a constant λ value = 0.533 (which is the average of all λ values obtained from the random sets produced for this study) can be used.

Implementing Γ

Two groups of series are selected to test the use of Γ as a measure of complexity. First, a group with known λs consisting of 28 simulations from series produced by the logistic and Hénon maps and three other pseudorandom sets of data are employed to test if the model succeeds in reproducing their designed λs. Their results are in Table 21-3, where L and H are abbreviations indicating the map used and the integer following each L or H is the series' λ by design. In the first column of the table, pairs of identical noise contamination levels of logistic and Hénon series are listed together for comparison. Each pair displayed similar θ levels, and θ continued to decrease until 20 < λ < 30 and stabilized thereafter. (This explains testing data with a maximum λ = 50.) Estimates of ω are in the third column. They produce the λ calculations in the fourth. It is clear that the estimated λs are very close to their real values. Γ, in the last column, shows that when the signal is equal to noise, i.e., λ = 1, the estimated λ is approximately equal to 1 and Γ is a logical 50 percent relative complexity. Γ decreases until the signal is 30 times the noise where complexity reaches a low 1 percent. Further, relative complexity of pseudorandom data is at 100 percent as should be expected. Given such results, the Γ measure was then used to calculate complexity of the second group of series, which includes processes not used in estimating the equation in Table 21-1 and whose λs are unknown. We tested nonlinear processes known to be chaotic, nonlinear stochastic processes, linear stochastic processes, and real-world data—stock market prices.

Complexity measures from series not used in estimating the equation in Table 21-1 are included in Table 21-4. These series are divided into four different groups. Three groups are series artificially generated from known systems, and the fourth group has data with unknown structures, stock market data. The first group consists of four nonlinear deterministic processes. Two are the logistic and Hénon maps already defined in Equations 4 and 5, and the third is the tent map [in Wolf and Vastomous (1986)]:

$$Y_t = 2\,Y_{t-1}, \qquad\qquad \text{if } Y_{t-1} \le 0.5 \tag{13}$$

$$Y_t = 2 - 1.9999\ Y_{t-1} \quad \text{if } Y_{t-1} > 0.5.$$

The fourth process considered is the Mackey-Glass equation [in Grassberger and Procaccia (1983)]. This process is different from the previous three. It is described by a delay differential equation of infinite dimension. Specifically,

$$\dot{X}_t = \frac{0.2\,X_{t-c}}{1 + [X_{t-c}]^{10}} - 0.1\,X_t, \tag{14}$$

where $\dot{X}$ represents the first derivative of X. To measure its complexity, Equation 14 was converted to a p-dimensional set of difference equations, where p is any large positive integer. Using p = 600 (similar to Grassberger and Procaccia) three series are generated with time steps Δt = 0.03, 0.05, and 0.1667, where Δt = c/p and c is a positive constant integer. The results are in Table 21-4 identified respectively as MG=18, MG=30, and MG=100.

The second group consists of three nonlinear stochastic processes. These systems combine deterministic with stochastic processes dynamically. "Dynamical" combinations are substantially different from the nonlinear stochastic combination processes that generated the data used to estimate the equation in Table 21-1 and obtain the results in Table 21-3. Those combine deterministic with stochastic processes "statically." The difference is that dynamic combinations incorporate the effect of noise shocks on subsequent solutions from the deterministic process while static combinations do not (or are unable to) adjust to external shocks. (Intuitively, systems dynamically combined should have higher complexity indexes than those statically combined, if the same ε_t set is used. Undoubtedly, further investigation is necessary.) Both dynamic and static combinations may occur in the real world. An example of the first is as in the case of stock prices that adjust to shocks instantly. An example of static combinations is the case of external shocks imposed on preplanned production process that cannot be altered and production continues to follow the prescribed course. The difference between the two also parallels economic outcomes in free markets versus centrally planned systems.

Simulations of the nonlinear stochastic group were possible after generating different sets of ε_t such that $\varepsilon_t \sim N(0,1)$. Here are formal definitions of the processes:

Table 21-3

Estimates of the Relative Complexity Index

Series	Theta	Omega	Lambda	Gamma
L-1	0.960	0.218	1.051	0.507
H-1	0.966	0.136	1.032	0.517
L-2	0.915	3.231	2.104	0.253
H-2	0.925	3.096	2.040	0.261
L-3	0.892	4.586	2.875	0.185
H-3	0.883	4.708	2.956	0.180
L-4	0.820	6.638	4.611	0.116
H-4	0.836	6.421	4.387	0.122
L-5	0.789	7.058	5.079	0.105
H-5	0.753	7.546	5.683	0.094
L-6	0.727	7.898	6.163	0.087
H-6	0.735	7.790	6.011	0.089
L-7	0.685	8.467	7.026	0.076
H-7	0.701	8.250	6.684	0.080
L-8	0.648	8.968	7.885	0.068
H-8	0.653	8.900	7.763	0.069
L-9	0.598	9.645	9.216	0.058
H-9	0.610	9.483	8.877	0.060
L-10	0.548	10.323	10.771	0.049
H-10	0.562	10.133	10.311	0.052
L-20	0.345	13.072	20.288	0.026
H-20	0.360	12.869	19.360	0.028
L-30	0.328	14.911	30.978	0.017
H-30	0.325	14.951	31.269	0.017
L-40	0.321	16.103	40.762	0.013
H-40	0.321	16.103	40.762	0.013
L-50	0.319	17.037	50.553	0.011
H-50	0.317	17.065	50.870	0.010
RAND1	1.067	−2.908	0.512	1.041
RAND2	1.054	−2.731	0.533	1.000
RAND3	1.061	−2.826	0.522	1.022

Table 21-4

Predicting Relative Complexity

Series	Theta	Omega	Lambda	Gamma
		Nonlinear Deterministic		
Logistic	0.302	17.268	53.306	0.010
Henon	0.315	17.092	51.188	0.010
Tent	0.390	12.463	17.631	0.030
MG-18	0.370	12.734	18.766	0.028
MG-30	0.450	11.650	14.622	0.036
MG-100	0.640	9.076	8.084	0.066
		Nonlinear Stochastic		
NAARX	0.910	3.299	2.137	0.249
GARCH	0.910	3.299	2.137	0.249
TAR	0.650	8.941	7.836	0.068
		Linear Stochastic		
AR1	0.769	7.329	5.406	0.099
(Filtered)	0.955	0.285	1.068	0.499
AR2	0.591	9.740	9.419	0.057
(Filtered)	0.763	7.410	5.508	0.097
MA1	0.927	3.068	2.027	0.263
(Filtered)	0.996	−1.946	0.639	0.835
		Stock Price Returns		
Abbott	0.969	0.098	1.023	0.521
DuPont	0.934	2.978	1.985	0.269
IBM	0.952	0.321	1.077	0.495
S&P 500	0.991	−1.874	0.649	0.821

1. NAARX [Chen and Tsay (1993)]:

$$X_t = 0.8 \ Log \ (1 + 3 \ X_{t-1}^2) - 0.6 \ Log \ (1 + 3 \ X_{t-3}^2) + \varepsilon_t. \tag{15}$$

2. GARCH(1,1) [in Hsieh (1989)]:

$$X_t = \sqrt{h_t} \ \varepsilon_t, \tag{16}$$

$$h_t = 1 + 0.25 \ X_{t-1}^2 + 0.7 \ h_{t-1}.$$

3.   TAR [Tong and Lim (1980)]:

$$X_t = 0.9 \ X_{t-1} + \varepsilon_t, \qquad if \ | \ X_{t-1} \ | \leq 1,$$

$$X_t = -0.3 \ X_{t-1} + \varepsilon_t \qquad if \ | \ X_{t-1} \ | > 1. \tag{17}$$

The third group consists of three linear stochastic functions, with $\varepsilon_t \sim$ N(0,1), specifically,

1.   AR1:

$$X_t = 2.4 - 0.8 \ X_{t-1} + \varepsilon_t. \tag{18}$$

2.   AR2:

$$X_t = 6.0 + 1.4 \ X_{t-1} - 0.8 \ X_{T-2} + \varepsilon_t. \tag{19}$$

3.   MA1:

$$X_t = 0.5 \ \varepsilon_{t-1} + \varepsilon_t. \tag{20}$$

The fourth group includes real-world data. These series are stock price returns, and their complexity measures are shown at the bottom of Table 21-4. Returns are conventionally defined as $\ln(P_t/P_{t-1})$ or the natural logarithm of the ratio of today's closing price relative to yesterday's. We employed 1,000 consecutive trading returns starting February 1982 and ending prior to the 1987 crash. As shown, only three stock returns and the S&P 500 are investigated.

Here are a few comments on the results in Table 21-4:

1.   Series that are strictly nonlinear deterministic and known to be chaotic produced low relative complexity index estimates. Most of these processes have a relative complexity index between 1 and 2 percent. These levels are similar to those from systems with known signal-to-noise ratios of 30 and higher (L-30, -40, and -50 and H-30, -40, and -50 in Table 21-3). The only exception is MG-100, the series that was simulated using the Mackey-Glass equation with the largest lag structure. This should not be surprising since it is logical that complexity would increase due to information loss when lag is increased from one point to the next in the data selected to represent the process.

2.   Nonlinear stochastic processes showed higher relative complexities than those of the nonlinear deterministic as should be expected. NAARX and GARCH(1,1) displayed relative complexity similar to the levels observed in Table 21-3 when the signal-to-noise ratio is approximately 2 (L-2 and H-2). TAR displayed a level of complexity similar to series in Table 21-3, with signal-to-noise ratio of 8.

3. Complexity of linear stochastic processes was measured twice for each system tested and yielded different before and after filtering results. As shown, complexity of linear stochastic systems increased after filtering. In addition to the differences detected due to filtering, whether only before or only after filtering, these systems differ substantially in their complexity. This is because these processes have different signal-to-noise ratios. These differences do not change the main conclusion reached concerning the identification of the structure underlying each process. What is important is the fact that if the complexity indexes measured before and after filtering are significantly different, the process studied has some form of linear stochastic structure.

4. The relative complexity indexes of stock returns are definitely far more complex than chaotic nonlinear deterministic systems. They possess complexity levels similar to systems with signals tarnished by almost equally loud noise. There was no linearity detected in any of the four series tested, and the levels of complexity of different stock returns are not identical. Du Pont seems to be the result of a system that is almost half the complexity of the ones generating IBM and Abbott Labs returns. Du Pont returns revealed a relative complexity of about 27 percent. This level of complexity is similar to systems known to have $\lambda = 2$ (i.e., L-2 and H-2 in Table 21-3). A similar comparison of IBM's and Abbott Labs' complexities shows that they are similar to systems with $\lambda = 1$. The S&P 500 is most complex at 82 percent and $\lambda = 0.65$. Such a ratio is close to that of a pseudorandom process. It is logical to find the S&P 500 at such a high level of complexity, since it averages the dynamics of many stock prices. These results are new evidence against the efficient market hypothesis. Given the low complexity level found for Du Pont relative to those of IBM and Abbott Labs returns, and given that stock returns have a much lower complexity level altogether than the S&P 500, randomness is easily ruled out. Also, it seems that Du Pont's returns have a complexity level very similar to that found for the GARCH-in-mean type model. The complexity of the returns is very similar to the GARCH(1,1) specification tested earlier.

Concluding Remarks

This chapter proposed a relative complexity index Γ to help diagnose the dynamical structure of observed series. Γ is a quantitative measure of any series' complexity relative to that of a stochastic process. From the results documented in this study, if $\Gamma \leq 4$ percent the process under consideration is probably a deterministic signal and it may be possible to reasonably approximate its underlying model. Distinguishing between linear and other (nonlinear or stochastic) processes seems clearly feasible. If there is a difference between the pre- and post-filtering θ estimates, the magnitude of the linear signal may be identifiable even if the noise is fairly loud, as demonstrated by the cases considered above. As for other structures, the results show that most chaotic series from discrete systems seem to possess $\Gamma < 2$ percent, while nonlinear stochastic series' $\Gamma > 4$ percent, which increases with noise relative to signal. White noise's $\Gamma \approx 100$ percent.

The proposed measure was applied to stock returns. Our findings indicate that stock price returns are not random, not chaotic (or nonlinear deterministic), not linear or linear stochastic. They are, most probably, nonlinear stochastic with different levels of complexity. Measuring the complexity of individual stocks revealed that stocks have lower complexity levels than the S&P 500, probably due to averaging. Our results also suggest that intradaily stock returns may be less complex than interdaily price returns. Although premature, this conclusion is based on the results that the Mackey-Glass data revealed when the lag structure was increased. MG-18, the one with the lowest lag structure, showed the lowest level of complexity. MG-100 showed the highest level of complexity. This may mean that the larger the number of movements omitted from the sequence under investigation, the greater will be the level of complexity obtained. Interdaily prices represent sequences with too many movements omitted.

These preliminary results appear natural and intuitive and provide information not available using a single test alone. However, the proposed routine provides only a possible new avenue to follow in the quest for modeling time series. Much research remains to be explored. Future research will include more statistical testing of the three estimated parameters θ, λ, and Γ, which are statistical approximations. Further, the examples considered above include only discrete time series (except for MG series) and have yet to be applied to continuous processes.

References

Akgiray, V. "Conditional Heteroscedasticity in Time Series of Stock Returns: Evidence and Forecasts." *Journal of Business*, 62 (1989), pp. 55–80.

Albano, A. M., A. Passamante, T. Hediger, and M. E. Farrel. "Using Neural Nets to Look for Chaos." *Physica D*, 58 (1992), pp. 1–9.

Aleksic, Z. "Estimating the Embedding Dimension." *Physica D*, 52 (1991), pp. 362–368.

Brock, W., D. Dechert, and J. Scheinkman. "A Test of Independence Based on the Correlation Dimension." SSRI Report #8702, Department of Economics, University of Wisconsin, Madison, University of Houston, and University of Chicago, 1987.

Brock, W., J. Lakonishok, and B. LeBaron. "Simple Technical Trading Rules and the Stochastic Properties of Stock Returns." SSRI Report #9022, Department of Economics, University of Wisconsin, Madison, 1990.

Chen, R., and S. Tsay. "Nonlinear Additive ARX Models." *Journal of the American Statistical Association*, 88 (1993), pp. 955–967.

Eckmann, J.-P., and D. Ruelle. "Fundamental Limitations for Estimating Dimensions and Lyapunov Exponents in Dynamical Systems." *Physica D*, 56 (1992), pp. 185–187.

Efron, B. *The Jackknife, the Bootstrap, and Other Resampling Plans*. Philadelphia: Society for Industrial and Applied Mathematics, 1982.

Frank, M., and T. Stengos. "Chaotic Dynamics in Economic Time Series." *Journal of Economic Surveys*, 2 (1988), pp. 103–133.

Grabec, I. "Prediction of Chaotic Dynamical Phenomena by a Neural Network," in *Dynamic, Genetic, and Chaotic Programming: The Sixth-Generation*, eds. B. Soucek and the IRIS Group. New York: John Wiley & Sons, Inc., 1992, pp. 471–500.

Grassberger, P., and I. Procaccia. "Measuring the Strangeness of Strange Attractors." *Physica D*, 9 (1983), pp. 189–208.

Hinich, M. "Testing for Gaussianity and Linearity of Stationary Time Series." *Journal of Time Series Analysis*, 3 (1982), pp. 169–176.

Hinich, M., and D. Patterson. "Evidence of Nonlinearity in Daily Stock Returns." *Journal of Business and Economic Statistics*, 3 (1985), pp. 69–77.

Hsieh, D. "Testing for Nonlinear Dependence in Daily Foreign Exchange Rates." *Journal of Business*, 62 (1989), pp. 339–368.

Hsieh, D. "Testing for Nonlinear Dynamics." *Journal of Finance* (1991), pp. 1839–1877.

Jegadeesh, N. "Evidence of Predictable Behavior of Security Returns." *Journal of Finance*, XLV, 3 (1990), pp. 881–898.

Jensen, C. "Some Anomalous Evidence Regarding Market Efficiency." *Journal of Financial Economics*, 6 (1978), pp. 95–101.

Kaboudan, M. "A Complexity Test Based on the Correlation Integral." *Physics Letters A*, 181 (1993), pp. 381–386.

Keenan, D. "A Tukey Nonadditivity Type Test for Time Series Nonlinearity." *Biometrika*, 72 (1985), pp. 39–44.

Lee, T., H. White, and C. Granger. "Testing for Neglected Nonlinearity in Time Series Models." *Journal of Econometrics*, 56 (1993), pp. 269–290.

Liu, T., C. Granger, and W. Heller. "Using the Correlation Exponent to Decide If an Economic Series Is Chaotic." Discussion paper, University of California, San Diego, 1991.

Lo, A., and C. MacKinlay. "Stock Market Prices Do Not Follow Random Walks: Evidence from a Sample Specification Test." *The Review of Financial Studies*, 1 (1988), pp. 41–66.

May, R. "Simple Mathematical Models with Very Complicated Dynamics." *Nature*, 261 (1976), pp. 459–467.

Provenzale, A., L. Smith, R. Vio, and G. Murante. "Distinguishing Between Low-Dimensional Dynamics and Randomness in Measured Time Series." *Physica D*, 58 (1992), pp. 31–49.

Ramsey, J. B., and H. Yuan. "The Statistical Properties of Dimension Calculation Using Small Data Sets." *Nonlinearity*, 3 (1990), pp. 155–176.

Ruelle, D. "Deterministic Chaos: The Science and the Fiction." *Proc. Roy. Soc. Lond. A*, 427 (1990), pp. 241–248.

Scheinkman, J. A., and B. LeBaron. "Nonlinear Dynamics and Stock Returns." *Journal of Business*, 62 (1989), pp. 311–337.

Takens, F. *Dynamical Systems and Turbulence, Lecture Notes in Mathematics No. 898.* New York: Springer–Verlag, 1980.

Theiler, J., S. Eubank, A. Longtin, B. Galdrikian, and D. Farmer. "Testing for Nonlinearity in Time Series: The Method of Surrogate Data." *Physica D*, 58 (1992), pp. 77–94.

Tong, H., and K. Lim. "Threshold Autoregression, Limit Cycles and Cyclical Data." *Journal of the Royal Statistical Society*, Ser. B. 42 (1980), pp. 245–292.

Tong, H. *Non-Linear Time Series: A Dynamical System Approach.* Oxford: Clarendon Press, 1990.

Tsay, R. "Nonlinearity Tests for Time Series." *Biometrika*, 73 (1986), pp. 461–466.

Wayland, R., D. Bromley, D. Pickett, and A. Passamante. "Recognizing Determinism in a Time Series." *Physical Review Letters*, 70 (1993), pp. 580–582.

White, H. "Specification Testing in Dynamic Models," in *Advances in Econometrics, Fifth World Congress*, Vol. 1, Chapter 1, ed. T. F. Bewley. Cambridge University Press, 1987.

White, H. "Economic Prediction Using Neural Networks: The Case of IBM Stock Returns." USCD Department of Economics Working Paper #88–20, 1988.

Willey, T. "Testing for Nonlinear Dependence in Daily Stock Indices." *Journal of Economics and Business*, 44 (1992), pp. 63–74.

Wolf, A., and J. Vastomous. "Intermediate Length Scale Effects in Lyapunov Exponent Estimation," in *Dimensions and Entropies in Chaotic Systems*, ed. G. Mayer–Kress, Berlin: Springer–Verlag, 1986.

Zeng, X., R. Pielke, and R. Eykholt. "Estimating the Fractal Dimension and the Predictability of the Atmosphere." *Journal of the Atmospheric Sciences*, 49 (1992), pp. 649–659.

22

NONLINEARITIES AND CHAOTIC EFFECTS IN OPTIONS PRICES

By Robert Savit

I. Introduction

Recently, a good deal of evidence has been accumulated that suggests that prices in certain markets and over certain time horizons may be correlated in subtle ways that elude even common statistical tests. Although there are exceptions, such correlations may be induced by an underlying nonlinear process, and in particular, one that is chaotic, or nearly chaotic. Such nonlinear processes are expected to occur generically in self-regulating systems. Indeed, studies in a wide range of fields have indicated the important role that such processes play in systems as diverse as the human heart, the heating of water in a teapot, animal populations, and the availability of production parts in manufacturing. Insofar as the financial and commodities markets are self-regulating systems with intricate feedback and feed-forward loops, one may expect to find effects of these nonlinearities in the prices generated by those markets.[1]

Reprinted with permission from *The Journal of Futures Markets*, Vol. 9, No. 6 (December 1989): 507–18. © 1989 by John Wiley & Sons, Inc.

In one important development, Brock, Dechert, and Scheinkman[2] have developed a new statistical test (the BDS statistic), based on the idea of the correlation dimension, a notion developed in the physical sciences in the study of nonlinear dynamical systems. The BDS statistic and related methods of analysis[3] are explicitly constructed to be sensitive to the kinds of higher dimensional correlations that are typically induced by nonlinear processes, and against which many common statistical tests have little power. Using the BDS statistic, various detrended macroeconomic data sets[4] as well as more market-specific data[5], including the price movements of certain fixed-income instruments[6], have been shown to have a significant nonrandom structure, common statistical tests to the contrary notwithstanding. Specifically, the BDS test is a test against the null hypothesis that a sequence of numbers is IID. The failure of detrended economic and financial data to pass this test, despite their consistency with other more common tests of randomness, strongly suggests that such data may be produced by processes in which there are underlying dynamics with at least a partially deterministic character. Understanding the nature of the subtle deterministic correlations in this kind of data is certainly of great importance, both for honing investment strategies and for gaining a more basic understanding of economic dynamics. Equally important, however, is understanding the effects of these correlations on derivative market instruments such as options. This work is a first step in that direction.

The standard options price formula, the Black-Scholes result, or one of its close cousins, is based on two assumptions: (1) the options price is determined by the arbitrage condition that there be no riskless profitable arbitrage opportunities, and (2) the price of the underlying asset follows a random walk in the logarithm of the price as a function of time. In the limit of continuous trading, this random walk just means that the logarithm of the price of the underlying security is driven by a diffusive process. This chapter examines the effect on options prices of altering the standard random walk assumption to consider the possibility that the underlying instrument's price time series is only apparently random, and is actually driven by a noisy nonlinear process. In the specific case considered, the nonlinear process is chaotic but, as shall be explained, most conclusions apply also to other nonchaotic nonlinear price sequences.

The calculations will show that a noisy chaotic sequence, which generates a price path that looks completely random, and which in any case has only short-term higher dimensional correlations, alters the value of the usual expression for a call option in a risk-neutral economy for all times to expiration. This result has far-reaching implications for the construction of hedging strategies in the presence of nonlinear price movements, as will be discussed in Section IV. It should be emphasized that the price path generated by this noisy chaotic map is indistinguishable from any random path when subjected to standard statistical tests. Nonetheless, when folded into the options calculation, its subtle short-term correlations can significantly alter the evaluation of the correct, arbitrage-free options price. The model presented herein is not necessarily intended to be a realistic model of price movements in financial markets. Rather, it is a simple model introduced to show the effects that nonlinear dynamics in the trading of the underlying asset can have, in general, on options calculations.

The rest of this chapter is organized as follows: In Section II we describe the general strategy of the calculation and introduce the tent map, a very simple chaotic map that will be used as a model of a nonlinear process. In Section III the specific calculation will be described and the results presented. Section IV consists of a summary, comments about the implications of this work, and suggestions for future study.

II. The Options Formula and the Tent Map

Consider a risk-neutral economy in which an underlying asset moves according to a random walk. The standard options pricing formula, either in its continuum, Black-Scholes manifestation, or in a discrete time version, calculates the value of, say, a call option by computing the expectation value of the price of the underlying asset at expiration, and subtracting from that the striking price.[7] (This chapter, for simplicity, always considers European options. Most of the qualitative conclusions are expected to be valid for American options also.) It is convenient to cast the calculations in terms of a discrete binary pricing model. That is, it is assumed that at each time step in a discrete process, the value of the underlying asset can move up by a factor of u or down by a factor of d. Then the value of a call option that can be exercised (and expires) at time T is given by

$$C(T) = r^{-T} \sum_{n=0}^{T} P(n) \text{Max} \left[u^n d^{T-n} S - K; 0 \right] \tag{1}$$

where S is the initial stock price, K is the striking price, r is the "riskless" interest rate, and $P(n)$ is the probability that at expiration the price will have suffered exactly n upward movements.

Since the underlying asset is assumed to execute a random multiplicative walk in price space, $P(n)$ is just given by the binomial coefficient,

$$P(n) = \frac{T!}{n!(T-n)!} \, q^n (1-q)^{T-n}. \tag{2}$$

Here q is the probability that the asset price rises by a factor of u at any given time, and according to the assumption of risk-neutrality has the value $q = (r-d)/(u-d)$.

With these assumptions it is quite easy to do the sum in Equation 1, and one thus arrives at the standard result. Another way of describing this calculation is to say that Equation 1 represents a sum over all possible paths in price space, starting at the price S. According to the random walk assumption, each distinct path is weighted equally in the sum. Operationally, one can imagine that a given price path is generated in the following way: Divide the interval $(0,1)$ into two segments $(0, 1-q)$ and $(1-q, 1)$. Generate random numbers uniformly distributed on the interval $(0,1)$. If a given random number is less than $1-q$, then the price falls by a factor of d at that time step, otherwise the price rises by a factor of u.

Consider, now, an investor who wishes to price options on some asset. He observes the price movements of the asset for some period of time and computes the autocorrelation functions of the price movements and the probability distribution of asset prices. He finds that the autocorrelation functions are zero and that the price distribution is, over long times, lognormal. Moreover, he observes that the probability of up and down price movements satisfies the condition for risk neutrality. On the basis of this information he concludes that the asset price is executing a random multiplicative walk in price space, and he calculates the value of a call option using Equations 1 and 2.

Although this investor's conclusions concerning the price behavior of the underlying asset seem reasonable, it is possible that the price movements of the underlying asset are not at all random, while still having the same values for the autocorrelation functions and unconditional price distribution as prices generated by simple random walk dynamics. Such a situation may occur if the asset price is driven by a nonlinear chaotic process (either with or without noise). In that case, the subsequent price movements of the underlying asset would not be those expected by the investor, and the correct evaluation of the right-hand side of Equation 1 could be different. This in turn would render the investor's pricing of the option unreliable, and a new options price would have to be derived.

An example of a chaotic process that will give the same autocorrelation functions and price distributions as the random walk is the tent map.[8] The tent map is a nonlinear map, which expresses the $(m+1)^{\text{th}}$ value of an iterate, y, in terms of the mth value.

$$y(m + 1) = f[y(m)] = \begin{cases} 2y(m) & \text{if } 0 < y(m) < \dfrac{1}{2} \\[2mm] 2 - 2y(m) & \text{if } \dfrac{1}{2} < y(m) < 1 \end{cases} \tag{3}$$

The tent map is shown in Figure 22-1. Note that all the y's are between 0 and 1.

The tent map is a very simple example of a chaotic map and has the following important properties:

1. For almost all initial values, $y(0)$, the iterates $y(m)$ are uniformly distributed on the interval $(0,1)$ as m gets large.

2. The autocorrelation functions

$$\sum_{j=1}^{L} \left[<y(j)y(j + b)> - \frac{1}{4} \right] \tag{4}$$

go to zero as L gets large for any b not equal to zero.

Figure 22-1

The Tent Map Described in Equation 3

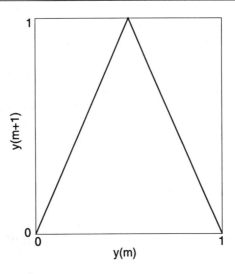

3. Suppose there is some small uncertainty, δ, in the value of $y(0)$. This uncertainty gets magnified exponentially fast. That is, consider two sequences $y(m)$ and $z(m)$. If $y(0)$ and $z(0)$ are identical, then for all m $y(m) = z(m)$ exactly. But if $z(0) = y(0) + \delta$ then, generically, $|y(m) - z(m)|$ will be of order $\exp(\gamma m)$, where, for the tent map, $\gamma = \ln 2$. (Subject, of course to the condition that z and y are always between 0 and 1.) That is, even if there is some small uncertainty in the value of y, that small uncertainty quickly becomes magnified, until the subsequent y's are completely unpredictable. This exponential growth of uncertainty is typical of chaotic systems. The quantity γ is called the Lyapunov exponent.

Using the tent map, a price sequence with the same autocorrelation functions and unconditional distributions as the random walk can be produced in the following way:

Let the sequence of up and down price movements be determined by the sequence of the values of the iterates $y(m)$ generated by Equation 3, rather than by a random number. If $y(m)$ is less than $q - 1$, then the asset price moves down at time m by a factor of d, otherwise it moves up by a factor of u. It is clear, from properties 1 and 2 above, that any particular realization of the price path would look completely random. On the other hand, if one happened to know with arbitrary accuracy the value $y(0)$, it is also clear that the value of the underlying asset could be predicted with certainty at any time, and so one would (trivially) be able to derive the correct arbitrage-free value of the options price.[9]

Of course, in the real world, one cannot predict with absolute certainty the price movements for all time. Even if the endogenous dynamics of some market were completely understood, that market is continually subject to exogenous influences as new information affecting the market becomes known. To model this more reasonable situation, suppose that each $y(m)$ is determined by the tent map (Equation 3), only to within some uncertainty. Specifically, we consider the sequence of iterates given by

$$y(m + 1) = f[y(m)] + \delta\zeta(m) \tag{5}$$

where $\zeta(m)$ is a random number uniformly distributed between 0 and 1. δ is then a parameter that controls the size of the noise in this stochastic chaotic map, and is a measure of the degree to which new information affects the price dynamics of the system. If, for example, $\delta = 0.1$, then we can say that the iterates are determined by the tent map to within about a 10 percent accuracy[10] at each time step. From property 3 above, it is clear that these errors will accumulate very quickly, and after a few iterates, the sequence $y(m)$ will bear no resemblance to the one that would have been generated by the noiseless case with the same starting value, $y(0)$. In fact, given only the value of $y(0)$ the price movements will be essentially unpredictable after only a few time steps. These noisy iterates again satisfy the same unconditional distributional properties and autocorrelation functions as a sequence of random numbers uniformly distributed on $(0,1)$. Thus, if the noisy $y(m)$'s are used to generate the price paths of the underlying asset, and hence the $P(n)$'s in Equation 1, one might suppose that for all but very short times-to-expiration, T, the evaluation of the right-hand side of Equation 1, using Equation 5 to determine the price movements, would be indistinguishable from the standard Black-Scholes or binomial price result. As will be shown in the next section, this is not the case.

III. Results

To see the effect of noisy chaotic trajectories on the options price, computer simulations were performed using the following strategy: Values of S, K, r, q, u, d, and δ were chosen, with q chosen to satisfy the conditions for a risk-neutral economy. Then an initial value $y(0)$ was chosen and a sequence of values $y(m)$ for $m = 1$ to T was generated using Equation 5 with a good random number generator for the $\zeta(m)$'s. This sequence of $y(m)$'s was used to determine a path in price space by associating a price increase at time m if $y(m)$ was greater than $1 - q$, and a price drop otherwise. Using the same initial $y(0)$, another sequence was generated in the same way, and associated with another path. In our calculations, 2,000 paths were generated and used to determine $P(n)$ (which in the risk-neutral economy is the distribution of prices of the underlying asset at time T).

Figure 22-2 shows the right-hand side of Equation 1 as a function of time to expiration for various values of δ. Look first at Figure 22-2(a), in which results are presented for $\delta = 0.1$. Notice that the two sample options results computed with different values of $y(0)$ differ significantly from each other and from the standard binomial pricing model result, which is plotted on the same graph. Notice, in particular, that significant differences are apparent for times to expiration that greatly exceed the time scale over which the underlying asset price can be said to be reasonably predictable. With $\delta = 0.1$ this time of predictability is only of the order of 5 to 10 time steps or less. The error on the individual option price curves is about 2 percent. It is clear that these examples differ from the standard binomial pricing model result by much more than that. Figures 22-2(b) and 22-2(c) present the same kind of plots for the same values of the parameters S, K,

r, u, d, and q, and for δ = 0.25 and δ = 1.0, respectively. In Figure 22-2(b) one again sees significant differences between Equation 1 evaluated under the assumption of a noisy chaotic map, and those evaluated under the standard random walk assumption with the same distributional properties. In this case, however, the differences, although significant, are smaller than in Figure 22-2(a). Finally, in Figure 22-2(c), all the cases seem to be quite similar. In fact, this is what one expects, since when δ = 1.0 it is easy to see that the sequence of iterates, $y(m)$, is just a set of random numbers uniformly distributed on $(0, 1)$.

Although the results in Figure 22-2 convincingly illustrate that a noisy chaotic price sequence can alter the evaluation of Equation 1 when compared to a similarly distributed random walk, it is useful to make these

---

Figure 22-2a

The value of the right-hand side of Equation 1 as a function of time to expiration, assuming that the price movements of the underlying asset are driven by a noisy (chaotic) tent map, as described in the text. In each graph two examples of the evaluation for different starting values, $y(0)$, of the tent map iterate are shown. Also shown for comparison is the Black–Scholes result (dashed line). All graphs are compared with the values $S = 100$, $K = 95$, $u = 1.02$, $d = 0.98$, $r = 1.0$, and $q = 0.5$. (a) δ = 0.1, (b) δ = 0.25, and (c) δ = 1.0.

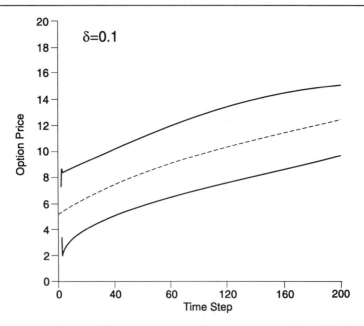

Figure 22-2b

Same as 22-2a, Except That δ = .25

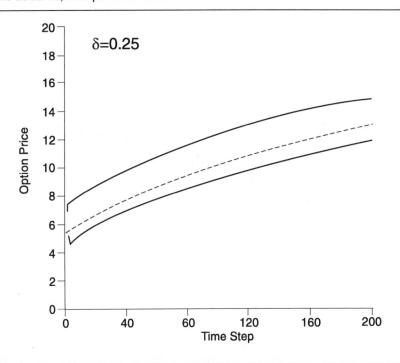

results somewhat more quantitative. Table 22-1 lists the average fractional deviation as a function of time to expiration between the noisy chaotic evaluation of Equation 1 for various values of δ and the purely random (Black-Scholes) result. Specifically, this table lists values of

$$\Psi(T) = \frac{\left[\dfrac{1}{N}\sum_i (C_i(T) - C_R(T)^2\right]^{1/2}}{C_R(T)} \tag{6}$$

where $C_R(T)$ is the standard random (Black–Scholes) options price and $C_i(T)$ is the noisy chaotic value of Equation 1 computed for some starting value, $y_i(0)$ of the tent map. The sum over i is a sum over N (in Table 22-1, $N = 100$) noisy chaotic evaluations computed with the same values of the options parameters and the same value of δ, but with different (randomly chosen) initial values, $y_i(0)$, of the tent map iterates.

Figure 22-2c

Same as 22-2a, Except That δ = 1.0

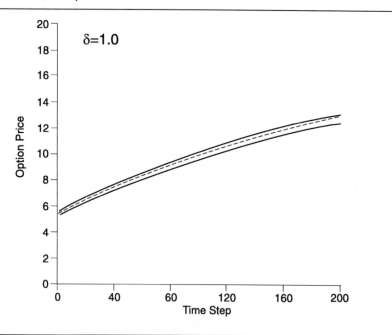

It is apparent that there is a persistent difference between the random and chaotic cases for all times to expiration. For example, if δ = 0.25, there is about an 8 percent difference between a typical noisy tent map evaluation of Equation 1 and the Black–Scholes result even for very long times. For shorter times the typical difference is, of course, much greater. Notice also that the difference between the chaotic and random results decreases as the noise increases, as one expects. In the case δ = 1.0, the values of Ψ are consistent with the values obtained by computing Ψ between different Monte-Carlo-generated samples of the standard binomial pricing formula with the same statistics. That is, for δ = 1.0 the C_i (T)'s are indistinguishable from the Black–Scholes result, given the statistical accuracy of the Monte Carlo calculations, as expected.

IV. Discussion

Perhaps the most startling result of the calculation is the observation that the evaluation of Equation 1, based on the assumption of a noisy chaotic

Table 22-1

Fractional difference between the Binomial Pricing Model and the right-hand side of Equation 1 when evaluated using the tent map for various strengths of the noise, as a function of time.

	Ψ		
T	$\delta = 0.1$	$\delta = 0.25$	$\delta = 1.0$
1	.34	.24	.01
2	.41	.26	.01
3	.42	.25	.02
4	.40	.24	.02
5	.38	.22	.02
6	.36	.21	.02
7	.35	.20	.02
8	.34	.20	.02
9	.33	.19	.02
10	.31	.19	.02
25	.22	.15	.02
50	.18	.11	.03
75	.15	.10	.03
100	.13	.10	.04
125	.12	.09	.04
150	.11	.07	.04
175	.11	.07	.04
200	.11	.07	.04

process for the underlying asset, differs from the usual random-walk-based options price for all times to expiration. To better appreciate why this is so unexpected, recall the following facts:

1. The chaotic tent map used in this model produces, even in the absence of noise, time series that are (linearly) indistinguishable from the corresponding random series of price movements, in the sense that (a) the unconditional distributions of the price movements are the same and (b) their autocorrelation functions are the same.

2. In the presence of noise, knowledge of the initial value of the map is quickly lost (the map has a positive Lyapunov exponent), and so, *given only the value y(0)* the paths that contribute to the evaluation of Equation 1 are, after a very short time, no more predictable than a random series.

On the basis of these facts, an apparently reasonable expectation would have been that the chaotic and random evaluations of Equation 1 differ significantly only for a very short initial period.

In fact, it is not difficult to understand the persistence of this difference. Recall that the usual binomial (or Black-Scholes) option formula has a strong dependence on the initial stock price, S. (If the striking price, K, is less than S, then this dependence is nearly linear for a broad range of values of the parameters in the options formula.) If one looks at the paths in price space generated by the noisy chaotic process, one sees that with a given $y(0)$, the paths are relatively similar for the first few time steps, and after that look like a collection of random walks. (The initial time over which the paths appear to be similar is determined by a combination of δ and the value of the Lyapunov exponent, which for the tent map is ln 2.) Thus, the distribution of prices, S', a few time steps into the future is less random than the one that would result from a random walk (with the same starting asset price, S, and the same values of u, d, r, and q), and so we have some predictive power for the price of the underlying asset over this time scale. In general, the expectation value (and certainly the distribution) of S' will not be the same as the initial starting price, S. Therefore, Equation 1 evaluated for a noisy chaotic process will resemble the random walk options price but with a different effective starting price, which will be close to the expectation value of S', the price at the time at which the set of noisy chaotic paths begins to appear random. Thus, if the underlying asset undergoes price movements generated by a noisy chaotic process, the value of Equation 1 will differ for all times from that associated with an underlying asset whose price path is generated by a random process, even though all initial parameters defining the option are the same and all the unconditional distributions and autocorrelations of the price movements are the same.[11] This heuristic explanation of these results is also consistent with the observation that as δ approaches 1, the nonlinear chaotic evaluation of Equation 1 approaches the Black–Scholes result. The point is that for larger δ, the set of paths in price space appear random sooner, so that S', the distribution of prices of the underlying asset at the time at which the set of price paths begins to look random, becomes closer to the original starting price, S.

A few more comments should be made concerning this result:

1. The fundamental origin of the discrepancy between the binomial pricing evaluation of Equation 1 and the tent map evaluation can be traced to the fact that processes with different conditional distributions may have the same unconditional distributions. The tent map has the same unconditional distributions as a sequence of random

numbers uniformly distributed on the unit interval, but has different conditional distributions. In a random process the $(n + 1)^{st}$ number is, by definition, unrelated to the nth number. In the noisy tent map this is not the case. Because $y(0)$ is the same for a given evaluation of Equation 1 with the noisy tent map, the evaluation of Equation 1 depends on the conditional distributions for this stochastic nonlinear process. The unexpected result of this chapter is that this dependence persists for all times-to-expiration, T.

2. This chapter does not intend to suggest that the noisy tent map is a realistic model of the price movements of some asset. Rather, it is a simple example of a chaotic map that illustrates the expected effects of nonlinearities on options calculations. Qualitatively, the behavior found can be expected in most situations in which an underlying asset's price contains some deterministic nonlinear component. It is not necessary that the nonlinearities be chaotic. In fact, in the presence of nonchaotic nonlinear price movements, it is expected that the evaluation of Equation 1 will differ even more strongly from the standard Black–Scholes result than in the chaotic case discussed here. The reason is that, generally, nonchaotic behavior has a greater degree of predictability than chaotic behavior.

   Although the noisy tent map is not necessarily a realistic model for asset price movements, it does contain ingredients that are likely to be a part of a more complete description of financial markets. Since the financial markets are complex self-regulating systems, they have their own internal dynamics, which affect the behavior of price movements in a constant external environment. It is of course possible that such dynamics lead to a simple equilibrium (or fixed-point) distribution of prices in the absence of new external information. This fixed-point behavior is the simplest kind of behavior a complex system can manifest. But it is not the only possible behavior, nor (as studies of self-regulating systems in the physical sciences reveal) is it the most common. Fortified by the empirical studies cited in Notes 2–5, one can be encouraged to consider behaviors for financial markets other than fixed-point behavior. In that case, the use of a noisy nonlinear iterative map to describe price movements is appropriate: The deterministic aspect of the map models the internal market dynamics, and the stochastic noise models the influence on the market of new, exogenous information.

3. Notice that even though the *set* of noisy chaotic paths appears random only after some initial time period, any one of the paths will still appear to be random for *all* times when analyzed according to tests based on

autocorrelation functions and unconditional price distributions. Since one can observe only one price history, one might (mistakenly) believe that the process producing that sequence is random even if it is not. Under such as assumption, one's expectation of the value of the right-hand side of Equation 1 would be wrong for all T. To distinguish properly between randomness and chaos, one must have recourse to methods of analysis based on ideas from the study of nonlinear systems.

4. Two important effects, of considerable significance for investment strategies, follow from the observation that a single price history that appears random may, in fact, be driven by a noisy nonlinear process. First, there may be unrecognized short-term price predictability, and second, as shown in this chapter, there may be systematic mispricing of the associated options *over all time scales*. Chaotic price movements are predictable only over short times. Nonetheless, using options may allow one to gain a long-term advantage from this short-term information.

These observations indicate the need for further examination of the problem of options pricing in the presence of a nonlinear process for asset price movements. This work has shown that the evaluation of the usual expression for an option based on a reasonable expectation that price movements are random may be quite inaccurate if the real price process is nonlinear, even though all unconditional distributions and autocorrelation functions are the same. On the other hand, a derivation of the arbitrage-free options price for chaotic price movements requires a study of the construction and evolution of a properly hedged portfolio in a nonlinear market. It is important to stress that the evaluation of Equation 1 for a noisy chaotic process may not be the same as the correct arbitrage-free options price in a nonlinear market. Work on this problem is in progress.

Contrary to naive expectations, a noisy nonlinear process for the price movements of an asset may affect the calculation of the price of an option written on that asset for all times-to-expiration. The origin of this effect is the fact that in the presence of nonlinear effects, the expectations of future price movements are dependent on conditional distributions of the underlying process. Thus, an option computed for a nonlinear process may differ from that computed for the random process with the same unconditional distributions.

Given a knowledge of the underlying nonlinear process, the correct arbitrage-free options price requires the construction of a hedged portfolio. But on the basis of the work in this chapter, such an options price may differ from the Black–Scholes expression for all times to expiration. In this context, knowledge of conditional price distributions is tantamount to the ability to make short-term predictions in the asset price. Such knowledge may result in improvements in the calculation of long-term options prices.

Many financial sequences have been shown to have significant nonlinear components. Using the techniques of nonlinear analysis, it is possible in those cases to better understand short-term price movements. Such an analysis may improve short-term price predictability and, with the use of options, may allow one to realize long-term improvement in investment strategies.

Acknowledgment

I am grateful to the Center for the Studies of Futures Markets at Columbia University for partial support for this work. I also thank Mark Powers for his encouragement, David Hirschfeld for comments on the manuscript, and Matthew Green for help with the numerical simulations.

Notes

1 For a pedagogical review of nonlinear dynamics and chaos, and its applicability to finance, see R. Savit (1988a). This is also Chapter 2 of this book.

2 See W. Brock, W. Dechert, and J. Scheinkman (1986); W. Brock and W. Dechert (1987); W. Brock (1986).

3 The BDS test is a test against an IID null. The tests of Savit and Green provide more specific information about the nature of the dependencies within a data set. See R. Savit and M. Green (1991 a) and (1991b).

4 See W. Brock and C. Sayers (1985); W. Brock (1988), and references therein.

5 J. Scheinkman and B. LeBaron (1986); D. Hsieh (1987).

6 R. Savit (1988b).

7 For clarity, the effects of nonlinearities are discussed in the context of a risk-neutral economy. In other environments the interpretation of the option price is somewhat different, but still involves a sum, the argument of which is still related to the expected price movements of the underlying assets. As will become clear, therefore, similar nonlinear effects may be expected in these other environments also. Furthermore, for convenience, the calculations will be carried out in the context of a discrete binomial version of the options pricing formula. But the dis-

tinction between the continuum Black-Scholes result and its various discrete time versions is unimportant here, and so these differences will be ignored in our discussion.

8 H. Sakai and H. Tokumaru (1980).

9 Observation of the price movement at time m contains information about the value of $y(m)$ but in a discrete process does not determine it, even in the absence of noise. In the limit that the price movements take on continuous values, however, it is possible to relate the size of the price movement to the value of $y(m)$, and so, in the absence of noise, determine the y's directly from the price movements. Of course, such a determination requires an analysis that goes beyond the study of ordinary autocorrelation functions.

10 Adding noise to the tent map as in Equation 5 will sometimes produce an iterate that is greater than 1 or less than zero. It is assumed, therefore, that there are periodic boundary conditions on the tent map, so that if $y(m + 1)$ is greater than 1, it is reset according to $y(m + 1) \rightarrow y(m + 1) - 1$, and if $y(m)$ is less than 1, it is reset according to $y(m + 1) \rightarrow y(m + 1) + 1$. The iterates are then always between zero and 1. A little thought will reveal that this procedure still results in y's that uniformly distributed on the interval $(0,1)$.

11 The early time behavior of the noisy chaotic price paths depends on $y(0)$. For some values of $y(0)$, the options price computed using Equation 3 will be fairly close to the standard random walk result. However, these are special cases, and as shown in Table 22-1, generally the noisy chaotic and random evaluations of Equation 1 are significantly different.

References

Brock, W., *Journal of Economic Theory* (1986), 40, 168 and references therein.

Brock, W., W. Dechert, and J. Scheinkman. "A Test for Independence Based on the Correlation Dimension." Unpublished, 1986.

Brock, W., and W. Dechert. "Theorems on Distinguishing Deterministic from Random Systems." University of Wisconsin preprint, unpublished, 1987.

Brock, W., and C. Sayers. "Is the Business Cycle Characterized by Deterministic Chaos?" University of Wisconsin preprint, 1985.

Brock, W. "Nonlinearity and Complex Dynamics in Economics and Finance," in *The Economy as an Evolving Complex System*, D. Pines, ed. New York: Addison-Wesley, 1988.

Hsieh, D. "Testing for Nonlinear Dependence in Foreign Exchange Rates: 1974–1983." University of Chicago preprint, 1987.

Sakai, H., and H. Tokumaru. IEEE Trans. Acoust. Speech Signal Process, V.I. ASSP-28 (1980), 588.

Savit, R., and M. Green. *Physica* D50 (1991a), 95.

Savit, R. and M. Green, *Physica* D50 (1991b), 521.

Savit, R. "When Random Is Not Random: An Introduction to Chaos in Market Prices." *The Journal of Futures Markets*, 8 (1988a), 271–291. This is also Chapter 2 of this book.

Savit, R. "Notes on the Price Behavior of Fixed Income Instruments." Unpublished (1988b).

Scheinkman, J., and B. LeBaron. "Nonlinear Dynamics and Stock Returns." University of Chicago preprint, 1986.

23

CHAOS, TAXES, STABILIZATION, AND TURNOVER

By Sherrill Shaffer

Introduction

One shortcoming of chaos theory that has hindered its economic applications to date has been its relative dearth of new insights on appropriate public policy. For this reason, Scheinkman (1990) evaluates chaos theory as having advanced too little to affect the work of economic practitioners. Bullard and Butler (1993) raise the more specific criticism that no new rationale for stabilization policy has thus far emerged from chaos theory that leads to different conclusions than previous, more conventional theories of the economy, even though stabilization policy rules are often more efficacious in chaotic models than in linear stochastic models.

The contribution of this chapter is threefold. First, fixed points of chaotic systems—or, to some extent, orbits in the neighborhood of fixed points—can yield higher mean or present value outcomes than other orbits in addition to more stable outcomes. Thus, the stable outcome in a chaotic system, unlike that in a typical linear stochastic model, can benefit even risk-neutral agents, thereby providing a qualitatively new rationale for stabilization policy. Second, some simple policy instruments, even if implemented uniformly rather than countercyclically, can modify the chaotic time path of economic variables and thereby serve either as potential stabilization tools or, if misapplied, as unintended sources of destabilization. Thus, chaotic models can lead to new stabilization tools, including previously unrecognized stabilization implications of existing tools. This point is illustrated for the specific case of a proportional corporate income tax in an extension of a simple model of Shaffer (1991). Third, such models may provide a hitherto missing theoretical basis for the long-standing notion that, apart from tacit collusion or first-mover advantages enjoyed by dominant firms, the ranking of firms by size or market share will normally fluctuate substantially over time.

The Model

Consider a firm that invests in each period a fixed fraction of its profits from the previous period:

$$I_t = \beta \pi_{t-1} \tag{1}$$

where β is a positive constant not exceeding unity.[1] Assume that the marginal efficiency of investment (MEI) is declining. Here we assume a linear form for convenience, although qualitatively similar results can be obtained for more general forms. Investment earns a marginal return of:

$$R(I_t) = a - bI_t \tag{2}$$

where $a > 0$ and $b > 0$. The corresponding total return in the same period is:

$$E_t = \int_0^{I_t} R(i)\, di = aI_t - bI_t^2 /2. \tag{3}$$

In subsequent periods these returns continue but in successively smaller amounts, depreciating at the rate d. All profits are taxed at the proportional rate τ, so the firm's *after-tax* profit in each period equals:

$$\pi_t = (1 - d)\pi_{t-1} + (1 - \tau)E_t$$

$$= [1 - d + (1 - \tau)a\beta]\pi_{t-1} - (1 - \tau)b\beta^2\pi_{t-1}^2 /2 \tag{4}$$

after substituting from Equations 1 and 3.[2]

   Now setting $A = 1 - d + (1 - \tau)a\beta$ and $\gamma = (1 - \tau)b\beta^2/(2A)$, we express Equation 4 in the form:

$$x_t = Ax_{t-1}(1 - x_{t-1}) \tag{5}$$

where x_t is defined as $\gamma \pi_t$, and π_t is expressed in units such that x_t is bounded between 0 and 1.[3] Equation 5, the logistic equation, is a form that has been widely studied and is known to generate chaotic time paths for certain values of A [see, for example, May (1976), Feigenbaum (1978), and Collet and Eckmann (1980)]. Shaffer (1991) has shown that small changes in the value of A can lead to large changes in the volatility of x over time, corresponding to changes in the value of the associated average Lyapunov exponent as a function of A. For example, small changes of A in the range 3.73–3.74 or in the range 3.82–3.83 can lead to changes in the sign of the average Lyapunov exponent, reflecting transitions of the system between chaotic and periodic time paths [see Jensen (1987)].[4] Although this model is purely deterministic, previous research has shown that deterministic chaos can still be clearly distinguished even if embedded in stochastic noise [see, for example, Schuster (1984), p. 109].

First-Moment Effects

The first property we wish to explore is the effect on the mean outcome, or on the present value of the stream of outcomes, of changes in initial values or parameters in the model. This line of inquiry departs from previous studies by focusing on the first moment rather than the second moment of the time path. Having shown how Equation 4 maps into Equation 5, and in particular that π_t is monotonically related to x_t, it suffices (and is simpler) to analyze the latter. Table 23-1 illustrates for particular parameter values that the mean outcome is about $1/2$ for all initial values other than the fixed point $x_0 = 1 - 1/A = 0.75$ for $A = 4$; or the degenerate point $x_0 = 1/2 \pm (1/4 - 1/A)^{1/2}$, which yields $x = 0$ after the second iteration. The present value of the outcomes is likewise highest at the fixed point (for $A > 2$) and, interestingly, is modestly higher in the neighborhood of the fixed point as well, suggesting that the fixed point need not be exactly attained in order to generate a first-moment benefit. The reason is that initial values near the fixed point tend to persist during the first few periods. Similar results obtain using different values of A and the discount rate r.

To see that such results are not limited to the logistic model, consider the chaotic Hénon map (see Ott et al. [1990]) given by:

$$x_{t+1} = 1.4 + 0.3x_{t-1} - x_t^2. \tag{6}$$

This system generates values of x between roughly –1.8 and 1.8 with a mean value less than 0.36; it also has a fixed point at roughly $x = 0.88$,

Table 23-1

Mean and Present Value of Chaotic Series Generated by Equation 5 with A = 4

Initial Value	Mean Value	Present Value	
		(r = 0.1)	(r = 0.05)
0.1	0.500	5.14	9.72
0.2	0.501	5.49	10.02
0.3	0.499	5.50	10.51
0.4	0.500	5.26	10.39
0.5	2.5×10^{-5}	1.41	1.45
0.6	0.500	5.46	10.59
0.7	0.498	5.90	11.03
0.72	0.499	6.10	10.74
0.74	0.502	6.47	11.32
0.75	0.750	8.25	15.75
0.76	0.501	6.39	10.86
0.78	0.500	6.12	11.83
0.8	0.501	6.10	10.69
0.9	0.501	5.94	10.46

Calculated numerically through 60,000 periods (to machine precision convergence); mean and present value for $x_0 = 0.75$ and $x_0 = 0.5$ confirmed analytically. Present value calculations discount in period t by $1/(1 + r)^t$.

greater than the mean. There may be other chaotic systems for which the fixed point is less than the mean value of non-steady-state orbits; if so, the more general lesson would be that transition to a fixed point may entail significant first-moment effects in chaotic systems, unlike in conventional linear stochastic systems.

Taxes

We next study the effect of a constant proportional income tax. Since A is defined in our model as a function of the tax rate τ—or, more generally, because $\partial \pi_t / \partial \pi_{t-1}$ is a function of τ from Equation 4—the immediate conclusion is that the level of the tax rate has a direct impact on the time path of profits and investment. Moreover, within some ranges of A, small changes in τ can trigger qualitative transitions of the profit and investment streams from periodic to chaotic behavior or vice versa, with associated changes in volatility.

As such behavior does not typify stochastic or nonchaotic deterministic models of the economy, we have here an example in which a chaotic model implies qualitatively and quantitatively different effects of a common policy tool. In particular, if the economy is chaotic, a judiciously chosen tax rate may be employed in some circumstances as a stabilization tool; conversely, a tax rate that is chosen for other purposes without regard to its dynamic implications may unintentionally increase the volatility of profits and investment over time. Moreover, unlike previously analyzed stabilization policy tools, the effect of the corporate income tax on the time path results from its *level* rather than from a countercyclically chosen pattern of *variations*.

The depreciation rate d also affects the time path of profits and investment through A. Thus, for instance, if an accelerated pace of R&D or product imitation by rivals increases d, then τ would need to be reduced to maintain the same time path; otherwise, even small changes in d can prove either stabilizing or destabilizing. However, the amount by which the tax rate should be changed is a function of profits, since d enters the intertemporal time dependence of profits in a fundamentally different way than does the tax rate. In particular, note that:

$$\partial \pi_t / \partial \pi_{t-1} = 1 - d + (1 - \tau)a\beta - b\beta^2(1 - \tau)\pi_{t-1} \qquad (7)$$

so the change in τ needed to offset a given change in d, leaving $\partial \pi_t / \partial \pi_{t-1}$ unchanged, is $\Delta \tau / \Delta d = 1/(b\beta^2 \pi_{t-1} - a\beta)$. This dependence of $\Delta \tau / \Delta d$ on profits implies that tax policy is not a practical method of neutralizing the dynamic impact of changes in the depreciation rate.

The proportional tax can affect stability only indirectly, by altering the current outcome, the fixed point of the system, and consequently the gap between the current outcome and the fixed point. As shown in the previous section, such changes can affect the first moment as well as the second moment of the time path. More complex techniques developed by Ott et al. (1990) and Auerbach et al. (1992), which in an economic context would correspond to dynamic lump sum tax formulas or the equivalent, can stabilize a chaotic system at arbitrary levels chosen within the feasible range—again with first-moment implications.

Asymmetries and Rank Turnover

The simple model above does not reflect asymmetries across firms in either the profit rate or the MEI schedule. But those features can be addressed within the same model, by noting that a uniform tax rate applied across firms of different sizes or facing different MEI schedules will yield different time paths of profits and investment for each firm. This result, in turn, may corroborate the long-held belief that competition produces substantial turnover in firm rank or instability of market shares [see, for example, Caves and Porter (1978) or Rhoades and Rutz (1981)], even though traditional stochastic modeling fails to provide a basis for that belief [see Shaffer (1986)].

Table 23-2 reports simulations of a duopoly characterized by Equation 5 for combinations of different starting values and different MEI schedules for each firm. If we interpret the x values as monotonically associated with each firm's output levels, then we may infer relative size rankings of firms across columns and observe how those rankings change over time. With one notable exception, comparisons across *pairs* of columns indicate that duopolists following the respective time paths would have exchanged rank nearly half of the maximum possible number of times: four out of eight times in columns 1 versus 3; four out of nine times in columns 1 versus 4, 2 versus 3, or 3 versus 4; and three out of eight times in columns 2 versus 4. These results support the notion of rapid churning in active markets.

By contrast, in a random walk model, the probability of as many as three rank changes out of eight possible changes between two firms is only 0.14, while the probability of as many as four out of eight possible rank changes is less than 0.05, if the market shares follow a random walk and the firms start with equal shares [see Shaffer (1986)]. These probabilities

---

Table 23-2

Rank Turnover in a Chaotic Duopoly

Period	$x_t = 4x_{t-1}(1 - x_{t-1})$		$x_t = 3.9x_{t-1}(1 - x_{t-1})$	
1	.1	.2	.1	.2
2	.36	.64	.351	.624
3	.922	.922	.888	.915
4	.289	.289	.387	.303
5	.822	.822	.925	.824
6	.585	.585	.271	.566
7	.971	.971	.771	.958
8	.113	.113	.690	.156
9	.402	.402	.835	.514
10	.962	.962	.538	.974

are even smaller if the random walk is in sizes rather than market shares, or if the firms begin with unequal sizes (ibid.).

A different phenomenon characterizes columns 1 versus 2. In the second period, the value of x_2 in column 1 equals the value of $1 - x_2$ in column 2. As a result, the subsequent time path is identical for both columns in every period thereafter, and no rank turnover could ever occur. Again, while not supporting the frequent turnover hypothesis, this outcome stands in contrast with that obtained under a random walk.

Table 23-3 extends this comparison between the chaotic and random walk models to a longer time horizon in which as many as 50 changes of rank are possible. The chaotic process generally produces about one rank change every other turn. By contrast, a random walk in market shares will generate this high a frequency of turnover with a probability of 10^{-6} or less.

The reason why chaos implies much more frequent turnover than does a linear stochastic model is that, when size or shares follow a random walk, the most likely outcome lies along the 45° line in a delay plot (as shown in Figure 23-1), which indicates no turnover.[5] Deviations from this locus are nonsystematic (the result of random noise only) and nonpersistent (since the expected outcome in the period following the deviation is back on the 45° line). By contrast, any chaotic attractor implies systematic, persistent deviations from the 45° line in a delay plot, as shown in Figure 23-1 for the specific case of Equation 5.[6] Such deviations translate into frequent turnover. Consequently, if we observe frequent turnover in a particular market, those observations might constitute indirect evidence of chaotic behavior as opposed to a linear stochastic dynamic process.

One policy implication of this contrast is that, to the extent that chaotic models imply radically more frequent turnover than do traditional linear

Table 23-3

Comparison of Chaotic versus Random Turnover
out of 50 Possible Changes in Rank

Starting Values	Values of A in Eq. 3	# Changes	Prob. that Random Walk Yields at Least as Many Changes
.1, .1	4, 3.9	24	3.7×10^{-7}
.2, .2	4, 3.9	24	3.7×10^{-7}
.1, .2	4, 3.9	25	1.2×10^{-7}
.2, .1	4, 3.9	23	1.1×10^{-6}
.1, .2	3.9, 3.9	33	1.5×10^{-12}

Figure 23-1

Delay Plot for Random Walk versus Chaotic Process

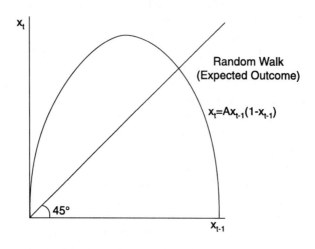

x_t

Random Walk
(Expected Outcome)

$x_t = Ax_{t-1}(1-x_{t-1})$

45°

x_{t-1}

---

models, an externally imposed stabilization policy would be needed in the former to achieve the same level of stability that naturally characterizes the latter. This is another way in which a chaotic model can imply a greater need for stabilization policy.

Conclusion

Recent criticisms of chaos theory have focused on its lack of new policy implications. This chapter has derived three such implications. First, stabilization policy can confer a first-moment benefit in a chaotic model, unlike in a linear stochastic model. Second, simple traditional policy tools can affect the time path of outcomes, including in some cases both the first and second moments, even when applied in a fixed rather than explicitly countercyclical manner. Third, frequent rank turnover of firms in a market—sometimes observed in practice but not consistent with linear stochastic models—can be explained by chaotic models. Each of these three results warrants additional research, and further points to the possibility of other overlooked implications of chaos theory for the behavior of markets and regulatory policy.

Acknowledgment

This chapter embodies the views of the author and does not necessarily reflect the views of the Federal Reserve System or of the Federal Reserve Bank of Philadelphia. The author is grateful to Adrian Tschoegl for helpful comments.

Notes

1 If $\beta < 1$, the remainder of profits may be distributed as dividends, retained as cash, etc.

2 Since π is defined as after-tax profits, π_{t-1} in Equation 4 already incorporates the $(1 - \tau)$ factor implicitly and only E_t must be explicitly multiplied by $(1 - \tau)$.

3 Note that this form does not depend qualitatively on the assumption of gradual depreciation of returns. For example, if $d = 1$, each dollar invested yields returns only in the current period, yet the time path of profits is still described by Equation 5. Similarly, if $d = 0$ (no depreciation), Equation 5 still holds.

4 Sensitivity of the time path to parameter values, as well as to initial conditions, is a generic property of chaotic systems rather than a unique property of the particular functional form used here.

5 If there is drift in sizes, then the line would have a slope of 1 plus the drift term rather than 45°. Alternatively, stochastic IID market shares or sizes would uniformly fill the space in a delay plot, but such outcomes are not realistic.

6 In certain other chaotic processes the structure of the attractor would involve periods t versus t + k for some k > 1; over the corresponding lag, the stochastic process would generate the same delay plot in expectation as in Figure 23-1.

References

Auerbach, D., C. Grebogi, E. Ott, and J. A. Yorke. "Controlling Chaos in High-Dimensional Systems." *Physical Review Letters* 69 (24) (1992), 3479–3482.

Bullard, J., and A. Butler. "Nonlinearity and Chaos in Economic Models: Implications for Policy Decisions." *Economic Journal* 103 (July 1993), 849–867.

Caves, R. E., and M. E. Porter. "Market Structure, Oligopoly, and Stability of Market Shares." *Journal of Industrial Economics* 26 (1978), 289–313.

Collet, P., and J. P. Eckmann. *Iterated Maps on the Unit Interval as Dynamical Systems*. Boston: Birkhauser, 1980.

Feigenbaum, M. J. "Quantitative Universality for a Class of Nonlinear Transformations." *Journal of Statistical Physics* 19 (1978), 25–52.

Jensen. "Classical Chaos." *American Scientist* 75 (1987), 168–181.

May, R. M. "Simple Mathematical Models with Very Complicated Dynamics." *Nature* 261 (1976), 459.

Ott, E., C. Grebogi, and J. A. Yorke. "Controlling Chaos." *Physical Review Letters* 64 (11) (1990), 1196–1199.

Rhoades, S. A., and R. D. Rutz. "A Reexamination and Extension of the Relationship between Concentration and Firm Rank Stability." *Review of Economics and Statistics* 63 (1981), 446–451.

Scheinkman, J. "Nonlinearities in Economic Dynamics." *Economic Journal* 100 (Conference) (1990), 33–48.

Schuster, H. G. *Deterministic Chaos: An Introduction*. New York: VCH Publishers, 1984.

Shaffer, S. "Does Competition Imply Frequent Rank Turnover?" *Scandinavian Journal of Economics* 88 (1986), 511–527.

Shaffer, S. "Structural Shifts and the Volatility of Chaotic Markets." *Journal of Economic Behavior and Organization* 15 (1991), 201–214.

24

Neural Learning of Chaotic Time Series Invariants

By Gustavo Deco, Bernd Schuermann, and Robert R. Trippi

1. Introduction

The most common assumption in analyzing prices of securities and other market-traded financial instruments is that successive price changes are independent of the history of previous price changes. In ex post analyses based on this assumption, price fluctuations are assumed to be purely stochastic, generated by one of several common noise processes. Until recently, empirical support for this (weak) form of the efficient markets hypothesis, in the form of numerous published statistical tests, has been compelling. For example, serial correlations of the returns on stocks and stock indexes are typically so small as to be unable to be exploited to achieve abnormal returns [for a survey of this literature see Lorie, Dodd, and Hamilton, Ch. 4 (1985) and Fama (1970)].

Within the past decade, however, there has been a growing interest in applying nonlinear models to identify deterministic components of price time series that may have eluded conventional tests, mainly those based on linear statistical models. For example, Scheinkman and LeBaron (1989) attribute a significant portion of stock index movements to deterministic nonlinear phenomena, Blank (1991) comes to much the same conclusion with respect to financial and commodity futures contracts, Hsieh (1989) found significant nonlinear dependence in foreign exchange rates, and Brock and Sayers (1988) examine deterministic nonlinear dependence in macroeconomic time series. In the type of nonlinear dependence found in these and in many other economic studies, the series mimics one that might be generated by a stochastic process. Such pseudostochastic processes are referred to as chaotic processes.

The major problem in such research is the difficulty of distinguishing between deterministic chaos and a purely random process. The most important characteristic of chaotic dynamical systems is their short-term predictability. It is well understood by now that long-term forecasting of the behavior of chaotic systems is not possible due to the exponential divergence of trajectories in such systems [Eckmann and Ruelle (1985)], typified by simple bifurcation. However, a great variety of conventional models that yield very accurate results for short-term prediction [Crutchfield and McNamara (1987), Abarbanel et al. (1989, 1990)] have been developed in the last decade.

Nonlinear modeling with neural networks offers a promising approach for studying the prediction of chaotic time series. An appreciable amount of recent literature deals with this subject [e.g., Farmer and Sidorovich (1987), Lapedes and Farber (1989), Casdagli (1989), Weigend et al. (1990), Wolpert and Miall (1990), Albano et al. (1992)] but the comparisons performed therein are restricted to comparisons of prediction errors. Principe et al. (1992) analyzed the modeling of chaotic time series with feedforward neural networks as well as the dynamical invariants of the real time series and of the trained model. The authors claimed that the backpropagation learning rule employed to train the neural network by minimizing the prediction error does not consistently indicate that the neural-network-based model has indeed captured the dynamics of the system. They demonstrated empirically for the Hénon map that the largest Lyapunov exponent and the Correlation Dimension are not captured by the neural model they used.

In this chapter [elaborating on Deco and Schuermann (1994)] we analyze neural network models of chaotic time series by comparing two dynamical invariants that characterize the chaotic attractor—the largest Lyapunov exponent and the Correlation Dimension. This approach permits us to claim that a learning algorithm really captures "chaos" if it learns the dynamical invariants of a chaotic dynamical system. Our work differs from that of Principe et al. in that we make a more thorough investigation for feedforward neural nets, and that we employ and analyze recurrent neural architectures. The trained networks are employed as recurrent models that generate a "learned" time series. Only if the dynamics of the original data were captured are the dynamic invariants resulting from these data reproduced. For further checks, Poincaré maps and Fourier power spectra are employed for dynamical comparison between models and data as well.

A stable learning algorithm for the recurrent architectures is presented for modeling chaotic time series. The learning algorithm is based on the recurrent algorithm "Backpropagation through Time" [Pearlmutter (1989)]. It consists of a gradient correction through time for a neural network that includes recurrences only in those variables that in the real dynamical system are also recurrent. The idea is that when the neural model begins to learn the real system in an accurate form, then it is itself chaotic and updates of the weights are therefore unstable ("to model something chaotic you should be also chaotic"). In order to avoid this effect, typical of chaotic time series, a stochastic "sample-by-sample" update of the weights with a forgetting function given by the largest Lyapunov exponent is introduced. In this fashion, learning consistent with the inherent limit of predictability is performed by a chaotic recurrent neural network. A recurrent architecture is introduced that captures very efficiently the dynamics of strange attractors. As a special case of the recurrent models we recover the feedforward model of Principe et al. We show for various examples that, contrary to the claim of Principe et al., the dynamics is indeed captured by this feedforward model as soon as enough hidden units and enough training data are used.

In this chapter we note a novel type of overtraining, which corresponds to the forgetting of the largest Lyapunov exponent during learning. We call this phenomenon dynamical overtraining. A novel penalty term is introduced in the cost function that involves the Lyapunov exponent of the network and eliminates dynamical overtraining (forgetting of the Lyapunov exponent) discovered in this study. We include also a thorough numerical study performed on the Hénon and Belousov–Zhabotinskii maps.

2. Dynamical Modeling of Deterministic Chaotic Systems

In this section we describe the standard methods for nonlinear modeling and the essential dynamical invariants of chaotic dynamic systems.

Takens Embedding Method

Given a time series of a single (one-dimensional) measured variable of a multidimensional dynamical system, the aim of forecasting is to predict the future evolution of this variable. On the other hand, good forecasting is related to good modeling, which implies the extraction of the dynamics (dynamical invariants) of the real system. It has been shown that in nonlinear deterministic chaotic systems it is possible to determine the dynamical invariants and geometric structure of the many-variable dynamic system that produces the single measurement [Takens (1980), Sauer et al. (1991)] from the observation of a single dynamical variable. The method is called *phase-space reconstruction* and results in a d-dimensional "embedding space" in which the dynamics of the multidimensional attractor is captured.

Given is a chaotic dynamic system

$$\vec{y}(t + 1) = \vec{g}\,[\vec{y}\,(t)\,]\,. \tag{2.1}$$

Let us define an observable measurement

$$x\,(t) = f[\vec{y}(t)]. \tag{2.2}$$

The Takens Theorem [Takens (1980)] assures that for an embedding

$$\vec{\xi}(t) = [x\,(t)\,,x\,(t - \tau)\,,...,\,x\,(t - d\tau)\,] \tag{2.3}$$

a map

$$\vec{\xi}(t + 1) = \vec{F}\,[\vec{\xi}(t)\,] \tag{2.4}$$

exists and has the same dynamical characteristics as the original system $\vec{y}\,(t)$ if $d = 2D+1$, where D is the dimension of the strange attractor. This sufficient condition may be relaxed to $d > 2D$ [cf. Sauer et al. (1991)]. This means that all the coordinate-independent properties of g(.) and F(.) will be identical. The proper choice of d and τ is an important topic of investigation [see Buzug and Pfister (1992), Liebert and Schuster (1989), Liebert et al. (1991), Pawelzik and Schuster (1991)]. In this chapter we will experiment with benchmark examples for which these two variables are well known. The goal of neural network modeling is to learn the map given by $\vec{F}(.)$ in Equation 2.4 so that the dynamical invariants of the neural model and of the embedded map (or original multidimensional dynamic system) are the same.

Dynamical Invariant 1: Lyapunov Exponents

The largest Lyapunov exponent contains information on how far in the future predictions are possible. The Lyapunov spectrum has proven to be one of the most useful dynamical invariants that characterize chaotic dynamic systems. The Lyapunov exponents provide us with a measure of the averaged exponential rates of divergence or convergence of neighbor orbits in phase space [Wolf et al. (1985)]. If at least one positive Lyapunov exponent exists, the dynamical system is said to be chaotic, and the initial small differences between two trajectories will diverge exponentially. We will concentrate our study on the largest Lyapunov exponent λ_m. The value of the largest Lyapunov exponent reflects the time scale on which system dynamics become unpredictable. Let us consider an embedding n-dimensional space. After some iterations, a small n-sphere becomes an n-ellipsoid. The i-th one-dimensional Lyapunov exponent is then defined in terms of the length of the ellipsoidal principal axis $p_i(t)$:

$$\lambda_i = \lim_{t \to \infty} \frac{1}{t} \ln \left(\frac{p_i(t)}{p_i(0)} \right). \tag{2.5}$$

The Lyapunov exponents reflect the deformation (expansion or contraction) of the map in the different directions of phase space.

In cases where only experimental data are given but not the function that generates the map, we have used the algorithm of Wolf et al. (1985) based on the Gram-Schmidt orthonormalization method and on the definition given by Equation 2.5. When the analytical form of the map is known (e.g., by neural networks after learning) the Lyapunov coefficient can be calculated directly. In the case of a one-dimensional map $x(t+1) = f([x(t)]$ the largest Lyapunov coefficient can be calculated by [Beck and Schlogl (1993)]

$$\lambda_m = \int dx\, P(x) \ln \left(\frac{\partial f}{\partial x} \right) \tag{2.6}$$

where $P(x)$ is the probability distribution of the measurements x.

Dynamical Invariant 2: Fractal and Grassberger–Procaccia Correlation Dimension

The Fractal or Correlation Dimension gives an indication of the complexity of the dynamical system. Chaotic attractors can be characterized by the

Haussdorff fractal dimension, which is smaller than the number of degrees of freedom [Froehling et al. (1980)]. A more reliable measurement of the dimension of a strange attractor was introduced by Grassberger and Procaccia (1983) and is defined as the slope

$$v = \frac{\partial}{\partial \ln (r)} \, ln \, [C \, (r)] \tag{2.7}$$

where $C \, (r)$ is the correlation integral given by

$$C \, (r) = lim_{N \to \infty} \frac{1}{N^2} \sum_{i,j}^{N} \theta \, (r - | \vec{x_i} - \vec{x_j} |) \tag{2.8}$$

with the Heaviside function $\theta \, (.)$. This measure takes into account the different frequency with which a region in an attractor is visited and therefore is more sensitive to the dynamics of the process than the Haussdorff fractal dimension. An interesting information-theoretic interpretation of v by entropy is also shown in the paper of Grassberger and Procaccia (1983). In the present study we will use v as one of the dynamical invariants to be compared between the real system and the model.

Power Spectrum

The power spectrum $S(\omega)$ of a scalar signal $x(t)$ is defined as the square of its Fourier amplitude per unit time, which can also be interpreted as the Fourier transform of the time correlation function; i.e.,

$$S \, (\omega) = lim_{T \to \infty} \frac{1}{T} \left| \int_0^T dt \; e^{i \omega t} x \, (t) \right|^2$$

$$= \int_{-\infty}^{\infty} dt \; e^{i \omega t} lim_{\tau \to \infty} \int_0^{\tau} d\tau' \; x(\tau') \, x \, (\tau' + 1) \; . \tag{2.9}$$

The power spectrum indicates whether the system is periodic, quasiperiodic, or chaotic. Strange attractors are characterized by broadband power spectra [Eckmann and Ruelle (1985)]. Comparing the power spectrum obtained from experimental data and data generated by trained neural nets gives a very close comparison of the dynamics of both iteration maps.

3. Neural Network Architectures and Learning Paradigms

In this section we introduce two different recurrent architectures. The essential idea is to reproduce the recurrences of Equation 2.4 by the structures of the nets. The two architectures are presented graphically in Figures 24-1a and 24-1b.

The update equations for the architecture of Figure 24-1a may be written as

$$\hat{\xi}_0 (t + 1) = \sum_i W_i \cdot \tanh \left[\sum_k \omega_{ik} \cdot \hat{\xi}_k (t) \right], \tag{3.1}$$

$$\hat{\xi}_j (t + 1) = \hat{\xi}_{j-1} (t), (j > 0) . \tag{3.2}$$

For the architecture of Figure 24-1b, the update equations are

$$\hat{\xi}_j (t + 1) = \sum_i W_{ji} \cdot \tanh \left[\sum_k \omega_{ik} \cdot \hat{\xi}_k (t) \right]. \tag{3.3}$$

For training the networks we use a modified version of *Backpropagation Through Time* (BTT) [Pearlmutter (1989)]. The modified learning paradigm consists in a gradient correction through time for a neural network that includes recurrences only in those variables that are also recurrent in the real dynamical system. The first architecture (Figure 24-1a) learns merely the first component F_0, while the second architecture (Figure 24-1b) learns components of F. A basic problem that arises in BTT when it is used for learning chaotic time series is that when the neural model begins to learn the real system in an accurate form, it is itself chaotic, and corrections to the weights are therefore unstable ("to model something chaotic you should be also chaotic"). Two modifications are introduced in this chapter in order to stabilize the learning process of chaotic systems:

1. Stochastic sampling of orbits

2. Lyapunov weighted backpropagation through time

Since the series to be learned is chaotic, only short-term predictions are possible. We generate samplings of sequences defining the sampling set by

$$S (\hat{t}) = [\vec{\xi}(\hat{t}) ,... \vec{\xi}(\hat{t} + \Delta)] \tag{3.4}$$

Figure 24-1(a)

Recurrent Architecture Corresponding to Equation 3.1

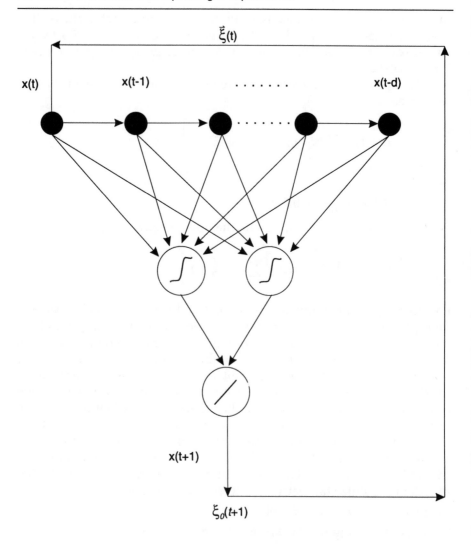

of the embedding vector and use this sampling for training the recurrent neural network with BTT through Δ cycles. The value of Δ depends on the largest Lyapunov coefficient. The samplings at different initial times $\vec{\Gamma}$ are presented stochastically during training. The update of the weights has

Figure 24-1(b)

Recurrent Architecture Corresponding to Equation 3.3

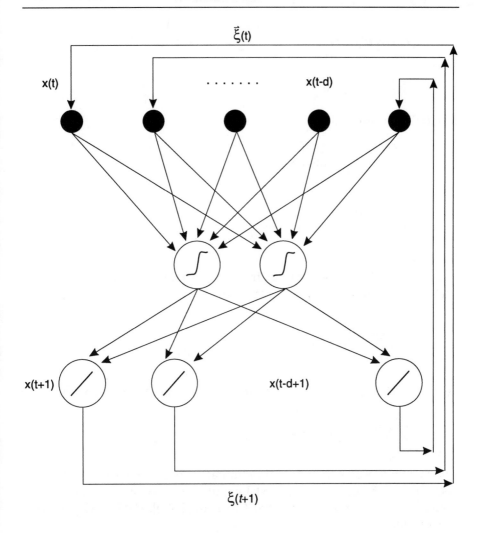

been done "sampling-by-sampling." In fact, when $\Delta=0$ standard stochastic backpropagation learning for feedforward networks is recovered.

Also due to the chaotic character of the sequence to be learned, the significance of the backpropagated error is progressively deteriorated during iteration. The distortion in each iteration is given by $exp(\lambda_m)$.

Therefore, we introduce a forgetting function in the update of the weights (i.e., in the learning rule of BTT) that takes into account the distortion of the errors,

$$\delta_i(t) = \sigma'_i(t-1) \left[E_i(t)\, e^{\lambda_m(\hat{t}-t)} + \sum_j w_{ji}\delta_j\,(t+1) \right] ; t = \hat{t} + 1 + \Delta, \ldots \hat{t} \quad (3.5)$$

$$\delta_i(\hat{t} + 2 + \Delta) = 0 \,.$$

The BTT-learning rule is

$$\Delta W_{ji} = - \sum_{\hat{t}}^{\hat{t}+1+\Delta} \tanh \left[\sum_k \omega_{ik} \cdot \hat{\xi}_k\,(t-1) \right] \delta_j\,(t) \,, \quad (3.6)$$

$$\Delta \omega_{ji} = - \sum_{\hat{t}}^{\hat{t}+1+\Delta} \hat{\xi}_i\,(t-1)\, \delta_j\,(t) \,. \quad (3.7)$$

Equation 3.5 can be obtained from the standard derivation of BTT, but instead of minimizing the cost function

$$\sum_{t=0}^{T} \left[\sum_k (\hat{\xi}_k\,(t) - \xi_k\,(t)) \right]^2 \quad (3.8)$$

for the total interval $(0,T)$ where data exist, we minimize the cost function

$$\sum_{\hat{t}}^{\hat{t}+\Delta} \{ e^{\lambda_m(\hat{t}-t)} \sum_k [\hat{\xi}_k\,(t) - \xi_k\,(t)]^2 \} \quad (3.9)$$

which compensates the prediction limitation due to the exponential distortion introduced by the largest Lyapunov exponent in a chaotic time series [Eckmann and Ruelle (1985), Casdagli (1989)]. The learning is stable in this sense.

4. Results and Simulations

We analyze three different chaotic series. The Hénon and logistic maps have been hypothesized in a number of empirical studies of financial time series [e.g., see Hsieh (1991)]. The Belousov-Zhabotinskii map may be useful for the modeling of post-innovation behavior of series that are asymptotic or mean-reverting, such as the ARCH process [see Engle (1982) and Engle and Gonzalez-Rivera (1991)].

1. The 2-D Hénon map [Hénon (1976)]:

$$x_{n+1} = 1 - 1.4x_n^2 + y_n ,$$ (4.1)

$$y_{n+1} = 0.3x_n .$$ (4.2)

2. 1-D Belousov-Zhabotinskii:
    This map originated empirically in the field of chemistry [Roux et al. (1983)]. The concentration of an ion in a reactive solution was measured and parameterized by the exponential map

$$c_{n+1} = a \cdot e^{-bc_n} (1 + \upsilon) .$$ (4.3)

where υ is randomly generated from a Gaussian distribution such that 5 percent multiplicative Gaussian noise is introduced.

3. The logistic map:

$$x_{n+1} = 4x_n (1 - x_n) + \upsilon .$$ (4.4)

where 5 percent Gaussian noise υ is added.

The neural networks were trained with the learning algorithm described in the previous section. After training, the networks are used in an iterative mode in order to generate a series of $\hat{\xi}$, and the dynamical invariants are measured and compared with the dynamical invariants measured for the original series $\overrightarrow{\xi}$.

Correlation Dimension, largest Lyapunov exponent, Poincare maps, and spectral power spectrum of the modeled series are compared with the values corresponding to the true strange attractor. In order to test the influence of recurrent learning in long-term prediction, we define a "long-term error" as the averaged error ELT between model and real series for M iterations in the future measured on a test set; i.e.,

$$ELT = \frac{1}{N} \sum_n \frac{1}{M} \sum_i^M [\hat{\xi}(n+i) - \xi(n+i)]^2$$ (4.5)

where N is the number of patterns in the test set. In the simulations we chose $M = 10$.

Experiments with Feedforward Learning

When the architecture of Figure 24-1.b is used with the learning algorithm described in Section 3 with $\Delta = 0$, standard stochastic backpropagation is obtained. In this section we study whether feedforward learning is sufficient to capture the dynamical invariants of the strange attractor. We use noise-free (Hénon map) and noisy data (Belousov–Zhabotinskii). The influences of dimension of input space, number of hidden units, and number of training patterns in feedforward architectures are studied. It turns out that, contrary to the claim of Principe et al., a feedforward net is capable of learning the Lyapunov exponent and Correlation Dimension as soon as the numbers of input dimension, hidden units, and training data are large enough. The results for the Hénon map are summarized in Tables 24-1a, 24-1b, and 24-1c. In the tables, N is the number of training patterns, h is the number of hidden neurons, and d is the dimension of the input layer.

For the case of noisy data (Belousov–Zhabotinskii) it is also possible to perfectly learn the Lyapunov exponent and the correlation dimension when 1,000 data and 15 hidden units are used. For the Belousov-Zhabotinskii (BZ) map the Lyapunov exponent is 0.35 (data and network) and the Procaccia-Grassberger correlation dimension is 0.82 (data and network). In the case of noisy data it is very important to take into account the dynamical overtraining reported above, which can only be observed during training by plotting the Lyapunov exponent of the neural network.

Experiments with Recurrent Learning

Recurrent networks may be trained for learning chaos. The multi-delayed architecture introduced here yields very good results. Dynamical invariants are learned and long-term prediction and power spectrum are improved. Figure 24-2 shows the dependence of the long-term error ELT on Δ for the Hénon map. For this experiment $N = 2,000$, $h = 15$, and $d = 5$. The improvement obtained when longer recurrent learning is used is clearly seen. Figure 24-3 shows the results of the learned largest Lyapunov exponent for the same experiment. We have purposely fixed a combination of N and h such that feedforward learning does not learn the Lyapunov exponent (in this case the number of patterns, 2,000, was not big enough for a network with 15 hidden units). When recurrent learning is applied even with a small amount of data, learning of the largest Lyapunov exponent is improved.

Table 24-1

Dynamical invariants from trained neural networks for the Hénon map in dependence on the embedding dimension d, the number of training patterns N, and the number of hidden units h, respectively. The largest Lyapunov exponent of the examples data is 0.l6 and the correlation dimension 1.22.

(a)

N=2,000 h=10	Test Error	Largest Lyapunov Exponent	Correlation Dimension
d=7	0.0014	0.60	1.26
d=5	0.00055	0.57	1.20
d=2	0.00018	0.55	1.20
d=1	0.079	0.52	0.91

(b)

d=5 h=15	Largest Lyapunov Exponent	Correlation Dimension
N=50	−0.05	0.034
N=100	0.53	1.32
N=500	0.60	1.25
N=1,000	0.60	1.21

(c)

d=5 N=500	Largest Lyapunov Exponent	Correlation Dimension
h=5	0.462	1.024
h-10	0.485	1.09
h=12	0.57	1.237
h=15	0.59	1.22

Figures 24-4 and 24-5 show the power spectrum of data and model for the Belousov-Zhabotinskii map for $\Delta = 0$ and $\Delta = 3$, respectively. A closer estimate of the spectrum is obtained with recurrent learning.

Dynamical Overtraining and Lyapunov Penalty Term

In this subsection we deal with nonrecurrent learning of the noisy Belousov-Zhabotinskii series. We train a network architecture with 1 input, 15 hidden units, and 1 output, using 3,000 training data points and 10,000

Figure 24-2

Long-term test error as function of the number of iterations Δ for BTT during recurrent learning of the Hénon map. Dashed line: recurrent architecture of Figure 24-1a; solid line: recurrent architecture of Figure 24-1b.

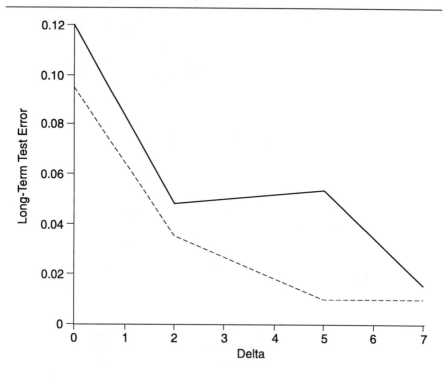

test data points. During learning we plot the evolution of the training error, the generalization error, and the Lyapunov exponent of the network calculated with Equation 2.6, with $f(.)$ being the neural network function

$$f(x) = \sum_i W_i \sigma \, (\omega_i \cdot x) \ . \tag{4.6}$$

A "dynamical overtraining" is observed when noisy data are used. This type of overtraining consists in forgetting the learned Lyapunov exponent. The network during training learns the correct value of the largest Lyapunov exponent, but when the training process continues, the network begins to forget it without overtraining the error. In other words, the sensitivity with respect to overtraining of the Lyapunov exponent is

Figure 24-3

Solid line: largest Lyapunov exponent as a function of the number of iterations Δ for BTT during recurrent learning of the Hénon map; dashed line: true largest Lyapunov exponent.

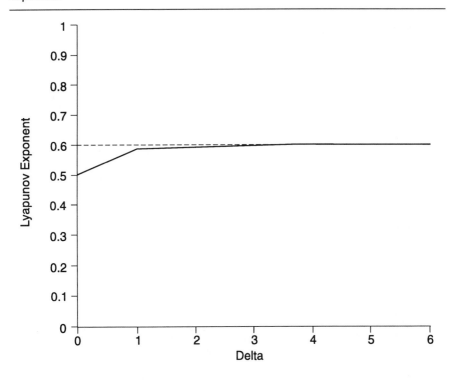

greater than that of the prediction error. Therefore we observe in the experiments a forgetting of the Lyapunov coefficient without observing an increase (overtraining) in the generalization error, which is normally the criterion for overtraining. In conclusion, for neural modeling of chaotic series the Lyapunov exponent during training provides us with a more reliable method for control of overfitting than the cross-validation method.

In order to avoid dynamical overtraining a novel penalty term is introduced. The cost function is defined by the sum of the squared error and the squared difference between the true largest Lyapunov exponent and the Lyapunov exponent of the network. In the one-dimensional case for a neural network $f(x)$, the cost function reads

Figure 24-4

Dashed line: power spectrum of the original data of the Belousov–Zhabotinskii map; solid line: power spectrum of the trained network with feedforward training (BTT with $\Delta = 0$).

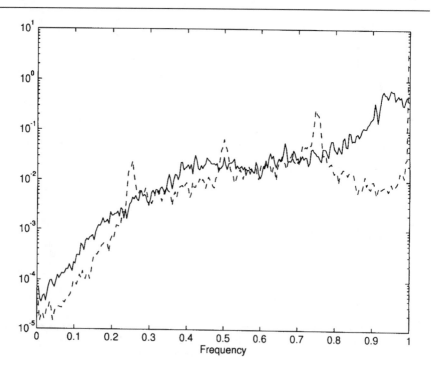

$$E = \left(\sum_{p=1}^{N} \| O^{(p)} - f(x^{(p)}) \|^2 \right) + \left(\lambda_m^{true} - \frac{1}{N} \sum_{p=1}^{N} \ln \left| \frac{\partial f}{\partial x}(x) \mid_{(p)} \right| \right)^2 . \quad (4.7)$$

In Equation 4.7, λ_m^{true} is the largest Lyapunov exponent of the time series to be modeled, σ is the sigmoid function, and N is the number of patterns. The new update rule can be obtained by the gradient method. The correction due to the penalty term is obtained in batch mode and can be written as

Figure 24-5

Same as Figure 24-4 but for (BTT with Δ = 3).

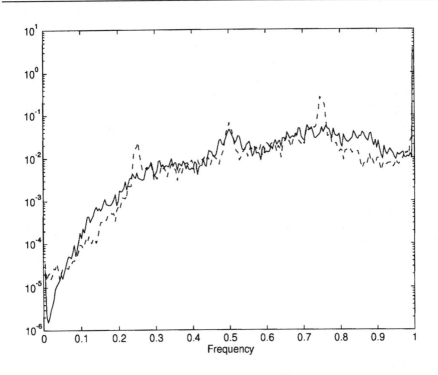

$$\Delta W_i = \varepsilon \left(\lambda_m^{true} - \frac{1}{n} \sum_{p=1}^{N} ln \left| \frac{\partial f}{\partial x}(x) \mid_{(p)} \right| \right) \frac{\sigma'_i \omega_i}{\left| \frac{\partial f}{\partial x}(x) \mid_{(p)} \right|}, \tag{4.8}$$

$$\Delta \omega_i = \varepsilon \left(\lambda_m^{true} - \frac{1}{N} \sum_{p=1}^{N} ln \left| \frac{\partial f}{\partial x}(x) \mid_{(p)} \right| \right) \frac{\sigma'_i W_i}{\left| \frac{\partial f}{\partial x}(x) \mid_{(p)} \right|}. \tag{4.9}$$

In Equations 4.8 and 4.9, σ'_i is the derivative of the activation function at hidden unit i and ε is the learning rate.

In Figure 24-6, a typical result for dynamical overtraining and its remedy by introducing the penalty term of Equation 4.7 is displayed, the reaction considered being 1-D Belousov-Zhabotinskii. According to Roux et al., the largest Lyapunov exponent is $\lambda_m^{true} = .3 \pm .1$. It is seen that without penalty term, λ_m does not saturate, whereas with penalty term a plateau is reached after a sufficient number of epochs.

Figure 24-7 shows the same experiment for the case of the logistic map with noise. In this figure the generalization error is also plotted. It is very important to remark that no overtraining (increase of generalization error) is observed. When the penalty term is added, stable learning of the largest Lyapunov exponent $\lambda_m^{true} = .52$ is obtained. Without penalty term dynamical overtraining occurs and the true largest Lyapunov exponent is forgot-

Figure 24-6

Dynamical overtraining and its correction by using the Lyapanov penalty term (Equation 4.6) for noisy Belonsov-Zhabotinskii map.

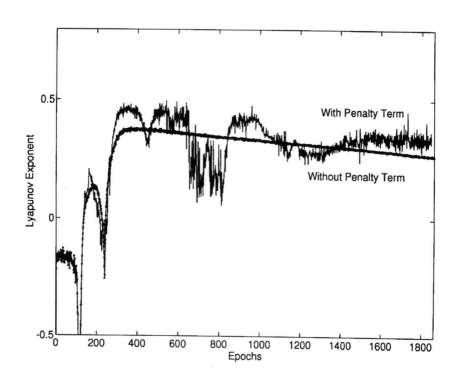

Figure 24-7

Same as Figure 24-6 but for a noisy logistic map.

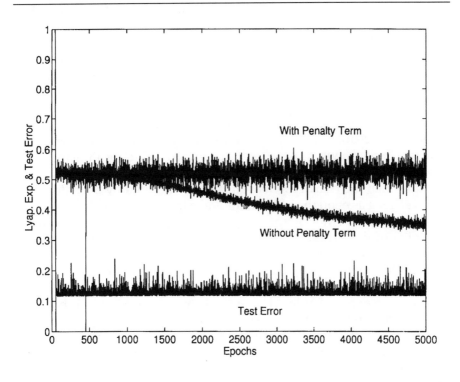

ten during learning. In both cases the same evolution of generalization error is obtained (the figures are indistinguishable).

5. Summary and Conclusions

In this chapter, neural network models of chaotic time series were analyzed by comparing the dynamical invariants that characterize the chaotic attractor with the dynamical invariants of the trained neural network models. The observed invariants are the largest Lyapunov exponent and the Correlation Dimension. An additional noninvariant quantity, the power spectrum, was also examined. Our analysis permits us to claim that neural networks capture "chaos" because they learn the dynamical invariants of a chaotic dynamical system.

We employed feedforward and two different recurrent neural architectures in this chapter. The trained networks were employed as recurrent models that generate a "learned" time series. A stable learning algorithm for the recurrent architecture is presented for modeling chaotic time series. Stability is needed for the following reason: When the neural model begins to learn the real system in an accurate form, then it is itself chaotic and updates of the weights are therefore unstable. In order to avoid this effect, which is typical of chaotic time series, we employed a stochastic "sample-by-sample" updating of the weights with a forgetting function given by the largest Lyapunov exponent. In this manner a consistent learning process incorporating the inherent limit of predictability could be performed by a chaotic recurrent neural network. As a special case of the recurrent models, we recover the feedforward model of Principe et al. (1992). Contrary to the claims of Principe et al., we demonstrate for several examples that the dynamics may already be captured by a feedforward model so long as enough hidden units and enough training data are used.

We examined a novel type of overtraining, which corresponds to the forgetting of the largest Lyapunov exponent during learning, which we call "dynamical overtraining." A penalty term is introduced into the cost function that involves the largest Lyapunov exponent of the network, eliminating the observed dynamical overtraining (i.e., forgetting of the Lyapunov exponent). Numerical analyses were performed on both the Hénon and Belousov-Zhabotinskii maps.

We believe that the encouraging results obtained herein with respect to the neural modeling of chaotic systems, in combination with existing nonlinear dynamic techniques, has great potential for the modeling of financial, economic, and other time series generated by complex market-driven systems.

References

Abarbanel, H. D. I., R. Brown, and J. B. Kadtke. "Prediction and System Identification in Chaotic Time Series with Broadband Fourier Spectra." *Phys. Lett. A*, 138 (1989), 401–408.

Abarbanel, H. D. I., R. Brown, and J. B. Kadtke. "Prediction in Chaotic Nonlinear Systems: Methods for Time Series with Broadband Fourier Spectra." *Phys. Rev. A*, 41 (1990), 1782–1807.

Albano, A., A. Passamante, T. Hediger, and M. E. Farell. "Using Neural Nets to Look for Chaos." *Physica D*, 58 (1992), 1.

Beck, C., and F. Schlogl. "Thermodynamics of Chaotic Systems." Cambridge Nonlinear Science Series, Cambridge University Press, 1993.

Blank, Steven C. "Chaos in Futures Markets? A Nonlinear Dynamical Analysis." *The Journal of Futures Markets,* 11:6 (1991), 711–728.

Brock, W., and C. Sayers. "Is the Business Cycle Characterized by Deterministic Chaos?" *Journal of Monetary Economics,* 22 (1988), 71–90.

Buzug, T. and G. Pfister. "Optimal Delay Time and Embedding Dimension for Delay-Time Coordinates by Analysis of the Global Static and Local Dynamical Behavior of Strange Attractors." *Phys. Rev. A,* 45 (1992), 7073–7084.

Casdagli, M. "Nonlinear Prediction of Chaotic Time Series." *Physica D,* 35 (1989), 335–356.

Crutchfield, J. , and McNamara. "Equations of Motion from Data Series." *Complex Systems,* 1 (1987), 417–452.

Deco, G., and B. Schuermann. "Learning the Dynamical Invariants of Chaotic Time Series by Recurrent Neural Networks." *Proc. World Congress on Neural Networks,* Lawrence Erlbaum Associates, Inc., Vol. IV (1994), 722–726.

Engle, R. F. "Autoregressive Conditional Heteroskedasticity with Estimates of the Variance of United Kingdom Inflation," *Econometrica* 50 (1982), pp. 987–1997.

Engle, R. F., and G. Gonzalez-Rivera, "Semiparametric ARCH Models." *Journal of Business and Economic Statistics,* 9:4 (1991), 345–359.

Eckmann, J. P., and D. Ruelle. "Ergodic Theory of Chaos and Strange Attractors." *Rev. Mod. Phys.,* 57 (1985), 617–656.

Fama, E. "Efficient Capital Markets: A Review of Theory and Empirical Work." *Journal of Finance,* 25 (1970), 383–417.

Farmer, J., and J. Sidorowich. "Predicting Chaotic Time Series." *Phys. Rev. Letters,* 59 (1987), 845.

Froehling, H., J. Crutchfield, D. Farmer, N. H. Packard, and R. Shaw. "On Determining the Dimension of Chaotic Flow." *Physica* (Utrecht), 3D (1981), 605.

Grassberger, P., and I. Procaccia. "Characterization of Strange Attractors." *Phys. Rev. Lett.,* 50 (1983), 346.

Henon, M. "A Two-Dimensional Mapping with a Strange Attractor." *Comm. Math. Phys.,* 50 (1976), 69.

Hsieh, D. A. "Testing for Nonlinear Dependence in Daily Foreign Exchange Rates." *The Journal of Business* 62 (1989), 339–368.

Hsieh, D. A. "Chaos and Nonlinear Dynamics—Application to Financial Markets," *The Journal of Finance*, 6:5 (1991), 1839–1877.

Lapedes, A., and R. Farber. "Nonlinear Signal Processing Using Neural Networks: Prediction and System Modeling." Tech. Rep. n LA–UR–87–2662, Los Alamos National Laboratory, Los Alamos, NM (1987).

Liebert, W., and H. G. Schuster. "Proper Choice of the Time Delay for the Analysis of Chaotic Time Series." *Phys. Lett. A*, 142 (1989), 107–111.

Liebert, W., K. Pawelzik, and H. G. Schuster. "Optimal Embedding of Chaotic Attractors from Topological Considerations." *Europhysics Lett.*, 14 (1991), 521–526.

Lorie, J. H., P. Dodd, and M. J. Hamilton. *The Stock Market: Theories and Evidence*. New York: Irwin, 1985.

Pawelzik, K., and H. G. Schuster. "Unstable Periodic Orbits and Prediction." *Phys. Rev. A*, 43 (1991), 1808–1812.

Pearlmutter, B. "Learning State Space Trajectories in Recurrent Neural Networks." *Neural Computation*, 1 (1989), 239–269.

Principe, J., A. Rathie, and J. Kuo. "Prediction of Chaotic Time Series with Neural Networks and the Issue of Dynamic Modeling." *Bifurcation and Chaos*, 2 (1992), n. 4, 989.

Roux, J.–C., R. H. Simoyi, and H. L. Swinney. "Observation of a Strange Attractor." *Physica D*, 8 (1983), 257–266.

Sauer, T., J. Yorke, and M. Casdagli. "Embedology." *J. Stat. Phys.*, 65 (1991), 579–616.

Scheinkman, J. A., and B. LeBaron. "Nonlinear Dynamics and Stock Returns," *Journal of Business*, 62 (1989), 311–337.

Takens, F. "Detecting Strange Attractors in Turbulence," in *Dynamical Systems and Turbulence* (Warwick, 1980), D. A. Rand and L. S. Young, eds. *Lecture Notes in Mathematics*, 898. New York: Springer–Verlag, 1980, 366–381.

Weigend, A., D. Rumelhart, and B. Huberman. "Back–Propagation, Weight Elimination and Time Series Prediction," in *Connectionist Models, Proc. 1990*, Touretzky, Elman, Sejnowski and Hinton, eds. M. Kaufman Publishing Co., 1990, 105–116.

Wolf, A., J. B. Swift, H. L. Swinney, and J. A. Vastano. "Determining Lyapunov Exponents from a Time Series." *Physica D*, 16 (1985), 285–317.

Wolpert, D. M., and R. C. Miall. "Detecting Chaos with Neural Networks." *Phil. Trans. R. Soc. Lond. B*, 242 (1990), 82–86.

NAME INDEX

A

Abarbanel, H., 468, 486
Abraham, N., 204, 205, 220
Akgiray, V., 226, 242, 418, 435
Albano, A., 274, 289, 418, 435, 486
Aleksic, Z., 420, 435
Anderson, R., 227, 242
Aradhyula, S., 209, 220
Arnott, R., 174
Artstein, Z., 64, 70
Ashley, R., 90, 101, 139, 147, 202, 220
Auerbach, D., 461, 465

B

Babloyantz, A., 291
Baek, E., 348, 355, 387, 412
Baillie, R., 209, 220
Bajo-Rubio, O., 288, 290, 327, 328, 333
Baldauf, B., 226, 242
Barenblatt, G., 148
Barnett, W., 106, 107, 119, 180, 193, 194, 201, 202, 220, 250, 263, 288, 290, 337, 355, 384, 411
Baumol, W., 71, 91, 93, 101, 108, 119, 138, 147, 194, 200, 207, 220, 383, 412
Bear, R., 181, 197, 202, 223
Beck, C., 471, 487
Beck, E., 365, 368, 369, 372, 373, 374, 379

Benhabib, J., 36, 84, 85, 89, 91, 93, 101, 108, 119, 138, 147, 194, 200, 207, 220, 383, 412
Bernanke, B., 336, 355
Berndt, E., 228, 242, 306, 323
Bernhardt, C., 137
Bhatt, S., 88, 101
Bickel, P., 262, 263
Birkhoff, G., 6
Blank, S., 106, 114, 119, 180, 194, 199, 217, 220, 225, 226, 242, 276, 288, 290, 468, 487
Blattberg, R., 321, 323
Boldrin, M., 269, 290
Bollerslev, T., 209, 220, 226, 227, 242, 255, 263, 277, 290, 306, 307, 323, 324
Booth, G., 202, 220, 226, 242
Booth, P., 321, 324
Box, G., 114, 120, 239
Brandstater, A., 415
Brealey, R., 245, 263
Brock, W., 36, 61, 62, 90, 93, 97, 101, 106, 108, 109, 114, 118, 119, 120, 139, 144, 147, 153, 159, 180, 184, 194, 195, 200, 201, 203, 204, 205, 207, 208, 209, 221, 225, 228, 229, 230, 232, 233, 240, 242, 245, 246, 247, 248, 249, 250, 257, 261, 262, 263, 269, 290, 298, 307, 321, 324, 348, 355, 362, 365, 368, 370, 372,

Subject Index

A

Adaptive learning
and the cobweb model, 63-69
Adaptive price expectations, 69
Attracting hyperbolic point, 17-18
Attractor(s), 5, 134, 203, 271, 471
chaotic, 123-124, 126, 132, 249
chaotic, for the S&P 500, 121-133
defining an, 122-123, 134, 249
foreign-exchange markets and, 278
fractal (chaotic), 28, 58, 123
limit cycle, 122
low-dimensional, 126, 132, 271, 287, 353
low-dimensional fractal, 269
point, 122, 123
strange, 28, 139, 204, 249, 379, 385, 386, 388, 390, 399, 401, 472, 477
two mechanisms responsible for strange, 385
ARCH (autoregressive conditional heteroskedasticity) process
commodity futures prices and, 185, 190, 192
daily futures prices and, 226
EGARCH vs. GARCH and, in risk analysis, 306
foreign-exchange markets analysis and, 270
measuring gold/silver rates of return and, 255, 257, 258

nonlinear dependence in stock indices and, 111

B

Backpropagation through time (BTT), 469, 473
BBT-learning rule, 476
Lyapunov weighted, 473-476
Basis of attraction, 5, 47, 203, 249
BDS (Brock, Dechert, and Scheinkman) test, 408
daily futures prices and the, 229-239, 240
daily stock indices and the, 108-109, 118
economic series and the, 372-377, 378
EGARCH and, 307, 311
options prices and the, 440
in the test of IID, 296, 297-299, 320
Belousov-Zhabotinskii map, 469, 477, 478, 479, 484, 486
Best linear unbiased estimate (BLUE), 200
Black Monday, 57, 218
See also Stock
Black-Scholes result, 440, 441, 445, 447, 448, 450, 451, 452
Bootstrapping, 215, 257, 311
and shuffling procedure, 108
Box-Pierce statistic, 299
Brock's residual test